DATA WAREHOUSING FUNDAMENTALS FOR IT PROFESSIONALS

DATA WAREHOUSING FUNDAMENTALS FOR IT PROFESSIONALS

Second Edition

PAULRAJ PONNIAH

A JOHN WILEY & SONS, INC., PUBLICATION

Library of Congress Cataloging-in-Publication Data:

Ponniah, Paulraj.
  Data warehousing fundamentals for IT professionals / Paulraj Ponniah.—2nd ed.
    p. cm.
  Previous ed. published under title: Data warehousing fundamentals.
  Includes bibliographical references and index.
  ISBN 978-0-470-46207-2 (cloth)
  1. Data warehousing. I. Ponniah, Paulraj. Data warehousing fundamentals. II. Title.
  QA76.9.D37P66 2010
  005.74′5—dc22

                                                                      2009041789

10 9 8 7 6 5 4 3 2 1

To
Vimala, my loving wife
and to
Joseph, David, and Shobi,
my dear children

CONTENTS

11 DIMENSIONAL MODELING: ADVANCED TOPICS   249

PART 6 IMPLEMENTATION AND MAINTENANCE   461

18 THE PHYSICAL DESIGN PROCESS   463

PREFACE

THIS BOOK IS FOR YOU

Are you an information technology professional watching, with great interest, the massive unfolding and spreading of the data warehouse movement during the past decade? Are you contemplating a move into this fast-growing area of opportunity? Are you a systems analyst, programmer, data analyst, database administrator, project leader, or software engineer eager to grasp the fundamentals of data warehousing? Do you wonder how many different books you may have to study to learn the underlying principles and the current practices? Are you lost in the maze of the literature and products on the subject? Do you wish for a single publication on data warehousing, clearly and specifically designed for IT professionals? Do you need a textbook that helps you learn the fundamentals in sufficient depth? If you answered "yes" to any of the above, this book is written specially for you.

This is the *one* definitive book on data warehousing clearly intended for IT professionals. The organization and presentation of the book are specially tuned for IT professionals. This book does not presume to target anyone and everyone remotely interested in the subject for some reason or another, but is written to address the specific needs of IT professionals like you. It does not tend to emphasize certain aspects and neglect other critical ones. The book takes you over the entire spectrum of data warehousing.

As a veteran IT professional with wide and intensive industry experience, as a successful database and data warehousing consultant for many years, and as one who teaches data warehousing fundamentals in the college classroom and at public seminars, I have come to appreciate the precise needs of IT professionals. In every chapter I have incorporated these requirements of the IT community.

THE SCENARIO

Why have companies rushed into data warehousing? Why is there a tremendous surge in interest? Data warehousing is no longer a purely novel idea just for research and experimentation. It has become a mainstream phenomenon. True, the data warehouse is not in every doctor's office yet, but neither is it confined to only high-end businesses. More than half of all U.S. companies and a large percentage of worldwide businesses have made a commitment to data warehousing.

In every industry across the board, from retail chain stores to financial institutions, from manufacturing enterprises to government departments, and from airline companies to utility businesses, data warehousing has revolutionized the way people perform business analysis and make strategic decisions. Every company that has a data warehouse is realizing the enormous benefits translated into positive results at the bottom line. These companies, now incorporating Web-based technologies, are enhancing the potential for greater and easier delivery of vital information.

Over the past decade, a large number of vendors have flooded the market with numerous data warehousing products. Vendor solutions and products run the gamut of data warehousing and business intelligence—data modeling, data acquisition, data quality, data analysis, metadata, information delivery, and so on. The market is large, mature, and continues to grow.

CHANGED ROLE OF IT

In this scenario, information technology departments of all progressive companies have perceived a radical change in their roles. IT is no longer required to create every report and present every screen for providing information to the end-users. IT is now charged with the building of information delivery systems and letting the end-users themselves retrieve information in innovative ways for analysis and decision making. Data warehousing and business intelligence environments are proving to be just that type of successful information delivery system.

IT professionals responsible for building data warehouses had to revise their mindsets about building applications. They had to understand that a data warehouse is not a one-size-fits-all proposition. First, they had to get a clear understanding about data extraction from source systems, data transformations, data staging, data warehouse architecture, infrastructure, and the various methods of information delivery. In short, IT professionals, like you, must get a strong grip on the fundamentals of data warehousing.

WHAT THIS BOOK CAN DO FOR YOU

The book is comprehensive and detailed. You will be able to study every significant topic in planning, requirements, architecture, infrastructure, design, data preparation, information delivery, deployment, and maintenance. The book is specially designed for IT professionals; you will be able to follow the presentation easily because it is built upon the foundation of your background as an IT professional, your knowledge, and the technical terminology familiar to you. It is organized logically, beginning with an overview of concepts, moving on to planning and requirements, then to architecture and infrastructure, on to data design, then to information delivery, and concluding with deployment and maintenance. This progression is typical of what you are most familiar with in your IT experience and day-to-day work.

The book provides an interactive learning experience. It is not just a one-way lecture. You participate through the review questions and exercises at the end of each chapter. For each chapter, the objectives at the beginning set the theme and the summary at the end highlights the topics covered. You can relate each concept and technique presented in the book to the data warehousing industry and marketplace. You will benefit from the substantial number of industry examples. Although intended as a first course on the fundamentals, this book provides sufficient coverage of each topic so that you can comfortably proceed to the next step of specialization for specific roles in a data warehouse project.

Featuring all the significant topics in appropriate measure, this book is eminently suitable as a textbook for serious self-study, a college course, or a seminar on the essentials. It provides an opportunity for you to become a data warehouse expert.

ENHANCEMENTS IN THIS SECOND EDITION

This greatly enhanced edition captures the developments and changes in the data warehousing landscape during the past nearly ten years. The underlying purposes and principles of data warehousing have remained the same. However, we notice definitive changes in the details, some finer aspects, and in product innovations. Although this edition succeeds in incorporating all the significant revisions, I have been careful not to disturb the overall logical arrangement and sequencing of the chapters.

The term "business intelligence" has gained a lot more currency. Many practitioners now consider data warehousing to refer to populating the warehouse with data, and business intelligence to refer to using the warehouse data. Data warehousing has made inroads into areas such as Customer Relationship Management, Enterprise Application Integration, Enterprise Information Integration, Business Activity Monitoring, and so on. The size of corporate data warehouses has been rising higher and higher. Some progressive businesses have reaped enormous benefits from data warehouses that are almost in the 500 terabyte range (five times the size of the U.S. Library of Congress archive). The benefits from data warehouses are no longer limited to a selected core of executives, managers, and analysts. Pervasive data warehousing has become the operative principle, providing access and usage to staff at multiple levels. Information delivery through traditional reports and queries is being replaced by interactive dashboards and scorecards.

More specifically, among topics on recent trends and changes, this enhanced edition includes the following:

- Evolution of business intelligence
- Real-time business intelligence
- Data warehouse appliances
- Data warehouse: architectural types
- Data visualization enhancements
- Enterprise application integration (EAI)
- Enterprise information integration (EII)
- Agile data warehouse development

- Data warehousing and KM (knowledge management)
- Data warehousing and ERP (enterprise resource planning)
- Data warehousing and CRM (customer relationship management)
- Improved requirements gathering methods
- Business activity monitoring (BAM)
- Interactive information delivery through dashboards and scorecards
- Additional STAR schema examples
- Master data management
- Examples of typical OLAP (online analytical processing) implementations
- Data mining applications
- Web clickstream analysis
- Highlights of vendors and products
- Real-world examples of best practices

ACKNOWLEDGMENTS

I wish to acknowledge my indebtedness and to express my gratitude to the authors listed in the reference section at the end of the book. Their insights and observations have helped me cover every topic adequately.

I must also express my appreciation to my students and professional colleagues. My interactions with them have enabled me to shape this textbook according to the needs of IT professionals.

My special thanks are due to the wonderful staff and editors at Wiley, my publishers, who have worked with me and supported me for more than a decade in the publication and promotion of my books.

PAULRAJ PONNIAH, PH.D.

Milltown, New Jersey
October 2009

PART 1

OVERVIEW AND CONCEPTS

CHAPTER 1

THE COMPELLING NEED FOR DATA WAREHOUSING

CHAPTER OBJECTIVES

- Understand the desperate need for strategic information
- Recognize the information crisis at every enterprise
- Distinguish between operational and informational systems
- Learn why all past attempts to provide strategic information failed
- Clearly see why data warehousing is the viable solution
- Understand business intelligence for an enterprise

As an information technology (IT) professional, you have worked on computer applications as an analyst, programmer, designer, developer, database administrator, or project manager. You have been involved in the design, implementation, and maintenance of systems that support day-to-day business operations. Depending on the industries you have worked in, you must have been involved in applications such as order processing, general ledger, inventory, human resources, payroll, in-patient billing, checking accounts, insurance claims, and so on.

These applications are important systems that run businesses. They process orders, maintain inventory, keep the accounting books, service the clients, receive payments, and process claims. Without these computer systems, no modern business can survive. Companies started building and using these systems in the 1960s and have become completely dependent on them. As an enterprise grows larger, hundreds of computer applications are needed to support the various business processes. These applications are effective in what they are designed to do. They gather, store, and process all the data needed to successfully perform the daily routine operations. They provide online information and produce a variety of reports to monitor and run the business.

Data Warehousing Fundamentals for IT Professionals, Second Edition. By Paulraj Ponniah
Copyright © 2010 John Wiley & Sons, Inc.

Organizations achieve competitive advantage:

◆ Retail
  ◆ Customer Loyalty
  ◆ Market Planning
◆ Financial
  ◆ Risk Management
  ◆ Fraud Detection
◆ Airlines
  ◆ Route Profitability
  ◆ Yield Management

◆ Manufacturing
  ◆ Cost Reduction
  ◆ Logistics Management
◆ Utilities
  ◆ Asset Management
  ◆ Resource Management
◆ Government
  ◆ Manpower Planning
  ◆ Cost Control

Figure 1-1   Organizations' use of data warehousing.

In the 1990s, as businesses grew more complex, corporations spread globally, and competition became fiercer, business executives became desperate for information to stay competitive and improve the bottom line. The operational computer systems did provide information to run the day-to-day operations but what the executives needed were different kinds of information that could be used readily to make strategic decisions. The decision makers wanted to know which geographic regions to focus on, which product lines to expand, and which markets to strengthen. They needed the type of information with proper content and format that could help them make such strategic decisions. We may call this type of information strategic information as different from operational information. The operational systems, important as they were, could not provide strategic information. Businesses, therefore, were compelled to turn to new ways of getting strategic information.

Data warehousing is a new paradigm specifically intended to provide vital strategic information. In the 1990s, organizations began to achieve competitive advantage by building data warehouse systems. Figure 1-1 shows a sample of strategic areas where data warehousing had already produced results in different industries.

At the outset, let us now examine the crucial question: why do enterprises really need data warehouses? This discussion is important because unless we grasp the significance of this critical need, our study of data warehousing will lack motivation. So, please pay close attention.

ESCALATING NEED FOR STRATEGIC INFORMATION

While we discuss the clamor by enterprises for strategic information, we need to look at the prevailing information crisis that was holding them back, as well as the technology trends of the past few years that are working in our favor, enabling us to provide strategic information. Our discussion of the need for strategic information will not be complete unless we study the opportunities provided by strategic information and the risks facing a company without such information.

Who needs strategic information in an enterprise? What exactly do we mean by strategic information? The executives and managers who are responsible for keeping the enterprise competitive need information to make proper decisions. They need information to formulate the business strategies, establish goals, set objectives, and monitor results.

Here are some examples of business objectives:

- Retain the present customer base
- Increase the customer base by 15% over the next 5 years
- Improve product quality levels in the top five product groups
- Gain market share by 10% in the next 3 years
- Enhance customer service level in shipments
- Bring three new products to market in 2 years
- Increase sales by 15% in the North East Division

For making decisions about these objectives, executives and managers need information for the following purposes: to get in-depth knowledge of their company's operations, review and monitor key performance indicators and note how these affect one another, keep track of how business factors change over time, and compare their company's performance relative to the competition and to industry benchmarks. Executives and managers need to focus their attention on customers' needs and preferences, emerging technologies, sales and marketing results, and quality levels of products and services. The types of information needed to make decisions in the formulation and execution of business strategies and objectives are broad-based and encompass the entire organization. All these types of essential information may be combined under the broad classification called strategic information.

Strategic information is not for running the day-to-day operations of the business. It is not intended to produce an invoice, make a shipment, settle a claim, or post a withdrawal from a bank account. Strategic information is far more important for the continued health and survival of the corporation. Critical business decisions depend on the availability of proper strategic information in an enterprise. Figure 1-2 lists the desired characteristics of strategic information.

INTEGRATED	Must have a single, enterprise-wide view.
DATA INTEGRITY	Information must be accurate and must conform to business rules.
ACCESSIBLE	Easily accessible with intuitive access paths, and responsive for analysis.
CREDIBLE	Every business factor must have one and only one value.
TIMELY	Information must be available within the stipulated time frame.

Figure 1-2   Characteristics of strategic information.

The Information Crisis

You may be working in the IT department of a large conglomerate or you may be part of a medium-sized company. Whatever may be the size of your company, think of all the various computer applications in your company. Think of all the databases and the quantities of data that support the operations of your company. How many years' worth of customer data is saved and available? How many years' worth of financial data is kept in storage? Ten years? Fifteen years? Where is all this data? On one platform? In legacy systems? In client/server applications?

We are faced with two startling facts: (1) organizations have lots of data, (2) information technology resources and systems are not effective at turning all that data into useful strategic information. Over the past two decades, companies have accumulated tons and tons of data about their operations. Mountains of data exist. Information is said to double every 18 months.

If we have such huge quantities of data in our organizations, why can't our executives and managers use this data for making strategic decisions? Lots and lots of information exists. Why then do we talk about an information crisis? Most companies are faced with an information crisis not because of lack of sufficient data, but because the available data is not readily usable for strategic decision making. These large quantities of data are very useful and good for running the business operations but hardly amenable for use in making decisions about business strategies and objectives.

Why is this so? First, the data of an enterprise is spread across many types of incompatible structures and systems. Your order processing system might have been developed 25 years ago and is still running on an old mainframe. Possibly, some of the data may still be on VSAM files. Your later credit assignment and verification system might be on a client/server platform and the data for this application might be in relational tables. The data in a corporation resides in various disparate systems, multiple platforms, and diverse structures. The more technology your company has used in the past, the more disparate the data of your company will be. But, for proper decision making on overall corporate strategies and objectives, we need information integrated from all systems.

Data needed for strategic decision making must be in a format suitable for easy analysis to spot trends. Executives and managers need to look at trends over time and steer their companies in the proper direction. The tons of available operational data cannot be readily used to discern trends. Operational data is event-driven. You get snapshots of transactions that happen at specific times. You have data about units of sale of a single product in a specific order on a given date to a certain customer. In the operational systems, you do not readily have the trends of a single product over the period of a month, a quarter, or a year.

For strategic decision making, executives and managers must be able to review data from different business viewpoints. For example, they must be able to review and analyze sales quantities by product, salesperson, district, region, and customer groups. Can you think of operational data being readily available for such analysis? Operational data is not directly suitable for review from different viewpoints.

Technology Trends

Those of us who have worked in the information technology field for two or three decades have witnessed the breathtaking changes that have taken place. First, the name of the computer department in an enterprise went from "data processing" to "management information systems," then to "information systems," and more recently to "information technology." The entire spectrum of computing has undergone tremendous changes. The computing focus itself has changed over the years. Old practices could not meet new needs. Screens and preformatted reports are no longer adequate to meet user requirements.

Over the years, the price of MIPS (million instructions per second) is continuing to decline, digital storage is costing less and less, and network bandwidth is increasing as its price decreases. Specifically, we have seen explosive changes in these critical areas:

- Computing technology
- Human–machine interface
- Processing options

Figure 1-3 illustrates these waves of explosive growth.

What is our current position in the technology revolution? Hardware economics and miniaturization allow a workstation on every desk and provide increasing power at reducing costs. New software provides easy-to-use systems. Open systems architecture creates cooperation and enables the use of multivendor software. Improved connectivity, networking, and the Internet open up interaction with an enormous number of systems and databases.

All of these improvements in technology are meritorious. These have made computing faster, cheaper, and widely available. But what is their relevance to the escalating need for strategic information? Let us understand how the current state of the technology is conducive to providing strategic information.

Providing strategic information requires collection of large volumes of corporate data and storing it in suitable formats. Technology advances in data storage and reduction in storage costs readily accommodate data storage needs for strategic decision-support systems. Analysts, executives, and managers use strategic information interactively to analyze and spot business trends. The user will ask a question and get the results, then ask another question, look at the results, and ask yet another question. This interactive process continues. Tremendous advances in interface software make such interactive analysis possible.

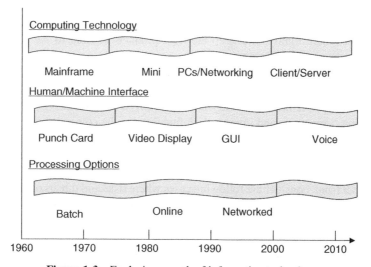

Figure 1-3   Explosive growth of information technology.

Processing large volumes of data and providing interactive analysis requires extra computing power. The explosive increase in computing power and its lower costs make provision of strategic information feasible. What we could not accomplish a few years earlier for providing strategic information is now possible with the current advanced stage of information technology.

Opportunities and Risks

We have looked at the information crisis that exists in every enterprise and grasped that in spite of lots of operational data in the enterprise, data suitable for strategic decision making is not available. Yet, the current state of the technology can make it possible to provide strategic information. While we are still discussing the escalating need for strategic information by companies, let us ask some basic questions. What are the opportunities available to companies resulting from the possible use of strategic information? What are the threats and risks resulting from the lack of strategic information available in companies?

Here are some examples of the opportunities made available to companies through the use of strategic information:

* A business unit of a leading long-distance telephone carrier empowers its sales personnel to make better business decisions and thereby capture more business in a highly competitive, multibillion-dollar market. A Web-accessible solution gathers internal and external data to provide strategic information.
* Availability of strategic information at one of the largest banks in the United States with assets in the $250 billion range allows users to make quick decisions to retain their valued customers.
* In the case of a large health management organization, significant improvements in health care programs are realized, resulting in a 22% decrease in emergency room visits, 29% decrease in hospital admissions for asthmatic children, potentially sight-saving screenings for hundreds of diabetics, improved vaccination rates, and more than 100,000 performance reports created annually for physicians and pharmacists.
* At one of the top five U.S. retailers, strategic information combined with Web-enabled analysis tools enables merchants to gain insights into their customer base, manage inventories more tightly, and keep the right products in front of the right people at the right place at the right time.
* A community-based pharmacy that competes on a national scale with more than 800 franchised pharmacies coast to coast gains in-depth understanding of what customers buy, resulting in reduced inventory levels, improved effectiveness of promotions and marketing campaigns, and improved profitability for the company.
* A large electronics company saves millions of dollars a year because of better management of inventory.

On the other hand, consider the following cases where risks and threats of failures existed before strategic information was made available for analysis and decision making:

* With an average fleet of about 150,000 vehicles, a nationwide car rental company can easily get into the red at the bottom line if fleet management is not effective. The fleet is the biggest cost in that business. With intensified competition, the potential for failure is immense if the fleet is not managed effectively. Car idle time must be kept to an

absolute minimum. In attempting to accomplish this, failure to have the right class of car available in the right place at the right time, all washed and ready, can lead to serious loss of business.

- For a world-leading supplier of systems and components to automobile and light truck equipment manufacturers, serious challenges faced included inconsistent data computations across nearly 100 plants, inability to benchmark quality metrics, and time-consuming manual collection of data. Reports needed to support decision making took weeks. It was never easy to get company-wide integrated information.

- For a large utility company that provided electricity to about 25 million consumers in five mid-Atlantic states in the United States, deregulation could result in a few winners and lots of losers. Remaining competitive and perhaps even just surviving depended on centralizing strategic information from various sources, streamlining data access, and facilitating analysis of the information by the business units.

FAILURES OF PAST DECISION-SUPPORT SYSTEMS

Assume a specific scenario. The marketing department in your company has been concerned about the performance of the West Coast region and the sales numbers from the monthly report this month are drastically low. The marketing vice president is agitated and wants to get some reports from the IT department to analyze the performance over the past two years, product by product, and compared to monthly targets. He wants to make quick strategic decisions to rectify the situation. The CIO wants your boss to deliver the reports as soon as possible. Your boss runs to you and asks you to stop everything and work on the reports. There are no regular reports from any system to give the marketing department what they want. You have to gather the data from multiple applications and start from scratch. Does this sound familiar?

At one time or another in your career in information technology, you must have been exposed to situations like this. Sometimes, you may be able to get the information required for such ad hoc reports from the databases or files of one application. Usually this is not so. You may have to go to several applications, perhaps running on different platforms in your company environment, to get the information. What happens next? The marketing department likes the ad hoc reports you have produced. But now they would like reports in a different format, containing more information that they did not think of originally. After the second round, they find that the contents of the reports are still not exactly what they wanted. They may also find inconsistencies among the data obtained from different applications.

The fact is that for nearly two decades or more, IT departments have been attempting to provide information to key personnel in their companies for making strategic decisions. Sometimes an IT department could produce ad hoc reports from a single application. In most cases, the reports would need data from multiple systems, requiring the writing of extract programs to create intermediary files that could be used to produce the ad hoc reports.

Most of these attempts by IT in the past ended in failure. The users could not clearly define what they wanted in the first place. Once they saw the first set of reports, they wanted more data in different formats. The chain continued. This was mainly because of the very nature of the process of making strategic decisions. Information needed for strategic decision making has to be available in an interactive manner. The user must be able to query online, get results, and query some more. The information must be in a format suitable for analysis.

In order to appreciate the reasons for the failure of IT to provide strategic information in the past, we need to consider how IT was attempting to do this all these years. Let us, therefore, quickly run through a brief history of decision support systems.

History of Decision-Support Systems

Depending on the size and nature of the business, most companies have gone through the following stages of attempts to provide strategic information for decision making.

Ad hoc Reports. This was the earliest stage. Users, especially from marketing and finance, would send requests to IT for special reports. IT would write special programs, typically one for each request, and produce the ad hoc reports.

Special Extract Programs. This stage was an attempt by IT to anticipate somewhat the types of reports that would be requested from time to time. IT would write a suite of programs and run the programs periodically to extract data from the various applications. IT would create and keep the extract files to fulfill any requests for special reports. For any reports that could not be run off the extracted files, IT would write individual special programs.

Small Applications. In this stage, IT formalized the extract process. IT would create simple applications based on the extracted files. The users could stipulate the parameters for each special report. The report printing programs would print the information based on user-specific parameters. Some advanced applications would also allow users to view information through online screens.

Information Centers. In the early 1970s, some major corporations created what were called information centers. The information center typically was a place where users could go to request ad hoc reports or view special information on screens. These were predetermined reports or screens. IT personnel were present at these information centers to help the users to obtain the desired information.

Decision-Support Systems. In this stage, companies began to build more sophisticated systems intended to provide some semblance of strategic information. Again, similar to the earlier attempts, these systems were supported by extracted files. The systems were menu-driven and provided online information and also the ability to print special reports. Many such decision-support systems were for marketing.

Executive Information Systems. This was an attempt to bring strategic information to the executive desktop. The main criteria were simplicity and ease of use. The system would display key information every day and provide the ability to request simple, straightforward reports. However, only preprogrammed screens and reports were available. After seeing the total countrywide sales, if the executive wanted to see the analysis by region, by product, or by another dimension, it was not possible unless such breakdowns were already preprogrammed. This limitation caused frustration and executive information systems did not last long in many companies.

Inability to Provide Information

Every one of the past attempts at providing strategic information to decision makers was unsatisfactory. Figure 1-4 depicts the inadequate attempts by IT to provide strategic information. As IT professionals, we are all familiar with the situation.

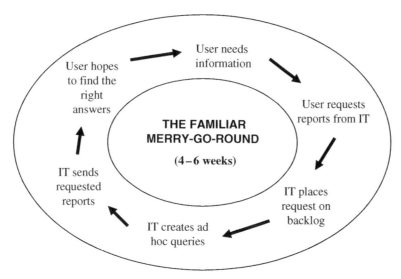

Figure 1-4   Inadequate attempts by IT to provide strategic information.

Here are some of the factors relating to the inability to provide strategic information:

- IT receives too many ad hoc requests, resulting in a large overload. With limited resources, IT is unable to respond to the numerous requests in a timely fashion.
- Requests are too numerous; they also keep changing all the time. The users need more reports to expand and understand the earlier reports.
- The users find that they get into the spiral of asking for more and more supplementary reports, so they sometimes adapt by asking for every possible combination, which only increases the IT load even further.
- The users have to depend on IT to provide the information. They are not able to access the information themselves interactively.
- The information environment ideally suited for strategic decision making has to be very flexible and conducive for analysis. IT has been unable to provide such an environment.

OPERATIONAL VERSUS DECISION-SUPPORT SYSTEMS

Is there an underlying reason for the failure of all the previous attempts by IT to provide strategic information? What has IT been doing all along? The fundamental reason for the inability to provide strategic information is that we have been trying all along to provide strategic information from the operational systems. These operational systems such as order processing, inventory control, claims processing, outpatient billing, and so on are not designed or intended to provide strategic information. If we need the ability to provide strategic information, we must get the information from altogether different types of systems. Only specially designed decision support systems or informational systems can provide strategic information. Let us understand why.

Get the data in

Making the wheels of business turn

◆ Take an order

◆ Process a claim

◆ Make a shipment

◆ Generate an invoice

◆ Receive cash

◆ Reserve an airline seat

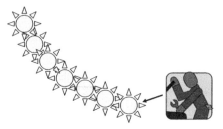

Figure 1-5   Operational systems.

Making the Wheels of Business Turn

Operational systems are online transaction processing (OLTP) systems. These are the systems that are used to run the day-to-day core business of the company. They are the so-called bread-and-butter systems. Operational systems make the wheels of business turn (see Fig. 1-5). They support the basic business processes of the company. These systems typically get the data into the database. Each transaction processes information about a single entity such as a single order, a single invoice, or a single customer.

Watching the Wheels of Business Turn

On the other hand, specially designed and built decision-support systems are not meant to run the core business processes. They are used to watch how the business runs, and then make strategic decisions to improve the business (see Fig. 1-6).

Decision-support systems are developed to get strategic information *out of* the database, as opposed to OLTP systems that are designed to put the data *into* the database. Decision-support systems are developed to provide strategic information.

Different Scope, Different Purposes

Therefore, we find that in order to provide strategic information we need to build informational systems that are different from the operational systems we have been building to run the basic business. It will be worthless to continue to dip into the operational systems for

Get the information out

Watching the wheels of business turn

◆ Show me the top-selling products

◆ Show me the problem regions

◆ Tell me why (drill down)

◆ Let me see other data (drill across)

◆ Show the highest margins

◆ Alert me when a district sells below target

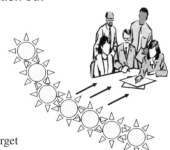

Figure 1-6   Decision-support systems.

How are they different?

	OPERATIONAL	INFORMATIONAL
Data Content	Current values	Archived, derived, summarized
Data Structure	Optimized for transactions	Optimized for complex queries
Access Frequency	High	Medium to low
Access Type	Read, update, delete	Read
Usage	Predictable, repetitive	Ad hoc, random, heuristic
Response Time	Sub-seconds	Several seconds to minutes
Users	Large number	Relatively small number

Figure 1-7   Operational and informational systems.

strategic information as we have been doing in the past. As companies face fiercer competition and businesses become more complex, continuing the past practices will only lead to disaster.

We need to design and build informational systems

- That serve different purposes
- Whose scopes are different
- Whose data content is different
- Where the data usage patterns are different
- Where the data access types are different

Figure 1-7 summarizes the differences between the traditional operational systems and the newer informational systems that need to be built.

DATA WAREHOUSING—THE ONLY VIABLE SOLUTION

At this stage of our discussion, we now realize that we do need different types of decision-support systems to provide strategic information. The type of information needed for strategic decision making is different from that available from operational systems. We need a new type of system environment for the purpose of providing strategic information for analysis, discerning trends, and monitoring performance.

Let us examine the desirable features and processing requirements of this new type of system environment. Let us also consider the advantages of this type of system environment designed for strategic information.

A New Type of System Environment

The desired features of the new type of system environment are:

- Database designed for analytical tasks
- Data from multiple applications
- Easy to use and conducive to long interactive sessions by users

- Read-intensive data usage
- Direct interaction with the system by the users without IT assistance
- Content updated periodically and stable
- Content to include current and historical data
- Ability for users to run queries and get results online
- Ability for users to initiate reports

Processing Requirements in the New Environment

Most of the processing in the new environment for strategic information will have to be analytical. There are at least four levels of analytical processing requirements:

1. Running of simple queries and reports against current and historical data.
2. Ability to perform "what if" analysis in many different ways.
3. Ability to query, step back, analyze, and then continue the process to any desired length.
4. Ability to spot historical trends and apply them in future interactive processes.

Strategic Information from the Data Warehouse

This new system environment that users desperately need to obtain strategic information happens to be the new paradigm of data warehousing. Beginning with the late 1980s and into the 1990s enterprises began building such system environments. This new environment, known as the data warehouse environment, is kept separate from the system environment that supports the routine day-to-day operations. The data warehouse essentially has become the source of strategic information for the enterprise to enable strategic decision making. The data warehouse has proved to be the only viable solution. We have clearly seen that solutions based on the data extracted from operational systems have all been totally unsatisfactory. Figure 1-8 shows the general overview of the data warehouse as the source of strategic information for the enterprise.

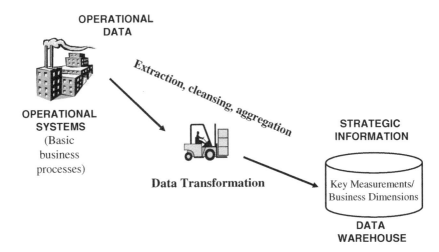

Figure 1-8   General overview of the data warehouse.

At a high level of interpretation, the data warehouse contains critical metrics of the business processes stored along business dimensions. For example, a data warehouse might contain units of sales, by product, day, customer group, sales district, sales region, and promotion. Here the business dimensions are product, day, customer group, sales district, sales region, and sales promotion type. Unit sales represent the metrics being measured across products, days, customer groups, sales districts, sales regions, and sales promotion types.

From where does the data warehouse get its data? The data is derived from the operational systems that support the basic business processes of the organization. In between the operational systems and the data warehouse, there is a data staging area. In this staging area, the operational data is cleansed and transformed into a form suitable for placement in the data warehouse for easy retrieval.

DATA WAREHOUSE DEFINED

We have reached the strong conclusion that data warehousing is the only viable solution for providing strategic information. We arrived at this conclusion based on the functions of the new system environment called the data warehouse. So, let us try to come up with a functional definition of the data warehouse.

The data warehouse is an informational environment that:

- Provides an integrated and total view of the enterprise.
- Makes the enterprise's current and historical information easily available for strategic decision making.
- Makes decision-support transactions possible without hindering operational systems.
- Renders the organization's information consistent.
- Presents a flexible and interactive source of strategic information.

A Simple Concept for Information Delivery

In the final analysis, data warehousing is a simple concept. It is born out of the need for strategic information and is the result of the search for a new way to provide such information. The methods of the previous decades using the operational computing environment were unsatisfactory. The new concept is not to generate fresh data, but to make use of the large volumes of existing data and to transform it into forms suitable for providing strategic information.

The data warehouse exists to answer questions users have about the business, the performance of the various operations, the business trends, and about what can be done to improve the business. The data warehouse exists to provide business users with direct access to data, to provide a single unified version of the key performance indicators, to record the past accurately, and to provide the ability for viewing the data from many different perspectives. In short, the data warehouse is there to support decisional processes.

Data warehousing is really a simple concept: Take all the data you already have in the organization, clean and transform it, and then provide useful strategic information. What could be simpler than that?

An Environment, Not a Product

A data warehouse is not a single software or hardware product you purchase to provide strategic information. It is, rather, a computing environment where users can find strategic information, an environment where users are put directly in touch with the data they need to make better decisions. It is a user-centric environment.

Let us summarize the characteristics of this new computing environment called the data warehouse:

* An ideal environment for data analysis and decision support
* Fluid, flexible, and interactive
* 100% user-driven
* Very responsive and conducive to the ask–answer–ask again pattern
* Provides the ability to discover answers to complex, unpredictable questions

A Blend of Many Technologies

Let us reexamine the basic concept of data warehousing. The basic concept of data warehousing is:

* Take all the data from the operational systems.
* Where necessary, include relevant data from outside, such as industry benchmark indicators.
* Integrate all the data from the various sources.
* Remove inconsistencies and transform the data.
* Store the data in formats suitable for easy access for decision making.

Different technologies are, therefore, needed to support these functions. Figure 1-9 shows how a data warehouse is a blend of the many technologies needed for the various functions.

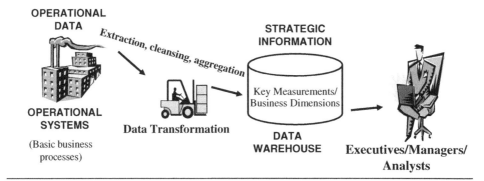

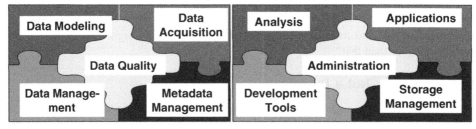

Figure 1-9   The data warehouse: a blend of technologies.

Although many technologies are in use, they all work together in a data warehouse. The end result is the creation of a new computing environment for the purpose of providing the strategic information every enterprise needs desperately.

THE DATA WAREHOUSING MOVEMENT

As enterprises began to realize the effectiveness of data warehousing, more and more organizations jumped on the bandwagon and data warehousing began to spread at a rapid rate. First the large companies that were able to quickly afford the outlay of resources began to launch data warehousing projects. Medium-sized companies also entered the data warehousing arena. Soon several businesses began to reap the benefits provided by data warehousing. Much research began to be focused on this new phenomenon. Many vendors began to offer hardware and software products to support the different functions within the data warehouse.

Prior to the data warehousing concept with an architectural model for the movement of data from operational systems to decision support environments, companies attempted multiple decision-support environments within their organizations. This had to be done with enormous costs fraught with large amounts of data redundancies and inconsistencies. Each decision-support environment was intended to serve specific groups of users for limited purposes. The adoption of data warehousing changed all of this. Similar to industrial warehouses, data warehouses are intended for large-scale collection and storage of corporate data to provide strategic information for the overall needs. Just as products stored in industrial warehouses are distributed to retail stores or marts, data stored in data warehouses may be channeled to data marts for specific users.

Data Warehousing Milestones

As data warehousing gained acceptance during the 1980s and 1990s, we may trace some of the highlights of the movement. Listed below are the significant milestones during the initial phase of the movement:

- 1983—Teradata introduces a database management system (DBMS) designed for decision-support systems.
- 1988—The article *An Architecture for a Business and Information Systems* introducing the term "business data warehouse" is published by Barry Devlin and Paul Murphy in the *IBM Systems Journal*.
- 1990—Red Brick Systems introduces Red Brick Warehouse, a DBMS specifically for data warehousing.
- 1991—Bill Inmon publishes his book *Building the Data Warehouse* (he is generally considered the father of data warehousing).
- 1991—Prism Solutions introduces Prism Warehouse Manager software for developing a data warehouse.
- 1995—The Data Warehousing Institute, a premier institution that promotes data warehousing is founded. (This institution has since emerged as the leading voice in the data warehousing and business intelligence arena providing education, research, and support.)

- 1996—Ralph Kimball publishes a seminal book *The Data Warehousing Toolkit*. (He is among the top authorities in the field of data warehousing and decision support systems.)
- 1997—Oracle 8, with support for STAR schema queries, is released.

Initial Challenges

As the adoption of data warehousing by organizations continued, even those companies that implemented data warehouses faced significant challenges that promoted a moderate shift from the original implementations. Here is a list of the key challenges that had to be overcome:

- Customers had become more sophisticated and savvy, pressing for greater service, improved quality, and innovative customization.
- Government deregulation of industries exposed companies to fiercer competition and the need for leaner operation.
- Expansion of globalization opened the arena for competitors, more in number and greater in power.
- New privacy regulations created the need to revise methods of collection and use of information.
- Improper architecture of some initial data warehousing systems produced fragmented views of corporate data and tended to produce disparate information silos.
- Query, reporting, and analysis tools provided to the users in the early data warehousing environments for self-service proved to be too complex and overwhelming for use by the users themselves.
- The promises of early data warehouse environments to provide user-friendly tools for the masses remained unfulfilled.

EVOLUTION OF BUSINESS INTELLIGENCE

The initial challenges following the adoption of early data warehousing systems forced companies to take a second look at providing decision support. Companies began to perceive that the goal of decision-support systems is twofold: transformation of data to information; derivation of knowledge from information. Each of these two aspects needs to be emphasized and strengthened appropriately to provide the necessary results. Business intelligence for an organization requires two environments, one to concentrate on transformation of data into information and the other to deal with transformation of information into knowledge.

Business intelligence (BI), therefore, is a broad group of applications and technologies. First, the term refers to the systems and technologies for gathering, cleansing, consolidating, and storing corporate data. Next, business intelligence relates to the tools, techniques, and applications for analyzing the stored data. The Gartner Group popularized BI as an umbrella term to include concepts and methods to improve business decision making by fact-based support systems. The Data Warehousing Institute compares BI to a data refinery. Similar to an oil refinery, a BI setting takes data as the raw material, collects it, refines it, and processes it into several information products.

BI: Two Environments

When you consider all that BI encompasses, you may view BI for an enterprise as composed of two environments:

Data to Information. In this environment data from multiple operational systems are extracted, integrated, cleansed, transformed and stored as information in specially designed repositories.

Information to Knowledge. In this environment analytical tools are made available to users to access and analyze the information content in the specially designed repositories and turn information into knowledge.

BI: Data Warehousing and Analytics

As some of the early challenges indicated, sufficient and separate attention needs to be given to the two environments that BI encompasses. In today's businesses, extraction, consolidation, transformation, and storing of data as strategic information is a formidable task. Again, using this information with sophisticated tools for proper decision making is equally challenging. Therefore, the trend is to consider these as two distinct environments for corporate BI. Vendors also tend to specialize in tools appropriate for these two distinct environments.

However, the two environments are complementary and need to work together. Figure 1-10 shows the two complementary environments, the data warehousing environment, which transforms data into information, and the analytical environment, which produces knowledge from information. As we proceed from chapter to chapter, we will keep expanding and intensifying our discussion of these two environments.

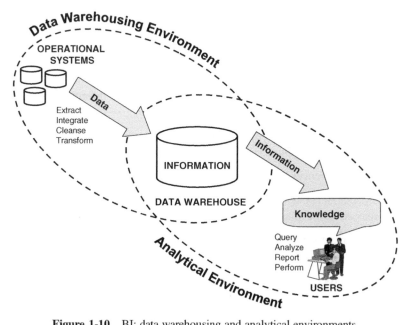

Figure 1-10   BI: data warehousing and analytical environments.

CHAPTER SUMMARY

- Companies are desperate for strategic information to counter fiercer competition, extend market share, and improve profitability.
- In spite of tons of data accumulated by enterprises over the past decades, every enterprise is caught in the middle of an information crisis. Information needed for strategic decision making is not readily available.
- All the past attempts by IT to provide strategic information have been failures. This was mainly because IT has been trying to provide strategic information from operational systems.
- Informational systems are different from the traditional operational systems. Operational systems are not designed for strategic information.
- We need a new type of computing environment to provide strategic information. The data warehouse promises to be this new computing environment.
- Data warehousing is the viable solution. There is a compelling need for data warehousing in every enterprise.
- The challenges faced in early data warehouse implementations led the movement towards maturity.
- The notion of business intelligence for an enterprise has evolved as an umbrella concept embracing data warehousing and analytics to transform data into information and information into knowledge.

REVIEW QUESTIONS

1. What do we mean by strategic information? For a commercial bank, name five types of strategic objectives.

2. Do you agree that a typical retail store collects huge volumes of data through its operational systems? Name three types of transaction data likely to be collected by a retail store in large volumes during its daily operations.

3. Examine the opportunities that can be provided by strategic information for a medical center. Can you list five such opportunities?

4. Why were all the past attempts by IT to provide strategic information failures? List three concrete reasons and explain.

5. Describe five differences between operational systems and informational systems.

6. Why are operational systems not suitable for providing strategic information? Give three specific reasons and explain.

7. Name six characteristics of the computing environment needed to provide strategic information.

8. What types of processing take place in a data warehouse? Describe.

9. A data warehouse is an environment, not a product. Discuss.

10. Data warehousing is the only viable means to resolve the information crisis and to provide strategic information. List four reasons to support this assertion and explain them.

EXERCISES

1. Match the columns:

1. information crisis	**A.** OLTP applications
2. strategic information	**B.** produce ad hoc reports
3. operational systems	**C.** explosive growth
4. information center	**D.** despite lots of data
5. data warehouse	**E.** data cleaned and transformed
6. order processing	**F.** users go to get information
7. executive information	**G.** used for decision making
8. data staging area	**H.** environment, not product
9. extract programs	**I.** for day-to-day operations
10. information technology	**J.** simple, easy to use

2. The current trends in hardware/software technology make data warehousing feasible. Explain with some examples how exactly technology trends do help.

3. You are the IT director of a nationwide insurance company. Write a memo to the executive vice president explaining the types of opportunities that can be realized with readily available strategic information.

4. For an airline company, how can strategic information increase the number of frequent flyers? Discuss giving specific details.

5. You are a senior analyst in the IT department of a company manufacturing automobile parts. The marketing VP is complaining about the poor response by IT in providing strategic information. Draft a proposal to him introducing the concept of business intelligence and how data warehousing and analytics as part of business intelligence for your company would be the optimal solution.

CHAPTER 2

DATA WAREHOUSE: THE BUILDING BLOCKS

CHAPTER OBJECTIVES

- Review formal definitions of a data warehouse
- Discuss the defining features
- Distinguish between data warehouses and data marts
- Review the evolved architectural types
- Study each component or building block that makes up a data warehouse
- Introduce metadata and highlight its significance

As we have seen in the last chapter, data warehousing has evolved as part of business intelligence for the enterprise. In the data warehouse you integrate and transform enterprise data into information suitable for strategic decision making. You take all the historic data from the various operational systems, combine this internal data with any relevant data from outside sources, and pull them together. You resolve any conflicts in the way data resides in different systems and transform the integrated data content into a format suitable for providing information to the various classes of users. Finally, you supplement with information delivery methods.

In order to set up this information delivery system, you need different components or building blocks. These building blocks are arranged together in the most optimal way to serve the intended purpose. They are arranged in a suitable architecture. Before we get into the individual components and their arrangement in the overall architecture, let us first look at some fundamental features of the data warehouse.

Bill Inmon (1996, p. 33), considered to be the father of data warehousing as noted in the previous chapter, provides the following definition: "A Data Warehouse is a subject oriented, integrated, nonvolatile, and time variant collection of data in support of management's decisions."

Data Warehousing Fundamentals for IT Professionals, Second Edition. By Paulraj Ponniah
Copyright © 2010 John Wiley & Sons, Inc.

Sean Kelly, another leading data warehousing practitioner, defines the data warehouse in the following way. The data in the data warehouse is:

Separate
Available
Integrated
Time stamped
Subject oriented
Nonvolatile
Accessible

DEFINING FEATURES

Let us examine some of the key defining features of the data warehouse based on these definitions. What about the nature of the data in the data warehouse? How is this data different from the data in any operational system? Why does it have to be different? How is the data content in the data warehouse used?

Subject-Oriented Data

In operational systems, we store data by individual applications. In the data sets for an order processing application, we keep the data for that particular application. These data sets provide the data for all the functions for entering orders, checking stock, verifying customer's credit, and assigning the order for shipment. But these data sets contain only the data that is needed for those functions relating to this particular application. We will have some data sets containing data about individual orders, customers, stock status, and detailed transactions, but all of these are structured around the processing of orders.

Similarly, for a banking institution, data sets for a consumer loans application contain data for that particular application. Data sets for other distinct applications for checking accounts and savings accounts relate to those specific applications. Again, in an insurance company, different data sets support individual applications such as automobile insurance, life insurance, and workers' compensation insurance.

In every industry, data sets are organized around individual applications to support those particular operational systems. These individual data sets have to provide data for the specific applications to perform the specific functions efficiently. Therefore, the data sets for each application need to be organized around that specific application.

In striking contrast, in the data warehouse, data is stored by real-world business subjects or events, not by applications. The data in a data warehouse is organized in such a way that all the data sets relating to the same real-world business subject or event is tied together. We have said that data is linked and stored by business subjects. Well, what are business subjects? Business subjects differ from enterprise to enterprise. These are the subjects critical for the enterprise. For a manufacturing company, sales, shipments, and inventory are critical business subjects. For a retail store, sales at the check-out counter would be a critical business subject.

Figure 2-1 distinguishes between how data is stored in operational systems and in the data warehouse. In the operational systems shown, data for each application is organized separately by application: order processing, consumer loans, customer billing, accounts

In the data warehouse, data is not stored by operational applications, but by business subjects.

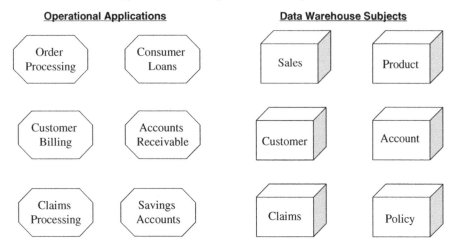

Figure 2-1   The data warehouse is subject oriented.

receivable, claims processing, and savings accounts. For example, *claims* is a critical business subject for an insurance company. Claims under automobile insurance policies are processed in the auto insurance application. Claims data for automobile insurance is organized in that application. Similarly, claims data for workers' compensation insurance is organized in the workers' comp insurance application. But in the data warehouse for an insurance company, data about *claims* is organized around the subject of *claims* and not by *individual* applications of auto insurance and workers' comp.

In a data warehouse, there is no application flavor. The data in a data warehouse cuts across applications.

Integrated Data

For proper decision making, you need to pull together all the relevant data from the various applications. The data in the data warehouse comes from several operational systems. Source data reside in different databases, files, and data segments. These are disparate applications, so the operational platforms and operating systems could be different. The file layouts, character code representations, and field naming conventions all could be different.

In addition to data from internal operational systems, for many enterprises, data from outside sources is likely to be very important. Companies such as Metro Mail, A. C. Nielsen, and IRI specialize in providing vital data on a regular basis. Your data warehouse may need data from such sources. This is one more variation in the mix of source data for a data warehouse.

Figure 2-2 illustrates a simple process of data integration for a banking institution. Here the data fed into the subject area of *account* in the data warehouse comes from three different operational applications. Even within just three applications, there could be several variations. Naming conventions could be different; attributes for data items could be different. The account number in the savings account application could be eight bytes long, but only six bytes in the checking account application.

Before the data from various disparate sources can be usefully stored in a data warehouse, you have to remove the inconsistencies. You have to standardize the various data elements

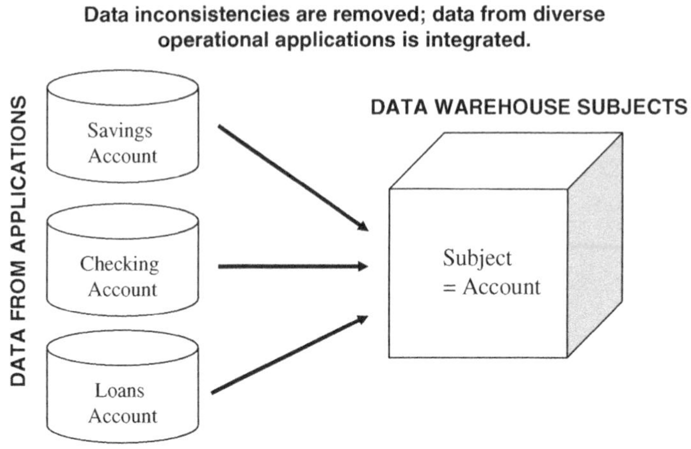

Data inconsistencies are removed; data from diverse operational applications is integrated.

Figure 2-2   The data warehouse is integrated.

and make sure of the meanings of data names in each source application. Before moving the data into the data warehouse, you have to go through a process of transformation, consolidation, and integration of the source data.

Here are some of the items that would need to standardized and made consistent:

- Naming conventions
- Codes
- Data attributes
- Measurements

Time-Variant Data

For an operational system, the stored data contains the *current* values. In an accounts receivable system, the balance is the current outstanding balance in the customer's account. In an order entry system, the status of an order is the current status of the order. In a consumer loans application, the balance amount owed by the customer is the current amount. Of course, we store some past transactions in operational systems, but, essentially, operational systems reflect current information because these systems support day-to-day current operations.

On the other hand, the data in the data warehouse is meant for analysis and decision making. If a user is looking at the buying pattern of a specific customer, the user needs data not only about the current purchase, but on the past purchases as well. When a user wants to find out the reason for the drop in sales in the North East division, the user needs all the sales data for that division over a period extending back in time. When an analyst in a grocery chain wants to promote two or more products together, that analyst wants sales of the selected products over a number of past quarters.

A data warehouse, because of the very nature of its purpose, has to contain historical data, not just current values. Data is stored as snapshots over past and current periods. Changes to data are tracked and recorded so that, if necessary, reports can be produced to show changes over time. Every data structure in the data warehouse contains the time element. You will find historical snapshots of the operational data in the data warehouse. This aspect of the data warehouse is quite significant for both the design and the implementation phases.

For example, in a data warehouse containing units of sale, the quantity stored in each file record or table row relates to a specific time element. Depending on the level of the details in the data warehouse, the sales quantity in a record may relate to a specific date, week, month, or quarter.

The time-variant nature of the data in a data warehouse

- Allows for analysis of the past
- Relates information to the present
- Enables forecasts for the future

Nonvolatile Data

Data extracted from the various operational systems and pertinent data obtained from outside sources are transformed, integrated, and stored in the data warehouse. The data in the data warehouse is not intended for running of the day-to-day business. When you want to process the next order received from a customer, you do not look into the data warehouse to find the current stock status. The operational order entry application is meant for that purpose. In the data warehouse, you keep the extracted stock status data as snapshots over time. You do not update the data warehouse every time you process a single order.

Data from the operational systems are moved into the data warehouse at specific intervals. Depending on the requirements of the business, these data movements take place twice a day, once a day, once a week, or maybe once in two weeks. In fact, in a typical data warehouse, data movements to different data sets may take place at different frequencies. The changes to the attributes of the products may be moved once a week. Any revisions to geographical setup may be moved once a month. The units of sales may be moved once a day. You plan and schedule the data movements or data loads based on the requirements of your users.

As illustrated in Fig. 2-3, every business transaction does not update the data in the data warehouse. The business transactions update the operational system databases in real time. We add, change, or delete data from an operational system as each transaction happens but do not usually update the data in the data warehouse. You do not delete the data in the data

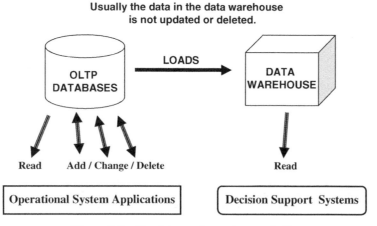

Figure 2-3   The data warehouse is nonvolatile.

warehouse in real time. Once the data is captured and committed in the data warehouse, you do not run individual transactions to change the data there. Data updates are commonplace in an operational database; not so in a data warehouse. The data in a data warehouse is not as volatile as the data in an operational database is. The data in a data warehouse is primarily for query and analysis.

Data Granularity

In an operational system, data is usually kept at the lowest level of detail. In a point-of-sale system for a grocery store, the units of sale are captured and stored at the level of units of a product per transaction at the check-out counter. In an order entry system, the quantity ordered is captured and stored at the level of units of a product per order received from the customer. Whenever you need summary data, you add up the individual transactions. If you are looking for units of a product ordered this month, you read all the orders entered for the entire month for that product and add up. You do not usually keep summary data in an operational system.

When a user queries the data warehouse for analysis, he or she usually starts by looking at summary data. The user may start with total sale units of a product in an entire region. Then the user may want to look at the breakdown by states in the region. The next step may be the examination of sale units by the next level of individual stores. Frequently, the analysis begins at a high level and moves down to lower levels of detail.

In a data warehouse, therefore, you find it efficient to keep data summarized at different levels. Depending on the query, you can then go to the particular level of detail and satisfy the query. Data granularity in a data warehouse refers to the level of detail. The lower the level of detail, the finer is the data granularity. Of course, if you want to keep data in the lowest level of detail, you have to store a lot of data in the data warehouse. You will have to decide on the granularity levels based on the data types and the expected system performance for queries. Figure 2-4 shows examples of data granularity in a typical data warehouse.

THREE DATA LEVELS IN A BANKING DATA WAREHOUSE

Daily Detail	Monthly Summary	Quarterly Summary
Account	Account	Account
Activity Date	Month	Quarter
Amount	Number of transactions	Number of transactions
Deposit/Withdrawal	Withdrawals	Withdrawals
	Deposits	Deposits
	Beginning Balance	Beginning Balance
	Ending Balance	Ending Balance

Data granularity refers to the level of detail. Depending on the requirements, multiple levels of detail may be present. Many data warehouses have at least dual levels of granularity.

Figure 2-4   Data granularity.

DATA WAREHOUSES AND DATA MARTS

Those who had been following the literature on data warehouses in the early years of the subject no doubt came across the terms "data warehouse" and "data mart." Many who were new to this paradigm were confused about these terms. Some authors and vendors used the two terms synonymously. Some made distinctions that were not clear enough. At this point, it would be worthwhile for us to examine these two terms and take our position.

Writing in a leading trade magazine in 1998, the early days of data warehousing, Bill Inmon stated, "The single most important issue facing the IT manager this year is whether to build the data warehouse first or the data mart first." This statement is somewhat true even today. Let us examine this statement and tackle the definitions.

Before deciding to build a data warehouse for your organization, you need to ask the following basic and fundamental questions and address the relevant issues:

- Top-down or bottom-up approach?
- Enterprise-wide or departmental?
- Which first—data warehouse or data mart?
- Build pilot or go with a full-fledged implementation?
- Dependent or independent data marts?

These are critical issues requiring careful examination and planning.

Should you look at the big picture of your organization, take a top-down approach, and build a mammoth data warehouse? Or, should you adopt a bottom-up approach, look at the individual local and departmental requirements, and build bite-size departmental data marts?

Should you build a large data warehouse and then let that repository feed data into local, departmental data marts? On the other hand, should you build individual local data marts, and combine them to form your overall data warehouse? Should these local data marts be independent of one another? Or should they be dependent on the overall data warehouse for data feed? Should you build a pilot data mart? These are crucial questions.

How Are They Different?

Let us take a close look at Fig. 2-5. Here are the two different basic approaches: (1) overall data warehouse feeding dependent data marts, and (2) several departmental or local data marts combining into a data warehouse. In the first approach, you extract data from the operational systems; you then transform, clean, integrate, and keep the data in the data warehouse. So, which approach is best in your case, the top-down or the bottom-up approach? Let us examine these two approaches carefully.

Top-Down Versus Bottom-Up Approach

Top-Down Approach   Bill Inmon is one of the leading proponents of the top-down approach. He has defined a data warehouse as a centralized repository for the entire enterprise. In this approach the data in the data warehouse is stored at the lowest level of granularity based on a normalized data model. In the Inmon vision the data warehouse is at the center of the "Corporate Information Factory" (CIF) providing the logical framework for delivering business intelligence to the enterprise. Business operations provide data to

DATA WAREHOUSE	DATA MART
◆ Corporate/Enterprise-wide	◆ Departmental
◆ Union of all data marts	◆ A single business process
◆ Data received from staging area	◆ STARjoin (facts & dimensions)
◆ Queries on presentation resource	◆ Technology optimal for data
◆ Structure for corporate view of	access and analysis
data	◆ Structure to suit the
◆ Organized on E-R model	departmental view of data

Figure 2-5   Data warehouse versus data mart.

drive the CIF. The centralized data warehouse would feed the dependent data marts that may be designed based on a dimensional data model.
The advantages of this approach are:

- A truly corporate effort, an enterprise view of data
- Inherently architected, not a union of disparate data marts
- Single, central storage of data about the content
- Centralized rules and control
- May see quick results if implemented with iterations

The disadvantages are:

- Takes longer to build even with an iterative method
- High exposure to risk of failure
- Needs high level of cross-functional skills
- High outlay without proof of concept

This is the big-picture approach in which you build the overall, big, enterprise-wide data warehouse. Here you do not have a collection of fragmented islands of information. The data warehouse is large and integrated. This approach, however, would take longer to build and has a high risk of failure. If you do not have experienced professionals on your team, this approach could be hazardous. Also, it will be difficult to sell this approach to senior management and sponsors. They are not likely to see results soon enough.

Bottom-Up Approach   Ralph Kimball, another leading author and expert practitioner in data warehousing, is a proponent of the approach that has come to be known as the bottom-up approach. Kimball (1996) envisions the corporate data warehouse as a collection of conformed data marts. The key consideration is the conforming of the dimensions among the separate data marts. In this approach data marts are created first to provide analytical and reporting capabilities for specific business subjects based on the dimensional data model.

Data marts contain data at the lowest level of granularity and also as summaries depending on the needs for analysis. These data marts are joined or "unioned" together by conforming the dimensions. We will discuss this process of conforming the dimensions in great detail in subsequent chapters.

The advantages of this approach are:

- Faster and easier implementation of manageable pieces
- Favorable return on investment and proof of concept
- Less risk of failure
- Inherently incremental; can schedule important data marts first
- Allows project team to learn and grow

The disadvantages are:

- Each data mart has its own narrow view of data
- Permeates redundant data in every data mart
- Perpetuates inconsistent and irreconcilable data
- Proliferates unmanageable interfaces

In this bottom-up approach, you build your departmental data marts one by one. You would set a priority scheme to determine which data marts you must build first. The most severe drawback of this approach is data fragmentation. Each independent data mart will be blind to the overall requirements of the entire organization.

A Practical Approach

In order to formulate an approach for your organization, you need to examine what exactly your organization wants. Is your organization looking for long-term results or fast data marts for only a few subjects for now? Does your organization want quick, proof-of-concept, throw-away implementations? Or, do you want to look into some other practical approach?

Although the top-down and the bottom-up approaches each have their own advantages and drawbacks, a compromise approach accommodating both views appears to be practical. In this approach we do not lose sight of the overall big picture for the entire enterprise. We base our planning on this overall big picture. This aspect is from the top-down approach. Then we adopt the principles of the bottom-up approach and build the conformed data marts based on a priority scheme. The steps in this practical approach are as follows:

1. Plan and define requirements at the overall corporate level
2. Create a surrounding architecture for a complete warehouse
3. Conform and standardize the data content
4. Implement the data warehouse as a series of supermarts, one at a time

In this practical approach, you go to the basics and determine what exactly your organization wants in the long term. The key to this approach is that you first plan at the enterprise level. You gather requirements at the overall level. You establish the architecture for the complete warehouse. Then you determine the data content for each supermart. Supermarts are carefully architected data marts. You implement these supermarts, one at a time. Before implementation, you make sure that the data content among the various supermarts are conformed in terms of data types, field lengths, precision, and semantics. A certain data element must mean the same thing in every supermart. This will avoid spread of disparate data across several data marts.

A data mart, in this practical approach, is a logical subset of the complete data warehouse, a sort of pie-wedge of the whole data warehouse. A data warehouse, therefore, is a conformed union of all data marts. Individual data marts are targeted to particular business groups in the enterprise, but the collection of all the data marts form an integrated whole, called the enterprise data warehouse.

When we refer to data warehouses and data marts in our discussions here, we use the meanings as understood in this practical approach. For us, a data warehouse means a collection of the constituent data marts.

ARCHITECTURAL TYPES

We have now reviewed the basic definitions and features of data warehouses and data marts and completed a significant discussion of them. We have established our position on what the terms data warehouse and data mart mean to us. Now we are almost ready to examine the individual components.

Over the years, in practice, several arrangements of data warehouses and data marts have evolved based on the individual requirements of organizations. Before we proceed to study the individual components within a data warehouse, let us briefly discuss the leading architectural types and note how individual data marts feature in these architectural types. For each of these architectural types we will indicate how data is stored in the data warehouse and the relationships between the data warehouse and the data marts. Figure 2-6 illustrates each of these architectural types.

Centralized Data Warehouse

This architectural type takes into account the enterprise-level information requirements. An overall infrastructure is established. Atomic level normalized data at the lowest level of granularity is stored in the third normal form. Occasionally, some summarized data is included. Queries and applications access the normalized data in the central data warehouse. There are no separate data marts.

Independent Data Marts

This architectural type evolves in companies where the organizational units develop their own data marts for their own specific purposes. Although each data mart serves the particular organizational unit, these separate data marts do not provide "a single version of the truth." The data marts are independent of one another. As a result, these different data marts are likely to have inconsistent data definitions and standards. Such variances hinder analysis of data across data marts. For example, if there are two independent data marts, one for sales and the other for shipments, although sales and shipments are related subjects, the independent data marts would make it difficult to analyze sales and shipments data together.

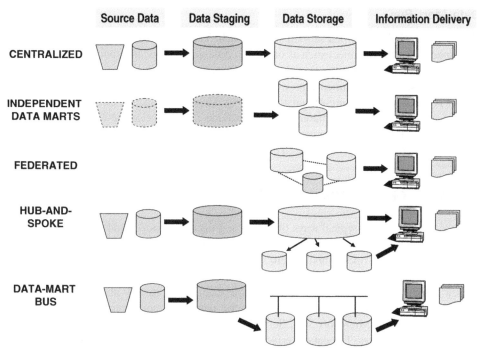

Figure 2-6 Data warehouse architectural types.

Federated

Some companies get into data warehousing with an existing legacy of an assortment of decision-support structures in the form of operational systems, extracted datasets, primitive data marts, and so on. For such companies, it may not be prudent to discard all that huge investment and start from scratch. The practical solution is a federated architectural type where data may be physically or logically integrated through shared key fields, overall global metadata, distributed queries, and such other methods. In this architectural type, there is no one overall data warehouse.

Hub-and-Spoke

This is the Inmon Corporate Information Factory approach. Similar to the centralized data warehouse architecture, here too is an overall enterprise-wide data warehouse. Atomic data in the third normal form is stored in the centralized data warehouse. The major and useful difference is the presence of dependent data marts in this architectural type. Dependent data marts obtain data from the centralized data warehouse. The centralized data warehouse forms the hub to feed data to the data marts on the spokes. The dependent data marts may be developed for a variety of purposes: departmental analytical needs, specialized queries, data mining, and so on. Each dependent dart mart may have normalized, denormalized, summarized, or dimensional data structures based on individual requirements. Most queries are directed to the dependent data marts although the centralized data warehouse may itself be used for querying. This architectural type results from adopting a top-down approach to data warehouse development.

Data-Mart Bus

This is the Kimbal conformed supermarts approach. You begin with analyzing requirements for a specific business subject such as orders, shipments, billings, insurance claims, car rentals, and so on. You build the first data mart (supermart) using business dimensions and metrics. These business dimensions will be shared in the future data marts. The principal notion is that by conforming dimensions among the various data marts, the result would be logically integrated supermarts that will provide an enterprise view of the data. The data marts contain atomic data organized as a dimensional data model. This architectural type results from adopting an enhanced bottom-up approach to data warehouse development.

OVERVIEW OF THE COMPONENTS

Having reviewed a few typical ways of organizing data warehouses and data marts, we are now ready to launch a general discussion of the components of the data warehouse.

When we build an operational system such as order entry, claims processing, or savings account, we put together several components to make up the system. The front-end component consists of the GUI (graphical user interface) to interface with the users for data input. The data storage component includes the database management system, such as Oracle, Informix, or Microsoft SQL Server. The display component is the set of screens and reports for the users. The data interfaces and the network software form the connectivity component. Depending on the information requirements and the framework of our organization, we arrange these components in the most optimum way.

Architecture is the proper arrangement of the components. You build a data warehouse with software and hardware components. To suit the requirements of your organization you arrange these building blocks in a certain way for maximum benefit. You may want to lay special emphasis on one component; you may want to bolster up another component with extra tools and services. All of this depends on your circumstances.

Figure 2-7 shows the basic components of a typical warehouse. You see the *Source Data* component shown on the left. The *Data Staging* component serves as the next building block. In the middle, you see the *Data Storage* component that manages the data warehouse data. This component not only stores and manages the data, it also keeps track of the data by means of the metadata repository. The *Information Delivery* component shown on the right consists of all the different ways of making the information from the data warehouse available to the users.

Whether you build a data warehouse for a large manufacturing company on the Fortune 500 list, a leading grocery chain with stores all over the country, or a global banking institution, the basic components are the same. Each data warehouse is put together with the same building blocks. The essential difference for each organization is in the way these building blocks are arranged. The variation is in the manner in which some of the blocks are made stronger than others in the architecture.

We will now take a closer look at each of the components. At this stage, we want to know what the components are and how each fits into the architecture. We also want to review specific issues relating to each particular component.

Source Data Component

Source data coming into the data warehouse may be grouped into four broad categories, as discussed here.

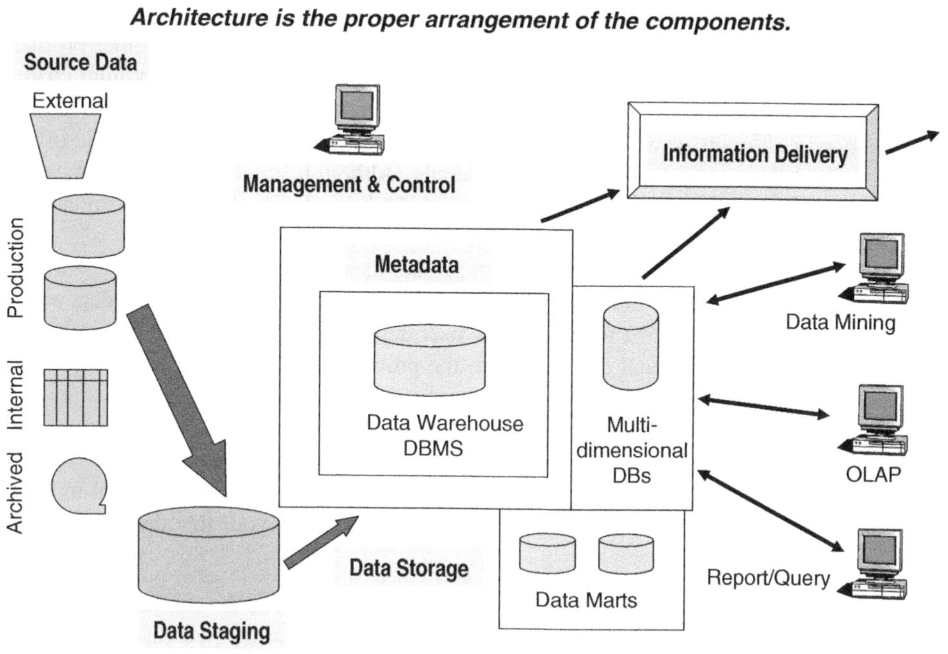

Architecture is the proper arrangement of the components.

Figure 2-7   Data warehouse: building blocks or components.

Production Data   This category of data comes from the various operational systems of the enterprise. These normally include financial systems, manufacturing systems, systems along the supply chain, and customer relationship management systems. Based on the information requirements in the data warehouse, you choose segments of data from the different operational systems. While dealing with this data, you come across many variations in the data formats. You also notice that the data resides on different hardware platforms. Further, the data is supported by different database systems and operating systems. This is data from many vertical applications.

In operational systems, information queries are narrow. You query an operational system for information about specific instances of business objects. You may want just the name and address of a single customer. Or, you may need the orders placed by a single customer in a single week. Or, you may just need to look at a single invoice and the items billed on that single invoice. In operational systems, you do not have broad queries. You do not query the operational system in unexpected ways. The queries are all predictable. Again, you do not expect a particular query to run across different operational systems. What does all of this mean? Simply this: there is no conformance of data among the various operational systems of an enterprise. A term like *an account* may have different meanings in different systems.

The significant and disturbing characteristic of production data is disparity. Your great challenge is to standardize and transform the disparate data from the various production systems, convert the data, and integrate the pieces into useful data for storage in the data warehouse. It is really the integration of these various sources that provide the value to the data in the data warehouse.

Internal Data   In every organization, users keep their "private" spreadsheets, documents, customer profiles, and sometimes even departmental databases. This is the internal data, parts of which could be useful in a data warehouse.

If your organization does business with customers on a one-to-one basis and the contribution of each customer to the bottom line is significant, then detailed customer profiles with ample demographics are important in a data warehouse. Profiles of individual customers become very important for consideration. When your account representatives talk to their assigned customers or when your marketing department wants to make specific offerings to individual customers, you need the details. Although much of this data may be extracted from production systems, a lot of it is held by individuals and departments in their private files.

You cannot ignore the internal data held in private files in your organization. It is a collective judgment call on how much of the internal data should be included in the data warehouse. The IT department must work with the user departments to gather the internal data.

Internal data adds additional complexity to the process of transforming and integrating the data before it can be stored in the data warehouse. You have to determine strategies for collecting data from spreadsheets, find ways of taking data from textual documents, and tie into departmental databases to gather pertinent data from those sources. Again, you may want to schedule the acquisition of internal data. Initially, you may want to limit yourself to only some significant portions before going live with your first data mart.

Archived Data   Operational systems are primarily intended to run the current business. In every operational system, you periodically take the old data and store it in archived files. The circumstances in your organization dictate how often and which portions of the operational databases are archived for storage. Some data is archived after a year. Sometimes data is left in the operational system databases for as long as five years. Much of the archived data comes from old legacy systems that are nearing the end of their useful lives in organizations.

Many different methods of archiving exist. There are staged archival methods. At the first stage, recent data is archived to a separate archival database that may still be online. At the second stage, the older data is archived to flat files on disk storage. At the next stage, the oldest data is archived to tape cartridges or microfilm and even kept off-site.

As mentioned earlier, a data warehouse keeps historical snapshots of data. You essentially need historical data for analysis over time. For getting historical information, you look into your archived data sets. Depending on your data warehouse requirements, you have to include sufficient historical data. This type of data is useful for discerning patterns and analyzing trends.

External Data   Most executives depend on data from external sources for a high percentage of the information they use. They use statistics relating to their industry produced by external agencies and national statistical offices. They use market share data of competitors. They use standard values of financial indicators for their business to check on their performance.

For example, the data warehouse of a car rental company contains data on the current production schedules of the leading automobile manufacturers. This external data in the data warehouse helps the car rental company plan for its fleet management.

The purposes served by such external data sources cannot be fulfilled by the data available within your organization itself. The insights gleaned from your production data and your archived data are somewhat limited. They give you a picture based on what you are doing or have done in the past. In order to spot industry trends and compare performance against other organizations, you need data from external sources.

Usually, data from outside sources do not conform to your formats. You have to devise ways to convert data into your internal formats and data types. You have to organize the data transmissions from the external sources. Some sources may provide information at regular, stipulated intervals. Others may give you the data on request. You need to accommodate the variations.

Data Staging Component

After you have extracted data from various operational systems and from external sources, you have to prepare the data for storing in the data warehouse. The extracted data coming from several disparate sources needs to be changed, converted, and made ready in a format that is suitable to be stored for querying and analysis.

Three major functions need to be performed for getting the data ready. You have to extract the data, transform the data, and then load the data into the data warehouse storage. These three major functions of extraction, transformation, and preparation for loading take place in a staging area. The data staging component consists of a workbench for these functions. Data staging provides a place and an area with a set of functions to clean, change, combine, convert, deduplicate, and prepare source data for storage and use in the data warehouse.

Why do you need a separate place or component to perform the data preparation? Can you not move the data from the various sources into the data warehouse storage itself and then prepare the data? When we implement an operational system, we are likely to pick up data from different sources, move the data into the new operational system database, and run data conversions. Why can't this method work for a data warehouse? The essential difference here is this: in a data warehouse you pull in data from many source operational systems. Remember that data in a data warehouse is subject-oriented and cuts across operational applications. A separate staging area, therefore, is a necessity for preparing data for the data warehouse. Occasionally, particularly with old legacy systems, you may need a separate literal staging area. What you have in this literal staging area would be literal copies of source system content but in a more convenient environment (such as an ODBC accessible relational database). This literal staging area then acts as a surrogate for the particular source systems.

Now that we have clarified the need for a separate data staging component, let us understand what happens in data staging. We will now briefly discuss the three major functions that take place in the staging area.

Data Extraction   This function has to deal with numerous data sources. You have to employ the appropriate technique for each data source. Source data may be from different source machines in diverse data formats. Part of the source data may be in relational database systems. Some data may be on other legacy network and hierarchical data models. Many data sources may still be in flat files. You may want to include data from spreadsheets and local departmental data sets. Data extraction may become quite complex.

Tools are available on the market for data extraction. You may want to consider using outside tools suitable for certain data sources. For the other data sources, you may want to develop in-house programs to do the data extraction. Purchasing outside tools may entail high initial costs. In-house programs, on the other hand, may mean ongoing costs for development and maintenance.

After you extract the data, where do you keep the data for further preparation? You may perform the extraction function in the legacy platform itself if that approach suits your framework. More frequently, data warehouse implementation teams extract the source into a separate physical environment from which moving the data into the data warehouse would be easier. In the separate environment, you may extract the source data into a group of flat files, or a data-staging relational database, or a combination of both.

Data Transformation   In every system implementation, data conversion is an important function. For example, when you implement an operational system such as a magazine subscription application, you have to initially populate your database with data from the prior system records. You may be converting over from a manual system. Or, you may be moving from a file-oriented system to a modern system supported with relational database tables. In either case, you will convert the data from the prior systems. So, what is so different for a data warehouse? How is data transformation for a data warehouse more involved than for an operational system?

Again, as you know, data for a data warehouse comes from many disparate sources. If data extraction for a data warehouse poses great challenges, data transformation presents even greater challenges. Another factor in the data warehouse is that the data feed is not just an initial load. You will have to continue to pick up the ongoing changes from the source systems. Any transformation tasks you set up for the initial load will be adapted for the ongoing revisions as well.

You perform a number of individual tasks as part of data transformation. First, you clean the data extracted from each source. Cleaning may just be correction of misspellings, or may include resolution of conflicts between state codes and zip codes in the source data, or may deal with providing default values for missing data elements, or elimination of duplicates when you bring in the same data from multiple source systems.

Standardization of data elements forms a large part of data transformation. You standardize the data types and field lengths for same data elements retrieved from the various sources. Semantic standardization is another major task. You resolve synonyms and homonyms. When two or more terms from different source systems mean the same thing, you resolve the synonyms. When a single term means many different things in different source systems, you resolve the homonym.

Data transformation involves many forms of combining pieces of data from the different sources. You combine data from a single source record or related data elements from many source records. On the other hand, data transformation also involves purging source data that is not useful and separating out source records into new combinations. Sorting and merging of data takes place on a large scale in the data staging area.

In many cases, the keys chosen for the operational systems are field values with built-in meanings. For example, the product key value may be a combination of characters indicating the product category, the code of the warehouse where the product is stored, and some code to show the production batch. Primary keys in the data warehouse cannot have built-in meanings. We will discuss this further in Chapter 10. Data transformation also includes the assignment of surrogate keys derived from the source system primary keys.

A grocery chain point-of-sale operational system keeps the unit sales and revenue amounts by individual transactions at the check-out counter at each store. But in the data warehouse, it may not be necessary to keep the data at this detailed level. You may want to summarize the totals by product at each store for a given day and keep the summary totals of the sale units and revenue in the data warehouse storage. In such cases, the data transformation function would include appropriate summarization.

◆ This function is time-consuming

◆ Initial load moves very large volumes of data

◆ The business conditions determine the refresh cycles

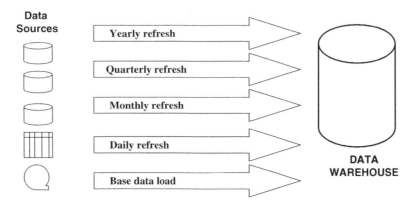

Figure 2-8 Data movements to the data warehouse.

When the data transformation function ends, you have a collection of integrated data that is cleaned, standardized, and summarized. You now have data ready to load into each data set in your data warehouse.

Data Loading Two distinct groups of tasks form the data loading function. When you complete the design and construction of the data warehouse and go live for the first time, you do the initial loading of the data into the data warehouse storage. The initial load moves large volumes of data using up substantial amounts of time. As the data warehouse starts functioning, you continue to extract the changes to the source data, transform the data revisions, and feed the incremental data revisions on an ongoing basis. Figure 2-8 illustrates the common types of data movements from the staging area to the data warehouse storage.

Data Storage Component

The data storage for the data warehouse is a separate repository. The operational systems of your enterprise support the day-to-day operations. These are online transaction processing applications. The data repositories for the operational systems typically contain only the current data. Also, these data repositories contain the data structured in highly normalized formats for fast and efficient processing. In contrast, in the data repository for a data warehouse, you need to keep large volumes of historical data for analysis. Further, you have to keep the data in the data warehouse in structures suitable for analysis, and not for quick retrieval of individual pieces of information. Therefore, the data storage for the data warehouse is kept separate from the data storage for operational systems.

In your databases supporting operational systems, the updates to data happen as transactions occur. These transactions hit the databases in a random fashion. How and when the transactions change the data in the databases is not completely within your control. The data in the operational databases could change from moment to moment. When your analysts use the data in the data warehouse for analysis, they need to know that the data is stable and that it represents snapshots at specified periods. As they are working with the data, the data storage must not be in a state of continual updating. For this reason, the data warehouses are "read-only" data repositories.

Generally, the database in your data warehouse must be open. Depending on your requirements, you are likely to use tools from multiple vendors. The data warehouse must be open to different tools. Most of the data warehouses employ relational database management systems.

Many data warehouses also employ multidimensional database management systems. Data extracted from the data warehouse storage is aggregated in many ways and the summary data is kept in the multidimensional databases (MDDBs). Such multidimensional database systems are usually proprietary products.

Information Delivery Component

Who are the users that need information from the data warehouse? The range is fairly comprehensive. The novice user comes to the data warehouse with no training and, therefore, needs prefabricated reports and preset queries. The casual user needs information once in a while, not regularly. This type of user also needs prepackaged information. The business analyst looks for ability to do complex analysis using the information in the data warehouse. The power user wants to be able to navigate throughout the data warehouse, pick up interesting data, format his or her own queries, drill through the data layers, and create custom reports and ad hoc queries.

In order to provide information to the wide community of data warehouse users, the information delivery component includes different methods of information delivery. Figure 2-9 shows the different information delivery methods. Ad hoc reports are predefined reports primarily meant for novice and casual users. Provision for complex queries, multidimensional (MD) analysis, and statistical analysis cater to the needs of the business analysts and power users. Information fed into executive information systems (EIS) is meant for senior

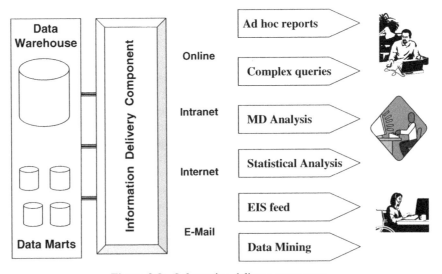

Figure 2-9   Information delivery component.

executives and high-level managers. Some data warehouses also provide data to data-mining applications. Data-mining applications are knowledge discovery systems where the mining algorithms help you discover trends and patterns from the usage of your data.

In your data warehouse, you may include several information delivery mechanisms. Most commonly, you provide for online queries and reports. The users will enter their requests online and will receive the results online. You may set up delivery of scheduled reports through e-mail or you may make adequate use of your organization's intranet for information delivery. Recently, information delivery over the Internet has been gaining ground.

Metadata Component

Metadata in a data warehouse is similar to the data dictionary or the data catalog in a database management system. In the data dictionary, you keep the information about the logical data structures, the information about the files and addresses, the information about the indexes, and so on. The data dictionary contains data about the data in the database.

Similarly, the metadata component is the data about the data in the data warehouse. This definition is a commonly used definition. We need to elaborate on this definition. Metadata in a data warehouse is similar to a data dictionary, but much more than a data dictionary. Later, in a separate section in this chapter, we will devote more time to the discussion of metadata. Here, for the sake of completeness, we just want to list metadata as one of the components of the data warehouse architecture.

Management and Control Component

This component of the data warehouse architecture sits on top of all the other components. The management and control component coordinates the services and activities within the data warehouse. This component controls the data transformation and the data transfer into the data warehouse storage. On the other hand, it moderates the information delivery to the users. It works with the database management systems and enables data to be properly stored in the repositories. It monitors the movement of data into the staging area and from there into the data warehouse storage itself.

The management and control component interacts with the metadata component to perform the management and control functions. As the metadata component contains information about the data warehouse itself, the metadata is the source of information for the management module.

METADATA IN THE DATA WAREHOUSE

Think of metadata as the Yellow Pages® of your town. Do you need information about the stores in your town, where they are, what their names are, and what products they specialize in? Go to the Yellow Pages. The Yellow Pages is a directory with data about the institutions in your town. Almost in the same manner, the metadata component serves as a directory of the contents of your data warehouse.

Because of the importance of metadata in a data warehouse, we have set apart all of Chapter 9 for this topic. At this stage, we just want to get an introduction to the topic and highlight that metadata is a key architectural component of the data warehouse.

Types of Metadata

Metadata in a data warehouse fall into three major categories:

- Operational metadata
- Extraction and transformation metadata
- End-user metadata

Operational Metadata   As you know, data for the data warehouse comes from several operational systems of the enterprise. These source systems contain different data structures. The data elements selected for the data warehouse have various field lengths and data types. In selecting data from the source systems for the data warehouse, you split records, combine parts of records from different source files, and deal with multiple coding schemes and field lengths. When you deliver information to the end-users, you must be able to tie that back to the original source data sets. Operational metadata contain all of this information about the operational data sources.

Extraction and Transformation Metadata   Extraction and transformation metadata contain data about the extraction of data from the source systems, namely, the extraction frequencies, extraction methods, and business rules for the data extraction. Also, this category of metadata contains information about all the data transformations that take place in the data staging area.

End-User Metadata   The end-user metadata is the navigational map of the data warehouse. It enables the end-users to find information from the data warehouse. The end-user metadata allows the end-users to use their own business terminology and look for information in those ways in which they normally think of the business.

Special Significance

Why is metadata especially important in a data warehouse?

- First, it acts as the glue that connects all parts of the data warehouse.
- Next, it provides information about the contents and structures to the developers.
- Finally, it opens the door to the end-users and makes the contents recognizable in their own terms.

CHAPTER SUMMARY

- Defining features of the data warehouse are: separate, subject-oriented, integrated, time-variant, and nonvolatile.
- You may use a top-down approach and build a large, comprehensive, enterprise data warehouse, or you may use a bottom-up approach and build small, independent,

departmental data marts. In spite of some advantages, both approaches have serious shortcomings.

- A viable practical approach is to build conformed data marts, which together form the corporate data warehouse.
- Data warehouse building blocks or components are source data, data staging, data storage, information delivery, metadata, and management and control.
- In a data warehouse, metadata is especially significant because it acts as the glue holding all the components together and serves as a roadmap for the end-users.

REVIEW QUESTIONS

1. Name at least six characteristics or features of a data warehouse.

2. Why is data integration required in a data warehouse, more so than in an operational application?

3. Every data structure in the data warehouse contains the time element. Why?

4. Explain data granularity and how it is applicable to the data warehouse.

5. How are the top-down and bottom-up approaches for building a data warehouse different? List the major types of architectures and highlight the features of any two of these.

6. What are the various data sources for the data warehouse?

7. Why do you need a separate data staging component?

8. Under data transformation, list five different functions you can think of.

9. Name any six different methods for information delivery.

10. What are the three major types of metadata in a data warehouse? Briefly mention the purpose of each type.

EXERCISES

1. Match the columns:

1.	nonvolatile data	A.	roadmap for users
2.	dual data granularity	B.	subject-oriented
3.	dependent data mart	C.	knowledge discovery
4.	disparate data	D.	private spreadsheets
5.	decision support	E.	application flavor
6.	data staging	F.	because of multiple sources
7.	data mining	G.	details and summary
8.	metadata	H.	read-only
9.	operational systems	I.	workbench for data integration
10.	internal data	J.	data from main data warehouse

2. A data warehouse is subject-oriented. What would be the major critical business subjects for the following companies?

   a. an international manufacturing company
   b. a local community bank
   c. a domestic hotel chain

3. You are the data analyst on the project team building a data warehouse for an insurance company. List the possible data sources from which you will bring the data into your data warehouse. State your assumptions.

4. For an airlines company, identify three operational applications that would feed into the data warehouse. What would be the data load and refresh cycles?

5. Prepare a table showing all the potential users and information delivery methods for a data warehouse supporting a large national grocery chain.

CHAPTER 3

TRENDS IN DATA WAREHOUSING

CHAPTER OBJECTIVES

- Review the continued growth in data warehousing
- Learn how data warehousing has become mainstream
- Discuss several major trends, one by one
- Grasp the need for standards and review the progress
- Understand Web-enabled data warehouse

In the previous chapters, we have seen why business intelligence along with the underlying data warehouses is essential for enterprises of all sizes in all industries. We have reviewed how businesses are reaping major benefits from data warehousing. We have also discussed the building blocks of a data warehouse. You now have a fairly good idea of the features and functions of the basic components and a reasonable definition of data warehousing. You have understood that it is a fundamentally simple concept; at the same time, you know it is also a blend of many technologies. Several business and technological drivers have moved data warehousing forward in the past few years.

Before we proceed further, we are at the point where we want to ask some relevant questions. What is the current scenario and state of the market? What businesses have adopted data warehousing? What are the technological advances? In short, what are the significant trends?

Are you wondering if it is too early in our discussion of the subject to talk about trends? The usual practice is to include a chapter on future trends towards the end, almost as an afterthought. The reader typically glosses over the discussion on future trends. This chapter is not so much like looking into the crystal ball for possible future happenings; we want to deal with the important trends that are happening now.

Data Warehousing Fundamentals for IT Professionals, Second Edition. By Paulraj Ponniah
Copyright © 2010 John Wiley & Sons, Inc.

It is important for you to keep the knowledge about current trends as a backdrop in your mind as you continue the in-depth study of the subject. When you gather the informational requirements for your data warehouse, you need to be aware of current trends. When you get into the design phase, you need to be cognizant of the trends. When you implement your data warehouse, you need to ensure that your data warehouse is in line with the trends. Knowledge of trends is important and necessary even at a fairly early stage of your study.

In this chapter, we will touch upon most of the major trends. You will understand how and why data warehousing continues to grow and become more and more pervasive. We will discuss trends in vendor solutions and products. We will relate data warehousing with other technological phenomena such as the Internet and the World Wide Web. Wherever more detailed discussions are necessary, we will revisit some of the trends in later chapters.

CONTINUED GROWTH IN DATA WAREHOUSING

Data warehousing is no longer a purely novel idea for study and experimentation. It has become mainstream. True, the data warehouse is not in every dentist's office yet, but neither is it confined only to high-end businesses. More than half of all U.S. companies have made a commitment to data warehousing. About 90% of multinational companies have data warehouses or are planning to implement data warehouses in the next few months.

In every industry across the board, from retail chain stores to financial institutions, from manufacturing enterprises to government departments, from airline companies to pharmaceuticals, data warehousing has revolutionized the way people perform business analysis and make strategic decisions. Every company that has a data warehouse continues to realize enormous benefits that get translated into positive results at the bottom line. Many of these companies, incorporating Web-based technologies, have enhanced the potential for greater and easier delivery of vital information.

Even during the first few years of data warehousing in the late 1990s, hundreds of vendors had flooded the market with numerous products. Vendor solutions and products run the gamut of data warehousing: data modeling, data acquisition, data quality, data analysis, metadata, and so on. A buyer's guide published by the Data Warehousing Institute at that time featured no fewer than 105 leading products. The market is huge and continues to grow in revenue dollars.

Data Warehousing has Become Mainstream

In the early stages, four significant factors drove many companies to move into data warehousing:

- Fierce competition
- Government deregulation
- Need to revamp internal processes
- Imperative for customized marketing

Telecommunications, banking, and retail were the first industries to adopt data warehousing. That was largely because of government deregulation in telecommunications and banking. Retail businesses moved into data warehousing because of fiercer competition. Utility companies joined the group as that sector was deregulated. The next wave of businesses to get into data warehousing consisted of companies in financial services, health care, insurance, manufacturing, pharmaceuticals, transportation, and distribution.

Today, telecommunications and financial services continue to lead in data warehouse spending. As much as 15% of technology budgets in these industries is spent on data warehousing. Companies in these industries collect large volumes of transaction data. Data warehousing is able to transform such large volumes of data into strategic information useful for decision making.

At present, data warehouses exist in every conceivable industry. Figure 3-1 lists the industries in the order of the average salaries paid to data warehousing professionals. In 2008, pharmaceuticals was at the top of the list, with the highest average salary.

In the early stages of data warehousing, it was, for the most part, used exclusively by global corporations. It was expensive to build a data warehouse and the tools were not quite adequate. Only large companies had the resources to spend on the new paradigm. Now we have begun to see a strong presence of data warehousing in medium-sized and smaller companies, which are now able to afford the cost of building data warehouses or buying turnkey data marts. Take a look at the database management systems (DBMSs) you have been using in the past. You will find that the database vendors have now added features to assist you in building data warehouses using these DBMSs. Packaged solutions have also become less expensive and operating systems robust enough to support data warehousing functions.

Data Warehouse Expansion

Although earlier data warehouses concentrated on keeping summary data for high-level analysis, we now see larger and larger data warehouses being built by different businesses. Now companies have the ability to capture, cleanse, maintain, and use the vast amounts of data generated by their business transactions. The quantities of data kept in data warehouses continue to swell to the terabyte range. Data warehouses storing several terabytes of data are not uncommon in retail and telecommunications.

For example, take the telecommunications industry. A telecommunications company generates hundreds of millions of call-detail transactions in a year. For promoting the

Annual average salary in $ 000			
Pharmaceuticals	117	Manufacturing (non-computer)	100
Consulting/professional	112	Telecommunications	98
Software/Internet	107	Healthcare	98
Government (federal)	105	Retail/wholesale/distribution	92
Financial Services	105	Insurance	90
Media/entertainment/publishing	103	Education	85
Computer manufacturing	103	Government (state/local)	82

Source: 2008 Data Warehousing Salary Survey by the Data Warehousing Institute

Figure 3-1   Industries using data warehousing.

proper products and services, the company needs to analyze these detailed transactions. The data warehouse for the company has to store data at the lowest level of detail.

Similarly, consider a retail chain with hundreds of stores. Every day, each store generates many thousands of point-of-sale transactions. Again, another example is a company in the pharmaceutical industry that processes thousands of tests and measurements for getting product approvals from the government. Data warehouses in these industries tend to be very large.

Finally, let us look at the potential size of a typical Medicaid fraud control unit of a large state. This organization is exclusively responsible for investigating and prosecuting health care fraud arising out of billions of dollars spent on Medicaid in that state. The unit also has to prosecute cases of patient abuse in nursing homes and monitor fraudulent billing practices by physicians, pharmacists, and other health care providers and vendors. Usually there are several regional offices. A fraud scheme detected in one region must be checked against all other regions. Can you imagine the size of the data warehouse needed to support such a fraud control unit? There could be many terabytes of data.

Vendor Solutions and Products

As an information technology professional, you are familiar with database vendors and database products. In the same way, you are familiar with most of the operating systems and their vendors. How many leading database vendors are there? How many leading vendors of operating systems are there? A handful? The number of database and operating system vendors pales in comparison with data warehousing products and vendors. There are hundreds of data warehousing vendors and thousands of data warehousing products and solutions.

In the beginning, the market was filled with confusion and vendor hype. Every vendor, small or big, that had any product remotely connected to data warehousing jumped on the bandwagon. Data warehousing meant what each vendor defined it to be. Each company positioned its own products as the proper set of data warehousing tools. Data warehousing was a new concept for many of the businesses that adopted it. These businesses were at the mercy of the marketing hype of the vendors.

Over the past decade, the situation has improved tremendously. The market is reaching maturity, to the extent of producing off-the-shelf packages and becoming increasingly stable. Figure 3-2 shows the current state of the data warehousing market as compared to how the market was in the beginning stages.

What do we normally see in any maturing market? We expect to find a process of consolidation. And that is exactly what is taking place in the data warehousing market. Data warehousing vendors are merging to form stronger and more viable companies. Some major players in the industry are extending the range of their solutions by acquisition of other companies. Some vendors are positioning suites of products, their own or ones from groups of other vendors, piecing them together as integrated data warehousing solutions.

Now the traditional database companies are also in the data warehousing market. They have begun to offer data warehousing solutions built around their database products. On the one hand, data extraction and transformation tools are packaged with the database management system. On the other hand, inquiry and reporting tools are enhanced for data warehousing. Some database vendors take the enhancement further by offering sophisticated products such as data mining tools.

With so many vendors and products, how can we classify the vendors and products, and thereby make sense of the market? It is best to separate the market broadly into two distinct

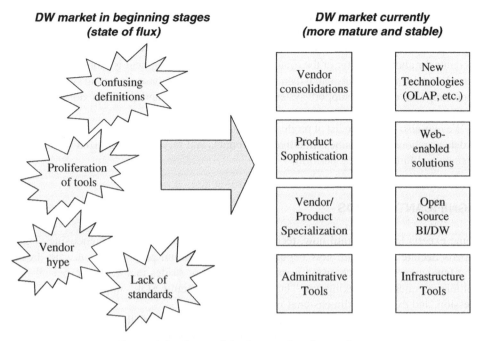

Figure 3-2   Status of the data warehousing market.

Administration & Operations: System/network administration, backup/restore, disaster recovery, performance/usage management, capacity planning, security, database management

Analytics: Business Activity Monitoring, Query/Reporting, OLAP, Forecasting, Data Mining, Dashboards/Scorecards, Visualization, Text Analysis, Analytic Application Development

BI Services: Analytic Service Providers (ASP), BI Software, Consultants, Systems Integrators, Industry Associations/Consortia, Research

Data Integration: Business Process Management, Data Profiling/Cleaning/Conversion/Movement, Data Mapping/Transformation, Master Data Management, Metadata Management

DW Design: Data Analysis, Data Modeling (Dimensional Modeling/Entity-Relationship Modeling), Data Warehousing Toolset

Information Delivery: Broadcasting, Collaboration, Content Management, Document Management, Enterprise Information Portals, Wireless Data Analysis

Infrastructure: Data Accelerators, Data Warehouse Appliances, Database Management Systems, Multidimensional Databases, Servers, Storage Management Systems

Open Source BI/DW: Business Intelligence, Data Integration, Databases, Consultants, Systems Integrators

Source: The Data Warehousing Institute

Figure 3-3   Categories of products and services.

groups. The first group consists of data warehouse vendors and products catering to the needs of corporate data warehouses in which all enterprise data is integrated and transformed. This segment has been referred to as the market for strategic data warehouses. This segment accounts for about a quarter of the total market. The second segment is more loose and dispersed, consisting of departmental data marts, fragmented database marketing systems, and a wide range of decision support systems. Specific vendors and products dominate each segment.

We may also look at the list of products in another way. Figure 3-3 shows a list of the types of data warehouse and business intelligence products and services, categorized based on the features and functions they perform.

SIGNIFICANT TRENDS

Some experts feel that, until now, technology has been driving data warehousing. These experts declare that we are now beginning to see important progress in software. In the next few years, data warehousing is expected make big strides in software, especially for optimizing queries, indexing very large tables, enhancing SQL, improving data compression, and expanding dimensional modeling.

Let us separate out the significant trends and discuss each briefly. Be prepared to visit each trend, one by one—each has a serious impact on data warehousing. As we walk through each trend, try to grasp its significance and be sure that you perceive its relevance to your company's data warehouse. Be prepared to answer the question: What must you do to take advantage of the trend in your data warehouse?

Real-Time Data Warehousing

Business intelligence systems and the supporting data warehouses have been used mainly for strategic decision making. The data warehouse was kept separate from operational systems. Recently industry momentum is swinging towards using business intelligence for tactical decision making for day-to-day business operations. Data warehousing is progressing rapidly to the point that real-time data warehousing is the focus of senior executives.

Traditional data warehousing is passive, providing historical trends, whereas real-time data warehousing is dynamic, providing the most up-to-date view of the business in real time. A real-time data warehouse gets refreshed continuously, with almost zero latency.

Real-time information delivery increases productivity tremendously by sharing information with more people. Companies are, therefore, coming under a lot of pressure to provide information, in real time, to everyone connected to critical business processes. However, extraction, transformation, and integration of data for real-time data warehousing have several challenges. We will discuss these in detail in a later chapter.

Multiple Data Types

When you build the first iteration of your data warehouse, you may include just numeric data. But soon you will realize that including structured numeric data alone is not enough. Be prepared to consider other data types as well.

Traditionally, companies included structured data, mostly numeric, in their data warehouses. From this point of view, decision support systems were divided into two camps: data warehousing dealt with structured data, knowledge management involved unstructured data. This distinction is being blurred. For example, most marketing data consists of structured data in the form of numeric values. Marketing data also contains unstructured data in the form of images. Let us say a decision maker is performing an analysis to find the top-selling product types. The decision maker arrives at a specific product type in the course of the analysis. He or she would now like to see images of the products in that type to make further decisions. How can this be made possible? Companies are realizing there is a need to integrate both structured and unstructured data in their data warehouses.

What are the types of data we call unstructured data? Figure 3-4 shows the different types of data that need to be integrated in the data warehouse to support decision making more effectively.

Let us now turn to the progress made in the industry for including some of the types of unstructured data. You will gain an understanding of what must be done to include these data types in your data warehouse.

Adding Unstructured Data   Some vendors are addressing the inclusion of unstructured data, especially text and images, by treating such multimedia data as just another data type. These are defined as part of the relational data and stored as binary large objects (BLOBs) up to 2 GB in size. User-defined functions (UDFs) are used to define these as user-defined types (UDTs).

Not all BLOBs can be stored simply as another relational data type. For example, a video clip would require a server supporting delivery of multiple streams of video at a given rate and synchronization with the audio portion. For this purpose, specialized servers are being provided.

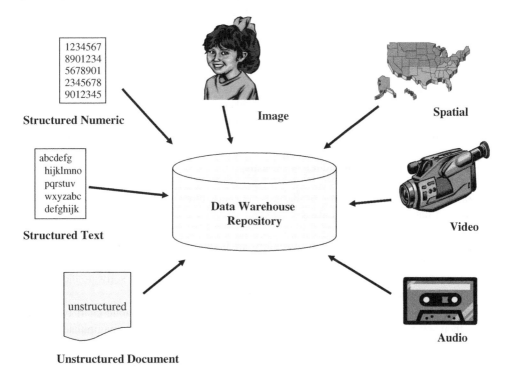

Figure 3-4   Multiple data types in a data warehouse.

Searching Unstructured Data   You have enhanced your data warehouse by adding unstructured data. Is there anything else you need to do? Of course, without the ability to search unstructured data, integration of such data is of little value. Vendors are now providing new search engines to find the information the user needs from unstructured data. Query by image content is an example of a search mechanism for images. The product allows you to preindex images based on shapes, colors, and textures. When more than one image fits the search argument, the selected images are displayed one after the other.

For free-form text data, retrieval engines preindex the textual documents to allow searches by words, character strings, phrases, wild cards, proximity operators, and Boolean operators. Some engines are powerful enough to substitute corresponding words and search. A search with a word *mouse* will also retrieve documents containing the word *mice*.

Searching audio and video data directly is still in the research stage. Usually, these are described with free-form text, and then searched using textual search methods that are currently available.

Spatial Data   Consider one of your important users, maybe the marketing director, being online and performing an analysis using your data warehouse. The marketing director runs a query: show me the sales for the first two quarters for all products compared to last year in store XYZ. After reviewing the results, he or she thinks of two other questions. What is the average income of people living in the neighborhood of that store? What is the average driving distance for those people to come to the store? These questions may be answered only if you include spatial data in your data warehouse.

Adding spatial data will greatly enhance the value of your data warehouse. Address, street block, city quadrant, county, state, and zone are examples of spatial data. Vendors have begun to address the need to include spatial data. Some database vendors are providing spatial extenders to their products using SQL extensions to bring spatial and business data together.

Data Visualization

When a user queries your data warehouse and expects to see results only in the form of output lists or spreadsheets, your data warehouse is already outdated. You need to display results in the form of graphics and charts as well. Every user now expects to see the results of a query shown as charts. Visualization of data in the result sets boosts the process of analysis for the user, especially when the user is looking for trends over time. Data visualization helps the user to interpret query results quickly and easily.

Major Visualization Trends   In the last few years, three major trends have shaped the direction of data visualization software.

> *More Chart Types.* Most data visualizations are in the form of some standard chart type. The numerical results are converted into a pie chart, a scatter plot, or another chart type. Now the list of chart types supported by data visualization software has grown much longer.
>
> *Interactive Visualization.* Visualizations are no longer static. Dynamic chart types are themselves user interfaces. Your users can review a result chart, manipulate it, and then see newer views online.
>
> *Visualization of Complex and Large Result Sets.* Your users can view a simple series of numeric result points as a rudimentary pie or bar chart. But newer visualization software can visualize thousands of result points and complex data structures.

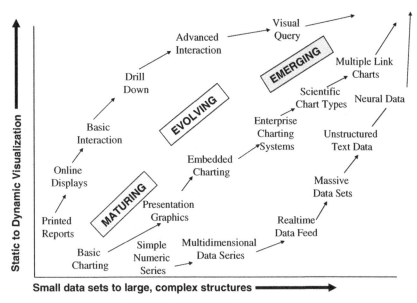

Figure 3-5 Data visualization trends.

Figure 3-5 summarizes these major trends. See how the technologies are maturing, evolving, and emerging.

Visualization Types   Visualization software now supports a large array of chart types. Gone are the days of simple line graphs. The current needs of users vary enormously. Business users demand pie and bar charts. Technical and scientific users need scatter plots and constellation graphs. Analysts looking at spatial data need maps and other three-dimensional representations. In the last few years, major trends have shaped the direction of data visualization software.

Advanced Visualization Techniques   The most remarkable advance in visualization techniques is the transition from static charts to dynamic interactive presentations.

Chart Manipulation. A user can rotate a chart or dynamically change the chart type to get a clearer view of the results. With complex visualization types such as constellation and scatter plots, a user can select data points with a mouse and then move the points around to clarify the view.

Drill Down. The visualization first presents the results at the summary level. The user can then drill down the visualization to display further visualizations at subsequent levels of detail.

Advanced Interaction. These techniques provide a minimally invasive user interface. The user simply double clicks a part of the visualization and then drags and drops representations of data entities. Or the user simply right clicks and chooses options from a menu. Visual query is the most advanced of user interaction features. For example, the user may see the outlying data points in a scatter plot, then select a few of them with the mouse and ask for a brand new visualization of just those selected points. The data visualization software generates the appropriate query from the selection, submits the query to the database, and then displays the results in another representation.

Dashboards and Scorecards Within the past few years many companies have adopted dashboards and scorecards as their preferred method of viewing performance information. In a certain sense, these means of obtaining information represent the culmination of business intelligence. Executives and managers, who need to monitor performance metrics, like digital dashboards that allow them to visualize the metrics as in speedometers, thermometers, or traffic lights. A dashboard informs users about what is happening; a scorecard informs users how well it is happening.

Dashboards monitor and measure processes. A dashboard provides real-time information like the dashboard in an automobile, enabling drivers to check current speed, engine temperature, fluid level, and so on. Dashboards are linked directly to real-time systems that capture events as they happen. Dashboards warn users with alerts or exception conditions. Industry vendors have improved dashboards to a very large extent and made them interactive and comprehensive.

Scorecards track progress compared to objectives. A scorecard displays periodic snapshots of performance viewed against an organization's strategic objectives and targets. Users select key performance indicators and have the progress displayed on the scorecards.

Parallel Processing

You know that the data warehouse is a user-centric and query-intensive environment. Your users will constantly be executing complex queries to perform all types of analyses. Each query would need to read large volumes of data to produce result sets. Analysis, usually performed interactively, requires the execution of several queries, one after the other, by each user. If the data warehouse is not tuned properly for handling large, complex, simultaneous queries efficiently, the value of the data warehouse will be lost. Performance is of primary importance.

The other functions for which performance is crucial are the functions of loading data and creating indexes. Because of large volumes, loading of data can be slow. Indexing in a data warehouse is usually elaborate because of the need to access the data in many different ways. Because of large numbers of indexes, index creation can also be slow.

How do you speed up query processing, data loading, and index creation? A very effective way to do this is to use parallel processing. Both hardware configurations and software techniques go hand in hand to accomplish parallel processing. A task is divided into smaller units and these smaller units are executed concurrently.

Parallel Processing Hardware Options In a parallel processing environment, you will find these characteristics: multiple CPUs, memory modules, one or more server nodes, and high-speed communication links between interconnected nodes.

Essentially, you can choose from three architectural options. Figure 3-6 indicates the three options and their comparative merits. Note the advantages and disadvantages so that you may choose the proper option for your data warehouse.

Parallel Processing Software Implementation You may choose the appropriate parallel processing hardware configuration for your data warehouse. Hardware alone would be worthless if the operating system and the database software cannot make use of the parallel features of the hardware. You will have to ensure that the software can allocate units of a larger task to the hardware components appropriately.

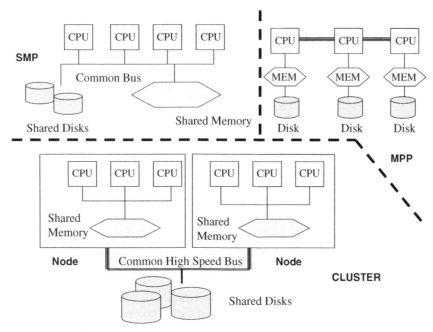

Figure 3-6 Hardware options for parallel processing.

Parallel processing software must be capable of performing the following steps:

- Analyzing a large task to identify independent units that can be executed in parallel
- Identifying which of the smaller units must be executed one after the other
- Executing the independent units in parallel and the dependent units in the proper sequence
- Collecting, collating, and consolidating the results returned by the smaller units

Database vendors usually provide two options for parallel processing: parallel server option and parallel query option. You may purchase each option separately. Depending on the provisions made by the database vendors, these options may be used with one or more of the parallel hardware configurations.

The parallel server option allows each hardware node to have its own separate database instance, and enables all database instances to access a common set of underlying database files. The parallel query option supports key operations such as query processing, data loading, and index creation.

Implementing a data warehouse without parallel processing options is almost unthinkable in the current state of the technology. In summary, you will realize the following significant advantages when you adopt parallel processing in your data warehouse:

- Performance improvement for query processing, data loading, and index creation
- Scalability, allowing the addition of CPUs and memory modules without changes to the existing application

- Fault tolerance so that the database is available even when some of the parallel processors fail
- A single logical view of the database even though the data may reside on the disks of multiple nodes

Data Warehouse Appliances

In the previous section we discussed how adoption of parallel processing has become a necessity in a data warehouse environment. More recently companies are realizing that fully adopting business intelligence could make or break the business. Vast quantities need to be retrieved for the decision-making process. Timeliness and depth of analysis have become crucial. Terabyte-sized data warehouses have become common.

Until recently vendors and users have handled this rapid growth in database size and complexity in analysis with very expensive and constant upgrading of hardware and software. Now it is becoming clearer that existing infrastructures are unable to handle the continued growth. The objective is to find a new approach to data warehousing infrastructure that is flexible, expandable, and specifically applicable to an organization. The result is the advent of data warehouse appliances.

The data warehouse appliance is designed specifically to take care of the workload of business intelligence. It is built with hardware and software components specifically architected for this purpose. Through its architecture, a data warehouse appliance integrates hardware, storage, and DBMS into one unified device. It combines the best elements of SMP and MPP to enable queries to be processed in the most optimal manner. Appliances from most vendors are designed to interface seamlessly with standardized applications and tools available on the business intelligence market.

A data warehouse appliance is quite scalable. Because all parts of the appliance, hardware and software, come from the same vendor, it is designed to be homogeneous and reliable. For the administrator, a data warehouse appliance provides simplicity because of its integrated nature.

Data warehouse appliances are already supporting data warehouse and business intelligence deployments at major corporations. This is especially true in telecommunications and retail where data volumes are enormous and queries and analysis more complex and demanding.

Query Tools

In a data warehouse, if there is one set of functional tools that is most significant, it is the set of query tools. The success of your data warehouse depends on your query tools. Because of this, data warehouse vendors have improved query tools during the past few years.

We will discuss query tools in greater detail in Chapter 14. At this stage, just note the following functions for which vendors have greatly enhanced their query tools.

- *Flexible presentation*—Easy to use and able to present results online and in reports, in many different formats.
- *Aggregate awareness*—Able to recognize the existence of summary or aggregate tables and automatically route queries to the summary tables when summarized results are desired.
- *Crossing subject areas*—Able to cross over from one subject data mart to another automatically.

- *Multiple heterogeneous sources*—Capable of accessing heterogeneous data sources on different platforms.
- *Integration*—Able to integrate query tools for online queries, batch reports, and data extraction for analysis, and provide seamless interface to go from one type of output to another.
- *Overcoming SQL limitations*—Able to provide SQL extensions to handle requests that cannot usually be done through standard SQL.

Browser Tools

Here we are using the term "browser" in a generic sense, not limiting it to Web browsers. Your users will be running queries against your data warehouse. They will be generating reports from your data warehouse. They will be performing these functions directly and not with the assistance of someone like you in IT. This is expected to be one of the major advantages of the data warehouse approach.

If the users have to go to the data warehouse directly, they need to know what information is available there. Users need good browser tools to browse through the informational metadata and search to locate the specific pieces of information they want to receive. Similarly, when you are part of the IT team to develop your company's data warehouse, you need to identify the data sources, the data structures, and the business rules. You also need good browser tools to browse through the information about the data sources. Here are some recent trends in enhancements to browser tools:

- Tools are extensible to allow definition of any type of data or informational object.
- Open APIs (application program interfaces) are included.
- Several types of browsing functions, including navigation through hierarchical groupings, are provided.
- Users are able to browse the catalog (data dictionary or metadata), find an informational object of interest, and proceed further to launch the appropriate query tool with the relevant parameters.
- Web browsing and search techniques are available to browse through the information catalogs.

Data Fusion

A data warehouse is a place where data from numerous sources is integrated to provide a unified view of the enterprise. Data may come from the various operational systems running on multiple platforms, where it may be stored in flat files or in databases supported by different DBMSs. In addition to internal sources, data from external sources is also included in the data warehouse. In the data warehouse repository, you may also find various types of unstructured data in the form of documents, images, audio, and video.

In essence, various types of data from multiple disparate sources need to be integrated or fused together and stored in the data warehouse. Data fusion is a technology dealing with the merging of data from disparate sources. It has a wider scope and includes real-time merging of data from instruments and monitoring systems. Serious research is being conducted in the technology of data fusion. The principles and techniques of data fusion technology have a direct application in data warehousing.

Data fusion not only deals with the merging of data from various sources, it also has another application in data warehousing. In present-day warehouses, we tend to collect data in astronomical proportions. The more information stored, the more difficult it is to find the right information at the right time. Data fusion technology is expected to address this problem also.

By and large, data fusion is still in the realm of research. Vendors are not rushing to produce data fusion tools yet. At this stage, all you need to do is to keep your eyes open and watch for developments.

Data Integration

In the previous section we touched upon the need for and challenges of combining data from disparate sources in a data warehouse. Integrating disparate data has been a challenge for data warehouse developers. This task is not becoming any easier given the data explosion in most businesses. Data integration has become a top priority and challenge for many companies. In this section we will consider the trends for integration being adopted in progressive organizations.

Data integration is not just confined to data warehousing projects, but is also important for companies to develop an enterprise-wide strategy for integration. The Data Warehousing Institute conducted a study on data integration approaches across the board. They noticed that large organizations are leaning towards an enterprise-wide integration architecture while medium-sized companies are dealing with data integration primarily from a business intelligence viewpoint.

Integration is viewed in a few different ways: Enterprise Information Integration (EII), Enterprise Application Integration (EAI), and so on. In general, integration can be brought about at four different levels in an information technology system: data integration, application integration, business process integration, and user interaction integration. An integration architecture must incorporate all these different levels.

> *Data Integration.* The objective is to provide a single, unified view of the business data scattered across the various systems in an organization. This unified view may be a physical one that has been combined and consolidated from multiple disparate sources into a single repository such as a data warehouse or an operational data store. On the other hand, this may a virtual federated view of disparate data pulled together dynamically at the time of data access. Another technique for data integration is the straightforward approach of merging data from one database to another, for example, merging customer data from a CRM database into a manufacturing system database.
>
> *Application Integration.* Here the objective is to provide a unified view of business applications used in the organization. The flow of transactions, messages, and data between applications is controlled and managed to obtain a unified view.
>
> *Business Process Integration.* The objective is to provide a unified view of the organization's business processes. This type of integration is achieved through business process design tools and business process management tools.
>
> *User Interaction Integration.* The objective is to provide users with a single, personalized interface to the business processes and data for performing their organizational functions. This type of integration fosters data sharing and user collaboration. An enterprise portal is an example of a technique for user interaction integration.

Analytics

Data warehousing and business intelligence is all about analysis of data. During the past few years, vendors have made tremendous strides in providing effective tools for analysis. Companies are concentrating on two areas of analysis more than others.

Multidimensional Analysis   Today, every data warehouse environment provides for multidimensional analysis. This is becoming an integral part of the information delivery system of the data warehouse. Provision of multidimensional analysis to your users simply means that they will be able to analyze business measurements in many different ways. Multidimensional analysis is also synonymous with online analytical processing (OLAP).

Because of the enormous importance of OLAP, we will discuss this topic in greater detail in Chapter 15. At this stage, just note that vendors have made tremendous progress in OLAP tools. Now vendor products are evaluated to a large extent by the strength of their OLAP components.

Predictive Analytics   Already many organizations are reaping tremendous benefits by using predictive analytics in their business intelligence environment. Predictive analytics assist the organizations greatly by improving their understanding of their customer behaviors, by optimizing their business processes, by enabling them to anticipate problems before they arise, and by helping them to recognize opportunities well ahead of time.

Agent Technology

A software agent is a program that is capable of performing a predefined programmable task on behalf of the user. For example, on the Internet, software agents can be used to sort and filter out e-mail according to rules defined by the user. Within the data warehouse, software agents are beginning to be used to alert users to predefined business conditions. They are also beginning to be used extensively in conjunction with data mining and predictive modeling techniques. Some vendors specialize in alert system tools. You should definitely consider software agent programs for your data warehouse.

As the size of data warehouses continues to grow, agent technology gets applied more and more. Let us say your marketing analyst needs to use your data warehouse at specific, invariable intervals to identify threat and opportunity conditions that can offer business advantages to the enterprise. The analyst has to run several queries and perform multilevel analysis to find these conditions. Such conditions are exception conditions. So the analyst has to step through very intense iterative analysis. Some threat and opportunity conditions may be discovered only after long periods of iterative analysis. This takes up a lot of the analyst's time, perhaps on a daily basis.

Whenever a threat or opportunity condition is discovered through elaborate analysis, it makes sense to describe the event to a software agent program. This program will then automatically signal to the analyst every time that condition is encountered in the future. This is the very essence of agent technology.

Software agents may even be used for routine monitoring of business performance. Your CEO may want to be notified every time the corporate-wide sales fall below the monthly targets, three months in a row. A software agent program may be used to alert him or her every time this condition happens. Your marketing VP may want to know every time the monthly sales promotions in all the stores are successful. Again, a software agent program may be used for this purpose.

Syndicated Data

The value of the data content is derived not only from the internal operational systems, but from suitable external data as well. With the escalating growth of data warehouse implementations, the market for syndicated data is expanding rapidly.

Examples of traditional suppliers of syndicated data are A. C. Nielsen and Information Resources, Inc. for retail data and Dun & Bradstreet and Reuters for financial and economic data. Some of the earlier data warehouses incorporated syndicated data from such traditional suppliers to enrich the data content.

Now data warehouse developers are looking at a host of new suppliers dealing with many other types of syndicated data. The more recent data warehouses receive demographic, psychographic, market research, and other kinds of useful data from new suppliers. Syndicated data is becoming big business.

Data Warehousing and ERP

Look around to see what types of applications companies have been implementing in the last few years. You will observe a predominant phenomenon. Many businesses are adopting ERP (enterprise resource planning) application packages offered by major vendors like SAP, Baan, JD Edwards, and PeopleSoft. The ERP market is huge, crossing the $50 billion mark.

Why are companies rushing into ERP applications? Most companies are plagued by numerous disparate applications that cannot present a single unified view of the corporate information. Many of the legacy systems are totally outdated. Reconciliation of data retrieved from various systems to produce meaningful and correct information is extremely difficult and, at some large corporations, almost impossible. Some companies were looking for alternative ways to circumvent the enormous undertaking of making old legacy systems Y2K-compliant. ERP vendors seemingly came to the rescue of such companies.

Data in ERP Packages   A remarkable feature of an ERP package is that it supports practically every phase of the day-to-day business of an enterprise, from inventory control to customer billing, from human resources to production management, from product costing to budgetary control. Because of this feature, ERP packages are huge and complex. The ERP applications collect and integrate lots of corporate data. As these are proprietary applications, the large volumes of data are stored in proprietary formats available for access only through programs written in proprietary languages. Usually, thousands of relational database tables arc needed to support all the various functions.

Integrating ERP and Data Warehouse   In the 1990s and beyond, when ERP was introduced, this grand solution promised to bring about the integrated corporate data repositories companies were looking for. Because all data was cleansed, transformed, and integrated in one place, the appealing vision was that decision making and action taking could take place from one integrated environment. Soon companies implementing ERP realized that the thousands of relational database tables, designed and normalized for running the business operations, were not at all suitable for providing strategic information. Moreover, ERP data repositories lacked data from external sources and from other operational systems in the company. If your company has ERP or is planning to acquire ERP, you need to consider the integration of ERP with data warehousing.

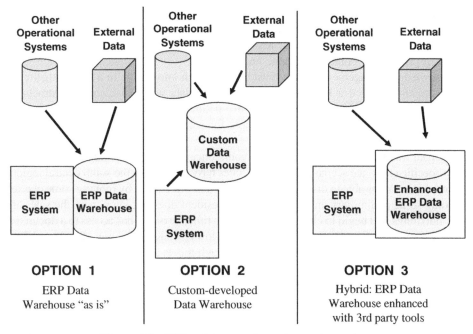

Figure 3-7   ERP and data warehouse integration options.

Integration Options   Corporations integrating ERP and the data warehouse initiatives usually adopt one of three options shown in Figure 3-7. ERP vendors have begun to complement their packages with data warehousing solutions. Companies adopting option 1 implement the data warehousing solution of the ERP vendor with currently available functionality and await enhancements. The downside to this approach is that you may be waiting forever for the enhancements. In option 2, companies implement customized data warehouses and use third-party tools to extract data from the ERP datasets. Retrieving and loading data from proprietary ERP datasets is not easy. Option 3 is a hybrid approach that combines the functionalities provided by the vendor's data warehouse with additional functionalities from third-party tools.

You need to examine these three approaches carefully and pick the one most suitable for your corporation.

Data Warehousing and KM

If 1998 marked the resurgence of ERP systems, 1999 marked the genesis of knowledge management (KM) systems in many corporations. Since then, into the 2000s, KM caught on very rapidly. Operational systems deal with data; informational systems such as data warehouses empower users by capturing, integrating, storing, and transforming the data into useful information for analysis and decision making. Knowledge management takes this to a higher level. It completes the process by providing users with knowledge to use the right information, at the right time, and at the right place,

Knowledge is actionable information. What do we mean by *knowledge management*? It is a systematic process for capturing, integrating, organizing, and communicating knowledge accumulated by employees. It is a vehicle to share corporate knowledge so that employees may be more effective and productive in their work. Where does the knowledge exist in a corporation? Corporate procedures, documents, reports analyzing exception conditions, objects, math models, what-if cases, text streams, video clips—all of these and many more such instruments contain corporate knowledge.

A knowledge management system must store all such knowledge in a knowledge repository, sometimes called a knowledge warehouse. A data warehouse contains structured information; a knowledge warehouse holds unstructured information. Therefore, a knowledge management framework must have tools for searching and retrieving unstructured information.

As a data warehouse developer, what are your concerns about knowledge management? Take a specific corporate scenario. Let us say sales have dropped in the south central region. Your marketing VP is able to discern this from your data warehouse by running some queries and doing some preliminary analysis. The vice president does not know why the sales are down, but things will begin to clear up if, just at that time, he or she has access to a document prepared by an analyst explaining why the sales are low and suggesting remedial action. That document contains the pertinent knowledge, although this is a simplistic example. The VP needs numeric information, but something more as well.

Knowledge, stored in a free unstructured format, must be linked to the sales results to provide context to the sales numbers from the data warehouse. With technological advances in organizing, searching, and retrieval of unstructured data, more knowledge philosophy will enter into data warehousing. Figure 3-8 shows how you can extend your data warehouse to include retrievals from the knowledge repository that is part of the knowledge management framework of your company.

Now, in the above scenario, the VP can get the information about the drop in sales from the data warehouse and then retrieve the relevant analyst's document from the knowledge repository. Knowledge obtained from the knowledge management system can provide

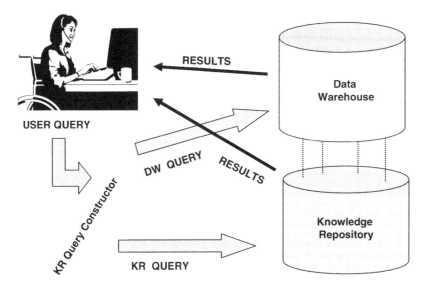

Integrated Data Warehouse—Knowledge Repository

Figure 3-8   Integration of KM and the data warehouse.

context to the information received from the data warehouse to understand the story behind the numbers.

Data Warehousing and CRM

Fiercer competition has forced many companies to pay greater attention to retaining customers and winning new ones. Customer loyalty programs have become the norm. Companies are moving away from mass marketing to one-on-one marketing. Customer focus has become the watchword. Concentration on customer experience and customer intimacy has become the key to better customer service. More and more companies are embracing customer relationship management (CRM) systems. A number of leading vendors offer turnkey CRM solutions that promise to enable one-on-one service to customers.

When your company is gearing up to be more attuned to high levels of customer service, what can you, as a data warehouse architect, do? If you already have a data warehouse, how must you readjust it? If you are building a new data warehouse, what are the factors for special emphasis? You will have to make your data warehouse more focused on the customer. You will have to make your data warehouse CRM-ready, not an easy task by any means. In spite of the difficulties, the payoff from a CRM-ready data warehouse is substantial.

Your data warehouse must hold details of every transaction at every touchpoint with each customer. This means every unit of every sale of every product to every customer must be gathered in the data warehouse repository. You need not only sales data in detail but also details of every other type of encounter with each customer. In addition to summary data, you have to load every encounter with every customer into the data warehouse. Atomic or detailed data provides maximum flexibility for the CRM-ready data warehouse. Making your data warehouse CRM-ready will increase the data volumes tremendously. Fortunately, today's technology facilitates large volumes of atomic data to be placed across multiple storage management devices that can be accessed through common data warehouse tools.

To make your data warehouse CRM-ready, you have to enhance some other functions also. For customer-related data, cleansing and transformation functions are more involved and complex. Before taking the customer name and address records to the data warehouse, you have to parse unstructured data to eliminate duplicates, combine them to form distinct households, and enrich them with external demographic and psychographic data. These are major efforts. Traditional data warehousing tools are not quite suited for the specialized requirements of customer-focused applications.

Agile Development

During the 1990s more and more organizations began to realize the problems encountered while adopting traditional methods of software development. The development methodology had been too structured, linear, and inflexible. Project delays and budget overruns became common and troublesome. Organizations suffered far-reaching consequences. Development efforts took too long and became too expensive. Users and stakeholders got frustrated. Ongoing feuds among groups in the development team resulted in rampant political maneuvers. Important issues slipped through the cracks. A radical new way of approaching software development was immediately called for.

Answering the clarion call for reformation, in February 2001 an initial group of 17 methodologists met in the city of Snowbird, Utah, and formed the Agile Software Development Alliance (briefly known as the Agile Alliance). The agile software development methodology was born. This group did not consist of professionals with exactly the same skills and background; the group spanned a panel of professionals with varied backgrounds and experience levels. They met with one primary goal: to dramatically improve the software development effort.

The initial members of the Agile Alliance agreed on a bold manifesto that enumerates preferential and underlying themes for successful software development: people and interactions, usable software, user collaboration, and acceptance of change. Agile software development is based on a set of well-defined principles and practices. It is not a set of software tools and mechanisms for software development.

Today, many organizations have embraced the principles and practices of agile development and have realized remarkable success in their software projects. More recently companies have begun to apply agile development to data warehousing and business intelligence projects. In later chapters, we will discuss this further.

Active Data Warehousing

So far we have discussed a number of significant trends that are very relevant to what you need to bear in mind while building your data warehouse. Why not end our discussion of the significant trends with a bang? Let us look at what is known as active data warehousing.

What do you think of opening your data warehouse to 30,000 users worldwide, consisting of employees, customers, and business partners, in addition to allowing about 15 million users public access to the information every day? What do you think about making it a 24-7 continuous service delivery environment with 99.9% availability? Your data warehouse quickly becomes mission-critical instead of just being strategic. You are into active data warehousing.

This is what one global company has accomplished with an active data warehouse. The company operates in more than 60 countries, manufactures in more than 40 countries, conducts research in nearly 30 countries, and sells over 50,000 products in 200 countries. The advantages of opening up the data warehouse to outside parties other than employees are enormous. Suppliers work with the company on improved demand planning and supply chain management; the company and its distributors cooperate on planning between different sales strategies; customers make expeditious purchasing decisions. The active data warehouse truly provides one-on-one service to customers and business partners.

EMERGENCE OF STANDARDS

Think back to our discussion in Chapter 1 of the data warehousing environment as a blend of many technologies. A combination of multiple types of technologies is needed for building a data warehouse. The range is wide: data modeling, data extraction, data transformation, database management systems, control modules, alert system agents, query tools, analysis tools, report writers, and so on.

Now in a hot industry such as data warehousing, there is no scarcity of vendors and products. In each of the multitude of technologies supporting the data warehouse, numerous vendors and products exist. The implication is that when you build your data warehouse, many choices are available to you to create an effective solution with the best-of-breed products. That is the good news. However, the bad news is that when you try to use multivendor products, the result could also be total confusion and chaos. These multivendor products have to cooperate and work together in your data warehouse.

Unfortunately, there are no elaborate and established standards for the various products to exchange information and function together. When you use the database product from one vendor, the query and reporter tool from another vendor, and the OLAP (online analytical processing) product from yet another vendor, these three products have no standard method for exchanging data. Standards are especially critical in two areas: metadata interchange and OLAP functions.

Metadata is like the total roadmap to the information contained in a data warehouse. Each product adds to the total metadata content; each product needs to use metadata created by the other products. Metadata is like the glue that holds all the functional pieces together.

No modern data warehouse is complete without OLAP functionality. Without OLAP, you cannot provide your users full capability to perform multidimensional analysis, to view the information from many perspectives, and to execute complex calculations. OLAP is crucial.

In the following sections, we will review the progress made so far in establishing standards in these two significant areas. Although much progress has been made, as of the late 2000s, we have not achieved fully adopted standards in either of the areas.

Metadata

Two separate bodies have been working on standards for metadata, the Meta Data Coalition and the Object Management Group.

The Meta Data Coalition (MDC) was formed as a consortium of about 50 vendors and interested parties in October 1995 to launch a metadata standards initiative. The coalition worked on a standard known as the Open Information Model (OIM). Microsoft joined the coalition in December 1998 and became a staunch supporter along with some other leading vendors. In July 1999, the Meta Data Coalition accepted the Open Information Model as the standard and began to work on extensions. In November 1999, the coalition was driving new key initiatives. However, in November 2000, Meta Data Coalition discontinued its independent operations and merged with the Object Management Group. This paved the way for a unified standard combining the results of the efforts of two independent bodies.

The Object Management Group (OMG) comprised another group of vendors, including Oracle, IBM, Hewlett-Packard, Sun, and Unisys, which sought metadata standards through the Object Management Group, a larger, established forum dealing with a wider array of standards in object technology. In June 2000, the Object Management Group unveiled the Common Warehouse Metamodel (CWM) as the standard for metadata interchange for data warehousing.

In April 2000, the Meta Data Coalition and the Object Management Group announced that they would cooperate in reaching consensus on a single standard. This goal was realized in November 2000 when both bodies merged. As most corporate data is managed with tools from Oracle, IBM, and Microsoft, cooperation between the two camps was all the more critical. Since the merger, OMG has worked on integrating the Meta Data Coalition's OIM into its CWM.

OLAP

The OLAP Council was established in January 1995 as a customer advocacy group to serve as an industry guide. Membership and participation are open to interested organizations. In early 2000 the council included 16 general members, mainly vendors of OLAP products.

JAN 1999	Council outlines areas of focus (2007 – Council/ASF defunct)
NOV 1998	Council releases Enhanced Analytical Processing benchmark
JAN 1998	Council announces Oracle-led, read-only MDAPI 2.0
	Council "re-born" as the Analytical Solutions Forum (ASF)
MAY 1997	NCR joins the Council
SEP 1996	Council releases MDAPI
JUL 1996	IQ Software company joins the Council
MAY 1996	IBM joins the Council
APR 1996	The Council releases first benchmark
MAR 1996	Business Objects company joins the Council
JAN 1995	OLAP Council established

Figure 3-9   OLAP Council: activities timeline.

Over the years, the council has worked on OLAP standards for the Multi-Dimensional Application Programmers Interface (MDAPI) and has come up with revisions. Figure 3-9 shows a timeline of the earlier activities of the council.

Several OLAP vendors, platform vendors, consultants, and system integrators had indicated their support for MDAPI 2.0. OLAP membership dwindled and soon the council was reborn as the Analytical Solutions Forum (ASF). In practice, MDAPI 2.0 never really got adopted by any substantial group of vendors. It appears the OLAP Council and its successor ASF have been long forgotten.

WEB-ENABLED DATA WAREHOUSE

We all know that the single most remarkable phenomenon that has impacted computing and communication during the last few years is the Internet. At every major industry conference and in every trade journal, most of the discussions relate to the Internet and the World Wide Web in one way or another.

Starting with a meager number of just four host computer systems in 1969, the Internet swelled to gigantic proportions, with nearly 95 million hosts by 2000. It is still growing exponentially. The number of World Wide Web sites escalated to nearly 26 million by 2000. Nearly 150 million global users get on the Internet. Making full use of the ever-popular Web technology, numerous companies have built Intranets and Extranets to reach their employees, customers, and business partners. The Web has become the universal information delivery system.

We are also aware of how the Internet has fueled the tremendous growth of electronic commerce in recent years. Annual volume of business-to-business e-commerce exceeds

$300 billion and total e-commerce will soon pass the $1 trillion mark. No business can compete or survive without a Web presence. The number of companies conducting business over the Internet had grown to 400,000 by 2003.

As a data warehouse professional, what are the implications for you? Clearly, you have to tap into the enormous potential of the Internet and Web technology for enhancing the value of your data warehouse. Also, you need to recognize the significance of e-commerce and enhance your warehouse to support and expand your company's e-business.

You have to transform your data warehouse into a Web-enabled data warehouse. On the one hand, you have to bring your data warehouse to the Web, and, on the other hand, you need to bring the Web to your data warehouse. In the next two subsections, we will discuss these two distinct aspects of a Web-enabled data warehouse.

The Warehouse to the Web

In early implementations, the corporate data warehouse was intended for managers, executives, business analysts, and a few other high-level employees as a tool for analysis and decision making. Information from the data warehouse was delivered to this group of users in a client-server environment. But today's data warehouses are no longer confined to a select group of internal users. Under present conditions, corporations need to increase the productivity of all the members in the corporation's value chain. Useful information from the corporate data warehouse must be provided not only to employees but also to customers, suppliers, and all other business partners.

So in today's business climate, you need to open your data warehouse to the entire community of users in the value chain, and perhaps also to the general public. This is a tall order. How can you accomplish this requirement to serve information to thousands of users in 24-7 mode? How can you do this without incurring exorbitant costs for information delivery? The Internet, along with Web technology, is the answer. The Web will be your primary information delivery mechanism.

This new delivery method will radically change the ways your users will retrieve, analyze, and share information from your data warehouse. The components of your information delivery will be different. The Internet interface will include a browser, search engine, push technology, home page, information content, hypertext links, and downloaded Java or ActiveX applets.

When you bring your data warehouse to the Web, from the point of view of the users, the key requirements are: self-service data access, interactive analysis, high availability and performance, zero-administration client (thin client technology such as Java applets), tight security, and unified metadata.

The Web to the Warehouse

Bringing the Web to the warehouse essentially involves capturing the clickstream of all the visitors to your company's Web site and performing all the traditional data warehousing functions. And you must accomplish this, near real-time, in an environment that has now come to be known as the data Webhouse. Your effort will involve extraction, transformation, and loading of the clickstream data to the Webhouse repository. You will have to build dimensional schemas from the clickstream data and deploy information delivery systems from the Webhouse.

Clickstream data tracks how people proceeded through your company's Web site, what triggers purchases, what attracts people, and what makes them come back. Clickstream data enables analysis of several key measures, including:

- Customer demand
- Effectiveness of marketing promotions
- Effectiveness of affiliate relationship among products
- Demographic data collection
- Customer buying patterns
- Feedback on Web site design

A clickstream Webhouse may be the single most important tool for identifying, prioritizing, and retaining e-commerce customers. The Webhouse can produce the following useful information:

- Site statistics
- Visitor conversions
- Ad metrics
- Referring partner links
- Site navigation resulting in orders
- Site navigation not resulting in orders
- Pages that are session killers

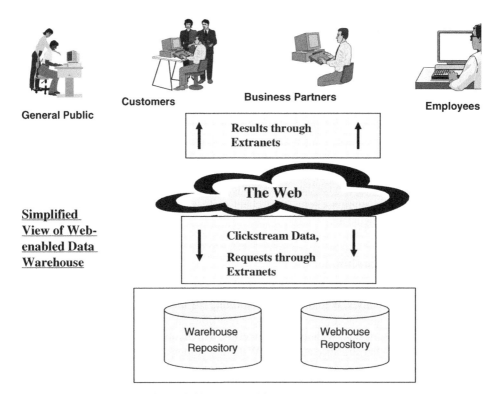

Figure 3-10   Web-enabled data warehouse.

- Relationships between customer profiles and page activities
- Best customer and worst customer analysis

The Web-Enabled Configuration

Figure 3-10 indicates an architectural configuration for a Web-enabled data warehouse. Notice the presence of the essential functional features of a traditional data warehouse. In addition to the data warehouse repository holding the usual types of information, the Webhouse repository contains clickstream data.

The convergence of the Web and data warehousing is of supreme importance to every corporation doing business in the twenty-first century. Because of its critical significance, we will discuss this topic in much greater detail in Chapter 16.

CHAPTER SUMMARY

- Data warehousing has become mainstream with the spread of high-volume data warehouses and the rapid increase in the number of vendor products.
- To be effective, modern data warehouses need to store multiple types of data: structured and unstructured, including documents, images, audio, and video.
- Data visualization deals with displaying information in several types of visual forms: text, numerical arrays, spreadsheets, charts, graphs, and so on. Tremendous progress has been made in data visualization, including information through dashboards and scorecards.
- Data warehouse performance may be improved by using parallel processing with appropriate hardware and software options. Many companies are opting for data warehouse appliances.
- It is critical to adapt data warehousing to work with ERP packages, knowledge management, and customer relationship systems.
- The data warehousing industry is seriously seeking agreed-upon standards for metadata and OLAP. The end is perhaps in sight.
- Web-enabling the data warehouse means using the Web for information delivery and integrating the clickstream data from the corporate Web site for analysis. The convergence of data warehousing and Web technology is crucial to every business in the twenty-first century.

REVIEW QUESTIONS

1. State any three factors that indicate the continued growth in data warehousing and business intelligence. Can you think of some examples?

2. Why do data warehouses continue to grow in size, storing huge amounts of data? Give any three reasons.

3. Why is it important to store multiple types of data in the data warehouse? Give examples of some nonstructured data likely to be found in the data warehouse of a health management organization (HMO).

4. What is meant by data fusion? Where does it fit in data warehousing?

5. Describe four types of charts you are likely to see in the delivery of information from a data mart supporting the finance department.

6. What is your understanding of data warehouse appliances? List some of the benefits of data warehouse appliances.

7. Explain what is meant by agent technology? How can this technology be used in a data warehouse?

8. Describe any one of the options available to integrate ERP with data warehousing.

9. What is CRM? How can you make your data warehouse CRM-ready?

10. What do we mean by a Web-enabled data warehouse? Describe three of its functional features.

EXERCISES

1. Indicate if true or false:

    A. Data warehousing helps in customized marketing.
    B. It is as important to include unstructured data as structured data in a data warehouse.
    C. Dynamic charts are themselves user interfaces.
    D. MPP is a shared-memory parallel hardware configuration.
    E. ERP systems may be substituted for data warehouses.
    F. Most of a corporation's knowledge base contains unstructured data.
    G. The traditional data transformation tools are quite adequate for a CRM-ready data warehouse.
    H. Metadata standards facilitate deploying a combination of best-of-breed products.
    I. MDAPI is a data fusion standard.
    J. A Web-enabled data warehouse stores only the clickstream data captured at the corporation's Web site.

2. As the senior analyst on the data warehouse project of a large retail chain, you are responsible for improving data visualization of the output results. Make a list of your recommendations.

3. Explain how and why parallel processing can improve performance for data loading and index creation.

4. Discuss three specific ways in which agent technology may be used to enhance the value of the data warehouse in a large manufacturing company.

5. Your company is in the business of renting DVDs and video tapes. The company has recently entered into e-business and the senior management wants to make the existing data warehouse Web-enabled. List and describe any three of the major tasks required for satisfying the management's directive.

PART 2

PLANNING AND REQUIREMENTS

CHAPTER 4

PLANNING AND PROJECT MANAGEMENT

CHAPTER OBJECTIVES

- Review the essentials of planning for a data warehouse
- Distinguish between data warehouse projects and OLTP system projects
- Learn how to adapt the life cycle approach for a data warehouse project
- Introduce agile development methodology for DW projects
- Discuss project team organization, roles, and responsibilities
- Consider the warning signs and success factors

As soon as you read the title of this chapter, you might hasten to conclude that this is a chapter intended for the project manager or the project coordinator. If you are not already a project manager or planning to be one in the near future, you might be inclined to just skim through the chapter. That would be a mistake. This chapter is very much designed for all IT professionals, irrespective of their roles in data warehousing projects. It will show you how best you can fit into your specific role in a project. If you want to be part of a team that is passionate about building a successful data warehouse, you need the details presented in this chapter. So please read on.

First read the following confession.

Consultant   So, your company is into data warehousing? How many data marts do you have?

Project Manager   Eleven.

Consultant   That's great. But why so many?

Project Manager   Ten mistakes.

Data Warehousing Fundamentals for IT Professionals, Second Edition. By Paulraj Ponniah
Copyright © 2010 John Wiley & Sons, Inc.

Although this conversation is a bit exaggerated, according to industry experts, more than 50% of data warehouse projects are considered failures. In many cases, the project is not completed and the system is not delivered. In a few cases, the project somehow gets completed but the data warehouse turns out to be a data basement. The project is improperly sized and architected. The data warehouse is not aligned with the business. Projects get abandoned in midstream.

Several factors contribute to the failures. When your company gets into data warehousing for the first time, the project will involve many organizational changes. At the present time, the emphasis is on enterprise-wide information analysis. Until now, each department and each user "owned" its data and was concerned with a set of its "own" computer systems. Data warehousing has changed all of that and made managers, data owners, and end-users uneasy. You are likely to uncover problems with the production systems as you build the data warehouse.

PLANNING YOUR DATA WAREHOUSE

More than any other factor, improper planning and inadequate project management tend to result in failures. First and foremost, determine if your company really needs a data warehouse. Is it really ready for one? You need to develop criteria for assessing the value expected from your data warehouse. Your company has to decide on the type of data warehouse to be built and where to keep it. You have to ascertain where the data is going to come from and even whether you have all the needed data. You have to establish who will be using the data warehouse, how they will use it, and at what times.

We will discuss the various issues related to the proper planning for a data warehouse. You will learn how a data warehouse project differs from the types of projects you were involved with in the past. We will study the guidelines for making your data warehouse project a success.

Key Issues

Planning for your data warehouse begins with a thorough consideration of the key issues. Answers to the key questions are vital for proper planning and successful completion of the project. Therefore, let us consider the pertinent issues, one by one.

Value and Expectations   Some companies jump into data warehousing and business intelligence projects without assessing the value to be derived from their proposed data warehouse. Of course, first you have to be sure that, given the culture and the current requirements of your company, a data warehouse is the most viable solution. After you have established the suitability of this solution, only then can you begin to enumerate the benefits and value propositions. Will your data warehouse help the executives and managers to do better planning and make better decisions? Is it going to improve the bottom line? Is it going to increase market share? If so, by how much? What are the expectations? What does the management want to accomplish through the data warehouse? As part of the overall planning process, make a list of realistic benefits and expectations. This is the starting point.

Risk Assessment   Planners generally associate project risks with the cost of the project. If the project fails, how much money will go down the drain? But the assessment of risks is more than calculating the loss from the project costs. What are the risks faced by the company without the benefits derivable from a data warehouse? What losses are likely to be incurred? What opportunities are likely to be missed? Risk assessment is broad and relevant to each business. Use the culture and business conditions of your company to assess the risks. Include this assessment as part of your planning document.

Top-Down or Bottom-Up In Chapter 2, we discussed the top-down and bottom-up approaches for building a data warehouse. The top-down approach is to start at the enterprise-wide data warehouse, and possibly build it iteratively. Then data from the overall, large enterprise-wide data warehouse flows into departmental and subject data marts. On the other hand, the bottom-up approach is to start by building individual data marts, one by one. The conglomerate of these data marts will make up the enterprise data warehouse.

We looked at the pros and cons of the two methods. We also discussed a practical approach of going bottom-up, but making sure that the individual data marts are conformed to one another so that they can be viewed as a whole. For this practical approach to be successful, you have to first plan and define requirements at the overall corporate level.

You have to weigh these options as they apply to your company. Do you have the large resources needed to build a corporate-wide data warehouse first and then deploy the individual data marts? This option may also take more time for implementation and delay the realization of potential benefits. But this option, by its inherent approach, will ensure a fully unified view of the corporate data.

It is possible that your company would be satisfied with quick deployment of a few data marts for specific reasons. At this time, it may be important to just quickly react to some market forces or ward off some fierce competitor. There may not be time to build an overall data warehouse. Or, you may want to examine and adopt the practical approach of conformed data marts. Whatever approach your company desires to adopt, scrutinize the options carefully and make the choice. Document the implications of the choice in the planning document.

Build or Buy This is a major issue for all organizations. No one builds a data warehouse totally from scratch by in-house programming. There is no need to reinvent the wheel every time. A wide and rich range of third-party tools and solutions are available. After nearly a decade of the data warehousing movement the market has matured, with suitable tools for data warehousing and business intelligence. The real question is how much of your data marts should you build yourselves? How much of these may be composed of ready-made solutions? What type of mix and match must be done?

In a data warehouse, there is a large range of functions. Do you want to write more in-house programs for data extraction and data transformation? Do you want to use in-house programs for loading the data warehouse storage? Do you want to use vendor tools completely for information delivery and business intelligence? You retain control over the functions wherever you use in-house software. On the other hand, the buy option could lead to quick implementation if managed effectively.

Be wary of the marts-in-the-box or the 15-minute data marts. There are no silver bullets out there. The bottom line is to do your homework and find the proper balance between in-house and vendor software. Do this at the planning stage itself.

Single Vendor or Best-of-Breed Vendors come in a variety of categories. There are multiple vendors and products catering to the many functions of the data warehouse. So what are the options? How should you decide? Two major options are: to use the products of a single vendor, or to use products from more than one vendor, selecting appropriate tools. Choosing a single vendor solution has a few advantages:

- High level of integration among the tools
- Constant look and feel
- Seamless cooperation among components
- Centrally managed information exchange
- Negotiable overall price

This approach will naturally enable your data warehouse to be well integrated and function coherently. However, only a few vendors such as IBM and NCR offer fully integrated solutions.

Reviewing this specific option further, here are the major advantages of the best-of-breed solution that combines products from multiple vendors:

- You can build an environment to fit your organization.
- There is no need to compromise between database and support tools.
- You can select products best suited for the specific function.

With the best-of-breed approach, compatibility among the tools from the different vendors could become a serious problem. If you are taking this route, make sure the selected tools are proven to be compatible. In this case, the staying power of individual vendors is crucial. Also, you will have less bargaining power with regard to individual products and may incur higher overall expense. Make a note of the recommended approach: have one vendor for the database and the information delivery functions, and pick and choose other vendors for the remaining functions. However, the multivendor approach is not advisable if your environment is not heavily technical.

Business Requirements, Not Technology

Let business requirements drive your data warehouse, not technology. Although this seems so obvious, you would not believe how many data warehouse projects grossly violate this maxim. Many data warehouse developers are interested in putting pretty pictures on the user's screen and pay little attention to the real requirements. They like to build snappy systems exploiting the depths of technology and merely demonstrating their prowess in harnessing the power of technology.

Remember, data warehousing is not about technology, it is about solving users' need for strategic information. Do not plan to build the data warehouse before understanding the requirements. Start by focusing on what information is needed and not on how to provide the information. Do not emphasize the tools. Tools and products come and go. The basic structure and the architecture to support the user requirements are more important.

So before making the overall plan, conduct a preliminary survey of requirements. How do you do that? No details are necessary at this stage. No in-depth probing is needed. Just try to understand the overall requirements of the users. Your intention is to gain a broad understanding of the business. The outcome of this preliminary survey will help you formulate the overall plan. It will be crucial to set the scope of the project. Also, it will assist you in prioritizing and determining the rollout plan for individual data marts. For example, you may have to plan on rolling out the marketing data mart first, the finance mart next, and only then consider the human resources one.

What types of information must you gather in the preliminary survey? At a minimum, obtain general information on the following from each group of users:

- Mission and functions of each user group
- Computer systems used by the group
- Key performance indicators
- Factors affecting success of the user group
- Who the customers are and how they are classified
- Types of data tracked for the customers, individually and as groups
- Products manufactured or sold
- Categorization of products and services
- Locations where business is conducted
- Levels at which profits are measured—per customer, per product, per district
- Levels of cost details and revenue
- Current queries and reports for strategic information

As part of the preliminary survey, include a source system audit. Even at this stage, you must have a fairly good idea from where the data is going to be extracted for the data warehouse. Review the architecture of the source systems. Find out about the relationships among the data structures. What is the quality of the data? What documentation is available? What are the possible mechanisms for extracting the data from the source systems? Your overall plan must contain information about the source systems.

Top Management Support

No major initiative in a company can succeed without support from senior management. This is very true in the case of the company's data warehouse project. The project must have the full support of the top management right from day one.

No other venture unifies the information view of the entire corporation as the corporation's data warehouse does. The entire organization is involved and positioned for strategic advantage. No one department or group can sponsor the data warehousing initiative in a company.

Make sure you have a sponsor from the highest levels of management to keep the focus. The data warehouse must often satisfy conflicting requirements. The sponsor must wield his or her influence to arbitrate and to mediate. In most companies that launch data warehouses, the CEO is also directly interested in its success. In some companies, a senior executive outside of IT becomes the primary sponsor. This person, in turn, nominates some of the senior managers to be actively involved in the day-to-day progress of the project. Whenever the project encounters serious setbacks, the sponsor jumps in to resolve the issues.

Justifying Your Data Warehouse

Even if your company is a medium-sized company, when everything is accounted for, the total investment in your data warehouse could run to a few million dollars. A rough breakdown of the costs is as follows: hardware, 31%; software, including the DBMS, 24%; staff and system integrators, 35%; administration, 10%. How do you justify the total cost by balancing the risks against the benefits, both tangible and intangible? How can you calculate the ROI and ROA? How can you make a business case?

It is not easy. Real benefits may not be known until after your data warehouse is built and put to use fully. Your data warehouse will allow users to run queries and analyze the variables in many different ways. Your users can run what-if analysis by moving into several hypothetical scenarios and make strategic decisions. They will not be limited in the ways in which they can query and analyze. Who can predict what queries and analysis they might run, what significant decisions they will be able to make, and how beneficially these decisions will impact the bottom line?

Many companies are able to introduce data warehousing without a full cost-justification analysis. Here the justification is based mainly on intuition and potential competitive pressures. In these companies, the top management is able to readily recognize the benefits of data integration, improved data quality, user autonomy in running queries and analyses, and the ease of information accessibility. If your company is such a company, good luck to you. Do some basic justification and jump into the project with both feet in.

Not every company's top management is so easy to please. In many companies, some type of formal justification is required. We want to present the typical approaches taken for justifying the data warehouse project. Review these examples and pick the approach that is closest to what will work in your organization. Here are some sample approaches for preparing the justification:

1. Calculate the current technology costs to produce the applications and reports supporting strategic decision making. Compare this with the estimated costs for the data warehouse and find the ratio between the current costs and proposed costs. See if this ratio is acceptable to senior management.

2. Calculate the business value of the proposed data warehouse with the estimated dollar values for profits, dividends, earnings growth, revenue growth, and market share growth. Review this business value expressed in dollars against the data warehouse costs and come up with the justification.

3. Do the full-fledged exercise. Identify all the components that will be affected by the proposed data warehouse and those that will affect the data warehouse. Start with the cost items, one by one, including hardware purchase or lease, vendor software, in-house software, installation and conversion, ongoing support, and maintenance costs. Then put a dollar value on each of the tangible and intangible benefits, including cost reduction, revenue enhancement, and effectiveness in the business community. Go further to do a cash flow analysis and calculate the ROI.

The Overall Plan

The seed for a data warehousing initiative gets sown in many ways. The initiative may get ignited simply because the competition has a data warehouse. Or the CIO makes a recommendation to the CEO or some other senior executive proposes a data warehouse as the solution for the information problems in a company. In some cases, a senior executive was exposed to the idea at a conference or seminar. Whatever may be the reason for your company to think about data warehousing, the real initiative begins with a well-thought-out

► INTRODUCTION

► MISSION STATEMENT

► SCOPE

► GOALS & OBJECTIVES

► KEY ISSUES & OPTIONS

► VALUES & EXPECTATIONS

► JUSTIFICATION

► EXECUTIVE SPONSORSHIP

► IMPLEMENTATION STRATEGY

► TENTATIVE SCHEDULE

► PROJECT AUTHORIZATION

Figure 4-1   Overall plan for data warehousing initiative.

formal plan that sets the direction, tone, and goals of the initiative. The plan lays down the motivation and the incentives. It considers the various options and reasons out the selection process. The plan discusses the type of data warehouse and enumerates the expectations. This is not a detailed project plan. It is an overall plan to lay the foundation, to recognize the need, and to authorize a formal project.

Figure 4-1 lists the types of content to be included in the formal overall plan. Review the list carefully and adapt it for your data warehouse initiative.

THE DATA WAREHOUSE PROJECT

As an IT professional, you have worked on application projects before. You know what goes on in these projects and are aware of the methods needed to build the applications from planning through implementation. You have been part of the analysis, the design, the programming, or the testing phases. If you have functioned as a project manager or a team leader, you know how projects are monitored and controlled. A project is a project. If you have seen one IT project, have you not seen them all?

The answer is not a simple yes or no. Data warehouse projects are different from projects building the transaction processing systems. If you are new to data warehousing, your first data warehouse project will reveal the major differences. We will discuss these differences and also consider ways to react to them. We will also ask a basic question about the readiness of the IT and user departments to launch a data warehouse project. How about the traditional system development life cycle (SDLC) approach? Can we use this approach to data warehouse projects as well? If so, what are the development phases in the life cycle?

How is it Different?

Let us understand why data warehouse projects are distinctive. You are familiar with application projects for OLTP systems. A comparison with an OLTP application project will help us recognize the differences.

Data Warehouse: Distinctive Features and Challenges for Project Management

DATA ACQUISITION	DATA STORAGE	INFO. DELIVERY
Large number of sources	Storage of large data volumes	Several user types
Many disparate sources		Queries stretched to limits
Different computing platforms	Rapid growth	Multiple query types
	Need for parallel processing	Web-enabled
Outside sources		Multidimensional analysis
Huge initial load	Data storage in staging area	OLAP functionality
Ongoing data feeds	Multiple index types	Metadata management
Data replication considerations	Several index files	Interfaces to DSS apps.
	Storage of newer data types	Feed into Data Mining
Difficult data integration	Archival of old data	Multi-vendor tools
Complex data transformations	Compatibility with tools	
Data cleansing	RDBMS & MDDBMS	

Figure 4-2   Differences between a data warehouse project and one on OLTP application.

Try to describe a data warehouse in terms of major functional pieces. First you have the data acquisition component. Next is the data storage component. Finally, there is the information delivery component. At a very general level, a data warehouse is made up of these three broad components. You will notice that a data warehouse project differs from a project on OLTP application in each of these three functional areas. Let us go over the differences. Figure 4-2 lists the differences and also describes them.

Data warehousing is a new paradigm. We almost expect a data warehouse project to be different from an OLTP system project. We can accept the differences. But more important is the discussion of the consequences of the differences. What must you do about the differences? How should the project phases be changed and enhanced to deal with them? The following suggestions address the differences:

- Consciously recognize that a data warehouse project has broader scope, tends to be more complex, and involves many different technologies.
- Allow for extra time and effort for newer types of activities.
- Do not hesitate to find and use specialists wherever in-house talent is not available. A data warehouse project has many out-of-the-ordinary tasks.
- Metadata in a data warehouse is so significant that it needs special treatment throughout the project. Pay extra attention to building the metadata framework properly.
- Typically, you will be using a few third-party tools during the development and for ongoing functioning of the data warehouse. In your project schedule, plan to include time for the evaluation and selection of tools.
- Allow ample time to build and complete the infrastructure.

- Include enough time for the architecture design.
- Involve the users in every stage of the project. Data warehousing could be completely new to both IT and the users in your company. A joint effort is imperative.
- Allow sufficient time for training the users in the query and reporting tools.
- Because of the large number of tasks in a data warehouse project, parallel development tracks are absolutely necessary. Be prepared for the challenges of running parallel tracks in the project life cycle.

Assessment of Readiness

Let us say you have justified the data warehouse project and received the approval and blessing of the top management. You have an overall plan for the data warehousing initiative. You have grasped the key issues and understood how a data warehouse project is different and what you have to do to handle the differences. Are you then ready to jump into the preparation of a project plan and get moving swiftly?

Not yet. You need to do a formal readiness assessment. Normally, to many of the project team members and to almost all of the users, data warehousing would be a brand new concept. A readiness assessment and orientation is important. Which person does the readiness assessment? The project manager usually does it with the assistance of an outside expert. By this time, the project manager would already be trained in data warehousing or he or she may have prior experience. Engage in discussions with the executive sponsor, users, and potential team members. The objective is to assess their familiarity with data warehousing in general, assess their readiness, and uncover gaps in their knowledge. Prepare a formal readiness assessment report before the project plan is firmed up.

The readiness assessment report is expected to serve the following purposes:

- Lower the risks of big surprises occurring during implementation
- Provide a proactive approach to problem resolution
- Reassess corporate commitment
- Review and reidentify project scope and size
- Identify critical success factors
- Restate user expectations
- Ascertain training needs

The Life-Cycle Approach

As an IT professional you are all too familiar with the traditional system development life cycle (SDLC). You know how to begin with a project plan, move into the requirements analysis phase, then into the design, construction, and testing phases, and finally into the implementation phase. The life cycle approach accomplishes all the major objectives in the system development process. It enforces orderliness and enables a systematic approach to building computer systems. The life cycle methodology breaks down the project complexity and removes any ambiguity with regard to the responsibilities of project team members. It implies a predictable set of tasks and deliverables.

That the life cycle approach breaks down the project complexity is reason enough for this approach to be considered for a data warehouse project. A data warehouse project is complex in terms of tasks, technologies, and team member roles. But a one-size-fits-all life cycle approach will not work for a data warehouse project. Adapt the life cycle approach to the special needs of your data warehouse project. Note that a life cycle for data warehouse development is not a waterfall method in which one phase ends and cascades into the next one.

The approach for a data warehouse project has to include iterative tasks going through cycles of refinement. For example, if one of your tasks in the project is identification of data sources, you might begin by reviewing all the source systems and listing all the source data structures. The next iteration of the task is meant to review the data elements with the users. You move on to the next iteration of reviewing the data elements with the database administrator and some other IT staff. The next iteration of walking through the data elements one more time completes the refinements and the task. This type of iterative process is required for each task because of the complexity and broad scope of the project.

Remember that the broad functional components of a data warehouse are data acquisition, data storage, and information delivery. Make sure the phases of your development life cycle wrap around these functional components. Figure 4-3 shows how to relate the functional components to SDLC.

As in any system development life cycle, the data warehouse project begins with the preparation of a project plan. The project plan describes the project, identifies the specific objectives, mentions the crucial success factors, lists the assumptions, and highlights the critical issues. The plan includes the project schedule, lists the tasks and assignments, and provides for monitoring progress. Figure 4-4 provides a sample outline of a data warehouse project plan.

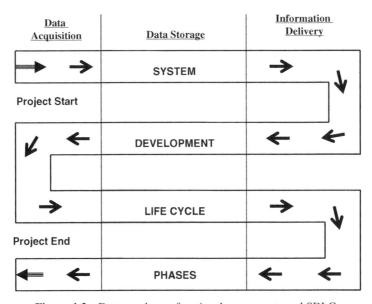

Figure 4-3   Date warehouse functional components and SDLC.

▶ INTRODUCTION

▶ PURPOSE

▶ ASSESSMENT OF READINESS

▶ GOALS & OBJECTIVES

▶ STAKEHOLDERS

▶ ASSUMPTIONS

▶ CRITICAL ISSUES

▶ SUCCESS FACTORS

▶ PROJECT TEAM

▶ PROJECT SCHEDULE

▶ DEPLOYMENT DETAILS

Figure 4-4   Sample outline of a data warehouse project plan.

THE DEVELOPMENT PHASES

In the previous section, we again referred to the overall functional components of a data warehouse as data acquisition, data storage, and information delivery. These three functional components form the general architecture of the data warehouse. There must be the proper technical infrastructure to support these three functional components. Therefore, when we formulate the development phases in the life cycle, we have to ensure that the phases include tasks relating to the three components. The phases must also include tasks to define the architecture as composed of the three components and to establish the underlying infrastructure to support the architecture. The design and construction phase for these three components may run somewhat in parallel.

Refer to Figure 4-5 and notice the three tracks of the development phases. In the development of every data warehouse, these tracks are present with varying sets of tasks. You may change and adapt the tasks to suit your specific requirements. You may want to emphasize one track more than the others. If data quality is a problem in your company, you need to pay special attention to the related phase. The figure shows the broad division of the project life cycle into the traditional phases:

- Project plan
- Requirements definition
- Design
- Construction
- Deployment
- Growth and maintenance

Interwoven within the design and construction phases are the three tracks along with the definition of the architecture and the establishment of the infrastructure. Each of the boxes shown in the diagram represents a major activity to be broken down further into individual

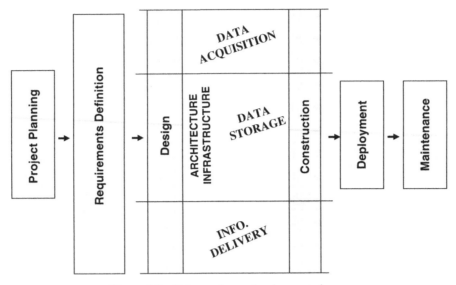

Figure 4-5   Data warehouse development phases.

tasks and assigned to the appropriate team members. Use the diagram as a guide for listing the activities and tasks for your data warehouse project. Although the major activities may remain the same for most warehouses, the individual tasks within each activity are likely to vary for your specific data warehouse.

In the following chapters, we will discuss these development activities in greater detail. When you get to those chapters, you may want to refer back to this diagram.

Adopting Agile Development

In the previous chapter we introduced the use of agile development principles and practices for software development. This is a recent phenomenon, more recent for data warehouse development than for other types of applications. Companies are beginning to adopt agile development for data warehouse and business intelligence projects. Agile development methodology encourages collaboration among project team members and users, and promotes iterative and incremental development efforts. The entire methodology rests on the adoption of certain core values, principles, and practices in every aspect of data warehouse development and implementation.

Core Values. Values that are emphasized include striving for simplicity and not being bogged down in complexity, providing and obtaining constant feedback on individual development tasks, fostering free and uninhibited communication, and rewarding courage to learn from mistakes.

Core Principles. Principles that are followed include encouraging quality, embracing change, changing incrementally, adopting simplicity, and providing rapid feedback.

Core Practices. Practices that are implemented include creating short releases of application components, performing development tasks jointly ("pair programming"), working the 40-hour work week intensively, not expanding the time for ineffective pursuits, and having user representatives on site with the project team.

Variables. Control variables that can be manipulated for trade-offs to achieve results are
time, quality, scope, and cost.

THE PROJECT TEAM

As in any type of project, the success of a data warehouse project rides on the shoulders of
the project team. The best team wins. A data warehouse project is similar to other software
projects in that it is human-intensive. It takes several trained and specially skilled persons
to form the project team. Organizing the project team for a data warehouse project has to
do with matching diverse roles with proper skills and levels of experience. That is not an
easy feat to accomplish.

Two things can break a project: complexity overload and responsibility ambiguity. In a
life cycle approach, the project team minimizes the complexity of the effort by sharing
and performing. When the right person on the team, with the right type of skills and with
the right level of experience, does an individual task, this person is really resolving the
complexity issue.

In a properly constituted project team, each person is given specific responsibilities or a
particular role based on his or her skill and experience level. In such a team, there is no
confusion or ambiguity about responsibilities.

In the following sections, we will discuss the fitting of the team members into suitable
roles. We will also discuss the responsibilities associated with the roles. Further, we will
discuss the skills and experience levels needed for each of these roles. Pay close attention
and learn how to determine project roles for your data warehouse. Also, try to match your
project roles with the responsibilities and tasks in your warehouse project.

Organizing the Project Team

Organizing a project team involves putting the right person in the right job. If you are organizing and putting together a team to work on an OLTP system development, you know that
the required skills set is of a reasonable size and is manageable. You would need specialized
skills in the areas of project management, requirements analysis, application design, database design, and application testing. But a data warehouse project calls for many other
roles. How then do you fill all these varied roles?

A good starting point is to list all the project challenges and specialized skills needed.
Your list may run like this: planning, defining data requirements, defining types of queries,
data modeling, tools selection, physical database design, source data extraction, data validation and quality control, setting up the metadata framework, and so on. As the next
step, using your list of skills and anticipated challenges, prepare a list of team roles
needed to support the development work.

Once you have a list of roles, you are ready to assign individual persons to the team roles.
It is not necessary to assign one or more persons to each of the identified roles. If your data
warehouse effort is not large and your company's resources are meager, try making the
same person wear many hats. In this personnel allocation process, remember that the user
representatives must also be considered as members of the project team. Do not fail to
recognize the users as part of the team and to assign them to suitable roles.

Skills, experience, and knowledge are important for team members. However, attitude,
team spirit, passion for the data warehouse effort, and strong commitment are equally important, if not more so. Do not neglect to look for these critical traits.

Executive Sponsor	Data Provision Specialist
Project Director	Business Analyst
Project Manager	System Administrator
User Representative Manager	Data Migration Specialist
Data Warehouse Administrator	Data Grooming Specialist
Organizational Change Manager	Data Mart Leader
Database Administrator	Infrastructure Specialist
Metadata Manager	Power User
Business Requirements Analyst	Training Leader
Data Warehouse Architect	Technical Writer
Data Acquisition Developer	Tools Specialist
Data Access Developer	Vendor Relations Specialist
Data Quality Analyst	Web Master
Data Warehouse Tester	Data Modeler
Maintenance Developer	Security Architect

Figure 4-6   Job titles in a data warehouse project.

Roles and Responsibilities

Project team roles are designated to perform one or more related tasks. In many data warehouse projects, the team roles are synonymous with the job titles given to the team members. If you review an OLTP system development project, you will find that the job titles for the team members are more or less standardized. In the OLTP system project, you will find the job titles of project manager, business analyst, systems analyst, programmer, data analyst, database administrator, and so on. However, data warehouse projects are not yet standardized as far as job tiles go. There still is an element of experimentation and exploration.

So what are the prevailing job titles? Let us first look at the long list shown in Figure 4-6. Do not be alarmed by the length of the list. Unless your data warehouse is of mammoth proportions, you will not need all these job titles. This list just indicates the possibilities and variations. Responsibilities of the same role may be attached to different job titles in different projects. In many projects, the same team member will fulfill the responsibilities of more than one role.

Data warehousing authors and practitioners tend to classify roles or job titles in various ways. They first come up with broad classifications and then include individual job titles within these classifications. Here are some of the classifications of the roles:

- Staffing for initial development, staffing for testing, staffing for ongoing maintenance, staffing for data warehouse management
- IT and end-users, then subclassifications within each of the two broad classifications, followed by further subclassifications
- Front office roles, back office roles
- Coaches, regular lineup, special teams
- Management, development, support
- Administration, data acquisition, data storage, information delivery

In your data warehouse project, you may want to come up with broad classifications that are best suited for your environment. How do you come up with the broad classifications? You will have to reexamine the goals and objectives. You will have to assess the areas in the development phases that would need special attention. Is data extraction going to be your greatest challenge? Then support that function with specialized roles. Is your information delivery function going to be complex? Then have special project team roles strong in information delivery. Once you have determined the broad classifications, then work on the individual roles within each classification. If it is your first data warehouse project, you may not come up with all the necessary roles up front. Do not be too concerned. You may keep supporting the project with additional team roles here and there as the project moves along.

You have read the long list of possible team roles and the ways the roles may be classified. This may be your first data warehouse project and you may be the one responsible to determine the team roles for the project. You want to get started and have a basic question: Is there a standard set of basic roles to get the project rolling? Not really. There is no such standard set. If you are inclined to follow traditional methodology, follow the classifications of management, development, and support. If you want to find strengths for the three major functional areas, then adopt the classifications of data acquisition, data storage, and information delivery. You may also find that a combination of these two ways of classifying would work for your data warehouse.

Despite the absence of a standard set of team roles, we would suggest the following basic set:

- Executive sponsor
- Project manager
- User liaison manager
- Lead architect
- Infrastructure specialist
- Business analyst
- Data modeler
- Data warehouse administrator
- Data transformation specialist
- Quality assurance analyst
- Testing coordinator
- End-user applications specialist
- Development programmer
- Lead trainer

Figure 4-7 lists the usual responsibilities attached to the suggested set of roles. Review the descriptions of the responsibilities. Add or modify the descriptions to make them applicable to the special circumstances of your data warehouse.

Skills and Experience Levels

We discussed the guidelines for determining the broad classifications of the team roles. After you figure out the classifications relevant to your data warehouse project, you will come up with the set of team roles appropriate to your situation. We reviewed some examples of

Executive Sponsor	**Data Warehouse Administrator**
Direction, support, arbitration.	DBA functions.
Project Manager	**Data Transformation Specialist**
Assignments, monitoring, control.	Data extraction, integration, transformation.
User Liaison Manager	**Quality Assurance Analyst**
Coordination with user groups.	Quality control for warehouse data.
Lead Architect	**Testing Coordinator**
Architecture design.	Program, system, tools testing.
Infrastructure Specialist	**End-User Applications Specialist**
Infrastructure design/construction.	Confirmation of data meanings/relationships.
Business Analyst	**Development Programmer**
Requirements definition.	In-house programs and scripts.
Data Modeler	**Lead Trainer**
Relational and dimensional modeling.	Coordination of User and Team training.

Figure 4-7   Roles and responsibilities of a data warehouse project team.

typical roles. The roles may also be called job titles in a project. Moving forward, you will write down the responsibilities associated with the roles you have established. You have established the roles and you have listed the responsibilities. Are you then ready to match the people to fill into these roles? There is one more step needed before you can do that.

To fit into the roles and discharge the responsibilities, the selected persons must have the right abilities. They should possess suitable skills and the proper work experience. So you have to come up with a list of skills and experience required for the various roles. Figure 4-8 describes the skills and experience levels for our sample set of team roles. Use the descriptions found in the figure as examples to compose the descriptions for the team roles in your data warehouse project.

It is not easy to find IT professionals to fill all the roles established for your data warehouse. OLTP systems are ubiquitous. All IT professionals have assumed some role or the other in an OLTP system project. This is not the case with data warehouse projects. Not too many professionals have direct hands-on experience in the development of data warehouses. Outstanding skills and abilities are in short supply.

If people qualified to work on data warehouse projects are not readily available, what is your recourse? How can you fill the roles in your project? This is where training becomes important. Train suitable professionals in data warehousing concepts and techniques. Let them learn the fundamentals and specialize for the specific roles. In addition to training your in-house personnel, use external consultants in specific roles for which you are unable to find people from the inside. However, as a general rule, consultants must not be used in leading roles. The project manager or the lead administrator must come from within the organization.

User Participation

In a typical OLTP application, the users interact with the system through GUI screens. They use the screens for data input and for retrieving information. The users receive any

Executive Sponsor

Senior level executive, in-depth knowledge of the business, enthusiasm and ability to moderate and arbitrate as necessary.

Project Manager

People skills, project management experience, business and user oriented, ability to be practical and effective.

User Liaison Manager

People skills, respected in user community, organization skills, team player, knowledge of systems from user viewpoint.

Lead Architect

Analytical skills, ability to see the big picture, expertise in interfaces, knowledge of data warehouse concepts.

Infrastructure Specialist

Specialist in hardware, operating systems, computing platforms, experience as operations staff.

Business Analyst

Analytical skills, ability to interact with users, sufficient industry experience as analyst.

Data Modeler

Expertise in relational and dimensional modeling with case tools, experience as data analyst.

Data Warehouse Administrator

Expert in physical database design and implementation, experience as relational DBA, MDDBMS experience a plus.

Data Transformation Specialist

Knowledge of data structures, in-depth knowledge of source systems, experience as analyst.

Quality Assurance Analyst

Knowledge of data quality techniques, knowledge of source systems data, experience as analyst.

Testing Coordinator

Familiarity with testing methods and standards, use of testing tools, knowledge of some data warehouse information delivery tools, experience as programmer/analyst.

End-User Applications Specialist

In-depth knowledge of source applications.

Development Programmer

Programming and analysis skills, experience as programmer in selected language and DBMS.

Lead Trainer

Training skills, experience in IT/User training, coordination and organization skills.

Figure 4-8   Skills and experience levels required for a data warehouse project team.

additional information through reports produced by the system at periodic intervals. If the users need special reports, they have to get IT involved to write ad hoc programs that are not part of the regular application.

In striking contrast, user interaction with a data warehouse is direct and intimate. Usually, there are no or just a few set reports or queries. When the implementation is complete, your users will begin to use the data warehouse directly with no mediation from IT. There is no predictability in the types of queries they will be running, the types of reports they will be requesting, or the types of analysis they will be performing. If there is one major difference between OLTP systems and data warehousing systems, it is in the usage of the system by the users.

What is the implication of this major difference in project team composition and data warehouse development? The implication is extremely consequential. What does this mean? This means that if the users will be using the data warehouse directly in unforeseen ways, they must have a strong voice in its development. They must be part of the project team all the way. More than an OLTP system project, a data warehouse project calls for serious joint application development (JAD) techniques.

Your data warehouse project will succeed only if appropriate members of the user community are accepted as team members with specific roles. Make use of their expertise and knowledge of the business. Tap into their experience in making business decisions. Actively involve them in the selection of information delivery tools. Seek their help in testing the system before implementation.

Project Planning

Provide goals, objectives, expectations, business information during preliminary survey; grant active top management support; initiate project as executive sponsor.

Requirements Definition

Actively participate in meetings for defining requirements; identify all source systems; define metrics for measuring business success, and business dimensions for analysis; define information needed from data warehouse.

Design

Review dimensional data model, data extraction and transformation design; provide anticipated usage for database sizing; review architectural design and metadata; participate in tool selection; review information delivery design.

Construction

Actively participate in user acceptance testing; test information delivery tools; validate data extraction and transformation functions; confirm data quality; test usage of metadata; benchmark query functions; test OLAP functions; participate in application documentation.

Deployment

Verify audit trails and confirm initial data load; match deliverables against stated expectations; arrange and participate in user training; provide final acceptance.

Maintenance

Provide input for enhancements; test and accept enhancements.

Figure 4-9   User participation in data warehouse development.

Figure 4-9 illustrates how and where in the development process users must be made to participate. Review each development phase and clearly decide how and where your users need to participate. This figure relates user participation to stages in the development process. Here is a list of a few team roles that users can assume to participate in the development:

- Project sponsor—responsible for supporting the project effort all the way (must be an executive)
- User department liaison representatives—help IT to coordinate meetings and review sessions and ensure active participation by the user departments
- Subject area experts—provide guidance in the requirements of the users in specific subject areas and clarify semantic meanings of business terms used in the enterprise
- Data review specialists—review the data models prepared by IT; confirm the data elements and data relationships
- Information delivery consultants—examine and test information delivery tools; assist in the tool selection
- User support technicians—act as the first-level, front-line support for the users in their respective departments

PROJECT MANAGEMENT CONSIDERATIONS

Your project team was organized, the development phases were completed, the testing was done, the data warehouse was deployed, and the project was pronounced completed on time and within budget. Has the effort been successful? In spite of the best intentions of the

Data Basement

Poor quality data
without proper access.

Data Shack

Pathetic data dump
collapsing even
before completion.

Data Mausoleum

An expensive data
basement with poor
access and
performance.

Data Cottage

Stand-alone, aloof,
fragmented, island
data mart.

Data Tenement

Built by a legacy
system vendor or an
ignorant consultant
with no idea of
what users want.

Data Jailhouse

Confined and invisible
data system keeping
data imprisoned so
that users cannot get at
the data.

Figure 4-10   Possible scenarios of failure.

project team, it is likely that the deployed data warehouse turns out to be anything but a data warehouse. Figure 4-10 shows possible scenarios of failure. How will your data warehouse turn out in the end?

Effective project management is critical to the success of a data warehouse project. In this section, we will consider project management issues as they apply especially to data warehouse projects, review some basic project management principles, and list the possible success factors. We will review a real-life successful project and examine the reasons for its success. When all is said and done, you cannot always run your project totally by the book. Adopt a practical approach that produces results without getting bogged down in unnecessary drudgery.

Guiding Principles

Having worked on OLTP system projects, you are already aware of some of the guiding principles of project management—do not give into analysis paralysis, do not allow scope creep, monitor slippage, keep the project on track, and so on. Although most of those guiding principles also apply to data warehouse project management, we do not want to repeat them here. On the other hand, we want to consider some guiding principles that pertain to data warehouse projects exclusively. At every stage of the project, you have to keep the guiding principles as a backdrop so that these principles can condition each project management decision and action. The major guiding principles are:

Sponsorship. No data warehouse project succeeds without strong and committed executive sponsorship.

Project Manager. It is a serious mistake to have a project manager who is more technology-oriented than user-oriented and business-oriented.

New Paradigm. Data warehousing is new for most companies; innovative project management methods are essential to deal with the unexpected challenges.

Team Roles. Team roles are not to be assigned arbitrarily; the roles must reflect the needs of each individual data warehouse project.

Data Quality. Three critical aspects of data in the data warehouse are: quality, quality, and quality.

User Requirements. Although obvious, user requirements alone form the driving force of every task on the project schedule.

Building for Growth. Number of users and number of queries increase very quickly after deployment; data warehouses not built for growth will crumble swiftly.

Project Politics. The first data warehouse project in a company poses challenges and threats to users at different levels; trying to handle project politics is like walking the proverbial tightrope, to be trodden with extreme caution.

Realistic Expectations. It is easy to promise the world in the first data warehouse project; setting expectations at the right and attainable levels is the best course.

Dimensional Data Modeling. A well-designed dimensional data model is a required foundation and blueprint.

External Data. A data warehouse does not live by internal data alone; data from relevant external sources is an absolutely necessary ingredient.

Training. Data warehouse user tools are different and new. If the users do not know how to use the tools, they will not use the data warehouse. An unused data warehouse is a failed data warehouse.

Warning Signs

As the life cycle of your data warehouse project runs its course and the development phases are moving along, you must keep a close watch for any warning signs that may spell disaster. Constantly be looking for any indicators suggesting doom and failure. Some of the warning signs may just point to inconveniences calling for little action. But there are likely to be other warning signs indicative of wider problems that need corrective action to ensure final success. Some warning signs may portend serious drawbacks that require immediate remedial action.

Whatever might be the nature of the warning sign, be vigilant and keep a close watch. As soon as you spot an omen, recognize the potential problem, and take corrective action. Figure 4-11 presents a list of typical warning signs and suggested corrective action. The list in the figure is just a collection of examples. In your data warehouse project, you may find other types of warning signs. Your corrective action for potential problems may be different depending on your circumstances.

Success Factors

You have followed the tenets of effective project management and your data warehouse is completed. How do you know that your data warehouse is a success'? Do you need three or five years to see if you get the ROI (return on investment) proposed in your plan? How long do you have to wait before you can assert that your data warehouse effort is successful. Or, are there some immediate signs indicating success?

WARNING SIGN	INDICATION	ACTION
The Requirements Definition phase is well past the target date.	Suffering from "analysis paralysis."	Stop the capturing of unwanted information. Remove any problems by meeting with users. Set firm final target date.
Need to write too many in-house programs.	Selected third party tools running out of steam.	If there is time and budget, get different tools. Otherwise increase programming staff.
Users not cooperating to provide details of data.	Possible turf concerns over data ownership.	Very delicate issue. Work with executive sponsor to resolve the issue.
Users not comfortable with the query tools.	Users not trained adequately.	First, ensure that the selected query tool is appropriate. Then provide additional training.
Continuing problems with data brought over to the staging area.	Data transformation and mapping not complete.	Revisit all data transformation and integration routines. Ensure that no data is missing. Include the user representative in the verification process.

Figure 4-11 Warning signs for a data warehouse project.

There are some such indications of success that can be observed within a short time after implementation. The following happenings generally indicate success:

- Queries and reports—rapid increase in the number of queries and reports requested by the users directly from the data warehouse
- Query types—queries becoming more sophisticated
- Active users—steady increase in the number of users
- Usage—users spending more and more time in the data warehouse looking for solutions
- Turnaround times—marked decrease in the times required for obtaining strategic information

Figure 4-12 provides a list of key factors for a successful data warehouse project. By no means is this list an exhaustive compilation of all possible ingredients for success. Nor is it a magic wand to guarantee success in every situation. You know very well that a good part of ensuring success depends on your specific project, its definite objectives, and its unique project management challenges. Therefore, use the list for general guidance.

Anatomy of a Successful Project

No matter how many success factors you review, and no matter how many guidelines you study, you get a better grasp of the success principles by analyzing the details of what really made a real-world project a success. We will now do just that. Let us review a case study of an actual business in which the data warehouse project was a tremendous success.

✳ Ensure continued, long-term, committed support from the executive sponsors.

✳ Up front, establish well-defined, real, and agreed business value from your data warehouse. Manage user expectations realistically.

✳ Get the users enthusiastically involved throughout the project.

✳ The data extraction, transformation, and loading (ETL) function is the most time-consuming, labor-intensive activity. Do not under-estimate the time and effort for this activity.

✳ Remember architecture first, then technology, then tools. Select an architecture that is right for your environment.

✳ The right query and information tools for the users are extremely critical. Select the most useful and easy-to-use ones, not the glamorous. Avoid bleeding-edge technology.

✳ Plan for growth and evolution. Be mindful of performance considerations.

✳ Assign a user-oriented project manager.

✳ Focus the design on queries, not transactions.

✳ Define proper data sources. Only load the data that is needed.

Figure 4-12   Key success factors for a data warehouse project.

The warehouse met the goals and produced the desired results. Figure 4-13 depicts this data warehouse, indicating the success factors and benefits. A fictional name is used for the business.

Adopt a Practical Approach

After the entire project management principles are enunciated, numerous planning methods are described, and several theoretical nuances are explored, a practical approach is still best for achieving results. Do not get bogged down in the strictness of the principles, rules, and methods. Adopt a practical approach to managing the project. Results alone matter; just being active and running around chasing the theoretical principles will not produce the desired outcome.

A practical approach is simply a common-sense approach that has a nice blend of practical wisdom and hard-core theory. While using a practical approach, you are totally results oriented. You constantly balance the significant activities against the less important ones and adjust the priorities. You are not driven by technology just for the sake of technology itself; you are motivated by business requirements.

In the context of a data warehouse project, here are a few tips on adopting a practical approach:

• Running a project in a pragmatic way means constantly monitoring the deviations and slippage, and making in-flight corrections to stay the course. Rearrange the priorities as and when necessary.

• Let project schedules act as guides for smooth workflow and achieving results, not just to control and inhibit creativity. Please do not try to control each task to the minutest

Business Context

BigCom, Inc., world's leading supplier of data, voice, and video communication technology with more than 300 million customers and significant recent growth.

Challenges

Limited availability of global information; lack of common data definitions; critical business data locked in numerous disparate applications; fragmented reporting needing elaborate reconciliation; significant system downtime for daily backups and updates.

Technology and Approach

Deploy large-scale corporate data warehouse to provide strategic information to 1,000 users for making business decisions; use proven tools from single vendor for data extraction and building data marts; query and analysis tool from another reputable vendor.

Success Factors

Clear business goals; strong executive support; user departments actively involved; selection of appropriate and proven tools; building of proper architecture first; adequate attention to data integration and transformation; emphasis on flexibility and scalability.

Benefits Achieved

True enterprise decision support; improved sales measurement; decreased cost of ownership; streamlined business processes; improved customer relationship management; reduced IT development; ability to incorporate clickstream data from company's Web site.

Figure 4-13   Analysis of a successful data warehouse.

detail. You will then only have time to keep the schedules up to date, with less time to do the real job.

- Review project task dependencies continuously. Minimize wait times for dependent tasks.
- There really is such a thing as "too much planning." Do not give into the temptation. Occasionally, *ready – fire – aim* may be a worthwhile principle for a practical approach.
- Similarly, too much analysis can produce "analysis paralysis."
- Avoid "bleeding edge" and unproven technologies. This is very important if the project is the first data warehouse project in your company.
- Always produce early deliverables as part of the project. These deliverables will sustain the interest of users and also serve as proof-of-concept systems.
- Build the architecture first, and only then the tools. Do not choose the tools and then build your data warehouse around the selected tools. Build the architecture first, based on business requirements, and then pick the tools to support the architecture.

Review these suggestions and use them appropriately in your data warehouse project. Especially if this is their first data warehouse project, the users will be interested in quick and easily noticeable benefits. You will soon find out that they are never interested in your fanciest project scheduling tool that empowers them to track each task by the hour or minute. They are satisfied only by results. They are attracted to the data warehouse only by how useful and easy to use it is.

CHAPTER SUMMARY

- While planning for your data warehouse, key issues to be considered include setting proper expectations, assessing risks, deciding between top-down or bottom-up approaches, choosing from vendor solutions.
- Business requirements, not technology, must drive your project.
- A data warehouse project without the full support of the top management and without a strong and enthusiastic executive sponsor is doomed to failure from day one.
- Benefits from a data warehouse accrue only after the users put it to full use. Justification through stiff ROI calculations is not always easy. Some data warehouses are justified and the projects started by just reviewing the potential benefits.
- A data warehouse project is much different from a typical OLTP system project. The traditional life cycle approach of application development must be changed and adapted for the data warehouse project. Also, consider making use of agile development methodology.
- Standards for organization and assignment of team roles are still in the experimental stage in many projects. Modify the roles to match what is important for your project.
- Participation of the users is mandatory for success of the data warehouse project. Users can participate in a variety of ways.
- Consider the warning signs and success factors: in the final analysis, adopt a practical approach to build a successful data warehouse.

REVIEW QUESTIONS

1. Name four key issues to be considered while planning for a data warehouse.
2. Explain the difference between the top-down and bottom-up approaches for building data warehouses. Do you have a preference? If so, why?
3. List three advantages for each of the single-vendor and multivendor solutions.
4. What is meant by a preliminary survey of requirements? List six types of information you will gather during a preliminary survey.
5. How are data warehouse projects different from OLTP system projects? Describe four such differences.
6. List and explain any four of the development phases in the life cycle of a data warehouse project.
7. What do you consider to be a core set of team roles for a data warehouse project? Describe the responsibilities of three roles from your set.
8. List any three warning signs likely to be encountered in a data warehouse project. What corrective actions will you need to take to resolve the potential problems indicated by these three warning signs?
9. Name and describe any five of the success factors in a data warehouse project.
10. What is meant by "taking a practical approach" to the management of a data warehouse project? Give any two reasons why you think a practical approach is likely to succeed.

EXERCISES

1. Match the columns:

1. top-down approach	**A.** tightrope walking
2. single-vendor solution	**B.** not standardized
3. team roles	**C.** requisite for success
4. team organization	**D.** enterprise data warehouse
5. role classifications	**E.** consistent look and feel
6. user support technician	**F.** front office, back office
7. executive sponsor	**G.** part of overall plan
8. project politics	**H.** right person in right role
9. active user participation	**I.** front-line support
10. source system structures	**J.** guide and support project

2. As the recently assigned project manager, you are required to work with the executive sponsor to write a justification without detailed ROI calculations for the first data warehouse project in your company. Write a justification report to be included in the planning document.

3. You are the data transformation specialist for the first data warehouse project in an airlines company. Prepare a project task list to include all the detailed tasks needed for data extraction and transformation.

4. Why do you think user participation is absolutely essential for success? As a member of the recently formed data warehouse team in a banking business, your job is to write a report on how the user departments can best participate in the development. What specific responsibilities for the users will you include in your report?

5. As the lead architect for a data warehouse in a large domestic retail store chain, prepare a list of project tasks relating to designing the architecture. In which development phases will these tasks be performed?

CHAPTER 5

DEFINING THE BUSINESS REQUIREMENTS

CHAPTER OBJECTIVES

- Discuss how and why defining requirements is different for a data warehouse
- Understand the role of business dimensions
- Learn about information packages and their use in defining requirements
- Review methods for gathering requirements
- Grasp the significance of a formal requirements definition document

A data warehouse is an information delivery system for business intelligence. It is not about technology, but about solving users' problems and providing strategic information to the user. In the phase of defining requirements, you need to concentrate on what information the users need, not so much on how you are going to provide the required information. The actual methods for providing information will come later, not while you are collecting requirements.

Before we proceed, let us clarify the scope and content of this chapter. In this chapter, we will focus on determining requirements for what was referred to as the practical approach in Chapter 2. As we discussed in that chapter, we plan for an enterprise-wide solution; then we gather requirements for each data mart, subject by subject. These requirements will enable us to implement conformed data marts, one by one, on a priority basis; eventually to cover the needs of the entire enterprise.

On the other hand, if the goal is to take a strictly top-down approach and build an enterprise-wide data warehouse first, determining the requirements will be different from what is discussed in this chapter. With the purely top-down approach, the data warehouse will be developed based on the third normal form relational data model. This relational database will form the data warehouse. In turn this enterprise data warehouse will feed the

Data Warehousing Fundamentals for IT Professionals, Second Edition. By Paulraj Ponniah
Copyright © 2010 John Wiley & Sons, Inc.

dependent data marts. However, these dependent data marts will be developed based on the requirements determination elaborated on in this chapter.

Now, on with our discussion of requirements determination for the data marts—the outcome of either the practical approach or the derived products of the purely top-down approach.

Most of the developers of data warehouses come from a background of developing operational or OLTP (online transactions processing) systems. OLTP systems are primarily data capture systems. On the other hand, data warehouse systems are information delivery systems. When you begin to collect requirements for your proposed data warehouse, your mindset will have to be different. You have to go from a data capture model to an information delivery model. This difference will have to show through all phases of the data warehouse project.

The users also have a different perspective about a data warehouse system. Unlike an OLTP system, which is needed to run the day-to-day business, no immediate payout is seen in a decision support system. The users do not immediately perceive a compelling need to use a decision support system, whereas they cannot refrain from using an operational system, without which they cannot run their business.

DIMENSIONAL ANALYSIS

In several ways, building a data warehouse is very different from building an operational system. This becomes notable especially in the requirements gathering phase. Because of this difference, the traditional methods of collecting requirements that work well for operational systems cannot be directly applied to data warehouses.

Usage of Information Unpredictable

Let us imagine you are building an operational system for order processing in your company. For gathering requirements, you interview the users in the order processing department. The users will list all the functions that need to be performed. They will inform you how they receive the orders, check stock, verify customers' credit arrangements, price the order, determine the shipping arrangements, and route the order to the appropriate warehouse. They will show you how they would like the various data elements to be presented on the GUI (graphical user interface) screen for the application. The users will also give you a list of reports they would need from the order processing application. They will be able to let you know how, when, and where they would use the application daily.

In providing information about the requirements for an operational system, the users are able to give you precise details of the required functions, information content, and usage patterns. In striking contrast, for a data warehousing system, the users are generally unable to define their requirements clearly. They cannot define precisely what information they really want from the data warehouse, nor can they express how they would like to use the information or process it.

For most of the users, this could be the very first data warehouse they are being exposed to. The users are familiar with operational systems because they use these in their daily work, so they are able to visualize the requirements for other new operational systems. They cannot relate a data warehouse system to anything they have used before.

If, therefore, the whole process of defining requirements for a data warehouse is so nebulous, how can you proceed as one of the analysts in the data warehouse project? You are in a quandary. To be on the safe side, do you then include every piece of data in the data warehouse you think the users will be able to use? How can you build something the users are unable to define clearly and precisely?

Initially, you may collect data on the overall business of the organization. You may check on the industry's best practices. You may gather some business rules guiding the day-to-day decision making. You may find out how products are developed and marketed. But these are generalities and are not sufficient to determine detailed requirements.

Dimensional Nature of Business Data

Fortunately, the situation is not as hopeless as it seems. Even though the users cannot fully describe what they want in a data warehouse, they can provide you with very important insights into how they think about the business. They can tell you what measurement units are important for them. Each user department can let you know how they measure success in that particular department. The users can give you insights into how they combine the various pieces of information for strategic decision making.

Managers think of the business in terms of business dimensions. Figure 5-1 shows the kinds of questions managers are likely to ask for decision making. The figure shows what questions a typical marketing vice president, a marketing manager, and a financial controller may ask.

Let us briefly examine these questions. The marketing vice president is interested in the revenue generated by her new product, but she is not interested in a single number. She is interested in the revenue numbers by month, in a certain division, by customer demographics, by sales office, relative to the previous product version, and compared to plan. So the marketing vice president wants the revenue numbers broken down by month, division, customer demographics, sales office, product version, and plan. These are her business dimensions along which she wants to analyze her numbers.

Marketing Vice President

> How much did my new product generate
>   month by month, in the southern division, by customer demographic, by
>   sales office, relative to the previous version, and compared to plan?

Marketing Manager

> Give me sales statistics
>   by products, summarized by product categories, daily, weekly, and
>   monthly, by sale districts, by distribution channels.

Financial Controller

> Show me expenses
>   listing actual vs budget, by months, quarters, and annual, by budget line
>   items, by district, division, summarized for the whole company.

Figure 5-1   Managers think in business dimensions.

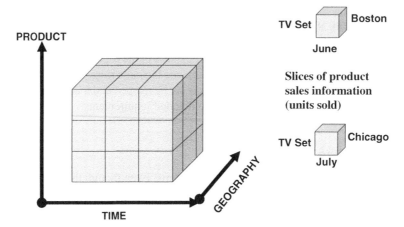

Figure 5-2 Dimensional nature of business data.

Similarly, for the marketing manager, his business dimensions are product, product category, time (day, week, month), sales district, and distribution channel. For the financial controller, the business dimensions are budget line, time (month, quarter, year), district, and division.

If your users of the data warehouse think in terms of business dimensions for decision making, you should also think of business dimensions while collecting requirements. Although the actual proposed usage of a data warehouse could be unclear, the business dimensions used by the managers for decision making are not nebulous at all. The users will be able to describe these business dimensions to you. You are not totally lost in the process of requirements definition. You can find out about the business dimensions.

Let us try to get a good grasp of the dimensional nature of business data. Figure 5-2 shows the analysis of sales units along the three business dimensions of product, time, and geography. These three dimensions are plotted against three axes of coordinates. You will see that the three dimensions form a collection of cubes. In each of the small dimensional cubes, you will find the sales units for that particular slice of time, product, and geographical division. In this case, the business data of sales units is three dimensional because there are just three dimensions used in this analysis. If there are more than three dimensions, we extend the concept to multiple dimensions and visualize multidimensional cubes, also called hypercubes.

Examples of Business Dimensions

The concept of business dimensions is fundamental to the requirements definition for a data warehouse. Therefore, we want to look at some more examples of business dimensions in a few other cases. Figure 5-3 displays the business dimensions in four different cases.

Let us quickly look at each of these examples. For the supermarket chain, the measurements that are analyzed are the sales units. These are analyzed along four business dimensions. When you are looking for the hypercubes, the sides of such cubes are time, promotion, product, and store. If you are the marketing manager for the supermarket chain, you would want your sales broken down by product, at each store, in time sequence, and in relation to the promotions that take place.

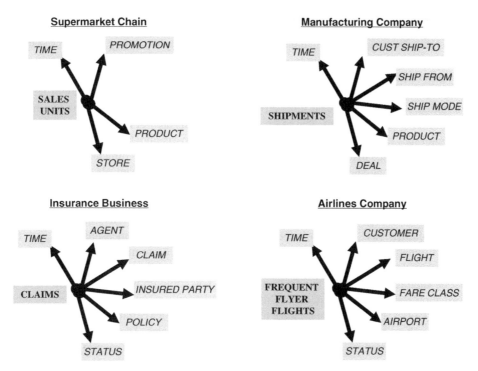

Figure 5-3 Examples of business dimensions.

For the insurance company, the business dimensions are different and appropriate for that business. Here you would want to analyze the claims data by agent, individual claim, time, insured party, individual policy, and status of the claim. The example of the airlines company shows the dimensions for analysis of frequent flyer data. Here the business dimensions are time, customer, specific flight, fare class, airport, and frequent flyer status.

The example analyzing shipments for a manufacturing company shows some other business dimensions. In this case, the business dimensions used for the analysis of shipments are the ones relevant to that business and the subject of the analysis. Here you see the dimensions of time, ship-to and ship-from locations, shipping mode, product, and any special deals.

What we find from these examples is that the business dimensions are different and relevant to the industry and to the subject for analysis. We also find the time dimension to be a common dimension in all examples. Almost all business analyses are performed over time.

INFORMATION PACKAGES—A USEFUL CONCEPT

We will now introduce a novel idea for determining and recording information requirements for a data warehouse. This concept helps us to give a concrete form to the various insights, nebulous thoughts, and opinions expressed during the process of collecting requirements. The information packages, put together while collecting requirements, are very useful for taking the development of the data warehouse to the next phases.

Requirements Not Fully Determinate

As we have discussed, the users are unable to describe fully what they expect to see in the data warehouse. You are unable to get a handle on what pieces of information you want to keep in the data warehouse. You are unsure of the usage patterns. You cannot determine how each class of users will use the new system. So, when requirements cannot be fully determined, we need a new and innovative concept to gather and record the requirements. The traditional methods applicable to operational systems are not adequate in this context. We cannot start with the functions, screens, and reports. We cannot begin with the data structures. We have noted that the users tend to think in terms of business dimensions and analyze measurements along such business dimensions. This is a significant observation and can form the very basis for gathering information.

The new methodology for determining requirements for a data warehouse system is based on business dimensions. It flows out of the need of the users to base their analysis on business dimensions. The new concept incorporates the basic measurements and the business dimensions along which the users analyze these basic measurements. Using the new methodology, you come up with the measurements and the relevant dimensions that must be captured and kept in the data warehouse. You come up with what is known as an information package for the specific subject.

Let us look at an information package for analyzing sales for a certain business. Figure 5-4 contains such an information package. The subject here is sales. The measured facts or the measurements that are of interest for analysis are shown in the bottom section of the package diagram. In this case, the measurements are actual sales, forecast sales, and budget sales. The business dimensions along which these measurements are to be analyzed are shown at the top of the diagram as column headings. In our example, these dimensions are time, location, product, and demographic age group. Each of these business dimensions contains a hierarchy or levels. For example, the time dimension has the hierarchy going from year down to the level of individual day. The other intermediary levels in the time dimension could be quarter,

Information Subject: Sales Analysis

Dimensions

Time Periods	Locations	Products	Age Groups		
Year	Country	Class	Group 1		

Measured Facts: Forecast Sales, Budget Sales, Actual Sales

Hierarchies

Figure 5-4   An information package.

month, and week. These levels or hierarchical components are shown in the information package diagram.

Your primary goal in the requirements definition phase is to compile information packages for all the subjects for the data warehouse. Once you have firmed up the information packages, you'll be able to proceed to the other phases.

Essentially, information packages enable you to:

- Define the common subject areas
- Design key business metrics
- Decide how data must be presented
- Determine how users will aggregate or roll up
- Decide the data quantity for user analysis or query
- Decide how data will be accessed
- Establish data granularity
- Estimate data warehouse size
- Determine the frequency for data refreshing
- Ascertain how information must be packaged

Business Dimensions

As we have seen, business dimensions form the underlying basis of the new methodology for requirements definition. Data must be stored to provide for the business dimensions. The business dimensions and their hierarchical levels form the basis for all further development phases. So we want to take a closer look at business dimensions. We should be able to identify business dimensions and their hierarchical levels. We must be able to choose the proper and optimal set of dimensions related to the measurements.

We begin by examining the business dimensions for an automobile manufacturer. Let us say that the goal is to analyze sales. We want to build a data warehouse that will allow the user to analyze automobile sales in a number of ways. The first obvious dimension is the product dimension. Again for the automaker, analysis of sales must include analysis by breaking the sales down by dealers. Dealer, therefore, is another important dimension for analysis. As an automaker, you would want to know how your sales break down along customer demographics. You would want to know who is buying your automobiles and in what quantities. Customer demographics would be another useful business dimension for analysis. How do the customers pay for the automobiles? What effect does financing for the purchases have on the sales? These questions can be answered by including the method of payment as another dimension for analysis. What about time as a business dimension? Almost every query or analysis involves the time element. In summary, we have come up with the following dimensions for the subject of sales for an automaker: product, dealer, customer demographic, method of payment, and time.

Let us take one more example. In this case, we want to come up with an information package for a hotel chain. The subject in this case is hotel occupancy. We want to analyze occupancy of the rooms in the various branches of the hotel chain. We want to analyze the occupancy by individual hotels and by room types. So, hotel and room type are critical business dimensions for the analysis. As in the other case, we also need to include the time dimension. In the hotel occupancy information package, the dimensions to be included are hotel, room type, and time.

Dimension Hierarchies and Categories

When a user analyzes the measurements along a business dimension, the user usually would like to see the numbers first in summary and then at various levels of detail. What the user does here is to traverse the hierarchical levels of a business dimension for getting the details at various levels. For example, the user first sees the total sales for the entire year. Then the user moves down to the level of quarters and looks at the sales by individual quarters. After this, the user moves down further to the level of individual months to look at monthly numbers. What we notice here is that the hierarchy of the time dimension consists of the levels of year, quarter, and month. The dimension hierarchies are the paths for drilling down or rolling up in our analysis.

Within each major business dimension there are categories of data elements that can also be useful for analysis. In the time dimension, you may have a data element to indicate whether a particular day is a holiday. This data element would enable you to analyze by holidays and see how sales on holidays compare with sales on other days. Similarly, in the product dimension, you may want to analyze by type of package. The package type is one such data element within the product dimension. The holiday flag in the time dimension and the package type in the product dimension do not necessarily indicate hierarchical levels in these dimensions. Such data elements within the business dimension may be called categories.

Hierarchies and categories are included in the information packages for each dimension. Let us go back to the two examples in the previous section and find out which hierarchical levels and categories must be included for the dimensions. Let us examine the product dimension. Here, the product is the basic automobile. Therefore, we include the data elements relevant to product as hierarchies and categories. These would be model name, model year, package styling, product line, product category, exterior color, interior color, and first model year. Looking at the other business dimensions for the auto sales analysis, we summarize the hierarchies and categories for each dimension as follows:

> *Product*: Model name, model year, package styling, product line, product category, exterior color, interior color, first model year
>
> *Dealer*: Dealer name, city, state, single brand flag, date of first operation
>
> *Customer Demographics*: Age, gender, income range, marital status, household size, vehicles owned, home value, own or rent
>
> *Payment Method*: Finance type, term in months, interest rate, agent
>
> *Time*: Date, month, quarter, year, day of week, day of month, season, holiday flag

Let us go back to the hotel occupancy analysis. We have included three business dimensions. Let us list the possible hierarchies and categories for the three dimensions.

> *Hotel*: Hotel line, branch name, branch code, region, address, city, state, zip code, manager, construction year, renovation year

Room Type: Room type, room size, number of beds, type of bed, maximum occupants, suite, refrigerator, kitchenette

Time: Date, day of month, day of week, month, quarter, year, holiday flag

Key Business Metrics or Facts

So far we have discussed the business dimensions in the above two examples. These are the business dimensions relevant to the users of these two data marts for performing analysis. The respective users think of their business subjects in terms of these business dimensions for obtaining information and for doing analysis.

But using these business dimensions, what exactly are the users analyzing? What numbers are they analyzing? The numbers the users analyze are the measurements or metrics that measure the success of their departments. These are the facts that indicate to the users how their departments are doing in fulfilling their departmental objectives.

In the case of the automaker, these metrics relate to the sales. These are the numbers that tell the users about their performance in sales. These are numbers about the sale of each individual automobile. The set of meaningful and useful metrics for analyzing automobile sales is as follows:

Actual sale price

MSRP

Options price

Full price

Dealer add-ons

Dealer credits

Dealer invoice

Amount of down payment

Manufacturer proceeds

Amount financed

In the second example of hotel occupancy, the numbers or metrics are different. The nature of the metrics depends on what is being analyzed. For hotel occupancy, the metrics would therefore relate to the occupancy of rooms in each branch of the hotel chain. Here is a list of metrics for analyzing hotel occupancy:

Occupied rooms

Vacant rooms

Unavailable rooms

Number of occupants

Revenue

Now putting it all together, let us discuss what goes into the information package diagrams for these two examples. In each case, the metrics or facts go into the bottom section of the information package. The business dimensions will be the column headings. In each column, you will include the hierarchies and categories for the business dimensions.

Figures 5-5 and 5-6 show the information packages for the two examples we just discussed.

Information Subject: Automaker Sales

Dimensions

Time	Product	Payment Method	Customer Demo-graphics	Dealer	
Year	Model Name	Finance Type	Age	Dealer Name	
Quarter	Model Year	Term (Months)	Gender	City	
Month	Package Styling	Interest Rate	Income Range	State	
Date	Product Line	Agent	Marital Status	Single Brand Flag	
Day of Week	Product Category		House-hold Size	Date First Operation	
Day of Month	Exterior Color		Vehicles Owned		
Season	Interior Color		Home Value		
Holiday Flag	First Year		Own or Rent		

Facts: Actual Sale Price, MSRP, Options Price, Full Price, Dealer Add-ons, Dealer Credits, Dealer Invoice, Down Payment, Proceeds, Finance

(left margin label: Hierarchies/Categories)

Figure 5-5 Information package: automaker sales.

Information Subject: Hotel Occupancy

Dimensions

Time	Hotel	Room Type			
Year	Hotel Line	Room Type			
Quarter	Branch Name	Room Size			
Month	Branch Code	Number of Beds			
Date	Region	Type of Bed			
Day of Week	Address	Max. Occupants			
Day of Month	City/State /Zip	Suite			
Holiday Flag	Construction Year	Refrigerator			
	Renovation Year	Kichennette			

Facts: Occupied Rooms, Vacant Rooms, Unavailable Rooms, Number of Occupants, Revenue

(left margin label: Hierarchies/Categories)

Figure 5-6 Information package: hotel occupancy.

REQUIREMENTS GATHERING METHODS

Now that we have a way of formalizing requirements definition through information package diagrams, let us discuss the methods for gathering requirements. Remember that a data warehouse is an information delivery system for providing information for strategic decision making. It is not a system for running the day-to-day business. Who are the users that can make use of the information in the data warehouse? Where do you go for getting the requirements?

Broadly, we can classify the users of the data warehouse as follows:

Senior executives (including the sponsors)

Key departmental managers

Business analysts

Operational system database administrators (DBAs)

Others nominated by the above

Executives will give you a sense of direction and scope for your data warehouse. They are the ones closely involved in the focused area. The key departmental managers are the ones who report to the executives in the area of focus. Business analysts are the ones who prepare reports and analyses for the executives and managers. The operational system DBAs and IT applications staff will give you information about the data sources for the warehouse.

What requirements do you need to gather? Here is a broad list:

Data elements: fact classes, dimensions

Recording of data in terms of time

Data extracts from source systems

Business rules: attributes, ranges, domains, operational records

You will have to go to different groups of people in the various departments to gather the requirements. Three basic techniques are universally adopted for obtaining information from groups of people: (1) interviews, one-on-one or in small groups; (2) joint application development (JAD) sessions; (3) questionnaires.

One-on-one interviews are the most interactive of the three methods. JAD or group sessions are a little less interactive. Questionnaires are not interactive. An interactive method has several advantages of getting confirmed information.

A few thoughts about these three basic approaches follow.

Interviews

- Two or three persons at a time
- Easy to schedule
- Good approach when details are intricate
- Some users are comfortable only with one-on-one interviews
- Need good preparation to be effective
- Always conduct pre-interview research

- Establish objectives for each interview
- Decide on the question types
- Also encourage users to prepare for the interview

Group Sessions

- Groups of 20 or fewer persons at a time
- Use only after getting a baseline understanding of the requirements
- Not good for initial data gathering
- Use when free flow of ideas is essential
- Useful for confirming requirements
- Efficient when users are scattered across locations
- Need to be very well organized

Questionnaires

- Can gather lots of requirements quickly
- Useful when people to be questioned are widely dispersed
- Good in exploration phase to get overall reactions
- May be used for people whose work schedule is too tight for interviews
- However, questionnaires do not permit interactive responses like interviews

Types of Questions

In all these three different methods of gathering requirements we use questions to elicit information. It is, therefore, very important to understand the types of questions that may be used and the effectiveness of each.

Open-Ended Questions. These open up options for interviewees to respond. The benefits of using open-ended questions are they put interviewees at ease, allow insights into values and beliefs, provides exposure to interviewees' vocabulary, opens up opportunities for more questioning, and are interesting and spontaneous. Drawbacks are that they could result in too much unnecessary detail, the risk of losing control in the interview, they may take too much time, not proportional to the information gathered.

Closed Questions. These allow limited responses to interviewees. Some closed questions are bipolar in the sense that these look for "Yes or No" type answers. Closed questions enable you to save time and get to the point quickly and easily. Closed questions allow for interviews to be compared, provide control over the interview and the ability to cover a lot of ground quickly, and are likely to gather only the relevant information. Drawbacks are the inability to get rich details, less chance for building trust and rapport between interviewer and interviewee, and they may become boring and dull.

Probes. These are really follow-up questions. Probes may be used after open-ended or closed questions. The intention would be to go beyond the initial questions and answers. Probes are useful in drawing out an interviewee's point of view.

Arrangement of Questions

For information gathering using the proper types of questions alone is not enough. You must be able to arrange the questioning in an effective sequence to suit the audience and the purpose. The following structures for arranging questions are used in practice.

Pyramid Structure. This is an inductive method of arranging the questions. You begin with very specific closed questions and then expand the topics with open-ended questions. This structure is useful when the interviewee needs to warm up to the topics being discussed. Use this structure when general views of the topics are to be extracted at the end.

Funnel Structure. This is a deductive method. Begin with general open-ended questions and then narrow the topics with specific, closed questions. This structure is useful when the interviewee is emotional about the topics under discussion. Use this structure when gradual levels of details are needed at the end.

Diamond-Shaped Structure. In this case, you warm up the interview with specific closed questions. You then proceed towards broad, general, open-ended questions. Finally you narrow the interview and achieve closure with specific closed questions. Usually, this structure is better than the other two. However, this structure may lengthen the interview.

Interview Techniques

The interview sessions can use up a good percentage of the project time. Therefore, these will have to be organized and managed well. Before your project team launches the interview process, make sure the following major tasks are completed.

- Select and train the project team members conducting the interviews
- Assign specific roles for each team member (lead interviewer/scribe)
- Prepare a list of users to be interviewed and prepare a broad schedule
- List your expectations from each set of interviews
- Complete pre-interview research
- Prepare interview questionnaires
- Prepare the users for the interviews
- Conduct a kick-off meeting of all users to be interviewed

Most of the users you will be interviewing fall into three broad categories: senior executives, departmental managers/analysts, and IT department professionals. What are the expectations from interviewing each of these categories? Figure 5-7 shows the baseline expectations.

Pre-interview research is important for the success of the interviews. Here is a list of some key research topics:

- History and current structure of the business unit
- Number of employees and their roles and responsibilities
- Locations of the users

<u>**Senior Executives**</u>

- Organization objectives
- Criteria for measuring success
- Key business issues, current & future
- Problem identification
- Vision and direction for the organization
- Anticipated usage of the DW

<u>**Dept. Managers / Analysts**</u>

- Departmental objectives
- Success metrics
- Factors limiting success
- Key business issues
- Products & Services
- Useful business dimensions for analysis
- Anticipated usage of the DW

<u>**IT Dept. Professionals**</u>

- Key operational source systems
- Current information delivery processes
- Types of routine analysis
- Known quality issues
- Current IT support for information requests
- Concerns about proposed DW

Figure 5-7   Expectations from interviews.

- Primary purpose of the business unit in the enterprise
- Relationship of the business unit to the strategic initiatives of the enterprise
- Secondary purposes of the business unit
- Relationship of the business unit to other units and to outside organizations
- Contribution of the business unit to corporate revenues and costs
- The company's market
- Competition in the market

Some tips on the nature of questions to be asked in the interviews follow.

Current Information Sources   Which operational systems generate data about important business subject areas? What are the types of computer systems that support these subject areas? What information is currently delivered in existing reports and online queries? How about the level of details in the existing information delivery systems?

Subject Areas

Which subject areas are most valuable for analysis?

What are the business dimensions? Do these have natural hierarchies?

What are the business partitions for decision making?

Do the various locations need global information or just local information for decision making? What is the mix?

Are certain products and services offered only in certain areas?

Key Performance Metrics

How is the performance of the business unit currently measured?

What are the critical success factors and how are these monitored?

How do the key metrics roll up?

Are all markets measured in the same way?

Information Frequency

How often must the data be updated for decision making?

What is the time frame?

How does each type of analysis compare the metrics over time?

What is the timeliness requirement for the information in the data warehouse?

As initial documentation for the requirements definition, prepare interview write-ups using this general outline:

1. User profile
2. Background and objectives
3. Information requirements
4. Analytical requirements
5. Current tools used
6. Success criteria
7. Useful business metrics
8. Relevant business dimensions

Adapting the JAD Methodology

If you are able to gather a lot of baseline data up front from different sources, group sessions may be a good substitute for individual interviews. In this method, you are able to get a number of interested users to meet together in group sessions. On the whole, this method could result in fewer group sessions than individual interview sessions. The overall time for requirements gathering may prove to be less and, therefore, shorten the project. Also, group sessions may be more effective if the users are dispersed in remote locations.

Joint application development (JAD) techniques were successfully utilized to gather requirements for operational systems in the 1980s. Users of computer systems had grown to be more computer-savvy and their direct participation in the development of applications proved to be very useful.

As the name implies, JAD is a joint process, with all the concerned groups getting together for a well-defined purpose. It is a methodology for developing computer applications jointly by the users and the IT professionals in a well-structured manner. JAD centers around discussion workshops lasting a certain number of days under the direction of a facilitator. Under suitable conditions, the JAD approach may be adapted for building a data warehouse.

JAD consists of a five-phased approach:

Project definition
    Complete high-level interviews
    Conduct management interviews
    Prepare management definition guide
Research
    Become familiar with the business area and systems
    Document user information requirements
    Document business processes
    Gather preliminary information
    Prepare agenda for the sessions
Preparation
    Create working document from previous phase
    Train the scribes
    Prepare visual aids
    Conduct presession meetings
    Set up a venue for the sessions
    Prepare a checklist for objectives
JAD sessions
    Open with a review of the agenda and purpose
    Review assumptions
    Review data requirements
    Review business metrics and dimensions
    Discuss dimension hierarchies and roll-ups
    Resolve all open issues
    Close sessions with lists of action items
Final document
    Convert the working document
    Map the gathered information
    List all data sources
    Identify all business metrics
    List all business dimensions and hierarchies
    Assemble and edit the document
    Conduct review sessions
    Get final approvals
    Establish procedure to change requirements

The success of a project using the JAD approach very much depends on the composition of the JAD team. The size and mix of the team will vary based on the nature and purpose of the data warehouse. The typical composition, however, must have pertinent roles present in the team. For each of the following roles, usually one or more persons are assigned.

Executive sponsor—Person controlling the funding, providing the direction, and empowering the team members

Facilitator—Person guiding the team throughout the JAD process

Scribe—Person designated to record all decisions

Full-time participants—Everyone involved in making decisions about the data warehouse

On-call participants—Persons affected by the project, but only in specific areas

Observers—Persons who would like to sit in on specific sessions without participating in the decision making

Using Questionnaires

Because using questionnaires is not interactive, questionnaires must be designed with much care. We note important points relating to significant aspects of administering questionnaires. If properly done, questionnaires may form an important method for gathering requirements for your data warehouse.

Type and Choice of Questions. You may use both open-ended and closed questions in a questionnaire. Choice of language is important. Use the language of the respondents, not cryptic technical jargon. Be specific, not vague. Keep questions short and precise. Avoid objectionable, politically incorrect language. Avoid talking down to the respondents. Target the questions to the appropriate respondent group.

Application of Scales. Questionnaires usually contain nominal and interval scales. These make it easy to respond. Nominal scales are used to classify things. Interval scales are used for quantitative analysis.

Questionnaire Design. The order of the questions is important. Start the questionnaire with less controversial, highly important questions. Cluster questions with similar content. The design must be inviting and pleasing. Allow ample white space. Provide sufficient space for responses. Make it easy to mark or indicate responses while using scales. Maintain a consistent style.

Administering Questionnaires. Carefully decide on who gets the questionnaire. Ensure that there are no omissions. Some ways of administering the questionnaires include at an initial group session, through personal delivery and later collection, self-administration by respondents, by mail to respondent locations, and electronically via e-mail.

Review of Existing Documentation

Although most of the requirements gathering will be done through interviews, group sessions, and questionnaires, you will be able to gather useful information from the review of existing documentation. Review of existing documentation can be done by the project team without too much involvement from the users of the business units. Scheduling of the review of existing documentation involves only the members of the project team.

Documentation from User Departments What can you get out of the existing documentation? First, let us look at the reports and screens used by the users in the business areas that will be using the data warehouse. You need to find out everything about the functions of the business units, the operational information gathered and used by these users, what is important to them, and whether they use any of the existing reports for analysis. You need to look at the user documentation for all the operational systems used. You need to grasp what is important to the users.

The business units usually have documentation on the processes and procedures in those units. How do the users perform their functions? Review in detail all the processes and procedures. You are trying to find out what types of analyses the users in these business units are likely to be interested in. Review the documentation and then augment what you have learned from the documentation prepared from the interview sessions.

Documentation from IT The documentation from the users and the interviews with the users will give you information on the metrics used for analysis and the business dimensions along which the analysis gets done. But from where do you get the data for the metrics and business dimensions? These will have to come from internal operational systems. You need to know what is available in the source systems.

Where do you turn for information available in the source systems? This is where the operational system DBAs and application experts from IT become very important for gathering data. The DBAs will provide you with all the data structures, individual data elements, attributes, value domains, and relationships among fields and data structures. From the information you have gathered from the users, you will then be able to relate the user information to the source systems as ascertained from the IT personnel.

Work with your DBAs to obtain copies of the data dictionary or data catalog entries for the relevant source systems. Study the data structures, data fields, and relationships. Eventually, you will be populating the data warehouse from these source systems, so you need to understand completely the source data, the source platforms, and the operating systems.

Now let us turn to the IT application experts. These professionals will give you the business rules and help you to understand and appreciate the various data elements from the source systems. You will learn about data ownership, about people responsible for data quality, and how data is gathered and processed in the source systems. Review the programs and modules that make up the source systems. Look at the copy books inside the programs to understand how the data structures are used in the programs.

REQUIREMENTS DEFINITION: SCOPE AND CONTENT

Formal documentation is often neglected in computer system projects. The project team goes through the requirements definition phase. They conduct the interviews and group sessions. They review the existing documentation. They gather enough material to support the next phases in the system development life cycle. But they skip the detailed documentation of the requirements definition.

There are several reasons why you should commit the results of your requirements definition phase to writing. First of all, the requirements definition document is the basis for the next phases. If project team members have to leave the project for any reason at all, the project will not suffer from people walking away with the knowledge they have gathered. The formal documentation will also validate your findings when reviewed with the users.

We will come up with a suggested outline for the formal requirements definition document. Before that, let us look at the types of information this document must contain.

Data Sources

This piece of information is essential in the requirements definition document. Include all the details you have gathered about the source systems. You will be using the source system data in the data warehouse. You will collect the data from these source systems, merge and integrate it, transform the data appropriately, and populate the data warehouse.

Typically, the requirements definition document should include the following information:

- Available data sources
- Data structures within the data sources
- Location of the data sources
- Operating systems, networks, protocols, and client architectures
- Data extraction procedures
- Availability of historical data

Data Transformation

It is not sufficient just to list the possible data sources. You will list relevant data structures as possible sources because of the relationships of the data structures with the potential data in the data warehouse. Once you have listed the data sources, you need to determine how the source data will have to be transformed appropriately into the type of data suitable to be stored in the data warehouse.

In your requirements definition document, include details of data transformation. This will necessarily involve mapping of source data to the data in the data warehouse. Indicate where the data about your metrics and business dimensions will come from. Describe the merging, conversion, and splitting that need to take place before moving the data into the data warehouse.

Data Storage

From your interviews with the users, you would have found out the level of detailed data you need to keep in the data warehouse. You will have an idea of the number of data marts you need for supporting the users. Also, you will know the details of the metrics and the business dimensions.

When you find out about the types of analyses the users will usually do, you can determine the types of aggregations that must be kept in the data warehouse. This will give you information about additional storage requirements.

Your requirements definition document must include sufficient details about storage requirements. Prepare preliminary estimates on the amount of storage needed for detailed and summary data. Estimate how much historical and archived data needs to be in the data warehouse.

Information Delivery

Your requirements definition document must contain the following requirements on information delivery to the users:

- Drill-down analysis
- Roll-up analysis
- Drill-through analysis
- Slicing and dicing analysis
- Ad hoc reports
- Online monitoring tools such as dashboards and scorecards

Information Package Diagrams

The presence of information package diagrams in the requirements definition document is the major and significant difference between operational systems and data warehouse systems. Remember that information package diagrams are the best approach for determining requirements for a data warehouse.

The information package diagrams crystallize the information requirements for the data warehouse. They contain the critical metrics measuring the performance of the business units, the business dimensions along which the metrics are analyzed, and the details of how drill-down and roll-up analyses are done.

Spend as much time as needed to make sure that the information package diagrams are complete and accurate. Your data design for the data warehouse will be totally dependent on the accuracy and adequacy of the information package diagrams.

Requirements Definition Document Outline

1. *Introduction.* State the purpose and scope of the project. Include broad project justification. Provide an executive summary of each subsequent section.
2. *General Requirements Descriptions.* Describe the source systems reviewed. Include interview summaries. Broadly state what types of information requirements are needed in the data warehouse.
3. *Specific Requirements.* Include details of source data needed. List the data transformation and storage requirements. Describe the types of information delivery methods needed by the users.
4. *Information Packages.* Provide as much detail as possible for each information package. Include this in the form of package diagrams.
5. *Other Requirements.* Cover miscellaneous requirements such as data extract frequencies, data loading methods, and locations to which information must be delivered.

6. *User Expectations.* State the expectations in terms of problems and opportunities. Indicate how the users expect to use the data warehouse.

7. *User Participation and Sign-Off.* List the tasks and activities in which the users are expected to participate throughout the development life cycle.

8. *General Implementation Plan.* At this stage, give a high-level plan for implementation.

CHAPTER SUMMARY

- Unlike the requirements for an operational system, the requirements for a data warehouse are quite nebulous.
- Business data is dimensional in nature and the users of the data warehouse think in terms of business dimensions.
- A requirements definition for the data warehouse can, therefore, be based on business dimensions such as product, geography, time, and promotion.
- Information packages—a new and useful concept—are the backbone of the requirements definition. An information package records the critical measurements or facts and business dimensions along which the facts are normally analyzed.
- Interviews, group sessions, and questionnaires are standard methods for collecting requirements.
- Key people to be interviewed or to be included in group sessions are senior executives (including the sponsors), departmental managers, business analysts, and operational systems DBAs.
- Review all existing documentation of related operational systems.
- Scope and content of the requirements definition document include data sources, data transformation, data storage, information delivery, and information package diagrams.

REVIEW QUESTIONS

1. What are the essential differences between defining requirements for operational systems and for data warehouses?

2. Explain business dimensions. Why and how can business dimensions be useful for defining requirements for the data warehouse?

3. What data does an information package contain?

4. What are dimension hierarchies? Give three examples.

5. Explain business metrics or facts with five examples.

6. List the types of users who must be interviewed for collecting requirements. What information can you expect to get from them?

7. In which situations can JAD methodology be successful for collecting requirements?

8. Why are reviews of existing documents important? What can you expect to get out of such reviews?

9. Various data sources feed the data warehouse. What are the pieces of information you need to get about data sources?

10. Name any five major components of the formal requirements definition document. Describe what goes into each of these components.

EXERCISES

1. Indicate if true or false:

   A. Requirements definitions for a sales processing operational system and a sales analysis data warehouse are very similar.

   B. Managers think in terms of business dimensions for analysis.

   C. Unit sales and product costs are examples of business dimensions.

   D. Dimension hierarchies relate to drill-down analysis.

   E. Categories are attributes of business dimensions.

   F. JAD is a methodology for one-on-one interviews.

   G. Questionnaires provide the least interactive method for gathering requirements.

   H. The departmental users provide information about the company's overall direction.

   I. Departmental managers are very good sources for information on data structures of operational systems.

   J. Information package diagrams are essential parts of the formal requirements definition document.

2. You are the vice president of marketing for a nation-wide appliance manufacturer with three production plants. Describe any three different ways you will tend to analyze your sales. What are the business dimensions for your analysis?

3. BigBook, Inc. is a large book distributor with domestic and international distribution channels. The company orders from publishers and distributes publications to all the leading booksellers. Initially, you want to build a data warehouse to analyze shipments that are made from the company's many warehouses. Determine the metrics or facts and the business dimensions. Prepare an information package diagram.

4. You are on the data warehouse project of AuctionsPlus.com, an Internet auction company selling upscale works of art. Your responsibility is to gather requirements for sales analysis. Find out the key metrics, business dimensions, hierarchies, and categories. Draw the information package diagram.

5. Create a detailed outline for the formal requirements definition document for a data warehouse to analyze product profitability of a large department store chain.

CHAPTER 6

REQUIREMENTS AS THE DRIVING FORCE FOR DATA WAREHOUSING

CHAPTER OBJECTIVES

- Understand why business requirements are the driving force
- Discuss how requirements drive every development phase
- Specifically learn how requirements influence data design
- Review the impact of requirements on architecture
- Note the special considerations for ETL and metadata
- Examine how requirements shape information delivery

In the previous chapter, we discussed the requirements definition phase in detail. You learned that gathering requirements for a data warehouse is not the same as defining the requirements for an operational system. We arrived at a new way of creating information packages to express the requirements. Finally, we put everything together and produced the requirements definition document.

When you design and develop any system, it is obvious that the system must reflect exactly what the users need to perform their business processes. They should have the proper GUI screens, the system must have the correct logic to perform the functions, and the users must receive the required outputs including screens and reports. Requirements definition guides the whole process of system design and development.

What about the requirements definition for a data warehouse? If accurate requirements definition is important for any operational system, it is many times more important for a data warehouse. Why? The data warehouse environment is an information delivery system where the users themselves will access the data warehouse repository and create their own outputs. In an operational system, you provide the users with predefined outputs.

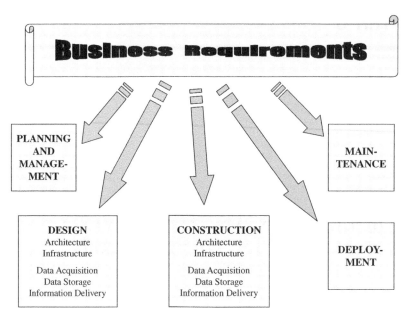

Figure 6-1   Business requirements as the driving force.

It is therefore extremely important that your data warehouse contains the right elements of information in the most optimal formats. Your users must be able to find all the strategic information they would need in exactly the way they want it. They must be able to access the data warehouse easily, run their queries, get results painlessly, and perform various types of data analysis without any problems.

In a data warehouse, business requirements of the users form the single and most powerful driving force. Every task that is performed in every phase in the development of the data warehouse is determined by the requirements. Every decision made during the design phase—whether it may be the data design, the design of the architecture, the configuration of the infrastructure, or the scheme of the information delivery methods—is totally influenced by the requirements. Figure 6-1 depicts this fundamental principle.

Because requirements form the primary driving force for every phase of the development process, you need to ensure especially that your requirements definition contains adequate details to support each phase. This chapter particularly highlights a few significant development activities and specifies how requirements must guide, influence, and direct these activities. Why is this kind of special attention necessary? When you gather business requirements and produce the requirements definition document, you must always bear in mind that what you are doing in this phase of the project is of immense importance to every other phase. Your requirements definition will drive every phase of the project, so please pay special attention.

DATA DESIGN

In the data design phase you come up with the data model for the following data repositories:

- The staging area where you transform, cleanse, and integrate the data from the source systems in preparation for loading into the data warehouse repository
- The data warehouse repository itself

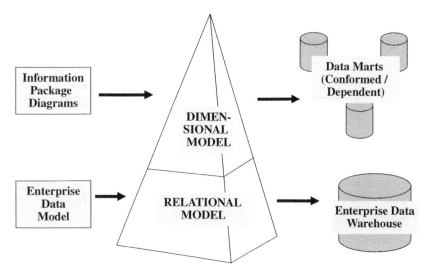

Figure 6-2 Requirements driving the data model.

If you are adopting the practical approach of building your data warehouse as a conglomeration of conformed data marts, your data model at this point will consist of the dimensional data model for your first set of data marts. On the other hand, your company may decide to build the large corporate-wide data warehouse first along with the initial data mart fed by the large data warehouse. In this case, your data model will include both the data model for the large data warehouse and the data model for the initial data mart.

These data models will form the blueprint for the physical design and implementation of the data repositories. You will be using these models for communicating among the team members on what data elements will be available in the data warehouse and how they will all fit together. You will be walking through these data models with the users to inform them of the data content and the data relationships. The data models for individual data marts play a strong and useful role in communication with the users.

Which portions of the requirements definition drive the data design? To understand the impact of requirements on data design, imagine the data model as a pyramid of data contents as shown in Figure 6-2. The base of the pyramid represents the data model for the enterprise-wide data repository and the top half of the pyramid denotes the dimensional data model for the data marts. What do you need in the requirements definition to build and meld the two halves of the pyramid? Two basic pieces of information are needed: the source system data models and the information package diagrams.

The data models of the current source systems will be used for the lower half. Therefore, ensure that your requirements definition document contains adequate information about the components and the relationships of the source system data. In the previous chapter, we discussed information package diagrams in sufficient detail. Please take special care that the information package diagrams that are part of the requirements definition document truly reflect the actual business requirements. Otherwise, your data model will not signify what the users really want to see in the data warehouse.

Structure for Business Dimensions

In the data models for the data marts, the business dimensions along which the users analyze the business metrics must be featured prominently. In the last chapter, while discussing

Information Package Diagram: Automaker Sales

Dimensions

DIMENSIONAL DATA MODEL

Time	Product	Payment Method	Customer Demographics	Dealer	
Year	Model Name	Finance Type	Age	Dealer Name	
Quarter	Model Year	Term (Months)	Gender	City	
Month	Package Styling	Interest Rate	Income Range	State	
Date	Product Line	Agent	Marital Status	Single Brand Flag	
Day of Week	Product Category		House-hold Size	Date First Operation	
Day of Month	Exterior Color		Vehicles Owned		
Season	Interior Color		Home Value		
Holiday Flag	First Year		Own or Rent		

Metrics: Actual Sale Price, MSRP, Options Price, Full Price, Dealer Add-ons, Dealer Credits, Dealer Invoice, Down Payment

Figure 6-3   Business dimensions in the data model.

information package diagrams, we reviewed a few examples. In an information package diagram, the business dimensions are listed as column headings. For example, look at the business dimensions for Automaker Sales in Figure 6-3, which is a partial reproduction of the earlier Figure 5-5.

If you create a data model for this data mart, the business dimensions as shown in the figure must necessarily be included in the model. The usefulness of the data mart is directly related to the accuracy of the data model. Where does this lead you? It leads you to the paramount importance of having the appropriate dimensions and the right contents in the information package diagrams.

Structure for Key Measurements

Key measurements are the metrics or measures that are used for business analysis and monitoring. Users measure performance by using and comparing key measurements. For automaker sales, the key measurements include actual sale price, MSRP, options price, full price, and so on. Users measure their success in terms of the key measurements. They tend to make calculations and summarizations in terms of such metrics.

In addition to getting query results based on any combination of the dimensions, the facts or metrics are used for analysis. When your users analyze the sales along the product, time, and location dimensions, they see the results displayed in the metrics such as sale units, revenue, cost, and profit margin. In order for the users to review the results in proper key measurements, you have to guarantee that the information package diagrams you include as part of the requirements definition contain all the relevant key measurements.

Business dimensions and key measures form the backbone of the dimensional data model. The structure of the data model is directly related to the number of business dimensions. The data content of each business dimension forms part of the data model. For example, if an information package diagram has product, customer, time, and location as the business dimensions, these four dimensions will be four distinct components in the structure of the data model. In addition to the business dimensions, the group of key measurements also forms another distinct component of the data model.

Levels of Detail

What else must be reflected in the data model? To answer this question, let us scrutinize how your users plan to use the data warehouse for analysis. Let us take a specific example. The senior analyst wants to analyze the sales in the various regions. First he or she starts with the total countrywide sales by product in this year. Then the next step is to view total countrywide sales by product in individual regions during the year. Moving on, the next step is to get a breakdown by quarters. After this step, the user may want to get comparisons with the budget and with the prior year performance.

What we observe is that in this kind of analysis you need to provide drill-down and roll-up facilities for analysis. Do you want to keep data at the lowest level of detail? If so, when your user desires to see countrywide totals for the full year, the system must do the aggregation during analysis while the user is waiting at the workstation. On the other hand, do you have to keep the details for displaying data at the lowest levels, and summaries for displaying data at higher levels of aggregation?

This discussion brings us to another specific aspect of requirements definition as it relates to the data model. If you need summaries in your data warehouse, then your data model must include structures to hold details as well as summary data. If you can afford to let the system sum up on the fly during analysis, then your data model need not have summary structures. Find out about the essential drill-down and roll-up functions and include enough particulars about the types of summary and detail levels of data your data warehouse must hold.

THE ARCHITECTURAL PLAN

You know that data warehouse architecture refers to the proper arrangement of the architectural components for maximum benefit. How do you plan your data warehouse architecture? Basically, every data warehouse is composed of pretty much the same components. Therefore, when you are planning the architecture, you are not inventing any new components to go into your particular warehouse. You are really sizing up each component for your environment. You are planning how all the components must be knit together so that they will work as an integrated system.

Before we proceed further, let us recap the major architectural components as discussed in Chapter 2:

Source data
    Production data
    Internal data
    Archived data
    External data

Data staging
   Data extraction
   Data transformation
   Data loading
Data storage
Information delivery
Metadata
Management and control

When you plan the overall architecture for your data warehouse, you will be setting the scope and contents of each of these components. For example, in your company all of the source data might fortunately reside on a single computing platform and also on a single relational database. If this were the case, then the data extraction component in the architecture would be substantially smaller and straightforward. Again, if your company decides on using just the facilities provided by the DBMS, such as alias definition and comments features, for metadata storage, then your metadata component would be simple.

Planning the architecture, therefore, involves reviewing each of the components in the light of your particular context, and setting the parameters. Also, it involves the interfaces among the various components. How can the management and control module be designed to coordinate and control the functions of the different components? What is the information you need to do the planning? How will you know to size up each component and provide the appropriate infrastructure to support it? Of course, the answer is *business requirements.* All the information you need to plan the architecture must come from the requirements definition. In the following subsections, we will explore the importance of business requirements for the architectural plan. We will take each component and review how proper requirements drive the size and content of the data warehouse.

Composition of the Components

Let us review each component and ascertain what exactly is needed in the requirements definition to plan for the data warehouse architecture. Again, remember that planning for the architecture involves the determination of the size and content of each component. In the following list, the bulleted points under each component indicate the type of information that must be contained in the requirements definition to drive the architectural plan.

- Source Data
  - Operational source systems
  - Computing platforms, operating systems, databases, files
  - Departmental data such as files, documents, and spreadsheets
  - External data sources
- Data Staging
  - Data mapping between data sources and staging area data structures
  - Data transformations
  - Data cleansing
  - Data integration

- Data Storage
    - Size of extracted and integrated data
    - DBMS features
    - Growth potential
    - Centralized for enterprise data warehouse
    - Data marts—conformed, dependent, independent, federated
- Information Delivery
    - Types and number of users
    - Types of queries and reports
    - Classes of analysis
    - Dashboards/scorecards
    - Data mining operations
    - Front-end DSS applications
- Metadata
    - Operational metadata
    - ETL (data extraction, transformation, and loading) metadata
    - End-user metadata
    - Metadata storage
- Management and Control
    - Data loading
    - External sources
    - Alert systems
    - End-user information delivery

Figure 6-4 provides a useful summary of the architectural components driven by requirements. The figure indicates the impact of business requirements on the data warehouse architecture.

Special Considerations

Having reviewed the impact of requirements on the architectural components in some detail, we now turn our attention to a few functions that deserve special consideration. We need to bring out these special considerations because if these are missed in the requirements definition, serious consequences will follow. When you are in the requirements definition phase, you have to pay special attention to these factors.

Data Extraction, Transformation, and Loading (ETL)   The activities that relate to ETL in a data warehouse are by far the most time-consuming and human-intensive. Special recognition of the extent and complexity of these activities in the requirements will go a long way in easing the pain while setting up the architecture. If you are planning for real time data warehousing, then ETL functions need special attention. Techniques must be adopted for real time data extraction, rapid transformation and integration of data, and updates to the data warehouse in real time with near-zero latency. Let us separate out the functions and state the special considerations needed in the requirements definition.

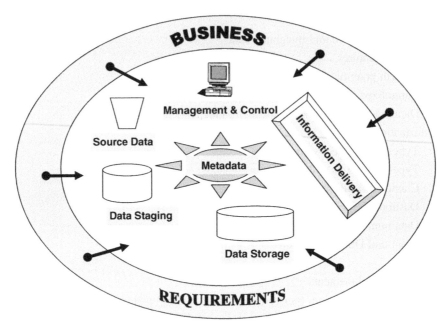

Figure 6-4   Impact of requirements on architecture.

Data Extraction   Clearly identify all the internal data sources. Specify all the computing platforms and source files from which the data is to be extracted. If you are going to include external data sources, determine the compatibility of your data structures with those of the outside sources. Also indicate the methods for data extraction.

Data Transformation   Many types of transformation functions are needed before data can be mapped and prepared for loading into the data warehouse repository. These functions include input selection, separation of input structures, normalization and denormalization of source structures, aggregation, conversion, resolving of missing values, and conversions of names and addresses. In practice, this turns out to be a long and complex list of functions. Examine each data element planned to be stored in the data warehouse against the source data elements and ascertain the mappings and transformations.

Data Loading   Define the initial load. Determine how often each major group of data must be kept up-to-date in the data warehouse. How much of the updates will be nightly updates? Does your environment warrant more than one update cycle in a day? How are the changes going to be captured in the source systems? Define how the daily, weekly, and monthly updates will be initiated and carried out. If your plan includes real time data warehousing, specify the method for real time updates.

Data Quality   Bad data leads to bad decisions. No matter how well you tune your data warehouse, and no matter how adeptly you provide for queries and analysis functions to the users, if the data quality of your data warehouse is suspect, the users will quickly lose confidence and flee the data warehouse. Even simple discrepancies can result in serious repercussions while making strategic decisions with far-reaching consequences. Data quality in a data warehouse is sacrosanct. Therefore, right in the early phase of requirements definition, identify potential sources of data pollution in the source systems. Also, be aware of all the possible types of data quality problems likely to be encountered in your operational systems. Note the following tips.

> Data Pollution Sources
>> System conversions and migrations
>> Heterogeneous systems integration
>> Inadequate database design of source systems
>> Data aging
>> Incomplete information from customers
>> Input errors
>> Internationalization/localization of systems
>> Lack of data management policies/procedures
> Types of Data Quality Problems
>> Dummy values in source system fields
>> Absence of data in source system fields
>> Multipurpose fields
>> Cryptic data
>> Contradicting data
>> Improper use of name and address lines
>> Violation of business rules
>> Reused primary keys
>> Nonunique identifiers

Metadata   You already know that metadata in a data warehouse is not merely data dictionary entries. Metadata in a data warehouse is much more than details that can be carried in a data dictionary or data catalog. Metadata acts as a glue to tie all the components together. When data moves from one component to another, that movement is governed by the relevant portion of metadata. When a user queries the data warehouse, metadata acts as the information resource to connect the query parameters with the database components.

Earlier, we had categorized the metadata in a data warehouse into three groups: operational, data extraction and transformation, and end-user. Figure 6-5 displays the impact of business requirements on the metadata architectural component.

It is needless to reiterate the significance of the metadata component. Study the figure and apply it to your data warehouse project. For each type of metadata, figure out how much detail would be necessary in your requirements definition. Have sufficient detail to enable vital decisions such as choosing the type of metadata repository and reckoning whether the repository must be centralized or distributed.

Tools and Products

When tools are mentioned in the data warehousing context, you probably think only of end-user tools. Many people do so. But for building and maintaining your data warehouse, you need many types of tools to support the various components of the architecture.

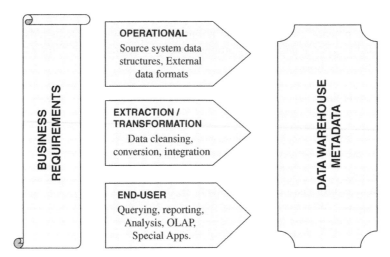

Figure 6-5   Impact of requirements on metadata.

As we discuss the impact of requirements on the data warehouse architecture in this section, we want to bring up the subject of tools and products for two reasons. First, requirements do not directly impact the selection of tools. Do not select the tools based on requirements and then adjust the architecture to suit the tools. This is like putting the cart before the horse. Design the data warehouse architecture and then look for the proper tools to support the architecture. A specific tool, ideally suited for the functions in one data warehouse, may be a complete misfit in another data warehouse. That is because the architectures are different. What do we mean by the statement that the architectures are different? Although the architectural components are generally the same in both data warehouses, the scope, size, content, and the make-up of each component are not the same.

The second reason for mentioning tools and products is this. While collecting requirements to plan the architecture, sometimes you may feel constrained to make the architecture suit the requirements. You may think that you will not be able to design the type of architecture dictated by the requirements because appropriate tools to support that type of architecture may not be available. Please note that there are numerous production-worthy tools available in the market. We want to point out that once your architectural design is completed, you can obtain the most suitable third-party tools and products.

In general, tools are available for the following functions:

- Data Extraction and Transformation
    Middleware
    Data extraction
    Data transformation
    Data quality assurance
    Load image creation
- Warehouse Storage
    Data marts
    Meta data

- Information Access/Delivery
    Report writers
    Query processors
    Alert systems
    Dashboards
    Scorecards
    DSS applications
    Data mining

DATA STORAGE SPECIFICATIONS

If your company is adopting the top-down approach of developing the data warehouse, then you have to define the storage specifications for

- The data staging area
- The overall corporate data warehouse
- Each of the dependent data marts, beginning with the first
- Any multidimensional databases for OLAP

Alternatively, if your company opts for the bottom-up approach, you need specifications for

- The data staging area
- Each of the conformed data marts, beginning with the first
- Any multidimensional databases for OLAP

Typically, the overall corporate data warehouse will be based on the relational model supported by a relational database management system (RDBMS). The data marts are usually structured on the dimensional model implemented using an RDBMS. Many vendors offer proprietary multidimensional database systems (MDDBs). Specification for your MDDB will be based on your choice of vendor. The extent and sophistication of the staging area depends on the complexity and breadth of data transformation, cleansing, and conversion. The staging area may just be a bunch of flat files or, at the other extreme, a fully developed relational database.

Whatever your choice of the database management system may be, that system will have to interact with back-end and front-end tools. The back-end tools are the products for data transformation, data cleansing, and data loading. The front-end tools relate to information delivery to the users. If you are trying to find the best tools to suit your environment, the chances are these tools may not be from the same vendors who supplied the database products. Therefore, one important criterion for the database management system is that the system must be open. It must be compatible with the chosen back-end and front-end tools. More recently many composite data warehouse appliance products are available. These are integrated hardware/software bundles.

So what are we saying about the impact of business requirements on the data storage specifications? Business requirements determine how robust and how open the database systems must be. While defining requirements, bear in mind their influence on data storage specifications and collect all the necessary details about the back-end and the front-end architectural components.

We will next examine the impact of business requirements on the selection of the DBMS and on estimating storage for the data warehouse.

DBMS Selection

In the requirements definition phase, when you are interviewing the users and having formal meetings with them, you are not particularly discussing the type of DBMS to be selected. However, many of the user requirements affect the selection of the proper DBMS. The relational DBMS products on the market are usually bundled with a set of tools for processing queries, writing reports, interfacing with other products, and so on. Your choice of the DBMS may be conditioned by its tool kit component. And the business requirements are likely to determine the type of tool kit component needed. Broadly, the following elements of business requirements affect the choice of the DBMS:

Level of User Experience. If the users are totally inexperienced with database systems, the DBMS must have features to monitor and control runaway queries. On the other hand, if many of your users are power users, then they will be formulating their own queries. In this case, the DBMS must support an easy SQL-type language interface.

Types of Queries. The DBMS must have a powerful optimizer if most of the queries are complex and produce large result sets. Alternatively, if there is an even mix of simple and complex queries, there must be some sort of query management in the database software to balance the query execution.

Need for Openness. The degree of openness depends on the back-end and front-end architectural components and those, in turn, depend on the business requirements.

Data Loads. The data volumes and load frequencies determine the strengths in the areas of data loading, recovery, and restart.

Metadata Management. If your metadata component does not have to be elaborate, then a DBMS with an active data dictionary may be sufficient. Let your requirements definition reflect the type and extent of the metadata framework.

Data Repository Locations. Is your data warehouse going to reside in one central location, or is it going to be distributed? The answer to this question will establish whether the selected DBMS must support distributed databases.

Data Warehouse Growth. Your business requirements definition must contain information on the estimated growth in the number of users, and in the number and complexity of queries. The growth estimates will have a direct relation to how the selected DBMS supports scalability.

Storage Sizing

How big will your data warehouse be? How much storage will be needed for all the data repositories? What is the total storage size? Answers to these questions will impact the type and size of the storage medium. How do you find answers to these questions? Again, it goes back to business requirements. In the requirements definition, you must have enough information to answer these questions.

Let us summarize. You need to estimate the storage sizes for the following in the requirements definition phase:

Data Staging Area. Calculate storage estimates for the data staging area of the overall corporate data warehouse from the sizes of the source system data structures for each business subject. Figure the data transformations and mapping into your calculation. For the data marts, initially estimate the staging area storage based on the business dimensions and metrics for the first data mart.

Overall Corporate Data Warehouse. Estimate the storage size based on the data structures for each business subject. You know that data in the data warehouse is stored by business subjects. For each business subject, list the various attributes, estimate their field lengths, and arrive at the calculation for the storage needed for that subject.

Data Marts—Conformed, Independent, Dependent, or Federated. While defining requirements, you create information diagrams. A set of these diagrams constitutes a data mart. Each information diagram contains business dimensions and their attributes. The information diagram also holds the metrics or business measurements that are meant for analysis. Use the details of the business dimensions and business measures found in the information diagrams to estimate the storage size for the data marts. Begin with your first data mart.

Multidimensional Databases. These databases support OLAP or multidimensional analysis. How much online analytical processing (OLAP) is necessary for your users? The corporate data warehouse or the individual conformed or dependent data mart supplies the data for the multidimensional databases. Work out the details of OLAP planned for your users and then use those details to estimate storage for these multidimensional databases.

INFORMATION DELIVERY STRATEGY

The impact of business requirements on the information delivery mechanism in a data warehouse is straightforward. During the requirements definition phase, users tell you what information they want to retrieve from the data warehouse. You record these requirements in the requirements definition document. You then provide all the desired features and content in the information delivery component. Does this sound simple and straightforward? Although the impact appears to be straightforward and simple, there are several issues to be considered. Many different aspects of the requirements impact various elements of the information delivery component in different ways.

The composition of the user community that is expected to use the business intelligence from the data warehouse affects the information delivery strategy. Are most of the potential users of the data warehouse power users and analysts? Then the information strategy must be slanted toward providing potent analytical tools. Are many of the users expecting to receive preformatted reports and to run precomposed queries? Then query and reporting facilities in the information delivery component must be strengthened.

The broad areas of the information delivery component directly impacted by business requirements are:

- Queries and reports
- Types of analysis

- Information distribution
- Real time information delivery
- Decision support applications
- Growth and expansion

Figure 6-6 shows the impact of business requirements on information delivery.

A data warehouse exists for one reason and one reason alone—to provide strategic information to users. Information delivery tops the list of architectural components. Most of the other components are transparent to the users, but they see and experience what is made available to them in the information delivery component. The importance of business requirements relating to information delivery cannot be overemphasized.

The following subsections contain some valuable tips for requirements definition in order to make the highly significant information delivery component effective and useful. Study these carefully.

Queries and Reports

Find out who will be using predefined queries and preformatted reports. Get the specifications. Also, get the specifications for the production and distribution frequency for the reports. How many users will be running the predefined queries? How often? The second type of queries is not a set of predefined ones. In this case, the users formulate their own queries and they themselves run the queries. Also in this class is the set of reports in which the users supply the report parameters and print fairly sophisticated reports themselves. Get as many details of this type of queries and this type of report sets as you can.

Power users may run complex queries, most of the time as part of an interactive analysis session. Apart from analysis, do your power users need the ability to run single complex queries? Find out.

Types of Analysis

Most data warehouse and business intelligence environments provide several features to run interactive sessions and perform complex data analysis. Analysis encompassing drill-down

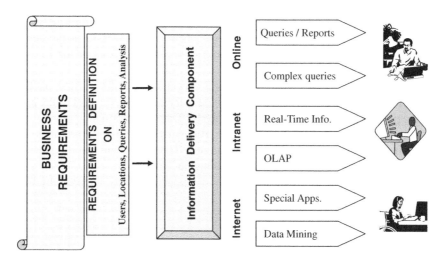

Figure 6-6 Impact of business requirements on information delivery.

and roll-up methods is fairly common. Review with your users all the types of analysis they would like to perform. Get information on the anticipated complexity of the types of analysis.

In addition to the analysis performed directly on the data marts, most of today's data warehouse and business intelligence environments equip users with OLAP. Using the OLAP facilities, users can perform multidimensional analysis and obtain multiple views of the data from multidimensional databases. This type of analysis is called slicing and dicing. Estimate the nature and extent of the drill-down and roll-up facilities to be provided for. Determine how much slicing and dicing has to be made available.

Most of today's business intelligence environments provide information through dashboards and scorecards. So, your information requirements must include details about the composition of these two means of information delivery. Users may work with dashboards interactively and perform various types of analysis.

Information Distribution

Where are your users? Are they in one location? Are they in one local site connected by a local area network (LAN)? Are they spread out on a wide area network (WAN)? These factors determine how information must be distributed to your users. Clearly indicate these details in the requirements definition.

In many companies, users get access to information through the corporate intranet. Web-based technologies are used. If this is the case in your company, Web-based technologies must be incorporated into the information delivery component. Let your requirements definition be explicit about these factors.

Real Time Information Delivery

If your data warehouse is configured to be a real time data warehouse where data updates are carried out in real time or near real time, then your information requirements must have special considerations for real time information delivery. Real time information delivery right away implies more information with more people. Your data warehouse must enable people with the information they need to make critical decisions all day, every day, and must deliver this information in a way that is cost effective. To meet this challenge, you must be able to deploy information delivery systems to very large numbers of people across the enterprise, rapidly and at a low cost of ownership. You must be able to provide information, in real time, to everyone who impacts key business processes: employees, management, suppliers, partners, and customers. How do you do this? Collect the details in the requirements gathering phase.

The following factors need special considerations in your requirements definition: delivery of information to people the way they want it—in the most commonly used formats, e-mail, Web pages, Excel, PDF, and word-processing documents; implementation of a personalized and organized approach to business intelligence that delivers information broadly throughout the enterprise; use of Web-based technology to meet the ever-growing demands for strategic information.

Decision Support Applications

These are specialized applications designed to support individual groups of users for specific purposes. An executive information system provides decision support to senior executives.

A data mining application is a special-purpose system to discover new patterns of relationships and predictive possibilities. We will discuss data mining in more detail in Chapter 17.

The data warehouse supplies data for these decision support applications. Sometimes the design and development of these ad hoc applications are outside the scope of the data warehouse project. The only connection with the data warehouse is the feeding of the data from the data warehouse repository.

Whatever may be the development strategy for the specialized decision support applications in your company, make sure that the requirements definition spells out the details. If the data warehouse will be used just for data feeds, define the data elements and the data movement frequencies.

Growth and Expansion

Let us say your data warehouse is deployed. You have provided your users with the ability to run queries, print reports, perform analysis, use OLAP for complex analysis, and feed the specialized applications with data. The information delivery component is complete and working well. Is that then the end of the effort? Yes, maybe just for the first iteration.

The information delivery component continues to grow and expand. It continues to grow in the number and complexity of queries and reports. It expands in the enhancements to each part of the component. In your original requirements definition you need to anticipate the growth and expansion. Enough details about the growth and expansion can influence the proper design of the information delivery component, so collect enough details to estimate the growth and enhancements.

CHAPTER SUMMARY

- Accurate requirements definition in a data warehouse project is many times more important than in other types of projects. Clearly understand the impact of business requirements on every development phase.
- Business requirements condition the outcome of the data design phase.
- Every component of the data warehouse architecture is strongly influenced by the business requirements.
- In order to provide data quality, identify the data pollution sources, the prevalent types of quality problems, and the means to eliminate data corruption early in the requirements definition phase itself.
- Data storage specifications, especially the selection of the DBMS, are determined by business requirements. Make sure you collect enough relevant details during the requirements phase.
- Business requirements strongly influence the information delivery mechanism. Requirements define how, when, and where the users will receive information from the data warehouse.

REVIEW QUESTIONS

1. "In a data warehouse, business requirements of the users form the single and most powerful driving force." Do you agree? If you do, state four reasons why. If not, is there any other such driving force?

2. How do accurate information diagrams turn into sound data models for your data marts? Explain briefly.

3. Name five architectural components that are strongly impacted by business requirements. Explain the impact of business requirements on any one of those five components.

4. What is the impact of requirements on the selection of vendor tools and products? Do requirements directly determine the choice of tools?

5. List any four aspects of information delivery that are directly impacted by business requirements. For two of those aspects, describe the impact.

6. How do business requirements affect the choice of DBMS? Describe any three of the ways in which the selection of DBMS is affected.

7. What are MDDBs? What types of business requirements determine the use of MDDBs in a data warehouse?

8. How do requirements affect the choice of the metadata framework? Explain very briefly.

9. What types of user requirements dictate the granularity or the levels of detail in a data warehouse?

10. How do you estimate the storage size? What factors determine the size?

EXERCISES

1. Match the columns:

1. information package diagrams	**A.** determine data extraction
2. need for drill-down	**B.** provide OLAP
3. data transformations	**C.** provide data feed
4. data sources	**D.** influences load management
5. data aging	**E.** query management in DBMS
6. sophisticated analysis	**F.** low levels of data
7. simple and complex queries	**G.** larger staging area
8. data volume	**H.** influence data design
9. specialized DSS	**I.** possible pollution source
10. corporate data warehouse	**J.** data staging design

2. It is a known fact that data quality in the source systems is poor in your company. You are assigned to be the data quality assurance specialist on the project team. Describe what details you will include in the requirements definition document to address the data quality problem.

3. As the analyst responsible for data loads and data refreshes, describe all the details you will look for and document during the requirements definition phase.

4. You are the manager for the data warehouse project at a retail chain with stores all across the country and users in every store. How will you ensure that all the details necessary to decide on the DBMS are gathered during the requirements phase? Write a memo to the senior analyst directly responsible to coordinate the requirements definition phase.

5. You are the query tools specialist on the project team for a manufacturing company with the primary users based in the main office. These power users need sophisticated tools for analysis. How will you determine what types of information delivery methods are needed? What kinds of details are to be gathered in the requirements definition phase?

PART 3

ARCHITECTURE AND INFRASTRUCTURE

CHAPTER 7

ARCHITECTURAL COMPONENTS

CHAPTER OBJECTIVES

- Understand data warehouse architecture
- Learn about the architectural components
- Review the distinguishing characteristics of data warehouse architecture
- Examine how the architectural framework supports the flow of data
- Comprehend what technical architecture means
- Study the functions and services of the architectural components
- Revisit the five major architectural types

UNDERSTANDING DATA WAREHOUSE ARCHITECTURE

In Chapter 2, you were introduced to the building blocks of the data warehouse. At that stage, we quickly looked at the list of components and reviewed each very briefly. In Chapter 6, we revisited the data warehouse architecture and established that the business requirements form the principal driving force for all design and development, including the architectural plan.

In this chapter, we want to review the data warehouse architecture from different perspectives. You will study the architectural components in the order in which they enable the flow of data from the sources as business intelligence to the end-users. Then you will be able to look at each area of the architecture and examine the functions, procedures, and features in that area. That discussion will lead you into the technical architecture in those architectural areas.

Data Warehousing Fundamentals for IT Professionals, Second Edition. By Paulraj Ponniah
Copyright © 2010 John Wiley & Sons, Inc.

Architecture: Definitions

The structure that brings all the components of a data warehouse together is known as the architecture. For example, take the case of the architecture of a school building. The architecture of the building is not just the visual style. It includes the various classrooms, offices, library, corridors, gymnasiums, doors, windows, roof, and a large number of other such components. When all of these components are brought and placed together, the structure that ties all of the components together is the architecture of the school building. If you can extend this comparison to a data warehouse, the various components of the data warehouse together form the architecture of the data warehouse.

While building the school building, let us say that the builders were told to make the classrooms large. So they made the classrooms larger but eliminated the offices altogether, thus constructing the school building with a faulty architecture. What went wrong with the architecture? For one thing, all the necessary components were not present. Probably, the arrangement of the remaining components was also not right. Correct architecture is critical for the success of your data warehouse. Therefore, in this chapter, we will take another close look at data warehouse architecture.

In your data warehouse, architecture includes a number of factors. Primarily, it includes the integrated data that is the centerpiece. The architecture includes everything that is needed to prepare the data and store it. On the other hand, it also includes all the means for delivering information from your data warehouse. The architecture is further composed of the rules, procedures, and functions that enable your data warehouse to work and fulfill the business requirements. Finally, the architecture is made up of the technology that empowers your data warehouse.

What is the general purpose of the data warehouse architecture? The architecture provides the overall framework for developing and deploying your data warehouse; it is a comprehensive blueprint. The architecture defines the standards, measurements, general design, and support techniques.

Architecture in Three Major Areas

As you already know, the three major areas in the data warehouse are:

- Data acquisition
- Data storage
- Information delivery

In Chapter 2, we identified the following major building blocks of the data warehouse:

- Source data
- Data staging
- Data storage
- Information delivery
- Metadata
- Management and control

Figure 7-1 groups these major architectural components into the three areas. In this chapter, we will study the architecture as it relates to these three areas. In each area, we

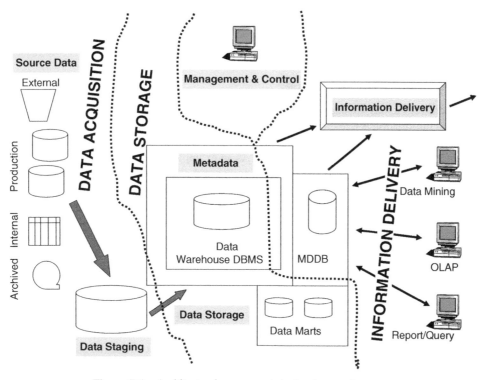

Figure 7-1   Architectural components in the three major areas.

will consider the supporting architectural components. Each of the components has definite functions and provides specific services. We will probe these functions and services and also examine the underlying technical architecture of the individual components in these three areas.

Because of the importance of the architectural components, you will also receive additional details in later chapters. For now, for the three data warehouse areas, let us concentrate on the functions, services, and technical architecture in these major areas as highlighted in Figure 7-1.

DISTINGUISHING CHARACTERISTICS

As an IT professional, when you were involved in the development of an OLTP system such as order processing or inventory control, or sales reporting, were you considering an architecture for each system? Although the term architecture is not usually mentioned in the context of operational systems, nevertheless, an underlying architecture does exist for these systems as well. For example, the architectural considerations for such a system would include the file conversions, initial population of the database, methods for data input, information delivery through online screens, and the entire suite of online and batch reporting. But for such systems we do not deal with architectural considerations in much detail. The data warehouse is different and distinctive in that it compels us to consider architecture in elaborate detail.

Data warehouse architecture is wide, complex, and expansive. In a data warehouse, the architecture consists of distinct components. The architecture has distinguishing characteristics worth considering in detail. Before moving on to discuss the architectural framework itself, let us review the distinguishing characteristics of data warehouse architecture.

Different Objectives and Scope

The architecture has to support the requirements for providing strategic information. Strategic information is markedly different from information obtained from operational systems. When you provide information from an operational application, the information content and quantity per user session is limited. As an example, at a particular time, the user is interested only in information about one customer and all the related orders. From a data warehouse, however, the user is interested in obtaining large result sets. An example of a large result set from your data warehouse is all sales for the year broken down by quarters, products, and sales regions.

Primarily, therefore, the data warehouse architecture must have components that will work to provide data to the users in large volumes in a single session. Basically, the extent to which a decision support system is different from an operational system directly translates into just one essential principle: a data warehouse must have a different and more elaborate architecture.

Defining the scope for a data warehouse is also difficult. How do you scope an operational system? You consider the group of users, the range of functions, the data repository, and the output screens and reports. For a data warehouse with the architecture as the blueprint, what are all the factors you must consider for defining the scope?

There are several sets of factors to consider. First, you must consider the number and extent of the data sources. How many legacy systems are you going to extract the data from? What are the external sources? Are you planning to include departmental files, spreadsheets, and private databases? What about including the archived data? Scope of the architecture may again be measured in terms of the data transformations and integration functions. In a data warehouse, data granularity and data volumes are also important considerations.

Yet another serious consideration is the impact of the data warehouse on the existing operational systems. Because of the data extractions, comparisons, and reconciliation, you have to determine how much negative impact the data warehouse will have on the performance of operational systems. When will your batch extracts be run and how will they affect the production source systems? On the other hand, if yours is going to be a real time data warehouse, data capture functions will become elaborate and complex.

Data Content

The "read-only" data in the data warehouse sits in the middle as the primary component in the architecture. In an operational system, although the database is important, it is not as important as the data repository in a data warehouse. Before data is brought into your data warehouse and stored as read-only data, a number of functions must be performed. These exhaustive and critical functions do not compare with the data conversion that happens in an operational system.

In your data warehouse, you keep data integrated from multiple sources. After extracting the data, which by itself is an elaborate process, you transform the data, cleanse it, and integrate it in a staging area. Only then do you move the integrated data into the data warehouse repository as read-only data. Operational data is not "read-only" data.

Further, your data warehouse architecture must support the storing of data grouped by business subjects, not grouped by applications as in the case of operational systems. The data in your data warehouse does not represent a snapshot containing the values of the variables as they are at the current time. This is different and distinct from most operational systems.

When we mention historical data stored in the data warehouse, we are talking about very high data volumes. Most companies opt to keep data going back 10 years in the data warehouse. Some companies want to keep even more, if the data is available. This is another reason why the data warehouse architecture must support high data volumes.

Complex Analysis and Quick Response

Your data warehouse architecture must support complex analysis of the strategic information by the users. Information retrieval processes in an operational system dwindle in complexity when compared to the use of information from a data warehouse. Most of the online information retrieval during a session by a user in a data warehouse is interactive analysis. A user does not run an isolated query, go away from the data warehouse, and come back much later for the next single query. A session by the user is continuous and lasts a long time because the user usually starts with a query at a high level, reviews the result set, initiates the next query looking at the data in a slightly different way, and so on.

Your data warehouse architecture must, therefore, support variations for providing analysis. Users must be able to drill down, roll up, slice and dice data, and play with "what-if" scenarios. Users must have the capability to review the result sets in different output options. Users are no longer content with textual result sets or results displayed in tabular formats. Every result set in tabular format must be translated into graphical charts.

Provision of strategic information is meant for making rapid decisions and to deal with situations quickly. For example, let us say your vice president of marketing wants to quickly discover the reasons for the drop in sales for three consecutive weeks in the central region and make prompt decisions to remedy the situation. Your data warehouse must give him or her the tools and information for a quick response to the problem.

Your data warehouse architecture must make it easy to make strategic decisions quickly. There must be appropriate components in the architecture to support quick response by the users to deal with situations by using the information provided by your data warehouse.

If your data warehouse supports real time information retrieval, the architecture has to expand to accommodate real time data capture and the ability to obtain strategic information in real time to make on-the-spot decisions. Real time data warehousing means delivery of information to a larger number of users both inside and outside the organization.

Flexible and Dynamic

Especially in the case of the design and development of a data warehouse, you do not know all business requirements up front. Using the technique for creating information packages, you are able to assess most of the requirements and dimensionally model the data requirements. Nevertheless, the missing parts of the requirements show up after your users begin to use the data warehouse. What is the implication of this? You have to make sure your data warehouse architecture is flexible enough to accommodate additional requirements as and when they surface.

Additional requirements surface to include the missed items in the business requirements. Moreover, business conditions themselves change. In fact, they keep on changing. Changing business conditions call for additional business requirements to be included in the data warehouse. If the data warehouse architecture is designed to be flexible and dynamic, then your data warehouse can cater to the supplemental requirements as and when they arise.

Metadata-Driven

As the data moves from the source systems to the end-users as useful, strategic information, metadata surrounds the entire movement. The metadata component of the architecture holds data about every phase of the movement, and, in a certain sense, guides the data movement.

In an operational system, there is no component that is equivalent to metadata in a data warehouse. The data dictionary of the DBMS of the operational system is just a faint shadow of the metadata in a data warehouse. So, in your data warehouse architecture, the metadata component interleaves with and connects the other components. Metadata in a data warehouse is so important that we have dedicated Chapter 9 to a discussion of metadata.

ARCHITECTURAL FRAMEWORK

Earlier in a previous section of this chapter, we grouped the architectural components as building blocks in the three distinct areas of data acquisition, data storage, and information delivery. In each of these broad areas of the data warehouse, the architectural components serve specific purposes.

Architecture Supporting Flow of Data

Now we want to associate the components as forming a framework to condition and enable the flow of data from beginning to end. As you know very well, data that finally reaches the end-user as useful strategic information begins as disparate data elements in the various data sources. This collection of data from the various sources moves to the staging area. What happens next? The extracted data goes through a detailed preparation process in the staging area before it is sent forward to the data warehouse to be properly stored. From the data warehouse storage, data transformed into useful information is retrieved by the users or delivered to the user desktops as required. In a basic sense, what then is data warehousing? Do you agree that data warehousing just means taking all the necessary source data, preparing it, storing it in suitable formats, and then delivering useful information to the end-users?

Figure 7-2 shows the flow of data from beginning to end and also highlights the architectural components enabling the flow of data as the data moves along.

Let us now follow the flow of the data and identify the architectural components. Some of the architectural components govern the flow of data from beginning to end. The management and control module is one such component. This module touches every step along the data movement path.

What happens at critical points of the flow of data? What are the architectural components, and how do these components enable the data flow?

At the Data Source   Here the internal and external data sources form the *source data* architectural component. Source data governs the extraction of data for preparation and storage in the data warehouse. The *data staging* architectural component governs the transformation, cleansing, and integration of data.

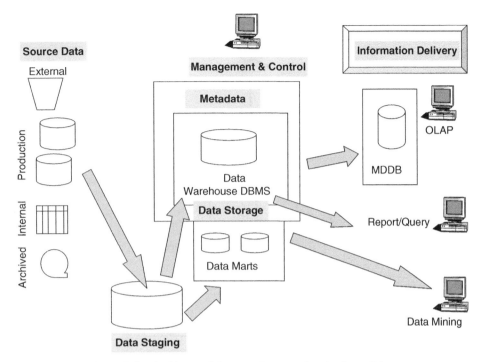

Figure 7-2   Architectural framework supporting the flow of data.

In the Data Warehouse Repository   The *data storage* architectural component includes the loading of data from the staging area and also storing the data in suitable formats for information delivery. The *metadata* architectural component is also a storage mechanism to contain data about the data at every point of the flow of data from beginning to end.

At the User End   The *information delivery* architectural component includes dependent data marts, special multidimensional databases, and a full range of query and reporting facilities, including dashboards and scorecards.

The Management and Control Module

This architectural component is an overall module managing and controlling the entire data warehouse environment. It is an umbrella component working at various levels and covering all the operations. This component has two major functions: first to constantly monitor all the ongoing operations, and next to step in and recover from problems when things go wrong. Figure 7-3 shows how the management component relates to and manages all of the data warehouse operations.

At the outset in your data warehouse, you have operations relating to data acquisition. These include extracting data from the source systems either for full refresh or for incremental loads. Moving the data into the staging area and performing the data transformation functions is also part of data acquisition. The management architectural component manages and controls these data acquisition functions, ensuring that extracts and transformations are carried out correctly and in a timely fashion.

The management module also manages backing up significant parts of the data warehouse and recovering from failures. Management services include monitoring the growth

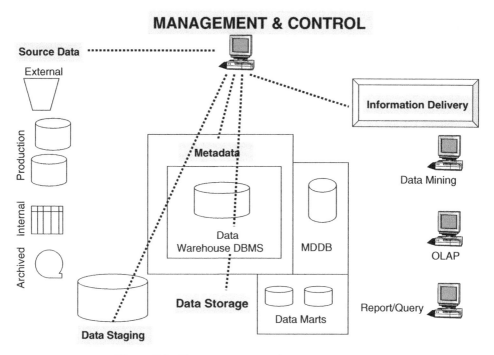

Figure 7-3 The management and control component.

and periodically archiving data from the data warehouse. This architectural component also governs data security and provides authorized access to the data warehouse. Also, the management component interfaces with the end-user information delivery component to ensure that information delivery is carried out properly.

Only a few tools specially designed for data warehouse administration arc presently available. Generally, data warehouse administrators perform the functions of the management and control component by using the tools available in the data warehouse DBMS.

TECHNICAL ARCHITECTURE

We have already reviewed the various components of the data warehouse architecture in a few different ways. First, we grouped the components into the three major areas of data acquisition, data storage, and information delivery. Then, we explored the distinguishing characteristics of the data warehouse architecture. We examined the architecture and highlighted the distinguishing characteristics of the data warehouse architecture in comparison with that of any operational system. We also traced the flow of data through the data warehouse and linked individual architectural components to stations along the passage of data.

You now have a good grasp of how we have applied the term architecture to the data warehouse. We have indicated that each component of the architecture is there to perform a set of definite functions and provide a group of specific services. When all the components perform their predefined functions and provide the required services, then the whole architecture supports the data warehouse to fulfill the goals and business requirements.

We denote the technical architecture of a data warehouse as the complete set of functions and services provided within its component structures. The technical architecture also includes the procedures and rules that are required to perform the functions and provide the services. The technical architecture also encompasses the data stores needed for each component to provide the services.

Let us now make another significant distinction. The architecture is not the set of tools needed to perform the functions and provide the services. When we refer to the data extraction function within one of the architectural components, we are simply mentioning the function itself and the various tasks associated with that function. Also, we are relating the data store for the staging area to the data extraction function because extracted data is moved to the staging area. Notice that there is no mention of any tools for performing the function. Where do the tools fit in? What are the tools for extracting the data? What are tools in relation to the architecture? *Tools are the means to implement the technical architecture.* That is why you must remember that architecture comes first and the tools follow.

You will be selecting the tools most appropriate for the architecture of your data warehouse. Let us take a very simple, perhaps unrealistic, example. Suppose the only data source for your data warehouse is just four tables from a single centralized relational database. If so, what is the extent and scope of the data source component? What is the magnitude of the data extraction function? They are extremely limited. Do you then need sophisticated third-party tools for data extraction? Obviously not. Taking the other extreme position, suppose your data sources consist of databases and files from 50 or more legacy systems running on multiple platforms at remote sites. In this case, your data source architectural component and the data extraction function have a very broad and complex scope. You certainly need to augment your in-house effort with proper data extraction tools from vendors.

In the remaining sections of this chapter, we will consider the technical architecture of the components. We will discuss and elaborate on the types of functions, services, procedures, and data stores that are relevant to each architectural component. These are guidelines. You have to take these guidelines and review and adapt them for establishing the architecture for your data warehouse. When you establish the architecture for your data warehouse, you will prepare the architectural plan that will include all the components. The plan will also state in detail the extent and complexity of all the functions, services, procedures, and data stores related to each architectural component. The architectural plan will serve as a blueprint for the design and development of the data warehouse. It will also serve as a master checklist for your tool selection.

Let us now consider the technical architecture in each of the three major areas of the data warehouse.

Data Acquisition

This area covers the entire process of extracting data from the data sources, moving all the extracted data to the staging area, and preparing the data for loading into the data warehouse repository. The two major architectural components identified earlier as part of this area are *source data* and *data staging*. The functions and services in this area relate to these two architectural components. The variations in the data sources have a direct impact on the extent and scope of the functions and services.

What happens in this area is of great importance in the development of your data warehouse. The processes of data extraction, transformation, and loading are time-consuming, human-intensive, and very important. Chapter 12 treats these processes in great depth.

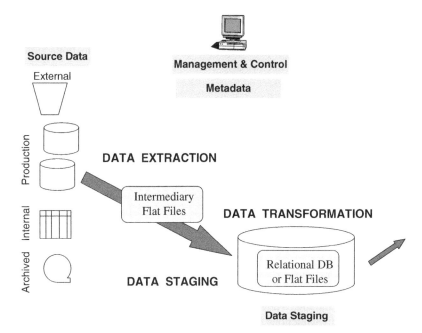

Figure 7-4 Data acquisition: technical architecture.

However, at this time, we will deal with these in sufficient length for you to place all the architectural components in proper perspective. Figure 7-4 summarizes the technical architecture for data acquisition.

Data Flow

Flow In the data acquisition area, the data flow begins at the data sources and pauses at the staging area. After transformation and integration, the data is ready for loading into the data warehouse repository.

Data Sources For the majority of data warehouses, the primary data source consists of the enterprise's operational systems. In many organizations, some operational systems are still legacy systems. Legacy data resides on hierarchical or network databases. You have to use the appropriate fourth generation language of the particular DBMS to extract data from these databases. However, most of the recent operational systems run on the client/server architecture. Usually, these systems are supported by relational DBMSs. Here you may use an SQL-based language for extracting data.

A fairly large number of companies have adopted ERP (enterprise resource planning) systems. ERP data sources provide an advantage in that the data from these sources is already consolidated and integrated. There could, however, be a few drawbacks to using ERP data sources. You will have to use the ERP vendor's proprietary tool for data extraction. Also, most of the ERP offerings contain very large numbers of source data tables.

For including data from outside sources, you will have to create temporary files to hold the data received from the outside sources. After reformatting and rearranging the data elements, you will have to move the data to the staging area.

Intermediary Data Stores   As data gets extracted from the data sources, it moves through temporary files. Sometimes, extracts of homogeneous data from several source applications are pulled into separate temporary files and then merged into another temporary file before moving it to the staging area.

The opposite process is also common. From each application, one or two large flat files are created and then divided into smaller files and merged appropriately before moving the data to the staging area. Typically, the general practice is to use flat files to extract data from operational systems.

Staging Area   This is the place where all the extracted data is put together and prepared for loading into the data warehouse. The staging area is like an assembly plant or a construction area. In this area, you examine each extracted file, review the business rules, perform the various data transformation functions, sort and merge data, resolve inconsistencies, and cleanse the data. When the data is finally prepared either for an enterprise-wide data warehouse or one of the conformed data marts, the data temporarily resides in the staging area repository waiting to be loaded into the data warehouse repository.

In many data warehouses, data in the staging area is kept in sequential or flat files. These flat files, however, contain the fully integrated and cleansed data in appropriate formats ready for loading. Typically, these files are in the formats that could be loaded by the utility tools of the data warehouse RDBMS. Now more and more staging area data repositories are becoming relational databases. The data in such staging areas are retained for longer periods. Although extracts for loading may be easily obtained from relational databases with proper indexes, creating and maintaining these relational databases involves overhead for index creation and data migration from the source systems.

The staging area may contain data at the lowest grain to populate tables containing business measurements. It is also common for aggregated data to be kept in the staging area for loading. The other types of data kept in the staging area relate to business dimensions such as product, time, sales region, customer, and promotional schemes.

Functions and Services   The list of functions and services in this section relates to the data acquisition area and is broken down into three groups. This is a general list. It does not indicate the extent or complexity of each function or service. For the technical architecture of your data warehouse, you have to determine the content and complexity of each function or service.

List of Functions and Services

Data Extraction

Select data sources and determine the types of filters to be applied to individual sources.

Generate automatic extract files from operational systems using replication and other techniques.

Create intermediary files to store selected data to be merged later.

Transport extracted files from multiple platforms.

Provide automated job control services for creating extract files.

Reformat input from outside sources.

Reformat input from departmental data files, databases, and spreadsheets.

Generate common application codes for data extraction.

Resolve inconsistencies for common data elements from multiple sources.

Data Transformation

Map input data to data for data warehouse repository.

Clean data, deduplicate, and merge/purge.

Denormalize extracted data structures as required by the dimensional model of the data warehouse.

Convert data types.

Calculate and derive attribute values.

Check for referential integrity.

Aggregate data as needed.

Resolve missing values.

Consolidate and integrate data.

Data Staging

Provide backup and recovery for staging area repositories.

Sort and merge files.

Create files as input to make changes to dimension tables.

If data staging storage is a relational database, create and populate database.

Preserve audit trail to relate each data item in the data warehouse to input source.

Resolve and create primary and foreign keys for load tables.

Consolidate datasets and create flat files for loading through DBMS utilities.

If staging area storage is a relational database, extract load files.

Data Storage

This covers the process of loading the data from the staging area into the data warehouse repository. All functions for transforming and integrating the data are completed in the data staging area. The prepared data in the data warehouse is like the finished product that is ready to be stacked in an industrial warehouse.

Even before loading data into the data warehouse, metadata, which is another component of the architecture, is already active. During the data extraction and data transformation stages themselves, the metadata repository gets populated. Figure 7-5 shows a summarized view of the technical architecture for data storage.

Data Flow

Flow   For data storage, the data flow begins at the data staging area. The transformed and integrated data is moved from the staging area to the data warehouse repository.

If the data warehouse is an enterprise-wide data warehouse being built in a top-down fashion, then there could be movements of data from the enterprise-wide data warehouse repository to the repositories of the dependent data marts. Alternatively, if the data warehouse is a conglomeration of conformed data marts being built in a bottom-up manner, then the data movements stop with the appropriate conformed data marts.

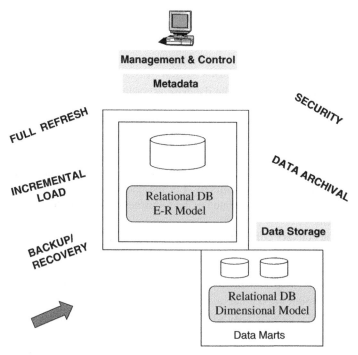

Figure 7-5   Data storage: technical architecture.

Data Groups   Prepared data waiting in the data staging area fall into two groups. The first group is the set of files or tables containing data for a full refresh. This group of data is usually meant for the initial loading of the data warehouse. Occasionally, some data warehouse tables may be refreshed fully.

The other group of data is the set of files or tables containing ongoing incremental loads. Most of these relate to nightly loads. Some incremental loads of dimension data may be performed at less frequent intervals.

The Data Repository   Almost all of today's data warehouse databases are relational databases. All the power, flexibility, and ease of use capabilities of the RDBMS become available for the processing of data.

Functions and Services   The general list of functions and services given in this section is for your guidance. The list relates to the data storage area and covers the broad functions and services. This is a general list. It does not indicate the extent or complexity of each function or service. For the technical architecture of your data warehouse, you have to determine the content and complexity of each function or service.

List of Functions and Services

- Load data for full refreshes of data warehouse tables.
- Perform incremental loads at regular prescribed intervals.
- Support loading into multiple tables at the detailed and summarized levels.
- Optimize the loading process.

- Provide automated job control services for loading the data warehouse.
- Provide backup and recovery for the data warehouse database.
- Provide security.
- Monitor and fine-tune the database.
- Periodically archive data from the database according to preset conditions.

Information Delivery

This area spans a broad spectrum of methods for making information available to users. For your users, the information delivery component is the data warehouse. They do not come into contact with the other components directly. For the users, the strength of your data warehouse architecture is mainly concentrated in the robustness and flexibility of the information delivery component.

The information delivery component makes it easy for the users to access the information either directly from the enterprise-wide data warehouse, from the dependent data marts, or from the set of conformed data marts. Most of the information access in a data warehouse is through online queries and interactive analysis sessions. Nevertheless, your data warehouse will also be producing regular and ad hoc reports.

Almost all modern data warehouses provide for online analytical processing (OLAP). In this case, the primary data warehouse feeds data to proprietary multidimensional databases (MDDBs) where summarized data is kept as multidimensional cubes of information. The users perform complex multidimensional analysis using the information cubes in the MDDBs. Refer to Figure 7-6 for a summarized view of the technical architecture for information delivery.

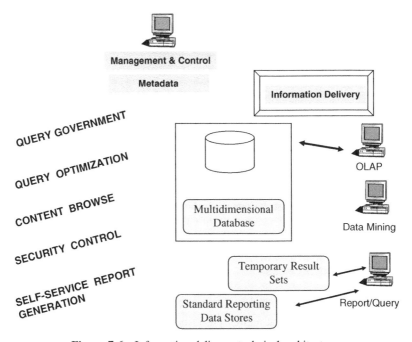

Figure 7-6   Information delivery: technical architecture.

Data Flow

Flow   For information delivery, the data flow begins at the enterprise-wide data warehouse and the dependent data marts when the design is based on the top-down technique. When the design follows the bottom-up method, the data flow starts at the set of conformed data marts. Generally, data transformed into information flows to user desktops during query sessions. Also, information printed on regular or ad hoc reports reaches the users. Sometimes, the result sets from individual queries or reports are held in proprietary data stores of the query or reporting tool vendors. The stored information may be put to faster repeated use.

Recently progressive organizations implement dashboards and scorecards as part of information delivery. Dashboards are real time or near real time information display devices. Data flows to the dashboards in real time from the data warehouse.

In many data warehouses, data also flows into specialized downstream decision support applications such as executive information systems (EIS) and data mining. The other more common flow of information is to proprietary multidimensional databases for OLAP.

Service Locations   In your information delivery component, you may provide query services from the user desktop, from an application server, or from the database itself. This will be one of the critical decisions for your architecture design.

For producing regular or ad hoc reports you may want to include a comprehensive reporting service. This service will allow users to create and run their own reports. It will also provide for standard reports to be run at regular intervals.

Data Stores   For information delivery, you may consider the following intermediary data stores:

- Proprietary temporary stores to hold results of individual queries and reports for repeated use
- Data stores for standard reporting
- Data stores for dashboards
- Proprietary multidimensional databases

Functions and Services   Review the general list of functions and services given below and use it as a guide to establish the information delivery component of your data warehouse architecture. The list relates to information delivery and covers the broad functions and services. Again, this is a general list. It does not indicate the extent or complexity of each function or service. For the technical architecture of your data warehouse, you have to determine the content and complexity of each function or service.

- Provide security to control information access.
- Monitor user access to improve service and for future enhancements.
- Allow users to browse data warehouse content.
- Simplify access by hiding internal complexities of data storage from users.
- Automatically reformat queries for optimal execution.
- Enable queries to be aware of aggregate tables for faster results.
- Govern queries and control runaway queries.

- Provide self-service report generation for users, consisting of a variety of flexible options to create, schedule, and run reports.
- Store result sets of queries and reports for future use.
- Provide multiple levels of data granularity.
- Provide event triggers to monitor data loading.
- Make provision for the users to perform complex analysis through online analytical processing (OLAP).
- Enable data feeds to downstream, specialized decision support systems such as EIS and data mining.

In this chapter we have looked at the data warehouse architecture and the components from various points of view. We discussed the architecture as it relates to the three major areas of data acquisition, data storage, and information delivery. Then we considered the overall architectural framework and focused on how the architecture supports the flow of data. We reviewed the management and control component in the architecture.

Our coverage detailed the technical architecture in each of the three major areas. In each of these three areas, we studied the architecture in relation to the data flow and listed the functions and services. All of this discussion has provided you with a strong and clear understanding of data warehouse architectural components, their arrangement, and their functions.

ARCHITECTURAL TYPES

In Chapter 2, we introduced five common and major types of architecture. As indicated earlier, these types essentially differ in the way data is integrated and stored and also in the way "data warehouses" and "data marts" are related.

At this point, we would like to revisit these architectural types so that you may view our entire discussion of architecture in this chapter and see how it would apply to each of these five common types of architecture. Note the arrangement and linkage of the "data warehouse" and "data marts" in each case wherever applicable. Also, notice how the architectural arrangements facilitate the intended data flows as discussed earlier in this chapter.

Centralized Corporate Data Warehouse

In this architecture type, a centralized enterprise data warehouse is present. There are no data marts, whether dependent or independent. Therefore all information delivery is from the centralized data warehouse.

See Figure 7-7 for a high-level overview of the components. Note the flow of data from source systems to staging area, then to the normalized central data warehouse, and thereafter to end-users as business intelligence.

Independent Data Marts

In this architecture type, the data warehouse is really a collection of unconnected, disparate data marts, each serving a specific department or purpose. These data marts in such organizations usually evolve over time without any overall planning. Each data mart delivers information to its own group of users.

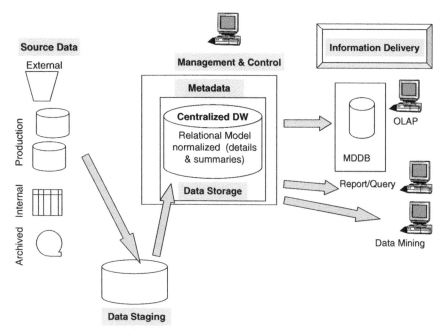

Figure 7-7   Overview of the components of a centralized data warehouse.

See Figure 7-8 for a high-level overview of the components. Note the flow of data from source systems to staging area, then to the various independent data marts, and thereafter to individual groups of end-users as business intelligence. In many cases, data staging functions and movement to each data mart may be carried out separately.

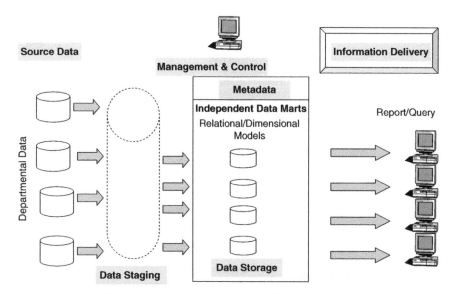

Figure 7-8   Overview of the components of independent data marts.

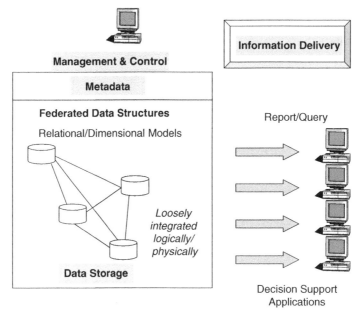

Figure 7-9 Overview of the components of a federated data warehouse.

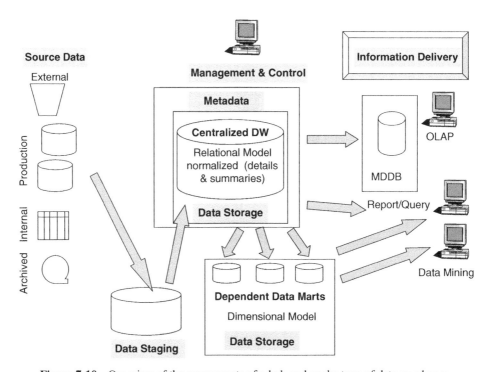

Figure 7-10 Overview of the components of a hub-and-spoke type of data warehouse.

Federated

This architecture type appears to be similar to the type with independent data marts. But there is one big difference. In the federated architectural type, common data elements in the various data marts and even data warehouses that compose the federation are integrated physically or logically. The goal is to strive for a single version of truth for the organization; a centralized enterprise data warehouse is present. There are no data marts, whether dependent or independent. Therefore all information delivery is from the centralized data warehouse.

See Figure 7-9 for a high-level overview of the components. Note the flow of data from the federation of data marts, data warehouses, and other sources to the end-users as business intelligence. In between, logical or physical integration of common data elements takes place.

Hub-and-Spoke

In this architecture type, a centralized enterprise data warehouse is present. In addition, there are data marts that depend on the enterprise data warehouse for data feed. Information delivery can, therefore, be both from the centralized data warehouse and the dependent data marts.

See Figure 7-10 for a high-level overview of the components. Note the flow of data from source systems to the staging area, then to the normalized central data warehouse, and thereafter to end-users as business intelligence from both the central data warehouse and the dependent data marts.

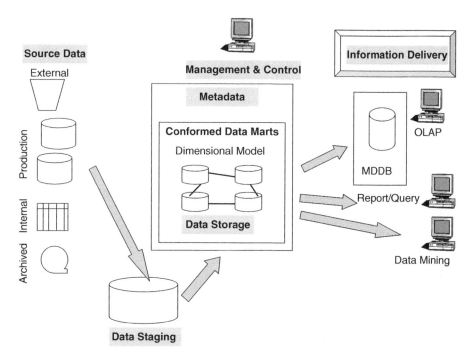

Figure 7-11   Overview of the components of a data-mart bus.

Data-Mart Bus

In this architecture type, no distinct, single data warehouse exists. The collection of all the data marts form the data warehouse because the data marts are conformed "super-marts" because the business dimensions and measured facts are conformed and linked among the data marts. All information delivery is from the conglomeration of the conformed data marts. These data marts may serve the entire enterprise, not just single departments.

See Figure 7-11 for a high-level overview of the components. Note the flow of data from source systems to staging area, then to the various conformed data marts, thereafter to end-users as business intelligence from the conformed data marts.

CHAPTER SUMMARY

- Architecture is the structure that brings all the components together.
- Data warehouse architecture consists of distinct components with the read-only data repository as the centerpiece.
- A few typical data warehouse architectural types are in use at various organizations. Broadly these types reflect how data is stored and made available—centrally as the single enterprise data warehouse database or as a collection cohesive data marts.
- The architectural components support the functioning of the data warehouse in the three major areas of data acquisition, data storage, and information delivery.
- Data warehouse architecture is wide, complex, expansive, and has several distinguishing characteristics.
- The architectural framework enables the flow of data from the data sources at one end to the user's desktop at the other.
- The technical architecture of a data warehouse is the complete set of functions and services provided within its components. It includes the procedures and rules needed to perform the functions and to provide the services. It encompasses the data stores needed for each component to provide the services.
- The flow of data from the source systems to end-users as business intelligence depends on the architectural type.

REVIEW QUESTIONS

1. What is your understanding of data warehouse architecture? Describe in one or two paragraphs.

2. What are the three major areas in the data warehouse? Is this a logical division? If so, why do you think so? Relate the architectural components to the three major areas.

3. Name four distinguishing characteristics of data warehouse architecture. Describe each briefly.

4. Trace the flow of data through the data warehouse from beginning to end.

5. For information delivery, what is the difference between top-down and bottom-up approaches to data warehouse implementation?

6. In which architectural component does OLAP fit? What is the function of OLAP?

7. Define the technical architecture of the data warehouse. How does it relate to the individual architectural components?

8. List five major functions and services in the data storage area.

9. What are the types of storage repositories in the data staging area?

10. List four major functions and services for information delivery. Describe each briefly.

EXERCISES

1. Indicate if true or false:

   A. Data warehouse architecture is just an overall guideline. It is not a blueprint for the data warehouse.

   B. In a data warehouse, the metadata component is unique, with no truly matching component in operational systems,

   C. Normally, data flows from the data warehouse repository to the data staging area.

   D. The management and control component does not relate to all operations in a data warehouse.

   E. Technical architecture simply means the vendor tools.

   F. SQL-based languages are used to extract data from hierarchical databases.

   G. Sorts and merges of files are common in the staging area.

   H. MDDBs are generally relational databases.

   I. Sometimes, results of individual queries are held in temporary data stores for repeated use.

   J. Downstream specialized applications are fed directly from the source data component.

2. You have been recently promoted to administrator for the data warehouse of a nationwide automobile insurance company. You are asked to prepare a checklist for selecting a proper vendor tool to help you with the data warehouse administration. Make a list of the functions in the management and control component of your data warehouse architecture. Use this list to derive the tool-selection checklist.

3. As the senior analyst responsible for data staging, you are responsible for the design of the data staging area. If your data warehouse gets input from several legacy systems on multiple platforms, and also regular feeds from two external sources, how will you organize your data staging area? Describe the data repositories you will have for data staging.

4. You are the data warehouse architect for a leading national department store chain. The data warehouse has been up and running for nearly a year. Now the management has decided to provide power users with OLAP facilities. How will you alter the information delivery component of your data warehouse architecture? Make realistic assumptions and proceed.

5. You recently joined as the data extraction specialist on the data warehouse project team developing a conformed data mart for a local but progressive pharmacy. Make a detailed list of functions and services for data extraction, data transformation, and data staging.

CHAPTER 8

INFRASTRUCTURE AS THE FOUNDATION FOR DATA WAREHOUSING

CHAPTER OBJECTIVES

- Understand the distinction between architecture and infrastructure
- Find out how the data warehouse infrastructure supports its architecture
- Gain an insight into the components of the physical infrastructure
- Review hardware and operating systems for the data warehouse
- Study parallel processing options as applicable to the data warehouse
- Discuss the server options in detail
- Learn how to select the DBMS
- Review the types of tools needed for the data warehouse
- Study the concept and use of data warehouse appliances

What is data warehouse infrastructure in relation to its architecture? What is the distinction between architecture and infrastructure? In what ways are they different? Why do we have to study the two separately?

In the previous chapter, we discussed data warehouse architecture in detail. We looked at the various architectural components and studied them by grouping them into the three major areas of the data warehouse, namely, data acquisition, data storage, and information delivery. You learned the elements that composed the technical architecture of each architectural component. You also reviewed the prevalent distinct architectural types and how flow of data is supported in each type.

In this chapter, let us find out what infrastructure means and what it includes. We will discuss each part of the data warehouse infrastructure. You will understand the significance of infrastructure and master the techniques for creating the proper infrastructure for your data warehouse.

INFRASTRUCTURE SUPPORTING ARCHITECTURE

Consider the architectural components. For example, let us take the technical architecture of the data staging component. This part of the technical architecture for your data warehouse does a number of things. First of all, it indicates that there is a section of the architecture relevant to data staging. Then it notes that this section of the architecture contains an area where data is staged before it is loaded into the data warehouse repository. Next, it denotes that this section of the architecture performs certain functions and provides specific services in the data warehouse. Among others, the functions and services include data transformation and data cleansing.

Let us now ask a few questions. Where exactly is the data staging area? What are the specific files and databases? How do the functions get performed? What enables the services to be provided? What is the underlying base? What is the foundational structure? Infrastructure is the foundation supporting the architecture. Figure 8-1 expresses this fact in a simple manner.

What are the various elements needed to support the architecture? The foundational infrastructure includes many elements. First, it consists of the basic computing platform. The platform includes all the required hardware and the operating system. Next, the database management system (DBMS) is an important element of the infrastructure. All other types of software and tools are also part of the infrastructure. What about the people and the procedures that make the architecture come alive? Are these also part of the infrastructure? In a sense, they are.

Data warehouse infrastructure includes all the foundational elements that enable the architecture to be implemented. In summary, the infrastructure includes several elements such as server hardware, operating system, network software, database software, the LAN and WAN, vendor tools for every architectural component, people, procedures, and training.

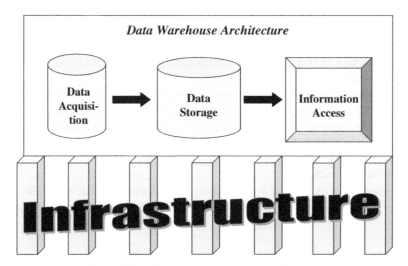

Figure 8-1   Infrastructure supporting architecture.

The elements of the data warehouse infrastructure may be classified into two categories: operational infrastructure and physical infrastructure. This distinction is important because elements in each category are different in their nature and features compared to those in the other category. First, we will go over the elements that may be grouped as operational infrastructure. The physical infrastructure is much wider and more fundamental.

After gaining a basic understanding of the elements of the physical architecture, we will spend a large portion of this chapter examining specific elements in greater detail.

Operational Infrastructure

To understand operational infrastructure, let us once again take the example of data staging. One part of the foundational infrastructure refers to the computing hardware and the related software. You need the hardware and software to perform the data staging functions and render the appropriate services. You need software tools to perform data transformations. You need software to create the output files. You need disk hardware to place the data in the staging area files. But what about the people involved in performing these functions? What about the business rules and procedures for the data transformations? What about the management software to monitor and administer the data transformation tasks?

Operational infrastructure to support each architectural component consists of

- People
- Procedures
- Training
- Management software

These are not the people and procedures needed for developing the data warehouse. These are needed to keep the data warehouse going. These elements are as essential as the hardware and software that keep the data warehouse running. They support the management of the data warehouse and maintain its efficiency.

Data warehouse developers pay a lot of attention to the hardware and system software elements of the infrastructure. It is right to do so. But operational infrastructure is often neglected. Even though you may have the right hardware and software, your data warehouse needs the operational infrastructure in place for proper functioning. Without appropriate operational infrastructure, your data warehouse is likely to just limp along and cease to be effective. Pay attention to the details of your operational infrastructure.

Physical Infrastructure

Let us begin with a diagram. Figure 8-2 highlights the major elements of the physical infrastructure. What do you see in the diagram? As you know, every system, including your data warehouse, must have an overall platform on which to reside. Essentially, the platform consists of the basic hardware components, the operating system with its utility software, the network, and the network software. Along with the overall platform is the set of tools that run on the selected platform to perform the various functions and services of individual architectural components.

We will examine the elements of physical infrastructure in the next few sections. Decisions about the hardware top the list of decisions you have to make about the

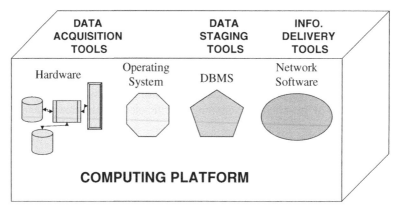

Figure 8-2 Physical infrastructure.

infrastructure of your data warehouse. Hardware decisions are not easy. You have to consider many factors. You have to ensure that the selected hardware will support the entire data warehouse architecture.

Perhaps we can go back to our mainframe days and get some helpful hints. As newer models of the corporate mainframes were announced and as we ran out of steam on the current configuration, we stuck to two principles. First, we leveraged as much of the existing physical infrastructure as possible. Next, we kept the infrastructure as modular as possible. When needs arose and when newer versions became available at cheaper prices, we unplugged an existing component and plugged in the replacement.

In your data warehouse, try to adopt these two principles. You already have the hardware and operating system components in your company supporting the current operations, How much of this can you use for your data warehouse? How much extra capacity is available? How much disk space can be spared for the data warehouse repository? Find answers to these questions.

Applying the modular approach, can you add more processors to the server hardware? Explore if you can accommodate the data warehouse by adding more disk or other storage units. Take an inventory of individual hardware components. Check which of these components needs to be replaced with more potent versions. Also, make a list of the additional components that have to be procured and plugged in.

HARDWARE AND OPERATING SYSTEMS

Hardware and operating systems make up the computing environment for your data warehouse. All the data extraction, transformation, integration, and staging jobs run on the selected hardware under the chosen operating system. When you transport the consolidated and integrated data from the staging area to your data warehouse repository, you make use of the server hardware and the operating system software. When the queries are initiated from the client workstations, the server hardware, in conjunction with the database software, executes the queries and produces the results.

Here are some general guidelines for hardware selection, not entirely specific to hardware for the data warehouse.

Scalability. Ensure that your selected hardware can be scaled up when your data warehouse grows in terms of the number of users, the number of queries, and the complexity of the queries.

Support. Vendor support is crucial for hardware maintenance. Make sure that the support from the hardware vendor is at the highest possible level.

Vendor Reference. It is important to check vendor references with other sites using hardware from this vendor. You do not want to be caught with your data warehouse being down because of hardware malfunctions when the CEO wants some critical analysis to be completed.

Vendor Stability. Check on the stability and staying power of the vendor.

Next let us quickly consider a few general criteria for the selection of the operating system. First of all, the operating system must be compatible with the hardware. A list of criteria follows.

Scalability. Again, scalability is first on the list because this is one common feature of every data warehouse. Data warehouses grow, and they grow very fast. Along with the hardware and database software, the operating system must be able to support the increase in the number of users and applications.

Security. When multiple client workstations access the server, the operating system must be able to protect each client and associated resources. The operating system must provide each client with a secure environment.

Reliability. The operating system must be able to protect the environment from application malfunctions.

Availability. This is a corollary to reliability. The computing environment must continue to be available after abnormal application terminations.

Preemptive Multitasking. The server hardware must be able to balance the allocation of time and resources among the multiple tasks. Also, the operating system must be able to let a higher priority task preempt or interrupt another task as and when needed.

Use a Multithreaded Approach. The operating system must be able to service multiple requests concurrently by distributing threads to multiple processors in a multiprocessor hardware configuration. This feature is very important because multiprocessor configurations are architectures of choice in a data warehouse environment.

Memory Protection. Again, in a data warehouse environment, large numbers of queries are common. That means that multiple queries will be executing concurrently. A memory protection feature in an operating system prevents one task from violating the memory space of another.

Having reviewed the requirements for hardware and operating systems in a data warehouse environment, let us try to narrow down the choices. What are the possible options? Review the following list of three common options.

Mainframes

- Leftover hardware from legacy applications
- Primarily designed for OLTP and not for decision support applications

- Not cost effective for data warehousing
- Not easily scalable
- Rarely used for data warehousing; only used when too much spare resources are available for smaller data marts

Open System Servers

- UNIX servers, the choice medium for most data warehouses
- Generally robust
- Adapted for parallel processing

NT Servers

- Support medium-sized data warehouses
- Limited parallel processing capabilities
- Cost-effective for medium-sized and small data warehouses

Platform Options

Let us now turn our attention to the computing platforms that are needed to perform the several functions of the various components of the data warehouse architecture. A computing platform is the set of hardware components, the operating system, the network, and the network software. Whether it is a function of an OLTP system or a decision support system like the data warehouse, the function has to be performed on a computing platform.

Before we get into a deeper discussion of platform options, let us get back to the functions and services of the architectural components in the three major areas. Here is a quick summary recap:

Data Acquisition: data extraction, data transformation, data cleansing, data integration, and data staging.
Data Storage: data loading, archiving, and data management.
Information Delivery: report generation, query processing, and complex analysis.

We will now discuss platform options in terms of the functions in these three areas. Where should each function be performed? On which platforms? How could you optimize the functions?

Single Platform Option   This is the most straightforward and simplest option for implementing the data warehouse architecture. In this option, all functions from the back-end data extraction to the front-end query processing are performed on a single computing platform. This was perhaps the earliest approach, when developers were implementing data warehouses on existing mainframes, minicomputers, or single UNIX-based servers.

Because all operations in the data acquisition, data storage, and information delivery areas take place on the same platform, this option hardly ever encounters any compatibility or interface problems. The data flows smoothly from beginning to end without any platform-to-platform conversions. No middleware is needed. All tools work in a single computing environment.

In many companies, legacy systems are still running on mainframes or minicomputers. Some of these companies have migrated to UNIX-based servers and others have moved over to ERP systems in client/server environments. Most legacy systems still reside on mainframes, minis, or UNIX-based servers. What is the relationship of the legacy systems to the data warehouse? Remember, the legacy systems contribute the major part of the data warehouse data. If these companies wish to adopt a single-platform solution, that platform of choice has to be a mainframe, mini, or a UNIX-based server.

If the situation in your company warrants serious consideration of the single-platform option, then analyze the implications before making a decision. The single-platform solution appears to be an ideal option. If so, why are not many companies adopting this option now? Let us examine the reasons.

Legacy Platform Stretched to Capacity   In many companies, the existing legacy computing environment may have been around for many years and be already fully stretched to capacity. The environment may be at a point where it can no longer be upgraded further to accommodate your data warehouse.

Nonavailability of Tools   Software tools form a large part of the data warehouse infrastructure. You will clearly grasp this fact from the last few subsections of this chapter. Most of the tools provided by the numerous data warehouse vendors do not support the mainframe or minicomputer environment. Without the appropriate tools in the infrastructure, your data warehouse will fall apart.

Multiple Legacy Platforms   Although we have surmised that the legacy mainframe or minicomputer environment may be extended to include data warehousing, the practical fact points to a different situation. In most corporations, a combination of a few mainframe systems, an assortment of minicomputer applications, and a smattering of the newer PC-based systems exist side by side. The path most companies have taken is from mainframes to minis and then to PCs. Figure 8-3 highlights the typical configuration.

If your corporation is one of the typical enterprises, what can you do about a single-platform solution? Not much. With such a conglomeration of disparate platforms, a single-platform option having your data warehouse alongside all the other applications is just not tenable.

Company's Migration Policy   This is another important consideration. You very well know the varied benefits of the client/server architecture for computing. You are also aware of the fact that every company has been changing to embrace this computing paradigm by moving the applications from the mainframe and minicomputer platforms. In most companies, the policy on the usage of information technology does not permit the perpetuation of the old platforms. If your company has a similar policy, then you will not be permitted to add another significant system such as your data warehouse on the old platforms.

Hybrid Option   After examining the legacy systems and the more modern applications in your corporation, it is most likely that you will decide that a single-platform approach is not workable for your data warehouse. This is the conclusion most companies come to. On the other hand, if your company falls in the category where the legacy platform will accommodate your data warehouse, then, by all means, take the approach of a single-platform solution. Again, the single-platform solution, if feasible, is an easier solution.

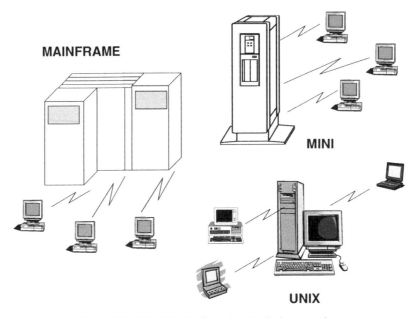

MAINFRAME

MINI

UNIX

Figure 8-3   Multiple platforms in a typical corporation.

For the rest of us who are not that fortunate, we have to consider other options. Let us begin with data extraction, the first major operation, and follow the flow of data until it is consolidated into load images and waiting in the staging area. We will now step through the data flow and examine the platform options.

Data Extraction   In any data warehouse, it is best to perform the data extraction function from each source system on its own computing platform. If your telephone sales data resides in a minicomputer environment, create extract files on the minicomputer itself for telephone sales. If your mail order application executes on the mainframe using an IMS database, then create the extract files for mail orders on the mainframe platform. It is rarely prudent to copy all the mail order database files to another platform and then do the data extraction.

Initial Reformatting and Merging   After creating the raw data extracts from the various sources, the extracted files from each source are reformatted and merged into a smaller number of extract files. Verification of the extracted data against source system reports and reconciliation of input and output record counts take place in this step. Just like the extraction step, it is best to do this step of initial merging of each set of source extracts on the source platform itself.

Preliminary Data Cleansing   In this step, you verify the extracted data from each data source for any missing values in individual fields, supply default values, and perform basic edits. This is another step for the computing platform of the source system itself. However, in some data warehouses, this type of data cleansing happens after the data from all sources are reconciled and consolidated. In either case, the features and conditions of data from your source systems dictate when and where this step must be performed for your data warehouse.

Transformation and Consolidation   This step comprises all the major data transformation and integration functions. Usually, you will use transformation software tools for this purpose. Where is the best place to perform this step? Obviously, not in any individual legacy platform. You perform this step on the platform where your staging area resides.

Validation and Final Quality Check   This step of final validation and quality check is a strong candidate for the staging area. You will arrange for this step to happen on that platform.

Creation of Load Images   This step creates load images for individual database files of the data warehouse repository. This step almost always occurs in the staging area and, therefore, on the platform where the staging area resides.

Figure 8-4 summarizes the data acquisition steps and the associated platforms. You will notice the options for the steps. Relate this to your own corporate environment and determine where the data acquisition steps must take place.

Options for the Staging Area   In the discussion of the data acquisition steps, we have highlighted the optimal computing platform for each step. You will notice that the key steps happen in the staging area. This is the place where all data for the data warehouse come together and get prepared. What is the ideal platform for the staging area? Let us repeat that the platform most suitable for your staging area depends on the status of your source platforms. Nevertheless, let us explore the options for placing the staging area and come up with general guidelines. These will help you decide. Figure 8-5 shows the different

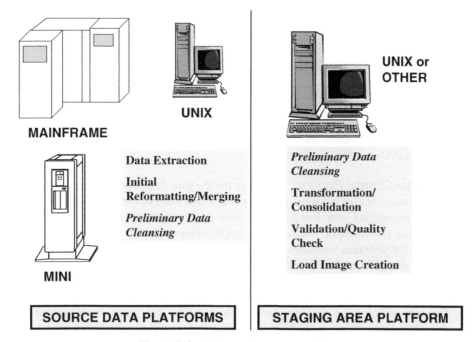

Figure 8-4   Platforms for data acquisition.

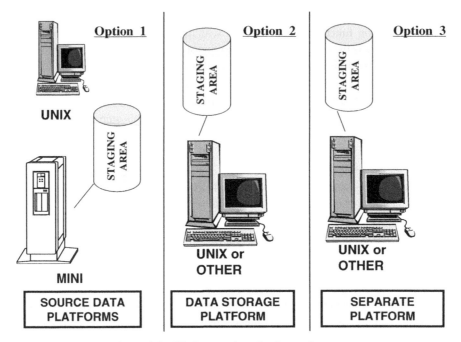

Figure 8-5 Platform options for the staging area.

options for the staging area. Study the figure and follow the amplification of the options given in the subsections below.

In One of the Legacy Platforms   If most of your legacy data sources are on the same platform and if extra capacity is readily available, then consider keeping your data staging area in that legacy platform. In this option, you will save time and effort in moving the data across platforms to the staging area.

On the Data Storage Platform   This is the platform on which the data warehouse DBMS runs and the database exists. When you keep your data staging area on this platform, you will realize all the advantages for applying the load images to the database. You may even be able to eliminate a few intermediary substeps and apply data directly to the database from some of the consolidated files in the staging area.

On a Separate Optimal Platform   You may review your data source platforms, examine the data warehouse storage platform, and then decide that none of these platforms are really suitable for your staging area. It is likely that your environment needs complex data transformations. It is possible that you need to work through your data thoroughly to cleanse and prepare it for your data warehouse. In such circumstances, you need a separate platform to stage your data before loading to the database.

Here are some distinct advantages of a separate platform for data staging:

- You can optimize the separate platform for complex data transformations and data cleansing. What do we mean by this? You can gear up the neutral platform with all the necessary tools for data transformation, data cleansing, and data formatting.

- While the extracted data is being transformed and cleansed in the data staging area, you need to keep the entire data content and ensure that nothing is lost on the way. You may want to think of some tracking file or table to contain tracking entries. A separate environment is most conducive for managing the movement of data.
- We talked about the possibility of having specialized tools to manipulate the data in the staging area. If you have a separate computing environment for the staging area, you could easily have people specifically trained on these tools running the separate computing equipment.

Data Movement Considerations On whichever computing platforms the individual steps of data acquisition and data storage happen, data has to move across platforms. Depending on the source platforms in your company and the choice of the platform for data staging and data storage, you have to provide for data transportation across different platforms.

Review the following options. Figure 8-6 summarizes the standard options. You may find that a single approach alone is not sufficient. Do not hesitate to have a balanced combination of the different approaches. In each data movement across two computing platforms, choose the option that is most appropriate for that environment. Brief explanations of the standard options follow.

Shared Disk This method goes back to the mainframe days. Applications running in different partitions or regions were allowed to share data by placing the common data on a shared disk. You may adapt this method to pass data from one step to another for data

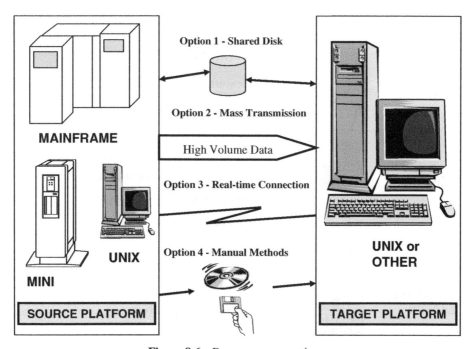

Figure 8-6 Data movement options.

acquisition in your data warehouse. You have to designate a disk storage area and set it up so that each of the two platforms recognizes the disk storage area as its own.

Mass Data Transmission   In this case, transmission of data across platforms takes place through data ports. Data ports are simply interplatform devices that enable massive quantities of data to be transported from one platform to the other. Each platform must be configured to handle the transfers through the ports. This option calls for special hardware, software, and network components. There must also be sufficient network bandwidth to carry high data volumes.

Real-Time Connection   In this option, two platforms establish connection in real time so that a program running on one platform may use the resources of the other platform. A program on one platform can write to the disk storage on the other. Also, jobs running on one platform can schedule jobs and events on the other. With the widespread adoption of TCP/IP, this option is very viable for your data warehouse. If your data warehouse is intended to be a real time or near real time data warehouse, then this is an important consideration.

Manual Methods   Perhaps these are the options of last resort. Nevertheless, these options are straightforward and simple. A program on one platform writes to an external medium such as tape or disk. Another program on the receiving platform reads the data from the external medium.

Client/Server Architecture for the Data Warehouse   Although mainframe and minicomputer platforms were utilized in the early implementations of data warehouses, by and large, today's warehouses are built using the client/server architecture. Most of

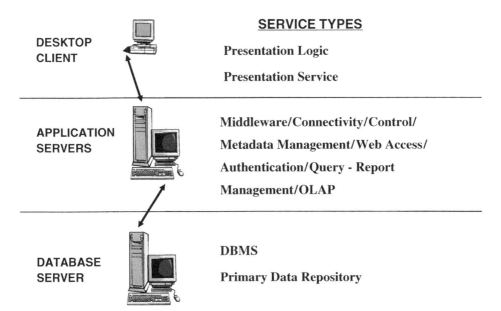

Figure 8-7   Client/server architecture for the data warehouse.

these are multitiered, second-generation client/server architectures. Figure 8-7 shows a typical client/server architecture for a data warehouse implementation.

The data warehouse DBMS executes on the data server component. The data repository of the data warehouse sits on this machine. This server component is a major component and it is discussed in detail in the next section.

As data warehousing technologies have grown substantially, you will now observe a proliferation of application server components in the middle tier. You will find application servers for a number of purposes. Here are the important ones:

- To run middleware and establish connectivity
- To execute management and control software
- To handle data access from the Web
- To manage metadata
- For authentication
- As front end
- For managing and running standard reports
- For sophisticated query management
- For OLAP applications

Generally, the client workstations still handle the presentation logic and provide the presentation services. Let us briefly address the significant considerations for the client workstations.

Considerations for Client Workstations   When you are ready to consider the configurations for the workstation machines, you will quickly come to realize that you need to cater to a variety of user types. We are only considering the needs at the workstation with regard to information delivery from the data warehouse. A casual user is perhaps satisfied with a machine that can run a Web browser to access HTML reports. A serious analyst, on the other hand, needs a larger and more powerful workstation machine. The other types of users between these two extremes need a variety of services.

Do you then come up with a unique configuration for each user? That will not be practical. It is better to determine a minimum configuration on an appropriate platform that would support a standard set of information delivery tools in your data warehouse. Apply this configuration for most of your users. Here and there, add a few more functions as necessary. For the power users, select another configuration that would support tools for complex analysis. Generally, this configuration for power users also supports OLAP. More recently, considerations are given to the ability to support presentation of dashboards for continuous monitoring.

The factors for consideration when selecting the configurations for your users' workstations are similar to the ones for any operating environment. However, the main consideration for workstations accessing the data warehouse is the support for the selected set of tools. This is the primary reason for the preference of one platform over another.

Use this checklist while considering workstations:

- Workstation operating system
- Processing power

- Memory
- Disk storage
- Network and data transport
- Tool support

Options as the Data Warehouse Matures   After all this discussion of the computing platforms for your data warehouse, you might reach the conclusion that the platform
choice is fixed as soon as the initial choices are made. It is interesting to note that as the
data warehouse in each enterprise matures, the arrangement of the platforms also evolves.
Data staging and data storage may start out on the same computing platform. As time
goes by and more of your users begin to depend on your data warehouse for strategic decision
making, you will find that the platform choices may have to be recast. Figure 8-8 shows you
what to expect as your data warehouse matures.

Options in Practice   Before we leave this section, it may be worthwhile to take a look
at the types of data sources and target platforms in use at different enterprises. An independent survey has produced some interesting findings. Figure 8-9 shows the approximate
percentage distribution for the first part of the survey about the principal data sources.
Figure 8-10 shows the distribution of the answers to question about the platforms the
respondents use for the data storage component of their data warehouses.

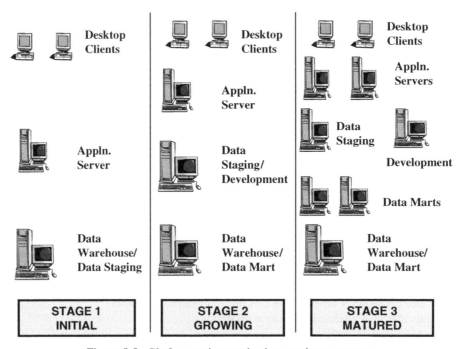

Figure 8-8   Platform options as the data warehouse matures.

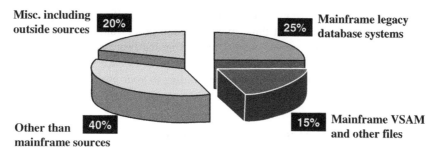

Figure 8-9   Principal data sources.

Server Hardware

Selecting the server hardware is among the most important decisions your data warehouse project team is faced with. Probably, for most warehouses, server hardware selection can be a "bet your bottom dollar" decision. Scalability and optimal query performance are the key phrases.

You know that your data warehouse exists for one primary purpose—to provide information to your users. Ad hoc, unpredictable, complex querying of the data warehouse is the most common method for information delivery. If your server hardware does not support faster query processing, the entire project is in jeopardy.

The need to scale is driven by a few factors. As your data warehouse matures, you will see a steep increase in the number of users and in the number of queries. The load will simply shoot up. Typically, the number of active users doubles in six months. Again, as your data warehouse matures, you will be increasing the content by including more business subject areas and adding more data marts. Corporate data warehouses start at approximately 200 to 300 GB and some shoot up to a terabyte within 18 to 24 months.

Hardware options for scalability and complex query processing consist of four types of parallel architecture. Initially, parallel architecture makes the most sense. Shouldn't a query complete faster if you increase the number of processors, each processor working on parts of the query simultaneously? Can you not subdivide a large query into separate tasks and spread the tasks among many processors? Parallel processing with multiple computing engines does provide a broad range of benefits, but no single processing option does everything right.

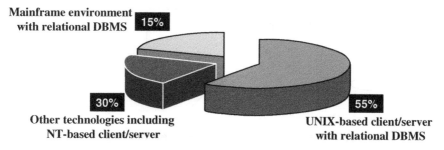

Figure 8-10   Target platforms for the data storage component.

In Chapter 3, we reviewed parallel processing as one of the significant trends in data warehousing. We also briefly looked at three more common processing architectures. In this section, let us summarize the current parallel processing hardware options. You will gain sufficient insight into the features, benefits, and limitations of each of these options. By doing so, you will be able contribute your understanding to your project team for selecting the proper server hardware.

SMP (Symmetric Multiprocessing)   Refer to Figure 8-11.

Features:
- This is a shared-everything architecture, the simplest parallel processing machine.
- Each processor has full access to the shared memory through a common bus.
- Communication between processors occurs through common memory.
- Disk controllers are accessible to all processors.

Benefits:
- This is a proven technology that has been used since the early 1970s.
- It provides high concurrency. You can run many concurrent queries.
- It balances workload very well.
- It gives scalable performance; simply add more processors to the system bus.
- Being a simple design, you can administer the server easily.

Limitations:
- Available memory may be limited.
- Performance may be limited by bandwidth for processor-to-processor communication, I/O, and bus communication.
- Availability is limited; like a single computer with many processors.

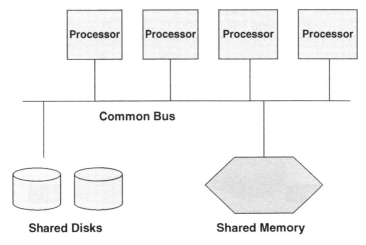

Figure 8-11   Server hardware option: SMP.

You may consider this option if the size of your data warehouse is expected to be about 200 or 300 GB and concurrency requirements are reasonable.

Clusters   Refer to Figure 8-12.

Features:
* Each node consists of one or more processors and associated memory.
* Memory is not shared among the nodes; it is shared only within each node.
* Communication occurs over a high-speed bus.
* Each node has access to the common set of disks.
* This architecture is a cluster of nodes.

Benefits:
* This architecture provides high availability; all data is accessible even if one node fails.
* It preserves the concept of one database.
* This option is good for incremental growth.

Limitations:
* Bandwidth of the bus could limit the scalability of the system.
* This option comes with a high operating system overhead.
* Each node has a data cache; the architecture needs to maintain cache consistency for internode synchronization. A cache is a "work area" holding currently used data; the main memory is like a big file cabinet stretching across the entire room.

You may consider this option if your data warehouse is expected to grow in well-defined increments.

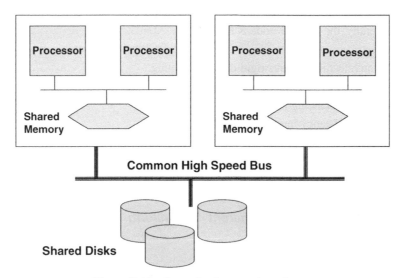

Figure 8-12   Server hardware option: cluster.

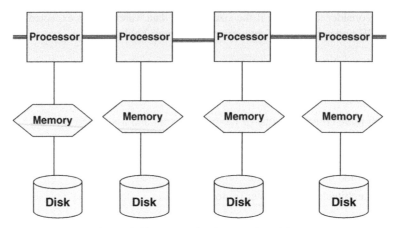

Figure 8-13 Server hardware option: MPP.

MPP (Massively Parallel Processing)   Refer to Figure 8-13.

Features:
- This is a shared-nothing architecture.
- This architecture is more concerned with disk access than memory access.
- It works well with an operating system that supports transparent disk access.
- If a database table is located on a particular disk, access to that disk depends entirely on the processor that owns it.
- Internode communication is by processor-to-processor connection.

Benefits:
- This architecture is highly scalable.
- The option provides fast access between nodes.
- Any failure is local to the failed node; this improves system availability.
- Generally, the cost per node is low.

Limitations:
- The architecture requires rigid data partitioning.
- Data access is restricted.
- Workload balancing is limited.
- Cache consistency must be maintained.

Consider this option if you are building a medium-sized or large data warehouse in the range of 400 to 500 GB. For larger warehouses in the terabyte range, look for special architectural combinations.

ccNUMA or NUMA (Cache-Coherent Nonuniform Memory Architecture)
Refer to Figure 8-14.

Features:
- This is the newest architecture; it was developed in the 1990s.
- The NUMA architecture is like a big SMP broken into smaller SMPs that are easier to build.

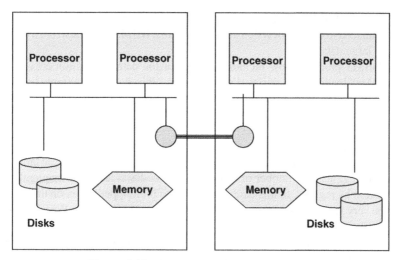

Figure 8-14 Server hardware option: NUMA.

- The hardware considers all memory units as one giant memory. The system has a single real memory address space over the entire machine; memory addresses begin with 1 on the first node and continue on the following nodes. Each node contains a directory of memory addresses within that node.
- In this architecture, the amount of time needed to retrieve a memory value varies because the first node may need the value that resides in the memory of the third node. That is why this architecture is called nonuniform memory access architecture.

Benefits:

- Provides maximum flexibility.
- Overcomes the memory limitations of SMP.
- Better scalability than SMP.
- If you need to partition your data warehouse database and run these using a centralized approach, you may want to consider this architecture. You may also place your OLAP data on the same server.

Limitations:

- Programming NUMA architecture is more complex than even with MPP.
- Software support for NUMA is fairly limited.
- The technology is still maturing.

This option is a more aggressive approach for you. You may decide on a NUMA machine consisting of one or two SMP nodes, but if your company is inexperienced in hardware technology, this option may not be for you.

DATABASE SOFTWARE

Examine the features of the leading commercial relational database management systems (RDBMSs). As data warehousing has become widely prevalent, you now see data warehouse features being included in software products. That is exactly what the database vendors have been doing during the past decade. Data warehouse-related add-ons have become part of the database offerings. Database software that started out for use in operational OLTP systems have been enhanced to cater to decision support systems. DBMSs have also been scaled up to support very large databases.

Some RDBMS products now include support for the data acquisition area of the data warehouse. Mass loading and retrieval of data from other database systems have become easier. Some vendors have paid special attention to the data transformation function. Replication features have been reinforced to assist in bulk refreshes and incremental loading of the data warehouse.

Bit-mapped indexes could be very effective in a data warehouse environment to index on fields that have a smaller number of distinct values. For example, in a database table containing geographic regions, the number of distinct region codes is few. But frequently, queries involve selection by regions. In this case, retrieval by a bit-mapped index on the region code values can be very fast. Vendors have strengthened this type of indexing. We will discuss bit-mapped indexing further in Chapter 18.

Apart from these enhancements, the more important ones relate to load balancing and query performance. These two features are critical in a data warehouse. Your data warehouse is query-centric. Everything that can be done to improve query performance is most desirable. The DBMS vendors have provided parallel processing features to improve query performance. Let us briefly review the parallel processing options within the DBMS that can take full advantage of parallel server hardware.

Parallel Processing Options

Parallel processing options in database software are intended only for machines with multiple processors. Most of the current database software can parallelize a large number of operations. These operations include the following: mass loading of data, full table scans, queries with exclusion conditions, queries with grouping, selection with distinct values, aggregation, sorting, creation of tables using subqueries, creating and rebuilding indexes, inserting rows into a table from other tables, enabling constraints, star transformation (an optimization technique when processing queries against a STAR schema), and so on. Notice that this is an impressive list of operations that the RDBMS can process in parallel.

Let us now examine what happens when a user initiates a query at the workstation. Each session accesses the database through a server process. The query is sent to the DBMS and data retrieval takes place from the database. Data is retrieved and the results are sent back, all under the control of the dedicated server process. The query dispatcher software is responsible for splitting the work, distributing the units to be performed among the pool of available query server processes, and balancing the load. Finally, the results of the query processes are assembled and returned as a single, consolidated result set.

Interquery Parallelization   In this method, several server processes handle multiple requests simultaneously. Multiple queries may be serviced based on your server configuration and the number of available processors. You may successfully take advantage of this feature of the DBMS on SMP systems, thereby increasing the throughput and supporting more concurrent users.

However, interquery parallelism is limited. Let us see what happens here. Multiple queries are processed concurrently, but each query is still being processed serially by a single server process. Suppose a query consists of index read, data read, join, and sort operations; these operations are carried out in this order. Each operation must finish before the next one can begin. Parts of the same query do not execute in parallel. To overcome this limitation, many DBMS vendors have come up with versions of their products to provide intraquery parallelization.

Intraquery Parallelization   We will use Figure 8-15 for our discussion of intraquery parallelization. Understanding this will help you to match your choice of server hardware with your selection of RDBMS.

Let us say a query from one of your users consists of an index read, a data read, a data join, and a data sort from the data warehouse database. A serial processing DBMS will process this query in the sequence of these base operations and produce the result set. However, while this query is executing on one processor in the SMP system, other queries can execute in parallel. This method is the interquery parallelization discussed above. The first group of operations in Figure 8-15 illustrates this method of execution.

Using the intraquery parallelization technique, the DBMS splits the query into the lower-level operations of index read, data read, data join, and data sort. Then each one of these basic operations is executed in parallel on a single processor. The final result set is the consolidation of the intermediary results. Let us review three ways a DBMS can provide intraquery parallelization, that is, parallelization of parts of the operations within the same query itself.

Horizontal Parallelism   The data is partitioned across multiple disks. Parallel processing occurs within each single task in the query; for example, data read, which is performed on multiple processors concurrently on different sets of data to be read from multiple disks. After the first task is completed from all of the relevant parts of the partitioned data, the next task of that query is carried out, and then the next one after that task, and so on. The

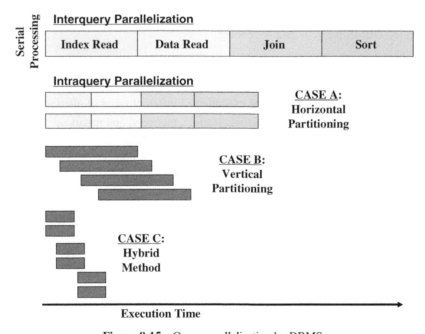

Figure 8-15   Query parallelization by DBMS.

problem with this approach is the resulting wait until all the needed data is read. Look at Case A in Figure 8-15.

Vertical Parallelism   This kind of parallelism occurs among different tasks, not just a single task in a query as in the case of horizontal parallelism. All component query operations are executed in parallel, but in a pipelined manner. This assumes that the RDBMS has the capability to decompose the query into subtasks; each subtask has all the operations of index read, data read, join, and sort. Then each subtask executes on the data in serial fashion. In this approach, the database records are ideally processed by one step and immediately given to the next step for processing, thus avoiding wait times. Of course, in this method, the DBMS must possess a very high level of sophistication in decomposing tasks. Now, look at Case B in Figure 8-15.

Hybrid Method   In this method, the query decomposer partitions the query both horizontally and vertically. Naturally, this approach produces the best results. You will realize the greatest utilization of resources, optimal performance, and high scalability. Case C in Figure 8-15 illustrates this method.

Selection of the DBMS

Our discussions of the server hardware and the DBMS parallel processing options must have convinced you that selection of the DBMS is most crucial. You must choose the server hardware with the appropriate parallel architecture. Your choice of the DBMS must match with the selected server hardware. These are critical decisions for your data warehouse.

While discussing how business requirements drive the design and development of the data warehouse in Chapter 6, we briefly mentioned how requirements influence the selection of the DBMS, Apart from the criteria that the selected DBMS must have load balancing and parallel processing options, the other key features listed below must be considered when selecting the DBMS for your data warehouse.

Query governor—to anticipate and abort runaway queries

Query optimizer—to parse and optimize user queries

Query management—to balance the execution of different types of queries

Load utility—for high-performance data loading, recovery, and restart

Metadata management—with an active data catalog or dictionary

Scalability—in terms of both number of users and data volumes

Extensibility—having hybrid extensions to OLAP databases

Portability—across platforms

Query tool Application Program Interfaces (APIs)—for tools from leading vendors

Administration—providing support for all DBA functions

COLLECTION OF TOOLS

Think about an OLTP application, perhaps a checking account system in a commercial bank. When you, as a developer, designed and deployed the application, how many third-party software tools did you use to develop such an application? Of course, do not count the programming language or the database software. We mean other third-party vendor tools for data modeling, GUI design software, and so on. You probably used just a few, if any, at all. Similarly, when the bank teller uses the application, she or he probably uses no third-party software tools.

But a data warehouse environment is different. When you, as a member of the project team, develop the data warehouse, you will use third-party tools for different phases of the development. You may use code-generators for preparing in-house software for data extraction. When the data warehouse is deployed, your users will be accessing information through third-party query tools and creating reports with report writers. Software tools are very significant parts of the infrastructure in a data warehouse environment.

Software tools are available for every architectural component of the data warehouse. As the data warehousing has matured over the past decade, vendors have produced more and more sophisticated and useful tools for all aspects. Figure 8-16 shows the tool groups that support the various functions and services in a data warehouse.

Software tools are extremely important in a data warehouse. As you have seen from this figure, tools cover all the major functions. Data warehouse project teams write in-house only a small part of the software needed to perform these functions. Because the data warehouse tools are so important, we will discuss these again in later chapters: data extraction and transformation tools in Chapter 12, data quality tools in Chapter 13, and query tools in Chapter 14. Also, Appendix C provides guidelines for evaluating vendor solutions. When you get to the point of selecting tools for your data warehouse project, that list could serve as a handy reference.

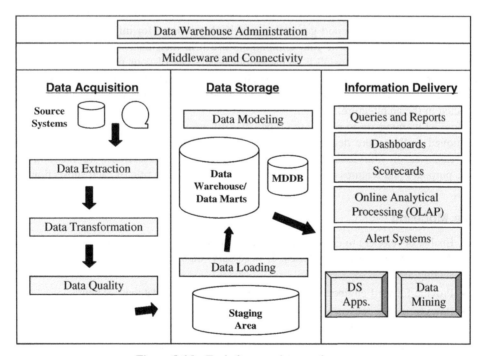

Figure 8-16   Tools for your data warehouse.

At this stage, let us introduce the types of software tools that are generally required in a data warehouse environment. For each type, we will briefly discuss the purpose and functions.

Before we get to the types of software tools, let us reiterate an important maxim that was mentioned earlier in the previous chapter. In that chapter we discussed the architectural components and studied the functions and services of individual components. Now go to the next subsection here and read about that important principle again.

Architecture First, Then Tools

The title of this subsection simply means this: ignore the tools; design the architecture first; then, and only then, choose the tools to match the functions and services stipulated for the architectural components. Do the architecture first; select the tools later.

Why is this principle sacred? Why is it not advisable to just buy the set of tools and then use the tools to build and to deploy your data warehouse? This appears to be an easy solution. The salespersons of the tool vendors promise success. Why would this not work in the end? Let us take an example.

Let us begin to design your information delivery architectural component. First of all, the business requirements are the driving force. Your largest group of users is the group of power users. They will be creating their own reports and run their own queries. These users will constantly perform complex analysis consisting of drilling down, slicing and dicing of data, and extensive visualization of result sets. You know these users are power users. They need the most sophisticated information delivery component. The functions and services of the information delivery component must be very involved and powerful. But you have not yet established the information delivery architectural component.

Hold it right there. Let us now say that the salesperson from XYZ Report Writer, Inc. has convinced you that their report generation tool is all you need for information delivery in your data warehouse. Two of your competitors use it in their data warehouses. You buy the tool and are ready to install it. What would be the fate of your power users? What is wrong with this scenario? The information delivery tool was selected before the architectural component was established. The tool did not meet the requirements as these would have been reflected in the architecture.

Now let us move on to review the types of software tools for your data warehouse. As mentioned earlier, more details will be added in the later chapters. These chapters will also elaborate on individual tool types. In the following subsections, we mention the basic purposes and features of the type of tool indicated by the title of each subsection.

Data Modeling

- Enable developers to create and maintain data models for the source systems and the data warehouse target databases. If necessary, data models may be created for the staging area.
- Provide forward engineering capabilities to generate the database schema.
- Provide reverse engineering capabilities to generate the data model from the data dictionary entries of existing source databases.
- Provide dimensional modeling capabilities to data designers for creating STAR schemas.

Data Extraction

- Two primary extraction methods are available: bulk extraction for full refreshes and change-based replication for incremental loads.
- Tool choices depend on the following factors: source system platforms and databases, and available built-in extraction and duplication facilities in the source systems.

Data Transformation

- Transform extracted data into appropriate formats and data structures.
- Provide default values as specified.
- Major features include field splitting, consolidation, standardization, and deduplication.

Data Loading

- Load transformed and consolidated data in the form of load images into the data warehouse repository.
- Some loaders generate primary keys for the tables being loaded.
- For load images available on the same RDBMS engine as the data warehouse, precoded procedures stored on the database itself may be used for loading.

Data Quality

- Assist in locating and correcting data errors.
- May be used on the data in the staging area or on the source systems directly.
- Help resolve data inconsistencies in load images.

Queries and Reports

- Allow users to produce canned, graphic-intensive, sophisticated reports.
- Help users to formulate and run queries.
- Two main classifications are report writers and report servers.

Dashboards

- Provide real-time or near real-time information to users in an interactive manner.
- Most real-time dashboards are linked directly to operational systems.
- Allow several capabilities for users such as drill down, parameter changes on the fly, different kinds of displays, and so on.

Scorecards

- Allow users to select key performance indicators easily for reporting.
- Provide comparison of current performance against targets and past performance.
- Focus on clarity and ease of use.

Online Analytical Processing (OLAP)

- Allow users to run complex dimensional queries.
- Enable users to generate canned queries.
- Two categories of online analytical processing are multidimensional online analytical processing (MOLAP) and relational online analytical processing (ROLAP). MOLAP works with proprietary multidimensional databases that receive data feeds from the main data warehouse. ROLAP provides online analytical processing capabilities from the relational database of the data warehouse itself.

Alert Systems

- Highlight and get user's attention based on defined exceptions.
- Provide alerts from the data warehouse database to support strategic decisions.
- Three basic alert types are: from individual source systems, from integrated enterprise-wide data warehouses, and from individual data marts.

Middleware and Connectivity

- Transparent access to source systems in heterogeneous environments.
- Transparent access to databases of different types on multiple platforms.
- Tools are moderately expensive but prove to be invaluable for providing interoperability among the various data warehouse components.

Data Warehouse Administration

- Assist data warehouse administrators in day-to-day management.
- Some tools focus on the load process and track load histories.
- Other tools track types and number of user queries.

DATA WAREHOUSE APPLIANCES

In Chapter 3 while discussing data warehousing trends, we introduced the recently prevalent trend of data warehouse appliances. In the present chapter we have reviewed data warehouse infrastructure. We have seen how server hardware and the concomitant operating system and database management system are crucial pieces of the infrastructure. Companies that are gaining more and more experience in data warehousing have realized the importance of parallel processing options for server hardware and accompanying software to support parallel processing. As their data warehouses grew in size and complexity, these companies addressed the challenges with constant upgrades to hardware and software.

More recently, with enormous emphasis on business intelligence, the older methods of constant upgrades do not seem to work. Upgrading hardware and software in a piecemeal fashion opened up problems of compatibility. This is because the hardware and software are not specially designed and tuned for data warehouses with massive data volumes and complex business intelligence delivery mechanisms. Consequently, organizations have begun to use what are known as data warehouse appliances.

A data warehouse appliance is a device with hardware and software components specifically designed and architected for data warehouses. Through its architecture, a data warehouse appliance integrates processor hardware, data storage, operating systems, and database software into one unified whole. Scalability all around is achieved easily as almost all the components come from a single vendor.

Evolution of DW Appliances

Beginning with the adoption of data warehouses by organizations, in many cases the business intelligence infrastructure remains a loosely coupled patchwork of hardware, software, and storage. Typically what we notice as the common configuration consists of the following:

- Hardware and operating system, generically put together, and continuously optimized and upgraded
- Database management system (DBMS), initially designed for transaction processing, now amended and enlarged to support unexpectedly large volumes of data in a data warehouse
- Storage units and storage management, ever expanding to suit the needs of a data warehouse

The only answer to increased demand for business intelligence seems to be just adding hardware, software, and storage up to the breaking point. In most companies the situation is getting worse.

In this context, the data warehouse appliance is crafted specifically to streamline business intelligence workload by integrating hardware, software, and storage components. The best features of SMP and MPP approaches are embedded into the appliance architecture to produce the best results.

Generally, Teradata's core product line is considered the mother of all data warehouse appliances, although the term was not associated with the product offering. Greater interest in data warehouse appliances surged with the emergence of Netezza in the early 2000s. This vendor did much to prove the concept and educate organizations in the data warehouse arena. The term data warehouse appliance was coined by Foster Hinshaw, a founder of Netezza.

As of 2009, we are into a second generation of data warehouse appliances resulting from mainstream vendor integration. Vendors have created DW appliances totally with their own products. Some other vendors have partnered with major hardware vendors to create bundles to constitute their DW appliance offerings.

As the data warehousing and business intelligence markets mature, we have noticed standardization of interfaces, protocols, features, and functionality of components. The data warehouse appliance, as it emerges in this climate of standardization, is easily being made to work seamlessly with tools and applications.

Benefits of DW Appliances

As data warehouse appliances gain popularity and usage, organizations acquiring these obtain a number of benefits. The following highlight the benefits of data warehouse appliances.

Cost Reduction   The total cost associated with a data warehouse mainly breaks down into initial set-up cost and ongoing maintenance cost. Data warehouse appliances incur less initial costs compared to the alternative options. Ongoing maintenance also costs less. As powerful, off-the-shelf components continue to drop in price, the data warehouse constructed with such components will reflect the price reduction. Wherever a data warehouse appliance is put together with components from a single vendor, the total cost of ownership is linked to just one vendor, with great reduction in support costs.

Performance Improvement   Favorable price/performance ratio stands out as a great benefit from data warehouse appliances. Most appliances support mixed workloads, enabling reports, queries, and complex analysis to be run simultaneously with ease. DW appliance vendors apply various partitioning and load distribution methods to achieve parallel processing. Improved performance opens up great possibilities to the user. Reports that took days for turnaround would now take hours; analysis that took hours would now take minutes; queries that ran for minutes would now take seconds.

High Availability   By building in selective redundancy, DW appliance vendors are able to provide high availability. Many vendors offer warm-standby servers, dual power supplies, backup networks, disk mirroring, and automatic solutions for server failures.

Reduced Administration   A DW appliance is an administrator's dream. The integrated nature of the components in an appliance translates into greatly reduced time for troubleshooting and maintenance. As most DW appliances are single-vendor devices, the design and responsibility for optimization rest with single vendors. The data warehouse administrator needs to spend a lot less time on administrative tasks. DW appliances reduce administrative costs through features such as automated space allocation, reduced index maintenance, and reduced performance tuning.

Scalability   Most DW appliances implement a modular design for each of the components. This makes it easy for the appliances to scale for both capacity and performance. For example, in MPP architectures, adding servers improves performance and capacity.

Reliability   The homogeneous nature of a DW appliance, usually with components from a single owner, contributes to its reliability. The users need not perform difficult and uncertain integration of disk storage, operating systems, DBMS, and processors and attempt to make them all work together. A DW appliance is a single, architected, cohesive device.

Faster Implementation   Because DW appliances may be implemented without regression or integration testing, the overall implementation time is greatly reduced. Also, rapid prototyping is possible with DW appliances. Faster implementation means ability to reap the benefits of business intelligence in the current business cycle itself.

CHAPTER SUMMARY

- Infrastructure acts as the foundation supporting the data warehouse architecture.
- The data warehouse infrastructure consists of operational infrastructure and physical infrastructure.
- Hardware and operating systems make up the computing environment for the data warehouse.
- Several options exist for the computing platforms needed to implement the various architectural components.
- Selecting the server hardware is a key decision. Invariably, the choice is one of four parallel server architectures.
- Parallel processing options are critical in the DBMS. Current database software products are able to perform interquery and intraquery parallelization.
- Software tools are used in the data warehouse for data modeling, data extraction, data transformation, data loading, data quality assurance, queries and reports, and online analytical processing (OLAP). Tools are also used as middleware, alert systems, and for data warehouse administration.
- A data warehouse appliance is an architected device consisting of integrated hardware processors, storage, operating systems, and DBMS, specifically preoptimized for data warehousing. Usually, these are single-vendor solutions, providing substantial benefits. DW appliances are becoming more and more popular.

REVIEW QUESTIONS

1. What is the composition of the operational infrastructure of the data warehouse? Why is the operational infrastructure as important as the physical infrastructure?

2. List the major components of the physical infrastructure. Write two or three sentences to describe each component.

3. Briefly describe any six criteria you will use for selecting the operating system for your data warehouse.

4. What are the platform options for the staging area? Compare the options and mention the advantages and disadvantages.

5. What are the four common methods for data movement within the data warehouse? Explain any two of these methods.

6. What are data warehouse appliances? List their benefits.

7. What are the four parallel server hardware options? List the features, benefits, and limitations of any one of these options.

8. How have RDBMS vendors enhanced their products for data warehousing? Describe briefly in one or two paragraphs.

9. What is intraquery parallelization by the DBMS? What are the three methods?

10. List any six types of software tools used in the data warehouse. Pick any three types from your list and describe the features and the purposes.

EXERCISES

1. Match the columns:

1. operational infrastructure	**A.** shared-nothing architecture
2. preemptive multitasking	**B.** provides high concurrency
3. shared disk	**C.** single memory address space
4. MPP	**D.** operating system feature
5. SMP	**E.** vertical parallelism
6. interquery parallelization	**F.** people, procedures, training
7. intraquery parallelization	**G.** easy administration
8. NUMA	**H.** choice data warehouse platform
9. UNIX-based system	**I.** optimize for data transformation
10. data staging area	**J.** data movement option

2. In your company, all the source systems reside on a single UNIX-based platform, except one legacy system on a mainframe computer. Analyze the platform options for your data warehouse. Would you consider the single-platform option? If so, why? If not, why not?

3. You are the manager for the data warehouse project of a nationwide car rental company. Your data warehouse is expected to start out in the 500 GB range. Examine the options for server hardware and write a justification for choosing one.

4. As the administrator of the proposed data warehouse for a hotel chain with a leading presence in 10 eastern states, write a proposal describing the criteria you will use to select the RDBMS for your data warehouse. Make your assumptions clear.

5. You are the senior analyst responsible for the tools in the data warehouse of a large local bank with branches in only one state. Make a list of the types of tools you will provide for use in your data warehouse. Include tools for developers and users. Describe the features you will be looking for in each tool type.

CHAPTER 9

THE SIGNIFICANT ROLE OF METADATA

CHAPTER OBJECTIVES

- Find out why metadata is so important
- Understand who needs metadata and what types they need
- Review metadata types by the three functional areas
- Discuss business metadata and technical metadata in detail
- Examine all the requirements metadata must satisfy
- Understand the challenges for metadata management
- Study options for providing metadata

We discussed metadata briefly in earlier chapters. In Chapter 2, we considered metadata as one of the major building blocks for a data warehouse. We grouped metadata into three types, namely, operational, extraction and transformation, and end-user metadata. While discussing the major data warehousing trends in Chapter 3, we reviewed the industry initiatives to standardize metadata.

This chapter deals with the topic of metadata in further depth. We will attempt to remove uncertainty you may have about the exact meaning, content, and characteristics of metadata. We will also get an appreciation for why metadata is vitally important. Further, we will look for practical methods to provide effective metadata in a data warehouse environment.

WHY METADATA IS IMPORTANT

Let us begin with a positive assumption. Assume that your project team has successfully completed the development of the first data mart. Everything was done according to

Data Warehousing Fundamentals for IT Professionals, Second Edition. By Paulraj Ponniah
Copyright © 2010 John Wiley & Sons, Inc.

schedule. Your management is pleased that the team finished the project under budget and comfortably before the deadline. All the results proved out in comprehensive testing. Your data warehouse is ready to be deployed. This is the big day.

One of your prominent users is sitting at the workstation poised to compose and run the first query. Before he or she touches the keyboard, several important questions come to mind.

- Are there any predefined queries I can look at?
- What are the various elements of data in the warehouse?
- Is there information about unit sales and unit costs by product?
- How can I browse and see what is available?
- From where did they get the data for the warehouse? From which source systems?
- How did they merge the data from the telephone orders system and the mail orders system?
- How old is the data in the warehouse?
- When was the last time fresh data was brought in?
- Are there any summaries by month and by product?

These questions and several more like them are very valid and pertinent. What are the answers? Where are the answers? Can your user see the answers? How easy is it for the user to get to the answers?

Metadata in a data warehouse contains the answers to questions about the data in the data warehouse. You keep the answers in a place generally called the metadata repository. Even if you ask just a few data warehousing practitioners or if you read just a few of the books on data warehousing, you will receive seemingly different definitions for metadata. Here is a sample list of definitions:

- Data about the data
- Table of contents for the data
- Catalog for the data
- Data warehouse atlas
- Data warehouse roadmap
- Data warehouse directory
- Glue that holds the data warehouse contents together
- Tongs to handle the data
- The nerve center

So, what exactly is metadata? Which one of these definitions comes closest to the truth? Let us take a specific example. Assume your user wants to know about the table or entity called *Customer* in your data warehouse before running any queries on customer data. What is the information content about *Customer* in your metadata repository? Let us review the metadata element for the *Customer entity* as shown in Figure 9-1.

What do you see in the figure? The metadata element describes the entity called *Customer* residing the data warehouse. It is not just a description. It tells you more. It gives more than the explanation of the semantics and the syntax. Metadata describes all the pertinent aspects

| **Entity Name:** Customer |
| **Alias Names:** Account, Client |

Definition:	A person or an organization that purchases goods or services from the company.
Remarks:	Customer entity includes regular, current, and past customers.
Source Systems:	Finished Goods Orders, Maintenance Contracts, Online Sales.

Create Date:	January 15, 2006
Last Update Date:	January 21, 2008
Update Cycle:	Weekly
Last Full Refresh Date:	December 29, 2007
Full Refresh Cycle:	Every six months
Data Quality Reviewed:	January 25, 2008
Last Deduplication:	January 10, 2008
Planned Archival:	Every six months
Responsible User:	Jane Brown

Figure 9-1   Metadata element for the entity *Customer.*

of the data in the data warehouse fully and precisely. Pertinent to whom? Pertinent primarily to the users and also to you as developer and part of the project team.

In this chapter, we will explore why metadata has a very significant role in the data warehouse. We will find out why and how metadata is vital to the users and the developers. Without metadata, your data warehouse will simply be a disjointed system. If metadata is so significant, how best can you provide it? We will discuss some available options and make some valid suggestions.

A Critical Need in the Data Warehouse

Let us first examine the need for metadata in a slightly general way. We will get more specific in later sections. In broad terms, proper metadata is absolutely necessary for using, building, and administering your data warehouse.

For Using the Data Warehouse   There is one big difference between a data warehouse and any operational system such as an order processing application. The difference is in the usage—the information access. In an order processing application, how do your users get information? You provide them with GUI screens and predefined reports. They get information about pending or back orders through the relevant screens. They get information about the total orders for the day from specific daily reports. You created the screens and you formatted the reports for the users. Of course, these were designed based on specifications from the users. Nevertheless, the users themselves do not create the screen formats or lay out the reports every time they need information.

In marked contrast, users themselves retrieve information from the data warehouse. By and large, users themselves create ad hoc queries and run these against the data warehouse.

They format their own reports. Because of this major difference, before they can create and run their queries, users need to know about the data in the data warehouse. They need metadata.

In our operational systems, however, we do not really have any easy and flexible methods for knowing the nature of the contents of the database. In fact, there is no great need for user-friendly interfaces to the database contents. The data dictionary or catalog is meant for IT uses only.

The situation for a data warehouse is totally different. Your data warehouse users need to receive maximum value from your data warehouse. They need sophisticated methods for browsing and examining the contents of the data warehouse. They need to know the meanings of the data items. You have to prevent them from drawing wrong conclusions from their analysis through their ignorance about the exact meanings.

Earlier data mart implementations were limited in scope to probably one subject area. Mostly, those data marts were used by small groups of users in single departments. The users of those data marts were able to get by with scanty metadata. Today's data warehouses are much wider in scope and larger in size. Without adequate metadata support, users of these larger data warehouses are totally handicapped.

For Building the Data Warehouse   Let us say you are the data extraction and transformation expert on the project team. You know data extraction methods very well. You can work with data extraction tools. You understand the general data transformation techniques. But, in order to apply your expertise, first you must know the source systems and their data structures. You need to know the structures and the data content in the data warehouse. Then you need to determine the mappings and the data transformations. So far, to perform your tasks in building the data extraction and data transformation component of the data warehouse, you need metadata about the source systems, source-to-target mappings, and data transformation rules.

Try to wear a different hat. You are now the database administrator (DBA) for the data warehouse database. You are responsible for the physical design of the database and for doing the initial loading. You are also responsible for periodic incremental loads. There are more responsibilities for you. Even ignoring all the other responsibilities for a moment, in order to perform just the tasks of physical design and loading, you need metadata about a number of things. You need the layouts in the staging area. You need metadata about the logical structure of the data warehouse database. You need metadata about the data refresh and load cycles. This is just the bare minimum information you need.

If you consider every activity and every task for building the data warehouse, you will come to realize that metadata is an overall compelling necessity and a very significant component in your data warehouse. Metadata is absolutely essential for building your data warehouse.

For Administering the Data Warehouse   Because of the complexities and enormous sizes of modern data warehouses, it is impossible to administer the data warehouse without substantial metadata. Figure 9-2 lists a series of questions relating to data warehouse administration. Review each question on the list carefully. You cannot administer your data warehouse without answers to these questions. Your data warehouse metadata must address these issues.

Figure 9-3 gives you an idea about who needs and uses metadata. We will elaborate on this in later sections.

Data Extraction/Transformation/Loading

How to handle data changes?

How to include new sources?

Where to cleanse the data? How to change the data cleansing methods?

How to cleanse data after populating the warehouse?

How to switch to new data transformation techniques?

How to audit the application of ongoing changes?

Data from External Sources

How to add new external data sources?

How to drop some external data sources?

When mergers and acquisitions happen, how to bring in new data to the warehouse?

How to verify all external data on ongoing basis?

Data Warehouse

How to add new summary tables?

How to control runaway queries?

How to expand storage?

When to schedule platform upgrades?

How to add new information delivery tools for the users?

How to continue ongoing training?

How to maintain and enhance user support function?

How to monitor and improve ad hoc query performance?

When to schedule backups?

How to perform disaster recovery drills?

How to keep data definitions up-to-date?

How to maintain the security system?

How to monitor system load distribution?

Figure 9-2   Data warehouse administration: questions and issues.

	IT Professionals	Power Users	Casual Users
Information Discovery	Databases, Tables, Columns, Server Platforms	Databases, Tables, Columns	List of Predefined Queries and Reports, Business Views
Meaning of Data	Data Structures, Data Definitions, Data Mapping, Cleansing Functions, Transformation Rules	Business Terms, Data Definitions, Data Mapping, Cleansing Functions, Transformation Rules	Business Terms, Data Definitions, Filters, Data Sources, Conversion , Data Owners
Information Access	Program Code in SQL, 3GL, 4GL, Front-end Applications, Security	Query Toolsets, Database Access for Complex Analysis	Authorization Requests, Information Retrieval into Desktop Applications such as Spreadsheets

Figure 9-3   Who needs metadata?

Imagine a filing cabinet stuffed with documents without any folders and labels. Without metadata, your data warehouse is like such a disorganized filing cabinet. It is probably filled with information very useful for your users and for IT developers and administrators. But without an easy means to know what is there, the data warehouse is of very limited value.

Metadata is Like a Nerve Center   Various processes during the building and administering of the data warehouse generate parts of the data warehouse metadata. Parts of metadata generated by one process are used by another. In the data warehouse, metadata assumes a key position and enables communication among various processes. It acts like a nerve center in the data warehouse. Figure 9-4 shows the location of metadata within the data warehouse. Use this figure to determine the metadata components that apply to your data warehouse environment. By examining each metadata component closely, you will also perceive that the individual parts of the metadata are needed by two groups of people: (1) end-users, and (2) IT developers and administrators. In the next two subsections, we will review why metadata is critical for each of these two groups.

Why Metadata Is Vital for End-Users

The following would be a typical use of your data warehouse by a key user, say, a business analyst. The marketing VP of your company has asked this business analyst to do a thorough analysis of a problem that recently surfaced. Because of the enormous sales potential in the midwest and northeast regions, your company has opened five new stores in each region. Although overall countrywide sales increased nicely for two months following the opening of the stores, after that the sales went back to the prior levels and remained flat. The marketing VP wants to know why, so that she can take appropriate action.

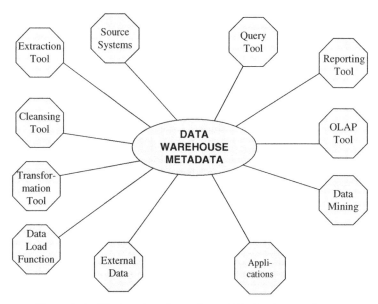

Figure 9-4   The location of metadata within the data warehouse.

As a user, the business analyst expects to find answers from the new data warehouse, but he does not know the details about the data in the data warehouse. Specifically, he does not know the answers to the following questions:

- Are the sale units and dollars stored by individual transactions or as summary totals, by product, for each day in each store?
- Can sales be analyzed by product, promotion, store, and month?
- Can current-month sales be compared to sales in the same month last year?
- Can sales be compared to targets?
- How is profit margin calculated? What are the business rules?
- What is the definition of a sales region? Which districts are included in each of the two regions being analyzed?
- Where did the sales come from? From which source systems?
- How old are the sales numbers? How often do these numbers get updated?

If the analyst is not sure of the nature of the data, he is likely to interpret the results of the analysis incorrectly. It is possible that the new stores are cannibalizing sales from other stores in their region and that is why the overall sales remain flat. But the analyst may not find the right reasons because of misinterpretation of the results.

The analysis will be more effective if you provide adequate metadata to help as a powerful roadmap of the data. If there is sufficient and proper metadata, the analyst does not have to get assistance from IT every time he needs to run an analysis. Easily accessible metadata is crucial for end-users.

Let us take the analogy of an industrial warehouse storing items of merchandise sold through a catalog. The customer refers to the catalog to find the merchandise to be ordered. The customer uses the item number in the catalog to place the order. Also, the catalog indicates the color, size, and shape of the merchandise item. The customer calculates the total amount to be paid from the price details in the catalog. In short, the catalog covers all the items in the industrial warehouse, describes the items, and facilitates the placing of the order.

In a similar way, the user of your data warehouse is like the customer. A query for information from the user is like an order for items of merchandise in the industrial warehouse. Just as the customer needs the catalog to place an order, so does your user need metadata to run a query on your data warehouse.

Figure 9-5 summarizes the vital need of metadata for end-users. The figure shows the types of information metadata provides to the end-users and the purposes for which they need these types of information.

Why Metadata Is Essential for IT

Development and deployment of your data warehouse is a joint effort between your IT staff and your user representatives. Nevertheless, because of the technical issues, IT is primarily responsible for the design and ongoing administration of the data warehouse. For performing the responsibilities for design and administration, IT must have access to proper metadata.

Throughout the entire development process, metadata is essential for IT. Beginning with the data extraction and ending with information delivery, metadata is crucial for IT. As the development process moves through data extraction, data transformation, data integration,

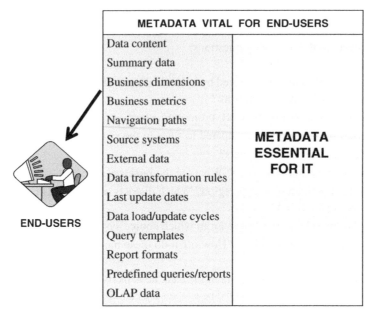

Figure 9-5   Metadata vital for end-users.

data cleansing, data staging, data storage, query and report design, and design for OLAF and other front-end systems, metadata is critical for IT to perform their development activities.

Here is a summary list of processes in which metadata is significant for IT:

- Data extraction from sources
- Data transformation
- Data scrubbing
- Data aggregation and summarization
- Data staging
- Data refreshment
- Database design
- Query and report design

Figure 9-6 summarizes the essential need for metadata for IT. The figure shows the types of information metadata provides IT staff and the purposes for which they need these types of information.

Automation of Warehousing Tasks

Maintaining metadata is no longer a form of glorified documentation. Traditionally, metadata has been created and maintained as documentation about the data for each process. Now metadata is assuming a new active role. Let us see how this is happening.

As you know, tools perform major functions in a data warehouse environment. For example, tools enable the extraction of data from designated sources. When you provide the mapping algorithms, data transformation tools transform data elements to suit the

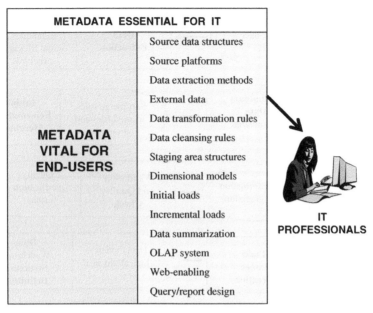

METADATA ESSENTIAL FOR IT	
METADATA VITAL FOR END-USERS	Source data structures
	Source platforms
	Data extraction methods
	External data
	Data transformation rules
	Data cleansing rules
	Staging area structures
	Dimensional models
	Initial loads
	Incremental loads
	Data summarization
	OLAP system
	Web-enabling
	Query/report design

IT PROFESSIONALS

Figure 9-6   Metadata essential for IT.

target data structures. You may specify valid values for data elements and the data quality tools will use these values to ensure the integrity and validity of data. At the front end, tools empower the users to browse the data content and gain access to the data warehouse. These tools generally fall into two categories: development tools for IT professionals, and information access tools for end-users.

When you, as a developer, use a tool for design and development, in that process, the tool lets you create and record a part of the data warehouse metadata. When you use another tool to perform another process in the design and development, this tool uses the metadata created by the first tool. When your end-user uses a query tool for information access at the front end, that query tool uses metadata created by some of the back-end tools. What exactly is happening here with metadata? Metadata is no longer passive documentation. Metadata takes part in the process. It aids in the automation of data warehouse processes.

Let us consider the back-end processes beginning with the defining of the data sources. As the data movement takes place from the data sources to the data warehouse database through the data staging area, several processes occur. In a typical data warehouse, appropriate tools assist in these processes. Each tool records its own metadata as data movement takes place. The metadata recorded by one tool drives one or more processes that follow. This is how metadata assumes an active role and assists in the automation of data warehouse processes.

Here is a list of back-end processes shown in the order in which they generally occur:

1. Source data structure definition
2. Data extraction
3. Initial reformatting/merging
4. Preliminary data cleansing

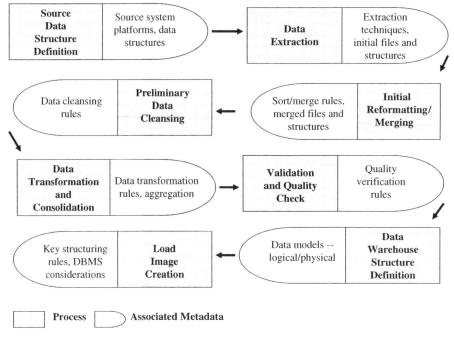

Figure 9-7 Metadata drives data warehouse processes.

5. Data transformation and consolidation
6. Validation and quality check
7. Data warehouse structure definition
8. Load image creation

Figure 9-7 shows each of these eight processes. The figure also indicates the metadata recorded by each process. Further, the figure points out how each process is able to use the metadata recorded in the earlier processes.

Metadata is important in a data warehouse because it drives the processes. However, our discussion above leads to the realization that each tool may record metadata in its own proprietary format. Again, the metadata recorded by each tool may reside on the platform where the corresponding process runs. If this is the case, how can the metadata recorded by one tool in a proprietary format drive the process for the next tool? This is a critical question. This is where standardization of metadata comes into play. We will get to the discussion on metadata standards later in the chapter.

Establishing the Context of Information

Imagine this scenario. One of your users wants to run a query to retrieve sales data for three products during the first seven days of April in the southern region. This user composes the query as follows:

Product = Widget-1 or Widget-2 or Widget-3, Region = 'SOUTH'
Period = 04-01-2009 to 04-07-2009

The result comes back:

	Sale Units	Amount
Widget-1	25,355	253,550
Widget-2	16,978	254,670
Widget-3	7,994	271,796

Let us examine the query and the results. In the specification for region, which territories does the region "SOUTH" include? Are these the territories your user is interested in? What is the context of the data item "SOUTH" in your data warehouse? Next, does the data item 04-01-2009 denote April 1, 2009 or January 4, 2009? What is the convention used for dates in your data warehouse?

Look at the result set. Are the numbers shown as sale units given in physical units of the products, or in some measure such as pounds or kilograms? What about the amounts shown in the result set? Are these amounts in dollars or in euros? This is a pertinent question if your user is accessing your data warehouse from Europe.

For the dates stored in your data warehouse, if the first two digits of the date format indicate the month and the next two digits denote the date, then 04-01-2009 means April 1, 2009. Only in this context is the interpretation correct. Similarly, context is important for the interpretation of the other data elements.

How can your user find out what exactly each data element in the query is and what the result set means? The answer is metadata. Metadata gives your user the meaning of each data element. Metadata establishes the context for the data elements. Data warehouse users, developers, and administrators interpret each data element in the context established and recorded in metadata.

METADATA TYPES BY FUNCTIONAL AREAS

So far in this chapter, we have discussed several aspects of metadata in a data warehouse environment. We have seen why metadata is a critical need for end-users as well as for IT professionals who are responsible for development and administration. We have established that metadata plays an active role in the automation of data warehouse processes.

At this stage, we can increase our understanding further by grouping the various types of metadata. When you classify each type, your appreciation for each type will increase and you can better understand the role of metadata within each group.

Different authors and data warehouse practitioners classify and group metadata in various ways: some by usage and some by who uses it. Let us look at some of the different methods for classification of metadata:

- Administrative/end-user/optimization
- Development/usage
- In the data mart/at the workstation
- Building/maintaining/managing/using
- Technical/business
- Back room/front room
- Internal/external

In an earlier chapter, we considered a way of dividing the data warehouse environment by means of the major functions. We can picture the data warehouse environment as being functionally divided into the three areas of *data acquisition, data storage*, and *information delivery*. All data warehouse processes occur in these three functional areas. As a developer, you design the processes in each of the three functional areas. Each of the tools used for these processes creates and records metadata and may also use and be driven by the metadata recorded by other tools.

First, let us group the metadata types by these three functional areas. Why? Because every data warehouse process occurs in one of just these three areas. Take into account all the processes happening in each functional area and then put together all the processes in all the three functional areas. You will get a complete set of the data warehouse processes without missing any one. Also, you will be able to compile a complete list of metadata types.

Let us move on to the classification of metadata types by the functional areas in the data warehouse:

1. Data acquisition
2. Data storage
3. Information delivery

Data Acquisition

In this area, the data warehouse processes relate to the following functions:

* Data extraction
* Data transformation
* Data cleansing
* Data integration
* Data staging

As the processes take place, the appropriate tools record the metadata elements relating to the processes. The tools record the metadata elements during the development phases as well as while the data warehouse is in operation after deployment.

As an IT professional and part of the data warehouse project team, you will be using development tools that record metadata relating to this area. Also, some other tools you will be using for other processes either in this area or in some other area may use the metadata recorded by other tools in this area. For example, when you use a query tool to create standard queries, you will be using metadata recorded by processes in the data acquisition area. As you will note, the query tool is meant for a process in a different area, namely, the information delivery area.

IT professionals will also be using metadata recorded by processes in the data acquisition area for administering and monitoring the ongoing functions of the data warehouse after deployment. You will use the metadata from this area to monitor ongoing data extraction and transformation. You will make sure that the ongoing load images are created properly by referring to the metadata from this area.

The users of your data warehouse will also be using the metadata recorded in the data acquisition area. When a user wants to find the data sources for the data elements in his or her query, he or she will look up the metadata from the data acquisition area. Again,

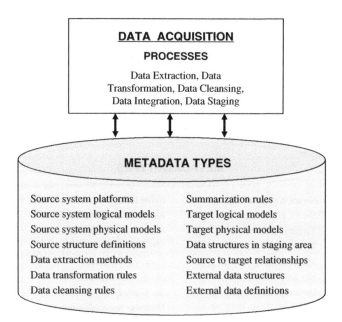

Figure 9-8   Data acquisition: metadata types.

when the user wants to know how the profit margin has been calculated and stored in the data warehouse, he or she will look up the derivation rules in the metadata recorded in the data acquisition area.

For metadata types recorded and used in the data acquisition area, refer to Fig. 9-8. This figure summarizes the metadata types and the relevant data warehouse processes. Try to relate these metadata types and processes to your data warehouse environment.

Data Storage

In this area, the data warehouse processes relate to the following functions:

- Data loading
- Data archiving
- Data management

Just as in the other areas, as processes take place in the data storage functional area, the appropriate tools record the metadata elements relating to the processes. The tools record the metadata elements during the development phases as well as while the data warehouse is in operation after deployment.

Similar to metadata recorded by processes in the data acquisition area, metadata recorded by processes in the data storage area is used for development, administration, and by the users. You will be using the metadata from this area for designing the full data refreshes and the incremental data loads. The DBA will be using metadata for the processes of backup, recovery, and tuning the database. For purging the data warehouse and for periodic archiving of data, metadata from this area will be used for data warehouse administration.

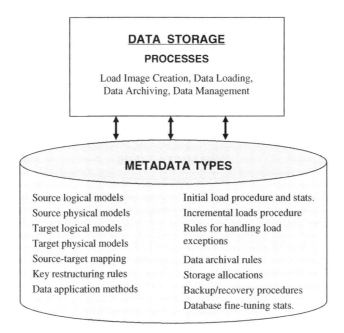

Figure 9-9   Data storage: metadata types.

Will the users be using metadata from the data storage functional area? To give you just one example, let us say one of your users wants to create a query breaking the total quarterly sales down by sale districts. Before the user runs the query, he or she would like to know when was the last time the data on district delineation was loaded. From where can the user get the information about load dates of the district delineation? Metadata recorded by the data loading process in the data storage functional area will give the user the latest load date for district delineation.

For metadata types recorded and used in the data storage area, refer to Fig. 9-9. This figure summarizes the metadata types and the relevant data warehouse processes. See how the metadata types and the processes relate to your data warehouse environment.

Information Delivery

In this area, the data warehouse processes relate to the following functions:

- Report generation
- Query processing
- Complex analysis

Mostly, the processes in this area are meant for end-users. While using the processes, end-users generally use metadata recorded in processes of the other two areas of data acquisition and data storage. When a user creates a query with the aid of a query processing tool, he or she can refer back to metadata recorded in the data acquisition and data storage areas and can look up the source data configurations, data structures, and data transformations from the metadata recorded in the data acquisition area. In the same way, from metadata recorded

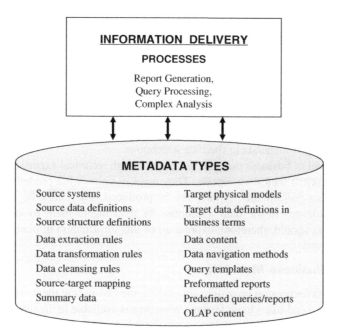

Figure 9-10   Information delivery: metadata types.

in the data storage area, the user can find the date of the last full refresh and the incremental loads for various tables in the data warehouse database.

Generally, metadata recorded in the information delivery functional area relate to predefined queries, predefined reports, and input parameter definitions for queries and reports. Metadata recorded in this functional area also include information for OLAP. The developers and administrators are involved in these processes.

For metadata types recorded and used in the information delivery area, see Fig. 9-10. This figure summarizes the metadata types and the relevant data warehouse processes. See how the metadata types and processes apply to your data warehouse environment.

Metadata types may also be classified as business metadata and technical metadata. This is another effective method of classifying metadata types because the nature and format of metadata in one group are markedly different from those in the other group. The next two sections deal with this method of classification.

BUSINESS METADATA

Business metadata connects your business users to your data warehouse. Business users need to know what is available in the data warehouse from a perspective different from that of IT professionals like you. Business metadata is like a roadmap or an easy-to-use information directory showing the contents and how to get there. It is like a tour guide for executives and a route map for managers and business analysts.

Content Overview

First of all, business metadata must describe the contents in plain language, giving information in business terms. For example, the names of the data tables or individual data elements must not be cryptic but be meaningful terms that business users are familiar with. The data item name *calc_pr_sle* is not acceptable. You need to rename this as *calculated-prior-month-sale.*

Business metadata is much less structured than technical metadata. A substantial portion of business metadata originates from textual documents, spreadsheets, and even business rules and policies not written down completely. Even though much of business metadata is from informal sources, it is as important as metadata from formal sources such as data dictionary entries. All of the informal metadata must be captured, put in a standard form, and stored as business metadata in the data warehouse.

A large segment of business users do not have enough technical expertise to create their own queries or format their own reports. They need to know what predefined queries are available and what preformatted reports can be produced. They must be able to identify the tables and columns in the data warehouse by referring to them by business names. Business metadata should, therefore, express all of this information in plain language.

Examples of Business Metadata

Business metadata focuses on providing support for the end-user at the workstation. It must make it easy for the end-users to understand what data is available in the data warehouse and how they can use it. Business metadata portrays the data warehouse purely from the perspective of the end-users. It is like an external view of the data warehouse designed and composed in simple business terms that users can easily understand.

Let us try to better understand business metadata by looking at a list of examples:

- Connectivity procedures
- Security and access privileges
- The overall structure of data in business terms
- Source systems
- Source-to-target mappings
- Data transformation business rules
- Summarization and derivations
- Table names and business definitions
- Attribute names and business definitions
- Data ownership
- Query and reporting tools
- Predefined queries
- Predefined reports
- Report distribution information
- Common information access routes
- Rules for analysis using OLAP
- Currency of OLAP data
- Data warehouse refresh schedule

The list is by no means all inclusive, but it gives a good basis for you to make up a similar list for your data warehouse. Use the list as a guide to ensure that business metadata is provided using business names and made easily understandable to your users.

Content Highlights

From the list of examples, let us highlight the contents of business metadata. What are all the various kinds of questions business metadata can answer? What types of information can the user get from business metadata?

Let us derive a list of questions business metadata can answer for the end-users. Although the following list does not include all possible questions by the users, it can be a useful reference:

- How can I sign onto and connect with the data warehouse?
- Which parts of the data warehouse can I access?
- Can I see all the attributes from a specific table?
- What are the definitions of the attributes I need in my query?
- Are there any queries and reports already predefined to give the results I need?
- Which source system did the data I want come from?
- What default values were used for the data items retrieved by my query?
- What types of aggregations are available for the metrics needed?
- How is the value in the data item I need derived from other data items?
- When was the last update for the data items in my query?
- On which data items can I perform drill-down analysis?
- How old is the OLAP data? Should I wait for the next update?

Who Benefits?

Business metadata primarily benefits end-users. This is a general statement. Who specifically benefits from business metadata? How does business metadata serve specific members of the end-user community? Look over the following list:

- Managers
- Business analysts
- Power users
- Regular users
- Casual users
- Senior managers/junior executives

TECHNICAL METADATA

Technical metadata is meant for the IT staff responsible for the development and administration of the data warehouse. The technical personnel need information to design each process. These are processes in every functional area of the data warehouse. You, as part of the technical group on the project team, must know the proposed structure and content of the data warehouse. Different members on the project team need different kinds of information from technical metadata. If business metadata is like a roadmap for the users to use the data warehouse, technical metadata is like a support guide for the IT professionals to build, maintain, and administer the data warehouse.

Content Overview

IT staff working on the data warehouse project need technical metadata for different purposes. If you are a data acquisition expert, your need for metadata is different from that of the information access developer on the team. As a whole, the technical staff on the project need to understand the data extraction, data transformation, and data cleansing processes. They have to know the output layouts from every extraction routine and must understand the data transformation rules.

IT staff require technical metadata for three distinct purposes. First, IT personnel need technical metadata for the initial development of the data warehouse. Let us say you are responsible for design and development of the data transformation process. For this purpose, the metadata from the earlier process of data extraction can assist in your development effort.

Second, technical metadata is absolutely essential for ongoing growth and maintenance of the data warehouse. If you are responsible for making changes to some data structures, or even for a second release of the data warehouse, where will you find the information on the contents and the various processes? You need technical metadata.

Technical metadata is also critical for the continuous administration of the production data warehouse. As an administrator, you have to monitor the ongoing data extractions. You have to ensure that the incremental loads are completed correctly and on time. Your responsibility may also include database backups and archiving of old data. Data warehouse administration is almost impossible without technical metadata.

Examples of Technical Metadata

Technical metadata concentrates on support for the IT staff responsible for development, maintenance, and administration. Technical metadata is more structured than business metadata. Technical metadata is like an internal view of the data warehouse showing the inner details in technical terms. Here is a list of examples of technical metadata:

- Data models of source systems
- Record layouts of outside sources
- Source to staging area mappings
- Staging area to data warehouse mappings
- Data extraction rules and schedules
- Data transformation rules and versioning
- Data aggregation rules
- Data cleansing rules
- Summarization and derivations
- Data loading and refresh schedules and controls
- Job dependencies

Program names and descriptions

- Data warehouse data model
- Database names
- Table/view names
- Column names and descriptions
- Key attributes

- Business rules for entities and relationships
- Mapping between logical and physical models
- Network/server information
- Connectivity data
- Data movement audit controls
- Data purge and archival rules
- Authority/access privileges
- Data usage/timings
- Query and report access patterns
- Query and reporting tools

Review the list and develop a comparable list for your data warehouse environment.

Content Highlights

The list of examples gives you an idea of the kinds of information technical metadata in a data warehouse environment must contain. Just as in the case of business metadata, let us derive a list of questions technical metadata can answer for developers and administrators. Review the following list:

- What databases and tables exist?
- What are the columns for each table?
- What are the keys and indexes?
- What are the physical files?
- Do the business descriptions correspond to the technical ones?
- When was the last successful update?
- What are the source systems and their data structures?
- What are the data extraction rules for each data source?
- What is the source to target mapping for each data item in the data warehouse?
- What are the data transformation rules?
- What default values were used for the data items while cleaning up missing data?
- What types of aggregations are available?
- What are the derived fields and their rules for derivation?
- When was the last update for the data items in my query?
- What are the load and refresh schedules?
- How often is data purged or archived? Which data items?
- What is the schedule for creating data for OLAP?
- What query and report tools are available?

Who Benefits?

The following list indicates the specific types of personnel who will benefit from technical metadata:

- Project manager
- Data warehouse administrator

- Database administrator
- Metadata manager
- Data warehouse architect
- Data acquisition developer
- Data quality analyst
- Business analyst
- System administrator
- Infrastructure specialist
- Data modeler
- Security architect

HOW TO PROVIDE METADATA

As your data warehouse is being designed and built, metadata needs to be collected and recorded. As you know, metadata describes your data warehouse from various points of view. You look into the data warehouse through the metadata to find the data sources, to understand the data extractions and transformations, to determine how to navigate through the contents, and to retrieve information. Most of the data warehouse processes are performed with the aid of software tools. The same metadata or true copies of the relevant subsets must be available to every tool.

In a study conducted by the Data Warehousing Institute in the early years of data warehousing, 86% of the respondents fully recognized the significance of having a metadata management strategy. However, only 9% had implemented a metadata solution. Another 16% had a plan and had begun to work on the implementation. This situation has improved somewhat in today's environment.

If most of the companies with data warehouses realized the enormous significance of metadata management, why is only a small percentage doing anything about it? Metadata management presents great challenges. The challenges are not in the capturing of metadata through the use of the tools during data warehouse processes but lie in the integration of the metadata from the various tools that create and maintain their own metadata.

We will explore the challenges. How can you find options to overcome the challenges and establish effective metadata management in your data warehouse environment? What is happening in the industry? While standards are being worked out in industry coalitions, are there interim options for you? First, let us establish the basic requirements for good metadata management. What are the requirements? Next, we will consider the sources for metadata before we examine the challenges.

Metadata Requirements

Very simply put, metadata must serve as a roadmap to the data warehouse for your users. It must also support IT in the development and administration of the data warehouse. Let us go beyond these simple statements and look at specifics of the requirements for metadata management.

Capturing and Storing Data The data dictionary in an operational system stores the structure and business rules as they are at the current time. For operational systems, it is not necessary to keep the history of the data dictionary entries. However, the history of the data in your data warehouse spans several years, typically 5 to 15 in most data warehouses. During this time, changes do occur in the source systems, data extraction methods, data transformation algorithms, and in the structure and content of the data warehouse database itself. Metadata in a data warehouse environment must, therefore, keep track of the revisions. As such, metadata management must provide means for capturing and storing metadata with proper versioning to indicate its time-variant feature.

Variety of Metadata Sources   Metadata for a data warehouse never comes from a single source. CASE tools, the source operational systems, data extraction tools, data transformation tools, the data dictionary definitions, and other sources all contribute to the data warehouse metadata. Metadata management, therefore, must be open enough to capture metadata from a large variety of sources.

Metadata Integration   We have looked at elements of business and technical metadata. You must be able to integrate and merge all these elements in a unified manner for them to be meaningful to your end-users. Metadata from the data models of the source systems must be integrated with metadata from the data models of the data warehouse databases. The integration must continue further to the front-end tools used by the end-users. All these are difficult propositions and very challenging.

Metadata Standardization   If your data extraction tool and the data transformation tool represent data structures, then both tools must record the metadata about the data structures in the same standard way. The same metadata in different metadata stores of different tools must be represented in the same manner.

Rippling Through of Revisions   Revisions will occur in metadata as data or business rules change. As the metadata revisions are tracked in one data warehouse process, the revisions must ripple throughout the data warehouse to the other processes.

Keeping Metadata Synchronized   Metadata about data structures, data elements, events, rules, and so on must be kept synchronized at all times throughout the data warehouse.

Metadata Exchange   While your end-users are using the front-end tools for information access, they must be able to view the metadata recorded by back-end tools like the data transformation tool. Free and easy exchange of metadata from one tool to another must be possible.

Support for End-Users   Metadata management must provide simple graphical and tabular presentations to end-users, making it easy for them to browse through the metadata and understand the data in the data warehouse purely from a business perspective.

The requirements listed are very valid for metadata management. Integration and standardization of metadata are great challenges. Nevertheless, before addressing these issues, you need to know the usual sources of metadata. A general list of metadata sources will help you establish a metadata management initiative for your data warehouse.

Sources of Metadata

As tools are used for the various data warehouse processes, metadata gets recorded as a byproduct. For example, when a data transformation tool is used, the metadata on the source to target mappings get recorded as a byproduct of the process carried out with that tool. Let us look at all the usual sources of metadata without any reference to individual processes.

Source Systems

- Data models of operational systems (manual or with CASE tools)
- Definitions of data elements from system documentation
- COBOL copybooks and control block specification
- Physical file layouts and field definitions
- Program specifications
- File layouts and field definitions for data from outside sources
- Other sources such as spreadsheets and manual lists

Data Extraction

- Data on source platforms and connectivity
- Layouts and definitions of selected data sources
- Definitions of fields selected for extraction
- Criteria for merging into initial extract files on each platform
- Rules for standardizing field types and lengths
- Data extraction schedules
- Extraction methods for incremental changes
- Data extraction job streams

Data Transformation and Cleansing

- Specifications for mapping extracted files to data staging files
- Conversion rules for individual files
- Default values for fields with missing values
- Business rules for validity checking
- Sorting and resequencing arrangements
- Audit trail for the movement from data extraction to data staging

Data Loading

- Specifications for mapping data staging files to load images
- Rules for assigning keys for each file
- Audit trail for the movement from data staging to load images
- Schedules for full refreshes
- Schedules for incremental loads
- Data loading job streams

Data Storage

- Data models for centralized data warehouse and dependent data marts
- Subject area groupings of tables
- Data models for conformed data marts
- Physical files
- Table and column definitions
- Business rules for validity checking

Information Delivery

- List of query and report tools
- List of predefined queries and reports
- Data model for special databases for OLAP
- Schedules for retrieving data for OLAP

Challenges for Metadata Management

Although metadata is so vital in a data warehouse environment, seamlessly integrating all the parts of metadata is a formidable task. Industry-wide standardization is far from being a reality. Metadata created by a process at one end cannot be viewed through a tool used at another end without going through convoluted transformations. These challenges force many data warehouse developers to abandon the requirements for proper metadata management.

Here are the major challenges to be addressed while providing metadata:

- Each software tool has its own propriety metadata. If you are using several tools in your data warehouse, how can you reconcile the formats?
- No industry-wide accepted standards exist for metadata formats.
- There are conflicting claims on the advantages of a centralized metadata repository as opposed to a collection of fragmented metadata stores.
- There are no easy and accepted methods of passing metadata along the processes as data moves from the source systems to the staging area and thereafter to the data warehouse storage.
- Preserving version control of metadata uniformly throughout the data warehouse is tedious and difficult.
- In a large data warehouse with numerous source systems, unifying the metadata relating to the data sources can be an enormous task. You have to deal with conflicting standards, formats, data naming conventions, data definitions, attributes, values, business rules, and units of measure. You have to resolve indiscriminate use of aliases and compensate for inadequate data validation rules.

Metadata Repository

Think of a metadata repository as a general-purpose information directory or cataloging device to classify, store, and manage metadata. As we have seen earlier, business metadata and technical metadata serve different purposes. The end-users need the business metadata;

data warehouse developers and administrators require the technical metadata. The structures of these two categories of metadata also vary. Therefore, the metadata repository can be thought of as two distinct information directories, one to store business metadata and the other to store technical metadata. This division may also be logical within a single physical repository.

Figure 9-11 shows the typical contents in a metadata repository. Notice the division between business and technical metadata. Did you also notice another component called the information navigator? This component is implemented in different ways in commercial offerings. The functions of the information navigator include the following:

Interface from Query Tools. This function attaches data warehouse data to third-party query tools so that metadata definitions inside the technical metadata may be viewed from these tools.

Drill Down for Details. The user of metadata can drill down and proceed from one level of metadata to a lower level for more information. For example, you can first get the definition of a data table, then go to the next level for seeing all attributes, and go further to get the details of individual attributes.

Review Predefined Queries and Reports. The user is able to review predefined queries and reports, and launch the selected ones with proper parameters.

A centralized metadata repository accessible from all parts of the data warehouse for your end-users, developers, and administrators appears to be an ideal solution for metadata management. But for a centralized metadata repository to be the best solution, the repository must meet some basic requirements. Let us quickly review these requirements. It is not easy to find a repository tool that satisfies every one of the requirements listed below.

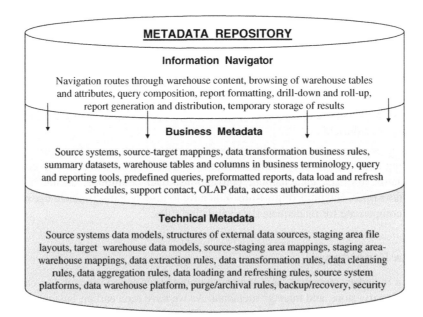

Figure 9-11 Metadata repository.

Flexible Organization. Allow the data administrator to classify and organize metadata into logical categories and subcategories, and assign specific components of metadata to the classifications.

Historical. Use versioning to maintain the historical perspective of the metadata.

Integrated. Store business and technical metadata in formats meaningful to all types of users.

Good Compartmentalization. Able to separate and store logical and physical database models.

Analysis and Look-up Capabilities. Capable of browsing all parts of metadata and also navigating through the relationships.

Customizable. Able to create customized views of metadata for individual groups of users and to include new metadata objects as necessary.

Maintain Descriptions and Definitions. View metadata in both business and technical terms.

Standardize Naming Conventions. Flexibility to adopt any type of naming convention and standardize throughout the metadata repository.

Synchronization. Keep metadata synchronized within all parts of the data warehouse environment and with the related external systems.

Open. Support metadata exchange between processes via industry-standard interfaces and be compatible with a large variety of tools.

Selection of a suitable metadata repository product is one of the key decisions the project team must make. Use the above list of criteria as a guide while evaluating repository tools for your data warehouse.

Metadata Integration and Standards

For a free interchange of metadata within the data warehouse between processes performed with the aid of software tools, the need for standardization is obvious. Our discussions so far must have convinced you of this. As mentioned in Chapter 3, the Meta Data Coalition and the Object Management Group had both been working on standards for metadata. The Meta Data Coalition had accepted a standard known as the Open Information Model (OIM). The Object Management Group had released the Common Warehouse Metamodel (CWM) as its standard. As mentioned earlier, in November 2000 these two bodies merged into the OMG. Since then some integration of the two standards have emerged for industry-wide acceptance.

You need to be aware of these efforts towards the worthwhile goal of metadata standards. Also, note the following highlights of these initiatives as they relate to data warehouse metadata:

- The standard model provides metadata concepts for database schema management, design, and reuse in a data warehouse environment. It includes both logical and physical database concepts.
- The model includes details of data transformations applicable to populating data warehouses.
- The model can be extended to include OLAP-specific metadata types capturing descriptions of data cubes.

- The standard model contains details for specifying source and target schemas and data transformations between those regularly found in the data acquisition processes in the data warehouse environment. This type of metadata can be used to support transformation design, impact analysis (which transformations are affected by a given schema change), and data lineage (which data sources and transformations were used to produce given data in the data warehouse).

- The transformation component of the standard model captures information about compound data transformation scripts. Individual transformations have relationships to the sources and targets of the transformation. Some transformation semantics may be captured by constraints and by code–decode sets for table-driven mappings.

Implementation Options

Enough has been said about the absolute necessity of metadata in a data warehouse environment. At the same time. we have noted the need for integration and standards for metadata. Associated with these two facts is the reality of the lack of universally accepted metadata standards. Therefore, in a typical data warehouse environment where multiple tools from different vendors are used, what are the options for implementing metadata management? In this section, we will explore a few random options. We have to hope, however, that the goal of universal standards will be met soon.

Review the following options and consider the ones most appropriate for your data warehouse environment.

- Select and use a metadata repository product with its business information directory component. Your information access and data acquisition tools that are compatible with the repository product will seamlessly interface with it. For the other tools that are not compatible, you will have to explore other methods of integration.

- In the opinion of some data warehouse consultants, a single centralized repository is a restrictive approach jeopardizing the autonomy of individual processes. Although a centralized repository enables sharing of metadata, it cannot be easily administered in a large data warehouse. In the decentralized approach, metadata is spread across different parts of the architecture with several private and unique metadata stores. Metadata interchange could be a problem.

- Some developers have come up with their own solutions. They have come up with a set of procedures for the standard usage of each tool in the development environment and provide a table of contents.

- Other developers create their own database to gather and store metadata and publish it on the company's intranet.

- Some adopt clever methods of integration of information access and analysis tools. They provide side-by-side display of metadata by one tool and display of the real data by another tool. Sometimes, the help texts in the query tools may be populated with the metadata exported from a central repository.

As you know, the current trend is to use Web technology for reporting and OLAP functions. The company's intranet is widely used as the means for information delivery. Figure 9-12 shows how this paradigm shift changes the way metadata may be accessed.

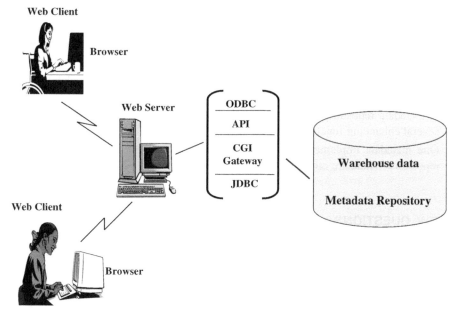

Figure 9-12   Metadata: Web-based access.

Business users can use their Web browsers to access metadata and navigate through the data warehouse and any data marts.

From the outset, pay special attention to metadata for your data warehouse environment. Prepare a metadata initiative to answer the following questions:

What are the goals for metadata in your enterprise? What metadata is required to meet the goals?

What are the sources for metadata in your environment?

Who will maintain it?

How will they maintain it?

What are the metadata standards?

How will metadata be used? By whom? What metadata tools will be needed?

Set your goals for metadata in your environment and follow through.

CHAPTER SUMMARY

- Metadata is a critical need for using, building, and administering the data warehouse.
- For end-users, metadata is like a roadmap to the data warehouse contents.
- For IT professionals, metadata supports development and administration functions.
- Metadata has an active role in the data warehouse and assists in the automation of the processes.
- Metadata types may be classified by the three functional areas of the data warehouse, namely, data acquisition, data storage, and information delivery. The types are linked to the processes that take places in these three areas.

- Business metadata connects the business users to the data warehouse. Technical metadata is meant for the IT staff responsible for development and administration.
- Effective metadata must meet a number of requirements. Metadata management is difficult; many challenges need to be faced.
- Universal metadata standardization is still an elusive goal. Lack of standardization inhibits seamless passing of metadata from one tool to another.
- A metadata repository is like a general-purpose information directory that includes several enhancing functions.
- One metadata implementation option includes the use of a commercial metadata repository. There are other possible home-grown options.

REVIEW QUESTIONS

1. Why do you think metadata is important in a data warehouse environment? Give a general explanation in one or two paragraphs.

2. Explain how metadata is critical for data warehouse development and administration.

3. Examine the concept that metadata is like a nerve center. Describe how the concept applies to the data warehouse environment.

4. List and describe three major reasons why metadata is vital for end-users.

5. Why is metadata essential for IT? List six processes in which metadata is significant for IT and explain why.

6. Pick three processes in which metadata assists in the automation of these processes. Show how metadata plays an active role in these processes.

7. What is meant by establishing the context of information? Briefly explain with an example of how metadata establishes the context of information in a data warehouse.

8. List four metadata types used in each of the three areas of data acquisition, data storage, and information delivery.

9. List any ten examples of business metadata.

10. List four major requirements that metadata must satisfy. Describe each of these four requirements.

EXERCISES

1. Indicate if true or false:
   A. The importance of metadata is the same in a data warehouse as it is in an operational system.
   B. Metadata is needed by IT for data warehouse administration.
   C. Technical metadata is usually less structured than business metadata.
   D. Maintaining metadata in a modern data warehouse is just for documentation.

E. Metadata provides information on predefined queries.

F. Business metadata comes from sources more varied than those for technical metadata.

G. Technical metadata is shared between business users and IT staff.

H. A metadata repository is like a general purpose directory tool.

I. Metadata standards facilitate metadata interchange among tools.

J. Business metadata is only for business users; business metadata cannot be understood or used by IT staff.

2. As the project manager for the development of the data warehouse for a domestic soft drinks manufacturer, your assignment is to write a proposal for providing metadata. Consider the options and come up with what you think is needed and how you plan to implement a metadata strategy.

3. As the data warehouse administrator, describe all the types of metadata you would need for performing your job. Explain how these types would assist you.

4. You are responsible for training the data warehouse end-users. Write a short procedure for your casual end-users to use the business metadata and run queries. Describe the procedure in user terms without using the word metadata.

5. As the data acquisition specialist, what types of metadata can help you? Choose one of the data acquisition processes and explain the role of metadata in that process.

PART 4

DATA DESIGN AND DATA PREPARATION

CHAPTER 10

PRINCIPLES OF DIMENSIONAL MODELING

CHAPTER OBJECTIVES

- Clearly unde rstand how the requirements definition determines data design
- Introduce dimensional modeling and contrast it with entity-relationship modeling
- Review the basics of the STAR schema
- Find out what is inside the fact table and inside the dimension tables
- Determine the advantages of the STAR schema for data warehouses
- Review examples of the STAR schema

FROM REQUIREMENTS TO DATA DESIGN

The requirements definition completely drives the data design for the data warehouse. Data design consists of putting together the data structures. A group of data elements form a data structure. Logical data design includes determination of the various data elements that are needed and combination of the data elements into structures of data. Logical data design also includes establishing the relationships among the data structures.

Let us look at Figure 10-1. Notice how the phases start with requirements gathering. The results of the requirements gathering phase is documented in detail in the requirements definition document. An essential component of this document is the set of information package diagrams. Remember that these are information matrices showing the metrics, business dimensions, and the hierarchies within individual business dimensions.

The information package diagrams form the basis for the logical data design for a data warehouse made up of data marts. The data design process results in a dimensional data model.

Data Warehousing Fundamentals for IT Professionals, Second Edition. By Paulraj Ponniah
Copyright © 2010 John Wiley & Sons, Inc.

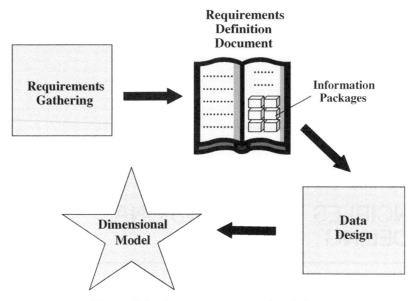

Figure 10-1 From requirements to data design.

Design Decisions

Before we proceed with designing the dimensional data model, let us quickly review some of the design decisions you have to make:

Choosing the Process. Selecting the subjects from the information packages for the first set of logical structures to be designed.

Choosing the Grain. Determining the level of detail for the data in the data structures.

Identifying and Conforming the Dimensions. Choosing the business dimensions (such as product, market, time, etc.) to be included in the first set of structures and making sure that each particular data element in every business dimension is conformed to one another.

Choosing the Facts. Selecting the metrics or units of measurements (such as product sale units, dollar sales, dollar revenue, etc.) to be included in the first set of structures.

Choosing the Duration of the Database. Determining how far back in time you should go for historical data.

Dimensional Modeling Basics

Dimensional modeling gets its name from the business dimensions we need to incorporate into the logical data model. It is a logical design technique to structure the business dimensions and the metrics that are analyzed along these dimensions. This modeling technique is intuitive for that purpose. The model has also proved to provide high performance for queries and analysis.

The multidimensional information package diagram we have discussed is the foundation for the dimensional model. Therefore, the dimensional model consists of the specific data structures needed to represent the business dimensions. These data structures also contain the metrics or facts.

In Chapter 5, we discussed information package diagrams in sufficient detail. We specifically looked at an information package diagram for automaker sales. Please go back and review Figure 5-5 in that chapter. What do you see? In the bottom section of the diagram, you observe the list of measurements or metrics that the automaker wants to use for analysis. Next, look at the column headings. These are the business dimensions along which the automaker wants to analyze the measurements or metrics. Under each column heading you see the dimension hierarchies and categories within that business dimension. What you see under each column heading are the attributes relating to that business dimension.

Reviewing the information package diagram for automaker sales, we notice three types of data entities: (1) measurements or metrics, (2) business dimensions, and (3) attributes for each business dimension. So, when we put together the dimensional model to represent the information contained in the automaker sales information package, we need to come up with data structures to represent these three types of data entities. Let us discuss how we can do this.

First, let us work with the measurements or metrics seen at the bottom of the information package diagram. These are the facts for analysis. In the automaker sales diagram, the facts are as follows:

Actual sale price

MSRP

Options price

Full price

Dealer add-ons

Dealer credits

Dealer invoice

Amount of down payment

Manufacturer proceeds

Amount financed

Each of these data items is a measurement or fact. Actual sale price is a fact about what the actual price was for the sale. Full price is a fact about what the full price was relating to the sale. As we review each of these factual items, we find that we can group all of these into a single data structure. In relational database terminology, you may call the data structure a relational table. So, the metrics or facts from the information package diagram will form the fact table. For the automaker sales analysis this fact table would be the automaker sales fact table.

Look at Figure 10-2 showing how the fact table is formed. The fact table gets its name from the subject for analysis; in this case, it is automaker sales. Each fact item or measurement goes into the fact table as an attribute for automaker sales.

We have determined one of the data structures to be included in the dimensional model for automaker sales and derived the fact table from the information package diagram. Let us now move on to the other sections of the information package diagram, taking the business dimensions, one by one. Look at the product business dimension in Figure 5-5.

The product business dimension is used when we want to analyze the facts by products. Sometimes our analysis could be a breakdown by individual models. Another analysis could

Dimensions

	Time	Product	Payment Method	Customer Demo-graphics	Dealer	
	Year	Model Name	Finance Type	Age	Dealer Name	
	Quarter	Model Year	Term (Months)	Gender	City	
	Month	Package Styling	Interest Rate	Income Range	State	
	Date	Product Line	Agent	Marital Status	Single Brand Flag	
	Day of Week	Product Category		House-hold Size	Date First Operation	
	Day of Month	Exterior Color		Vehicles Owned		
	Season	Interior Color		Home Value		
	Holiday Flag	First Year		Own or Rent		

Automaker Sales

Fact Table

Actual Sale Price
MSRP
Options Price
Full Price
Dealer Add-ons
Dealer Credits
Dealer Invoice
Down Payment
Proceeds Finance

Facts: Actual Sale Price, MSRP, Options Price, Full Price, Dealer Add-ons, Dealer Credits, Dealer Invoice, Down Payment, Proceeds, Finance

Figure 10-2   Formation of the automaker sales fact table.

be at a higher level by product lines. Yet another analysis could be at even a higher level by product categories. The list of data items relating to the product dimension are as follows:

    Model name
    Model year
    Package styling
    Product line
    Product category
    Exterior color
    Interior color
    First model year

What can we do with all these data items in our dimensional model? All of these relate to the product in some way. We can, therefore, group all of these data items in one data structure or one relational table. We can call this table the product dimension table. The data items in the above list would all be attributes in this table.

Looking further into the information package diagram, we note the other business dimensions shown as column headings. In the case of the automaker sales information package diagram, these other business dimensions are dealer, customer demographics, payment method, and time. Just as we formed the product dimension table, we can form the remaining dimension tables of dealer, customer demographics, payment method, and time. The data items shown within each column would then be the attributes for each corresponding dimension table.

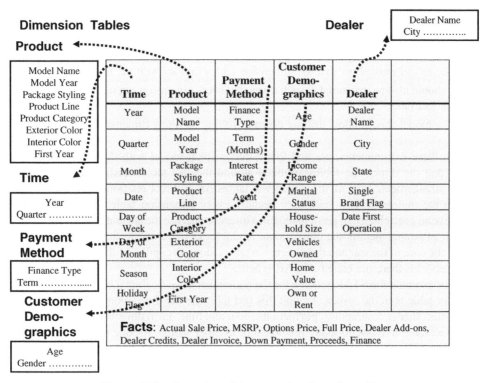

Figure 10-3   Formation of the automaker dimension tables.

Figure 10-3 puts all of this together. It shows how the various dimension tables are formed from the information package diagram. Look at the figure closely and see how each dimension table is formed.

So far we have formed the fact table and the dimension tables. How should these tables be arranged in the dimensional model? What are the relationships and how should we mark the relationships in the model? The dimensional model should primarily facilitate queries and analyses. What would be the types of queries and analyses? These would be queries and analyses where the metrics inside the fact table are analyzed across one or more dimensions using the dimension table attributes.

Let us examine a typical query against the automaker sales data. How much sales proceeds did the Jeep Cherokee, Year 2007 Model with standard options, generate in July 2007 at Big Sam Auto dealership for buyers who own their homes and who took 3-year leases, financed by Daimler-Chrysler Financing? We are analyzing actual sale price, MSRP, and full price. We are analyzing these facts along attributes in the various dimension tables. The attributes in the dimension tables act as constraints and filters in our queries. We also find that any or all of the attributes of each dimension table can participate in a query. Further, each dimension table has an equal chance to be part of a query.

Before we decide how to arrange the fact and dimension tables in our dimensional model and mark the relationships, let us go over what the dimensional model needs to achieve and what its purposes are. Here are some of the criteria for combining the tables into a dimensional model.

- The model should provide the best data access.
- The whole model must be query-centric.
- It must be optimized for queries and analyses.
- The model must show that the dimension tables interact with the fact table.
- It should also be structured in such a way that every dimension can interact equally with the fact table.
- The model should allow drilling down or rolling up along dimension hierarchies.

With these requirements, we find that a dimensional model with the fact table in the middle and the dimension tables arranged around the fact table satisfies the conditions. In this arrangement, each of the dimension tables has a direct relationship with the fact table in the middle. This is necessary because every dimension table with its attributes must have an even chance of participating in a query to analyze the attributes in the fact table.

Such an arrangement in the dimensional model looks like a star formation, with the fact table at the core of the star and the dimension tables along the spikes of the star. The dimensional model is therefore called a STAR schema.

Let us examine the STAR schema for the automaker sales as shown in Figure 10-4. The sales fact table is in the center. Around this fact table are the dimension tables of product, dealer, customer demographics, payment method, and time. Each dimension table is related to the fact table in a one-to-many relationship. In other words, for one row in the product dimension table, there are one or more related rows in the fact table.

E-R Modeling Versus Dimensional Modeling

We are familiar with data modeling for operational or OLTP systems. We adopt the Entity-Relationship (E-R) modeling technique to create the data models for these systems.

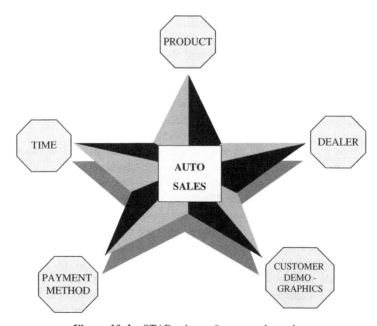

Figure 10-4   STAR schema for automaker sales.

◆ OLTP systems capture details of events or transactions

◆ OLTP systems focus on individual events

◆ An OLTP system is a window into micro-level transactions

◆ Picture at detail level necessary to run the business

◆ Suitable only for questions at transaction level

◆ Data consistency, non-redundancy, and efficient data
   storage critical

Entity-Relationship Modeling

Removes data redundancy
Ensures data consistency
Expresses microscopic
   relationships

Figure 10-5   E-R modeling for OLTP systems

Figure 10-5 lists the characteristics of OLTP systems and shows why E-R modeling is suitable for OLTP systems.

We have so far discussed the basics of the dimensional model and find that this model is most suitable for modeling the data for the data warehouse. Let us recapitulate the characteristics of the data warehouse information and review how dimensional modeling is suitable for this purpose. Study the features of dimensional modeling listed in Figure 10-6.

◆ DW meant to answer questions on overall process

◆ DW focus is on how managers view the business

◆ DW reveals business trends

◆ Information is centered around a business process

◆ Answers show how the business measures the process

◆ The measures to be studied in many ways along several
   business dimensions

Dimensional Modeling

Captures critical measures
Views along dimensions
Intuitive to business users

Figure 10-6   Dimensional modeling for the data warehouse.

Use of CASE Tools

Many case tools are available for data modeling. In Chapter 8, we introduced these tools and their features. You can use these tools for creating the logical schema and the physical schema for specific target database management systems (DBMSs).

You can use a case tool to define the tables, the attributes, and the relationships. You can assign the primary keys and indicate the foreign keys. You can form the entity-relationship diagrams. All of this is done very easily using graphical user interfaces and powerful drag-and-drop facilities. After creating an initial model, you may add fields, delete fields, change field characteristics, create new relationships, and make any number of revisions with utmost ease.

Another very useful function found in the case tools is the ability to forward-engineer the model and generate the schema for the target database system you need to work with. Forward-engineering is easily done with these case tools.

For modeling the data warehouse, we are interested in the dimensional modeling technique. Most of the existing vendors have expanded their modeling case tools to include dimensional modeling. You can create fact tables, dimension tables, and establish the relationships between each dimension table and the fact table. The result is a STAR schema for your model. Again, you can forward-engineer the dimensional STAR model into a relational schema for your chosen database management system.

THE STAR SCHEMA

Now that you have been introduced to the STAR schema, let us take a simple example and examine its characteristics in detail. Creating the STAR schema is the fundamental data design technique for the data warehouse. It is necessary to gain a good grasp of this technique.

Review of a Simple STAR Schema

We will take a simple STAR schema designed for order analysis. Assume this to be the schema for a manufacturing company and that the marketing department is interested in determining how they are doing with the orders received by the company.

Figure 10-7 shows this simple STAR schema. It consists of the orders fact table shown in the middle of the schema diagram. Surrounding the fact table are the four dimension tables of customer, salesperson, order date, and product. Let us begin to examine this STAR schema. Look at the structure from the point of view of the marketing department. The users in this department will analyze the orders using dollar amounts, cost, profit margin, and sold quantity. This information is found in the fact table of the structure. The users will analyze these measurements by breaking down the numbers in combinations by customer, salesperson, date, and product. All these dimensions along which the users will analyze are found in the structure. The STAR schema structure is a structure that can be easily understood by the users and with which they can comfortably work. The structure mirrors how the users normally view their critical measures along their business dimensions.

When you look at the order dollars, the STAR schema structure intuitively answers the questions of what, when, by whom, and to whom. From the STAR schema, the users can easily visualize the answers to these questions: For a given amount of dollars, what was

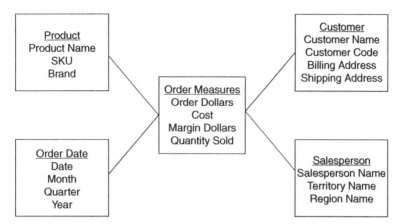

Figure 10-7   Simple STAR schema for orders analysis.

the product sold? Who was the customer? Which salesperson brought the order? When was the order placed?

When a query is made against the data warehouse, the results of the query are produced by combining or joining one of more dimension tables with the fact table. The joins are between the fact table and individual dimension tables. The relationship of a particular row in the fact table is with the rows in each dimension table. These individual relationships are clearly shown as the spikes of the STAR schema.

Take a simple query against the STAR schema. Let us say that the marketing department wants the quantity sold and order dollars for product *bigpart-1*, relating to customers in the

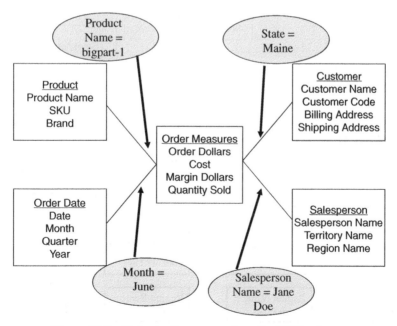

Figure 10-8   Understanding a query from the STAR schema.

state of *Maine*, obtained by salesperson *Jane Doe*, during the month of *June*. Figure 10-8 shows how this query is formulated from the STAR schema. Constraints and filters for queries are easily understood by looking at the STAR schema.

A common type of analysis is the drilling down of summary numbers to get at the details at the lower levels. Let us say that the marketing department has initiated a specific analysis by placing the following query: Show me the total quantity sold of product brand *big parts* to customers in the *northeast region for year 2008*. In the next step of the analysis, the marketing department now wants to drill down to the level of *quarters in 2008* for the *northeast region* for the same product brand, *big parts*. Next, the analysis goes down to the level of individual products in that brand. Finally, the analysis goes to the level of details by individual states in the northeast region. The users can easily discern all of this drill-down analysis by reviewing the STAR schema. Refer to Figure 10-9 to see how the drill-down is derived from the STAR schema.

Inside a Dimension Table

We have seen that a key component of the STAR schema is the set of dimension tables. These dimension tables represent the business dimensions along which the metrics are

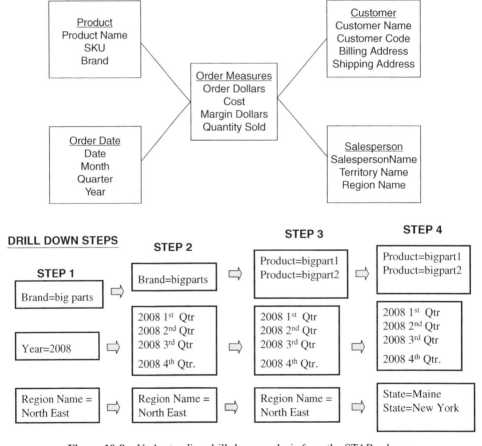

Figure 10-9   Understanding drill-down analysis from the STAR schema.

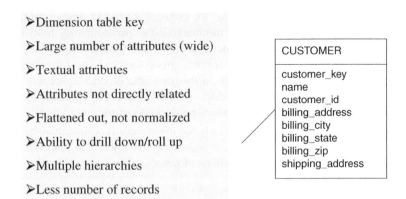

➤Dimension table key

➤Large number of attributes (wide)

➤Textual attributes

➤Attributes not directly related

➤Flattened out, not normalized

➤Ability to drill down/roll up

➤Multiple hierarchies

➤Less number of records

CUSTOMER
customer_key
name
customer_id
billing_address
billing_city
billing_state
billing_zip
shipping_address

Figure 10-10   Inside a dimension table.

analyzed. Let us look inside a dimension table and study its characteristics. See Figure 10-10 and review the following observations.

Dimension Table Key. The primary key of the dimension table uniquely identifies each row in the table.

Table is Wide. Typically, a dimension table has many columns or attributes. It is not uncommon for some dimension tables to have more than 50 attributes. Therefore, we say that the dimension table is wide. If you lay it out as a table with columns and rows, the table is spread out horizontally.

Textual Attributes. In the dimension table you will seldom find any numerical values used for calculations. The attributes in a dimension table are of textual format.

These attributes represent the textual descriptions of the components within the business dimensions. Users will compose their queries using these descriptors.

Attributes not Directly Related. Frequently you will find that some of the attributes in a dimension table are not directly related to the other attributes in the table. For example, package size is not directly related to product brand; nevertheless, package size and product brand could both be attributes of the product dimension table.

Not Normalized. The attributes in a dimension table are used over and over again in queries. An attribute is taken as a constraint in a query and applied directly to the metrics in the fact table. For efficient query performance, it is best if the query picks up an attribute from the dimension table and goes directly to the fact table and not through other intermediary tables. If you normalize the dimension table, you will be creating such intermediary tables and that will not be efficient. Therefore, a dimension table is flattened out, not normalized.

Drilling Down, Rolling Up. The attributes in a dimension table provide the ability to get to the details from higher levels of aggregation to lower levels of details. For example, the three attributes zip code, city, and state form a hierarchy. You may get the total sales by state, then drill down to total sales by city, and then by zip code. Going the other way, you may first get the totals by zip codes, and then roll up to totals by city and state.

Multiple Hierarchies. In the example of the customer dimension, there is a single hierarchy going up from individual customer to zip, city, and state. But dimension tables often provide for multiple hierarchies, so that drilling down may be performed along any of the multiple hierarchies. Take for example a product dimension table for a department store. In this business, the marketing department may have its way of classifying the products into product categories and product departments. On the other hand, the accounting department may group the products differently into categories and product departments. So in this case, the product dimension table will have the attributes of marketing–product–category, marketing–product–department, finance–product–category, and finance–product–department.

Fewer Records. A dimension table typically has fewer records or rows than the fact table. A product dimension table for an automaker may have just 500 rows. On the other hand, the fact table may contain millions of rows.

Inside the Fact Table

Let us now get into a fact table and examine the components. Remember this is where we keep the measurements. We may keep the details at the lowest possible level. In the department store fact table for sales analysis, we may keep the units sold by individual transactions at the cashier's checkout. Some fact tables may just contain summary data. These are called aggregate fact tables. Figure 10-11 lists the characteristics of a fact table. Let us review these characteristics.

Concatenated Key. A row in the fact table relates to a combination of rows from all the dimension tables. In this example of a fact table, you find quantity ordered as an attribute. Let us say the dimension tables are product, time, customer, and sales representative. For these dimension tables, assume that the lowest level in the dimension hierarchies are individual product, a calendar date, a specific customer, and a single sales representative. Then a single row in the fact table must relate to a particular product, a specific calendar date, a specific customer, and an individual sales representative. This means the row in the fact table must be identified by the primary keys of these four dimension tables. Thus, the primary key of the fact table must be the concatenation of the primary keys of all the dimension tables.

Data Grain. This is an important characteristic of the fact table. As we know, the data grain is the level of detail for the measurements or metrics. In this example, the metrics are at the detailed level. The quantity ordered relates to the quantity of a particular product on a single order, on a certain date, for a specific customer, and procured by a

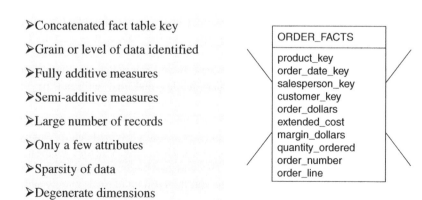

❯Concatenated fact table key

❯Grain or level of data identified

❯Fully additive measures

❯Semi-additive measures

❯Large number of records

❯Only a few attributes

❯Sparsity of data

❯Degenerate dimensions

ORDER_FACTS

product_key
order_date_key
salesperson_key
customer_key
order_dollars
extended_cost
margin_dollars
quantity_ordered
order_number
order_line

Figure 10-11   Inside a fact table.

specific sales representative. If we keep the quantity ordered as the quantity of a specific product for each month, then the data grain is different and is at a higher level.

Fully Additive Measures. Let us look at the attributes *order_dollars, extended_cost*, and *quantity_ordered*. Each of these relates to a particular product on a certain date for a specific customer procured by an individual sales representative. In a certain query, let us say that the user wants the totals for the particular product on a certain date, not for a specific customer, but for customers in a particular state. Then we need to find all the rows in the fact table relating to all the customers in that state and add the *order_dollars, extended_cost*, and *quantity_ordered* to come up with the totals. The values of these attributes may be summed up by simple addition. Such measures are known as fully additive measures. Aggregation of fully additive measures is done by simple addition. When we run queries to aggregate measures in the fact table, we will have to make sure that these measures are fully additive. Otherwise, the aggregated numbers may not show the correct totals.

Semiadditive Measures. Consider the margin_dollars attribute in the fact table. For example, if the *order_dollars* is 120 and *extended_cost* is 100, the *margin_percentage* is 20. This is a calculated metric derived from the *order_dollars* and *extended_cost*. If you are aggregating the numbers from rows in the fact table relating to all the customers in a particular state, you cannot add up the *margin_percentages* from all these rows and come up with the aggregated number. Derived attributes such as *margin_percentage* are not additive. They are known as semiadditive measures. Distinguish semiadditive measures from fully additive measures when you perform aggregations in queries.

Table Deep, Not Wide. Typically a fact table contains fewer attributes than a dimension table. Usually, there are about 10 attributes or less. But the number of records in a fact table is very large in comparison. Take a very simplistic example of 3 products, 5 customers, 30 days, and 10 sales representatives represented as rows in the dimension tables. Even in this example, the number of fact table rows will be 4500, very large in comparison with the dimension table rows. If you lay the fact table out as a two-dimensional table, you will note that the fact table is narrow, with a small number of columns, but very deep, with a large number of rows.

Sparse Data. We have said that a single row in the fact table relates to a particular product, a specific calendar date, a specific customer, and an individual sales representative. In other words, for a particular product, a specific calendar date, a specific customer, and an individual sales representative, there is a corresponding row in the fact table. What happens when the date represents a closed holiday and no orders are received and processed? The fact table rows for such dates will not have values for the measures. Also, there could be other combinations of dimension table attributes, values for which the fact table rows will have null measures. Do we need to keep such rows with null measures in the fact table? There is no need for this. Therefore, it is important to realize this type of sparse data and understand that the fact table could have gaps.

Degenerate Dimensions. Look closely at the example of the fact table. You find the attributes of *order_number* and *order_line*. These are not measures or metrics or facts. Then why are these attributes in the fact table? When you pick up attributes for the dimension tables and the fact tables from operational systems, you will be left with some data elements in the operational systems that are neither facts nor strictly dimension attributes. Examples of such attributes are reference numbers like order numbers, invoice numbers, order line numbers, and so on. These attributes are useful in some types of analyses. For example, you may be looking for average number of products per order. Then you will have to relate the products to the order number to calculate the average. Attributes such as *order_number* and *order_line* in the example are called degenerate dimensions and these are kept as attributes of the fact table.

The Factless Fact Table

Apart from the concatenated primary key, a fact table contains facts or measures. Let us say we are building a fact table to track the attendance of students. For analyzing student attendance, the possible dimensions are student, course, date, room, and professor. The attendance may be affected by any of these dimensions. When you want to mark the attendance relating to a particular course, date, room, and professor, what is the measurement you come up with for recording the event? In the fact table row, the attendance will be indicated with the number *one*. Every fact table row will contain the number *one* as attendance. If so, why bother to record the number *one* in every fact table row? There is no need to do this. The very presence of a corresponding fact table row could indicate the attendance. This type of situation arises when the fact table represents events. Such fact tables really do not need to contain facts. They are *factless* fact tables. Figure 10-12 shows a typical factless fact table.

Data Granularity

By now, we know that granularity represents the level of detail in the fact table. If the fact table is at the lowest grain, then the facts or metrics are at the lowest possible level at which they could be captured from the operational systems. What are the advantages of keeping the fact table at the lowest grain? What is the trade-off?

When you keep the fact table at the lowest grain, users can drill down to the lowest level of detail from the data warehouse without the need to go to the operational systems themselves. Base level fact tables must be at the natural lowest levels of all corresponding dimensions. By doing this, queries for drill down and roll up can be performed efficiently.

What then are the natural lowest levels of the corresponding dimensions? In the example with the dimensions of product, date, customer, and sales representative, the natural lowest levels are an individual product, a specific individual date, an individual customer, and an

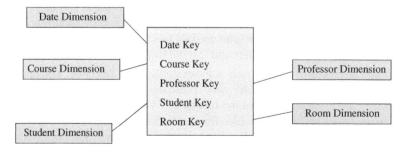

Measures or facts are represented in a fact table. However, there are business events or coverage that could be represented in a fact table, although no measures or facts are associated with these.

Tracks the attendance although no measured facts in the fact table

Figure 10-12   A factless fact table.

individual sales representative, respectively. So, in this case, a single row in the fact table should contain measurements at the lowest level for an individual product, ordered on a specific date, relating to an individual customer, and procured by an individual sales representative.

Let us say we want to add a new attribute of district in the sales representative dimension. This change will not warrant any changes in the fact table rows because these are already at the lowest level of individual sales representative. This is a "graceful" change because all the old queries will continue to run without any changes. Similarly, let us assume we want to add a new dimension of promotion. Now you will have to recast the fact table rows to include promotion dimensions. Still, the fact table grain will be at the lowest level.

Even here, the old queries will still run without any changes. This is also a "graceful" change. Fact tables at the lowest grain facilitate "graceful" extensions.

But we have to pay the price in terms of storage and maintenance for the fact table at the lowest grain. Lowest grain necessarily means large numbers of fact table rows. In practice, however, we build aggregate fact tables to support queries looking for summary numbers.

There are two more advantages of granular fact tables. Granular fact tables serve as natural destinations for current operational data that may be extracted frequently from operational systems. Further, the more recent data mining applications need details at the lowest grain. Data warehouses feed data into data mining applications.

STAR SCHEMA KEYS

Figure 10-13 illustrates how the keys are formed for the dimension and fact tables.

Primary Keys

Each row in a dimension table is identified by a unique value of an attribute designated as the primary key of the dimension. In a product dimension table, the primary key identifies each product uniquely. In the customer dimension table, the customer number identifies each

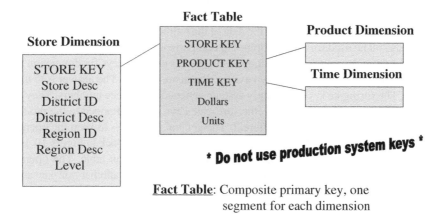

Fact Table: Composite primary key, one segment for each dimension

Dimension Table: Generated primary key

Figure 10-13   The STAR schema keys.

customer uniquely. Similarly, in the sales representative dimension table, the social security number of the sales representative identifies each sales representative.

We have picked these out as possible candidate keys for the dimension tables. Now let us consider some implications of these candidate keys. Let us assume that the product code in the operational system is an 8-position code, two of which positions indicate the code of the warehouse where the product is normally stored, and two other positions denote the product category. Let us see what happens if we use the operational system product code as the primary key for the product dimension table.

The data warehouse contains historic data. Assume that the product code gets changed in the middle of a year, because the product is now stored in a different warehouse of the company. So we have to change the product code in the data warehouse. If the product code is the primary key of the product dimension table, then the newer data for the same product will reside in the data warehouse with different key values. This could cause problems if we need to aggregate the data from before the change with the data from after the change to the product code. What really has caused this problem? The problem is the result of our decision to use the operational system key as the key for the dimension table.

Surrogate Keys

How do we resolve the problem faced in the previous section? Can we use production system keys as primary keys for dimension tables? If not, what are the other candidate keys?

There are two general principles to be applied when choosing primary keys for dimension tables. The first principle is derived from the problem caused when the product began to be stored in a different warehouse. In other words, the product key in the operational system has built-in meanings. Some positions in the operational system product key indicate the warehouse and some other positions in the key indicate the product category. These are built-in meanings in the key. The first principle to follow is: avoid built-in meanings in the primary key of the dimension tables.

In some companies, a few of the customers are no longer listed with the companies. They could have left their respective companies many years ago. It is possible that the customer numbers of such discontinued customers are reassigned to new customers. Now, let us say we had used the operational system customer key as the primary key for the customer dimension table. We will have a problem because the same customer number could relate to the data for the newer customer and also to the data of the retired customer. The data of the retired customer may still be used for aggregations and comparisons by city and state. Therefore, the second principle is: do not use production system keys as primary keys for dimension tables.

What then should we use as primary keys for dimension tables? The answer is to use surrogate keys. The surrogate keys are simply system-generated sequence numbers. They do not have any built-in meanings. Of course, the surrogate keys will be mapped to the production system keys. Nevertheless, they are different. The general practice is to keep the operational system keys as additional attributes in the dimension tables. Refer back to Figure 10-13. The STORE KEY is the surrogate primary key for the store dimension table. The operational system primary key for the store reference table may be kept as just another non-key attribute in the store dimension table.

Foreign Keys

Each dimension table is in a one-to-many relationship with the central fact table. So the primary key of each dimension table must be a foreign key in the fact table. If there are four dimension tables of product, date, customer, and sales representative, then the primary key of each of these four tables must be present in the orders fact table as foreign keys.

Let us reexamine the primary keys for the fact tables. There are three options:

1. *A single compound primary key whose length is the total length of the keys of the individual dimension tables.* Under this option, in addition to the compound primary key, the foreign keys must also be kept in the fact table as additional attributes. This option increases the size of the fact table.

2. *A concatenated primary key that is the concatenation of all the primary keys of the dimension tables.* Here you need not keep the primary keys of the dimension tables as additional attributes to serve as foreign keys. The individual parts of the primary keys themselves will serve as the foreign keys.

3. *A generated primary key independent of the keys of the dimension tables.* In addition to the generated primary key, the foreign keys must also be kept in the fact table as additional attributes. This option also increases the size of the fact table.

In practice, option (2) is used in most fact tables. This option enables you to easily relate the fact table rows with the dimension table rows.

ADVANTAGES OF THE STAR SCHEMA

When you look at the STAR schema, you find that it is simply a relational model with a one-to-many relationship between each dimension table and the fact table. What is so special about the arrangement of the STAR schema? Why is it declared to be eminently suitable for the data warehouse? What are the reasons for its wide use and success in providing optimization for processing queries?

Although the STAR schema is a relational model, it is not a normalized model. The dimension tables are purposely denormalized. This is a basic difference between the STAR schema and relational schemas for OLTP systems.

Before we discuss some very significant advantages of the STAR schema, we need to be aware that strict adherence to this arrangement is not always the best option. For example, if customer is one of the dimensions and if the enterprise has a very large number of customers, a denormalized customer dimension table is not desirable. A large dimension table may increase the size of the fact table correspondingly.

However, the advantages far outweigh any shortcomings. So, let us go over the advantages of the STAR schema.

Easy for Users to Understand

Users of OLTP systems interact with the applications through predefined GUI screens or preset query templates. There is practically no need for the users to understand the data structures behind the scenes. The data structures and the database schema remain in the realm of the IT professionals.

Users of decision support systems such as data warehouses are different. Here the users themselves will formulate queries. When they interact with the data warehouse through third-party query tools, the users should know what to ask for. They must gain a familiarity with what data is available to them in the data warehouse. They must have an understanding of the data structures and how the various pieces are associated with one another in the overall scheme. They must comprehend the connections without difficulty.

The STAR schema reflects exactly how the users think and need data for querying and analysis. They think in terms of significant business metrics. The fact table contains the metrics. The users think in terms of business dimensions for analyzing the metrics. The dimension tables contain the attributes along which the users normally query and analyze. When you explain to the users that the units of product A are stored in the fact table and point out the relationship of this piece of data to each dimension table, the users readily understand the connections. That is because the STAR schema defines the join paths in exactly the same way users normally visualize the relationships. The STAR schema is intuitively understood by the users.

Try to walk a user through the relational schema of an OLTP system. For them to understand the connections, you will have to take them through a maze of normalized tables, sometimes passing through several tables, one by one, to get even the smallest result set. The STAR schema emerges as a clear winner because of its simplicity. Users understand the structures and the connections very easily.

The STAR schema has definite advantages after implementation. However, the advantages even in the development stage cannot be overlooked. Because the users understand the STAR schema so very well, it is easy to use it as a vehicle for communicating with the users during the development of the data warehouse.

Optimizes Navigation

In a database schema, what is the purpose of the relationships or connections among the data entities? The relationships are used to go from one table to another for obtaining the information you are looking for. The relationships provide the ability to navigate through the database. You hop from table to table using the join paths.

If the join paths are numerous and convoluted, your navigation through the database gets difficult and slow. On the other hand, if the join paths are simple and straightforward, your navigation is optimized and becomes faster.

A major advantage of the STAR schema is that it optimizes the navigation through the database. Even when you are looking for a query result that is seemingly complex, the navigation is still simple and straightforward. Let us look at an example and understand how this works. Look at Figure 10-14 showing a STAR schema for analyzing defects in automobiles. Assume you are the service manager at an automobile dealership selling GM automobiles. You noticed a high incidence of chipped white paint on the Corvettes in January 2009. You need a tool to analyze such defects, determine the underlying causes, and resolve the problems.

In the STAR schema, the number of defects is kept as metrics in the middle as part of the defects fact table. The time dimension contains the model year. The component dimension has part information; for example, pearl white paint. The problem dimension carries the types of problems; for example, chipped paint. The product dimension contains the make, model, and trim package of the automobiles. The supplier dimension contains data on the suppliers of parts.

Now see how easy it is to determine the supplier causing the chipped paint on the pearl white Corvettes. Look at the four arrows pointing to the fact table from the four dimension tables. These arrows show how you will navigate to the rows in the fact table by isolating the Corvette from the product dimension, chipped paint from the problem dimension, pearl white paint from the component dimension, and January 2009 from the time dimension. From the fact table, the navigation goes directly to the supplier dimension to isolate the supplier causing the problem.

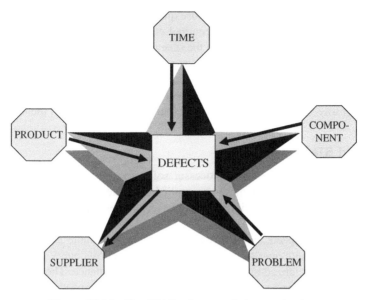

Figure 10-14   The STAR schema optimizes navigation.

Most Suitable for Query Processing

We have already mentioned a few times that the STAR schema is a query-centric structure. This means that the STAR schema is most suitable for query processing. Let us see how this is true.

Let us form a simple query on the STAR schema for the order analysis shown in Figure 10-7. What is the total extended cost of product A sold to customers in San Francisco during January 2009? This is a three-dimensional query. What should be the characteristics of the data structure or schema if it is to be most suitable for processing this query? The final result, which is the total extended cost, will come from the rows in the fact table. But from which rows? The answer is those rows relating to product A, relating to customers in San Francisco, and relating to January 2009.

Let us see how the query will be processed. First, select the rows from the customer dimension table where the city is San Francisco. Then, from the fact table, select only those rows that are related to these customer dimension rows. This is the first result set of rows from the fact tables. Next, select the rows in the Time dimension table where the month is January 2009. Select from the first result set only those rows that are related to these time dimension rows. This is now the second result set of fact table rows. Move on to the next dimension of product. Select the rows in the product dimension table where the product is product A. Select from the second result only those rows that are related to the selected product dimension rows. You now have the final result of fact table rows. Add up the extended cost to get the total.

Irrespective of the number of dimensions that participate in the query and irrespective of the complexity of the query, every query is simply executed first by selecting rows from the dimension tables using the filters based on the query parameters and then finding the corresponding fact table rows. This is possible because of the simple and straightforward join paths and because of the very arrangement of the STAR schema. There is no intermediary maze to be navigated to reach the fact table from the dimension tables.

Another important aspect of data warehouse queries is the ability to drill down or roll up. Let us quickly run through a drill-down scenario. Let us say we have queried and obtained the total extended cost for all the customers in the state of California. The result comes from the set of fact table rows. Then we want to drill down and look at the results by zip code ranges. This is obtained by making a further selection from the selected fact table rows relating to the chosen zip code ranges. Drill down is a process of further selection of the fact table rows. Going the other way, rolling up is a process of expanding the selection of the fact table rows.

STARjoin and STARindex

The STAR schema allows the query processor software to use better execution plans. It enables specific performance schemes to be applied to queries. The STAR schema arrangement is eminently suitable for special performance techniques such as the STARjoin and the STARindex.

STARjoin is a high-speed, single-pass, parallelizable, multitable join. It can join more than two tables in a single operation. This special scheme boosts query performance.

STARindex is a specialized index to accelerate join performance. These are indexes created on one or more foreign keys of the fact table. These indexes speed up joins between the dimension tables and the fact table.

Chapter 18 deals with the physical design and indexing methods for the data warehouse.

STAR SCHEMA: EXAMPLES

In this section we provide four examples of STAR schema relating to four different types of businesses. In each case, notice the following carefully and understand the STAR schema:

- The metrics or facts being analyzed
- The business dimensions used for analysis
- The hierarchy available within each dimension for drill down and roll up
- The primary and foreign keys

Video Rental

See Figure 10-15.

Supermarket

See Figure 10-16.

Wireless Phone Service

See Figure 10-17.

Auction Company

See Figure 10-18.

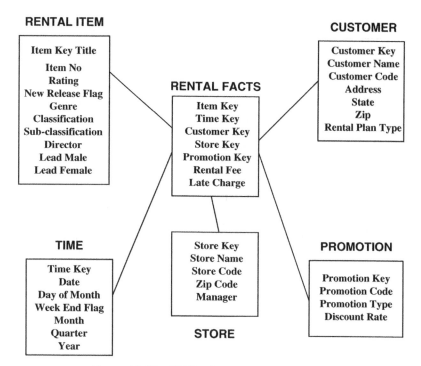

Figure 10-15   STAR schema example: video rental.

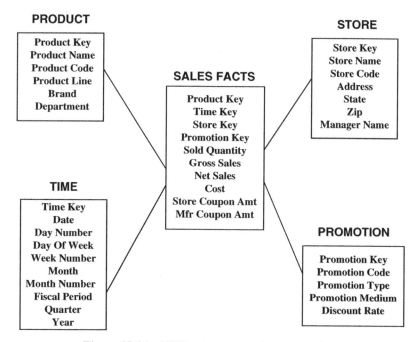

Figure 10-16   STAR schema example: supermarket.

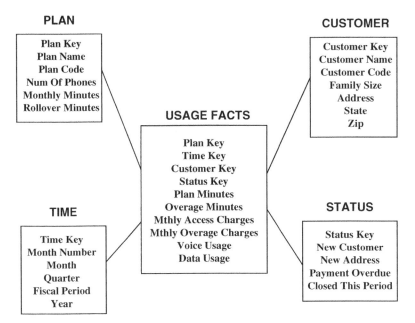

Figure 10-17 STAR schema example: wireless phone service.

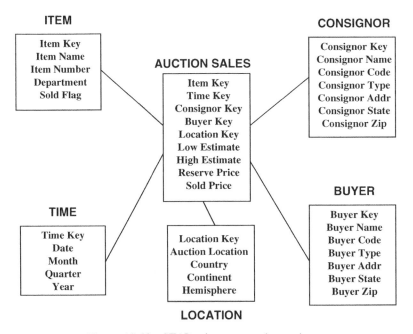

Figure 10-18 STAR schema example: auction company.

CHAPTER SUMMARY

• The components of the dimensional model are derived from the information packages in the requirements definition.

- The entity-relationship modeling technique is not suitable for data warehouses; the dimensional modeling technique is appropriate.
- The STAR schema used for data design is a relational model consisting of fact and dimension tables.
- The fact table contains the business metrics or measurements; the dimension tables contain the business dimensions. Hierarchies within each dimension table are used for drilling down to lower levels of data.
- STAR schema advantages are that it is easy for users to understand optimizes navigation, is most suitable for query processing, and enables specific performance schemes.

REVIEW QUESTIONS

1. Discuss the major design issues that need to be addressed before proceeding with the data design.

2. Why is the entity-relationship modeling technique not suitable for the data warehouse? How is dimensional modeling different?

3. What is the STAR schema? What are the component tables?

4. A dimension table is wide; the fact table is deep. Explain.

5. What are hierarchies and categories as applicable to a dimension table?

6. Differentiate between fully additive and semiadditive measures.

7. Explain the sparse nature of the data in the fact table.

8. Describe the composition of the primary keys for the dimension and fact tables.

9. Discuss data granularity in a data warehouse.

10. Name any three advantages of the STAR schema. Can you think of any disadvantages of the STAR schema?

EXERCISES

1. Match the columns:

1. information package	A. enable drill down
2. fact table	B. reference numbers
3. case tools	C. level of detail
4. dimension hierarchies	D. users understand easily
5. dimension table	E. semiadditive
6. degenerate dimensions	F. STAR schema components
7. profit margin percentage	G. used for dimensional modeling
8. data granularity	H. dimension attribute
9. STAR schema	I. contains metrics
10. customer demographics	J. wide

2. Refer back to the information package given for a hotel chain in Chapter 5 (Fig. 5.6). Use this information package and design a STAR schema.

3. What is a factless fact table? Design a simple STAR schema with a factless fact table to track patients in a hospital by diagnostic procedures and time.

4. You are the data design specialist on the data warehouse project team for a manufacturing company. Design a STAR schema to track the production quantities. Production quantities are normally analyzed along the business dimensions of product, time, parts used, production facility, and production run. State your assumptions.

5. In a STAR schema to track the shipments for a distribution company, the following dimension tables are found: (1) time, (2) customer ship-to, (3) ship-from, (4) product, (5) type of deal, and (6) mode of shipment. Review these dimensions and list the possible attributes for each of the dimension tables. Also, designate a primary key for each table.

CHAPTER 11

DIMENSIONAL MODELING: ADVANCED TOPICS

CHAPTER OBJECTIVES

- Discuss and get a good grasp of slowly changing dimensions
- Understand large dimensions and how to deal with them
- Examine the snowflake schema in detail
- Learn about aggregate tables and determine when to use them
- Completely survey families of STARS and their applications

From the previous chapter, you have learned the basics of dimensional modeling. You know that the STAR schema is composed of the fact table in the middle surrounded by the dimension tables. Although this is a good visual representation, it is still a relational model in which each dimension table is in a parent-child relationship with the fact table. The primary key of each dimension table, therefore, is a foreign key in the fact table.

You have also grasped the nature of the attributes within the fact table and the dimension tables. You have understood the advantages of the STAR schema in decision support systems. The STAR schema is easy for users to understand; it optimizes navigation through the data warehouse content and is most suitable for query-centric environments.

Our study of dimensional modeling will not be complete until we consider some more topics. In the STAR schema, the dimension tables enable analysis in many different ways. We need to explore the dimension tables in further detail. How about summarizing the metrics and storing aggregate numbers in additional fact tables? How much precalculated aggregation is necessary? The STAR schema is a denormalized design. Does this result in too much redundancy and inefficiency? If so, is there an alternative approach?

Let us now move beyond the basics of dimensional modeling and consider additional features and issues. Let us discuss the pertinent advanced topics and extend our study further.

Data Warehousing Fundamentals for IT Professionals, Second Edition. By Paulraj Ponniah
Copyright © 2010 John Wiley & Sons, Inc.

UPDATES TO THE DIMENSION TABLES

Going back to Figure 10-4 of the previous chapter, you see the STAR schema for automaker sales. The fact table *Auto Sales* contains the measurements or metrics such as *Actual Sale Price, Options Price*, and so on. Over time, what happens to the fact table? Every day as more and more sales take place, more and more rows get added to the fact table. Over time the number of rows in the fact table continues to grow. Very rarely are the rows in a fact table updated with changes. Even when there are adjustments to the prior numbers, these are also processed as additional adjustment rows and added to the fact table.

Now consider the dimension tables. Compared to the fact table, the dimension tables are more stable and less volatile. However, unlike the fact table, which changes through an increase in the number of rows, a dimension table does not change just through the increase in the number of rows, but also through changes to the attributes themselves.

Look at the product dimension table. Every year, rows are added as new models become available. But what about the attributes within the product dimension table? If a particular product is moved to a different product category, then the corresponding values must be changed in the product dimension table. Let us examine the types of changes that affect dimension tables and discuss the ways for dealing with these types.

Slowly Changing Dimensions

In the above example, we mentioned a change to the product dimension table because the product category for a product was changed. Consider the customer demographics dimension table. What happens when a customer's status changes from rental home to own home? The corresponding row in that dimension table must be changed. Next, look at the payment method dimension table. When finance type changes for one of the payment methods, this change must be reflected in the payment method dimension table.

From the consideration of the changes to the dimension tables, we can derive the following principles:

- Most dimensions are generally constant over time.
- Many dimensions, though not constant over time, change slowly.
- The product key of the source record does not change.
- The description and other attributes change slowly over time.
- In the source OLTP systems, the new values overwrite the old ones.
- Overwriting of dimension table attributes is not always the appropriate option in a data warehouse.
- The ways changes are made to the dimension tables depend on the types of changes and what information must be preserved in the data warehouse.

Techniques for making the changes fall into three distinct types. Data warehousing practitioners have come up with different techniques for applying the changes. They have also given names to these three types of dimension table changes. Yes, your guess in right. The given names are type 1 changes, type 2 changes, and type 3 changes.

We will study these three types by using a simple STAR schema for tracking orders for a distributor of industrial products, as shown in Figure 11-1. This STAR schema consists of

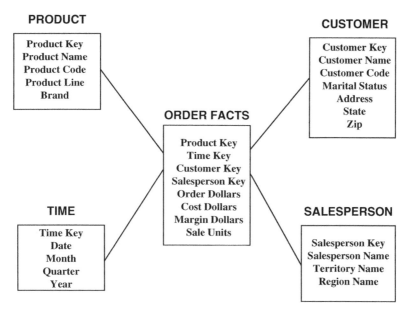

PRODUCT

| Product Key |
| Product Name |
| Product Code |
| Product Line |
| Brand |

CUSTOMER

| Customer Key |
| Customer Name |
| Customer Code |
| Marital Status |
| Address |
| State |
| Zip |

ORDER FACTS

| Product Key |
| Time Key |
| Customer Key |
| Salesperson Key |
| Order Dollars |
| Cost Dollars |
| Margin Dollars |
| Sale Units |

TIME

| Time Key |
| Date |
| Month |
| Quarter |
| Year |

SALESPERSON

| Salesperson Key |
| Salesperson Name |
| Territory Name |
| Region Name |

Figure 11-1   STAR schema for order tracking.

the fact table and four dimension tables. Let us assume some changes to these dimensions and review the techniques for applying the changes to the dimension tables.

Type 1 Changes: Correction of Errors

Nature of Type 1 Changes   These changes usually relate to the corrections of errors in the source systems. For example, suppose a spelling error in the customer name is corrected to read Michael Romano from the erroneous entry of Michel Romano, Also, suppose the customer name for another customer is changed from Kristin Daniels to Kristin Samuelson, and the marital status changed from single to married.

Consider the changes to the customer name in both cases. There is no need to preserve the old values. In the case of Michael Romano, the old name is erroneous and needs to be discarded. When a user needs to find all the orders from Michael Romano, he or she will use the correct name. The same principles apply to the change in customer name for Kristin Samuelson.

But the change in the marital status is slightly different. This change can be handled in the same way as the change in customer name only if that change is a correction of error. Otherwise, you will cause problems when the users want to analyze orders by marital status.

Here are the general principles for type 1 changes:

- Usually, the changes relate to correction of errors in source systems.
- Sometimes the change in the source system has no significance.
- The old value in the source system needs to be discarded.
- The change in the source system need not be preserved in the data warehouse.

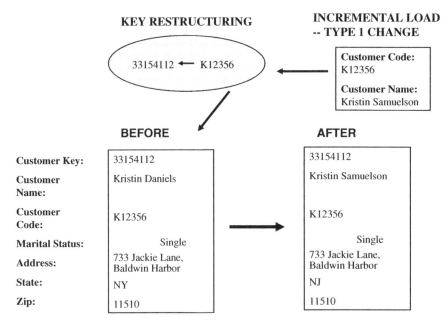

Figure 11-2   The method for applying type 1 changes.

Applying Type 1 Changes to the Data Warehouse   Figure 11-2 shows the application of type 1 changes to the customer dimension table. The method for applying type I changes is:

- Overwrite the attribute value in the dimension table row with the new value.
- The old value of the attribute is not preserved.
- No other changes are made in the dimension table row.
- The key of this dimension table or any other key values are not affected.
- This type is easiest to implement.

Type 2 Changes: Preservation of History

Nature of Type 2 Changes   Go back to the change in the marital status for Kristin Samuelson. Assume that in your data warehouse one of the essential requirements is to track orders by marital status in addition to tracking by other attributes. If the change to marital status happened on October 1, 2008, all orders from Kristin Samuelson before that date must be included under marital status: single, and all orders on or after October 1, 2008 should be included under marital status: married.

What exactly is needed in this case? In the data warehouse, you must have a way of separating the orders for the customer so that the orders before and after that date can be added up separately.

Now let us add another change to the information about Kristin Samuelson. Assume that she moved to a new address in California from her old address in New York on November 1, 2008. If it is a requirement in your data warehouse that you must be able to track orders by state, then this change must also be treated like the change to marital status. Any orders prior to November 1, 2008 will go under the state: NY.

The types of changes we have discussed for marital status and customer address are type 2 changes. Here are the general principles for this type of change:

- They usually relate to true changes in source systems.
- There is a need to preserve history in the data warehouse.
- This type of change partitions the history in the data warehouse.
- Every change for the same attribute must be preserved.

Applying Type 2 Changes to the Data Warehouse   Figure 11-3 shows the application of type 2 changes to the customer dimension table. The method for applying type 2 changes is:

- Add a new dimension table row with the new value of the changed attribute.
- An effective date field may be included in the dimension table.
- There are no changes to the original row in the dimension table.
- The key of the original row is not affected.
- The new row is inserted with a new surrogate key.

Type 3 Changes: Tentative Soft Revisions

Nature of Type 3 Changes   Almost all the usual changes to dimension values are either type 1 or type 2 changes. Of these two, type 1 changes are more common. Type 2 changes preserve the history. When you apply a type 2 change on a certain date, that date

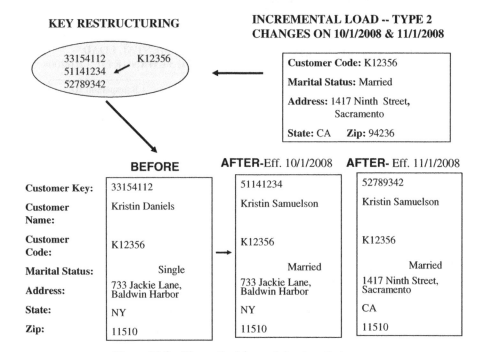

Figure 11-3   The method for applying type 2 changes.

is a cut-off point. In the above case of change to marital status on October 1, 2008, that date is the cut-off date. Any orders from the customer prior to that date fall into the older orders group; orders on or after that date fall into the newer orders group. An order for this customer has to fall in one or the other group; it cannot be counted in both groups for any period of time.

What if you have the need to count the orders on or after the cut-off date in both groups during a certain period after the cut-off date? You cannot handle this change as a type 2 change. Sometimes, though rarely, there is a need to track both the old and new values of changed attributes for a certain period, in both forward and backward directions. These types of changes are type 3 changes.

Type 3 changes are tentative or soft changes. An example will make this clearer. Assume your marketing department is contemplating a realignment of the territorial assignments for salespersons. Before making a permanent realignment, they want to count the orders in two ways: according to the current territorial alignment and also according to the proposed realignment. This type of provisional or tentative change is a type 3 change.

As an example, let us say you want to move salesperson Robert Smith from the New England territory to the Chicago territory with the ability to trace his orders in both territories. You need to track all orders through Robert Smith in both territories.

Here are the general principles for type 3 changes:

- They usually relate to "soft" or tentative changes in the source systems.
- There is a need to keep track of history with old and new values of the changed attribute.
- They are used to compare performances across the transition.
- They provide the ability to track forward and backward.

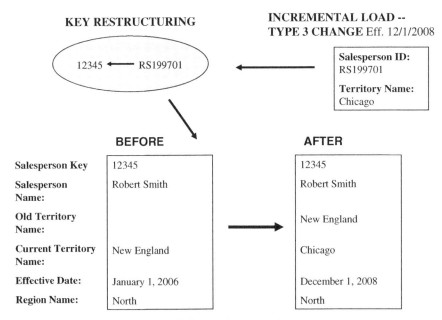

Figure 11-4 Applying type 3 changes.

Applying Type 3 Changes to the Data Warehouse   Figure 11-4 shows the application of type 3 changes to the customer dimension table. The methods for applying type 3 changes are:

- Add an "old" field in the dimension table for the affected attribute.
- Push down the existing value of the attribute from the "current" field to the "old" field.
- Keep the new value of the attribute in the "current" field.
- Also, you may add a "current" effective date field for the attribute.
- The key of the row is not affected.
- No new dimension row is needed.
- The existing queries will seamlessly switch to the "current" value.
- Any queries that need to use the "old" value must be revised accordingly.
- The technique works best for one "soft" change at a time.
- If there is a succession of changes, more sophisticated techniques must be devised.

MISCELLANEOUS DIMENSIONS

Having considered the types of changes to dimension attributes and the ways to handle the dimension changes in the data warehouse, let us now turn our attention to a few other important issues about dimensions. One issue relates to dimension tables that are very wide and very deep.

In our earlier discussion, we had assumed that dimension attributes do not change too rapidly. If the change is a type 2 change, you know that you have to create another row with the new value of the attribute. If the value of the attribute changes again, then you create another row with the newer value. What if the value changes too many times or too rapidly? Such a dimension is no longer a slowly changing dimension. What must you do about a not-so-slowly-changing dimension? We will complete our discussion of dimensions by considering such relevant issues.

Large Dimensions

You may consider a dimension large based on two factors. A large dimension is very deep; that is, the dimension has a very large number of rows. A large dimension may also be very wide; that is, the dimension may have a large number of attributes or columns. In either case, you may declare the dimension large. There are special considerations for large dimensions. You may have to attend to populating large-dimension tables in a special way. You may want to separate out some mini-dimensions from a large dimension. We will take a simple STAR schema designed for order analysis. Assume this to be the schema for a manufacturing company and that the marketing department is interested in determining how they are making progress with the orders received by the company.

In a data warehouse, typically the customer and product dimensions are likely to be large. Whenever an enterprise deals with the general public, the customer dimension is expected to be gigantic. The customer dimension of a national retail chain can approach the size of the number of U.S. households. Such customer dimension tables may have as many as 100 million rows. Next on the scale, the number of dimension table rows of companies in telecommunications and travel industries may also run in the millions. Having 10 or 20 million customer rows is not uncommon. The product dimension of large retailers is also quite huge.

Here are some typical features of large customer and product dimensions:

Customer
- Huge—in the range of 20 million rows
- Easily up to 150 dimension attributes
- Can have multiple hierarchies

Product
- Sometimes as many as 100,000 product variations
- Can have more than 100 dimension attributes
- Can have multiple hierarchies

Large dimensions call for special considerations. Because of the sheer size, many data warehouse functions involving large dimensions may be slow and inefficient. You need to address the following issues by using effective design methods, by choosing proper indexes, and by applying other optimizing techniques:

- Populating very large dimension tables
- Browse performance of unconstrained dimensions, especially where the cardinality of the attributes is low
- Browsing time for cross-constrained values of the dimension attributes
- Inefficiencies in fact table queries when large dimensions need to be used
- Additional rows created to handle type 2 slowly changing dimensions

Multiple Hierarchies   Large dimensions usually possess another distinct characteristic. They tend to have multiple hierarchies. Take the example of the product dimension for a large retailer. One set of attributes may form the hierarchy for the marketing department. Users from that department use these attributes to drill down or up. In the same way, the finance department may need to use its own set of attributes from the same product dimension to drill down or up. Figure 11-5 shows multiple hierarchies within a large product dimension.

Rapidly Changing Dimensions

As you know, when you deal with a type 2 change, you create an additional dimension table row with the new value of the changed attribute. By doing so, you are able to preserve the history. If the same attribute changes a second time, you create one more dimension table row with the latest value.

Most product dimensions change very infrequently, maybe once or twice a year. If the number of rows in such a product dimension is about 100,000 or so, using the approach of creating additional rows with the new values of the attributes is easily manageable. Even if the number of rows is in the range of several thousands, the approach of applying the changes as type 2 changes is still quite feasible.

However, consider another dimension, such as the customer dimension. Here the number of rows tends to be large, sometimes in the range of even a million or more rows. If the

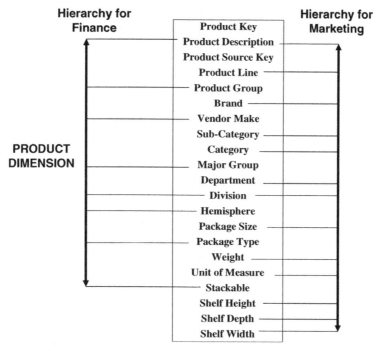

Figure 11-5   Multiple hierarchies in a large product dimension.

attributes of a large number of rows change, but change infrequently, the type 2 approach is not too difficult. But significant attributes in a customer dimension may change many times in a year. Rapidly changing large dimensions can be too problematic for the type 2 approach. The dimension table could be littered with a very large number of additional rows created every time there is an incremental load.

Before rushing to explore other options for handling rapidly changing large dimensions, deal with each large dimension individually. The type 2 approach is still good in a STAR schema design. Here are some reasons why the type 2 approach could work in many cases for rapidly changing dimensions:

- When the dimension table is kept flat, it allows symmetric cross-browsing among the various attributes of the dimension.
- Even when additional dimension table rows get created, the basic dimensional structure is still preserved. The fact table is connected to all the dimension tables by foreign keys. The advantages of the STAR schema are still available.
- Only when the end-user queries are based on a changed attribute does the existence of multiple rows for the same customer become apparent. For other queries, the existence of multiple rows is practically hidden.

What if the dimension table is too large and is changing too rapidly? Then seek alternatives to straightforward application of the type 2 approach. One effective approach is to break the large dimension table into one or more simpler dimension tables. How can you accomplish this?

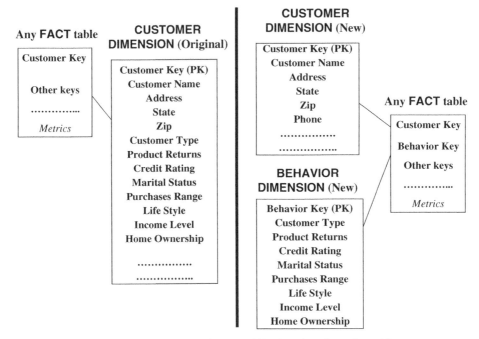

Figure 11-6   Dividing a large, rapidly changing dimension table.

Obviously, you need to break off the rapidly changing attributes into another dimension table, leaving the slowly changing attributes behind in the original table. Figure 11-6 shows how a customer dimension table may be separated into two dimension tables. The figure illustrates the general technique of separating out the rapidly changing attributes. Use this as a guide when dealing with large, rapidly changing dimensions in your data warehouse environment.

Junk Dimensions

Examine your source legacy systems and review the individual fields in source data structures for customer, product, order, sales territories, promotional campaigns, and so on. Most of these fields wind up in the dimension tables. You will notice that some fields like miscellaneous flags and textual fields are left in the source data structures. These include yes/no flags, textual codes, and free form texts.

A few of these flags and textual data may be too obscure to be of real value. These may be leftovers from past conversions from manual records created long ago. However, many of the flags and texts could be of value once in a while in queries. These may not be included as significant fields in the major dimensions. At the same time, these flags and texts cannot be discarded either. So, what are your options? Here are the main choices:

- Exclude and discard all flags and texts. Obviously, this is not a good option, for the simple reason that you are likely to throw away some useful information.
- Place the flags and texts unchanged in the fact table. This option is likely to swell up the fact table to no specific advantage.

- Make each flag and text a separate dimension table on its own. Using this option, the number of dimension tables will greatly increase.

- Keep only those flags and texts that are meaningful; group all the useful flags into a single "junk" dimension. "Junk" dimension attributes are useful for constraining queries based on flag/text values.

THE SNOWFLAKE SCHEMA

"Snowflaking" is a method of normalizing the dimension tables in a STAR schema. When you completely normalize all the dimension tables, the resultant structure resembles a snowflake with the fact table in the middle. First, let us begin with Figure 11-7, which shows a simple STAR schema for sales in a manufacturing company.

The sales fact table contains quantity, price, and other relevant metrics. Sales rep, customer, product, and time are the dimension tables. This is a classic STAR schema, denormalized for optimal query access involving all or most of the dimensions. The model is not in the third normal form.

Options to Normalize

Assume that there are 500,000 product dimension rows. These products fall under 500 product brands and these product brands fall under 10 product categories. Now suppose one of your users runs a query constraining just on product category. If the product dimension table is not indexed on product category, the query will have to search through 500,000 rows. On the other hand, even if the product dimension is partially normalized by separating out product brand and product category into separate tables, the initial search for the query will have to go through only 10 rows in the product category table. Figure 11-8 illustrates this reduction in the search process.

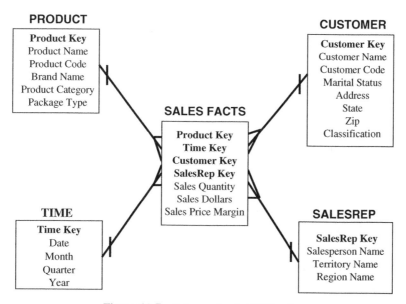

Figure 11-7 Sales: a simple STAR schema.

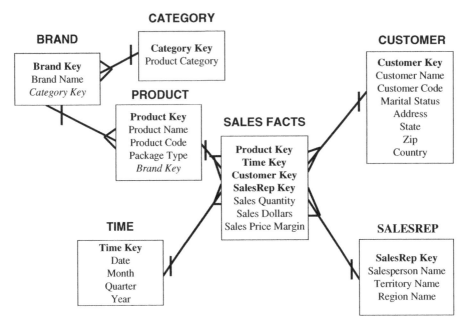

Figure 11-8   Product dimension: partially normalized.

In Figure 11-8, we have not completely normalized the product dimension. We can also move other attributes out of the product dimension table and form normalized structures. "Snowflaking" or normalization of the dimension tables can be achieved in a few different ways. When you want to "snowflake," examine the contents and the normal usage of each dimension table.

The following options indicate the different methods you may want to consider for normalization of the dimension tables:

- Partially normalize only a few dimension tables, leaving the others intact.
- Partially or fully normalize only a few dimension tables, leaving the rest intact.
- Partially normalize every dimension table.
- Fully normalize every dimension table.

Figure 11-9 shows the version of the snowflake schema for sales in which every dimension table is partially or fully normalized.

The original STAR schema for sales as shown in Figure 11-7 contains only 5 tables, whereas the normalized version now extends to 11 tables. You will notice that in the snowflake schema, the attributes with low cardinality in each original dimension table are removed to form separate tables. These new tables are linked back to the original dimension table through artificial keys.

Advantages and Disadvantages

You may want to snowflake for one obvious reason. By eliminating all the long text fields from the dimension tables, you expect to save storage space. For example, if you have "men's

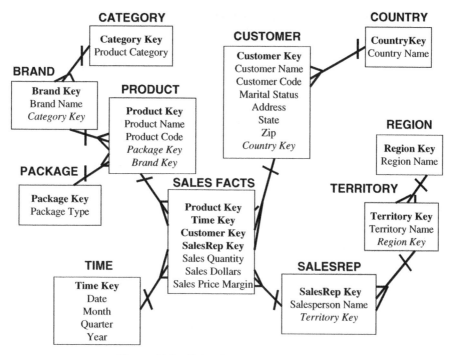

Figure 11-9   Sales: the "snowflake" schema.

furnishings" as one of the category names, that text will be repeated on every product row in that category. At first blush, removing such redundancies might appear to save significant storage space when the dimensions are large.

Let us assume that your product dimension table has 500,000 rows. By snowflaking you are able to remove 500,000 20-byte category names. At the same time, you have to add a 4-byte artificial category key to the dimension table. The net savings work out to be approximately 500,000 times 16, that is, about 8 MB. Your average 500,000-row product dimension table occupies about 200 MB of storage space and the corresponding fact table another 20 GB. The savings are just 4%. You will find that the small savings in space does not compensate for the other disadvantages of snowflaking.

Here is a brief summary of the advantages and limitations of snowflaking:

Advantages
  • Small savings in storage space
  • Normalized structures are easier to update and maintain
Disadvantages
  • Schema less intuitive and end-users are put off by the complexity
  • Ability to browse through the contents difficult
  • Degraded query performance because of additional joins

Snowflaking is not generally recommended in a data warehouse environment. Query performance takes the highest significance in a data warehouse and snowflaking hampers the performance.

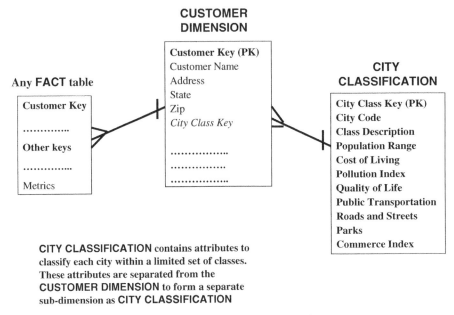

CITY CLASSIFICATION contains attributes to classify each city within a limited set of classes. These attributes are separated from the CUSTOMER DIMENSION to form a separate sub-dimension as CITY CLASSIFICATION

Figure 11-10   Forming a subdimension.

When to Snowflake

As an IT professional, you have an affinity for third normal form structures. We very well know all the problems unnormalized structures can cause. Further, wasted space could be another consideration for snowflaking.

In spite of the apparent disadvantages, are there any circumstances under which snowflaking may be permissible? The principle behind snowflaking is normalization of the dimension tables by removing low cardinality attributes and forming separate tables. In a similar manner, some situations provide opportunities to separate out a set of attributes and form a subdimension. This process is very close to the snowflaking technique. Figure 11-10 shows how a city classification subdimension is formed out of the customer dimension.

Although forming subdimensions may be construed as snowflaking, it makes a lot of sense to separate out the demographic attributes into another table. You usually load the demographic data at times different from the times when you load the other dimension attributes. The two sets of attributes differ in granularity. If the customer dimension is very large, running into millions of rows, the savings in storage space could be substantial, Another valid reason for separating out the demographic attributes relates to the browsing of attributes. Users may browse the demographic attributes more than the others in the customer dimension table.

AGGREGATE FACT TABLES

Aggregates are precalculated summaries derived from the most granular fact table. These summaries form a set of separate aggregate fact tables. You may create each aggregate fact table as a specific summarization across any number of dimensions. Let us begin by examining a sample STAR schema. Choose a simple STAR schema with the fact table at

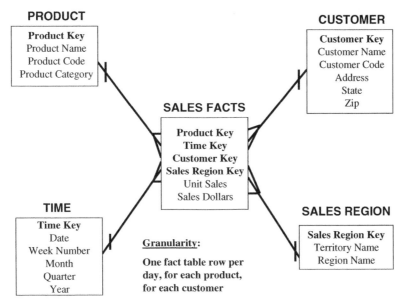

Figure 11-11   STAR schema with most granular fact table.

the lowest possible level of granularity. Assume there are four dimension tables surrounding this most granular fact table. Figure 11-11 shows the example we want to examine.

What is the essential difference between queries run in an operational system and those run in a data warehouse environment? When you run a query in an operational system, it produces a result set about a single customer, a single order, a single invoice, a single product, and so on. But, as you know, the queries in a data warehouse environment produce large result sets. Queries in a data warehouse retrieve hundreds and thousands of table rows, manipulate the metrics in the fact tables, and then produce the result sets. The manipulation of the fact table metrics may be a simple addition, an addition with some adjustments, a calculation of averages, or even an application of complex arithmetic algorithms.

Let us review a few typical queries against the sample STAR schema shown in Figure 11-11.

Query 1: Total sales for customer number 12345678 during the first week of December 2008 for product Widget-1.

Query 2: Total sales for customer number 12345678 during the first three months of 2009 for product Widget-1.

Query 3: Total sales for all customers in the south-central territory for the first two quarters of 2009 for product category Bigtools.

Scrutinize these queries and determine how the totals will be calculated in each case. The totals will be calculated by adding the sales quantities and sales dollars from the qualifying rows of the fact table. In each case, let us review the qualifying rows that contribute to the total in the result set.

Query 1: All fact table rows where the customer key relates to customer number 12345678, the product key relates to product Widget-1, and the time key relates to the seven days in the first week of December 2008. Assuming that a customer may make at most one purchase of a single product in a single day, only a maximum of seven fact table rows participate in the summation.

Query 2: All fact table rows where the customer key relates to customer number 12345678, the product key relates to product Widget-1, and the time key relates to about 90 days of the first quarter of 2009. Assuming that a customer may make at most one purchase of a single product in a single day, only about 90 fact table rows or less participate in the summation.

Query 3: All fact table rows where the customer key relates to all customers in the south-central territory, the product key relates to all products in the product category Bigtools, and the time key relates to about 180 days in the first two quarters of 2009. In this case, clearly a large number of fact table rows participate in the summation.

Obviously, Query 3 will run long because of the large number of fact table rows to be retrieved. What can be done to reduce the query time? This is where aggregate tables can be helpful. Before we discuss aggregate fact tables in detail, let us review the sizes of some typical fact tables in real-world data warehouses.

Fact Table Sizes

Figure 11-12 represents the STAR schema for sales of a large supermarket chain. There are about two billion rows of the base fact table with the lowest level of granularity. Study the calculations shown below:

Time dimension: 5 years $\times$ 365 days = 1825
Store dimension: 300 stores reporting daily sales
Product dimension: 40,000 products in each store (about 4000 sell in each store daily)
Promotion dimension: a sold item may be in only one promotion in a store on a given day
Maximum number of base fact table records: $1825 \times 300 \times 4000 \times 1 = 2$ billion

Here are a few more estimates of the fact table sizes in other typical cases:

Telephone call monitoring
  Time dimension: 5 years = 1825 days
  Number of calls tracked each day: 150 million
  Maximum number of base fact table records: 274 billion
Credit card transaction tracking
  Time dimension: 5 years = 60 months
  Number of credit card accounts: 150 million
  Average number of monthly transactions per account: 20
  Maximum number of base fact table records: 180 billion

From the above examples you see the typical enormity of the fact tables that are at the lowest level of granularity. Although none of the queries from the users would call for

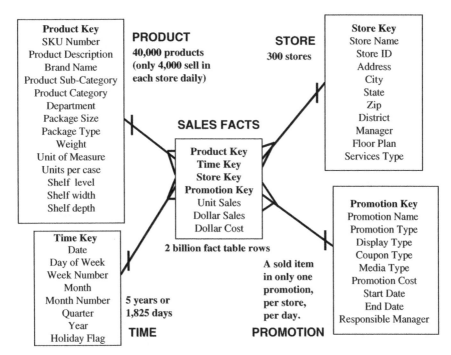

Figure 11-12 STAR schema: grocery chain.

data just from a single row in these fact tables, data at the lowest level of detail is needed. This is because when a user performs various forms of analysis, he or she must he able to get result sets comprising a variety of combinations of individual fact table rows. If you do not keep details by individual stores, you cannot retrieve result sets for products by individual stores. On the other hand, if you do not keep details by individual products, you cannot retrieve result sets for stores by individual products.

So, here is the question. If you need detailed data at the lowest level of granularity in the base fact tables, how do you deal with summations of huge numbers of fact table rows to produce query results? Consider the following queries related to a grocery chain data warehouse:

- How did the three new stores in Wisconsin perform during the last three months compared to the national average?
- What is the effect of the latest holiday sales campaign on meat and poultry?
- How do the July 4th holiday sales by product categories compare to last year?

Each of these three queries requires selections and summations from the fact table rows. For these types of summations, you need detailed data based on one or more dimensions, but only summary totals based on the other dimensions. For example, for the last query, you need detailed daily data based on the time dimension, but summary totals by product categories. In any case, if you had summary totals or precalculated aggregates readily available, the queries would run faster. With properly aggregated summaries, the performance of each of these queries can be dramatically improved.

Need for Aggregates

Refer to Figure 11-12 showing the STAR schema for a grocery chain. In those 300 stores, assume there are 500 products per brand. Of the 40,000 products, assume that there is at least one sale per product per store per week. Let us estimate the number of fact table rows to be retrieved and summarized for the following types of queries:

Query involves 1 product, 1 store, 1 week—retrieve/summarize only 1 fact table row

Query involves 1 product, all stores, I week—retrieve/summarize 300 fact table rows

Query involves 1 brand, 1 store, 1 week—retrieve/summarize 500 fact table rows

Query involves 1 brand, all stores, 1 year—retrieve/summarize 7,800,000 fact table rows

Suppose you had precalculated and created an aggregate fact table in which each row summarized the totals for a brand, per store, per week. Then the third query must retrieve only one row from this aggregate fact table. Similarly, the last query must retrieve only 15,600 rows from this aggregate fact table, much less than the 7 million rows.

Further, if you precalculate and create another aggregate fact table in which each row summarized the totals for a brand, per store, per year, the last query must retrieve only 300 rows.

Aggregates have fewer rows than the base tables. Therefore, when most of the queries are run against the aggregate fact tables instead of the base fact table, you notice a tremendous boost to performance in the data warehouse. Formation of aggregate fact tables is certainly a very effective method to improve query performance.

Aggregating Fact Tables

As we have seen, aggregate fact tables are merely summaries of the most granular data at higher levels along the dimension hierarchies. Figure 11-13 illustrates the hierarchies along three dimensions. Examine the hierarchies in the three dimensions. The hierarchy levels in the time dimension move up from day at the lowest level to year at the highest level. City is at the lowest level in the store dimension and product at the lowest level in the product dimension.

In the base fact table, the rows reflect the numbers at the lowest levels of the dimension hierarchies. For example, each row in the base fact table shows the sales units and sales dollars relating to one date, one store, and one product. By moving up one or more notches along the hierarchy in each dimension, you can create a variety of aggregate fact tables. Let us explore the possibilities.

Multi-Way Aggregate Fact Tables   Figure 11-14 illustrates the different ways aggregate fact tables may be formed. The following paragraphs describe possible aggregates.

One-Way Aggregates   When you rise to higher levels in the hierarchy of one dimension and keep the level at the lowest in the other dimensions, you create one-way aggregate tables. Review the following examples:

- Product category by store by date
- Product department by store by date

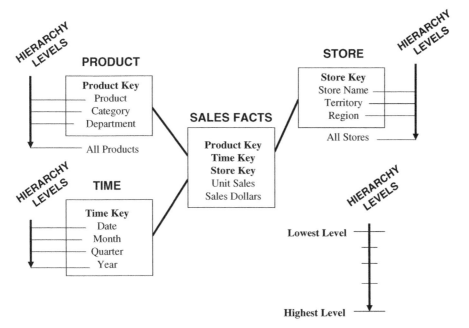

Figure 11-13 Dimension hierarchies.

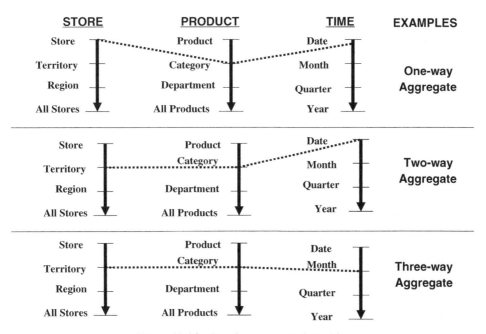

Figure 11-14 Forming aggregate fact tables.

- All products by store by date
- Territory by product by date
- Region by product by date
- All stores by product by date
- Month by store by product
- Quarter by store by product
- Year by store by product

Two-Way Aggregates   When you rise to higher levels in the hierarchies of two dimensions and keep the level at the lowest in the other dimension, you create two-way aggregate tables. Review the following examples:

- Product category by territory by date
- Product category by region by date
- Product category by all stores by date
- Product category by month by store
- Product category by quarter by store
- Product category by year by store
- Product department by territory by date
- Product department by region by date
- Product department by all stores by date
- Product department by month by store
- Product department by quarter by store
- Product department by year by store
- All products by territory by date
- All products by region by date
- All products by all stores by date
- All products by month by store
- All products by quarter by store
- All products by year by store
- District by month by product
- District by quarter by product
- District by year by product
- Territory by month by product
- Territory by quarter by product
- Territory by year by product
- Region by month by product
- Region by quarter by product
- Region by year by product
- All stores by month by product
- All stores by quarter by product
- All stores by year by product

Three-Way Aggregates   When you rise to higher levels in the hierarchies of all the three dimensions, you create three-way aggregate tables. Review the following examples:

- Product category by territory by month
- Product department by territory by month
- All products by territory by month
- Product category by region by month
- Product department by region by month
- All products by region by month
- Product category by all stores by month
- Product department by all stores by month
- Product category by territory by quarter
- Product department by territory by quarter
- All products by territory by quarter
- Product category by region by quarter
- Product department by region by quarter
- All products by region by quarter
- Product category by all stores by quarter
- Product department by all stores by quarter
- Product category by territory by year
- Product department by territory by year
- All products by territory by year
- Product category by region by year
- Product department by region by year
- All products by region by year
- Product category by all stores by year
- Product department by all stores by year
- All products by all stores by year

Each of these aggregate fact tables is derived from a single base fact table. The derived aggregate fact tables are joined to one or more derived dimension tables. Figure 11-15 shows a derived aggregate fact table connected to a derived dimension table.

Effect of Sparsity on Aggregation   Consider the case of the grocery chain with 300 stores, 40,000 products in each store, but only 4000 selling in each store in a day. As discussed earlier, assuming that you keep records for 5 years or 1825 days, the maximum number of base fact table rows is calculated as follows:

Product = 40,000
Store = 300
Time = 1825
Maximum number of base fact table rows = 22 billion

Figure 11-15   Aggregate fact table and derived dimension table.

Because only 4000 products sell in each store in a day, not all of these 22 billion rows are occupied. Because of this sparsity, only 10% of the rows are occupied. Therefore, the real estimate of the number of base table rows is 2 billion.

Now let us see what happens when you form aggregates. Scrutinize a one-way aggregate: brand totals by store by day. Calculate the maximum number of rows in this one-way aggregate.

Brand = 80
Store = 300
Time = 1825
Maximum number of aggregate table rows = 43,800,000

While creating the one-way aggregate, you will notice that the sparsity for this aggregate is not 10% as in the case of the base table. This is because when you aggregate by brand, more of the brand codes will participate in combinations with store and time codes. The sparsity of the one-way aggregate would be about 50%, resulting in a real estimate of 21,900,000. If the sparsity had remained as the 10% applicable to the base table, the real estimate of the number of rows in the aggregate table would be much less.

When you go for higher levels of aggregates, the sparsity percentage moves up and even reaches 100%. Because of the failure of sparsity to stay lower, you are faced with the question whether aggregates do improve performance that much. Do they reduce the number of rows that dramatically?

Experienced data warehousing practitioners have a suggestion. When you form aggregates, make sure that each aggregate table row summarizes at least 10 rows in the lower level table. If you increase this to 20 rows or more, it would be really remarkable.

Aggregation Options

Going back to our discussion of one-way, two-way, and three-way aggregates for a basic STAR schema with just three dimensions, you could count more than 50 different ways you may create aggregates. In the real world, the number of dimensions is not just three, but many more. Therefore, the number of possible aggregate tables escalates into the hundreds.

Further, from the reference to the failure of sparsity in aggregate tables, you know that the aggregation process does not reduce the number of rows proportionally. In other words, if the sparsity of the base fact table is 10%, the sparsity of the higher-level aggregate tables does not remain at 10%. The sparsity percentage increases more and more as your aggregate tables climb higher and higher in levels of summarization.

Is aggregation that much effective after all? What are some of the options? How do you decide what to aggregate? First, set a few goals for aggregation for your data warehouse environment.

Goals for Aggregation Strategy   Apart from the general overall goal of improving data warehouse performance, here are a few specific, practical goals:

- Do not get bogged down with too many aggregates. Remember, you have to create additional derived dimensions as well to support the aggregates.
- Try to cater to a wide range of user groups. In any case, provide for your power users.
- Go for aggregates that do not unduly increase the overall usage of storage. Look carefully into larger aggregates with low sparsity percentages.
- Keep the aggregates hidden from the end-users but be transparent to the end-user query. That is, it is the query tool that needs to be aware of the aggregates to direct the queries for proper access.
- Attempt to keep the impact on the data staging process as minimally intensive as possible.

Practical Suggestions   Before doing any calculations to determine the types of aggregates needed for your data warehouse environment, spend a good deal of time on determining the nature of the common queries. How do your users normally report results? What are the reporting levels? By stores? By months? By product categories? Go through the dimensions, one by one, and review the levels of the hierarchies. Check if there are multiple hierarchies within the same dimension. If so, find out which of these multiple hierarchies are more important. In each dimension, ascertain which attributes are used for grouping the fact table metrics. The next step is to determine which of these attributes are used in combinations and what the most common combinations are.

Once you determine the attributes and their possible combinations, look at the number of values for each attribute. For example, in a hotel chain schema, assume that hotel is at the lowest level and city is at the next higher level in the hotel dimension. Let us say there are 25,000 values for hotel and 15,000 values for city. Clearly, there is no big advantage of aggregating by cities. On the other hand, if city has only 500 values, then city is a level at which you may consider aggregation. Examine each attribute in the hierarchies within a dimension. Check the values for each of the attributes. Compare the values of attributes at different levels of the same hierarchy and decide which ones are strong candidates to participate in aggregation.

Develop a list of attributes that are useful candidates for aggregation, then work out the combinations of these attributes to come up with your first set of multi-way aggregate fact tables. Determine the derived dimension tables you need to support these aggregate fact tables. Go ahead and implement these aggregate fact tables as the initial set.

Bear in mind that aggregation is a performance tuning mechanism. Improved query performance drives the need to summarize, so do not be too concerned if your first set of aggregate tables do not perform perfectly. Your aggregates are meant to be monitored and revised as necessary. The nature of the bulk of the query requests is likely to change. As your users become more adept at using the data warehouse, they will devise new ways of grouping and analyzing data. So what is the practical advice? Do your preparatory work. Start with a reasonable set of aggregate tables, and continue to make adjustments as necessary.

FAMILIES OF STARS

When you look at a single STAR schema with its fact table and the surrounding dimension tables, you know that is not the extent of a data warehouse. Almost all data warehouses contain multiple STAR schema structures. Each STAR serves a specific purpose to track the measures stored in the fact table. When you have a collection of related STAR schemas, you may call the collection a family of STARS. Families of STARS are formed for various reasons. You may form a family by just adding aggregate fact tables and the derived dimension tables to support the aggregates. Sometimes, you may create a core fact table containing facts interesting to most users and customized fact tables for specific user groups. Many factors lead to the existence of families of STARS. First, look at the example provided in Figure 11-16.

The fact tables of the STARS in a family share dimension tables. Usually, the time dimension is shared by most of the fact tables in the group. In the above example, all three fact tables are likely to share the time dimension. Going the other way, dimension tables from multiple STARS may share the fact table of one STAR.

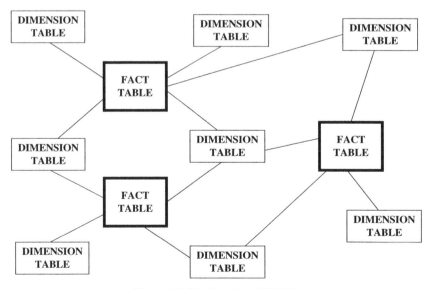

Figure 11-16   Family of STARS.

If you are in a business like banking or telephone services, it makes sense to capture individual transactions as well as snapshots at specific intervals. You may then use families of STARS consisting of transaction and snapshot schemas. If you are in a manufacturing company or a similar production-type enterprise, your company needs to monitor the metrics along the value chain. Some other institutions are like a medical center, where value is added not in a chain but at different stations within the enterprise. For these enterprises, the family of STARS supports the value chain or the value circle. We will get into details in the next few sections.

Snapshot and Transaction Tables

Let us review some basic requirements of a telephone company. A number of individual transactions make up a telephone customer's account. Many of the transactions occur during the hours of 6:00 a.m. to 10:00 p.m. of the customer's day. More transactions happen during the holidays and weekends for residential customers. Institutional customers use the phones on weekdays rather than over the weekends. A telephone company accumulates a very large collection of rich transaction data that can be used for many types of valuable analysis. The telephone company needs a schema capturing transaction data that supports strategic decision making for expansions, new service improvements, and so on. This transaction schema answers questions such as how does the revenue of peak hours over the weekends and holidays compare with peak hours over weekdays.

In addition, the telephone company needs to answer questions from the customers as to account balances. The customer service departments are constantly bombarded with questions on the status of individual customer accounts. At periodic intervals, the accounting department may be interested in the amounts expected to be received by the middle of next month. What are the outstanding balances for which bills will be sent this month-end? For these purposes, the telephone company needs a schema to capture snapshots at periodic intervals. Figure 11-17 shows the snapshot and transaction fact tables for a

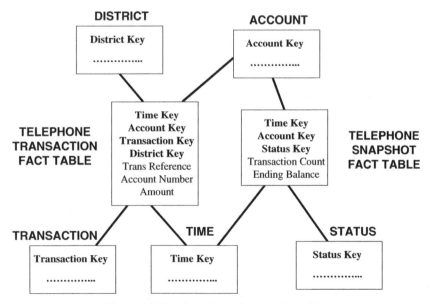

Figure 11-17   Snapshot and transaction tables.

telephone company. Make a note of the attributes in the two fact tables. One table tracks the individual phone transactions. The other table holds snapshots of individual accounts at specific intervals. Also, notice how dimension tables are shared between two fact tables.

Snapshots and transaction tables are also common for banks. For example, an ATM transaction table stores individual ATM transactions. This fact table keeps track of individual transaction amounts for the customer accounts. The snapshot table holds the balance for each account at the end of each day. The two tables serve two distinct functions. From the transaction table, you can perform various types of analysis of the ATM transactions. The snapshot table provides total amounts held at periodic intervals showing the shifting and movement of balances.

Financial data warehouses also require snapshot and transaction tables because of the nature of the analysis in these cases. The first set of questions for these warehouses relates to the transactions affecting given accounts over a certain period of time. The other set of questions centers around balances in individual accounts at specific intervals or totals of groups of accounts at the end of specific periods. The transaction table answers the questions of the first set; the snapshot table handles the questions of the second set.

Core and Custom Tables

Consider two types of businesses that are apparently dissimilar. First take the case of a bank. A bank offers a large variety of services all related to finance in one form or another. Most of the services are different from one another. The checking account service and the savings account service are similar in most ways. But the savings account service does not resemble the credit card service in any way. How do you track these dissimilar services?

Next, consider a manufacturing company producing a number of heterogeneous products. Although a few factors may be common to the various products, by and large the factors differ. What must you do to get information about heterogeneous products?

A different type of the family of STARS satisfies the requirements of these companies. In this type of family, all products and services connect to a core fact table and each product or service relates to individual custom tables. In Figure 11-18, you will see the core and custom tables for a bank. Note how the core fact table holds the metrics that are common to all types of accounts. Each custom fact table contains the metrics specific to that line of service. Also note the shared dimension and notice how the tables form a family of STARS.

Supporting Enterprise Value Chain or Value Circle

In a manufacturing business, a product travels through various steps, starting off as raw materials and ending as finished goods in the warehouse inventory. Usually, the steps include addition of ingredients, assembly of materials, process control, packaging, and shipping to the warehouse. From finished goods inventory, a product moves into shipments to distributor, distributor inventory, distributor shipment, retail inventory, and retail sales. At each step, value is added to the product. Several operational systems support the flow through these steps. The whole flow forms the supply chain or the value chain. Similarly, in an insurance company, the value chain may include a number of steps from sales of insurance through issuance of policy and then finally claims processing. In this case, the value chain relates to the service.

If you are in one of these businesses, you need to track important metrics at different steps along the value chain. You create STAR schemas for the significant steps and the complete

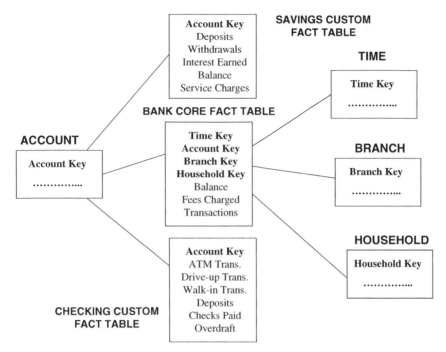

Figure 11-18   Core and custom tables.

set of related schemas forms a family of STARS. You define a fact table and a set of corresponding dimensions for each important step in the chain. If your company has multiple value chains, then you have to support each chain with a separate family of STARS.

A supply chain or a value chain runs in a linear fashion beginning with a certain step and ending at another step with many steps in between. Again, at each step, value is added. In some other kinds of businesses where value gets added to services, similar linear movements do not exist. For example, consider a health care institution where value gets added to patient service from different units almost as if they form a circle around the service. We perceive a value circle in such organizations. The value circle of a large health maintenance organization may include hospitals, clinics, doctor's offices, pharmacies, laboratories, government agencies, and insurance companies. Each of these units either provides patient treatments or measures patient treatments. Patient treatment by each unit may be measured in different metrics. But most of the units would analyze the metrics using the same set of conformed dimensions such as time, patient, health care provider, treatment, diagnosis, and payer. For a value circle, the family of STARS comprises multiple fact tables and a set of conformed dimensions.

Conforming Dimensions

While exploring families of STARS, you will have noticed that dimensions are shared among fact tables. Dimensions form common links between STARS. For dimensions to be conformed, you have to deliberately make sure that common dimensions may be used between two of more STARS. If the product dimension is shared between two fact tables of sales and inventory, then the attributes of the product dimension must have the same meaning in relation to each of the two fact tables. Figure 11-19 shows a set of conformed dimensions.

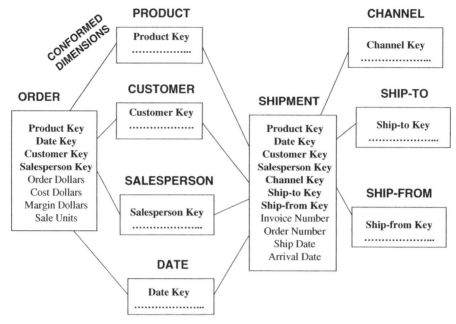

Figure 11-19 Conformed dimensions.

The order and shipment fact tables share the conformed dimensions of product, date, customer, and salesperson. A conformed dimension is a comprehensive combination of attributes from the source systems after resolving all discrepancies and conflicts. For example, a conformed product dimension must truly reflect the master product list of the enterprise and must include all possible hierarchies. Each attribute must be of the correct data type and must have proper lengths and constraints.

Conforming dimensions is a basic requirement in a data warehouse. Pay special attention and take the necessary steps to conform all your dimensions. This is a major responsibility of the project team. Conformed dimensions allow roll ups across data marts. User interfaces will be consistent irrespective of the type of query. Result sets of queries will be consistent across data marts. Of course, a single conformed dimension can be used against multiple fact tables.

Standardizing Facts

In addition to the task of conforming dimensions is the requirement to standardize facts. We have seen that fact tables work across STAR schemas. Review the following issues relating to the standardization of fact table attributes:

- Ensure the same definitions and terminology across data marts.
- Resolve homonyms and synonyms.
- Types of facts to be standardized include revenue, price, cost, and profit margin.
- Guarantee that the same algorithms are used for any derived units in each fact table.
- Make sure each fact uses the right unit of measurement.

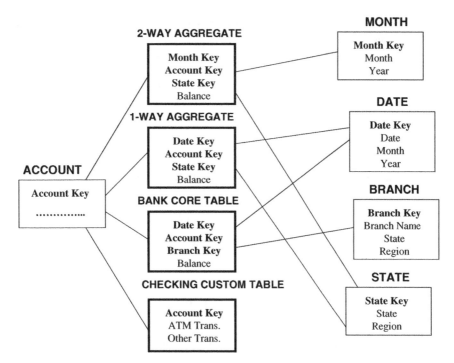

Figure 11-20   A comprehensive family of STARS.

Summary of Family of STARS

Let us end our discussion of the family of STARS with a comprehensive diagram showing a set of standardized fact tables and conformed dimension tables. Study Figure 11-20 carefully. Note the aggregate fact tables and the corresponding derived dimension tables. What types of aggregates are these? Which are the base fact tables? Notice the shared dimensions. Are these conformed dimensions? See how the various fact tables and the dimension tables are related.

CHAPTER SUMMARY

- Slowly changing dimensions may be classified into three different types based on the nature of the changes. Type 1 relates to corrections, type 2 to preservation of history, and type 3 to soft revisions. Applying each type of revision to the data warehouse is different.

- Large dimension tables such as customer or product need special considerations for applying optimizing techniques.

- "Snowflaking" or creating a snowflake schema is a method of normalizing the STAR schema. Although some conditions justify the snowflake schema, it is generally not recommended.

- Miscellaneous flags and textual data are thrown together in one table called a junk dimension table.

- Aggregate or summary tables improve performance. Formulate a strategy for building aggregate tables.
- A set of related STAR schemas make up a family of STARS. Examples are snapshot and transaction tables, core and custom tables, and tables supporting a value chain or a value circle. A family of STARS relies on conformed dimension tables and standardized fact tables.

REVIEW QUESTIONS

1. Describe slowly changing dimensions. What are the three types? Explain each type very briefly.

2. Compare and contrast type 2 and type 3 slowly changing dimensions.

3. Can you treat rapidly changing dimensions in the same way as type 2 slowly changing dimensions? Discuss.

4. What are junk dimensions? Are they necessary in a data warehouse?

5. How does a snowflake schema differ from a STAR schema? Name two advantages and two disadvantages of the snowflake schema.

6. Differentiate between slowly and rapidly changing dimensions.

7. What are aggregate fact tables? Why are they needed? Give an example.

8. Describe with examples snapshot and transaction fact tables. How are they related?

9. Give an example of a value circle. Explain how a family of STARS can support a value circle.

10. What is meant by conforming the dimension? Why is this important in a data warehouse?

EXERCISES

1. Indicate if true or false:

    A. Type 1 changes for slowly changing dimensions relate to correction of errors.

    B. To apply type 3 changes of slowly changing dimensions, overwrite the attribute value in the dimension table row with the new value.

    C. Large dimensions usually have multiple hierarchies.

    D. The STAR schema is a normalized version of the snowflake schema.

    E. Aggregates are precalculated summaries.

    F. The percentage of sparsity of the base table tends to be higher than that of aggregate tables.

    G. The fact tables of the STARS in a family share dimension tables.

    H. Core and custom fact tables are useful for companies with several lines of service.

    I. Conforming dimensions is not absolutely necessary in a data warehouse.

    J. A value circle usually needs a family of STARS to support the business.

2. Assume you are in the insurance business. Find two examples of type 2 slowly changing dimensions in that business. As an analyst on the project, write the specifications for applying the type 2 changes to the data warehouse with regard to the two examples.

3. You are the data design specialist on the data warehouse project team for a retail company. Design a STAR schema to track the sales units and sales dollars with three dimension tables. Explain how you will decide to select and build four two-way aggregates.

4. As the data designer for an international bank, consider the possible types of snapshot and transaction tables. Complete the design of one snapshot and one transaction table.

5. For a manufacturing company, design a family of three STARS to support the value chain.

CHAPTER 12

DATA EXTRACTION, TRANSFORMATION, AND LOADING

CHAPTER OBJECTIVES

- Survey broadly all the various aspects of the data extraction, transformation, and loading (ETL) functions
- Examine the data extraction function, its challenges, its techniques, and learn how to evaluate and apply the techniques
- Discuss the wide range of tasks and types of the data transformation function
- Understand the meaning of data integration and consolidation
- Perceive the importance of the data load function and probe the major methods for applying data to the warehouse
- Gain a true insight into why ETL is crucial, time consuming, and arduous

You may be convinced that the data in your organization's operational systems is totally inadequate for providing information for strategic decision making. As information technology professionals, we are fully aware of the futile attempts in the past decades to provide strategic information from operational systems. These attempts did not work. Data warehousing had begun to fulfill that pressing need for strategic information.

Mostly, the information contained in a warehouse flows from the same operational systems that could not be directly used to provide strategic information. What constitutes the difference between the data in the source operational systems and the information in the data warehouse? It is the set of functions that fall under the broad group of data extraction, transformation, and loading (ETL).

ETL functions reshape the relevant data from the source systems into useful information to be stored in the data warehouse. Without these functions, there would be no strategic information in the data warehouse. If the source data is not extracted correctly, cleansed, and

Data Warehousing Fundamentals for IT Professionals, Second Edition. By Paulraj Ponniah
Copyright © 2010 John Wiley & Sons, Inc.

integrated in the proper formats, query processing and delivery of business intelligence, the backbone of the data warehouse, could not happen.

In Chapter 2, when we discussed the building blocks of the data warehouse, we briefly looked at ETL functions as part of the data staging area. In Chapter 6 we revisited ETL functions and examined how the business requirements drive these functions as well. Further, in Chapter 8, we explored the hardware and software infrastructure options to support the data movement functions. Why, then, is additional review of ETL necessary?

ETL functions form the prerequisites for the data warehouse information content. ETL functions rightly deserve more consideration and discussion. In this chapter, we will delve deeper into issues relating to ETL functions. We will review many significant activities within ETL. In the next chapter, we need to continue the discussion by studying another important function that falls within the overall purview of ETL—data quality. Now, let us begin with a general overview of ETL.

ETL OVERVIEW

If you recall our discussion of the functions and services of the technical architecture of the data warehouse, you will see that we divided the environment into three functional areas. These areas are data acquisition, data storage, and information delivery. Data extraction, data transformation, and data loading encompass the areas of data acquisition and data storage. These are back-end processes that cover the extraction of data from the source systems. Next, they include all the functions and procedures for changing the source data into the exact formats and structures appropriate for storage in the data warehouse database. After the transformation of the data, these processes consist of all the functions for physically moving the data into the data warehouse repository.

Data extraction, of course, precedes all other functions. But what is the scope and extent of the data you will extract from the source systems? Do you not think that the users of your data warehouse are interested in all of the operational data for some type of query or analysis? So, why not extract all of the operational data and dump it into the data warehouse? This seems to be a straightforward approach. However, the approach for data extraction is driven by the user requirements. Your requirements definition should guide you as to what data you need to extract and from which source systems. Avoid creating a data junkhouse by dumping all the available data from the source systems and waiting to see what the users will do with it. Data extraction presupposes a selection process. Select the needed data based on the user requirements.

The extent and complexity of the back-end processes differ from one data warehouse to another. If your enterprise is supported by a large number of operational systems running on several computing platforms, the back-end processes in your case would be extensive and possibly complex as well. So, in your situation, data extraction becomes quite challenging. The data transformation and data loading functions may also be equally difficult. Moreover, if the quality of the source data is below standard, this condition further aggravates the back-end processes. In addition to these challenges, if only a few of the loading methods are feasible for your situation, then data loading could also be difficult. Let us get into specifics about the nature of the ETL functions.

Most Important and Most Challenging

Each of the ETL functions fulfills a significant purpose. When you want to convert data from the source systems into business information to be stored in the data warehouse, each of these functions is essential. For changing data into information you first need to capture the data. After you capture the data, you cannot simply dump that data into the data warehouse and call it strategic information. You have to subject the extracted data to all manner of transformations so that the data will be fit to be converted into strategic information. Once you have transformed the data, it is still not useful to the end-users until it is moved to the data warehouse repository. Data loading is an essential function. You must perform all three functions of ETL for successfully transforming data into strategic information or business intelligence.

Take as an example an analysis your user wants to perform. The user wants to compare and analyze sales by store, by product, and by month. The sales figures are available in the several sales applications in your company. Also, you have a product master file. Further, each sales transaction refers to a specific store. All these are pieces of data in the source operational systems. For doing the analysis, you have to provide information about the sales in the data warehouse database. You have to provide the sales units and dollars in a fact table, the products in a product dimension table, the stores in a store dimension table, and months in a time dimension table. How do you do this? Extract the data from each of the operational systems, reconcile the variations in data representations among the source systems, and transform all the sales of all the products. Then load the sales into the fact and dimension tables. Now, after completion of these three functions, the extracted data is sitting in the data warehouse, transformed into strategic information, ready for delivery as business intelligence for analysis. Notice that it is important for each function to be performed, and performed in sequence.

ETL functions are challenging primarily because of the nature of the source systems. Most of the challenges in ETL arise from the disparities among the source operational systems. Review the following list of reasons for the types of difficulties in ETL functions. Consider each carefully and relate it to your environment so that you may find proper resolutions.

- Source systems are very diverse and disparate.
- There is usually a need to deal with source systems on multiple platforms and different operating systems.
- Many source systems are older legacy applications running on obsolete database technologies.
- Generally, historical data on changes in values are not preserved in source operational systems. Historical information is critical in a data warehouse.
- Quality of data is dubious in many old source systems that have evolved over time.
- Source system structures keep changing over time because of new business conditions. ETL functions must also be modified accordingly.
- Gross lack of consistency among source systems is prevalent. Same data is likely to be represented differently in the various source systems. For example, data on salary may be represented as monthly salary, weekly salary, and bimonthly salary in different source payroll systems.
- Even when inconsistent data is detected among disparate source systems, lack of a means for resolving mismatches escalates the problem of inconsistency.
- Most source systems do not represent data in types or formats that are meaningful to the users. Many representations are cryptic and ambiguous.

Time Consuming and Arduous

When the project team designs the ETL functions, tests the various processes, and deploys them, you will find that these consume a very high percentage of the total project effort. It is not uncommon for a project team to spend as much as 50% to 70% of the project effort on ETL functions. You have already noted several factors that add to the complexity of the ETL functions.

Data extraction itself can be quite involved depending on the nature and complexity of the source systems. The metadata on the source systems must contain information on every database and every data structure that are needed from the source systems. You need very detailed information, including database size and volatility of the data. You have to know the time window during each day when you can extract data without impacting use of the operational systems. You also need to determine the mechanism for capturing the changes to data in each of the relevant source systems. These are strenuous and time-consuming activities.

Activities within the data transformation function can run the gamut of transformation methods. You have to reformat internal data structures, resequence data, apply various forms of conversion techniques, supply default values wherever values are missing, and you must design the whole set of aggregates that are needed for performance improvement. In many cases, you need to convert from EBCDIC to ASCII formats.

Now turn your attention to the data loading function. The sheer massive size of the initial loading can populate millions of rows in the data warehouse database. Creating and managing load images for such large numbers are not easy tasks. Even more difficult is the task of testing and applying the load images to actually populate the physical files in the data warehouse. Sometimes, it may take two or more weeks to complete the initial physical loading.

With regard to extracting and applying the ongoing incremental changes, there are several difficulties. Finding the proper extraction method for individual source datasets can be arduous. Once you settle on the extraction method, finding a time window to apply the changes to the data warehouse can be tricky if your data warehouse cannot suffer long downtimes.

ETL REQUIREMENTS AND STEPS

Before we highlight some key issues relating to ETL, let us review the functional steps. For initial bulk refresh as well as for the incremental data loads, the sequence is simply as noted here: triggering for incremental changes, filtering for refreshes and incremental loads, data extraction, transformation, integration, cleansing, and applying to the data warehouse database.

What are the major steps in the ETL process? Look at the list shown in Figure 12-1. Each of these major steps breaks down into a set of activities and tasks. Use this figure as a guide to come up with a list of steps for the ETL process of your data warehouse.

The following list enumerates the types of activities and tasks that compose the ETL process. This list is by no means complete for every data warehouse, but it gives a good insight into what is involved to complete the ETL process.

Plan for aggregate fact tables.

Determine data transformation and cleansing rules.

Establish comprehensive data extraction rules.

Prepare data mapping for target data elements from sources.

Integrate all the data sources, both internal and external.

Determine all the target data needed in the data warehouse.

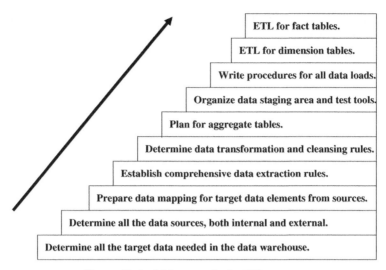

Figure 12-1   Major steps in the ETL process.

Combine several source data structures into a single row in the target database of the data warehouse.

Split one source data structure into several structures to go into several rows of the target database.

Read data from data dictionaries and catalogs of source systems.

Read data from a variety of file structures including flat files, indexed files (VSAM), and legacy system databases (hierarchical/network).

Load details for populating atomic fact tables.

Aggregate for populating aggregate or summary fact tables.

Transform data from one format in the source platform to another format in the target platform.

Derive target values for input fields (example: age from date of birth).

Change cryptic values to values meaningful to the users (example: 1 and 2 to male and female).

Key Factors

Before we move on, let us point out a couple of key factors. The first relates to the complexity of the data extraction and transformation functions. The second is about the data loading function.

Remember that the primary reason for the complexity of the data extraction and transformation functions is the tremendous diversity of the source systems. In a large enterprise, we could have a bewildering combination of computing platforms, operating systems, database management systems, network protocols, and source legacy systems. You need to pay special attention to the various sources and begin with a complete inventory of the source systems. With this inventory as a starting point, work out all the details of data extraction. The difficulties encountered in the data transformation function also relate to the heterogeneity of the source systems.

Now, turning your attention to the data loading function, you have a number of issues to be careful about. Usually, the mass refreshes, whether for initial load or for periodic refreshes, cause difficulties, not so much because of complexities, but because these load jobs run too long. You will have to find the proper time to schedule these full refreshes. Incremental loads have some other types of difficulties. First, you have to determine the best method to capture the ongoing changes from each source system. Next, you have to execute the capture without impacting the source systems. After that, at the other end, you have to schedule the incremental loads without impacting use of the data warehouse by the users.

Pay special attention to these key issues while designing the ETL functions for your data warehouse. Now let us take each of the three ETL functions, one by one, and study the details.

DATA EXTRACTION

As an IT professional, you must have participated in data extractions and conversions when implementing operational systems. When you went from a VSAM file-oriented order entry system to a new order processing system using relational database technology, you may have written data extraction programs to capture data from the VSAM files to get the data ready for populating the relational database.

Two major factors differentiate the data extraction for a new operational system from the data extraction for a data warehouse. First, for a data warehouse, you have to extract data from many disparate sources. Next, for a data warehouse, you have to extract data on the changes for ongoing incremental loads as well as for a one-time initial full load. For operational systems, all you need is one-time extractions and data conversions.

These two factors increase the complexity of data extraction for a data warehouse and, therefore, warrant the use of third-party data extraction tools in addition to in-house programs or scripts. Third-party tools are generally more expensive than in-house programs, but they record their own metadata. On the other hand, in-house programs increase the cost of maintenance and are hard to maintain as source systems change. If your company is in an industry where frequent changes to business conditions are the norm, then you may want to minimize the use of in-house programs. Third-party tools usually provide built-in flexibility. All you have to do is to change the input parameters for the third-party tool you are using.

Effective data extraction is a key to the success of your data warehouse. Therefore, you need to pay special attention to the issues and formulate a data extraction strategy for your data warehouse. Here is a list of data extraction issues:

- Source identification—identify source applications and source structures.
- Method of extraction—for each data source, define whether the extraction process is manual or tool-based.
- Extraction frequency—for each data source, establish how frequently the data extraction must be done: daily, weekly, quarterly, and so on.
- Time window—for each data source, denote the time window for the extraction process.
- Job sequencing—determine whether the beginning of one job in an extraction job stream has to wait until the previous job has finished successfully.
- Exception handling—determine how to handle input records that cannot be extracted.

Source Identification

Let us consider the first of the above issues, namely, source identification. We will deal with the other issues later as we move through the remainder of this chapter. Source identification, of course, encompasses the identification of all the proper data sources. It does not stop with just the identification of the data sources. It goes beyond that to include examination and verification that the identified sources will provide the necessary value to the data warehouse. Let us walk through the source identification process in some detail.

Assume that a part of your database, maybe one of your data marts, is designed to provide strategic information on the fulfillment of orders. For this purpose, you need to store historical information about the fulfilled and pending orders. If you ship orders through multiple delivery channels, you need to capture data about these channels. If your users are interested in analyzing the orders by the status of the orders as the orders go through the fulfillment process, then you need to extract data on the order statuses.

In the fact table for order fulfillment, you need attributes about the total order amount, discounts, commissions, expected delivery time, actual delivery time, and dates at different stages of the process. You need dimension tables for product, order disposition, delivery channel, and customer. First, you have to determine if you have source systems to provide you with the data needed for this data mart. Then, from the source systems, you have to establish the correct data source for each data element in the data mart. Further, you have to go through a verification process to ensure that the identified sources are really the right ones.

Figure 12-2 describes a stepwise approach to source identification for order fulfillment. Source identification is not as simple a process as it may sound. It is a critical first process in the data extraction function. You need to go through the source identification process for every piece of information you have to store in the data warehouse. As you might have already figured out, source identification needs thoroughness, lots of time, and exhaustive analysis.

Data Extraction Techniques

Before examining the various data extraction techniques, you must clearly understand the nature of the source data you are extracting or capturing. Also, you need to get an insight into how the extracted data will be used. Source data is in a state of constant flux.

Business transactions keep changing the data in the source systems. In most cases, the value of an attribute in a source system is the value of that attribute at that time. If you look at every data structure in the source operational systems, the day-to-day business transactions constantly change the values of the attributes in these structures. When a customer moves to another state, the data about that customer changes in the customer table in the source system. When two additional package types are added to the way a product may be sold, the product data changes in the source system. When a correction is applied to the quantity ordered, the data about that order gets changed in the source system.

Data in the source systems are said to be time-dependent or temporal. This is because source data changes with time. The value of a single variable varies over time. Again, take the example of the change of address of a customer who moves from New York to California. In the operational system, what is important is that the current address of the customer has CA as the state code. The actual change transaction itself, stating that the previous state code was NY and the revised state code is CA, need not be preserved. But think about how this change affects the information in the data warehouse. If the state

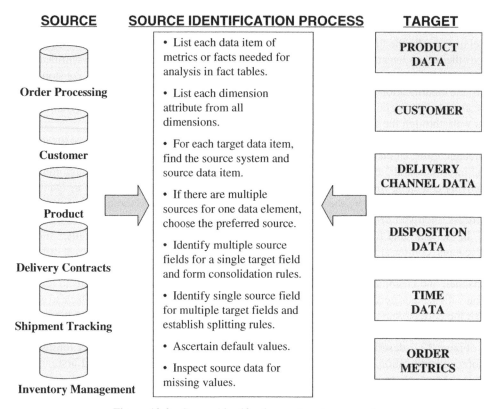

Figure 12-2   Source identification: a stepwise approach.

code is used for analyzing some measurements such as sales, the sales to the customer prior to the change must be counted in New York and those after the move must be counted in California. In other words, the history cannot be ignored in the data warehouse. This brings us to the question: how do you capture the history from the source systems? The answer depends on how exactly data is stored in the source systems. So let us examine and understand how data is stored in the source operational systems.

Data in Operational Systems   These source systems generally store data in two ways. Operational data in the source system may be thought of as falling into two broad categories. The type of data extraction technique you have to use depends on the nature of each of these two categories.

Current Value   Most of the attributes in the source systems fall into this category. Here the stored value of an attribute represents the value of the attribute at this moment of time. The values are transient or transitory. As business transactions happen, the values change. There is no way to predict how long the present value will stay or when it will get changed next. Customer name and address, bank account balances, and outstanding amounts on individual orders are some examples of this category.

What is the implication of this category for data extraction? The value of an attribute remains constant only until a business transaction changes it. There is no telling when it will get changed. Data extraction for preserving the history of the changes in the data warehouse gets quite involved for this category of data.

Periodic Status This category is not as common as the previous category. In this category, the value of the attribute is preserved as the status every time a change occurs. At each of these points in time, the status value is stored with reference to the time when the new value became effective. This category also includes events stored with reference to the time when each event occurred. Look at the way data about an insurance policy is usually recorded in the operational systems of an insurance company. The operational databases store the status data of the policy at each point of time when something in the policy changes. Similarly, for an insurance claim, each event, such as claim initiation, verification, appraisal, and settlement, is recorded with reference to the points in time.

For operational data in this category, the history of the changes is preserved in the source systems themselves. Therefore, data extraction for the purpose of keeping history in the data warehouse is relatively easier. Whether it is status data or data about an event, the source systems contain data at each point in time when any change occurred.

Study Figure 12-3 for an understanding of the two categories of data stored in the operational systems. Pay special attention to the examples.

Having reviewed the categories indicating how data is stored in the operational systems, we are now in a position to discuss the common techniques for data extraction. When you deploy your data warehouse, the initial data as of a certain time must be moved to the data warehouse to get it started. This is the initial load. After the initial load, your data warehouse must be kept updated so the history of the changes and statuses are reflected in the

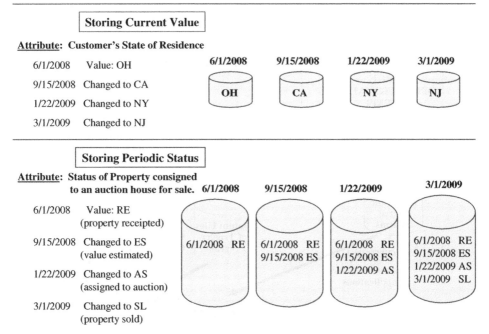

Figure 12-3 Data in operational systems.

data warehouse. Broadly, there are two major types of data extractions from the source operational systems: "as is" (static) data and data of revisions.

"As is" or static data is the capture of data at a given point in time. It is like taking a snapshot of the relevant source data at a certain point in time. For current or transient data, this capture would include all transient data identified for extraction. In addition, for data categorized as periodic, this data capture would include each status or event at each point in time as available in the source operational systems.

You will use static data capture primarily for the initial load of the data warehouse. Sometimes, you may want a full refresh of a dimension table. For example, assume that the product master of your source application is completely revamped. In this case, you may find it easier to do a full refresh of the product dimension table of the target data warehouse. So, for this purpose, you will perform a static data capture of the product data.

Data of revisions is also known as incremental data capture. Strictly, it is not incremental data but the revisions since the last time data was captured. If the source data is transient, the capture of the revisions is not easy. For periodic status data or periodic event data, the incremental data capture includes the values of attributes at specific times. Extract the statuses and events that have been recorded since the last data extraction.

Incremental data capture may be immediate or deferred. Within the group of immediate data capture there are three distinct options. Two separate options are available for deferred data capture.

Immediate Data Extraction   In this option, the data extraction is real-time. It occurs as the transactions happen at the source databases and files. Figure 12-4 shows the immediate data extraction options.

Now let us go into some details about the three options for immediate data extraction.

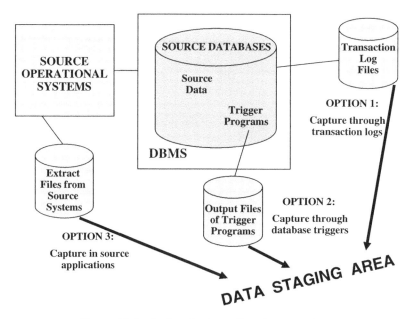

Figure 12-4   Options for immediate data extraction.

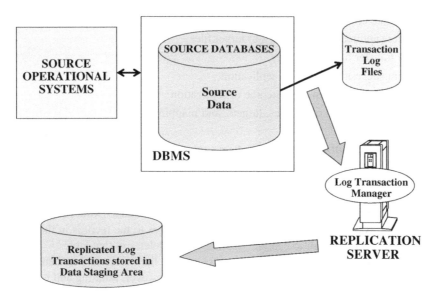

Figure 12-5   Data extraction using replication technology.

Capture through Transaction Logs   This option uses the transaction logs of the DBMSs maintained for recovery from possible failures. As each transaction adds, updates, or deletes a row from a database table, the DBMS immediately writes entries on the log file. This data extraction technique reads the transaction log and selects all the committed transactions. There is no extra overhead in the operational systems because logging is already part of the transaction processing.

You have to make sure that all transactions are extracted before the log file gets refreshed. As log files on disk storage get filled up, the contents are backed up on other media and the disk log files are reused. Ensure that all log transactions are extracted for data warehouse updates.

If all of your source systems are database applications, there is no problem with this technique. But if some of your source system data is on indexed and other flat files, this option will not work for these cases. There are no log files for these non-database applications. You will have to devise some other data extraction technique for these cases.

While we are on the topic of data capture through transaction logs, let us take a side excursion and look at the use of replication. Data replication is simply a method for creating copies of data in a distributed environment. Figure 12-5 illustrates how replication technology can be used to capture changes to source data.

The appropriate transaction logs contain all the changes to the various source database tables. Here are the broad steps for using replication to capture changes to source data:

- Identify the source system database table
- Identify and define target files in the staging area
- Create mapping between the source table and target files
- Define the replication mode
- Schedule the replication process

- Capture the changes from the transaction logs
- Transfer captured data from logs to target files
- Verify transfer of data changes
- Confirm success or failure of replication
- In metadata, document the outcome of replication
- Maintain definitions of sources, targets, and mappings

Capture through Database Triggers Again, this option is applicable to your source systems that are database applications. As you know, triggers are special stored procedures (programs) that are stored on the database and fired when certain predefined events occur. You can create trigger programs for all events for which you need data to be captured. The output of the trigger programs is written to a separate file that will be used to extract data for the data warehouse. For example, if you need to capture all changes to the records in the customer table, write a trigger program to capture all updates and deletes in that table.

Data capture through database triggers occurs right at the source and is therefore quite reliable. You can capture both before and after images. However, building and maintaining trigger programs puts an additional burden on the development effort. Also, execution of trigger procedures during transaction processing of the source systems puts additional overhead on the source systems. Further, this option is applicable only for source data in databases.

Capture in Source Applications This technique is also referred to as application-assisted data capture. In other words, the source application is made to assist in the data capture for the data warehouse. You have to modify the relevant application programs that write to the source files and databases. You revise the programs to write all adds, updates, and deletes to the source files and database tables. Then other extract programs can use the separate file containing the changes to the source data.

Unlike the previous two cases, this technique may be used for all types of source data irrespective of whether it is in databases, indexed files, or other flat files. But you have to revise the programs in the source operational systems and keep them maintained. This could be a formidable task if the number of source system programs is large. Also, this technique may degrade the performance of the source applications because of the additional processing needed to capture the changes on separate files.

Deferred Data Extraction In the cases discussed above, data capture takes place while the transactions occur in the source operational systems. The data capture is immediate or real-time. In contrast, the techniques under deferred data extraction do not capture the changes in real time. The capture happens later. Figure 12-6 shows the deferred data extraction options.

Now let us discuss the two options for deferred data extraction.

Capture Based on Date and Time Stamp Every time a source record is created or updated it may be marked with a stamp showing the date and time. The time stamp provides the basis for selecting records for data extraction. Here the data capture occurs at a later time, not while each source record is created or updated. If you run your data extraction program at midnight every day, each day you will extract only those with the date and time stamp later

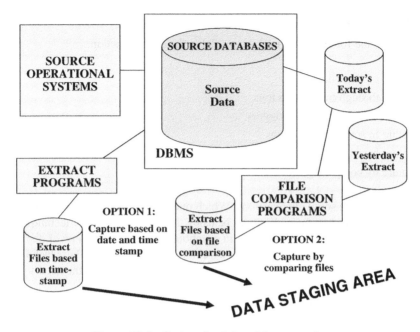

Figure 12-6   Options for deferred data extraction.

than midnight of the previous day. This technique works well if the number of revised records is small.

Of course, this technique presupposes that all the relevant source records contain date and time stamps. Provided this is true, data capture based on date and time stamp can work for any type of source file. This technique captures the latest state of the source data. Any intermediary states between two data extraction runs are lost.

Deletion of source records presents a special problem. If a source record gets deleted in between two extract runs, the information about the delete is not detected. You can get around this by marking the source record for delete first, do the extraction run, and then go ahead and physically delete the record. This means you have to add more logic to the source applications.

Capture by Comparing Files   If none of the above techniques are feasible for specific source files in your environment, then consider this technique as the last resort. This technique is also called the snapshot differential technique because it compares two snapshots of the source data. Let us see how this technique works.

Suppose you want to apply this technique to capture the changes to your product data. While performing today's data extraction for changes to product data, you do a full file comparison between today's copy of the product data and yesterday's copy. You also compare the record keys to find the inserts and deletes. Then you capture any changes between the two copies.

This technique necessitates the keeping of prior copies of all the relevant source data. Though simple and straightforward, comparison of full rows in a large file can be very inefficient. However, this may be the only feasible option for some legacy data sources that do not have transaction logs or time stamps on source records.

Evaluation of the Techniques

To summarize, the following options are available for data extraction:

- Capture of static data
- Capture through transaction logs
- Capture through database triggers
- Capture in source applications
- Capture based on date and time stamp
- Capture by comparing files

You are faced with some big questions. Which ones are applicable in your environment? Which techniques must you use? You will be using the static data capture technique at least in one situation when you populate the data warehouse initially at the time of deployment. After that, you will usually find that you need a combination of a few of these techniques for your environment. If you have old legacy systems, you may even have the need for the file comparison method.

Figure 12-7 highlights the advantages and disadvantages of the different techniques. Study it carefully and use it to determine the techniques you would need to use in your environment.

Let us make a few general comments. Which of the techniques are easy and inexpensive to implement? Consider the techniques of using transaction logs and database triggers. Both of these techniques are already available through the database products. Both are

Capture of static data

Good flexibility for capture specifications.
Performance of source systems not affected.
No revisions to existing applications.
Can be used on legacy systems.
Can be used on file-oriented systems.
Vendor products are used. No internal costs.

Capture in source applications

Good flexibility for capture specifications.
Performance of source systems affected a bit.
Major revisions to existing applications.
Can be used on most legacy systems.
Can be used on file-oriented systems.
High internal costs because of in-house work.

Capture through transaction logs

Not much flexibility for capture specifications.
Performance of source systems not affected.
No revisions to existing applications.
Can be used on most legacy systems.
Cannot be used on file-oriented systems.
Vendor products are used. No internal costs.

Capture based on date and time stamp

Good flexibility for capture specifications.
Performance of source systems not affected.
Major revisions to existing applications likely.
Cannot be used on most legacy systems.
Can be used on file-oriented systems.
Vendor products may be used.

Capture through database triggers

Not much flexibility for capture specifications.
Performance of source systems affected a bit.
No revisions to existing applications.
Cannot be used on most legacy systems.
Cannot be used on file-oriented systems.
Vendor products are used. No internal costs.

Capture by comparing files

Good flexibility for capture specifications.
Performance of source systems not affected.
No revisions to existing applications.
May be used on legacy systems.
May be used on file-oriented systems.
Vendor products are used. No internal costs.

Figure 12-7 Data capture techniques: advantages and disadvantages.

comparatively cheap and easy to implement. The technique based on transaction logs is perhaps the most inexpensive. There is no additional overhead on the source operational systems. In the case of database triggers, there is a need to create and maintain trigger programs. Even here, the maintenance effort and the additional overhead on the source operational systems are not that much compared to other techniques.

Data capture in source systems could be the most expensive in terms of development and maintenance. This technique needs substantial revisions to existing source systems. For many legacy source applications, finding the source code and modifying it may not be feasible at all. However, if the source data does not reside on database files and date and time stamps are not present in source records, this is one of the few available options.

What is the impact on the performance of the source operational systems? Certainly, the deferred data extraction methods have the least impact on the operational systems. Data extraction based on time stamps and data extraction based on file comparisons are performed outside the normal operation of the source systems. Therefore, these two are preferred options when minimizing the impact on operational systems is a priority. However, these deferred capture options suffer from some inadequacy. They track the changes from the state of the source data at the time of the current extraction as compared to its state at the time of the previous extraction. Any interim changes are not captured. Therefore, wherever you are dealing with transient source data, you can only come up with approximations of the history.

So, what is the bottom line? Use the data capture technique in source systems sparingly because it involves too much development and maintenance work. For your source data on databases, capture through transaction logs and capture through database triggers are obvious first choices. Between these two, capture through transaction logs is a better choice because of better performance. Also, this technique is also applicable to nonrelational databases. The file comparison method is the most time consuming for data extraction. Use it only if all others cannot be applied.

DATA TRANSFORMATION

By making use of the several techniques discussed in the previous section, you design the data extraction function. Now the extracted data is raw data and it cannot be applied to the data warehouse right away. First, all the extracted data must be made usable in the data warehouse. Having information that is usable for strategic decision making is the underlying principle of the data warehouse. You know that the data in the operational systems is not usable for this purpose. Next, because operational data is extracted from many old legacy systems, the quality of the data in those systems is less likely to be good enough for the data warehouse. You have to enrich and improve the quality of the data before it can be usable in the data warehouse.

Before moving the extracted data from the source systems into the data warehouse, you inevitably have to perform various kinds of data transformations. You have to transform the data according to standards because they come from many dissimilar source systems. You have to ensure that after all the data is put together, the combined data does not violate any business rules.

Consider the data structures and data elements that you need in your data warehouse. Now think about all the relevant data to be extracted from the source systems. From the variety of source data formats, data values, and the condition of the data quality, you know that you have to perform several types of transformations to make the source data suitable for your data warehouse. Transformation of source data encompasses a wide variety of manipulations to change all the extracted source data into usable information to be stored in the data warehouse.

Many organizations underestimate the extent and complexity of the data transformation functions. They start out with a simple departmental data mart as the pilot project. Almost all of the data for this pilot comes from a single source application. The data transformation just entails field conversions and some reformatting of the data structures. Do not make the mistake of taking the data transformation functions too lightly. Be prepared to consider all the different issues and allocate sufficient time and effort to the task of designing the transformations.

Data warehouse practitioners have attempted to classify data transformations in several ways, beginning with the very general and broad classifications of simple transformations and complex transformations. There is also some confusion about the semantics. One practitioner may refer to data integration as the process within the data transformation function that is some kind of preprocessing of the source data. To another practitioner, data integration may mean the mapping of the source fields to the target fields in the data warehouse. Resisting the temptation to generalize and classify, we will highlight and discuss the common types of major transformation functions. You may review each type and decide for yourself if that type is going to be simple or complex in your own data warehouse environment.

One major effort within data transformation is the improvement of data quality. In a simple sense, this includes filling in the missing values for attributes in the extracted data. Data quality is of paramount importance in the data warehouse because the effect of strategic decisions based on incorrect information can be devastating. Therefore, we will discuss data quality issues extensively in the next chapter.

Data Transformation: Basic Tasks

Irrespective of the variety and complexity of the source operational systems, and regardless of the extent of your data warehouse, you will find that most of your data transformation functions break down into a few basic tasks. Let us go over these basic tasks so that you can view data transformation from a fundamental perspective. Here is the set of basic tasks:

Selection. This takes place at the beginning of the whole process of data transformation. You select either whole records or parts of several records from the source systems. The task of selection usually forms part of the extraction function itself. However, in some cases, the composition of the source structure may not be amenable to selection of the necessary parts during data extraction. In these cases, it is prudent to extract the whole record and then do the selection as part of the transformation function.

Splitting/Joining. This task includes the types of data manipulation you need to perform on the selected parts of source records. Sometimes (uncommonly), you will be splitting the selected parts even further during data transformation. Joining of parts selected from many source systems is more widespread in the data warehouse environment.

Conversion. This is an all-inclusive task. It includes a large variety of rudimentary conversions of single fields for two primary reasons—one to standardize among the data extractions from disparate source systems, and the other to make the fields usable and understandable to the users.

Summarization. Sometimes you may find that it is not feasible to keep data at the lowest level of detail in your data warehouse. It may be that none of your users ever need data at the lowest granularity for analysis or querying. For example, for a grocery chain, sales data at the lowest level of detail for every transaction at the checkout may not be needed. Storing sales by product by store by day in the data warehouse may be quite adequate. So, in this case, the data transformation function includes summarization of daily sales by product and by store.

Enrichment. This task is the rearrangement and simplification of individual fields to make them more useful for the data warehouse environment. You may use one or more fields from the same input record to create a better view of the data for the data warehouse. This principle is extended when one or more fields originate from multiple records, resulting in a single field for the data warehouse.

Major Transformation Types

You have looked at the set of basic transformation tasks. When you consider a particular set of extracted data structures, you will find that the transformation functions you need to perform on this set may be done by a combination of the basic tasks discussed.

Now let us consider specific types of transformation functions. These are the most common transformation types:

Format Revisions. You will come across these quite often. These revisions include changes to the data types and lengths of individual fields. In your source systems, product package types may be indicated by codes and names in which the fields are numeric and text data types. Again, the lengths of the package types may vary among the different source systems. It is wise to standardize and change the data type to text to provide values meaningful to the users.

Decoding of Fields. This is also a common type of data transformation. When you deal with multiple source systems, you are bound to have the same data items described by a plethora of field values. The classic example is the coding for gender, with one source system using 1 and 2 for male and female and another system using M and F. Also, many legacy systems are notorious for using cryptic codes to represent business values. What do the codes AC, IN, RE, and SU mean in a customer file? You need to decode all such cryptic codes and change these into values that make sense to the users. Change the codes to Active, Inactive, Regular, and Suspended.

Calculated and Derived Values. What if you want to keep profit margin along with sales and cost amounts in your data warehouse tables? The extracted data from the sales system contains sales amounts, sales units, and operating cost estimates by product. You will have to calculate the total cost and the profit margin before data can be stored in the data warehouse. Average daily balances and operating ratios are examples of derived fields.

Splitting of Single Fields. Earlier legacy systems stored names and addresses of customers and employees in large text fields. The first name, middle initials, and last name were stored as a large text in a single field. Similarly, some earlier systems stored city, state, and zip code data together in a single field. You need to store individual components of names and addresses in separate fields in your data warehouse for two reasons. First, you may improve the operating performance by indexing on individual components. Second, your users may need to perform analysis by using individual components such as city, state, and zip code.

Merging of Information. This is not quite the opposite of splitting of single fields. This type of data transformation does not literally mean the merging of several fields to create a single field of data. For example, information about a product may come from different data sources. The product code and description may come from one data source. The relevant package types may be found in another data source. The cost data may be from yet another source. In this case, merging of information denotes the combination of the product code, description, package types, and cost into a single entity.

Character set conversion. This type of data transformation relates to the conversion of character sets to an agreed standard character set for textual data in the data warehouse. If you have mainframe legacy systems as source systems, the source data from these systems will be in EBCDIC characters. If PC-based architecture is the choice for your data warehouse, then you must convert the mainframe EBCDIC format to the ASCII format. When your source data is on other types of hardware and operating systems, you are faced with similar character set conversions.

Conversion of Units of Measurements. Many companies today have global branches. Measurements in many European countries are in metric units. If your company has overseas operations, you may have to convert the metrics so that the numbers are all in one standard unit of measurement.

Date/Time Conversion. This type relates to representation of date and time in standard formats. For example, the American and the British date formats may be standardized to an international format. The date of October 11, 2008 is written as $10/11/2008$ in the U.S. format and as $11/10/2008$ in the British format. This date may be standardized to be written as 11 OCT 2008.

Summarization. This type of transformation is the creating of summaries to be loaded in the data warehouse instead of loading the most granular level of data. For example, for a credit card company to analyze sales patterns, it may not be necessary to store in the data warehouse every single transaction on each credit card. Instead, you may want to summarize the daily transactions for each credit card and store the summary data instead of storing the most granular data by individual transactions.

Key Restructuring. While extracting data from your input sources, look at the primary keys of the extracted records. You will have to come up with keys for the fact and dimension tables based on the keys in the extracted records. See Figure 12-8. In the example shown in the figure, the product code in this organization is structured to have inherent meaning. If you use this product code as the primary key, there will be problems. If the product is moved to another warehouse, the warehouse part of the product key will have to be changed. This is a typical problem with legacy systems. When choosing keys for your data warehouse database tables, avoid such keys with built-in meanings. Transform such keys into generic keys generated by the system itself. This is called key restructuring.

Deduplication. In many companies, the customer files have several records for the same customer. Mostly, the duplicates are the result of creating additional records by mistake. In your data warehouse, you want to keep a single record for one customer and link all the duplicates in the source systems to this single record. This process is called deduplication of the customer file. Employee files and, sometimes, product master files have this kind of duplication problem.

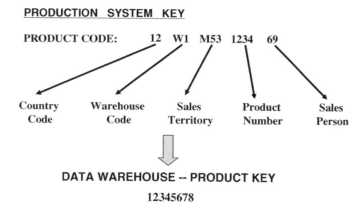

Figure 12-8 Data transformation: key restructuring.

Data Integration and Consolidation

The real challenge of ETL functions is the pulling together of all the source data from many disparate, dissimilar source systems. Even today, many data warehouses get data extracted from a combination of legacy mainframe systems and old minicomputer applications, in addition to newer client/server systems. Most of these source systems do not conform to the same set of business rules. Very often they follow different naming conventions and varied standards for data representation. Figure 12-9 shows a typical data source environment. Notice the challenging issues indicated in the figure.

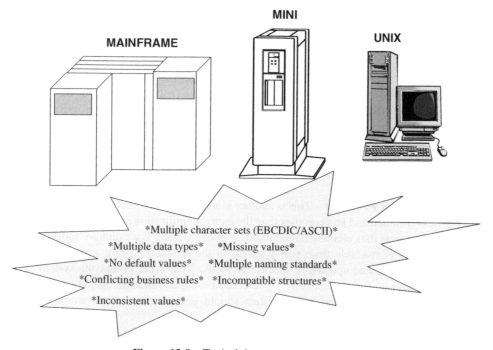

Figure 12-9 Typical data source environment.

Integrating the data involves combining all the relevant operational data into coherent data structures to be made ready for loading into the data warehouse. You may want to think of data integration and consolidation as a type of preprocess before other major transformation routines are applied. You have to standardize the names and data representations and resolve discrepancies in the ways in which the same data is represented in different source systems. Although time consuming, many of the data integration tasks can be managed. However, let us go over a couple of more difficult challenges.

Entity Identification Problem   If you have three different legacy applications developed in your organization at different times in the past, you are likely to have three different customer files supporting those systems. One system may be the old order entry system, another the customer service support system, and the third the marketing system. A very large number of the customers will be common to all three files. The same customer on each of the files may have a unique identification number. These unique identification numbers for the same customer may not be the same across the three systems.

This is a problem of identification in which you do not know which of the customer records relate to the same customer. But in the data warehouse you need to keep a single record for each customer. You must be able to get the activities of the single customer from the various source systems and then match up with the single record to be loaded to the data warehouse. This is a common but very difficult problem in many enterprises where applications have evolved over time from the distant past. This type of problem is prevalent where multiple sources exist for the same entities. Vendors, suppliers, employees, and sometimes products are the kinds of entities that are prone to this type of problem.

In the above example of the three customer files, you have to design complex algorithms to match records from all the three files and form groups of matching records. No matching algorithm can completely determine the groups. If the matching criteria are too tight, then some records will escape the groups. On the other hand, if the matching criteria are too loose, a particular group may include records of more than one customer. You need to get your users involved in reviewing the exceptions to the automated procedures. You have to weigh the issues relating to your source systems and decide how to handle the entity identification problem. Every time a data extract function is performed for your data warehouse, which may be every day, do you pause to resolve the entity identification problem before loading the data warehouse? How will this affect the availability of the data warehouse to your users? Some companies, depending on their individual situations, take the option of solving the entity identification problem in two phases. In the first phase, all records, irrespective of whether they are duplicates or not, are assigned unique identifiers. The second phase consists of reconciling the duplicates periodically through automatic algorithms and manual verification.

Multiple Sources Problem   This is another kind of problem affecting data integration, although less common and less complex than the entity identification problem. This problem results from a single data element having more than one source. For example, suppose unit cost of products is available from two systems. In the standard costing application, cost values are calculated and updated at specific intervals. Your order processing system also carries the unit costs for all products. There could be slight variations in the cost figures from these two systems. From which system should you get the cost for storing in the data warehouse?

A straightforward solution is to assign a higher priority to one of the two sources and pick up the product unit cost from that source. Sometimes, a straightforward solution such as this may not be compatible with the needs of the data warehouse users. You may have to select from either of the files based on the last update date. Or, in some other instances, your determination of the appropriate source depends on other related fields.

Transformation for Dimension Attributes

In Chapter 11, we discussed the changes to dimension table attributes. We reviewed the types of changes to these attributes. Also, we suggested ways to handle the three types of slowly changing dimensions. Type 1 changes are corrections of errors. These changes are applied to the data warehouse without any need to preserve history. Type 2 changes preserve the history in the data warehouse. Type 3 changes are tentative changes where your users need the ability to analyze the metrics in both ways—with the changes and without the changes.

In order to apply the changes correctly, you need to transform the incoming changes and prepare the changes to the data for loading into the data warehouse. Figure 12-10 illustrates how the data changes extracted from the source systems are transformed and prepared for data loading. This figure shows the handling of each type of change to dimension tables. Types 1, 2, and 3 are shown distinctly. Review the figure carefully to get a good grasp of the solutions. You will be faced with dimension table changes all the time.

How to Implement Transformation

The complexity and the extent of data transformation strongly suggest that manual methods alone will not be enough. You must go beyond the usual methods of writing conversion programs when you deployed operational systems. The types of data transformation are by far more difficult and challenging.

The methods you may want to adopt depend on some significant factors. If you are considering automating most of the data transformation functions, first consider if you have the time to select the tools, configure and install them, train the project team on the tools, and

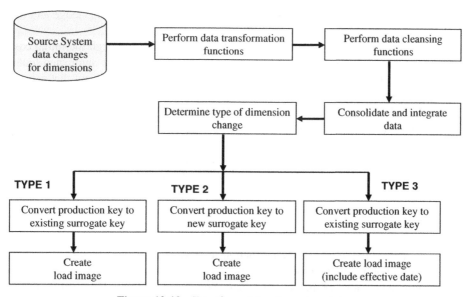

Figure 12-10 Transformed for dimension changes.

integrate the tools into the data warehouse environment. Data transformation tools can be expensive. If the scope of your data warehouse is modest, then the project budget may not have room for transformation tools.

Let us look at the issues relating to using manual techniques and to the use of data transformation tools. In many cases, a suitable combination of both methods will prove to be effective. Find the proper balance based on the available time frame and the money in the budget.

Using Transformation Tools In recent years, transformation tools have greatly increased in functionality and flexibility. Although the desired goal for using transformation tools is to eliminate manual methods altogether, in practice this is not completely possible. Even if you get the most sophisticated and comprehensive set of transformation tools, be prepared to use in-house programs here and there.

Use of automated tools certainly improves efficiency and accuracy. As a data transformation specialist, you just have to specify the parameters, the data definitions, and the rules to the transformation tool. If your input into the tool is accurate, then the rest of the work is performed efficiently by the tool.

You gain a major advantage from using a transformation tool because of the recording of metadata by the tool. When you specify the transformation parameters and rules, these are stored as metadata by the tool. This metadata then becomes part of the overall metadata component of the data warehouse. It may be shared by other components. When changes occur to transformation functions because of changes in business rules or data definitions, you just have to enter the changes into the tool. The metadata for the transformations get automatically adjusted by the tool.

Using Manual Techniques This was the predominant method in the early days of data warehousing when transformation tools began to appear in the market. Manual techniques may still be adequate for smaller data warehouses. In such cases, manually coded programs and scripts perform every data transformation. Mostly, these programs are executed in the data staging area. Analysts and programmers who already possess the knowledge and the expertise are able to produce the programs and scripts.

Of course, this method involves elaborate coding and testing. Although the initial cost may be reasonable, ongoing maintenance may escalate the cost. Unlike automated tools, the manual method is more likely to be prone to errors. It may also turn out that several individual programs are required in your environment.

A major disadvantage relates to metadata. Automated tools record their own metadata, but in-house programs have to be designed differently if you need to store and use metadata. Even if the in-house programs record the data transformation metadata initially, every time changes occur to transformation rules, the metadata has to be maintained. This puts an additional burden on the maintenance of manually coded transformation programs.

DATA LOADING

It is generally agreed that transformation functions end as soon as load images are created. The next major set of functions consists of the ones that take the prepared data, apply it to the data warehouse, and store it in the database there. You create load images to correspond to the target files to be loaded in the data warehouse database.

The whole process of moving data into the data warehouse repository is referred to in several ways. You must have heard the phrases applying the data, loading the data, and refreshing the data. For the sake of clarity we will use the phrases as indicated below:

Initial load—populating all the data warehouse tables for the very first time.

Incremental load—applying ongoing changes as necessary in a periodic manner.

Full refresh—completely erasing the contents of one or more tables and reloading with fresh data (initial load is a refresh of all the tables).

Because loading the data warehouse may take an inordinate amount of time, loads are generally causes for great concern. During the loads, the data warehouse has to be offline. You need to find a window of time when the loads may be scheduled without affecting your data warehouse users. Therefore, consider dividing up the whole load process into smaller chunks and populating a few files at a time. This will give you two benefits. You may be able to run the smaller loads in parallel. Also, you might be able to keep some parts of the data warehouse up and running while loading the other parts. It is hard to estimate the running times of the loads, especially the initial load or a complete refresh. Do test loads to verify the correctness and to estimate the running times.

When you are running a load, do not expect every record in the source load image file to be successfully applied to the data warehouse. For the record you are trying to load to the fact table, the concatenated key may be wrong and not correspond to the dimension tables. Provide procedures to handle the load images that do not load. Also, have a plan for quality assurance of the loaded records.

If the data staging area and the data warehouse database are on the same server that will save you the effort of moving the load images to the data warehouse server. But if you have to transport the load images to the data warehouse server, consider the options carefully and select the ones best suited for your environment. The Web, FTP, and database links are a few of the options. You have to consider the necessary bandwidth needed and also the impact of the transmissions on the network. Think of data compression and have contingency plans.

What are the general methods for applying data? The most straightforward method is writing special load programs. Depending on the size of your data warehouse, the number of load programs can be large. Managing the load runs of a large number of programs can be challenging. Further, maintaining a large suite of special load programs consumes a lot of time and effort. Load utilities that come with the DBMSs provide a fast method for loading. Consider this method as a primary choice. When the staging area files and the data warehouse repository are on different servers, database links are useful.

You are already aware of some of the concerns and difficulties in data loading. The project team has to be very familiar with the common challenges so that it can work out proper resolutions. Let us now move on to the details of the data loading techniques and processes.

Applying Data: Techniques and Processes

Earlier in this section, we defined three types of application of data to the data warehouse: initial load, incremental load, and full refresh. Consider how data is applied in each of these types. Let us take the example of product data. For the initial load, you extract the data for all the products from the various source systems, integrate and transform the data, and then create load images for loading the data into the product dimension table. For an incremental load, you collect the changes to the product data for those product records that have changed in the source systems since the previous extract, run the changes through the integration and transformation process, and create output records to be applied to the product dimension table. A full refresh is similar to the initial load.

In every case, you create a file of data to be applied to the product dimension table in the data warehouse. How can you apply the data to the warehouse? What are the modes? Data may be applied in the following four different modes: load, append, destructive merge, and constructive merge. Study Figure 12-11 for an understanding of the effect of applying data in each of these four modes. Let us explain how each mode works.

Load   If the target table to be loaded already exists and data exists in the table, the load process wipes out the existing data and applies the data from the incoming file. If the table is already empty before loading, the load process simply applies the data from the incoming file.

Append   You may think of the append as an extension of the load. If data already exists in the table, the append process unconditionally adds the incoming data, preserving the existing data in the target table. When an incoming record is a duplicate of an already existing record, you may define how to handle an incoming duplicate. The incoming record may be allowed to be added as a duplicate. In the other option, the incoming duplicate record may be rejected during the append process.

Destructive Merge   In this mode, you apply the incoming data to the target data. If the primary key of an incoming record matches with the key of an existing record, update the matching target record. If the incoming record is a new record without a match with any existing record, add the incoming record to the target table.

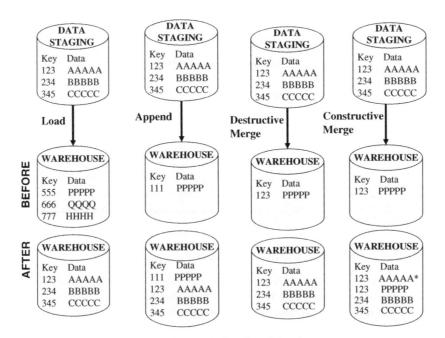

Figure 12-11   Modes of applying data.

Constructive Merge   This mode is slightly different from the destructive merge. If the primary key of an incoming record matches with the key of an existing record, leave the existing record, add the incoming record, and mark the added record as superseding the old record.

Let us now consider how these modes of applying data to the data warehouse fit into the three types of loads. We will discuss these one by one.

Initial Load   Let us say you are able to load the whole data warehouse in a single run. As a variation of this single run, let us say you are able to split the load into separate subloads and run each of these subloads as single loads. In other words, every load run creates the database tables from scratch. In these cases, you will be using the load mode discussed above.

If you need more than one run to create a single table, and your load runs for a single table must be scheduled to run on several days, then the approach is different. For the first run of the initial load of a particular table, use the load mode. All further runs will apply the incoming data using the append mode.

Creation of indexes on initial loads or full refreshes requires special consideration. Index creation on mass loads can be too time consuming. So drop the indexes prior to the loads to make the loads go quicker. You may rebuild or regenerate the indexes when the loads are complete.

Incremental Loads   These are the applications of ongoing changes from the source systems. Changes to the source systems are always tied to specific times, irrespective of whether or not they are based on explicit time stamps in the source systems. Therefore, you need a method to preserve the periodic nature of the changes in the data warehouse.

Let us review the constructive merge mode. In this mode, if the primary key of an incoming record matches with the key of an existing record, the existing record is left in the target table as is and the incoming record is added and marked as superseding the old record. If the time stamp is also part of the primary key or if the time stamp is included in the comparison between the incoming and the existing records, then constructive merge may be used to preserve the periodic nature of the changes. This is an oversimplification of the exact details of how constructive merge may be used. Nevertheless, the point is that the constructive merge mode is an appropriate method for incremental loads. The details will have to be worked out based on the nature of the individual target tables.

Are there cases in which the mode of destructive merge may be applied? What about a type 1 slowly changing dimension? In this case, the change to a dimension table record is meant to correct an error in the existing record. The existing record must be replaced by the corrected incoming record, so you may use the destructive merge mode. This mode is also applicable to any target tables where the historical perspective is not important.

Full Refresh   This type of application of data involves periodically rewriting the entire data warehouse. Sometimes, you may also do partial refreshes to rewrite only specific tables. Partial refreshes are rare because every dimension table is intricately tied to the fact table.

As far as the data application modes are concerned, full refresh is similar to the initial load. However, in the case of full refreshes, data exists in the target tables before incoming data is applied. The existing data must be erased before applying the incoming data. Just as in the case of the initial load, the load and append modes are applicable to full refresh.

Data Refresh Versus Update

After the initial load, you may maintain the data warehouse and keep it up to date by using two methods:

Update—application of incremental changes in the data sources. Refresh—complete reload at specified intervals.

Technically, refresh is a much simpler option than update. To use the update option, you have to devise the proper strategy to extract the changes from each data source. Then you have to determine the best strategy to apply the changes to the data warehouse. The refresh option simply involves the periodic replacement of complete data warehouse tables. But refresh jobs can take a long time to run. If you have to run refresh jobs every day, you may have to keep the data warehouse down for unacceptably long times. The case worsens if your database has large tables.

Is there some kind of a guideline as to when refresh is better than update or vice versa? Figure 12-12 shows a graph comparing refresh with update. The cost of refresh remains constant irrespective of the number of changes in the source systems. If the number of changes increases, the time and effort for doing a full refresh remain the same. On the other hand, the cost of update varies with the number of records to be updated.

If the number of records to be updated falls between 15% and 25% of the total number of records, the cost of loading per record tends to be the same whether you opt for a full refresh of the entire data warehouse or to do the updates. This range is just a general guide. If more than 25% of the source records change daily, then seriously consider full refreshes. Generally, data warehouse administrators use the update process. Occasionally, you may want to redo the data warehouse with a full refresh when some major restructuring or similar mass changes take place.

Procedure for Dimension Tables

In a data warehouse, dimension tables contain attributes that are used to analyze basic measurements such as sales and costs. As you know very well, customer, product, time,

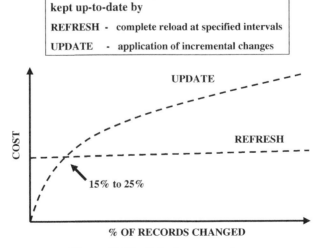

Figure 12-12   Refresh versus update.

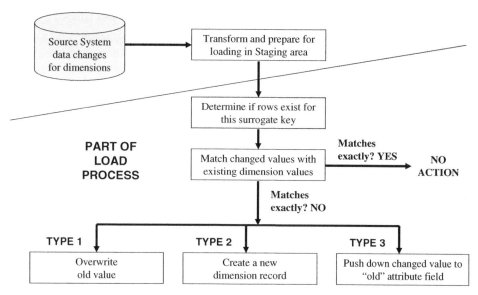

Figure 12-13 Loading changes to dimension tables.

and sales territory are examples of dimension tables. The procedure for maintaining the dimension tables includes two functions: first, the initial loading of the tables; thereafter, applying the changes on an ongoing basis. Let us consider two issues.

The first one is about the keys of the records in the source systems and the keys of the records in the data warehouse. For reasons discussed earlier, we do not use the production system keys for the records in the data warehouse. In the data warehouse, you use system-generated keys. The records in the source systems have their own keys. Therefore, before source data can be applied to the dimension tables, whether for the initial load or for ongoing changes, the production keys must be converted to the system-generated keys in the data warehouse. You may do the key conversion as part of the transformation functions or you may do it separately before the actual load functions. The separate key translation system is preferable.

The next issue relates to the application of the type 1, type 2, and type 3 dimension changes to the data warehouse. Figure 12-13 shows how these different types are handled.

Fact Tables: History and Incremental Loads

The key of the fact table is the concatenation of the keys of the dimension tables. Therefore, for this reason, dimension records are loaded first. Then, before loading each fact table record, you have to create the concatenated key for the fact table record from the keys of the corresponding dimension records.

Here are some tips for history loads of the fact tables:

- Identify historical data useful and interesting for the data warehouse.
- Define and refine extract business rules.
- Capture audit statistics to tie back to the operational systems.
- Perform fact table surrogate key look-up.
- Improve fact table content.
- Restructure the data.
- Prepare the load files.

Given below are a few useful remarks about incremental loads for fact tables:

- Incremental extracts for fact tables
  - Consist of new transactions
  - Consist of update transactions
  - Use database transaction logs for data capture
- Incremental loads for fact tables
  - Load as frequently as feasible
  - Use partitioned files and indexes
  - Apply parallel processing techniques

ETL SUMMARY

By now you should be fully convinced that the data extraction, transformation, and loading functions for a data warehouse cover very wide ground. The conversion functions normally associated with the development of any operational system bear no comparison to the extent and complexity of the ETL functions in a data warehouse environment. The data extraction function in a data warehouse spans several, varied source systems. As a data warehouse developer, you need to carefully examine the challenges the variety of your source systems pose and find appropriate data extraction methods. We have discussed most of the common methods. Data extraction for a data warehouse is not a one-time event; it is an ongoing function carried out at very frequent intervals.

There are many types of data transformation in a data warehouse with many different tasks. It is not just a field-to-field conversion. In our discussion, we considered many common types of data transformation. The list of types we were able to consider is by no means exhaustive or complete. In your data warehouse environment, you will come across additional types of data transformation.

What about the data loads in a data warehouse in comparison with the loads for a new operational system? For the implementation of a new operational system, you convert and load the data once to get the new system started. Loading of data in a data warehouse does not cease with the initial implementation. Just like extraction and transformation, data loading is not just an initial activity to get the data warehouse started. Apart from the initial data load, you have the ongoing incremental data loads and the periodic full refreshes.

Fortunately, many vendors have developed powerful tools for data extraction, data transformation, and data loading. You are no longer left to yourself to handle these challenges with unsophisticated manual methods. You have flexible and suitable vendor solutions. Vendor tools cover a wide range of functional options. You have effective tools to perform functions in every part of the ETL process. Tools can extract data from multiple sources, perform scores of transformation functions, and do mass loads as well as incremental loads. Let us review some of the options you have with regard to ETL tools.

ETL Tool Options

Vendors have approached the challenges of ETL and addressed them by providing tools falling into the following three broad functional categories:

1. *Data transformation engines*. These consist of dynamic and sophisticated data manipulation algorithms. The tool suite captures data from a designated set of

source systems at user-defined intervals, performs elaborate data transformations, sends the results to a target environment, and applies the data to target files. These tools provide you with maximum flexibility for pointing to various source systems, to select the appropriate data transformation methods, and to apply full loads and incremental loads. The functionality of these tools sweeps the full range of the ETL process.

2. *Data capture through replication.* Most of these tools use the transaction recovery logs maintained by the DBMS. The changes to the source systems captured in the transaction logs are replicated in near real time to the data staging area for further processing. Some of the tools provide the ability to replicate data through the use of database triggers. These specialized stored procedures in the database signal the replication agent to capture and transport the changes.

3. *Code generators.* These are tools that directly deal with the extraction, transformation, and loading of data. The tools enable the process by generating program code to perform these functions. Code generators create 3GL/4GL data extraction and transformation programs. You provide the parameters of the data sources and the target layouts along with the business rules. The tools generate most of the program code in some of the common programming languages. When you want to add more code to handle the types of transformation not covered by the tool, you may do so with your own program code. The code automatically generated by the tool has exits at which points you may add your code to handle special conditions.

Currently, several DBMS vendors include ETL capabilities in their database products at little or no extra cost. This option is attractive to many organizations because of the cost implications. Also, if ETL and database functionalities come from the same vendor, support issues are minimized.

More specifically, what can the ETL tools do? Review the following list and as you read each item consider if you need that feature in the ETL tool for your environment:

- Data extraction from various relational databases of leading vendors
- Data extraction from old legacy databases, indexed files, and flat files
- Data transformation from one format to another with variations in source and target fields
- Performing of standard conversions, key reformatting, and structural changes
- Provision of audit trails from source to target
- Application of business rules for extraction and transformation
- Combining of several records from the source systems into one integrated target record
- Recording and management of metadata

Reemphasizing ETL Metadata

Chapter 9 covered data warehouse metadata in great detail. We discussed the role and importance of metadata in the three major functional areas of the data warehouse. We reviewed the capture and use of metadata in the three areas of data acquisition, data storage, and information delivery. Metadata in data acquisition and data storage relate to the ETL functions.

When you use vendor tools for performing part or all of the ETL functions, most of these tools record and manage their own metadata. Even though the metadata is in the proprietary formats of the tools, it is usable and available. ETL metadata contains information about the source systems, mappings between source data and data warehouse target data structures, data transformations, and data loading.

But as you know, your selected tools may not exclusively perform all of the ETL functions. You will have to augment your ETL effort with in-house programs. In each of the data extraction, data transformation, and data loading functions, you may use programs written by the project team. Depending on the situation in your environment, these in-house programs may vary considerably in number. Although in-house programs give you more control and flexibility, there is one drawback. Unlike using ETL tools, in-house programs do not record or manage metadata. You have to make a special effort to deal with metadata. Although we have reviewed metadata extensively in the earlier chapter, we want to reiterate that you need to pay special attention and ensure that metadata is not overlooked when you use in-house programs for ETL functions. All the business rules, source data information, source-to-target mappings, transformation, and loading information must be recorded manually in the metadata directory. This is extremely important to make your metadata component complete and accurate.

ETL Summary and Approach

Let us summarize the functions covered in this chapter with Figure 12-14. Look at the figure and do a quick review of the major functions.

What do you think of the size of this chapter and the topics covered? If nothing else, the length of the chapter alone highlights the importance and complexity of the data extraction,

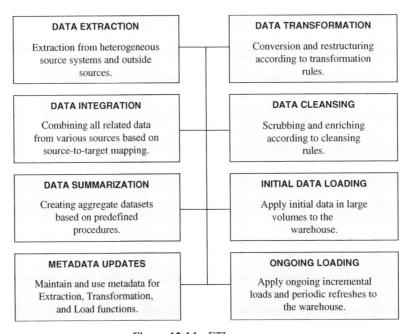

Figure 12-14   ETL summary.

transformation, and loading functions. Why so? Again and again, the variety and heterogeneous nature of the source systems comes to the forefront as the pressing reason to pay special attention to ETL. For one thing, the variety and heterogeneity add to the challenge of data extraction. But when you consider the number of different source systems, the more there are, the more intense and complex will be the transformation functions. More inconsistencies are likely to be present and more variations from standards are expected.

Nevertheless, what is required is a systematic and practical approach. Whenever you can break down a task into two, do so without hesitation. For example, look for ways to break down the initial load into several subloads. Additionally, detailed analysis is crucial. You cannot take any source system lightly. Every source system may pose its own challenges. Get down to the details. Spend enough time in the source-to-target mappings. Make an initial list of data transformations and let this list evolve. Do more analysis and add to the list.

You have to live with data loads every day. Frequent incremental loads are absolutely essential to keep your data warehouse up to date. Try to automate as much of incremental loading as possible. Keep in-house programming down to a reasonable level. Manual maintenance of metadata could impose a large burden. We realize ETL functions are time consuming, complex, and arduous; nevertheless, they are very important. Any flaws in the ETL process show up in the data warehouse. Your users will end up using faulty information. What kind of decisions do you think they will make with incorrect and incomplete information?

OTHER INTEGRATION APPROACHES

After considering all that was discussed in this chapter about data extraction, transforming, and loading, you can appreciate that ETL is a leading methodology for enterprise data integration. At the heart of ETL is the consolidation of enterprise data from, perhaps, many disparate sources. Nevertheless, as companies progress in information integration to provide a single unified corporate view, there are other integration approaches to be considered.

We will now review two leading approaches for information integration without getting too much into technical details. We will also compare each of these approaches to ETL in order to help you make choices in your own particular environment. The two other approaches are commonly known as Enterprise Information Integration (EII) and Enterprise Application Integration (EAI).

Enterprise Information Integration (EII)

This approach to integration is based on configuring and providing a unified view of dispersed corporate data. However, the integration is not physical but virtual. EII products strive to provide a virtual business view of dispersed data. The various collections of disparate data sources are deemed to be an information federation. The collections may include business transaction data, a data mart, and even some set of unstructured data content. EII supports an information federation approach to integration.

Applications needing to access data virtually see the dispersed data sets as though they all reside in a single database. A query is directed against a virtual view of the required data that may reside in various sources. EII products break the query down into subqueries. Each subquery is directed to the appropriate data set. When all the subqueries finish execution, the results are combined into a unified result and presented to the user. Relational DBMS and

XML technologies are driving the implementation of EII tools. These EII products support SQL and XML data interfaces.

EII compared to ETL

- EII may be applicable to a federated data warehouse; but a federated architecture is almost always not recommended for a new data warehouse. EII, therefore, is not generally a total substitute for ETL.
- When using ETL to capture and consolidate data, some latency is to be expected. However, if the operational data is highly volatile and real-time querying and analysis is absolutely essential, then EII may be considered as an option.
- Querying through EII implies data access to current operational systems as well as to historical data. If self-service business intelligence is opened up to unknown or less-trained users, erratic queries through EII may cause severe system degradation in operational systems.
- In cases where data volumes are too large for consolidation and only a fraction of the consolidated data is used regularly, retrieval and data consolidation using ETL may not be justified. EII may prove to be a viable alternative.
- Data transformation as part of ETL may sometimes be extremely complex. In these situations, complex data transformations of EII on the fly may result in very high system overhead.
- ETL enables the building of historical data over time in a systematic manner. Wherever historical trends and patterns are the focus of business intelligence, EII may not be the approach of choice.

Enterprise Application Integration (EAI)

In this approach, integration takes the form of linking application systems by allowing them to exchange data, messages, and transactions. A specific application may access the required data transparently without knowing the format of how the data is stored or where the data is stored. By its very nature, EAI is generally applied to real-time transaction processing in an operational system.

So, how does EAI fare as an integration approach? EAI may be used to move data from a real-time event to other data integration approaches such as ETL. EAI is designed to transport small amounts of data in real-time. Any data transformation in EAI is rudimentary. This approach is not meant for vast amounts of data retrieval, transformation, and delivery.

EAI compared to ETL

- First, EAI cannot be regarded as an integration approach competing with ETL. The two approaches may be combined to complement each other. EAI can be used as an input-producing mechanism for ETL; ETL may be considered as a service mechanism for EAI.
- Wherever ETL applications require low-latency data, EAI may be used to provide the EAI-to-ETL interface for real-time data extraction and consolidation.

- Although a dynamic EAI-to-ETL interface is desirable, most organizations are using EAI to create data sets that are subsequently input into ETL applications.

CHAPTER SUMMARY

- ETL functions in a data warehouse are most important, challenging, time consuming, and labor intensive.
- Data extraction is complex because of the disparate source systems; data transformation is difficult because of the wide range of tasks; data loading is challenging because of the volume of data.
- Several data extraction techniques are available, each with its advantages and disadvantages. Choose the right technique based on the conditions in your environment.
- The data transformation function encompasses data conversion, cleansing, consolidation, and integration. Implement the transformation function using a combination of specialized tools and in-house developed software.
- The data loading function relates to the initial load, regular periodic incremental loads, and full refreshes from time to time. Four methods to apply data are: load, append, destructive merge, and constructive merge.
- Tools for ETL functions fall into three broad functional categories: data transformation engines, data capture through replication, and code generators.
- Enterprise Information Integration (EII) and Enterprise Application Integration (EAI) are some other approaches to data integration.

REVIEW QUESTIONS

1. Give three reasons why you think ETL functions are most challenging in a data warehouse environment.
2. Name any five types of activities that are part of the ETL process. Which of these are time consuming?
3. The tremendous diversity of the source systems is the primary reason for their complexity. Do you agree? If so, explain briefly why.
4. What are the two general categories of data stored in source operational systems? Give two examples for each.
5. Name five types of the major transformation tasks. Give an example for each.
6. Describe briefly the entity identification problem in data integration and consolidation. How do you resolve this problem?
7. What is key restructuring? Explain why it is needed.
8. Define initial load, incremental load, and full refresh.

9. Explain the difference between destructive merge and constructive merge for applying data to the data warehouse repository. When do you use these modes?

10. When is a full data refresh preferable to an incremental load? Can you think of an example?

EXERCISES

1. Match the columns:

1. constructive merge	**A.** use static data capture
2. full refresh	**B.** EBCDIC to ASCII
3. character set conversion	**C.** technique of last resort
4. derived value	**D.** overwrite old value with new
5. immediate data extract	**E.** record supersedes
6. initial load	**F.** average daily balance
7. file comparison method	**G.** complete reload
8. data enrichment	**H.** make data more useful
9. Type 1 dimension changes	**I.** create extraction program
10. code generator	**J.** real-time data capture

2. As the ETL expert on the data warehouse project team for a telecommunications company, write a memo to your project leader describing the types of challenges in your environment, and suggest some practical steps to meet the challenges.

3. Your project team has decided to use the system logs for capturing the updates from the source operational systems. You have to extract data for the incremental loads from four operational systems all running on relational databases. These are four types of sales applications. You need data to update the sales data in the data warehouse. Make assumptions and describe the data extraction process.

4. In your organization, assume that customer names and addresses are maintained in three customer files supporting three different source operational systems. Describe the possible entity identification problem you are likely to face when you consolidate the customer records from the three files. Write a procedure outlining how you propose to resolve the problem.

5. You are the staging area expert on the data warehouse project team for a large toy manufacturer. Discuss the four modes of applying data to the data warehouse. Select the modes you want to use for your data warehouse and explain the reasons for your selection.

CHAPTER 13

DATA QUALITY: A KEY TO SUCCESS

CHAPTER OBJECTIVES

- Clearly understand why data quality is critical in a data warehouse
- Observe the challenges posed by corrupt data and learn the methods to deal with them
- Appreciate the benefits of quality data
- Review the various categories of data quality tools and examine their usage
- Study the implications of a data quality initiative and learn practical tips on data quality
- Review Master Data Management (MDM) and check its applicability to data quality in the data warehouse

Imagine a small error, seemingly inconsequential, creeping into one of your operational systems. While collecting data in that operational system about customers, let us say the user consistently entered erroneous region codes. The sales region codes of the customers are all messed up, but in the operational system, the accuracy of the region codes may not be that important because no invoices to the customers are going to be mailed out using region codes. These region codes were entered for marketing purposes.

Now take the customer data to the next step and move it into the data warehouse. What is the consequence of this error? All analyses performed by your data warehouse users based on region codes will result in serious misrepresentation. An error that seems to be so irrelevant in the operational systems can cause gross distortion in the results from the data warehouse. This example may not appear to be the true state of affairs in many data warehouses, but you will be surprised to learn how common these kinds of problems really are. Poor data quality in the source systems results in poor decisions by the users of the business intelligence from the data warehouse.

Data Warehousing Fundamentals for IT Professionals, Second Edition. By Paulraj Ponniah
Copyright © 2010 John Wiley & Sons, Inc.

Dirty data is among the top reasons for failure of a data warehouse. As soon as the users sense that the data is of unacceptable quality, they lose their confidence in the data warehouse. They will flee from the data warehouse in droves and all the effort of the project team will be down the drain. It will be impossible to get back the trust of the users.

Most companies overestimate the quality of the data in their operational systems. Very few organizations have procedures and systems in place to verify the quality of data in their various operational systems. As long as the quality of the data is acceptable enough to perform the functions of the operational systems, then the general conclusion is that all of the enterprise data is good. For some companies that are building data warehouses, data quality is not a high priority. These companies suspect that there may be a problem, but that it is not so pressing as to demand immediate attention.

Only when companies make an effort to ascertain the quality of their data are they amazed at the extent of data corruption. Even when companies discover a high level of data pollution, they tend to underestimate the effort needed to cleanse the data. They do not allocate sufficient time and resources for the clean-up effort. At best, the problem is addressed partially and intermittently.

If your enterprise has several disparate legacy systems from which your data warehouse must draw its data, start with the assumption that your source data is likely to be corrupt. Then ascertain the level of the data corruption. The project team must allow enough time and effort and have a plan for correcting the polluted data. In this chapter, we will define data quality in the context of the data warehouse. We will consider the common types of data quality problems so that when you analyze your source data, you can identify the types and deal with them. We will explore the methods for data cleansing and also review the features of the tools available to assist the project team in this crucial undertaking.

WHY IS DATA QUALITY CRITICAL?

Data quality in a data warehouse is critical (this sounds so obvious and axiomatic), more so than in an operational system. Strategic decisions made on the basis of business intelligence from the data warehouse are likely to be more far reaching in scope and consequences. Let us list some reasons why data quality is critical. Consider the following observations. Improved data quality:

- boosts confidence in decision making.
- enables better customer service.
- increases opportunity to add better value to the services.
- reduces risk from disastrous decisions.
- reduces costs, especially of marketing campaigns.
- enhances strategic decision making.
- improves productivity by streamlining processes.
- avoids compounding the effects of data contamination.

What Is Data Quality?

As an IT professional, you have heard of data accuracy quite often. Accuracy is associated with a data element. Consider an entity such as customer. The customer entity has attributes such as customer name, customer address, customer state, customer lifestyle, and so on. Each occurrence of the customer entity refers to a single customer. Data accuracy, as it relates to the attributes of the customer entity, means that the values of the attributes of a single occurrence accurately describe the particular customer. The value of the customer name for a single occurrence of the customer entity is actually the name of that customer. Data quality implies data accuracy, but it is much more than that. Most cleansing operations concentrate on just data accuracy. You need to go beyond data accuracy.

If the data is fit for the purpose for which it is intended, we can then say such data has quality. Therefore, data quality is to be related to the usage for the data item as defined by the users. Does the data item in an entity reflect exactly what the user is expecting to observe? Does the data item possess fitness of purpose as defined by the users? If it does, the data item conforms to the standards of data quality. Examine Fig. 13-1. This figure brings out the distinction between data accuracy and data quality.

What is considered to be data quality in operational systems? If the database records conform to the field validation edits, then we generally say that the database records are of good data quality. But such single field edits alone do not constitute data quality.

Data quality in a data warehouse is not just the quality of individual data items but the quality of the full, integrated system as a whole. It is more than the data edits on individual fields. For example, while entering data about the customers in an order entry application, you may also collect the demographics of each customer. The customer demographics are not directly germane to the order entry application and, therefore, they are not given too much attention. But you run into problems when you try to access the customer demographics in the data warehouse. The customer data as an integrated whole lacks data quality.

Figure 13-1 is just a clarification of the distinction between data accuracy and data quality. But how can you specifically define data quality? Can you know intuitively whether a data element is of high quality or not by examining it? If so, what kind of examination do you conduct, and how do you examine the data? As IT professionals, having worked with

DATA INTEGRITY	DATA QUALITY
Specific instance of an entity accurately represents that occurrence of the entity.	The data item is exactly fit for the purpose for which the business users have defined it.
Data element defined in terms of database technology.	Wider concept grounded in the specific business of the company.
Data element conforms to validation constraints.	Relates not just to single data elements but to the system as a whole.
Individual data items have the correct data types.	Form and content of data elements consistent across the whole system.
Traditionally relates to operational systems.	Essentially needed in a corporate-wide data warehouse for business users.

Figure 13-1 Data accuracy versus data quality.

data in our assignments, we have a sense of what corrupt data is and how to tell whether a data element is of high data quality or not. But a vague concept of data quality is not adequate to deal with data corruption effectively. So, let us get into some concrete ways of recognizing data quality in the data warehouse.

The following list is a survey of the characteristics or indicators of high-quality data. We will start with data accuracy, as discussed earlier. Study each of these data quality dimensions and use the list to recognize and measure the data quality in the systems that feed your data warehouse,

Accuracy. The value stored in the system for a data element is the right value for that occurrence of the data element. If you have a customer name and an address stored in a record, then the address is the correct address for the customer with that name. If you find the quantity ordered as 1000 units in the record for order number 12345678, then that quantity is the accurate quantity for that order.

Domain Integrity. The data value of an attribute falls in the range of allowable, defined values. The common example is the allowable values being "male" and "female" for the gender data element.

Data Type. Value for a data attribute is actually stored as the data type defined for that attribute. When the data type of the store name field is defined as "text," all instances of that field contain the store name shown in textual format and not numeric codes.

Consistency. The form and content of a data field is the same across multiple source systems. If the product code for product ABC in one system is 1234, then the code for this product is 1234 in every source system.

Redundancy. The same data must not be stored in more than one place in a system. If, for reasons of efficiency, a data element is intentionally stored in more than one place in a system, then the redundancy must be clearly identified and verified.

Completeness. There are no missing values for a given attribute in the system. For example, in a customer file, there must be a valid value for the "state" field for every customer. In the file for order details, every detail record for an order must be completely filled.

Duplication. Duplication of records in a system is completely resolved. If the product file is known to have duplicate records, then all the duplicate records for each product are identified and a cross-reference created.

Conformance to Business Rules. The values of each data item adhere to prescribed business rules. In an auction system, the hammer or sale price cannot be less than the reserve price. In a bank loan system, the loan balance must always be positive or zero.

Structural Definiteness. Wherever a data item can naturally be structured into individual components, the item must contain this well-defined structure. For example, an individual's name naturally divides into first name, middle initial, and last name. Values for names of individuals must be stored as first name, middle initial, and last name. This characteristic of data quality simplifies enforcement of standards and reduces missing values.

Data Anomaly. A field must be used only for the purpose for which it is defined. If the field Address-3 is defined for any possible third line of address for long addresses, then this field must be used only for recording the third line of address. It must not be used for entering a phone or fax number for the customer.

Clarity. A data element may possess all the other characteristics of quality data but if the users do not understand its meaning clearly, then the data element is of no value to the users. Proper naming conventions help to make the data elements well understood by the users.

Timely. The users determine the timeliness of the data. If the users expect customer dimension data not to be older than one day, the changes to customer data in the source systems must be applied to the data warehouse daily.

Usefulness. Every data element in the data warehouse must satisfy some requirements of the collection of users. A data element may be accurate and of high quality, but if it is of no value to the users, then it is totally unnecessary for that data element to be in the data warehouse.

Adherence to Data Integrity Rules. The data stored in the relational databases of the source systems must adhere to entity integrity and referential integrity rules. Any table that permits null as the primary key does not have entity integrity. Referential integrity forces the establishment of the parent–child relationships correctly. In a customer-to-order relationship, referential integrity ensures the existence of a customer for every order in the database.

Benefits of Improved Data Quality

Everyone generally understands that improved data quality is a critical goal, especially in a data warehouse. Bad data leads to bad decisions. At this stage, let us review some specific areas where data quality yields definite benefits.

Analysis with Timely Information Suppose a large retail chain is running daily promotions of many types in most of its 200 stores in the country. This is a major seasonal campaign. Promotion is one of the dimensions stored in the data warehouse. The marketing department wants to run various analyses using promotion as the primary dimension to monitor and tune the promotions as the season progresses. It is critical for the department to perform the analyses every day. Suppose the promotion details are fed into the data warehouse only once a week. Do you think the promotional data is timely for the marketing department? Of course not. Is the promotional data in the data warehouse of high quality for the data warehouse users? Not according to the characteristics of quality data listed in the previous section. Quality data produces timely information, a significant benefit for the users.

Better Customer Service The benefit of accurate and complete information for customer service cannot be overemphasized. Let us say the customer service representative at a large bank receives a call. The customer at the other end of the line wants to talk about the service charge on his checking account. The bank customer service representative notices a balance of $27.38 in the customer's checking account. Why is he making a big fuss about the service charge with almost nothing in the account? But let us say the customer service representative clicks on the customer's other accounts and finds that the customer has $35,000 in his savings accounts and CDs worth more than $120,000. How do you think the customer service representative will answer the call? Of course, with much respect. Complete and accurate information improves customer service tremendously.

Newer Opportunities   Quality data in a data warehouse is a great boon for marketing. It opens the doors to immense opportunities to cross-sell across product lines and departments. The users can select the buyers of one product and determine all the other products they are likely to purchase. Marketing departments can conduct well-targeted campaigns. This is just one example of the numerous opportunities that are made possible by quality data. On the other hand, if the data is of inferior quality, the campaigns will be failures.

Reduced Costs and Risks   What are some of the risks of poor data quality? The obvious risk is strategic decisions that could lead to disastrous consequences. Other risks include wasted time, malfunction of processes and systems, and sometimes even legal action by customers and business partners. One area where quality data reduces costs is in mailings to customers, especially in marketing campaigns. If the addresses are incomplete, inaccurate, or duplicated, most of the mailings are wasted.

Improved Productivity   Users get an enterprise-wide view of information from the data warehouse. This is a primary goal of the data warehouse. In areas where a corporate-wide view of information naturally enables the streamlining of processes and operations, you will see productivity gains. For example, a company-wide view of purchasing patterns in a large department store can result in better purchasing procedures and strategies.

Reliable Strategic Decision Making   This point is worth repeating. If the data in the warehouse is reliable and of high quality, then decisions based on the business intelligence from the data warehouse will be sound. No data warehouse can add value to a business until the data is clean and of high quality.

Types of Data Quality Problems

As part of the discussion on why data quality is critical in the data warehouse, we have explored the characteristics of quality data. The characteristics themselves have demonstrated the critical need for quality data. The discussion of the benefits of having quality data further strengthens the argument for cleaner data. Our discussion of the critical need for quality data is not complete until we quickly walk through the types of problems you are likely to encounter when the data is polluted. Description of the problem types will convince you even more that data quality is of critical importance.

If 4% of the sales amounts are wrong in the billing systems of a $2 billion company, what is the estimated loss in revenue? $80 million. What happens when a large catalog sales company mails catalogs to customers and prospects? If there are duplicate records for the same customer in the customer files, then, depending on how extensive the duplication problem is, the company will end up sending multiple catalogs to the same person.

In a recent independent survey, businesses with data warehouses were asked the question: What is the biggest challenge in data warehouse development and usage? Figure 13-2 shows the ranking of the answers. Nearly half of the respondents rated data quality as their biggest challenge. Data quality is the biggest challenge not just because of the complexity and extent of the problem of data pollution. More far-reaching is the effect of polluted data on strategic decisions made based on such data.

Many of today's data warehouses get their data feed from old legacy systems. Data in old systems undergo a decaying process. For example, consider the field for product codes in a retail chain store. Over the past few decades, the products sold must have changed many

DATA WAREHOUSE
CHALLENGES

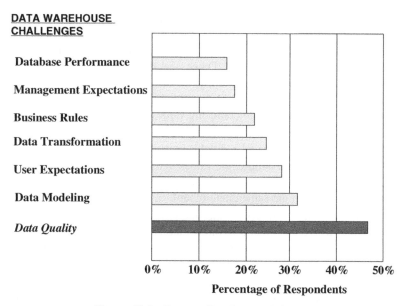

Figure 13-2   Data quality: the top challenge.

times and in many variations. The product codes must have been assigned and reassigned a number of times. The old codes must have decayed and perhaps some of the old codes could have been reassigned to newer products. This is not a problem in operational systems because these systems deal with current data. The old codes would have been right at that time in the past when they were current. But the data warehouse carries historical data and these old codes could cause problems in this repository.

Let us go over a list of explicit types of data quality problems. These are specific types of data corruption. This list is by no means exhaustive, but will give you an appreciation of the need for data quality.

Dummy Values in Fields. Are you aware of the practice of filling the Social Security number field temporarily with nines to pass the numerical edits? The intention is to enter the correct Social Security number when the data becomes available later on. Many times the correction does not happen and you are left with the nines in that field. Sometimes you may enter 88888 in the zip code field to pass the edit for an Asian customer or enter 77777 for a European customer.

Absence of Data Values. This is common in customer data. In operational systems, users are only concerned with the customer data that is needed to mail a billing statement, to send a follow-up letter, and to make a call about an overdue balance. Not too much attention is paid to demographic types of data that are not usable in operational systems. So, you are left with missing values in the demographic types of data that are very useful for analysis from the data warehouse. Absence of data values is also related to other types of data elements.

Unofficial Use of Fields. How many times have you asked your users to place their comments in the customer contact field because no field was provided for comments in the customer record? This is an unofficial use of the customer contact field.

Cryptic Values. This is a prevalent problem in legacy systems, many of which were not designed with end-users in mind. For example, the customer status codes could have been started with R = Regular and N = New. Then at one time, another code D = Deceased could have been added. Down the road, a further code A = Archive could have been included. More recently, the original R and N could have been discarded and R = Remove could have been added. Although this example is contrived to make a point, such cryptic and confusing values for attributes are not uncommon in old legacy systems.

Contradicting Values. There are related fields in the source systems in which the values must be compatible. For example, the values in the fields for state and zip code must agree. You cannot have a state value of CA (California) and a zip code of 08817 (a zip code in New Jersey) in the same client record.

Violation of Business Rules. In a personnel and payroll system, an obvious business rule is that the days worked in a year plus the vacation days, holidays, and sick days cannot exceed 365 or 366. Any employee record that comes up with the number of days more than 365 or 366 violates this basic business rule. In a bank loan system, the minimum interest rate cannot be more than the maximum rate for a variable rate loan.

Reused Primary Keys. Suppose a legacy system has a five-digit primary key field assigned for the customer record. This field will be adequate as long as the number of customers is less than 100,000. When the number of customers increases, some companies resolve the problem by archiving the older customer records and reassigning the key values so that the newer customers are assigned primary key values restarting with 1. This is not really a problem in the operational systems, but in the data warehouse, where you capture both present data from the current customer file and the past data from the archived customer file, you have a problem of duplication of the reused primary key values.

Nonunique Identifiers. There is a different complication with identifiers. Suppose the accounting systems have their own product codes used as identifiers but they are different from the product codes used in the sales and inventory systems. Product code 355 in the sales system may be identified as product code A226 in the accounting system. Here a unique identifier does not represent the same product in two different systems.

Inconsistent Values. Codes for policy type in different legacy systems in an expanding insurance company could have inconsistent values such as A = Auto, H = Home, F = Flood, W = Workers Comp in one system, and 1, 2, 3, and 4, respectively, in another system. Another variation of these codes could be AU, HO, FL, and WO, respectively.

Incorrect Values. Product code: 146, product name: crystal vase, and height: 486 inches in the same record point to some sort of data inaccuracy. The values for product name and height are not compatible. Perhaps the product code is also incorrect.

Multipurpose Fields. The same data value in a field entered by different departments may mean different things. A field could start off as a storage area code to indicate the back-room storage areas in stores. Later, when the company built its own warehouse to store products, it used the same field to indicate the warehouse. This type of problem is perpetuated because store codes and warehouse codes were residing in the same field. Warehouse codes went into the same field by redefining the store code field. This type of data pollution is hard to correct.

Erroneous Integration. In an auction company, buyers are the customers who bid at auctions and buy the items that are auctioned off. The sellers are the customers who sell their goods through the auction company. The same customer may be a buyer in the auction system and a seller in the property receipting system. Assume that customer number 12345 in the auction system is the same customer whose number is 34567 in the property receipting system. The data for customer number 12345 in the auction system must be integrated with the data for customer number 34567 in the property receipting system. The reverse side of the data integration problem is this: customer number 55555 in the auction system and customer number 55555 in the property receipting system are not the same customer but are different. These integration problems arise because, typically, each legacy system had been developed in isolation at different times in the past.

DATA QUALITY CHALLENGES

There is an interesting but strange aspect of the whole data cleansing initiative for the data warehouse. We are striving toward having clean data in the data warehouse. We want to ascertain the extent of the pollution. Based on the condition of the data, we plan data cleansing activities. What is strange about this whole set of circumstances is that the pollution of data occurs outside the data warehouse. As part of the data warehouse project team, you are taking measures to eliminate the corruption that arises in a place outside your control.

All data warehouses need historical data. A substantial part of the historical data comes from antiquated legacy systems. Frequently, the end-users use the historical data in the data warehouse for strategic decision making without knowing exactly what the data really means. In most cases, detailed metadata hardly exists for the old legacy systems. You are expected to fix the data pollution problems that emanate from the old operational systems without the assistance of adequate information about the data there.

Sources of Data Pollution

In order to come up with a good strategy for cleansing the data, it will be worthwhile to review a list of common sources of data pollution. Why does data get corrupted in the source systems? Study the following list of data pollution sources against the background of what data quality really is.

System Conversions. Trace the evolution of order processing in any company. The company must have started with a file-oriented order entry system in the early 1970s; orders were entered into flat files or indexed files. There was not much stock verification or customer credit verification during the entry of the order. Reports and hardcopy printouts were used to continue with the process of executing the orders. Then this system must have been converted into an online order entry system with VSAM files and IBM's CICS as the online processing monitor. The next conversion must have been to a hierarchical database system. Perhaps that is where your order processing system still remains, as a legacy application. Many companies have moved the system forward to a relational database application. In any case, what has happened to the order data through all these conversions? System conversions and migrations are prominent reasons for data pollution. Try to understand the conversions gone through by each of your source systems.

Data Aging. We have already dealt with data aging when we reviewed how over the course of many years the values in the product code fields could have decayed. The older values lose their meaning and significance. If many of your source systems are old legacy systems, pay special attention to the possibility of aged data in those systems.

Heterogeneous System Integration. The more heterogeneous and disparate your source systems are, the stronger is the possibility of corrupted data. In such a scenario, data inconsistency is a common problem. Consider the sources for each of your dimension tables and the fact table. If the sources for one table are several heterogeneous systems, be cautious about the quality of data coming into the data warehouse from these systems.

Poor Database Design. Good database design based on sound principles reduces the introduction of errors. DBMSs provide for field editing. RDBMSs enable verification of the conformance to business rules through triggers and stored procedures. Adhering to entity integrity and referential integrity rules prevents some kinds of data pollution.

Incomplete Information at Data Entry. At the time of the initial data entry about an entity, if all the information is not available, two types of data pollution usually occur. First, some of the input fields are not completed at the time of initial data entry. The result is missing values. Second, if the unavailable data is mandatory at the time of the initial data entry, then the person entering the data tries to force generic values into the mandatory fields. Entering N/A for not available in the field for city is an example of this kind of data pollution. Similarly, entry of all nines in the Social Security number field results in data pollution.

Input Errors. In the old days when data entry clerks entered data into computer systems, there was a second step of data verification. After the data entry clerk finished a batch, the entries from the batch were independently verified by another person. Now, users who are also responsible for the business processes enter the data. Data entry is not their primary vocation. Data accuracy is supposed to be ensured by sight verification and data edits planted on the input screens. Erroneous entry of data is a major source of data corruption.

Internationalization/Localization. Because of changing business conditions, the structure of the business gets expanded into the international arena. The company moves into wider geographic areas and newer cultures. As a company is internationalized, what happens to the data in the source systems? The existing data elements must adapt to newer and different values. Similarly, when a company wants to concentrate on a smaller area and localize its operations, some of the values for the data elements get discarded. This change in the company structure and the resulting revisions in the source systems are also sources of data pollution.

Fraud. Do not be surprised to learn that deliberate attempts to enter incorrect data are not uncommon. Here, the incorrect data entries are actually falsifications to commit fraud. Look out for monetary fields and fields containing units of products. Make sure that the source systems are fortified with tight edits for such fields.

Lack of Policies. In any enterprise, data quality does not just materialize by itself. Prevention of entry of corrupt data and preservation of data quality in the source systems are deliberate activities. An enterprise without explicit policies on data quality cannot be expected to have adequate levels of data quality.

Validation of Names and Addresses

Almost every company suffers from the problem of duplication of names and addresses. For a single person, multiple records can exist among the various source systems. Even within a single source system, multiple records can exist for one person. But in the data warehouse, you need to consolidate all the activities of each person from the various duplicate records that exist for that person in the multiple source systems. This type of problem occurs whenever you deal with people, whether they are customers, employees, physicians, or suppliers.

Take the specific example of an upscale auction company. Consider the different types of customers and the different purposes for which the customers seek the services of the auction company. Customers bring property items for sale, buy at auctions, subscribe to the catalogs for the various categories of auctions, and bring articles to be appraised by experts for insurance purposes and for estate dissolution. It is likely that there are different legacy systems at an auction house to service the customers in these different areas. One customer may come for all of these services and a record gets created for the customer in each of the different systems. A customer usually comes for the same service many times. On some of these occasions, it is likely that duplicate records are created for the same customer in one system. Entry of customer data happens at different points of contact of the customer with the auction company. If it is an international auction company, entry of customer data happens at many auction sites worldwide. Can you imagine the possibility for duplication of customer records and the extent of this form of data corruption?

Name and address data is captured in two ways (see Fig. 13-3). If the data entry is in the multiple field format, then it is easier to check for duplicates at the time of data entry. Here are a few inherent problems with entering names and addresses:

- No unique key
- Many names on one line
- One name on two lines
- Name and the address in a single line
- Personal and company names mixed
- Different addresses for the same person
- Different names and spellings for the same customer

Before attempting to deduplicate the customer records, you need to go through a preliminary step. First, you have to recast the name and address data into the multiple field format. This is not easy, considering the numerous variations in the way names and addresses are entered in free-form textual format. After this first step, you have to devise matching algorithms to match the customer records and find the duplicates. Fortunately, many good tools are available to assist you in the deduplication process.

Costs of Poor Data Quality

Cleansing the data and improving the quality of data takes money and effort. Although data cleansing is extremely important, you could justify the expenditure of money and effort by counting the costs of not having or using quality data. You can produce estimates with the help of the users. They are the ones who can really do estimates because the estimates are based on forecasts of lost opportunities and possible bad decisions.

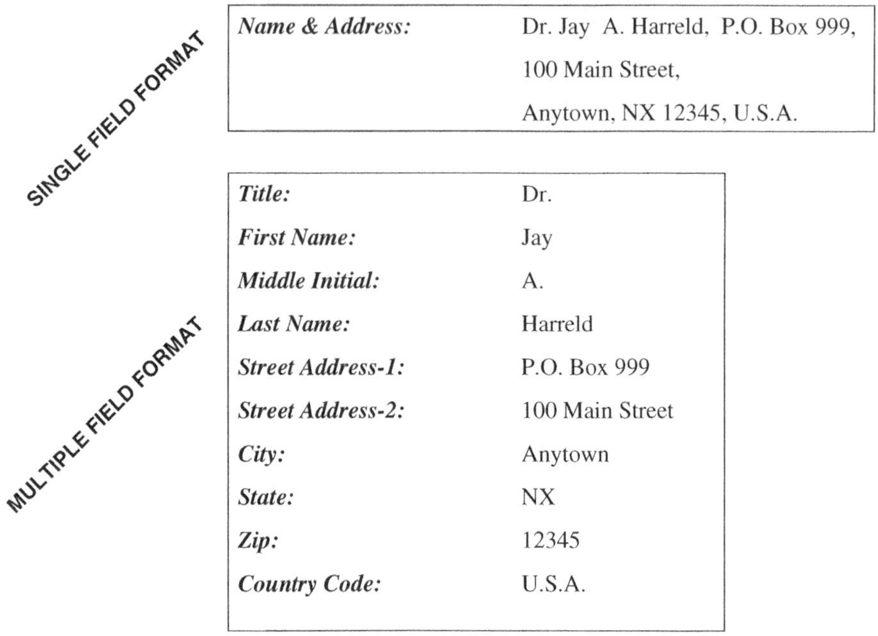

Name & Address:	Dr. Jay A. Harreld, P.O. Box 999, 100 Main Street, Anytown, NX 12345, U.S.A.

SINGLE FIELD FORMAT

MULTIPLE FIELD FORMAT

Title:	Dr.
First Name:	Jay
Middle Initial:	A.
Last Name:	Harreld
Street Address-1:	P.O. Box 999
Street Address-2:	100 Main Street
City:	Anytown
State:	NX
Zip:	12345
Country Code:	U.S.A.

Figure 13-3   Data entry: name and address formats.

The following is a list of categories for which cost estimates can be made. These are broad categories. You will have to get into the details for estimating the risks and costs for each category.

- Bad decisions based on routine analysis
- Lost business opportunities because of unavailable or "dirty" data
- Strain and overhead on source systems because of corrupt data causing reruns
- Fines from governmental agencies for noncompliance or violation of regulations
- Resolution of audit problems
- Redundant data unnecessarily using up resources
- Inconsistent reports
- Time and effort for correcting data every time data corruption is discovered

DATA QUALITY TOOLS

Based on our discussions in this chapter so far, you are at a point where you are convinced about the seriousness of data quality in the data warehouse. Companies have begun to recognize dirty data as one of the most challenging problems in a data warehouse.

You would, therefore, imagine that companies must be investing heavily in data clean-up operations. But according to experts, data cleansing is still not a very high priority for companies. This attitude is changing as useful data quality tools arrive on the market. You may choose to apply these tools to the source systems, in the staging area before the load images are created, or to the load images themselves. Many vendors have begun to provide a type of data cleansing tool-kit that can be integrated with other tools such as ETL.

Categories of Data Cleansing Tools

Generally, data cleansing tools assist the project team in two ways. Data error discovery tools work on the source data to identify inaccuracies and inconsistencies. Data correction tools help fix the corrupt data. These correction tools use a series of algorithms to parse, transform, match, consolidate, and correct the data.

Although data error discovery and data correction are two distinct parts of the data cleansing process, most of the tools on the market do a bit of both. The tools have features and functions that identify and discover errors. The same tools can also perform the cleaning up and correction of polluted data. In the following sections, we will examine the features of the two aspects of data cleansing as found in the available tools.

Error Discovery Features

Study the following list of error discovery functions that data cleansing tools are capable of performing.

- Quickly and easily identify duplicate records.
- Identify data items whose values are outside the range of legal domain values.
- Find inconsistent data.
- Check for range of allowable values.
- Detect inconsistencies among data items from different sources.
- Allow users to identify and quantify data quality problems.
- Monitor trends in data quality over time.
- Report to users on the quality of data used for analysis.
- Reconcile problems of RDBMS referential integrity.

Data Correction Features

The following list describes the typical error correction functions that data cleansing tools are capable of performing:

- Normalize inconsistent data.
- Improve merging of data from dissimilar data sources.
- Group and relate customer records belonging to the same household.
- Provide measurements of data quality.
- Standardize data elements to common formats.
- Validate for allowable values.

The DBMS for Quality Control

The database management system itself is used as a tool for data quality control in many ways. Relational database management systems have many features beyond the database engine (see list below). Later versions of RDBMS can easily prevent several types of errors creeping into the data warehouse.

Domain Integrity. Provide domain value edits. Prevent entry of data if the entered data value is outside the defined limits of value. You can define the edit checks while setting up the data dictionary entries.

Update Security. Prevent unauthorized updates to the databases. This feature will stop unauthorized users from updating data in an incorrect way. Casual and untrained users can introduce inaccurate or incorrect data if they happen to have authorization to update.

Entity Integrity Checking. Ensure that duplicate records with the same primary key value are not entered. Also prevent duplicates based on values of other attributes.

Minimize missing values. Ensure that nulls are not allowed in mandatory fields.

Referential Integrity Checking. Ensure that relationships based on foreign keys are preserved. Prevent deletion of related parent rows.

Conformance to Business Rules. Use trigger programs and stored procedures to enforce business rules. These are special scripts compiled and stored in the database itself. Trigger programs are automatically fired when the designated data items are about to be updated or deleted. Stored procedures may be coded to ensure that the entered data conforms to specific business rules. Stored procedures may be called from application programs.

DATA QUALITY INITIATIVE

In spite of the enormous importance of data quality, it seems as though many companies still ask the question whether to pay special attention to it and cleanse the data or not. In many instances, the data for the missing values of attributes cannot be recreated. In quite a number of cases, the data values are so convoluted that the data cannot really be cleansed. A few other questions arise. Should the data be cleansed? If so, how much of it can really be cleansed? Which parts of the data deserve higher priority for applying data cleansing techniques? The indifference and the resistance to data cleansing emerge from a few valid factors:

- Data cleansing is tedious and time consuming. The cleansing activity demands a combination of the use of vendor tools, writing of in-house code, and arduous manual tasks of examination and verification. Many companies are unable to sustain the effort. This is not the kind of work many IT professionals enjoy.

- The metadata on many source systems may be missing or nonexistent. It will be difficult or even impossible to probe into dirty data without the documentation.

- The users who are asked to ensure data quality have many other business responsibilities. Data quality probably receives the least attention.

- Sometimes, the data cleansing activity appears to be so gigantic and overwhelming that companies are terrified of launching a data cleansing initiative.

Once your enterprise decides to institute a data cleansing initiative, you may consider one of two approaches. You may opt to allow only clean data to go into your data warehouse. This means only data with a 100% quality can be loaded into the data warehouse. Data that is in any way polluted must be cleansed before it can be loaded. This is an ideal approach, but it takes a while to detect incorrect data and even longer to fix it. This approach is ideal from the point of view of data quality, but it will take a very long time before all data is cleaned up for data loading.

The second approach is a "clean as you go" method. In this method, you load all the data "as is" into the data warehouse and perform data cleansing operations in the data warehouse at a later time. Although you do not withhold data loads, the results of any query are suspect until the data gets cleansed. Questionable data quality at any time leads to losing user confidence that is extremely important for data warehouse success.

Data Cleansing Decisions

Before embarking on a data cleansing initiative, the project team, including the users, have to make a number of basic decisions. Data cleansing is not as simple as deciding to cleanse all data and to cleanse it now. Realize that absolute data quality is unrealistic in the real world. Be practical and realistic. Go for the fitness-for-purpose principle. Determine what the data is being used for and find the purpose. If the data from the warehouse has to provide exact sales dollars of the top 25 customers, then the quality of this data must be very high. If customer demographics are to be used to select prospects for the next marketing campaign, the quality of this data may be at a lower level.

In the final analysis, when it comes to data cleansing, you are faced with a few fundamental questions. You have to make some basic decisions. In the following subsections, we present the basic questions that need to be asked and the basic decisions that need to be made.

Which Data to Cleanse   This is the root decision. First of all, you and your users must jointly work out the answer to this question. It must primarily be the users' decision. IT will help the users make the decision. Decide on the types of questions the data warehouse is expected to answer. Find the source data needed for getting answers. Weigh the benefits of cleansing each piece of data. Determine how cleansing will help and how leaving the dirty data in will affect any analysis made by the users in the data warehouse.

The cost of cleaning up all data in the data warehouse is enormous. Users usually understand this. They do not expect to see 100% data quality and will usually settle for ignoring the cleansing of unimportant data as long as all the important data is cleaned up. But be sure of getting the definitions of what is important or unimportant from the users themselves.

Where to Cleanse   Data for your warehouse originates in the source operational systems, so does the data corruption. Then the extracted data moves into the staging area. From the staging area load images are loaded into the data warehouse. Therefore, theoretically, you may cleanse the data in any one of these areas. You may apply data cleansing techniques in the source systems, in the staging area, or perhaps even in the data warehouse. You may also adopt a method that splits the overall data cleansing effort into parts that can be applied in two of the areas, or even in all three areas.

You will find that cleansing the data after it has arrived in the data warehouse repository is impractical and results in undoing the effects of many of the processes for moving and loading the data. Typically, data is cleansed before it is stored in the data warehouse. So that leaves you with two areas where you can cleanse the data.

Cleansing the data in the staging area is comparatively easy. You have already resolved all the data extraction problems. By the time data is received in the staging area, you are fully aware of the structure, content, and nature of the data. Although this seems to be the best approach, there are a few drawbacks. Data pollution will keep flowing into the staging area from the source systems. The source systems will continue to suffer from the consequences of the data corruption. The costs of bad data in the source systems do not get reduced. Any reports produced from the same data from the source systems and from the data warehouse may not match and will cause confusion.

On the other hand, if you attempt to cleanse the data in the source systems, you are taking on a complex, expensive, and difficult task. Many legacy source systems do not have proper documentation. Some may not even have the source code for the production programs available for applying the corrections.

How to Cleanse   Here the question is about the use of vendor tools. Do you use vendor tools by themselves for all of the data cleansing effort? Do you integrate cleansing tool kits with other ETL tools? If not, how much of in-house programming is needed for your environment? Many tools are available in the market for several types of data cleansing functions.

If you decide to cleanse the data in the source systems, then you have to find the appropriate tools that can be applied to source system files and formats. This may not be easy if most of your source systems are fairly old. In that case, you have to fall back on in-house programs.

How to Discover the Extent of Data Pollution   Before you can apply data cleansing techniques, you have to assess the extent of data pollution. This is a joint responsibility shared among the users of operational systems, the potential users of the data warehouse, and IT. IT staff, supporting both the source systems and the data warehouse, have a special role in the discovery of the extent of data pollution. IT is responsible for installing the data cleansing tools and training the users in using those tools. IT must augment the effort with in-house programs.

In an earlier section, we discussed the sources of data pollution. Reexamine these sources. Make a list that reflects the sources of pollution found in your environment, then determine the extent of the data pollution with regard to each source of pollution. For example, in your case, data aging could be a source of pollution. If so, make a list of all the old legacy systems that serve as sources of data for your data warehouse. For the data attributes that are extracted, examine the sets of values. Check if any of these values do not make sense and have decayed. Similarly, perform detailed analysis for each type of data pollution source.

Figure 13-4 shows a few typical ways you can detect the possible presence and extent of data pollution. Use the list as a guide for your environment.

Setting Up a Data Quality Framework   You have to contend with so many types of data pollution. You need to make various decisions to embark on the cleansing of data. You must dig into the sources of possible data corruption and determine the pollution. Most companies serious about data quality pull all these factors together and establish a data quality framework. Essentially, the framework provides a basis for launching data quality initiatives. It embodies a systematic plan for action. The framework identifies the players, their roles, and responsibilities. In short, the framework guides the data quality improvement effort. Refer to Fig. 13-5. Notice the major functions carried out within the framework.

Who Should Be Responsible?

Data quality or data corruption originates in the source systems. Therefore, should not the owners of the data in the source systems alone be responsible for data quality? If these

➤ Operational systems converted from older versions are prone to the perpetuation of errors.

➤ Operational systems brought in house from outsourcing companies converted from their proprietary software may have missing data.

➤ Data from outside sources that is not verified and audited may have potential problems.

➤ When applications are consolidated because of corporate mergers and acquisitions, these may be error-prone because of time pressures.

➤ When reports from old legacy systems are no longer used, that could be because of erroneous data reported.

➤ If users do not trust certain reports fully, there may be room for suspicion because of bad data.

➤ Whenever certain data elements or definitions are confusing to the users, these may be suspect.

➤ If each department has its own copies of standard data such as Customer or Product, it is likely corrupt data exists in these files.

➤ If reports containing the same data reformatted differently do not match, data quality is suspect.

➤ Wherever users perform too much manual reconciliation, it may be because of poor data quality.

➤ If production programs frequently fail on data exceptions, large parts of the data in those systems are likely to be corrupt.

➤ Wherever users are not able to get consolidated reports, it is possible that data is not integrated.

Figure 13-4   Discovering the extent of data pollution.

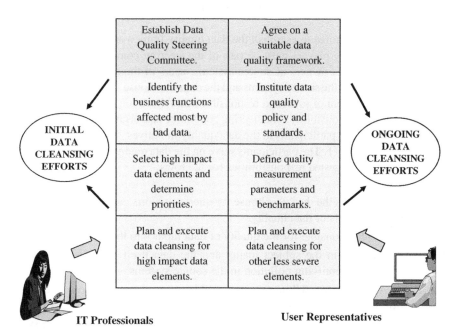

Figure 13-5   Data quality framework.

Figure 13-6 Data quality: participants and roles.

data owners are responsible for the data, should they also bear the responsibility for any data pollution that happens in the source systems? If data quality in the source systems is high, the data quality in the data warehouse will also be high. But, as you well know, in operational systems, there are no clear roles and responsibilities for maintaining data quality. This is a serious problem. Owners of data in the operational systems are generally not directly involved in the data warehouse. They have little interest in keeping the data clean in the data warehouse.

Form a steering committee to establish the data quality framework discussed in the previous section. All the key players must be part of the steering committee. You must have representatives of the data owners of source systems, users of the data warehouse, and IT personnel responsible for the source systems and the data warehouse. The steering committee is charged with assignment of roles and responsibilities. Allocation of resources is also the steering committee's responsibility. The steering committee also arranges data quality audits.

Figure 13-6 shows the participants in the data quality initiatives. These persons represent the user departments and IT. The participants serve on the data quality team in specific roles. Listed below are the suggested responsibilities for the roles:

Data Consumer. Uses the data warehouse for queries, reports, and analysis. Establishes the acceptable levels of data quality.

Data Producer. Responsible for the quality of data input into the source systems.

Data Expert. Expert in the subject matter and the data itself of the source systems. Responsible for identifying pollution in the source systems.

Data Policy Administrator. Ultimately responsible for resolving data corruption as data is transformed and moved into the data warehouse.

Data Integrity Specialist. Responsible for ensuring that the data in the source systems conforms to the business rules.

Data Correction Authority. Responsible for actually applying the data cleansing techniques through the use of tools or in-house programs.

Data Consistency Expert. Responsible for ensuring that all data within the data warehouse (various data marts) are fully synchronized.

The Purification Process

We all know that it is unrealistic to hold up the loading of the data warehouse until the quality of all data is at the 100% level. That level of data quality is extremely rare. So, how much of the data should you attempt to cleanse? When do you stop the purification process?

Again, we come to the issues of who will use the data and for what purposes. Estimate the costs and risks of each piece of incorrect data. Users usually settle for some measure of errors, provided these errors result in no serious consequences. But the users need to be kept informed of the extent of possible data corruption and exactly which parts of the data could be suspect.

How then could you proceed with the purification process? With the complete participation of your users, divide the data elements into priorities for the purpose of data cleansing. You may adopt a simple categorization by grouping the data elements into three priority categories: high, medium, and low. Achieving 100% data quality is critical for the high category. The medium-priority data requires as much cleansing as possible. Some errors may be tolerated when you strike a balance between the cost of correction and potential effect of bad data. The low-priority data may be cleansed if you have any time and remaining resources are still available. Begin your data cleansing efforts with the high-priority data. Then move on to the medium-priority data.

A universal data corruption problem relates to duplicate records. As we have seen earlier, for the same customer, there could be multiple records in the source systems. Activity records are related to each of these duplicate records in the source systems. Make sure your overall data purification process includes techniques for correcting the duplication problem. The techniques must be able to identify the duplicate records and then relate all the activities to this single customer. Duplication normally occurs in records relating to persons such as customers, employees, and business partners.

So far, we have not discussed data quality with regard to data obtained from external sources. Pollution can also be introduced into the data warehouse through errors in external data. Surely, if you pay for the external data and do not capture it from the public domain, then you have every right to demand a warranty on data quality. In spite of what the vendor might profess about the quality of the data, for each set of external data, set up some kind of data quality audit. If the external data fails the audit, be prepared to reject the corrupt data and demand a cleaner version.

Figure 13-7 illustrates the overall data purification process. Observe the process as shown in the figure and go through the following summary:

- Establish the importance of data quality.
- Form a data quality steering committee.
- Institute a data quality framework.
- Assign roles and responsibilities.
- Select tools to assist in the data purification process.
- Prepare in-house programs as needed.

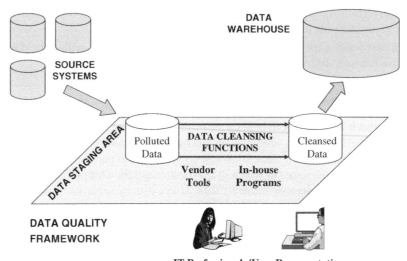

Figure 13-7 Overall data purification.

- Train the participants in data cleansing techniques.
- Review and confirm data standards.
- Prioritize data into high, medium, and low categories.
- Prepare a schedule for data purification beginning with the high priority data.
- Ensure that techniques are available to correct duplicate records and to audit external data.
- Proceed with the purification process according to the defined schedule.

Practical Tips on Data Quality

Before you run away to implement a comprehensive data quality framework and expend time and resources on data quality, let us pause to go over a few practical suggestions. Remember, ensuring data quality is a balancing act. You already know that 100% data quality is an unrealistic expectation. At the same time, overlooking errors that could potentially ruin the business is also not an option. You have to find the right balance between the data purification effort and the available time and resources. Here are a few practical tips:

- Identify high-impact pollution sources and begin your purification process with these.
- Do not try to do everything with in-house programs.
- Tools are good and useful. Select the proper tools.
- Agree on standards and reconfirm these.
- Link data quality with specific business objectives. By itself, data quality work is not attractive.
- Get the senior executive sponsor of your data warehouse project to be actively involved in backing the data cleansing initiative.
- Get users totally involved and keep them constantly informed of the developments.
- Wherever needed, bring in outside experts for specific assignments.

MASTER DATA MANAGEMENT (MDM)

More recently organizations are achieving data quality by adopting an overall master data management approach. MDM is an umbrella approach to provide consistent and comprehensive core information across the organization. Master data generally refers to data describing core business objects such as customers, products, locations, and financials. Sometimes data about other entities such as business partners, employees, sales contacts, and physical assets are also included as master data for an organization. These may be considered as nontransactional data entities or reference data.

MDM comprises a set of technologies, disciplines, and solutions to create and maintain consistent, accurate, and complete business data about the entities included within its ambit. MDM is as much about information strategy as it is about software. It cuts across business processes, software, data stewardship, data governance, and business information. At the most fundamental level, MDM is meant to ensure that an organization does not present multiple versions of the same master data in different operations and applications. It strives for a single version of high quality master data.

MDM Categories

When you consider how MDM is practiced and where it is applied, you can put MDM solutions into three broad categories. This categorization may vary from organization to organization. Again in some organizations, all three categories may not be relevant.

Operational MDM. This is integrated with and used with operational applications for CRM, ERP, financial systems, and such others.

Analytic MDM. This is predominant in data warehousing, useful for obtaining quality master data.

Enterprise MDM. This is much wider in scope than the other categories, attempting to encompass all aspects of master data within the enterprise.

MDM Benefits

Creating a master data service layer is a difficult undertaking for organizations. Nevertheless, businesses have begun to adopt MDM because of several benefits they expect to obtain. Here is a brief list of possible benefits from MDM.

- Reduction in cost and complexity of processes that use master data and provide internal efficiencies.
- Improvement in the ability to consolidate, share, and analyze business information in a timely manner, regionally and even globally.
- Possibility to rapidly assemble new, composite applications with accurate master data and reusable business processes.
- Reduction in time to market by having a single system for creating and maintaining product information, promotions, and consumer communications.
- Improvements to the supply chain with single, accurate, well-defined definitions of products and suppliers, eliminating duplications.
- Enhanced customer service, with a complete view of each customer designed to better anticipate customer needs and provide targeted offers.

- Better overall integration, eliminating information silos that may have developed across divisions within an organization.

MDM and Data Warehousing

As we have seen in this chapter, historically organizations have attempted to address data quality problems in the data warehouse by rectifying problems downstream. Source systems create inaccurate master data but in many organizations the trend has been to cleanse the inaccurate data not at the source. Nor do these organizations try to go back and propagate the corrections backward once the corrections are made in the data staging area or the data warehouse itself. MDM provides a way to correct bad master data at the source so that the data will be high quality when it reaches the data warehouse. The net result is accurate business intelligence.

Creation of a system of record (a trusted single data source) is the underlying theme across the many approaches to MDM. The intent is to establish an authenticated master copy from which entity definitions and physical data can flow among all applications integrated through the MDM initiative. Many enterprises build a central data warehouse or an operational data store as a hub through master data definitions, metadata, and content synchronized for all applications.

CHAPTER SUMMARY

- Data quality is critical because it boosts confidence, enables better customer service, enhances strategic decision making, and reduces risks from disastrous decisions.
- Data quality dimensions include accuracy, domain integrity, consistency, completeness, structural definiteness, clarity, and many more.
- Data quality problems run the gamut of dummy values, missing values, cryptic values, contradicting values, business rule violations, inconsistent values, and so on.
- Data pollution results from many sources in a data warehouse and this variety of sources of pollution intensifies the challenges faced when attempting to clean up the data.
- Poor data quality of names and addresses presents serious concerns to organizations. This area is one of the greatest challenges.
- Data cleansing tools contain useful error discovery and error correction features. Learn about them and make use of the tools applicable to your environment.
- The DBMS itself can be used for data cleansing.
- Set up a sound data quality initiative in your organization. Within that framework, make the data cleansing decisions.
- Master Data Management (MDM) initiatives provide a means for ensuring data quality in the data warehouse.

REVIEW QUESTIONS

1. List five reasons why you think data quality is critical in a data warehouse.

2. Explain how data quality is much more than just data accuracy. Give an example.

3. Briefly list three benefits of quality data in a data warehouse.

4. Give examples of four types of data quality problems.

5. What is the problem related to the reuse of primary keys? When does it usually occur?

6. Describe the functions of data correction in data cleansing tools.

7. Name five common sources of data pollution. Give an example for each type of source.

8. List six types of error discovery features found in data cleansing tools.

9. What is the "clean as you go" method? Is this a good approach for the data warehouse environment?

10. Name any three types of participants on the data quality team. What are their functions?

EXERCISES

1. Match the columns:

1. domain integrity	A. detect inconsistencies
2. data aging	B. better customer service
3. entity integrity	C. synchronize all data
4. data consumer	D. allowable values
5. poor quality data	E. used to pass edits
6. data consistency expert	F. uses warehouse data
7. error discovery	G. heterogeneous systems integration
8. data pollution source	H. lost business opportunities
9. dummy values	I. prevents duplicate key values
10. data quality benefit	J. decay of field values

2. Assume that you are the data quality expert on the data warehouse project team for a large financial institution with many legacy systems dating back to the 1970s. Review the types of data quality problems you are likely to have and make suggestions on how to deal with those.

3. Discuss the common sources of data pollution and provide examples.

4. You are responsible for the selection of data cleansing tools for your data warehouse environment. How will you define the criteria for selection? Prepare a checklist for evaluation and selection of these tools.

5. As a data warehouse consultant, a large bank with statewide branches has hired you to help the company set up a data quality initiative. List your major considerations. Produce an outline for a document describing the initiative, the policies, and the procedures.

PART 5

INFORMATION ACCESS AND DELIVERY

CHAPTER 14

MATCHING INFORMATION TO THE CLASSES OF USERS

CHAPTER OBJECTIVES

- Appreciate the enormous information potential of the data warehouse
- Carefully note all the users who will use the data warehouse and devise a practical way to classify them
- Delve deeply into the types of information delivery mechanisms
- Match each class of user to the appropriate information delivery method
- Understand the overall information delivery framework and study the components

Let us assume that your data warehouse project team has successfully identified all the pertinent source systems. You have extracted and transformed the source data. You have the best data design for the data warehouse repository. You have applied the most effective data cleansing methods and gotten rid of most of the pollution from the source data. Using the most optimal methods, you have loaded the transformed and cleansed data into your data warehouse database. Then what?

After performing all of these tasks most effectively, if your team has not provided the best possible mechanism for delivery of business intelligence to your users, you have really accomplished nothing from the users' perspective. As you know, the data warehouse exists for one reason and one reason alone. It is there just for providing strategic information to your users. For the users, the information delivery mechanism is the data warehouse. The user interface for information is what determines the ultimate success of your data warehouse. If the interface is intuitive, easy to use, and enticing, the users will keep coming back to the data warehouse. If the interface is difficult to use, cumbersome, and convoluted, your project team may as well leave the scene.

Data Warehousing Fundamentals for IT Professionals, Second Edition. By Paulraj Ponniah
Copyright © 2010 John Wiley & Sons, Inc.

Who are your users? What do they want? Your project team, of course, knows the answers and has designed the data warehouse based on the requirements of these users. How do you provide the needed information to your users? This depends on who your users are, what information they need, when and where they need the information, and in exactly what form they need the information. In this chapter, we will consider general classes of users of a typical warehouse and the methods for providing information to them.

A large portion of the success of your data warehouse rests on the information delivery tools made available to the users. Selecting the right tools is of paramount importance. You have to make sure that the tools are most appropriate for your environment. We will discuss in detail the selection of information delivery tools.

INFORMATION FROM THE DATA WAREHOUSE

As an IT professional, you have been involved in providing information to the user community. You must have worked on different types of operational systems that provide information to users. The users in enterprises make use of the information from the operational systems to perform their day-to-day work and run the business. If we have been involved in information delivery from operational systems and we understand what information delivery to the users entails, then what is the need for this special study on information delivery from the data warehouse?

Let us review how information delivery from a data warehouse differs from information delivery from an operational system. If the kinds of strategic information made available in a data warehouse were readily available from the source systems, then we would not really need the warehouse. Data warehousing enables the users to make better strategic decisions by obtaining data from the source systems and keeping it in a format suitable for querying and analysis.

Data Warehouse Versus Operational Systems

Databases already exist in operational systems for querying and reporting. If so, how do the databases in operational systems differ from those of the databases in the data warehouse? The difference relates to two aspects of the information contained in these databases. First, they differ in the usage of the information. Next, they differ in the value of the information. Figure 14-1 shows how the data warehouse differs from an operational system in usage and value.

Users go to the data warehouse to find information on their own. They navigate through the contents and locate what they want. The users formulate their own queries and run them. They format their own reports, run them, and receive the results. Some users may use predefined queries and preformatted reports but, by and large, the data warehouse is a place where the users are free to make up their own queries and reports. They move around the contents and perform their own analysis, viewing the data in ever so many different ways. Each time a user goes to the data warehouse, he or she may run different queries and different reports, not repeating the earlier queries or reports. The information delivery is intended to be interactive.

Compare this type of usage of the data warehouse to how an operational system is used for information delivery. How often are the users allowed to run their own queries and format their own reports from an operational system? From an inventory control application, do

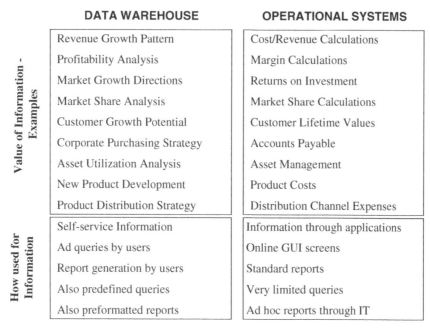

Figure 14-1   Data warehouse versus operational systems.

the users usually run their own queries and make up their own reports? Hardly ever. First of all, because of efficiency considerations, operational systems are not designed to let users loose on the systems. The users may impact the performance of the system adversely with runaway queries. Another important point is that the users of operational systems do not exactly know the contents of the databases; metadata or data dictionary entries are typically unavailable to them. Interactive analysis, which forms the bedrock of information delivery in the data warehouse, is almost never present in an operational system.

What about the value of the information from the data warehouse to the users? How does the value of information from an operational system compare to the value from the data warehouse? Take the case of information for analyzing the business operations. The information from an operational system shows the users how well the enterprise is doing for running the day-to-day business. The value of information from an operational system enables the users to monitor and control the current operations. On the other hand, information from the data warehouse gives the users the ability to analyze growth patterns in revenue, profitability, market penetration, and customer base. Based on such analysis, the users are able to make strategic decisions to keep the enterprise competitive and sound. Look at another area of the enterprise, namely, marketing. With regard to marketing, the value of information from the data warehouse is oriented to strategic matters such as market share, distribution strategy, predictability of customer buying patterns, and market penetration. Although this is the case of the value of information from the data warehouse for marketing, what is the value of information from operational systems? Mostly for monitoring sales against target quotas and for attempting to get repeat business from customers.

We see that the usage and value of information from the data warehouse differ from those of information from operational systems. What is the implication of the differences? First of all, because of the differences, as an IT professional, you should not try to apply the principles of information delivery from operational systems to the data warehouse. Information delivery from the data warehouse is markedly different. Different methods are needed. Further, you should take serious note of the interactive nature of information delivery from the data warehouse. Users are expected to gather information and perform analysis from the data in the data warehouse interactively on their own without the assistance of IT. IT staff supporting the users of the data warehouse do not run the queries and reports for the users; the users do that by themselves. So, make the information from the data warehouse easily and readily available to the users in their own terms.

Information Potential

Before we look at the different types of users and their information needs, we need to gain an appreciation of the enormous potential of the data warehouse for business intelligence. Because of this great potential, we have to pay adequate attention to information delivery from the data warehouse. We cannot treat information delivery in a special way unless we fully realize the significance of how the data warehouse plays a key role in the overall management of an enterprise.

Overall Enterprise Management   In every enterprise, three distinct processes govern the overall management. First, the enterprise is engaged in planning. Execution of the plans takes place next. Assessment of the results of the execution follows. Figure 14-2 indicates these plan–execute–assess processes.

Let us see what happens in this closed loop. Consider the planning for expansion into a specific geographic market for an enterprise. Let us say your company wants to increase its market share in the northwest region. Now this plan is translated into execution by means of

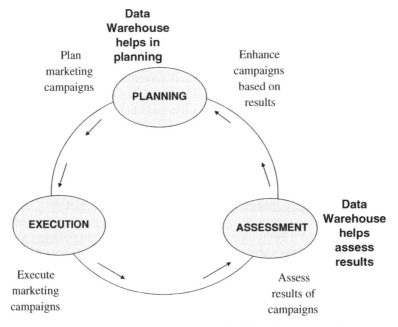

Figure 14-2   Plan–execute–assess closed loop for an enterprise.

promotional campaigns, improved services, and customized marketing. After the plan is executed, your company wants to find the results of the promotional campaigns and the marketing initiatives. Assessment of the results determines the effectiveness of the campaigns. Based on the assessment of the results, more plans may be made to vary the composition of the campaigns or launch additional ones. The cycle of planning, executing, and assessing continues.

It is very interesting to note that the data warehouse, with its specialized information potential, fits nicely into this plan−execute−assess loop. The data warehouse, with its business intelligence component, reports on the past and helps plan the future. First, the data warehouse assists in the planning. Once the plans are executed, the data warehouse is used to assess the effectiveness of the execution.

Let us go back to the example of your company wanting to expand in the northwest region. Here the planning consists of defining the proper customer segments in that region and also defining the products to concentrate on. Your data warehouse can be used effectively to separate out and identify the potential customer segments and product groups for the purpose of planning. Once the plan is executed with promotional campaigns, your data warehouse helps the users to assess and analyze the results of the campaigns. Your users can analyze the results by product and by individual districts in the northwest region. They can compare the sales to the targets set for the promotional campaigns, or the prior year's sales, or against industry averages. The users can estimate the growth in earnings due to the promotional campaigns. The assessment can then lead to further planning and execution. This plan−execute−assess loop is critical for the success of an enterprise.

Information Potential for Business Areas   We considered one isolated example of how the information potential of your data warehouse can assist in the planning for market expansion and in the assessment of the results of the execution of marketing campaigns for that purpose. Let us go through a few general areas of the enterprise where the data warehouse can assist in the planning and assessment phases of the management loop.

Profitability Growth   To increase profits, management has to understand how the profits are tied to product lines, markets, and services. Management must gain insights into which product lines and markets produce greater profitability. Business intelligence from the data warehouse is ideally suited to plan for profitability growth and to assess the results when the plans are executed.

Strategic Marketing   Strategic marketing drives business growth. When management studies the opportunities for up-selling and cross-selling to existing customers and for expanding the customer base, they can plan for business growth. The data warehouse has great information potential for strategic marketing.

Customer Relationship Management   A customer's interactions with an enterprise are captured in various operational systems. The order processing system contains the orders placed by the customer; the product shipment system, the shipments; the sales system, the details of the products sold to the customer; the accounts receivable system, the credit details and the outstanding balances. The data warehouse has all the data about the customer extracted from the various disparate source systems, transformed, and integrated. Thus, your management can "know" their customers individually from the information available in the data warehouse. This knowledge results in better customer relationship management.

Corporate Purchasing   From where can your management get the overall picture of corporate-wide purchasing patterns? Your data warehouse. This is where all data about products and vendors are collected after integration from the source systems. Your data warehouse empowers corporate management to plan for streamlining purchasing processes.

Realizing the Information Potential   What is the underlying significance of the information potential of the data warehouse? The data warehouse enables the users to view the data in the right business context. The various operational systems collect massive quantities of data on numerous types of business transactions. But these operational systems are not directly helpful for planning and assessment of results. The users need to assess the results by viewing the data in the proper business context. For example, when viewing the sales in the northwest region, the users need to view the sales in the business context of geography, product, promotion, and time. The data warehouse is designed for analysis of metrics such as sales along these dimensions. The users are able to retrieve the data, transform it into useful information, and leverage the information for planning and assessing the results.

The users interact with the data warehouse to obtain data, transform it into useful information, and realize the full potential. This interaction of the users generally goes through the six stages indicated in Figure 14-3 and summarized below.

1. Think through the business need and define it in terms of business rules as applicable to data in the data warehouse.
2. Harvest or select the appropriate subset of the data according to the stipulated business rules.
3. Enrich the selected subset with calculations such as totals or averages. Apply transformations to translate codes to business terms.

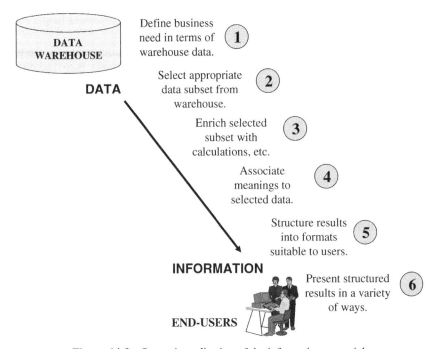

Figure 14-3   Stages in realization of the information potential.

4. Use metadata to associate the selected data with its business meaning.

5. Structure the result in a format useful to the users.

6. Present the structured information in a variety of ways, including tables, texts, graphs, and charts.

User–Information Interface

In order to pass through the six stages and realize the information potential of the data warehouse, you have to build a solid interface for information delivery to the users. Put the data warehouse on one side and the entire community of users on the other. The interface must be able to let the users realize the full information potential of the data warehouse.

The interface logically sits in the middle, enabling information delivery to the users. The interface could be a specific set of tools and procedures, tailored for your environment. At this point, we are not discussing the exact composition of the interface; we just want to specify its features and characteristics. Without getting into the details of the types of users and their specific information needs, let us define the general characteristics of the user–information interface.

Information Usage Modes   When you consider all the various ways the data warehouse may be used, you note that all the usage comes down to two basic modes or ways. Both modes relate to obtaining business intelligence. Remember, we are not considering information retrieved from operational systems.

Verification Mode. In this mode, the business user proposes a hypothesis and asks a series of questions to either confirm or repudiate it. Let us see how the use of the information in this mode works. Assume that your marketing department planned and executed several promotional campaigns on two product lines in the south-central region. Now the marketing department wants to assess the results of the campaign. The marketing department goes to the data warehouse with the hypothesis that sales in the south-central region have increased. Information from the data warehouse will help confirm the hypothesis.

Discovery Mode. When using the data warehouse in the discovery mode, the business analyst does not use a predefined hypothesis. In this case, the business analyst desires to discover new patterns of customer behavior or product demands. The user does not have any preconceived notions of what the result sets will indicate. Data mining applications with data feeds from the data warehouse are used for knowledge discovery.

We have seen that users interact with the data warehouse for information either in the hypothesis verification mode or in a knowledge discovery mode. What are the approaches for the interaction? In other words, do the users interact with the data warehouse in an informational approach, an analytical approach, or by using data mining techniques?

Informational Approach. In this approach, with query and reporting tools, users retrieve historical or current data and perform some standard statistical analysis. The data may be lightly or heavily summarized. The result sets may take the form of reports and charts.

Analytical Approach. As the name of this approach indicates, users make use of the data warehouse for performing analysis. They do the analysis along business dimensions using historical summaries or detailed data. The business users conduct the analysis using their own business terms. More complex analysis involves drill down, roll up, or slice and dice.

Data Mining Approach. Both the informational and analytical approaches work in the verification mode. The data mining approach, however, works in the knowledge discovery mode.

We have reviewed two modes and three approaches for information usage. What about the characteristics and structures of the data that is being used? How should the data be available through the user–information interface? Typically, the information made available through the user–information interface has the following characteristics:

Preprocessed Information. These include routine information automatically created and made readily available. Monthly and quarterly sales analysis reports, summary reports, and routine charts fall into this category. Users simply copy such preprocessed information.

Predefined Queries and Reports. This is a set of query templates and report formats kept ready for users. The users apply the appropriate parameters and run the queries and reports as and when needed. Sometimes, users are allowed to make minor modifications to the templates and formats.

Ad hoc Constructions. Users create their own queries and reports using appropriate tools. This category acknowledges the fact that not every need of the users can be anticipated. Generally, only power users and some regular users construct their own queries and reports.

Finally, let us list the essential features necessary for the user–information interface. The interface must

- Be easy to use, intuitive, and enticing to users.
- Support the ability to express the business need clearly.
- Convert the expressed need into a set of formal business rules.
- Be able to store these rules for future use.
- Provide the ability to the users to modify retrieved rules.
- Select, manipulate, and transform data according to the business rules.
- Have a set of data manipulation and transformation tools.
- Correctly link to data storage to retrieve the selected data.
- Be able to link with metadata.
- Be capable of formatting and structuring output in a variety of ways, both textual and graphical.
- Have the means of building a procedure for executing specific steps.
- Have a procedure management facility.

Industry Applications

So far in this section, we have clearly perceived the great information potential of the data warehouse. This enormous information potential drives the discussion that follows, where we get into more specifics and details. Before we do that, let us pause to refresh our minds on how the information potential of data warehouses is realized in a sample of industry sectors.

Manufacturing: Warranty and service management, product quality control, order fulfillment and distribution, supplier and logistics integration.

Retail and Consumer Goods: Store layout, product bundling, cross-selling, value chain analysis.

Banking and Finance: Relationship management, credit risk management.

WHO WILL USE THE INFORMATION?

You will observe that within six months after deployment of the data warehouse, the number of active users doubles. This is a typical experience for most data warehouses. Who are these new people arriving at the data warehouse for information? Unless you know how to anticipate who will come for business intelligence, you will not be able to cater to their needs appropriately and adequately.

Anyone who needs strategic information is expected to be part of the groups of users. That includes business analysts, business planners, departmental managers, and senior executives. It is likely that each of the data marts may be built for the specific needs of one segment of the user groups. In this case, you can identify the special groups and cater to their needs. At this stage, when we are discussing information delivery, we are not considering the information content so much but the actual mechanism of information delivery.

Each group of users has specific business needs for which they expect to get answers from the data warehouse. When we try to classify the user groups, it is best to understand them from the perspective of what they expect to get out of the warehouse. How are they going to use the information content in their job functions? Each user is performing a particular business function and needs information for support in that specific job function. Let us, therefore, base our classification of the users on their job functions and organizational levels.

Figure 14-4 suggests a way of classifying the user groups. When you classify the users by their job functions, their positions in the organizational hierarchy, and their computing proficiency, you get a firm basis for understanding what they need and how to provide information in the proper formats. If you are considering a user in accounting and finance, that user will be very comfortable with spreadsheets and financial ratios. For a user in customer service, a GUI screen showing consolidated information about each customer is most useful. For someone in marketing, a tabular format may be suitable.

Classes of Users

In order to make your information delivery mechanism best suited for your environment, you need to have a thorough understanding of the classes of users: First, let us start by associating the computing proficiency of the users with how each group based on this type of division interacts with the data warehouse.

Casual or Novice User. Uses the data warehouse occasionally, not daily. Needs a very intuitive information interface. Looks for the information delivery to prompt the user with available choices. Needs big button navigation.

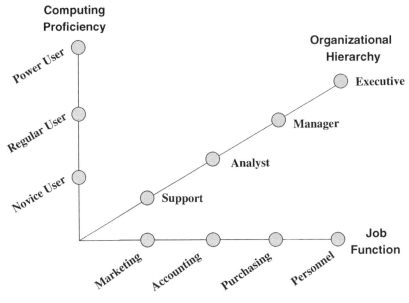

Figure 14-4 A method of classifying users.

Regular User. Uses the data warehouse almost daily. Comfortable with computing options but cannot create own reports and queries from scratch. Needs query templates and predefined reports.

Power User. Is highly proficient with technology. Can create reports and queries from scratch. Some can write their own macros and scripts. Can import data into spreadsheets and other applications.

Now let us change the perspective a bit and look at the user types by the way they wish to interact to obtain information.

Preprocessed Reports. Use routine reports run and delivered at regular intervals.

Predefined Queries and Templates. Enter own set of parameters and run queries with predefined templates and reports with predefined formats.

Limited ad hoc Access. Create from scratch and run limited number and simple types of queries and analysis.

Complex ad hoc Access. Create complex queries and run analysis sessions from scratch regularly. Provide the basis for preprocessed and predefined queries and reports.

Let us view the user groups from yet another perspective. Consider the users based on their job functions.

High-Level Executives and Managers. Need information for high-level strategic decisions. Standard reports on key metrics are useful. Customized and personalized information is preferable.

Technical Analysts. Look for complex analysis, statistical analysis, drill-down and slice-dice capabilities, and freedom to access the entire data warehouse.

Business Analysts. Although comfortable with technology, are not quite adept at creating queries and reports from scratch. Predefined navigation is helpful. Want to look at the results in many different ways. To some extent, can modify and customize predefined reports.

Business-Oriented Users. These are knowledge workers who like point-and-click GUIs. Desire to have standard reports and some measure of ad hoc querying.

We have considered a few ways of understanding how users may be grouped. Now, let us put it all together and label the user classes in terms of their access and information delivery practices and preferences. Figure 14-5 shows a way of classifying users adopted by many data warehousing experts and practitioners. This figure shows five broad classes of users. Within each class, the figure indicates the basic characteristics of the users in that class. The figure also assigns the users in the organizational hierarchy to specific classes.

Although the classification appears to be novel and interesting, you will find that it provides a good basis to understand the characteristics of each group of users. You can fit any user into one of these classes. When you observe the computing proficiency, the organizational level, the information requirements, or even the frequency of usage, you can readily identify the user as belonging to one of these groups. That will help you to satisfy the needs of each user who depends on your data warehouse for information. It comes down to this: if you provide proper information delivery to tourists, operators, farmers, explorers, and miners, then you would have taken care of the needs of every one of your users.

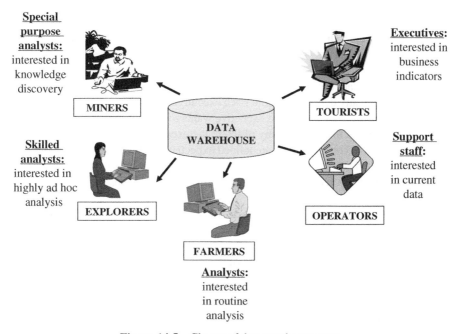

Figure 14-5   Classes of data warehouse users.

What They Need

By now we have formalized the broad classifications of data warehouse users. Let us pause and consider how we accomplished this. If you take two of your users with similar information access characteristics, computing proficiency, and scope of information needs, you may very well place both these users in the same broad class. For example, if you take two senior executives in different departments, they are similar in the way they would like to get information and in the level and scope of information they would like to have. You may place both of these executives in the tourist class or category.

Once you put both of these users in the tourist category, then it is easy for you to understand and formulate the requirements for information delivery to these two executives. The types of information needed by one user in a certain category are similar to the types needed by another user in the same category. An understanding of the needs of a category of users, generalized to some extent, provides insight into how best to provide the types of information needed. Formal classification leads to understanding the information needs. Understanding the information needs, in turn, leads to establishing proper ways for providing the information. Establishing the best methods and techniques for each class of users is the ultimate goal of information delivery.

What do the tourists need? What do the farmers need? What does each class of users need? Let us examine each class, one by one, review the information access characteristics, and arrive at the information needs.

Tourists   Imagine a tourist visiting an interesting place. First of all, the tourist has studied the broader features of the place he or she is visiting and is aware of the richness of the culture and the variety of sites at this place. Although many interesting sites are available, the tourist has to pick and choose the most worthwhile sites to visit. Once he or she has arrived at the place, the tourist must be able to select the sites to visit with utmost ease. At a particular site, if the tourist finds something very attractive, he or she will likely allocate additional time to that site.

Now let us apply the tourist story to the data warehouse. A senior-level executive arriving at the data warehouse for information is like a tourist visiting an interesting and useful place. The executive has a broad business perspective and knows about the overall information content of the data warehouse. However, the executive has no time to browse through the data warehouse in any detailed fashion. Each executive has specific key indicators. These are like specific sites to be visited. The executive wants to inspect the key indicators and if something interesting is found about any of them, the executive wants to spend some more time exploring further. The tourist has predefined expectations about each site being visited. If a particular site deviates from these expectations, the tourist wants to ascertain the reasons why. Similarly, if the executive finds indicators to be out of line, further investigation becomes necessary.

Let us, therefore, summarize what the users classified as tourists need from the data warehouse:

- Status of the indicators at routine intervals
- Capability to identify items of interest without any difficulty
- Selection of what is needed with utmost ease without wasting time in long navigation
- Ability to quickly move from one indicator of interest to another
- Wherever needed, additional information should be easily available about selected key indicators for further exploration

Operators   We have looked at some of the characteristics of users classified as operators. This class of users is interested in the data warehouse for one primary reason. They find the data warehouse to be the integrated source of information, not for historic data only but for current data as well. Operators are interested in current data at a detailed level. Operators are really monitors of current performance. Departmental managers, line managers, and section supervisors may all be classified as operators.

Operators are interested in today's performance and problems. They are not interested in historical data. Being extensive users of OLTP systems, operators expect fast response times and quick access to detailed data. How can they resolve the current bottleneck in the product distribution system? What are the currently available alternative shipment methods and which industrial warehouse is low on stock? Operators concern themselves with questions like these relating to current situations. Because the data warehouse receives and stores data extracted from disparate source systems, operators expect to find their answers there.

Note the following summary of what operators need.

- Immediate answers based on reliable current data
- Current state of the performance metrics
- Data as current as possible with daily or more frequent updates from source systems
- Quick access to very detailed information
- Rapid analysis of the most current data
- A simple and straightforward interface for information.

Farmers   What do some data warehouse users and farmers have in common? Consider a few traits of farmers. They are very familiar with the terrain. They know exactly what they want in terms of crops. Their requirements are consistent. The farmers know how to use the tools, work the fields, and get results. They also know the value of their crops. Now match these characteristics with the category of data warehouse users classified as farmers.

Typically, different types of analysts in an enterprise may be classified as farmers. These users may be technical analysts or analysts in marketing, sales, or finance. These analysts have standard requirements. The requirements may comprise estimating profitability by products or analyzing sales every month. Requirements rarely change. They are predictable and routine.

Let us summarize the needs of the users classified as farmers.

- Quality data properly integrated from source systems
- Ability to run predictable queries easily and quickly
- Capability to run routine reports and produce standard result types
- Ability to obtain the same types of information at predictable intervals
- Precise and smaller result sets
- Mostly current data with simple comparisons with historical data

Explorers   This class of users is different from the usual kind of routine users. Explorers do not have set ways of looking for information. They tend to go where very few others venture. Explorers often combine random probing with unpredictable investigation. Many times the investigation may not lead to any results, but the few that dig up useful patterns and unusual results produce nuggets of information that are solid gold. So the explorer continues his or her relentless search, using nonstandard procedures and unorthodox methods.

In an enterprise, researchers and highly skilled technical analysts may be classified as explorers. These users use the data warehouse in a highly random manner. The frequency of their use is quite unpredictable. They may use the data warehouse for several days of intense exploration and then stop using it for many months. Explorers analyze data in ways virtually unknown to other types of users. The queries run by explorers tend to encompass large data masses. These users work with lots of detailed data to discern desired patterns. These results are elusive, but the explorers continue until they find the patterns and relationships.

As in the other cases, let us summarize the needs of the users classified as explorers.

- Totally unpredictable and intensely ad hoc queries
- Ability to retrieve large volumes of detailed data for analysis
- Capability to perform complex analysis
- Provision for unstructured and completely new and innovative queries and analysis
- Long and protracted analysis sessions in bursts

Miners   People mining for gold dig to discover precious nuggets of great value. Users classified as miners also work in a similar manner. Before we get into the characteristics and needs of the miners, let us compare the miners with explorers, because both are involved in heavy analysis. Experts state that the role of the explorer is to create or suggest hypotheses, whereas the role of the miner is to prove or disprove hypotheses. This is one way of looking at the miner's role. The miner works to discover new, unknown, and unsuspected patterns in the data.

Miners are a special breed. In an enterprise, they are special purpose analysts with highly specialized training and skills. Many companies do not have users who might be called miners. Businesses employ outside consultants for specific data mining projects. Data miners adopt various techniques and perform specialized analysis that discovers clusters of related records, estimation of values for an unknown variable, grouping of products that would be purchased together, and so on.

Here is a summary of the needs of users classified as miners:

- Access to mountains of data to analyze and mine
- Availability of large volumes of historical data going back many years
- Ability to wade through large volumes to obtain meaningful correlations
- Capability of extracting data from the data warehouse into formats suitable for special mining techniques
- Ability to work with data in two modes: one to prove or disprove a stated hypothesis, the other to discover hypotheses without any preconceived notions

How to Provide Information

What is the point of all this discussion about tourists, operators, farmers, explorers, and miners? What is our goal? As part of a data warehouse project team, your objective is to provide each user exactly what that user needs in a data warehouse. The information delivery system must be wide enough and appropriate enough to suit the entire needs of your user community. What techniques and tools do your executives and managers need? How do your business analysts look for information? What about your technical analysts responsible for deeper and more intense analysis? How about the knowledge worker charged with monitoring day-to-day current operations? How are they going to interact with your data warehouse?

In order to provide the best information delivery system, you have to find answers to these questions. But how? Do you have to go to each individual user and determine how he or she plans to use the data warehouse? Do you then aggregate all these requirements and come up with the totality of the information delivery system? This would not be a practical approach. This is why we have come up with the broad classifications of users. If you are able to provide for these classifications of users, then you cover almost all of your user community. Maybe in your enterprise there are no data miners yet. If so, you do not have to cater to this group at the present time.

We have reviewed the characteristics of each class of users. We have also studied the needs of each of these classes, not in terms of the specific information content, but how and in what ways each class needs to interact with the data warehouse. Let us now turn our attention to the most important question: how to provide information.

Study Figure 14-6 very carefully. This figure describes three aspects of providing information to the five classes of users. The architectural implications state the requirements relating to components such as metadata and user–information interface. These are broad architectural needs. For each user class, the figure indicates the types of tools most useful for that class. These specify the types. When you select vendors and tools, you will use this as a guide. The "other considerations" listed in the figure include design issues, special techniques, and any out-of-the-ordinary technology requirements.

	Tourists	Operators	Farmers	Explorers	Miners
Architectural Implications	Strong Metadata interface including key word search.	Fast response times.	Reasonable response times.	Reasonable response times.	Special data repositories getting data feed from the warehouse.
Tool Features	Web-enabled user interface. Customized for individual needs. Intuitive navigation.	Scope of data content fairly large. Simple user interface to get current information. Simple queries and reports.	Multidimensional data models with business dimensions and metrics. Standard user interface for queries and reports.	Normalized data models. Special architecture including an exploration warehouse useful.	Normalized data models. Detailed data, summarized used hardly ever.
Other Considerations	Ability to provide interface through special icons. Limited drill-down. Very moderate OLAP capabilities. Simple applications for standard information.	Ability to create simple menu-driven applications. Provide key performance indicators routinely published. Small result sets.	Ability to create reports. Limited drill-down. Routine analysis with definite results. Usually work with summary data.	Provision for large queries on huge volumes of detailed data. A variety of tools to query and analyze. Support for long analysis sessions. Usually large result sets for study and further analysis.	Range of special data mining tools, statistical analysis tools, and data visualization tools. Discovery of unknown patterns and relationships. Ability to interpret results.

Figure 14-6 How to provide information.

INFORMATION DELIVERY

In all of our deliberations up to now, you have come to realize that there are four underlying methods for information delivery. You may be catering to the needs of any class of users. You may be constructing the information delivery system to satisfy the requirements of users with simple needs or those of power users. Still the principal means of delivery are the same.

The first method is the delivery of information through reports. Of course, the formats and content could be sophisticated. Nevertheless, these are reports. The method of information delivery through reports is a carry-over from operational systems. You are familiar with hundreds of reports distributed from legacy operational systems. The next method is also a perpetuation of a technique from operational systems. In operational systems, the users are allowed to run queries in a very controlled setup. However, in a data warehouse, query processing is the most common method for information delivery. The types of queries run the gamut from simple to very complex. As you know, the main difference between queries in an operational system and in the data warehouse is the extra capabilities and openness in the warehouse environment.

The method of interactive analysis is something special in the data warehouse environment. Rarely are any users provided with such an interactive method in operational systems. Lastly, the data warehouse is the source for providing integrated data for downstream decision support applications. The Executive Information System is one such application. But more specialized applications such as data mining make the data warehouse worthwhile. Figure 14-7 shows a comparison of information delivery methods between the data warehouse and operational systems.

The rest of this section is devoted to special considerations relating to these four methods. We will highlight some basic features of the reporting and query environments and provide details to be taken into account while designing these methods of information delivery.

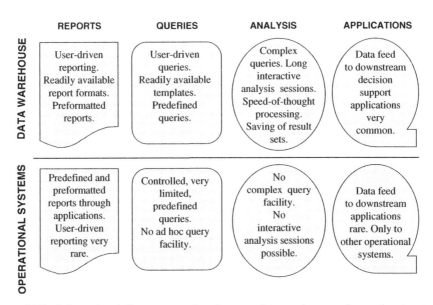

Figure 14-7 Information delivery: comparison between data warehouse and operational systems.

Queries

Query management ranks high in the provision of business intelligence from a data warehouse. Because most of the information delivery is through queries, query management is very important. The entire query process must be managed with utmost care. First, consider the features of a managed query environment:

- Query initiation, formulation, and results presentation are provided on the client machine.
- Metadata guides the query process.
- Ability for the users to navigate easily through the data structures is absolutely essential.
- Information is pulled by the users, not pushed to them.
- The query environment must be flexible to accommodate different classes of users.

Let us look at the arena in which queries are being processed. Essentially, there are three sections in this arena. The first section deals with the users who need the query management facility. The next section is about the types of queries themselves. Finally, you have the data that resides in the data warehouse repository. This is the data that is used for the queries. Figure 14-8 shows the query processing arena with the three sections. Please note the features in each section. When you establish the managed query environment, take into account the features and make proper provisions for them.

Let us now highlight a few important services to be made available in the managed query environment.

Query Definition. Make it easy to translate the business need into the proper query syntax.

Query Simplification. Make the complexity of data and query formulation transparent to the users. Provide simple views of the data structures showing tables and attributes. Make the rules for combining tables and structures easy to use.

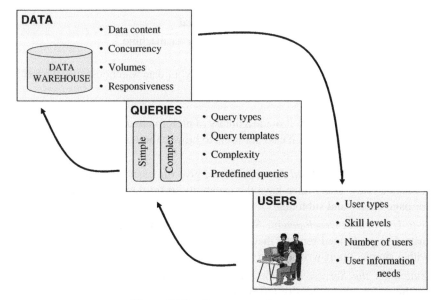

Figure 14-8   Query processing arena.

Query Recasting. Even simple-looking queries can result in intensive data retrieval and manipulation. Therefore, provide for parsing incoming queries and recasting them to work more efficiently.

Ease of Navigation. Use of metadata to browse through the data warehouse, easily navigating with business terminology and not technical phrases.

Query Execution. Provide ability for the user to submit the query for execution without intervention from IT.

Results Presentation. Present results of the query in a variety of ways.

Aggregate Awareness. Query processing mechanisms must be aware of aggregate fact tables and, whenever necessary, redirect the queries to the aggregate tables for faster retrieval.

Query Governance. Monitor and intercept runaway queries before they bring down the data warehouse operations.

Reports

In this subsection, let us observe the significant features of the reporting environment. Everyone is familiar with reports and how they are used. Without repeating what we already know, let us discuss reporting services by relating these to the data warehouse.

What can you say about the overall defining aspects of a managed reporting environment? Consider the following brief list.

- The information is pushed to the user, not pulled by the user as in the case of queries. Reports are published and the user subscribes to what he or she needs.
- Compared to queries, reports are inflexible and predefined.
- Most of the reports are preformatted and, therefore, rigid.
- The user has less control over the reports received than the queries he or she can formulate.
- A proper distribution system must be established.
- Report production normally happens on the server machine.

While constructing the reporting environment for your data warehouse, use the following as guidelines:

Set of Preformatted Reports. Provide a library of preformatted reports with clear descriptions of the reports. Make it easy for users to browse through the library and select the reports they need.

Parameter-Driven Predefined Reports. These give the users more flexibility than preformatted ones. Users must have the capability to set their own parameters and ask for page breaks and subtotals.

Easy-to-Use Report Development. When users need new reports in addition to preformatted or predefined reports, they must be able to develop their own reports easily with a simple report-writer facility.

Execution on the Server. Run the reports on the server machine to free the client machines for other modes of information delivery.

Report Scheduling. Users must be able to schedule their reports at a specified time or based on designated events.

Publishing and Subscribing. Users must have options to publish the reports they have created and allow other users to subscribe and receive copies.

Delivery Options. Provide various options to deliver reports, including mass distribution, e-mail, the Web, automatic fax, and so on. Allow users to choose their own methods for receiving the reports.

Multiple Data Manipulation Options. Allow the users to ask for calculated metrics, pivoting of results by interchanging the column and row variables, adding subtotals and final totals, changing the sort orders, and showing stoplight-style thresholds.

Multiple Presentation Options. Provide a rich variety of options, including graphs, tables, columnar formats, cross-tabs, fonts, styles, sizes, and maps.

Administration of Reporting Environment. Ensure easy administration to schedule, monitor, and resolve problems.

Analysis

Who are the users seriously interested in analysis? Business strategists, market researchers, product planners, production analysts—in short, all the users we have classified as explorers. Because of its rich historical data content, the data warehouse is very well suited for analysis. It provides these users with the means to search for trends, find correlations, and discern patterns.

In one sense, an analysis session is nothing but a session of a series of related queries. The user might start off with an initial query: What are the first quarter sales totals for this year by individual product lines? The user looks at the numbers and is curious about the sag in the sales of two of these product lines. The user then proceeds to drill down by individual products in those two product lines. The next query is for a breakdown by regions and then by districts. The analysis continues with comparison with the first quarterly sales of the two prior years. In analysis, there are no set predefined paths. Queries are formulated and executed at the speed of thought.

We have already covered the topic of query processing. Any provisions for query management apply to the queries executed as part of an analysis session. One significant difference is that each query in an analysis session is linked to the previous one. The queries in an analysis session form a linked series. Analysis is an interactive exercise.

Analysis can become extremely complex, depending on what the explorer is after. The explorer may take several steps in a winding navigational path. Each step may call for large masses of data. The data joins may involve several constraints. The explorer may want to view the results in many different formats and grasp the meaning of the results. Complex analysis falls in the domain of online analytical processing (OLAP). The next chapter is totally devoted to OLAP. There we will discuss complex analysis in detail.

Applications

A decision support application in relation to the data warehouse is any downstream system that gets its data feed from the data warehouse. In addition to letting the users access the data content of the warehouse directly, some companies create specialized applications for specific groups of users. Companies do this for various reasons. Some of the users may not be comfortable browsing through the data warehouse and looking for specific information. If the required data is extracted from the data warehouse at periodic intervals and specialized applications are built using the extracted data, these users have their needs satisfied.

How are the downstream applications different from an application driven with data extracted directly from the operational systems? Building an application with data from the warehouse has one major advantage. The data in the data warehouse is already consolidated, integrated, transformed, and cleansed. Any decision support applications built using individual operational systems directly may not have the enterprise view of the data.

A downstream decision support application may just start out to be nothing more than a set of preformatted and predefined reports. You add a simple menu for the users to select and run the reports and you have an application that may very well be useful to a number of your users. Executive Information Systems (EIS) are good candidates for downstream applications. EIS built with data from the warehouse proves to be superior to its counterparts of more than a decade ago when EIS were based on data directly from operational systems.

A more recent development is data mining, a major type of application that may get data feeds from the data warehouse. With more vendor products on the market to support data mining, this application has become more and more prevalent. Data mining deals with knowledge discovery. Refer to Chapter 17 for detailed coverage of data mining basics.

INFORMATION DELIVERY TOOLS

As we have indicated earlier, the success of your data warehouse rides on the strengths of the information delivery tools. If the tools are effective, usable, and enticing, your users will come to the data warehouse often. You have to select the information delivery tools with great care and thoroughness. We will discuss this very important consideration in detail.

Information delivery tools come in different formats to serve various purposes. The principal class of tools comprises query or data access tools. This class of tools enables users to define, formulate, and execute queries and obtain results. Other types are the report writers or reporting tools for formatting, scheduling, and running reports. Other tools specialize in complex analysis. A few tools combine the different features so that your users may learn to use a single tool for queries and reports. More commonly, you will find more than one information delivery tool used in a single data warehouse environment.

Information delivery tools typically perform two functions: they translate the user requests for queries or reports into SQL statements and send these to the DBMS; they receive results from the data warehouse DBMS, format the result sets in suitable outputs, and present the results to the users. Usually, the requests to the DBMS retrieve and manipulate large volumes of data. Compared to the volumes of data retrieved, the result sets contain much less data.

The Desktop Environment

In the client-server computing architecture, information delivery tools run in the desktop environment. Users initiate the requests on the client machines. When you select the query tools for your information delivery component, you are choosing software to run on the client workstations. What are the basic categories of information delivery tools?

TOOL CATEGORY	PURPOSE AND USAGE
Managed Query	Query templates and predefined queries. Users supply input parameters. Users can receive results on GUI screens or as reports.
Ad Hoc Query	Users can define the information needs and compose their own queries. May use complex templates. Results on screen or reports.
Preformatted Reporting	Users input parameters in predefined report formats and submit report jobs to be run. Reports may be run as scheduled or on demand.
Enhanced Reporting	Users can create own reports using report writer features. Used for special reports not previously defined. Reports run on demand.
Complex Analysis	Users write own complex queries. Perform interactive analysis usually in long sessions. Store intermediate results. Save queries for future use.
DSS Applications	Pre-designed standard decision support applications. May be customized. Example: Executive Information System. Data from the warehouse.
Application Builder	Software to build simple downstream applications for decision support applications. Proprietary language component. Usually menu-driven.
Knowledge Discovery	Set of data mining techniques. Tools used to discover patterns and relationships not apparent or previously known.

Figure 14-9 Information delivery: the desktop environment.

Grouping the tools into basic categories broadens your understanding of what types of tools are available and what types you need for your users.

Let us examine the array of information delivery tools you need to consider for selection. Study Figure 14-9 carefully. This figure lists the major categories for the desktop environment and summarizes the use and purpose of each category. Note the purpose of each category. The usage and functions of each category of tools help you match the categories with the classes of users.

Methodology for Tool Selection

Because of the enormous importance of the information delivery tools in a data warehouse environment, you must have a well thought out, formalized methodology for selecting the appropriate tools. A set of tools from certain vendors may be the best for a given environment, but the same set of tools could be a total disaster in another data warehouse environment. There is no one-size-fits-all proposition in the tool selection. The tools for your environment are for your users and must be the most suitable for them. Therefore, before formalizing the methodology for selection, do reconsider the requirements of your users.

Who are your users? At what organizational levels do they perform? What are the levels of their computing proficiency? How do they expect to interact with the data warehouse? What are their expectations? How many tourists are there? Are there any explorers at all? Ask all the pertinent questions and examine the answers.

Among the best practices in data warehouse design and development, a formal methodology ranks among the top. A good methodology certainly includes your user representatives. Make your users part of the process. Otherwise your tool selection methodology is doomed to failure. Have the users actively involved in setting the criteria for the tools and also in the evaluation activity itself. Apart from considerations of user preferences, technical compatibility with other components of the data warehouse must also be taken into account. Do not overlook technical aspects.

A good formal methodology promotes a staged approach. Divide the tool selection process into well-defined steps. For each step, declare the purpose and state the activities. Estimate the time needed to complete each step. Proceed from one stage to the next stage. The activities in each stage depend on the successful completion of the activities in the previous stage. Figure 14-10 illustrates the stages in the process for selecting information delivery tools.

The formal methodology you come up with for the selection of tools for your environment must define the activities in each stage of the process. Examine the following list suggesting the types of activities in each stage of the process. Use this list as a guide.

Form a Tool Selection Team. Include about four or five persons on the team. Because information delivery tools are important, ensure that the executive sponsor is part of the team. User representatives from the primary subject areas must be on the team. They will provide the user perspective and act as subject matter experts. Have someone experienced with information delivery tools on the team. If the data warehouse administrator is experienced in this area, let that person lead the team and drive the selection process.

Reassess User Requirements. Review the user requirements, not in a general way, but specifically in relation to information delivery. List the classes of users and put each potential user in the appropriate class. Describe the expectations and needs of each of your classes. Document the requirements so that you can match these up with the features of potential tools.

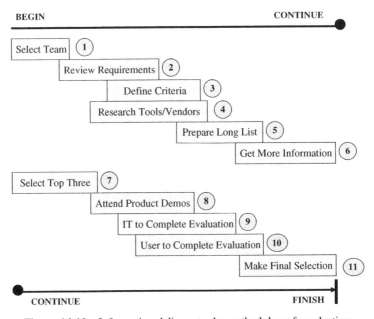

Figure 14-10   Information delivery tools: methodology for selection.

Stipulate Selection Criteria. For each broad group of tools such as query tools or reporting tools, specify the criteria. See the following subsection on Tool Selection Criteria.

Research Available Tools and Vendors. This stage can take a long time, so it is better to get a head start on this stage. Obtain product literature from the vendors. Trade shows can help for getting a first glimpse of potential tools. The Data Warehousing Institute is another good source. Although there are a few hundred tools on the market, narrow the list down to about 25 or less for preliminary research. At this stage, concentrate primarily on the functions and features of the tools on your list.

Prepare a Long List for Consideration. This follows from the research stage. Your research will result in the preliminary or long list of potential tools for consideration. For each tool on the preliminary list, document the functions and features. Also, note how these functions and features would match with the requirements.

Obtain Additional Information. In this stage, you want to do additional and more intensive research on the tools on your preliminary list. Talk to the vendors. Contact the installations the vendors suggest to you as references.

Select the Top Three Tools. Select the top three tools as possible candidates. If you are not very sure of the final outcome, choose more, but not more than five, because if you have another long list, it will take a lot longer to go through the rest of the selection process.

Attend Product Demonstrations. Now you want to know as much as possible about the tools on the short list. Call the vendors in for product demonstrations. You may go to the vendor sites if your computing configuration is not ready for the selected tools. Ask questions. During the demonstrations, constantly try to match the functions of the tools with the requirements of your users.

Complete Evaluation by IT. IT makes a separate evaluation, mainly for technical compatibility with your computing environment. Test features such as connectivity with your DBMS. Verify scalability.

Complete Evaluation by Users. This is a critical stage. User testing and acceptance is very important. Do not cut this stage short. This stage consists of a sufficient number of hands-on sessions. If it is feasible to prototype the actual usage, do so by all means. Especially if two products match the requirements to about the same extent, prototyping may bring out the essential differences.

Make the Final Selection. You are about ready to make the final selection. This stage gives you a chance to reevaluate the tools that come very close to the requirements. Also, in this stage check out the vendors. The tools may be excellent. But the current vendor could have acquired the tool from another company and the technical support may be inadequate. Or, the vendor may not be stable and enduring. Verify all the relevant issues about the vendor. Make the final selection, keeping the users in the loop all the while.

As you might have already realized, the tool selection process can be intense and may take a considerable length of time. Nevertheless, it must not be taken lightly. It is advisable to proceed in distinct stages, keeping the users involved from the beginning to the end of the process.

Let us end this subsection with the following practical tips:

- Nominate an experienced member of the team or the data warehouse administrator to lead the team and drive the process.
- Keep your users totally involved in the process.
- There is no substitute for hands-on evaluation. Do not be satisfied with just vendor demonstrations. Try the tools yourself.
- Consider prototyping a few typical information delivery interactions. Will the tool stand up to the load of multiple users?
- It is not easy to combine tools from multiple vendors.
- Remember, an information delivery tool must be compatible with the data warehouse DBMS.
- Continue to keep metadata considerations in the forefront.

Tool Selection Criteria

From the discussions on the needs of each class of users, you must have understood the criteria for selecting information delivery tools. For example, we referred to explorers and their need for complex analysis. This tells us that the tools for explorers must possess features suitable for performing complex analysis. For tourists, the tools must be easy and intuitive. By now, you have a reasonable insight into the criteria for selecting the information delivery tools. You have a good grasp of the criteria for selecting tools in the three main areas of information delivery, namely, reporting, queries, and analysis.

Let us now bring our thoughts together and provide a list of general criteria for selecting information delivery tools. This list is applicable to all three areas. You may use the list as a guide and prepare your own checklist that is specific to your environment.

Ease of Use. This is perhaps the most important way to make your users happy. Ease of use is specifically required for query creation, report building, and presentation flexibility.

Performance. Although system performance and response times are less critical in a data warehouse environment than in an OLTP system, still they rank high on the list of user requirements. Need for acceptable performance spans not only the information delivery system, but the entire environment.

Compatibility. The features of the information delivery tool must be exactly suited to the class of users it is intended for. For example, OLAP capability is not compatible with the class of users called tourists, nor are preformatted reports the precise requirement of explorers.

Functionality. This is an extension of compatibility. The profile of every user class demands certain indispensable functions in the tool. For example, miners need a full range of functions from data capture through discovery of unknown patterns.

Integrated. More commonly, querying, analyzing, and producing reports may be tied together in one user session. The user may start with an initial query whose results lead to drilling down or other forms of analysis. At the end of the session, the user is likely to capture the final result sets in the form of reports. If this type of usage is common in your environment, your information delivery tool must be able to integrate different functions.

Tool Administration. Centralized administration makes the task of the information delivery administrator easy. The tool must come with utility functions to configure and control the information delivery environment.

Web-Enabled. The Internet has become our window into the world. Today's data warehouses have a big advantage over the ones built before Web technology became popular. It is important for the information delivery tool to be able to publish Web pages over the Internet and your company's intranet.

Data Security. In most enterprises, safeguarding the warehouse data is as critical as providing security for data in operational systems. If your environment is a data-sensitive one, the information delivery tools must have security features.

Data Browsing Capability. The user must be able to browse the metadata and review the data definitions and meanings. Also, the tool must present data sets as GUI objects on the screen for the user to choose by clicking on the icons.

Data Selector Ability. The tool must provide the user with the means for constructing queries without having to perform specific joins of tables using technical terminology and methods.

Database Connectivity. The ability to connect to any of the leading database products is an essential feature needed in the information delivery tool.

Presentation Feature. It is important for the tool to present the result sets in a variety of formats, including texts, tabular formats, charts, graphs, maps, and so on.

Scalability. If your data warehouse is successful, you can be sure of a substantial increase in the number of users within a short time, as well as a marked expansion in the complexity of the information requests. The information delivery tool must be scalable to handle the larger volumes and extra complexity of the requests.

Vendor Dependability. As the data warehousing market matures you will notice many mergers and acquisitions. Also, some companies are likely to go out of business. The selected tool may be the best suited for your environment, but if the vendor is not stable, you may want to rethink your selection.

Information Delivery Framework

It is time for us to sum up everything we have discussed in this chapter. We classified the users and came up with standard classes of users. These are the classes into which you can fit every group of your users. Each class of users has specific characteristics when it comes to information delivery from the data warehouse. Classification of the users leads us to formalizing the information needs of each class. Once you understand what each class of users needs, you are able to derive the ways in which you must provide information to these classes. Our discussions moved on to the standard methods of information delivery and to the selection of information delivery tools. Figure 14-11 summarizes the discussions. The figure shows the classes of users. It indicates how the various users in the enterprise fit into this classification. The figure also matches each class of users with the common tool categories appropriate for the class. The figure brings everything together.

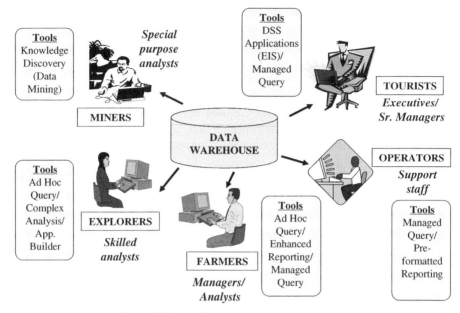

Figure 14-11   Information delivery framework.

INFORMATION DELIVERY: SPECIAL TOPICS

So far in this chapter we have covered a lot of ground on information delivery to the users. Provision of business intelligence from the data warehouse necessarily depends on the classes of users the data warehouse services. In this chapter, we reviewed, in detail, methods for classifying users. The classifications provided you great insight into the needs of the users.

You were able to see how the traditional information delivery methods of queries and reports may be adapted to satisfy the needs of the different classes of users. You were also able to notice the role of interactive analysis and down-stream decision support applications. Further, you were able to appreciate the usage and applicability of tools for information delivery.

We now want to turn our attention to two new trends in the demand and delivery of business intelligence. During the early years of data warehousing, the updates to the data warehouse were performed overnight, primarily in batch mode. And, usage of information from the data warehouse was mainly meant for strategic decision making, not for operational tasks. Now, the two new trends are real time business intelligence and pervasive business intelligence. Now the need is to update the data warehouses in real time. This is real time business intelligence. Also, the need is to make information available to a much larger population in the organization than anticipated earlier. This is pervasive business intelligence.

Business Activity Monitoring (BAM)

In recent years real-time business intelligence has gained a lot of ground. One way of providing real-time BI is to adapt the traditional data warehouse to be populated faster in real-time or near real-time instead of doing it overnight through batch ETL. However, a second approach is to provide means for business activity monitoring through middleware solutions using Web services or such monitoring methods. These software monitors or intelligent agents may be outside the data warehouse to recognize key events and measure key processes in operational systems in real time.

Although BAM may be outside the traditional data warehouse per se, it provides business intelligence to interested users. Therefore, we want to include BAM in the overall scheme of information delivery and consider a few of its aspects.

BAM is based on the notions of zero-latency and straight-through processing. Latency refers to the time-lag between when data is collected and when the resulting business intelligence is made available to the users. In straight-through processing inefficient intermediary steps are avoided.

BAM Features   These are real-time systems that alert decision makers to imminent problems and to potential opportunities. Data is collected from internal and external sources in real time, analyzed on the fly for specific patterns, and results are delivered to those who need to act immediately. Generally these users dependent on BAM solutions include line executives, departmental managers, financial officers, and heads of divisional facilities such as a factory or a warehouse.

BAM Technologies   Include (1) ETL to gather data from multiple sources, (2) process modeling to scope out relevant processes and activities, (3) rules engines to spot and recognize pertinent events in the activities, and (4) delivery mechanisms such as e-mails, portals, Web services, dashboards, and so on.

BAM Benefits   BAM empowers decision makers to quickly recognize critical events, respond promptly, and review results of timely actions. The most important benefit is real-time access to usable business intelligence in suitable formats. BAM tools enable decision makers to quickly model the problem, collaborate for action, weigh solution alternatives, and make faster and presumably better decisions. Further, real-time BI systems such as BAM may be made to interact directly with business applications. For example, if the inventory level of a product falls below a set threshold in a supply chain management (SCM) application, BAM can initiate replenishment of the inventory. Again, in a customer relationship management (CRM) application as soon as a customer places a substantially large online order, BAM can initiate intensive credit verification.

Dashboards and Scorecards

During the past five years or so, organizations have seriously begun to deploy dashboards and scorecards as their preferred mode of delivering business intelligence. Pervasive data warehousing and business intelligence became the catch phrases because the need to deliver operational, tactical, and strategic information was keenly felt. Further, organizations want to provide such information to large groups of users in real time.

Many organizations find their need fulfilled through what are known as dashboards and scorecards. Wayne Eckerson (2005), a leading researcher and business intelligence expert at the Data Warehousing Institute, writes, "In many ways, dashboards and scorecards represent the culmination of business intelligence." He continues, "To borrow a term from the telecommunications industry, dashboards and scorecards represent the 'last mile' of wiring that connects users to the data warehousing and analytical infrastructure that organizations have created during the past decade." Dashboards and scorecards greatly promote performance visibility and effectiveness. They provide visual displays of significant, consolidated information, nicely arranged and well presented on a single screen. With a single sweeping

	DASHBOARD	**SCORECARD**
PURPOSE	Measures performance	Charts progress
USERS	Specialists, supervisors	Executives, managers, staff
UPDATES	"Right-time" feeds	Periodic snapshots
DATA	Events	Summaries
DISPLAY	Visual graphs, raw data	Visual graphs, textual comments

Source: W. Eckerson, Performance Dashboards, Wiley, Hoboken, NJ, 2006

Figure 14-12   Differences between dashboards and scorecards.

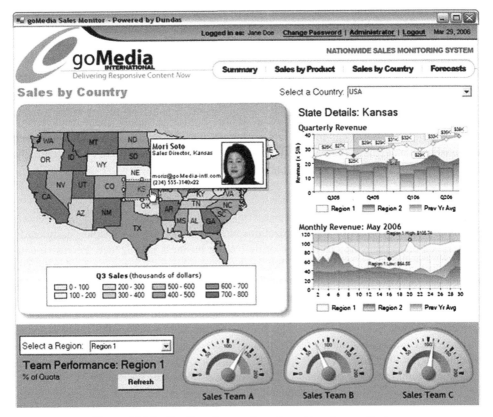

Figure 14-13   Dashboard example: nationwide sales monitoring.

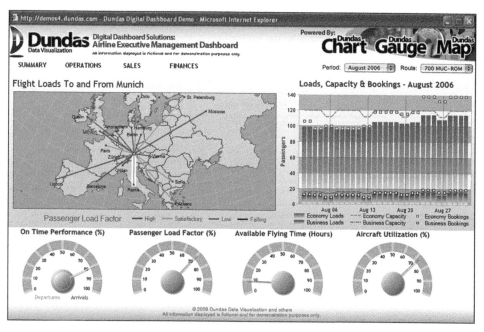

Figure 14-14   Dashboard example: airline executive management.

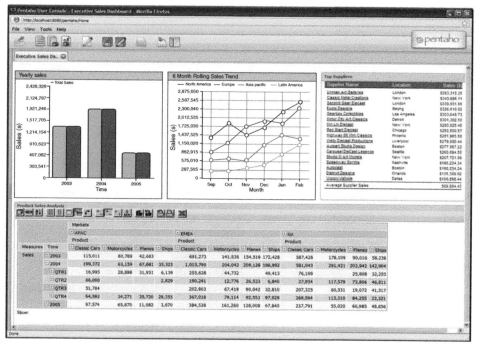

Figure 14-15   Dashboard example: executive sales.

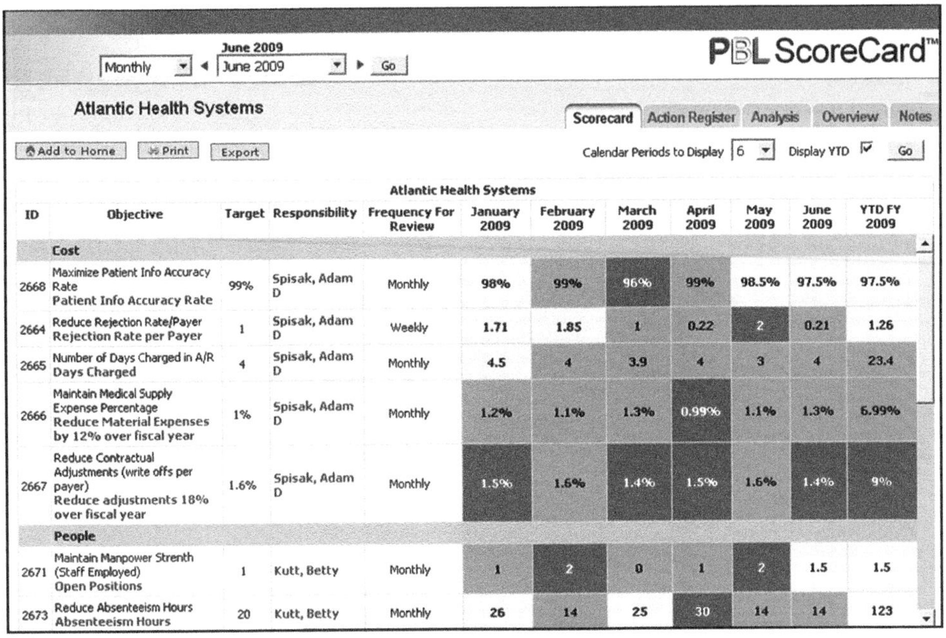

ID	Objective	Target	Responsibility	Frequency For Review	January 2009	February 2009	March 2009	April 2009	May 2009	June 2009	YTD FY 2009
	Cost										
2668	Maximize Patient Info Accuracy Rate Patient Info Accuracy Rate	99%	Spisak, Adam D	Monthly	98%	99%	96%	99%	98.5%	97.5%	97.5%
2664	Reduce Rejection Rate/Payer Rejection Rate per Payer	1	Spisak, Adam D	Weekly	1.71	1.85	1	0.22	2	0.21	1.26
2665	Number of Days Charged in A/R Days Charged	4	Spisak, Adam D	Monthly	4.5	4	3.9	4	3	4	23.4
2666	Maintain Medical Supply Expense Percentage Reduce Material Expenses by 12% over fiscal year	1%	Spisak, Adam D	Monthly	1.2%	1.1%	1.3%	0.99%	1.1%	1.3%	6.99%
2667	Reduce Contractual Adjustments (write offs per payer) Reduce adjustments 18% over fiscal year	1.6%	Spisak, Adam D	Monthly	1.5%	1.6%	1.4%	1.5%	1.6%	1.4%	9%
	People										
2671	Maintain Manpower Strenth (Staff Employed) Open Positions	1	Kutt, Betty	Monthly	1	2	0	1	2	1.5	1.5
2673	Reduce Absenteeism Hours Absenteeism Hours	20	Kutt, Betty	Monthly	26	14	25	30	14	14	123

Figure 14-16 Scorecard example: healthcare, cost and people.

glance user can obtain the gist of the presentation and explore the contents further. However, although dashboards and scorecards have much in common, some organizations do not fully comprehend the differences between them. Even in some trade journals the distinction is not clearly made.

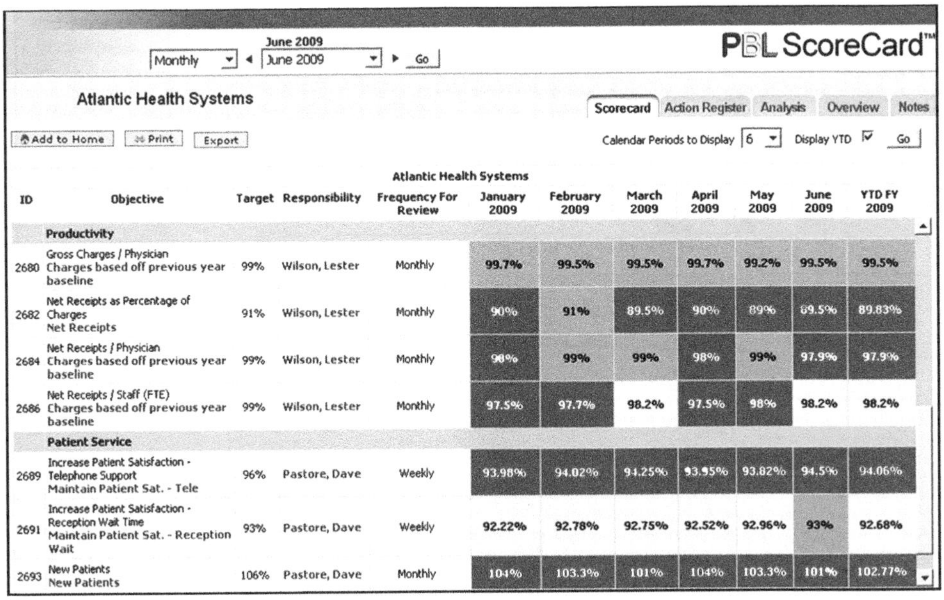

ID	Objective	Target	Responsibility	Frequency For Review	January 2009	February 2009	March 2009	April 2009	May 2009	June 2009	YTD FY 2009
	Productivity										
2680	Gross Charges / Physician Charges based off previous year baseline	99%	Wilson, Lester	Monthly	99.7%	99.5%	99.5%	99.7%	99.2%	99.5%	99.5%
2682	Net Receipts as Percentage of Charges Net Receipts	91%	Wilson, Lester	Monthly	90%	91%	89.5%	90%	89%	89.5%	89.83%
2684	Net Receipts / Physician Charges based off previous year baseline	99%	Wilson, Lester	Monthly	98%	99%	99%	98%	99%	97.9%	97.9%
2686	Net Receipts / Staff (FTE) Charges based off previous year baseline	99%	Wilson, Lester	Monthly	97.5%	97.7%	98.2%	97.5%	98%	98.2%	98.2%
	Patient Service										
2689	Increase Patient Satisfaction - Telephone Support Maintain Patient Sat. - Tele	96%	Pastore, Dave	Weekly	93.98%	94.02%	94.25%	93.95%	93.82%	94.5%	94.06%
2691	Increase Patient Satisfaction - Reception Wait Time Maintain Patient Sat. - Reception Wait	93%	Pastore, Dave	Weekly	92.22%	92.78%	92.75%	92.52%	92.96%	93%	92.68%
2693	New Patients New Patients	106%	Pastore, Dave	Monthly	104%	103.3%	101%	104%	103.3%	101%	102.77%

Figure 14-17 Scorecard example: healthcare, productivity and patient service.

Dashboards tell users what they are doing; scorecards tell them how well they are doing. Dashboards provide real-time readouts of various aspects of business performance as events occur. These are intended to inform, warn, caution, and alert users in a manner similar to an automobile dashboard. Scorecards, on the other hand, provide periodic snapshots of performance results. These measure business activities as compared to predefined targets and objectives. Figure 14-12 highlights the differences between dashboards and scorecards.

Dashboards These are designed to produce maximum visual impact with optimal arrangement of information for quick absorption. The display usually shows a combination of tables, graphs, dials, stoplights, gauges, threshold charts, odometers, and so on. Most dashboards allow the users to set parameters and select which pieces of information they would like to view. Dashboards are also presented as cascading dashboards from one view to another. Users may work with dashboards interactively. As dashboards have gained importance for information delivery, we have included three examples of dashboards. See Figures 14-13, 14-14, and 14-15.

Scorecards These are designed to provide visual representation of key performance indicators (KPIs). KPIs are preselected metrics intended to measure and manage performance. Scorecards display actual values of the KPIs at selected intervals as compared to targets or past periods. Figures 14-16 and 14-17 display two examples of scorecards for a healthcare organization.

CHAPTER SUMMARY

- Information content and usage in a data warehouse differ greatly from those in operational systems.
- The data warehouse possesses enormous information potential for the overall enterprise management as well as for individual business areas.
- You realize the information potential of the data warehouse through an effective user–information interface.
- Who will use the information? Understand the various users and their needs. The users may be classified into interest groups of tourists, operators, farmers, explorers, and miners.
- Provide information to each class according to its needs, skills, and business background.
- Queries, reports, analysis, and applications form the basis for information delivery. Each class of users needs variations of these information delivery methods.
- The success of your data warehouse rides on the effectiveness of the end-user information delivery tools. Carefully choose the tools by applying proven selection criteria.
- Dashboards and scorecards are gradually becoming preferred means of delivering business intelligence.

REVIEW QUESTIONS

1. How does the data warehouse differ from an operational system in usage and value?
2. Explain briefly how the information from the data warehouse promotes customer relationship management.

3. What are the two basic modes of usage of information from the data warehouse? Give an example for each mode.

4. List any five essential features necessary for the user–information interface.

5. Who are the power users? How do power users expect to use the data warehouse?

6. Who are the users classified as farmers? Name any three characteristics of this class of data warehouse users.

7. List any four essential features of a managed query environment.

8. List any four essential features of a managed reporting environment.

9. List and explain five criteria for selecting information delivery tools for your data warehouse.

10. Describe in less than four sentences your understanding of the information delivery framework.

EXERCISES

1. Match the columns:

1. information discovery mode	**A.** EIS
2. data warehouse tourists	**B.** needs intuitive interface
3. query recasting	**C.** plan, execute, assess
4. data warehouse explorers	**D.** confirm hypothesis
5. downstream application	**E.** information pull technique
6. overall enterprise management	**F.** analyze large data volumes
7. verification mode	**G.** need status of indicators
8. casual user	**H.** highly random access
9. data warehouse miners	**I.** parse and improve query
10. queries	**J.** data mining

2. Compare the usage and value of information in the data warehouse with those in operational systems. Explain the major differences. Discuss and give examples.

3. Examine the potential users of your data warehouse. Can you classify the users into casual users, regular users, and power users? If this method of simple classification is inadequate, discuss how your users may be classified.

4. Among the potential users in your data warehouse, whom can you classify as tourists? What are the characteristics of these tourists? How can you provide information for the tourists in your organization?

5. What do you understand about the information delivery framework in the data warehouse environment? As an end-user information delivery specialist, discuss how you will establish such a framework for a healthcare maintenance organization (HMO).

CHAPTER 15

OLAP IN THE DATA WAREHOUSE

CHAPTER OBJECTIVES

- Perceive the unqualified demand for online analytical processing (OLAP) and under-stand what drives this demand
- Review the major features and functions of OLAP in detail
- Grasp the intricacies of dimensional analysis and learn the meanings of hypercubes, drill-down and roll-up, and slice-and-dice
- Examine the different OLAP models and determine which model is suitable for your environment
- Consider OLAP implementation by studying the steps and the tools

In the earlier chapters we mentioned online analytical processing (OLAP) in passing. You had a glimpse of OLAP when we discussed the information delivery methods. You have some idea of what OLAP is and how it is used for complex analysis. As the name implies, OLAP has to do with the processing of data as it is manipulated for analysis. The data warehouse provides the best opportunity for analysis and OLAP is the vehicle for carrying out involved analysis. The data warehouse environment is also best for data access when analysis is carried out.

We now have the chance to explore OLAP in sufficient depth. In today's data warehous-ing environment, with such tremendous progress in analysis tools from various vendors, you cannot have a data warehouse without OLAP. It is unthinkable. Therefore, throughout this chapter, look out for the important topics in OLAP.

First, you have to perceive what OLAP is and why it is absolutely essential. This will help you to better understand the features and functions of OLAP. We will discuss the major features and functions so that your grasp of OLAP may be firmed up. There are two

Data Warehousing Fundamentals for IT Professionals, Second Edition. By Paulraj Ponniah
Copyright © 2010 John Wiley & Sons, Inc.

major models for OLAP. You should know which model is most suitable for your computing and user environments. We will highlight the significance of each model, learn how to implement OLAP in your data warehouse environment, investigate OLAP tools, and find out how to evaluate and procure them for your users. Finally, we will discuss the implementation steps for OLAP.

DEMAND FOR ONLINE ANALYTICAL PROCESSING

Recall our discussions in Chapter 2 of the top-down and bottom-up approaches for building a data warehouse. In the top-down approach, you build the overall corporate-wide data repository using the entity-relationship (E-R) data modeling technique. This enterprise-wide data warehouse feeds the departmental data marts that are designed using the dimensional modeling technique. In the bottom-up approach, you build several data marts using the dimensional modeling technique and the collection of these data marts forms the data warehouse environment for your company. Each of these two approaches has its advantages and shortcomings.

You also learned about a practical approach to building a conglomeration of supermarts with conformed and standardized data content. While adopting this approach, first you plan and define the requirements at the corporate level, build the infrastructure for the complete warehouse, and then implement one supermart at a time in a priority sequence. The supermarts are designed using the dimensional modeling technique.

As we have seen, a data warehouse is meant for performing substantial analysis using the available data. The analysis leads to strategic decisions that are the major reasons for building data warehouses in the first place. For performing meaningful analysis, data must be cast in a way suitable for analysis of the values of key indicators over time along business dimensions. Data structures designed using the dimensional modeling technique support such analysis.

In the three approaches referred to above, the data marts rest on the dimensional model. Therefore, these data marts must be able to support dimensional analysis. In practice, these data marts seem to be adequate for basic analysis. However, in today's business conditions, we find that users need to go beyond such basic analysis. They must have the capability to perform far more complex analysis in less time. Let us examine how the traditional methods of analysis provided in a data warehouse are not sufficient and perceive what exactly is demanded by the users to stay competitive and to expand.

Need for Multidimensional Analysis

Let us quickly review the business model of a large retail operation. If you just look at daily sales, you soon realize that the sales are interrelated with many business dimensions. The daily sales are meaningful only when they are related to the dates of the sales, the products, the distribution channels, the stores, the sales territories, the promotions, and a few more dimensions. Multidimensional views are inherently representative of any business model. Very few models are limited to three dimensions or less. For planning and making strategic decisions, managers and executives probe into business data through scenarios. For example, they compare actual sales against targets and against sales in prior periods. They examine the breakdown of sales by product, by store, by sales territory, by promotion, and so on.

Decision makers are no longer satisfied with one-dimensional queries such as "How many units of product A did we sell in the store in Edison, New Jersey?" Consider the following more useful query: "How much revenue did the new product X generate during the last three months, broken down by individual months, in the south central territory, by individual stores, broken down by promotions, compared to estimates, and compared to the previous version of the product?" The analysis does not stop with this single multidimensional query. The user continues to ask for further comparisons to similar products, comparisons among territories, and views of the results by rotating the presentation between columns and rows.

For effective analysis, your users must have easy methods of performing complex analysis along several business dimensions. They need an environment that presents a multidimensional view of data, providing the foundation for analytical processing through easy and flexible access to information. Decision makers must be able to analyze data along any number of dimensions, at any level of aggregation, with the capability of viewing results in a variety of ways. They must have the ability to drill down and roll up along the hierarchies of every dimension. Without a solid system for true multidimensional analysis, your data warehouse is incomplete.

In any analytical system, time is a critical dimension. Hardly any query is executed without having time as one of the dimensions along which analysis is performed. Further, time is a unique dimension because of its sequential nature—November always comes after October. Users monitor performance over time, as for example, performance this month compared to last month, or performance this month compared with performance the same month last year.

Another point about the uniqueness of the time dimension is the way in which the hierarchies of the dimension work. A user may look for sales in March and may also look for sales for the first four months of the year. In the second query for sales for the first four months, the implied hierarchy at the next higher level is an aggregation taking into account the sequential nature of time. No user looks for sales of the first four stores or the last three stores. There is no implied sequence in the store dimension. True analytical systems must recognize the sequential nature of time.

Fast Access and Powerful Calculations

Whether a user's request is for monthly sales of all products along all geographical regions or for year-to-date sales in a region for a single product, the query and analysis system must have consistent response times. Users must not be penalized for the complexity of their analysis. Both the size of the effort to formulate a query or the amount of time to receive the result sets must be consistent irrespective of the query types.

Let us take an example to understand how speed of the analysis process matters to users. Imagine a business analyst looking for reasons why profitability dipped sharply in recent months in the entire enterprise. The analyst starts this analysis by querying for the overall sales for the last five months for the entire company, broken down by individual months. The analyst notices that although the sales do not show a drop, there is a sharp reduction in profitability for the last three months. The analysis proceeds further when the analyst wants to find out which countries show reductions. The analyst requests a breakdown of sales by major worldwide regions and notes that the European region is responsible for the reduction in profitability. Now the analyst senses that clues are becoming more pronounced and looks for a breakdown of the European sales by individual countries. The analyst finds that the profitability has increased for a few countries, decreased sharply for some other countries, and been stable for the rest. At this point, the analyst introduces another dimension into the analysis. Now the analyst wants the breakdown of profitability for the European countries by country, month, and product. This step brings the analyst closer to the reason for the decline in the profitability. The analyst observes that the countries in the European Union (EU) show very sharp declines in profitability for the last two months. Further queries reveal that manufacturing and other direct costs remain at the usual levels but the indirect costs have shot up. The analyst is now able to determine that the decline is due to the additional tax levies on some products in the EU. The analyst has also determined the exact effect of the levies so far. Strategic decisions follow on how to deal with the decline in profitability.

Now look at Figure 15-1 showing the steps through the single analysis session. How many steps are there? Many steps, but one single analysis session with a necessary continuous train of thought. Each step in this train of thought constitutes a query. The analyst formulates each query, executes it, waits for the result set to appear on the screen, and studies the result set. Each query is interactive because the result set from one query forms the basis for the next query. In this manner of querying, the user cannot maintain the train of thought unless the momentum is preserved. Fast access is absolutely essential for an effective analytical processing environment.

Did you notice that none of the queries in the above analysis session included any serious calculations? This is not typical. In a real-world analysis session, many of the queries require calculations, sometimes complex calculations. What is the implication here? An effective analytical processing environment must not only be fast and flexible, but it must also support complex and powerful calculations.

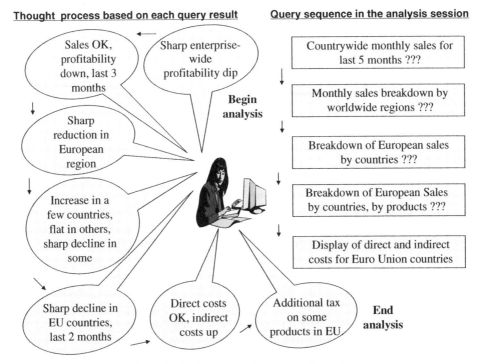

Figure 15-1 Query steps in an analysis session.

What follows is a list of typical calculations that get included in the query requests:

- Roll ups to provide summaries and aggregations along the hierarchies of the dimensions
- Drill downs from the top level to the lowest along the hierarchies of the dimensions, in combinations among the dimensions
- Simple calculations, such as computation of margins (sales minus costs)
- Share calculations to compute the percentage of parts to the whole
- Algebraic equations involving key performance indicators
- Moving averages and growth percentages
- Trend analysis using statistical methods

Limitations of Other Analysis Methods

You now have a fairly good grip on the types of requirements of users to execute queries and perform analysis. First and foremost, the information delivery system must be able to present multidimensional views of the data. Then the information delivery system must enable the users to use the data by analyzing it along multiple dimensions and their hierarchies in a myriad of ways. And this facility must be fast. It must be possible for users to perform complex calculations.

Let us understand why the traditional tools and methods are not up to the task when it comes to complex analysis and calculations. What information methods are we familiar with? Of course, the earliest method was the medium of reports. Then came spreadsheets with all their functionality and features. SQL has been the accepted interface for retrieving and manipulating data from relational databases. These methods are used in OLTP systems and in data warehouse environments. Now, when we discuss multidimensional analysis and complex calculations, how suitable are these traditional methods?

First, let us compare the characteristics of the OLTP and data warehouse environments. When we mention the data warehouse environment here, we are not referring to heavy multidimensional analysis and complex calculations. We are only referring to the environment with simple queries and routine reports. Figure 15-2 shows the characteristics of the OLTP and the basic data warehouse environments as they relate to information delivery needs.

Now consider information retrieval and manipulation in these two environments. What are the standard methods of information delivery? These are reports, spreadsheets, and online displays. What is the standard data access interface? SQL. Let us review these and determine if they are adequate for multidimensional analysis and complex calculations.

Report writers provide two key functions: the ability to point and click for generating and issuing SQL calls, and the capability to format the output reports. However, report writers do not support multidimensionality. With basic report writers, you cannot drill down to lower levels in the dimensions. That will have to come from additional reports. You cannot rotate the results by switching rows and columns. The report writers do not provide aggregate navigation. Once the report is formatted and run, you cannot alter the presentation of the result data sets.

If report writers are not the tools or methods we are looking for, how about spreadsheets for calculations and the other features needed for analysis? Spreadsheets, when they first appeared, were positioned as analysis tools. You can perform "what if" analysis with

CHARACTERISTICS	OLTP SYSTEMS	DATA WAREHOUSE
Analytical capabilities	Very low	Moderate
Data for a single session	Very limited	Small to medium size
Size of result set	Small	Large
Response time	Very fast	Fast to moderate
Data granularity	Detail	Detail and summary
Data currency	Current	Current and historical
Access method	Predefined	Predefined and ad hoc
Basic motivation	Collect and input data	Provide information
Data model	Design for data updates	Design for queries
Optimization of database	For transactions	For analysis
Update frequency	Very frequent	Generally read-only
Scope of user interaction	Single transactions	Throughout data content

Figure 15-2   OLTP and data warehouse environments.

spreadsheets. When you modify the values in some cells, the values in other related cells automatically change. What about aggregations and calculations?

Spreadsheets with their add-in tools can perform some forms of aggregations and also do a variety of calculations. Third-party tools have also enhanced spreadsheet products to present data in three-dimensional formats. You can view rows, columns, and pages on spreadsheets. For example, the rows can represent products, the columns represent stores, and the pages represent the time dimension in months. Modern spreadsheet tools offer pivot tables or n-way cross-tabs.

Even with enhanced functionality using add-ins, spreadsheets are still very cumbersome to use. Take an analysis involving the four dimensions of store, product, promotion, and time. Let us say each dimension contains an average of five hierarchical levels. Now try to build an analysis to retrieve data and present it as spreadsheets showing all the aggregation levels and multidimensional views, and also using even simple calculations. You can very well imagine how much effort it would take for this exercise. Now what if your user wants to change the navigation and do different roll ups and drill downs. The limitations of spreadsheets for multidimensional analysis and complex calculations are quite evident.

Let us now turn our attention to SQL (Structured Query Language). Although it might have been the original goal of SQL to be the end-user query language, now everyone agrees that the language is too abstruse even for sophisticated users. Third-party products attempt to extend the capabilities of SQL and hide the syntax from the users. Users can formulate their queries through GUI point-and-click methods or by using natural language syntax. Nevertheless, SQL vocabulary is ill-suited for analyzing data and exploring relationships. Even basic comparisons prove to be difficult in SQL.

Meaningful analysis such as market exploration and financial forecasting typically involve retrieval of large quantities of data, performing calculations, and summarizing the data on the fly. Perhaps, even the detailed analysis may be achieved by using SQL for retrieval and spreadsheets for presenting the results. But here is the catch: in a real-world analysis session, many queries follow one after the other. Each query may translate into a number of intricate SQL statements, with each of the statements likely to invoke full table scans, multiple joins, aggregations, groupings, and sorting. Analysis of the type we are discussing requires complex calculations and handling time series data. SQL is notably weak in these areas. Even if you can imagine an analyst accurately formulating such complex SQL statements, the overhead on the systems would still be enormous and seriously impact response times.

OLAP is the Answer

Users certainly need the ability to perform multidimensional analysis with complex calculations, but we find that the traditional tools of report writers, query products, spreadsheets, and language interfaces are distressfully inadequate. What is the answer? Clearly, the tools being used in the OLTP and basic data warehouse environments do not match up to the task. We need a different set of tools and products that are specifically meant for serious analysis. We need OLAP in the data warehouse.

In this chapter, we will thoroughly examine the various aspects of OLAP. We will come up with formal definitions and detailed characteristics. We will highlight all the features and functions. We will explore the different OLAP models. But now that you have an initial appreciation for OLAP, let us list the basic virtues of OLAP to justify our proposition.

- Enables analysts, executives, and managers to gain useful insights from the presentation of data.
- Can reorganize metrics along several dimensions and allow data to be viewed from different perspectives.
- Supports multidimensional analysis.
- Is able to drill down or roll up within each dimension.
- Is capable of applying mathematical formulas and calculations to measures.
- Provides fast response, facilitating speed-of-thought analysis.
- Complements the use of other information delivery techniques such as data mining.
- Improves the comprehension of result sets through visual presentations using graphs and charts.
- Can be implemented on the Web.
- Designed for highly interactive analysis.

Even at this stage, you will further appreciate the nature and strength of OLAP by studying a typical OLAP session (see Fig. 15-3). The analyst starts with a query requesting a high-level summary by product line. Next, the user moves to drilling down for details by year. In the following step, the analyst pivots the data to view totals by year rather than totals by product line. Even in such a simple example, you observe the power and features of OLAP.

OLAP Definitions and Rules

Where did the term OLAP originate? We know that multidimensionality is at the core of OLAP systems. We have also mentioned some other basic features of OLAP. Is it a vague collection of complex factors for serious analysis? Is there a formal definition and a set of fundamental guidelines identifying OLAP systems?

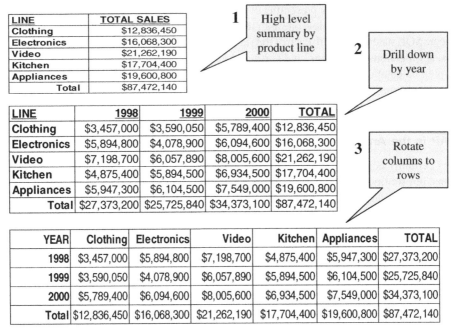

Figure 15-3 Simple OLAP session.

The term OLAP or online analytical processing was introduced in a paper entitled "Providing On-Line Analytical Processing to User Analysts," by Dr. E. F. Codd, the acknowledged father of the relational database model. The paper, published in 1993, defined 12 rules or guidelines for an OLAP system. Later, in 1995, six additional rules were included. We will discuss these rules. Before that, let us look for a short and precise definition for OLAP. Such a succinct definition comes from the OLAP council (www.olapcouncil.org), which provides membership, sponsors research, and promotes the use of OLAP. Here is the definition:

On-Line Analytical Processing (OLAP) is a category of software technology that enables analysts, managers and executives to gain insight into data through fast, consistent, interactive access in a wide variety of possible views of information that has been transformed from raw data to reflect the real dimensionality of the enterprise as understood by the user.

The definition from the OLAP council contains all the key ingredients. Speed, consistency, interactive access, and multiple dimensional views—all of these are principal elements. As one trade magazine described it as early as in 1995, OLAP is a fancy term for multidimensional analysis.

The guidelines proposed by Dr. Codd form the yardstick for measuring any sets of OLAP tools and products. A true OLAP system must conform to these guidelines. When your project team is looking for OLAP tools, it can prioritize these guidelines and select tools that meet the set of criteria at the top of your priority list. First, let us consider the initial 12 guidelines for an OLAP system:

Multidimensional Conceptual View. Provide a multidimensional data model that is intuitively analytical and easy to use. Business users' view of an enterprise is multidimensional in nature. Therefore, a multidimensional data model conforms to how the users perceive business problems.

Transparency. Make the technology, underlying data repository, computing architecture, and the diverse nature of source data totally transparent to users. Such transparency, supporting a true open system approach, helps to enhance the efficiency and productivity of the users through front-end tools that are familiar to them.

Accessibility. Provide access only to the data that is actually needed to perform the specific analysis, presenting a single, coherent, and consistent view to the users. The OLAP system must map its own logical schema to the heterogeneous physical data stores and perform any necessary transformations.

Consistent Reporting Performance. Ensure that the users do not experience any significant degradation in reporting performance as the number of dimensions or the size of the database increases. Users must perceive consistent run time, response time, or machine utilization every time a given query is run.

Client/Server Architecture. Conform the system to the principles of client/server architecture for optimum performance, flexibility, adaptability, and interoperability. Make the server component sufficiently intelligent to enable various clients to be attached with a minimum of effort and integration programming.

Generic Dimensionality. Ensure that every data dimension is equivalent in both structure and operational capabilities. Have one logical structure for all dimensions. The basic data structure or the access techniques must not be biased toward any single data dimension.

Dynamic Sparse Matrix Handling. Adapt the physical schema to the specific analytical model being created and loaded that optimizes sparse matrix handling. When encountering a sparse matrix, the system must be able to dynamically deduce the distribution of the data and adjust the storage and access to achieve and maintain consistent level of performance.

Multiuser Support. Provide support for end users to work concurrently with either the same analytical model or to create different models from the same data. In short, provide concurrent data access, data integrity, and access security.

Unrestricted Cross-Dimensional Operations. Provide ability for the system to recognize dimensional hierarchies and automatically perform roll-up and drill-down operations within a dimension or across dimensions. Have the interface language allow calculations and data manipulations across any number of data dimensions, without restricting any relations between data cells, regardless of the number of common data attributes each cell contains.

Intuitive Data Manipulation. Enable consolidation path reorientation (pivoting), drill down and roll up, and other manipulations to be accomplished intuitively and directly via point-and-click and drag-and-drop actions on the cells of the analytical model. Avoid the use of a menu or multiple trips to a user interface.

Flexible Reporting. Provide capabilities to the business user to arrange columns, rows, and cells in a manner that facilitates easy manipulation, analysis, and synthesis of information. Every dimension, including any subsets, must be able to be displayed with equal ease.

Unlimited Dimensions and Aggregation Levels. Accommodate at least 15, preferably 20, data dimensions within a common analytical model. Each of these generic dimensions must allow a practically unlimited number of user-defined aggregation levels within any given consolidation path.

In addition to these 12 basic guidelines, also take into account the following requirements, not all distinctly specified by Dr. Codd.

Drill-Through to Detail Level. Allow a smooth transition from the multidimensional, pre-aggregated database to the detail record level of the source data warehouse repository.

OLAP Analysis Models. Support Dr. Codd's four analysis models: exegetical (or descriptive), categorical (or explanatory), contemplative, and formulaic.

Treatment of Nonnormalized Data. Prohibit calculations made within an OLAP system from affecting the external data serving as the source.

Storing OLAP Results. Do not deploy write-capable OLAP tools on top of transactional systems.

Missing Values. Ignore missing values, irrespective of their source.

Incremental Database Refresh. Provide for incremental refreshes of the extracted and aggregated OLAP data.

SQL Interface. Seamlessly integrate the OLAP system into the existing enterprise environment.

OLAP Characteristics

Let us summarize in simple terms what we have covered so far. We explored why business users absolutely need online analytical processing. We examined why the other methods of information delivery do not satisfy the requirements for multidimensional analysis with powerful calculations and fast access. We discussed how OLAP is the answer to satisfy these requirements. We reviewed the definitions and authoritative guidelines for the OLAP system.

Before we get into a more detailed discussion of the major features of OLAP systems, let us list the most fundamental characteristics in plain language. OLAP systems

- Let business users have a multidimensional and logical view of the data in the data warehouse.
- Facilitate interactive query and complex analysis for the users.
- Allow users to drill down for greater details or roll up for aggregations of metrics along a single business dimension or across multiple dimensions.
- Provide the ability to perform intricate calculations and comparisons.
- Present results in a number of meaningful ways, including charts and graphs.

MAJOR FEATURES AND FUNCTIONS

Very often, you are faced with the question of whether OLAP is not just data warehousing in a nice wrapper? Can you not consider online analytical processing as just an information delivery technique and nothing more? Is it not another layer in the data warehouse, providing an interface between the data and the users? In some sense, OLAP is an information delivery system for the data warehouse. But OLAP is much more than that. A data warehouse stores data and provides simpler access to business intelligence. An OLAP system comp-lements the data warehouse by lifting the information delivery capabilities to new heights.

General Features

In this section, we will pay special attention to a few major features and functions of OLAP systems. You will gain greater insight into dimensional analysis, find deeper meanings about the necessity for drill downs and roll ups during analysis sessions and gain greater appreciation for the role of slicing and dicing operations in analysis. Before getting into greater details about these, let us recapitulate the general features of OLAP. Figure 15-4 summarizes these features. Also note the distinction between basic features and advanced features. The list shown in the figure includes the general features you observe in practice in most OLAP environments. Use the list as a quick checklist of features your project team must consider for your OLAP system.

Dimensional Analysis

By this time, you are perhaps tired of the term "dimensional analysis." We have used the term many times so far. You have been told that dimensional analysis is a strong suit in the arsenal of OLAP. Any OLAP system devoid of multidimensional analysis is utterly useless. So try to get a clear picture of the facility provided in OLAP systems for dimensional analysis.

Let us begin with a simple STAR schema. This STAR schema has three business dimen-sions, namely, product, time, and store. The fact table contains sales. Figure 15-5 shows the STAR schema and a three-dimensional representation of the model as a cube, with products on the X-axis, time on the Y-axis, and stores on the Z-axis. What are the values represented along each axis? For example, in the STAR schema, time is one of the dimensions and month is one of the attributes of the time dimension. Values of this attribute month are

BASIC FEATURES	Multidimensional analysis	Consistent performance	Fast response times for interactive queries
	Drill-down and roll-up	Navigation in and out of details	Slice-and-dice or rotation
	Multiple view modes	Easy scalability	Time intelligence (year-to-date, fiscal period)

ADVANCED FEATURES	Powerful calculations	Cross-dimensional calculations	Pre-calculation or pre-consolidation
	Drill-through across dimensions or details	Sophisticated presentation & displays	Collaborative decision making
	Derived data values through formulas	Application of alert technology	Report generation with agent technology

Figure 15-4 General features of OLAP.

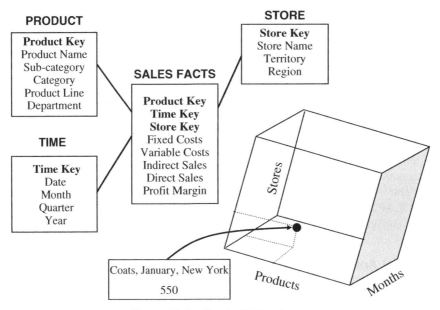

Figure 15-5   Simple STAR schema.

represented on the Y-axis. Similarly, values of the attributes product name and store name are represented on the other two axes.

This schema with just three business dimensions does not even look like a star. Nevertheless, it is a dimensional model. From the attributes of the dimension tables, pick the attribute product name from the product dimension, month from the time dimension, and store name from the store dimension. Now look at the cube representing the values of these attributes along the primary edges of the physical cube. Go further and visualize the sales for coats in the month of January at the New York store to be at the intersection of the three lines representing the product: coats, month: January, and store: New York.

If you are displaying the data for sales along these three dimensions on a spreadsheet, the columns may display the product names, the rows the months, and pages the data along the third dimension of store names. See Figure 15-6, which shows a screen display of a page of this three-dimensional data.

The page displayed on the screen shows a slice of the cube. Now look at the cube and move along a slice or plane passing through the point on the Z-axis representing store: New York. The intersection points on this slice or plane relate to sales along product and time business dimensions for store: New York. Try to relate these sale numbers to the slice on the cube representing store: New York.

Now we have a way of depicting three business dimensions and a single fact on a two-dimensional page and also on a three-dimensional cube. The numbers in each cell on the page are the sale numbers. What could be the types of multidimensional analysis on this particular set of data? What types of queries could be run during the course of analysis sessions? You could get sale numbers along the hierarchies of a combination of the three business dimensions of product, store, and time. You could perform various types of three-dimensional analysis of sales. The results of queries during analysis sessions will be displayed on the screen with the three dimensions represented in columns, rows, and

Store: New York

Products

PAGES: STORE dimension

COLUMNS: PRODUCT dimension

		Hats	Coats	Jackets	Dresses	Shirts	Slacks
	Jan	200	550	350	500	520	490
	Feb	210	480	390	510	530	500
ROWS: TIME dimension	Mar	190	480	380	480	500	470
	Apr	190	430	350	490	510	480
	May	160	530	320	530	550	520
	Jun	150	450	310	540	560	330
	Jul	130	480	270	550	570	250
	Aug	140	570	250	650	670	230
	Sep	160	470	240	630	650	210
	Oct	170	480	260	610	630	250
	Nov	180	520	280	680	700	260
Months	Dec	200	560	320	750	770	310

Figure 15-6   A three-dimensional display.

pages. The following is a sample of simple queries and the result sets during a multidimensional analysis session.

Query

Display the total sales of all products for past five years in all stores.

Display of Results

Rows: Year numbers 2009, 2008, 2007, 2006, 2005
Columns: Total Sales for all products
Page: One store per page

Query

Compare total sales for all stores, product by product, between years 2009 and 2008.

Display of Results

Rows: Year numbers 2009, 2008; difference; percentage increase or decrease
Columns: One column per product, showing all products
Page: All stores

Query

Show comparison of total sales for all stores, product by product, between years 2009 and 2008 only for those products with reduced sales.

Display of Results

Rows: Year numbers 2009, 2008; difference; percentage decrease
Columns: One column per product, showing only the qualifying products
Page: All stores

Query

Show comparison of sales by individual stores, product by product, between years 2009 and 2008 only for those products with reduced sales.

Display of Results

Rows: Year numbers 2009, 2008; difference; percentage decrease
Columns: One column per product, showing only the qualifying products
Page: One store per page

Query

Show the results of the previous query, but rotating and switching the columns with rows.

Display of Results

Rows: One row per product, showing only the qualifying products
Columns: Year numbers 2009, 2008; difference; percentage decrease
Page: One store per page

Query

Show the results of the previous query, but rotating and switching the pages with rows.

Display of Results

Rows: One row per store
Columns: Year numbers 2009, 2008; difference; percentage decrease
Page: One product per page, displaying only the qualifying products.

This multidimensional analysis can continue on until the analyst determines how many products showed reduced sales and which stores suffered the most.

In the above example, we had only three business dimensions and each of the dimensions could, therefore, be represented along the edges of a cube or the results displayed as columns, rows, and pages. Now add another business dimension, promotion. That will bring the number of business dimensions to four. When you have three business dimensions, you are able to represent these three as a cube with each edge of the cube denoting one dimension. You are also able to display the data on a spreadsheet with two dimensions as rows and columns and the third dimension as pages. But when you have four dimensions or more, how can you represent the data? Obviously, a three-dimensional cube does not work. And you also have a problem when trying to display the data on a spreadsheet as rows, columns, and pages. So what about multidimensional analysis when there are more than three dimensions? This leads us to a discussion of hypercubes.

What Are Hypercubes?

Let us begin with the two business dimensions of product and time. Usually, business users wish to analyze not just sales but other metrics as well. Assume that the metrics to be

PRODUCT: Coats

PAGES: PRODUCT dimension   <u>COLUMNS</u>: Metrics

	Fixed Cost	Variable Cost	Indirect Sales	Direct Sales	Profit Margin
Jan	340	110	230	320	100
Feb	270	90	200	260	100
Mar	310	100	210	270	70
Apr	340	110	210	320	80
May	330	110	230	300	90
Jun	260	90	150	300	100
Jul	310	100	180	300	70
Aug	380	130	210	360	60
Sep	300	100	180	290	70
Oct	310	100	170	310	70
Nov	330	110	210	310	80
Dec	350	120	200	360	90

ROWS: TIME dimension

Multidimensional Domain Structure

TIME	PRODUCT	METRICS
Jan	Hats	Fixed Cost
Feb		Variable
Mar	Coats	Cost
Apr		
May	Jackets	Indirect
Jun		Sales
Jul		
Aug	Dresses	Direct
Sep		Sales
Oct	Shirts	
Nov		Profit
Dec	Slacks	Margin

Figure 15-7   Display of columns, rows, and pages.

analyzed are fixed cost, variable cost, indirect sales, direct sales, and profit margin. These are five common metrics.

The data described here may be displayed on a spreadsheet showing metrics as columns, time as rows, and products as pages. Figure 15-7 shows a sample page of the spreadsheet display. In the figure, note the three straight lines, two of which represent the two business dimensions and the third, the metrics. You can independently move up or down along the straight lines. Some experts refer to this representation as a multidimensional domain structure (MDS).

The figure also shows a cube representing the data points along the edges. Relate the three straight lines to the three edges of the physical cube. Now the page you see in the figure is a slice passing through a single product and the divisions along the other two straight lines shown on the page as columns and rows. With three groups of data—two groups of business dimensions and one group of metrics—we can easily visualize the data as being along the three edges of a cube.

Now add another business dimension to the model. Let us add the store dimension. That results in three business dimensions plus the metrics data. How can you represent these four groups as edges of a three-dimensional cube? How do you represent a four-dimensional model with data points along the edges of a three-dimensional cube? How do you slice the data to display pages?

This is where an MDS diagram comes in handy. Now you need not try to perceive four-dimensional data as along the edges of the three-dimensional cube. All you have to do is draw four straight lines to represent the data as an MDS. These four lines represent the data (see Fig. 15-8). Looking at this figure, you realize that the metaphor of a physical cube to represent data breaks down when you try to represent four dimensions. But, as

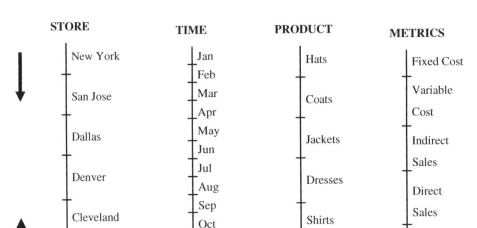

Figure 15-8   MDS for four dimensions.

you see, the MDS is well suited to represent four dimensions. Can you think of the four straight lines of the MDS intuitively to represent a "cube" with four primary edges? This intuitive representation is a hypercube, a representation that accommodates more than three dimensions. At a lower level of simplification, a hypercube can very well accommodate three dimensions. A hypercube is a general metaphor for representing multidimensional data.

You now have a way of representing four dimensions as a hypercube. The next question relates to display of four-dimensional data on the screen. How can you possibly show four dimensions with only three display groups of rows, columns, and pages? Please turn your attention to Figure 15-9. What do you notice about the display groups? How does the display resolve the problem of accommodating four dimensions with only three display groups? By combining multiple logical dimensions within the same display group. Notice how product and metrics are combined to display as columns. The displayed page represents the sales for store: New York.

Let us look at just one more example of an MDS representing a hypercube. Let us move up to six dimensions. Please study Figure 15-10 with six straight lines showing the data representations. The dimensions shown in this figure are product, time, store, promotion, customer demographics, and metrics.

There are several ways you can display six-dimensional data on the screen. Figure 15-11 illustrates one such six-dimensional display. Notice how product and metrics are combined and represented as columns, store and time are combined as rows, and demographics and promotion as pages.

We have reviewed two specific issues. First, we have noted a special method for representing a data model with more than three dimensions using an MDS. This method is an intuitive way of showing a hypercube. A model with three dimensions can be represented

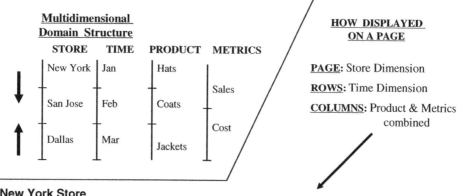

New York Store

	Hats:Sales	Hats:Cost	Coats:Sales	Costs:Cost	Jackets:Sales	Jackets:Cost
Jan	450	350	550	450	500	400
Feb	380	280	460	360	400	320
Mar	400	310	480	410	450	400

Figure 15-9   Page displays for four-dimensional data.

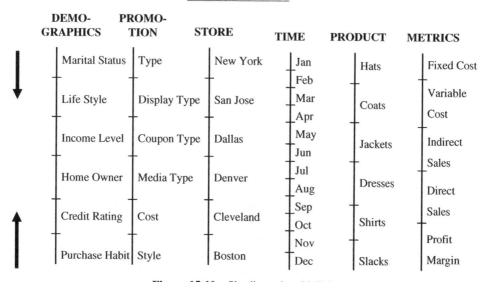

Figure 15-10   Six-dimensional MDS.

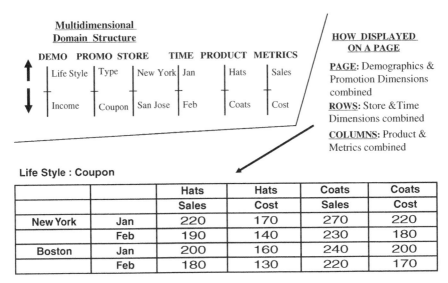

Figure 15-11   Page displays for six-dimensional data.

by a physical cube. But a physical cube is limited to only three dimensions or less. Second, we have also discussed the methods for displaying the data on a flat screen when the number of dimensions is three or more. Building on the resolution of these two issues, let us now move on to two very significant aspects of multidimensional analysis. One of these is the drill-down and roll-up exercise; the other is the slice-and-dice operation.

Drill Down and Roll Up

Return to Figure 15-5. Look at the attributes of the product dimension table of the STAR schema. In particular, note these specific attributes of the product dimension: product name, subcategory, category, product line, and department. These attributes signify an ascending hierarchical sequence from product name to department. A department includes product lines, a product line includes categories, a category includes subcategories, and each subcategory consists of products with individual product names. In an OLAP system, these attributes are called hierarchies of the product dimension.

OLAP systems provide drill-down and roll-up capabilities. Try to understand what we mean by these capabilities with reference to the above example. Figure 15-12 illustrates these capabilities with reference to the product dimension hierarchies. Note the different types of information given in the figure. It shows the rolling up to higher hierarchical levels of aggregation and the drilling down to lower levels of detail. Also note the sales numbers shown alongside. These are sales for one particular store in one particular month at these levels of aggregation. The sale numbers you notice as you go down the hierarchy are for a single department, a single product line, a single category, and so on. You drill down to get the lower level breakdown of sales. The figure also shows the drill across to another OLAP summarization using a different set of hierarchies of other dimensions. Notice also the drill through to the lower levels of granularity, as stored in the source data warehouse repository. Roll up, drill down, drill across, and drill through are extremely useful features of OLAP systems supporting multidimensional analysis.

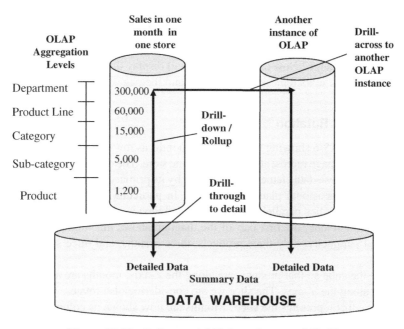

Figure 15-12   Roll-up and drill-down features of OLAP.

One more question remains. While you are rolling up or drilling down, how do the page displays change on the spreadsheets? For example, return to Figure 15-6 and look at the page display on the spreadsheet. The columns represent the various products, the rows represent the months, and the pages represent the stores. At this point, if you want to roll up to the next higher level of subcategory, how will the display in Figure 15-6 change? The columns on the display will have to change to represent subcategories instead of products. Figure 15-13 indicates this change.

Store: New York   Sub-categories

PAGES: STORE dimension   COLUMNS: PRODUCT dimension

	Outer	**Dress**	**Casual**
Jan	1,100	1,020	490
Feb	1,080	1,040	500
Mar	1,050	980	470
Apr	970	1,000	480
May	1,010	1,080	520
Jun	910	1,100	330
Jul	880	1,120	250
Aug	960	1,320	230
Sep	870	1,280	210
Oct	910	1,240	250
Nov	980	1,380	260
Dec	1,080	1,520	310

ROWS: TIME dimension

Months

Figure 15-13   Three-dimensional display with roll-up.

Let us ask just one more question before we leave this subsection. When you have rolled up to the subcategory level in the product dimension, what happens to the display if you also roll up to the next higher level of the store dimension, territory? How will the display on the spreadsheet change? Now the spreadsheet will display the sales with columns representing subcategories, rows representing months, and the pages representing territories.

Slice and Dice or Rotation

Let us revisit Figure 15-6 showing the display of months as rows, products as columns, and stores as pages. Each page represents the sales for one store. The data model corresponds to a physical cube with these data elements represented by its primary edges. The page displayed is a slice or two-dimensional plane of the cube. In particular, this display page for the New York store is the slice parallel to the product and time axes. Now look at Figure 15-14 carefully. On the left side, the first part of the diagram shows this alignment of the cube. For the sake of simplicity, only three products, three months, and three stores are chosen for illustration.

Now rotate the cube so that products are along the Z-axis, months are along the X-axis, and stores are along the Y-axis. The slice we are considering also rotates. What happens to the display page that represents the slice? Months are now shown as columns and stores as rows. The display page represents the sales of one product, namely product: hats.

You can go to the next rotation so that months are along the Z-axis, stores are along the X-axis, and products are along the Y-axis. The slice we are considering also rotates. What happens to the display page that represents the slice? Stores are now shown as columns and products as rows. The display page represents the sales of one month, namely month: January.

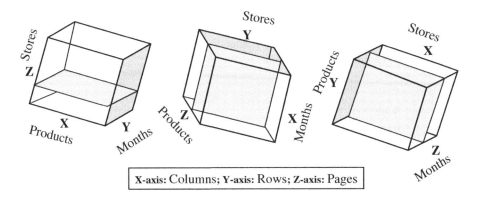

X-axis: Columns; Y-axis: Rows; Z-axis: Pages

Store: New York

	Hats	Coats	Jackets
Jan	200	550	350
Feb	210	480	390
Mar	190	480	380

Product: Hats

	Jan	Feb	Mar
New York	200	210	190
Boston	210	250	240
San Jose	130	90	70

Month: January

	New York	Boston	San Jose
Hats	200	210	130
Coats	550	500	200
Jackets	350	400	100

Figure 15-14   Slicing and dicing.

What is the great advantage of all of this for the users? Did you notice that with each rotation, the users can look at page displays representing different versions of the slices in the cube. The users can view the data from many angles, understand the numbers better, and arrive at meaningful conclusions.

Uses and Benefits

After exploring the features of OLAP in sufficient detail, you must have already deduced the enormous benefits of OLAP. We have discussed multidimensional analysis as provided in OLAP systems. The ability to perform multidimensional analysis with complex queries sometimes also entails complex calculations.

Let us summarize the benefits of OLAP systems:

- Increased productivity of business managers, executives, and analysts.
- Inherent flexibility of OLAP systems means that users may be self-sufficient in running their own analysis without IT assistance.
- Benefit for IT developers because using software specifically designed for the system development results in faster delivery of applications.
- Self-sufficiency for users, resulting in reduction in backlog.
- Faster delivery of applications following from the previous benefits.
- More efficient operations through reducing time on query executions and in network traffic.
- Ability to model real-world challenges with business metrics and dimensions.

OLAP MODELS

Have you heard of the terms ROLAP or MOLAP? How about the variation, DOLAP? A very simple explanation of the variations relates to the way data is stored for OLAP. The processing is still online analytical processing; basically, the storage methodology is different.

ROLAP. Refers to relational online analytical processing. In this case, the OLAP system is built on top of a relational database.

MOLAP. Refers to multidimensional online analytical processing. In this case, the OLAP system is implemented through a specialized multidimensional database.

HOLAP. Refers to hybrid online analytical processing. This models attempts to combine the strengths and features of ROLAP and MOLAP.

DOLAP. Refers for desktop online analytical processing. DOLAP is meant to provide portability to users of online analytical processing. In the DOLAP methodology, multidimensional datasets are created and transferred to the desktop machine, requiring only the DOLAP software to exist on that machine. DOLAP is a variation of ROLAP.

Database OLAP. Refers to a relational database management system (RDBMS) designated to support OLAP structures and to perform OLAP calculations.

Web OLAP. Refers to online analytical processing where OLAP data is accessible from a Web browser.

Overview of Variations

MOLAP and ROLAP are the fundamental models; therefore, we will discuss these in sufficient depth. In the MOLAP model, online analytical processing is best implemented by storing the data multidimensionally, that is, easily viewed in a multidimensional way. Here the data structure is fixed so that the logic to process multidimensional analysis can be based on well-defined methods of establishing data storage coordinates. Usually, multidimensional databases (MDDBs) are vendors' proprietary systems. On the other hand, the ROLAP model relies on the existing relational DBMS of the data warehouse. OLAP features are provided against the relational database.

See Figure 15-15 contrasting the two models. Notice the MOLAP model shown on the left side of the figure. The OLAP engine resides on a special server. Proprietary multidimensional databases (MDDBs) store data in the form of multidimensional hypercubes. You have to run special extraction and aggregation jobs from the relational database of the data warehouse to create these multidimensional data cubes in the MDDBs. The special server presents the data as OLAP cubes for processing by the users.

On the right side of the figure you see the ROLAP model. The OLAP engine resides on the desktop. Prefabricated multidimensional cubes are not created beforehand and stored in special databases. The relational data is presented as virtual multidimensional data cubes.

The MOLAP Model

As discussed, in the MOLAP model, data for analysis is stored in specialized multidimensional databases. Large multidimensional arrays form the storage structures. For example,

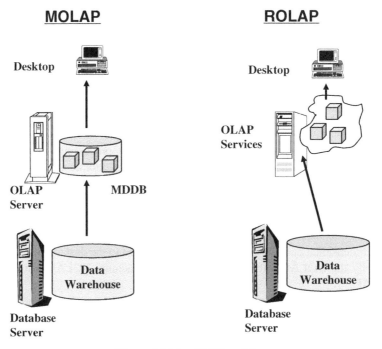

Figure 15-15   OLAP models.

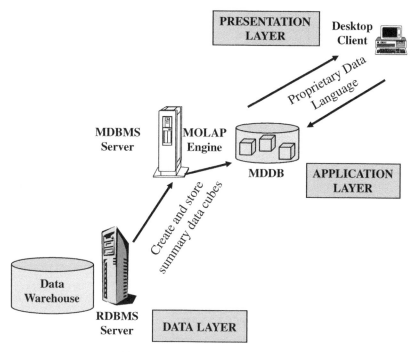

Figure 15-16 The MOLAP model.

to store sales number of 500 units for product ProductA, in month number 2009/01, in store StoreS1, under distributing channel Channe105, the sales number of 500 is stored in an array represented by the values (ProductA, 2009/01, StoreS1. Channe105).

The array values indicate the location of the cells. These cells are intersections of the values of dimension attributes. If you note how the cells are formed, you will realize that not all cells have values of metrics. If a store is closed on Sundays, then the cells representing Sundays will all be nulls.

Let us now consider the architecture for the MOLAP model. Please go over each part of Figure 15-16 carefully. Note the three layers in the multitier architecture. Precalculated and prefabricated multidimensional data cubes are stored in multidimensional databases. The MOLAP engine in the application layer pushes a multidimensional view of the data from the MDDBs to the users.

As mentioned earlier, multidimensional database management systems are proprietary software systems. These systems provide the capability to consolidate and fabricate summarized cubes during the process that loads data into the MDDBs from the main data warehouse. The users who need summarized data enjoy fast response times from the pre-consolidated data.

The ROLAP Model

In the ROLAP model, data is stored as rows and columns as in a relational data model. This model presents data to the users in the form of business dimensions. In order to hide the storage structure to the user and present data multidimensionally, a semantic layer of metadata is created. The metadata layer supports the mapping of dimensions to the relational

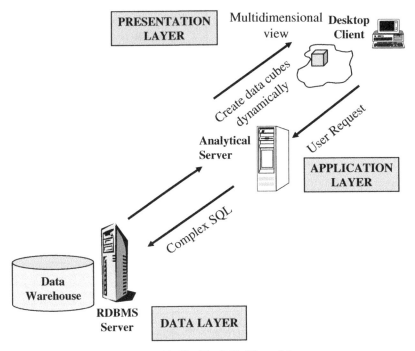

Figure 15-17 The ROLAP model.

tables. Additional metadata supports summarizations and aggregations. You may store the meta-data in relational databases.

Now see Figure 15-17. This figure shows the architecture of the ROLAP model. What you see is a three-tier architecture. The analytical server in the middle tier application layer creates multidimensional views on the fly. The multidimensional system at the presentation layer provides a multidimensional view of the data to the users. When the users issue complex queries based on this multidimensional view, the queries are transformed into complex SQL directed to the relational database. Unlike the MOLAP model, static multidimensional structures are not created and stored.

True ROLAP has three distinct characteristics:

- Supports all the basic OLAP features and functions discussed earlier
- Stores data in a relational form
- Supports some form of aggregation

Local hypercubing is a variation of ROLAP provided by vendors. This is how it works:

1 The user issues a query.
2 The results of the query get stored in a small, local, multidimensional database.
3 The user performs analysis against this local database.
4 If additional data is required to continue the analysis, the user issues another query and the analysis continues.

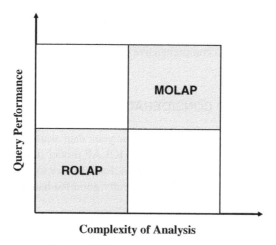

Figure 15-18   ROLAP or MOLAP?

ROLAP Versus MOLAP

Should you use the relational approach or the multidimensional approach to provide online analytical processing for your users? That depends on how important query performance is for your users. Again, the choice between ROLAP and MOLAP also depends on the complexity of the queries from your users. Figure 15-18 charts the solution options based

	Data Storage	Underlying Technologies	Functions and Features
ROLAP	Data stored as relational tables in the warehouse. Detailed and light summary data available. Very large data volumes. All data access from the warehouse storage.	Use of complex SQL to fetch data from warehouse. ROLAP engine in analytical server creates data cubes on the fly. Multidimensional views by presentation layer.	Known environment and availability of many tools. Limitations on complex analysis functions. Drill-through to lowest level easier. Drill-across not always easy.
MOLAP	Data stored as relational tables in the warehouse. Various summary data kept in proprietary databases (MDDBs) Moderate data volumes. Summary data access from MDDB, detailed data access from warehouse.	Creation of pre-fabricated data cubes by MOLAP engine. Propriety technology to store multidimensional views in arrays, not tables. High speed matrix data retrieval. Sparse matrix technology to manage data sparsity in summaries.	Faster access. Large library of functions for complex calculations. Easy analysis irrespective of the number of dimensions. Extensive drill-down and slice-and-dice capabilities.

Figure 15-19   ROLAP versus MOLAP.

on the considerations of query performance and complexity of queries. MOLAP is the choice for faster response and more intensive queries. These are just two broad considerations. Figure 15-19 provides a comprehensive comparison between the two.

OLAP IMPLEMENTATION CONSIDERATIONS

Before considering implementation of OLAP in your data warehouse, you have to take into account two key issues with regard to the MOLAP model running under MDDBMS. The first issue relates to the lack of standardization. Each vendor tool has its own client interface. Another issue is scalability. OLAP is generally good for handling summary data, but not good for volumes of detailed data.

On the other hand, highly normalized data in the data warehouse can give rise to processing overhead when you are performing complex analysis. You may reduce this by using a STAR schema multidimensional design. In fact, for some ROLAP tools, the multidimensional representation of data in a STAR schema arrangement is a prerequisite.

Consider a few choices of architecture. Look at Figure 15-20 showing four architectural options.

You have now studied the various implementation options for providing OLAP functionality in your data warehouse. These are important choices. Remember, without OLAP, your users have very limited means for analyzing data. Let us now examine some specific design considerations.

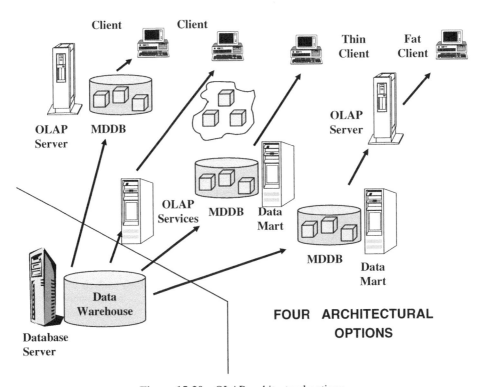

Figure 15-20   OLAP architectural options.

Data Design and Preparation

The data warehouse feeds data to the OLAP system. In the MOLAP model, separate proprietary multidimensional databases store the data fed from the data warehouse in the form of multidimensional cubes. On the other hand, in the ROLAP model, although no static intermediary data repository exists, data is still pushed into the OLAP system with cubes created dynamically on the fly. Thus, the sequence of the flow of data is from the operational source systems to the data warehouse and from there to the OLAP system.

Sometimes, you may have the desire to short-circuit the flow of data. You may wonder why you should not build the OLAP system on top of the operational source systems themselves. Why not extract data into the OLAP system directly? Why bother moving data into the data warehouse and then into the OLAP system? Here are a few reasons why this approach is flawed:

- An OLAP system needs transformed and integrated data. The system assumes that the data has been consolidated and cleansed somewhere before it arrives. The disparity among operational systems does not support data integration directly.
- The operational systems keep historical data only to a limited extent. An OLAP system needs extensive historical data. Historical data from the operational systems must be combined with archived historical data before it reaches the OLAP system.
- An OLAP system requires data in multidimensional representations. This calls for summarization in many different ways. Trying to extract and summarize data from the various operational systems at the same time is untenable. Data must be consolidated before it can be summarized at various levels and in different combinations.
- Assume there are a few OLAP systems in your environment. That is, one supports the marketing department, another supports the inventory control department, yet another supports the finance department, and so on. To accomplish this, you have to build a separate interface with the operational systems for data extraction into each OLAP system. Can you imagine how difficult this would be?

In order to help prepare the data for the OLAP system, let us first examine some significant characteristics of data in this system. Please review the following list:

- An OLAP system stores and uses much less data compared to a data warehouse.
- Data in the OLAP system is summarized. You will rarely find data at the lowest level of detail as in the data warehouse.
- OLAP data is more flexible for processing and analysis partly because there is much less data to work with.
- Every instance of the OLAP system in your environment is customized for the purpose that instance of the system serves.

In order words, OLAP data tends to be more departmentalized, whereas data in the data warehouse serves corporate-wide needs.

An overriding principle is that OLAP data is generally customized. When you build the OLAP system with system instances servicing different user groups, you need to keep this in mind. For example, one instance or specific set of summarizations would be meant for one group of users, say, the marketing department. Let us quickly go through the techniques for preparing OLAP data for a specific group of users or a particular department, for example, marketing.

Define Subset   Select the subset of detailed data the marketing department is interested in.

Summarize   Summarize and prepare aggregate data structures in the way the marketing department needs for summarizing. For example, summarize products along product categories as defined by marketing. Sometimes, marketing and accounting departments may categorize products in different ways.

Denormalize   Combine relational tables in exactly the same way the marketing department needs denormalized data. If marketing needs tables A and B joined, but finance needs tables B and C joined, go with the join for tables A and B for the marketing OLAP subset.

Calculate and Derive   If some calculations and derivations of the metrics are department-specific in your company, use the ones for marketing.

Index   Choose those attributes that are appropriate for marketing to build indexes.

What about data modeling for the OLAP data structure? The OLAP structure contains several levels of summarization and a few kinds of detailed data. How do you model these levels of summarization?

Please see Figure 15-21 indicating the types and levels of data in OLAP systems. These types and levels must be taken into consideration while performing data modeling for the OLAP systems. Pay attention to the different types of data in an OLAP system. When you model the data structures for your OLAP system, you need to provide for these types of data.

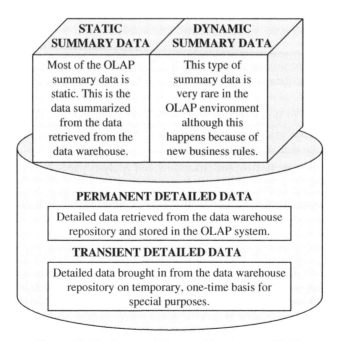

Figure 15-21   Data modeling considerations for OLAP.

Administration and Performance

Let us now turn our attention to two important though not directly connected issues.

Administration One of these issues is the matter of administration and management of the OLAP environment. The OLAP system is part of the overall data warehouse environment and, therefore, administration of the OLAP system is part of the data warehouse administration. Nevertheless, we must recognize some key considerations for administering and managing the OLAP system. Let us briefly indicate a few of these considerations.

- Expectations on what data will be accessed and how
- Selection of the right business dimensions
- Selection of the right filters for loading the data from the data warehouse
- Methods and techniques for moving data into the OLAP system (MOLAP model)
- Choosing the aggregation, summarization, and precalculation
- Developing application programs using the proprietary software of the OLAP vendor
- Size of the multidimensional database
- Handling of the sparse-matrix feature of multidimensional structures
- Drill down to the lowest level of detail
- Drill through to the data warehouse or to the source systems
- Drill across among OLAP system instances
- Access and security privileges
- Backup and restore facilities

Performance First you need to recognize that the presence of an OLAP system in your data warehouse environment shifts the workload. Some of the queries that usually must run against the data warehouse will now be redistributed to the OLAP system. The types of queries that need OLAP are complex and filled with involved calculations. Long and complicated analysis sessions consist of such complex queries. Therefore, when such queries get directed to the OLAP system, the workload on the main data warehouse becomes substantially reduced.

A corollary of shifting the complex queries to the OLAP system is the improvement in the overall query performance. The OLAP system is designed for complex queries. When such queries run in the OLAP system, they run faster. As the size of the data warehouse grows, the size of the OLAP system still remains manageable and comparably small.

Multidimensional databases provide a reasonably predictable, fast, and consistent response to every complex query. This is mainly because OLAP systems preaggregate and precalculate many, if not, all possible hypercubes and store these. The queries run against the most appropriate hypercubes. For instance, assume that there are only three dimensions. The OLAP system will calculate and store summaries as follows:

- A three-dimensional low-level array to store base data
- A two-dimensional array of data for dimension-1 and dimension-2
- A 2-dimensional array of data for dimension-2 and dimension-3
- A high-level summary array by dimension-1

- A high-level summary array by dimension-2
- A high-level summary array by dimension-3

All of these precalculations and preaggregations result in faster response to queries at any level of summarization. But this speed and performance do not come without any cost. You pay the price to some extent in the load performance. OLAP systems are not refreshed daily for the simple reason that load times for precalculating and loading all the possible hypercubes are exhorbitant. Enterprises use longer intervals between refreshes of their OLAP systems. Most OLAP systems are refreshed once a month.

OLAP Platforms

Where does the OLAP system physically reside? Should it be on the same platform as the main data warehouse? Should it be planned to be on a separate platform from the beginning? What about growth of the data warehouse and the OLAP system? How do the growth patterns affect the decision? These are some of the questions you need to answer as you provide OLAP capability to your users.

Usually, the data warehouse and the OLAP system start out on the same platform. When both are small, it is cost-justifiable to keep both on the same platform. Within a year, it is usual to find rapid growth in the main data warehouse. The trend normally continues. As this growth happens, you may want to think of moving the OLAP system to another platform to ease the congestion. But how exactly would you know whether to separate the platforms and when to do so? Here are some guidelines:

- When the size and usage of the main data warehouse escalate and reach the point where the warehouse requires all the resources of the common platform, start acting on the separation.
- If too many departments need the OLAP system, then the OLAP requires additional platforms to run.
- Users expect the OLAP system to be stable and perform well. The data refreshes to the OLAP system are much less frequent. Although this is true for the OLAP system, daily application of incremental loads and full refreshes of certain tables are needed for the main data warehouse. If these daily transactions applicable to the data warehouse begin to disrupt the stability and performance of the OLAP system, then move the OLAP system to another platform.
- Obviously, in decentralized enterprises with OLAP users spread out geographically, one or more separate platforms for the OLAP system become necessary.
- If users of one instance of the OLAP system want to stay away from the users of another, then separation of platforms needs to be looked into.
- If the chosen OLAP tools need a configuration different from the platform of the main data warehouse, then the OLAP system requires a separate platform, configured correctly.

OLAP Tools and Products

The OLAP market is becoming sophisticated. Many OLAP products have appeared and most of the recent products are quite successful. Quality and flexibility of the products have improved remarkably.

Before we provide a checklist to be used for evaluation of OLAP products, let us list a few broad guidelines:

- Let your applications and the users drive the selection of the OLAP products. Do not be carried away by flashy technology.
- Remember, your OLAP system will grow both in size and in the number of active users. Determine the scalability of the products before you choose.
- Consider how easy it is to administer the OLAP product.
- Performance and flexibility are key ingredients in the success of your OLAP system.
- As technology advances, the differences in the merits between ROLAP and MOLAP appear to be somewhat blurred. Do not worry too much about these two methods. Concentrate on the matching of the vendor product with your users' analytical requirements. Flashy technology does not always deliver.

Now let us get to the selection criteria for choosing OLAP tools and products. While you evaluate the products, use the following checklist and rate each product against each item on the checklist:

- Multidimensional representation of data
- Aggregation, summarization, precalculation, and derivations
- Formulas and complex calculations in an extensive library
- Cross-dimensional calculations
- Time intelligence such as year-to-date, current and past fiscal periods, moving averages, and moving totals
- Pivoting, cross-tabs, drill-down, and roll-up along single or multiple dimensions
- Interface of OLAP with applications and software such as spreadsheets, proprietary client tools, third-party tools, and 4GL environments.

Implementation Steps

At this point, perhaps your project team has been given the mandate to build and implement an OLAP system. You know the features and functions. You know the significance. You are also aware of the important considerations. How do you go about implementing OLAP? Let us summarize the key steps. These are the steps or activities at a very high level. Each step consists of several tasks to accomplish the objectives of that step. You will have to come up with the tasks based on the requirements of your environment. Here are the major steps:

- Dimensional modeling
- Design and building of the MDDB
- Selection of the data to be moved into the OLAP system
- Data acquisition or extraction for the OLAP system
- Data loading into the OLAP server
- Computation of data aggregation and derived data
- Implementation of application on the desktop
- Provision of user training

COMPANIES AND OLAP IMPLEMENTATION NOTES

Time Warner: Supports users in three continents with a strategic market planning and analysis system.

The World Bank: Performs complex statistical analyses on a mass of worldwide econometric data.

Hewlett-Packard: Provides speedy operational reports using a desktop OLAP over the corporate intranet to numerous users.

Sun Microsystems: Supports business planning with a networked OLAP tool, entirely Web-based.

Dun & Bradstreet: Provides a vital link between customers' corporate data and underlying detailed information.

British Airways: Reduces processing costs through better analysis using OLAP databases tied to new general ledger.

Barclays Bank: Manages risk on loans for maximum profit.

British Petroleum: Performs worldwide planning with its second generation OLAP application.

IBM Finance: Provides finance portal for cost-effective analysis, reporting, and performance management.

Subaru of America: Improves customer service through more effective allocation of inventory to franchised dealers.

GlaxoSmithKline: Performs international financial reporting through OLAP databases.

Deluxe Corp.: World's No. 1 check printer, performs more accurate forecasting through planning/analysis applications.

Source: Olapreport.com and vendor Web sites (paraphrased)

Figure 15-22   Typical OLAP implementations.

Examples of Typical Implementations

As OLAP is so very important for analysis to many organizations, we would like to list some examples of OLAP implementations. See Figure 15-22.

CHAPTER SUMMARY

- OLAP is critical because its multidimensional analysis, fast access, and powerful calculations exceed that of other analysis methods.
- OLAP is defined on the basis of Codd's initial twelve guidelines.
- OLAP characteristics include multidimensional view of the data, interactive and complex analysis facility, ability to perform intricate calculations, and fast response time.
- Dimensional analysis is not confined to three dimensions that can be represented by a physical cube. Hypercubes provide a method for representing views with more dimensions.
- ROLAP and MOLAP are the two major OLAP models. The difference between them lies in the way the basic data is stored. Ascertain which model is more suitable for your environment.
- OLAP tools have matured. Some RDBMSs include support for OLAP.

REVIEW QUESTIONS

1. Briefly explain multidimensional analysis.

2. Name any four key capabilities of an OLAP system.

3. State any five of Dr. Codd's guidelines for an OLAP system, giving a brief description for each.

4. What are hypercubes? How do they apply in an OLAP system?

5. What is meant by slice-and-dice? Give an example.

6. What are the essential differences between the MOLAP and ROLAP models? Also list a few similarities.

7. What are multidimensional databases? How do these store data?

8. Describe any one of the four OLAP architectural options.

9. Discuss two reasons why feeding data into the OLAP system directly from the source operational systems is not recommended.

10. Name any four factors for consideration in OLAP administration.

EXERCISES

1. Indicate if true or false:
   A. OLAP facilitates interactive queries and complex uses.
   B. A hypercube can be represented by the physical cube.
   C. Slice-and-dice is the same as the rotation of the columns and rows in presentation of data.
   D. DOLAP stands for departmental OLAP.
   E. ROLAP systems store data in multidimensional, proprietary databases.
   F. The essential difference between ROLAP and MOLAP is in the way data is stored.
   G. OLAP systems need transformed and integrated data.
   H. Data in an OLAP system is rarely summarized.
   I. Multidimensional domain structure (MDS) can represent only up to six dimensions.
   J. OLAP systems do not handle moving averages.

2. As a senior analyst on the project team of a publishing company exploring the options for a data warehouse, make a case for OLAP. Describe the merits of OLAP and how it will be essential in your environment.

3. Pick any six of Dr. Codd's initial guidelines for OLAP. Give your reasons why the selected six are important for OLAP.

4. You are asked to form a small team to evaluate the MOLAP and ROLAP models and make your recommendations. This is part of the data warehouse project for a large

manufacturer of heavy chemicals. Describe the criteria your team will use to make the evaluation and selection.

5. Your company is the largest producer of chicken products, selling to supermarkets, fast-food chains, and restaurants, and also exporting to many countries. The analysts from many offices worldwide expect to use the OLAP system when implemented. Discuss how the project team must select the platform for implementing OLAP for the company. Explain your assumptions.

CHAPTER 16

DATA WAREHOUSING AND THE WEB

CHAPTER OBJECTIVES

- Understand what Web-enabling the data warehouse means and examine the reasons for doing so
- Appreciate the implications of the convergence of Web technologies and those of the data warehouse
- Probe into all the facets of Web-based information delivery
- Study how OLAP and the Web connect and learn the different approaches to connecting them
- Examine the steps for building a Web-enabled data warehouse

What is the most dominant phenomenon in computing and communication that started in the 1990s? Undoubtedly, it is the Internet with the World Wide Web. The impact of the Web on our lives and businesses can hardly be matched by any other developments over the past years.

In the 1970s, we experienced a major breakthrough when the personal computer was ushered in with its graphical interfaces, pointing devices, and icons. Today's breakthrough is the Web, which is built on the earlier revolution. Making the personal computer useful and effective was our goal in the 1970s and 1980s. Making the Web useful and effective is our goal in the 1990s and onwards. The growth of the Internet and the use of the Web have overshadowed the earlier revolution. At the beginning of the year 2000, about 50 million households worldwide were estimated to be using the Internet. By the end of 2005, this number has grown 10-fold. More than 500 million households worldwide are browsing the Web.

Data Warehousing Fundamentals for IT Professionals, Second Edition. By Paulraj Ponniah
Copyright © 2010 John Wiley & Sons, Inc.

The Web changes everything, as they say. Data warehousing is no exception. In the 1980s, data warehousing was still being defined and growing. During the 1990s, it was maturing. Now, after the Web revolution of the 1990s, data warehousing has assumed a prominent place in the Web movement. Why?

What is the one major benefit of the Web revolution? Dramatically reduced communication costs. The Web has sharply diminished the cost of delivering information. What is the relevance of that? What is one major purpose of the data warehouse? It is the delivery of business intelligence. So they match perfectly. The data warehouse is for delivering strategic information; the Internet makes it cost effective to do so. We have arrived at the concept of a Web-enabled data warehouse or a "data Webhouse." The Web forces us to rethink data warehouse design and deployment.

In Chapter 3, we briefly considered the Web-enabled data warehouse. Specifically, we discussed two aspects of this topic. First, we considered how to use the Web as one of the information delivery channels. This is taking the warehouse to the Web, opening up the data warehouse to more than the traditional set of users. This chapter primarily focuses on this aspect of the relationship between the Web and the data warehouse.

The other aspect, briefly discussed in Chapter 3, deals with bringing the Web to the warehouse. This aspect relates to your company's e-commerce, where the clickstream data of your company's Web site is brought into the data Webhouse for analysis. In this chapter, we will briefly mention some points about this aspect of the Web–warehouse connection. Many articles by several authors and practitioners and a recent excellent book coauthored by Dr. Ralph Kimball do adequate justice to this aspect of the data Webhouse. The References section at the end of this book provides more information.

WEB-ENABLED DATA WAREHOUSE

A Web-enabled data warehouse uses the Web for information delivery and collaboration among users. In a maturing data warehousing environment, more and more data warehouses have been connected to the Web. Essentially, this means an increase in the access to information in the data warehouse. Increase in information access, in turn, means increase in the knowledge level of the enterprise. It is true that even before connecting to the Web, you could give access for information to more of your users, but with much difficulty and a proportionate increase in communication costs. The Web has changed all that. It is now a lot easier to add more users. The communications infrastructure is already there. Almost all of your users have Web browsers. No additional client software is required. You can leverage the Web that already exists. The exponential growth of the Web, with its networks, servers, users, and pages, has brought about the adoption of the Internet, intranets, and extranets as information transmission media. The Web-enabled data warehouse takes center stage in the Web revolution. Let us see why.

Why the Web?

It appears to be quite natural to connect the data warehouse to the Web. Why do we say this? For a moment, think of how your users view the Web. First, they view the Web as a tremendous source of information. They find the data content useful and interesting. Your internal users, customers, and business partners already use the Web frequently. They know how to get connected. The Web is everywhere. The sun never sets on the Web. The only client software needed is the Web browser, and almost everyone, young and old, has learned how to launch and use a browser. Almost all software vendors have already made their products Web-ready.

Now consider your data warehouse in relation to the Web. Your users need the data warehouse for information. Your business partners can use some of the specific information from the data warehouse. What do all of these have in common? Familiarity with the Web and ability to access it easily. These are strong reasons for a Web-enabled data warehouse.

How do you exploit the Web technology for your data warehouse? How do you connect the warehouse to the Web? Let us quickly review three information delivery mechanisms that companies have adopted based on Web technology. In each case, users access information with Web browsers.

Internet The first medium is, of course, the Internet, which provides low-cost transmission of information. You may exchange information with anyone within or outside the company. Because the information is transmitted over public networks, security concerns must be addressed.

Intranet Since the time the term *intranet* was coined in 1995, this concept of a private network has gripped the corporate world. An intranet is a private computer network based on the data communications standards of the public Internet. The applications posting information over the intranet all reside within the firewall and, therefore, are more secure. You can have all the benefits of the popular Web technology. In addition, you can manage security better on the intranet.

Extranet The Internet and the intranet have been followed by the extranet. An extranet is not completely open like the Internet, nor is it restricted just for internal use only like an intranet. An extranet is an intranet that is open to selective access by outside parties. From your intranet, in addition to looking inward and downward, you can look outward and upward to your customers, suppliers, and business partners.

Figure 16-1 illustrates how information from the data warehouse may be delivered over these information delivery mechanisms. Note how your data warehouse may be deployed over the Web. If you choose to restrict your data warehouse to internal users, then you adopt the intranet. If it has to be opened up to outside parties with proper authorization, you go with the extranet. In both cases, the information delivery technology and the transmission protocols are the same.

The intranet and the extranet come with several advantages. Here are a few:

- With a universal browser, your users will have a single point of entry for information.
- Minimal training is required to access information. Users already know how to use a browser.
- Universal browsers will run on any systems.
- Web technology opens up multiple information formats to the users. They can receive text, images, charts, even video and audio.
- It is easy to keep the intranet/extranet updated so that there will be one source of information.
- Opening up your data warehouse to your business partners over the extranet fosters and strengthens these partnerships.
- Deployment and maintenance costs are low for Web-enabling your data warehouse. Primarily, the network costs are less. Infrastructure costs are also low.

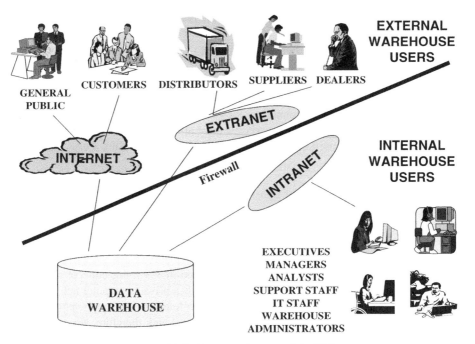

Figure 16-1 Data warehouse and the Web.

Convergence of Technologies

There is no getting away from the fact that Web technology and data warehousing have converged, and the bond is only getting stronger. If you do not Web-enable your data warehouse, you will be left behind. For the past two decades, vendors have been racing one another to release Web-enabled versions of their products. The Web offerings of the products are exceeding the client/server offerings for the first time since Web offerings began to appear. Indirectly, these versions are forcing the convergence of the Web and the data warehouse even further.

Remember that the Web is more significant than the data warehouse. The Web and its features will lead and the data warehouse has to follow. The Web has already pegged the expectations of the users at a high level. Users will therefore expect the data warehouse to perform at that high level. Consider some of the expectations promoted by the Web that are now expected to be adopted by data warehouses:

- Fast response, although some Web pages may be comparatively slower
- Extremely easy and intuitive to use
- Up 24 hours a day, 7 days a week
- More up-to-date content
- Graphical, dynamic, and flexible user interfaces
- Almost personalized display
- Expectation to connect to anywhere and drill across.

Over the last few years, the number of Web-enabled data warehouses has increased substantially. How have these Web-enabled data warehouses fared so far? To understand the effect of the convergence of the two technologies, we must consider the three orders of effects of decreasing costs as documented by Thomas W. Malone and John F. Rockart in the early 1990s:

First-Order Effect: Simple substitution of the new technology for the old.

Second-Order Effect: Increased demand for the functions provided by the new technology.

Third-Order Effect: The rise of new technology-intensive structures.

What has the convergence of the Web technology and data warehousing brought about so far? Web warehousing appears to have passed through the first two stages. Companies that have Web-enabled data warehouses have reduced costs by the substitution of the new methods of information delivery. Also, the demand for information has increased following the first stage. For most companies with Web-enabled data warehouses, progress stops when they reach the end of the second stage.

Adapting the Data Warehouse for the Web

Much is expected of a Web-enabled data warehouse. That means you have to reinvent your data warehouse. You have to carry out a number of tasks to adapt your data warehouse for the Web. Let us consider the specific provisions for Web-enabling your data warehouse.

First, let us get back to the discussion of the three stages following the introduction of a new technology. Apart from reducing costs from the substitution, demand for business intelligence has increased. Many companies seem to be stuck at the end of the second stage. Only a few companies have moved on to the next stage and have realized third-order results. What are these results? Some include extranet and consumer data marts, management by exception, and automated supply and value chains. When you adapt your data warehouse for the Web, make sure that you do not stay put at the second stage. Make plans to exploit the potential of the Web and move on to the third stage where the real benefits are found.

Study the following list of requisites for adapting the data warehouse to the Web.

Information "Push" Technique. The data warehouse was designed and implemented using the "pull" technique. The information delivery system pulls information from the data warehouse based on requests, and then provides it to the users. The Web offers another technique. The Web can "push" information to users without their asking for it every time. Your data warehouse must be able to adopt the "push" technique.

Ease of Usage. With the availability of clickstream data, you can very quickly check the behavior of the user at the site. Among other things, clickstream data reveals how easy or difficult it is for the users to browse the pages. Ease of use appears at the top of the list of requirements.

Speedy Response. Some data warehouses allow jobs to run long to produce the desired results. In the Web model, speed is expected and cannot be negotiated or compromised.

No Downtime. The Web model is designed so that the system is available all the time. Similarly, the Web-enabled data warehouse has no downtime.

Multimedia Output. Web pages have multiple data types: textual, numeric, graphics, sound, video, animation, audio, and maps. These types are expected to show as outputs in the information delivery system of the Web-enabled data warehouse.

Market of One. Web information delivery is tending to become highly personalized, with dynamically created XML pages replacing static HTML coding. Web-enabled data warehouses will have to follow suit.

Scalability. More access, more users, and more data—these are the results of Web-enabling the data warehouse. Therefore, scalability becomes a primary concern.

The Web as a Data Source

When you talk about Web-enabling the data warehouse, the first and perhaps the only thought that comes to mind is the use of Web technology as an information delivery mechanism. Ironically, it rarely crosses your mind that Web content is a valuable and potent data source for your data warehouse. You may hesitate before extracting data from the Web for your Web-enabled data warehouse.

Information content on the Web is so disparate and fragmented. You need to build a special search and extract system to sift through the mounds of information and pick up what is relevant for your data warehouse. Assume that your project team is able to build such an extraction system, then selection and extraction consists of a few distinct steps. Before extraction, you must verify the accuracy of the source data. Just because data was found on the Web, you cannot automatically assume it is accurate. You can get clues to accuracy from the types of sources. Figure 16-2 shows an arrangement of components for data selection and extraction from the Web.

How can you use Web content to enrich your data warehouse? Here are a few important uses:

- Add more descriptive attributes to the business dimensions.
- Include nominal or ordinal data about a dimension so that more options are available for pivoting and cross-tabulations.

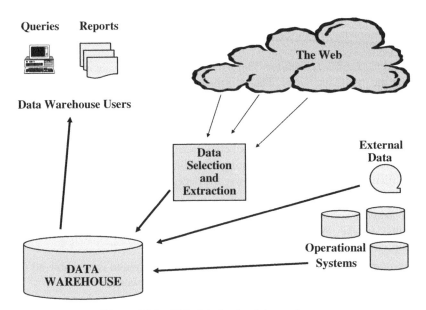

Figure 16-2 Web data for the data warehouse.

- Add linkage data to a dimension so that correlation analysis with other dimensions can be performed.
- Create a new dimension table.
- Create a new fact table.

What we have discussed here is much beyond the usual use of the Web as an information delivery medium. Data selection and data extraction from the Web is a radically new paradigm. If your project team is willing to try it in your data warehouse environment, the results will be worthwhile.

Clickstream Analysis

As you Web-enable your data warehouse, you find that enormous clickstream data of the visitors to your organization's Web site becomes available. This is valuable data. You can set up mechanisms to extract, transform, and load the clickstream data to the Webhouse repository. You may build this repository based on dimensional schemas and then deploy information delivery systems to the repository.

Considerations for Clickstream Data Retrieval   A few considerations regarding extracting and preparing clickstream data:

- Server logs usually contain multiple entries from a single page request.
- Proxy servers pose problems of confusing the identity of a session and why it ended.
- Basic clickstream data must be extracted from multiple servers.
- Retrieval of individual customer data is difficult as it gets buried in other data relating to pages served, browser types, hosts, etc.
- Identifying the separate sessions in a data stream is very involved requiring cookies or other session identification numbers.
- Clickstream data preparation is very time-consuming.

Usefulness of Clickstream Data   Clickstream data may be the most important source for identifying and retaining e-commerce customers. The following is a list of useful information derivable from clickstream data:

- Effectiveness of sales promotions
- Affinities between products that are likely to be bought together
- Customer demographics
- General buying patterns of customers
- Referring partner links
- Site statistics
- Site navigations resulting in sales
- Site navigations not producing sales
- Ability to differentiate between customer types

WEB-BASED INFORMATION DELIVERY

We have seen how the convergence of Web technology and data warehousing is inevitable. The two technologies deal with providing information. Web technology is able to deliver information more easily, around the clock. It is no wonder that companies want to Web-enable their data warehouses.

Other advantages and possibilities also emerge when you connect the warehouse to the Web. One such benefit is the ability to come up with newer ways of making the data warehouse more effective through extranet data marts and the like. We also looked at the possibility of using the Web as a data source for your warehouse.

Nevertheless, better information delivery remains the most compelling reason for adapting the data warehouse for the Web. The Web brings a new outlook on information delivery and revolutionizes the process. Let us, therefore, spend some time on Web-based information delivery. How does the Web escalate the usage of the data warehouse? What are the benefits and what are the challenges? How do you deal with the dramatic change in information delivery brought about by the Web?

Expanded Usage

No matter how you look at it, the advantages of connecting the data warehouse to the Web appear to be amazing. Users can use the browser to perform their queries easily and at any time during the day. There are no headaches associated with synchronizing distributed data warehouses present in client/server environments. Use of the data warehouse expands beyond internal users. Interested parties from outside can now be granted access to use the warehouse content. As the usage expands, scalability no longer poses a serious problem. What about the cost of training the users? Of course, training costs are minimal because of the use of the Web browser. Everything looks good and usage expands.

Let us understand what happens to the growth. Initially, your Web-enabled data warehouse may receive only 500 to 5000 hits a day, but depending on your audience, this number can skyrocket within a short time. What does more users imply? Simply, more information delivery. Also, more information delivery in a 24/7 environment. The Web never shuts down.

Examine this phenomenon of extraordinary growth. Universal access generates a whole set of challenges that must be faced. Primarily, this imposes additional strain on your Web-enabled data warehouse. Although scalability to accommodate more users and rapid expansion in the usage is no longer as strenuous as in a client/server environment, it is still a basic challenge.

Let us understand the pattern of this growth in usage. Two distinct factors foster the growth: first, a totally open window that never shuts, next, an easy and intuitive access mechanism via the ubiquitous Web browser. As a result, you have two challenges to contend with. The first is the increase in the user population. The second is the rapid acceleration of the growth. If you have opened your data warehouse to customers and business partners through an extranet, you will notice the steep expansion curve even more.

Let us call this extraordinary growth "supergrowth" and inspect the phenomenon. Refer to Figure 16-3, which charts this phenomenon. The striking feature of supergrowth manifests itself in your inability to scale up in time to contain the growth. The user base will grow faster than your ability to scale up your Web-enabled data warehouse to meet the expanding usage requirements. You cannot simply add processors, disk drives,

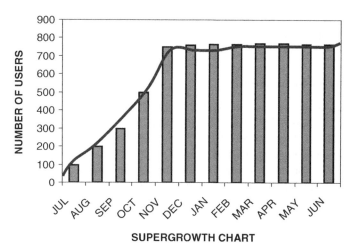

Figure 16-3   Supergrowth of a Web-enabled data warehouse.

or memory fast enough to meet the escalating demand, so how do you deal with supergrowth?

Let us propose an initial approach. Is it possible to anticipate the problem and avoid it altogether in the first place? In other words, can you control the growth and thereby come to grips with the problem. When you Web-enable your data warehouse, the first instinct is to become overenthusiastic and open the warehouse instantly to the public. This is like opening the floodgates without warning. But in order to control the growth, you have to contain your zeal and open up the warehouse in well-defined stages. This becomes absolutely necessary if the usage pattern is not very clear. Do not open the warehouse to the public at all, initially. First, let a few of your internal users have access. Then add some more users to the group. Include more and more in staged increments. In this manner, you can constantly monitor the growth pattern in usage. Adopt the same cautionary approach when it comes to opening up the data warehouse to the public in the second wave.

What if your circumstances warrant opening up the Web-enabled data warehouse in one swoop to all users, internal and external? What if the staged approach described above is not feasible in your case? What if you cannot avoid supergrowth? The key to answering these questions lies in a specific characteristic of the growth curve. Notice that supergrowth occurs only in the very initial stages. After the initial stages, the usage curve seems to level off, or at least the rate of increase becomes manageable. With this fact in mind, let us see how we can deal with supergrowth.

The secret lies in finding the point up to which the usage will grow and then level off. Go back to Figure 16-3 showing the supergrowth curve. The graph shows that the hypergrowth stage lasts until early December and is expected to level off at 750 users. Even if you start with 100 users, you are likely to hit the level of 750 users very soon. So, even if the intention is to start with just 100 users, let your initial offering of the Web-enabled data warehouse have enough resources to accommodate 750 users. But how do you come up with the number of 750 users and that the point of leveling off is early December? There are no industry-standard charts to predict the supergrowth pattern. The supergrowth pattern of your data warehouse depends entirely on the circumstances and conditions of your environment. You will have to define the graph for your environment by using the best techniques for estimation.

New Information Strategies

When the data warehouse and the Web technology converge, what are the expectations from the data warehouse? How should the user interface to the data warehouse be modified and enhanced on the Web model? Before your data warehouse was Web-enabled, user expectations were governed by a set of defined standards. Now, after Web-enabling, when users approach the warehouse using the same browser as they do for other Internet data, the yardstick is different. Now the users expect the same type of information interface as they are used to in an Internet session. Understanding these expectations will assist you in developing new information delivery strategies for your Web-enabled warehouse.

Information Delivery Guidelines Let us summarize the guidelines for formulating new information delivery strategies. Study the following list.

Performance. Industry experts agree on a less than 10-second response time for a page to deliver the first screen of useful contents. The page may keep loading for a longer time, provided useful contents can be seen within 10 seconds. Design for the modem with the lowest speed. Display navigation buttons immediately. Reveal contents in a planned order: the useful ones immediately, followed by the ones at the next levels of usefulness. Reconsider slow and redundant graphics. Use page caching techniques. Ensure that the physical database design enables fast response times.

User Options. Users are conditioned to expect to see a number of standard options when they arrive at a Web page. These include navigation selections. Navigation buttons for a Web-enabled data warehouse include drill-down options, home page, major subjects, website map, searches, and website sponsor details. Also, include warehouse-specific selections, help menus, and choices to communicate with the sponsoring company. More specifically, for a data warehouse, the user options must include navigation to a library of reports, selections to browse the business dimensions and the attributes within each dimension, and interface to business metadata.

User Experience. Every Web designer's fondest goal is to make each page a pleasing experience for the user. Users are eager to visit and stay on a page that is nicely formatted. If there are too many distractions and problems, users tend to shun the pages. Be judicious in the use of fonts, colors, blinking graphics, bold texts, underlines, audio clips, and video segments.

Processes. It is important that business processes be made to work smoothly and seamlessly on the Web. For the Web-enabled data warehouse, this requirement translates into streamlining Web interaction during an analysis session. Let the user be able to move from one step to the next, easily and gracefully.

User Support. In a lengthy process, a user must have the reassurance that nothing will be lost in the middle of the process. The user must know where he or she is in the process so that proceeding further will not be interrupted. During access to the Web-enabled data warehouse, let the user know the intermediary status information. For example, in running reports, provide the status of the reports to the users.

Resolving Problems. The user must be able to backtrack from a mistake, make corrections, and then proceed. The user must also be able to report problems.

Information in Context. Opening the data warehouse by means of the Web provides a new slant on how information may be viewed in broader contexts. Hitherto, queries could find answers to straight questions of "how much" and "how often." Answers to such questions were found within the narrow limits of the company's framework. With the opening of business intelligence through the Web, the circle widens to include the entire supply chain and some competitive concerns. Information may now be obtained within the larger strategic framework.

Personalized Information. It is almost impossible to provide predefined queries that will satisfy the requirements of everyone in the value chain. Therefore, strive to provide ad hoc capabilities for asking any type of question related to any type of data in the warehouse.

Self-Service Access. As the Web opens up the data warehouse to more users, both inside and outside the enterprise, tools must provide autonomous access to information. Users must be able to navigate and drill out to information sources. It must be practically an environment with self-service access where users may serve themselves.

HTML Files   In the Web-enabled data warehouse environment, the standard HTML document or file, also known as the Web page, is the principal means for communication. The Web page is the resource for displaying information on the Internet or an internal network. The information interface tool generates HTML files from the ad hoc user queries or from stored procedures in the database.

You can generate an HTML file one time or on a regular basis using triggers. As you know, a trigger is a special kind of stored procedure that is automatically executed when a specified data manipulation statement on a specific table is encountered. For example, a trigger program can automatically generate an exception report in the form of an HTML file when some predefined threshold values are exceeded. The users can then view the latest occurrence by calling up the corresponding Web page.

Database management systems offer publish-and-subscribe functions in their database engine. A subscription enables HTML pages to be created from scratch or refreshed whenever a trigger fires in the specified data source. A published HTML page can include filtered data directly from one or more tables, the result of a query translated internally into SQL statements, or an output from a stored procedure. However, the subscription facility is limited to the data within the particular database.

Reporting as a Strategic Tool   Next let us turn to reporting as a method of Web-based information delivery. On the Web, you are able to publish or distribute files via e-mail. These features open up enormous possibilities for reporting as a strategic tool. Now you can integrate business partners into the supply chain. Managers and executives may direct prescribed reports to be sent automatically to specific customers and suppliers. They may set thresholds on inventory levels and have reports sent only when the levels are outside the limits.

Report management can cover both types of reports. Routine reports and exception reports may be scheduled for distribution. You can create a number of parameter-driven reports that can be made available through the Web. You may even label the reports with business names and categorize them according to classes of users, depending on rank or security authorization levels.

Several report management techniques are possible; parameter-driven reports, customizable reports, exception reports, predefined reports, and so on. One technique can provide for OLAP drill down. In this technique, the user requests a first report showing results at high summary levels. This report may be used to proceed further with the analysis. When the first report comes back, that report serves as the launch pad for further analysis. The user changes the request parameters and drills down on the summary data for additional details without having to create a new report. Another useful technique relates to on-demand pages. When the report with several pages comes back, the user can navigate to the desired page via hyperlinks instead of paging through, one page at a time.

Browser Technology for the Data Warehouse

Web technology and browser technology are almost synonymous. Browsers are the common client software in a Web-enabled data warehouse environment. Your users will access information using a standard browser. Let us go over some details so that you can become familiar with browser technology. A browser-based application comes with many benefits. The user interface—the browser—is practically free. You need not configure and install a browser-based application on the client; the application runs on a server. Right away, you observe that deployment of the application becomes easy even when there are hundreds or thousands of desktops.

At present, four technologies are commonly used to build Web-enabled user interfaces. These are HTML, Java, ADO, and plug-ins. Look at Figure 16-4, which compares the four technologies in terms of strengths and weaknesses.

Study the following brief descriptions of the four technologies.

HTML   HTML, the simplest and easiest to manage technology, works on any browser regardless of the platform. Users can navigate by clicking on hyperlinks. HTML supports

	STRENGTHS	**WEAKNESSES**
HTML	Works with any browser. Platform-independent. Open standard. Static graphics.	Only moderately interactive. Static pages. Some platform limitations with dynamic HTML.
Java	Platform-independent. Increased popularity. Added security.	Long load times. Interpretive language. Could be a problem with older browsers.
ADO	Windows environment. Widely known and used. Compiled code. Better performance.	Exclusion of non-Windows platforms. Potential security problems and DLL glitches.
Plug-in	Tightly coupled with the browser. Compiled code and, therefore, better performance.	Sometimes plug-in size may be a problem for network traffic and download times. Browser-specific.

Figure 16-4   Web interface technologies.

graphics and forms. It is "stateless," meaning that the context of the network link between the browser and the application is not maintained between applications. You may simulate OLAP features such as pivoting and drill down by generating new HTML pages. But you have to pay the price of waiting for the result page to be generated and downloaded to the desktop. HTML is good for static reports. It is very suitable when your application does not know the features of the target platform.

Java   Do you need advanced three-dimensional visualization, drill through, drag and drop, or similar high-end functionality? Then Java is the technology for you. Java is available on all major client platforms. As Java applets are not allowed to write to hard drives or print to local printers, for some applications this could pose a problem. Because Java is an interpretive language, it is somewhat slower than compiled languages. The desktop must be equipped with a Java-enabled browser. As Java applets have to be downloaded from the server every time, sometimes the long download times may not be acceptable. Java is suitable for an interactive client, where long load times may not be a factor.

ADO   This is Microsoft's solution for distributed Web-based systems. ADO, implemented as Microsoft DLLs or data link libraries, can be installed by downloading from a server using a browser. As expected, ADO runs only on Windows platforms, thereby excluding UNIX and Mac configurations. Being a compiled interface, ADO is faster than Java. ADO/MD, Microsoft's extension to ADO as part of Pivot-Table Services, can be used to create ActiveX controls in Visual Basic to manipulate data in OLAP services from a Web page. ADO is restricted to Windows platforms where you have good control of DLLs.

Plug-Ins   These are browser-specific programs that execute within the browser itself. Plug-ins can be installed on local drives. Because each browser needs its own plug-in, you may want to standardize the browser in your environment if you choose this approach. OLAP clients on multiple platforms, especially those using Java, may have a problem because of limitations in bandwidth.

Security Issues

Without a doubt, when you open up your Web-enabled data warehouse to users throughout the enterprise via an intranet and to business partners outside via an extranet, you tend to maximize the value. Depending on your organization, you may even derive more value when you take the next step and open the warehouse to the public on the Internet. But these actions raise serious security issues. You may have to impose security restrictions at different levels.

At the network level, you may look into solutions that support data encryption and restricted transfer mechanisms. Security at the network level is just one piece in the protection scheme. Carefully institute a security system at the application level. At this level, the security system must manage authorizations regarding who is allowed to get into the application and what each user is allowed to access.

Have you heard of the information terrorist? This disloyal or undependable employee with authorization to access secured information is a great threat to the security of the warehouse. Plugging this hole is difficult and you need to address this aspect of security.

OLAP AND THE WEB

Large amounts of time and money are invested in building data warehouses in the hope that the enterprise will obtain the business intelligence it needs to make strategic decisions of lasting value. For maximizing the value potential, you need to cater to as large a user group as possible and tap into the potential of the warehouse. This includes the extension of OLAP capabilities to a larger group of analysts.

Enterprise OLAP

The early warehouses started as small-scale decision support systems for a selected handful of interested analysts. Early mainframe decision support systems provided powerful analytical capabilities although quite incomparable to today's OLAP systems. Because those systems were difficult to use, they seldom reached beyond a small group of analysts who could plough through the difficulties.

The next generation of decision support systems replaced complex mainframe computing with easy-to-use GUIs and point-and-click interfaces. These second-generation systems running on client/server architecture were gradually able to support OLAP in addition to simple querying and reporting. Still, deployment and maintenance costs prevented extension of decision support to larger number of users. OLAP and OLAP-like capabilities were still limited to a moderate number of users.

The Web has put a dramatically different slant on information delivery. Web-enabled data warehouses can open their doors to a large group of users both within and outside the enterprise, and OLAP services can be extended to more than a select group of analysts. The question arises: Can OLAP systems scale up to support a large number of concurrent users performing complex queries and intensive calculations? How can your project team ensure that OLAP is successful in your Web-enabled data warehouse?

Web-OLAP Approaches

The underlying combination for a successful implementation is comprised of Web technology, the data warehouse with its OLAP system, and a thin-client architecture. How do you implement OLAP in such an environment? How will the OLAP system work in your Web-enabled data warehouse? What kind of client and Web architecture will produce the optimum results? You may approach these questions in three different ways.

1. Browser plug-ins. In the first approach, you use plug-ins or browser extensions. This is just a slightly modified version of fat-client Windows implementation except that the client configuration is more like that of a thin client. Support issues creep in and this approach has scalability problems.
2. Pre-created HTML documents. In this next approach, you provide pre-created HTML documents along with the navigation tools to find these. The documents are result sets of analytical operations. This approach takes advantage of Web technology and thin-client economy, but users are confined to using predefined reports. The approach is devoid of on-demand analysis; users cannot do typical online analytical processing.
3. OLAP in the server. The best approach is to use the server to do all online analytical processing and present the results on a true thin-client information interface. This

approach realizes the economic benefits of the Web and thin-client architecture. At the same time, it provides an integrated server environment irrespective of the client machines. Maintenance is minimized because applications and logic are centralized on the server. Version control is also consistent. Everyone shares the same components: server, metadata, and reports. This approach works well in production environments.

OLAP Engine Design

When the data warehouse is Web-enabled and the level of OLAP operations elevated, the design of the OLAP engine determines possibilities for scaling up. In the OLAP product you choose for your Web-enabled data warehouse, OLAP engine design ranks high in criticality. A properly designed engine produces a performance curve that stays linear as the number of concurrent users increases. Let us consider some options:

Dependence on the RDBMS   The OLAP engine relies completely on the RDBMS to perform multidimensional processing, generating complex, multi-pass SQL to access summary data. Joins, aggregations, and calculations are all done within the database, posing serious problems for Web-enabled systems. A large number of temporary tables become necessary. The overhead for creating, inserting, dropping, allocating disk space, checking permissions, and modifying system tables for each calculation is enormous. Just five concurrent users may bring the OLAP system to its knees.

Dependence on the Engine   Here the engine generates SQL to access summary data and performs all processing on a middle tier. You will observe two problems with this approach. Heavy network traffic and large memory requirements make this approach undesirable. You may get a linear performance curve, but the curve is likely to be too steep because the potential of the DBMS is not being used.

Intelligent OLAP Engine   The engine has the intelligence to determine the type of request and where it will be performed optimally. Because of its intelligence, the engine is able to distribute the joins, aggregations, and calculations between the engine component and the RDBMS. In this model, you are able to separate the presentation, logic, and data layers both logically and physically. Therefore, system processing is balanced and network traffic is optimized. Currently, this seems to be the best approach, achieving a performance curve that remains linear with a gradual inclination as the number of concurrent users increases.

BUILDING A WEB-ENABLED DATA WAREHOUSE

Let us summarize what we have covered so far. We perceived how the Web has changed everything, including the design and deployment of data warehouses. We understood how Web technology and data warehousing have converged, opening up remarkable possibilities. The primary purpose of the data warehouse is to provide information, and the Web makes this easy. What a nice combination of technologies! Now the value of your data warehouse can be extended to a wider array of users.

When we match up the features of the data warehouse with the characteristics of the Web, we observe that we have to do a number of things to the design and deployment methods to adapt the warehouse to the Web. We went through most of the tasks. The Web has changed the way information is delivered from the data warehouse. Web-based information delivery is more inclusive, much easier to use, but also different from the traditional methods. We have spent some time on Web-based information delivery. We also touched on OLAP in relation to the Web. So, where are we now? We are now ready to review considerations for building a Web-enabled data warehouse.

Nature of the Data Webhouse

In mid-1999, Dr. Ralph Kimball popularized a new term, "data Webhouse," which included the notion of a Web-enabled data warehouse. He declared that the data warehouse is taking central stage in the Web revolution. He went on to state that this requires restating and adjusting our data warehouse thinking. How true!

In attempting to formulate the principles for building a Web-enabled data warehouse, let us first review the nature of the data Webhouse. We will use this knowledge to define the implementation considerations. Before going over the main features, look at Figure 16-5, which gives you a broad overview of a data Webhouse. Now let us review the features. Here is a list of the principal features of the data Webhouse:

- It is a fully distributed system. Many independent nodes make up the whole. As Dr. Kimball would say, there is no center to the data Webhouse.
- It is a Web-enabled system; it is beyond a client/server system. The distribution of tasks and the arrangement of the components are radically different.

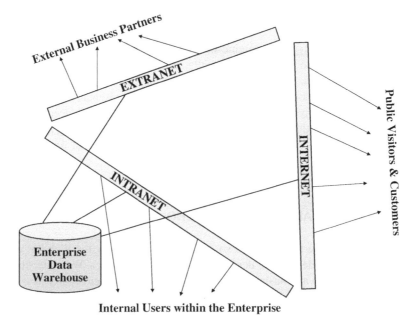

Figure 16-5   A broad overview of the data Webhouse.

- The Web browser is the key to information delivery. The system delivers the results of requests for information through remote browsers.
- Because of its openness, security is a serious concern.
- The Web supports all data types, including textual, numeric, graphical, photographic, audio, video, and more. It therefore follows that the data Webhouse supports many forms of data.
- The system provides results to information requests within reasonable response times.
- User interface design is of paramount importance for ease of use and for effective publication on the Web. Unlike the interfaces in other configurations, the Web has a definite method to measure the effectiveness of the user interface. The analysis of the clickstream data tells you how good the interface is.
- By nature, the data Webhouse necessitates a nicely distributed architecture comprising small-scale data marts.
- Because the arrangement of the components is based on a "bus" architecture of linked data marts, it is important to have fully conformed dimensions and completely conformed or standardized facts.
- The Web never sleeps. Your data Webhouse is expected to be up all the time.
- Finally, remember that the data Webhouse is meant to be open to all groups of users, both inside and outside the enterprise—employees, customers, suppliers, and other business partners.

Implementation Considerations

The major features described above lead us to factors you need to consider for implementing a Web-enabled data warehouse. Each feature listed above demands readjustment of the implementation principles. Mostly, by going through a list of features, you can derive what is required. We want to highlight just a few implementation considerations that are crucial.

If the data Webhouse is expected to be widely distributed, how could you manage it? How could you make all the components of the architecture work together and make sense? Do you not feel that without something in the middle, it seems impossible to make it work? In the real world, many of the connected groups may be using different technologies and different platforms. How could you tie them all together? From where?

Study the following observations carefully:

- In order to achieve basic architectural coherence among the distributed units, fully adopt dimensional modeling as the basic modeling technique.
- Use the data warehouse bus architecture. This architecture, with its fully conformed dimensions and completely standardized facts, is conducive to the flow of correct information.
- In a distributed environment, who conforms the dimensions and facts? In earlier chapters, we have already discussed the meaning of conforming the dimensions and facts. Basically, the implication is to have the same definitions throughout. One suggestion is to centralize the definitions of the conformed dimensions and the conformed facts. This need not be physical centralization; logical centralization will work. This centralization gives the semblance of a center to the data Webhouse.

- Still the question remains: who actually conforms the dimensions and facts? The answer depends on what will work for your environment. If feasible, assign the task of conforming the dimensions and facts to the local groups of participants. Each group gets the responsibility to come up with the definitions for a dimension or a set of facts.

- Well, how do all units become aware of the complete set of definitions for all dimensions and facts? This is where the Web comes in handy. You can have the definitions published on the Web; they then become the standards for conformed dimensions and facts.

- How do you physically implement the conformed dimension tables and the conformed fact tables? Dimension tables are often physically duplicated. Again, see what is feasible in your environment. Total physical centralization of all the dimension tables may not be practical, but the conformed fact tables are rarely duplicated. Generally, fact tables are very large in comparison to the dimension tables.

- One last consideration, now that we understand the data Webhouse as a distributed set of dimensions and facts based on possibly dissimilar database technologies. How can you make such a distributed collection work as a cohesive whole? This is what the query tool or the report writer is required to do in such a distributed configuration. Let us say one of the remote users executes a specific query. The query tool must establish connections to each of the required fact table providers and retrieve result sets that are constrained by the conformed dimensions. Then the tool must combine all the retrieved result sets in the application server using a single-pass sort-merge. The combination will produce the correct final result set simply because the dimensions are all conformed.

Putting the Pieces Together

In this subsection, let us go over the various components that need to be pulled together to make up the Web-enabled data warehouse. Consider the following list:

- The data Webhouse configuration is beyond client/server computing. The usual two-tier or three-tier technology is inadequate. As the number of users rise sharply, new servers must be added without any difficulty. Therefore, consider a distributed component architecture.

- With the user nodes spread out, you must strive for minimum administration on the client side. True thin-client technology like Java is likely to provide a zero-administration client setup.

- The client technology is expected to be a combination of thin clients and full clients. Ensure complete metadata integration. Both IT and the variety of user types will benefit from unified metadata.

- Select the right database to support the distributed environment. As you are likely to use Java, a RDBMS with the Java engine in the database would prove useful.

- In many Web applications, the HTTP server becomes a point of congestion as all data from a session is fed to the browser through this server. You will find scalability to be difficult unless you implement a CORBA model. CORBA provides distributed object computing and scalability because the server and the client communicate via CORBA.

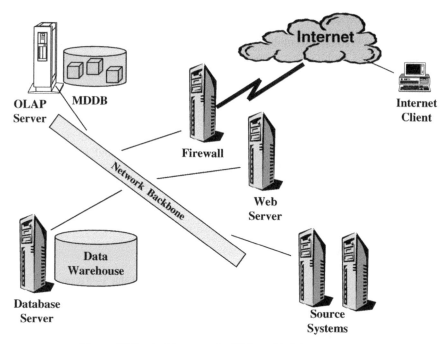

Figure 16-6   Architecture of a Web-enabled data warehouse.

- Ensure that you pay enough attention to administration and maintenance. This should include identification of the dimensions, hierarchies within dimensions, facts, and summaries. Summary management could be difficult.
- The Web interface consists of a browser, search engine, groupware, push technologies, home pages, hypertext links, and downloaded Java and ActiveX applets.
- Tools supporting HTML can be universally deployed. However, for complex analysis, HTML is cumbersome. Use HTML as much as possible and reserve Java or plug-ins for complex ad hoc analysis.

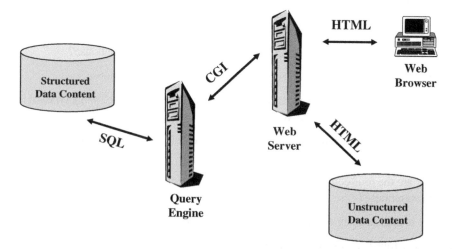

Figure 16-7   Web processing model.

Web Processing Model

First let us look at a Web architecture configuration. Figure 16-6 shows the overall arrangement. Notice that the architecture is more complex than a two-tier or three-tier client/server architecture. You need additional tiers to accommodate the requirements of Web computing. At a minimum, you need to have a Web server between the browser clients and the database. Also, note the firewall to protect your corporate applications from outside intrusions.

This covers the overall architecture. Figure 16-7 shows a model for delivering information. The model illustrates how HTML pages are translated into SQL queries passed on to the DBMS using CGI scripts. This model shows the components for information delivery through HTML pages. The model may be generalized to illustrate other technologies.

CHAPTER SUMMARY

- The Web is the most dominant computing phenomenon of the 1990s and beyond; its technology and data warehousing are converging to produce dramatic results.
- A Web-enabled data warehouse adapts the Web for information delivery and collaboration among the users.
- Adapting the data warehouse to the Web means including features such as the information "push" technique, ease of usage, speedy response, no downtime, multimedia output, and scalability.
- Web-based information delivery expands the data warehouse usage and opens up new information strategies.
- The combination of OLAP and Web technologies produces great benefits for users.
- Because of the open nature of the Web, adapting the data warehouse to the Web calls for serious implementation considerations.

REVIEW QUESTIONS

1. Describe briefly two major features of the Web-enabled data warehouse.
2. How do the Internet, intranet, and extranet apply to the data warehouse?
3. What are the expectations of users of a Web-enabled data warehouse?
4. How can you use the Web as a data source for your data warehouse? What types of information can you get from the Web?
5. Name any four standard options on a Web page delivering information from the data warehouse.
6. What are the four common technologies to build Web-enabled user interfaces for your data warehouse?
7. Why is data security a major concern for a Web-enabled data warehouse?
8. List any four features of the data Webhouse.

9. Name any two approaches for an OLAP system to function in a Web-enabled data warehouse.

10. What is a data warehouse bus architecture? How does it fit in a Web-enabled data warehouse?

EXERCISES

1. Indicate if true or false:

   A. The extranet excludes outside business partners from accessing the company's data warehouse.

   B. Web technology in a data warehouse opens up multiple information formats to users.

   C. Better information delivery to users is the only reason for Web-enabling your data warehouse.

   D. Supergrowth is a rare phenomenon in a Web-enabled data warehouse environment.

   E. The Web promotes "self-service" access.

   F. The data Webhouse necessitates a distributed architecture.

   G. Web technology makes it easier to add more users to the data warehouse.

   H. The Web and its features are not compatible with the data warehouse.

   I. For its information interface, the Web-enabled data warehouse is unable to use both "push" and "pull" techniques.

   J. In a Web-enabled data warehouse, the standard HTML or XML file is the principal means for communication.

2. Web-based information in a data warehouse results in "supergrowth." Discuss this phenomenal growth and describe how you will provide for supergrowth.

3. Your project team has been directed to provide all report generation and delivery over the Internet. Create a plan for adopting the Web technology for all reporting from your data warehouse. Discuss all the implications.

4. The Web-enabled data warehouse has no center. It is a distributed environment. Analyze the implications of these statements. From this perspective, what are the considerations for maintaining the dimension and fact tables?

5. As the Web specialist on the project team, prepare a document highlighting the major considerations for Web-enabling your data warehouse. Just list the considerations, not the implementation techniques.

CHAPTER 17

DATA MINING BASICS

CHAPTER OBJECTIVES

- Learn what exactly data mining is and examine its features
- Compare data mining with OLAP and understand the similarities and differences
- Notice the place for data mining in a data warehouse environment
- Carefully go through major data mining techniques and understand how each works
- Study a few data mining applications in different industries and perceive the application of the technology to your environment

In today's environment, almost everyone in IT has certainly heard about data mining. Most of you know that the technology has something to do with discovering knowledge. Some of you possibly know that data mining is used in applications such as marketing, sales, credit analysis, and fraud detection. All of you know vaguely that data mining is somehow connected to data warehousing. Data mining is used in just about every area of business from sales and marketing to new product development to inventory management and human resources.

There are perhaps as many variations in the definition of data mining as there are vendors and proponents. Some experts include a whole range of tools and techniques, from simple query mechanisms to statistical analysis in the definition. Others restrict the definition to knowledge discovery techniques. A workable data warehouse, although not a prerequisite, will give a practical boost to the data mining process.

Why is data mining being put to use in more and more businesses? Here are some basic reasons:

- In today's world, an organization generates more information in a week than most people can read in a lifetime. It is humanly impossible to study, decipher, and interpret all that data to find useful information.

- A data warehouse pools all the data after proper transformation and cleansing into well-organized data structures. Nevertheless, the sheer volume of data makes it impossible for anyone to use analysis and query tools to discern useful patterns.

- In recent times, many data mining tools suitable for a wide range of applications have appeared in the market. We are seeing the maturity of the tools and products.

- Data mining needs substantial computing power. Parallel hardware, databases, and other powerful components are becoming very affordable.

- As you are aware, organizations are placing enormous emphasis on building sound customer relationships, and for good reasons. Companies want to know how they can sell more to existing customers. Organizations are interested in determining which of their customers will prove to be of long-term value to them. Companies need to discover any existing natural classifications among their customers so that the classifications may be properly targeted with products and services. Data mining enables companies to find answers and discover patterns in their customer data.

- Finally, competitive considerations weigh heavily on your company to get into data mining. Perhaps your company's competition is already using data mining.

WHAT IS DATA MINING?

Before providing some formal definitions of data mining, let us try to understand the technology in a business context. Like all decision support systems, data mining delivers information. Figure 17-1 shows the progression of decision support. Note the earliest approach, when primitive types of decision support systems existed. Next came database systems providing more useful decision support information. Throughout the 1990s, data warehouses with query and report tools to assist users in retrieving the types of decision support information they need began to be the primary and valuable source of business intelligence. For more sophisticated analysis, OLAP tools became available. Up to this point, the approach for obtaining information was driven by the users. But the sheer volume of data renders it impossible for anyone to use analysis and query tools to discern useful patterns. For example, in marketing analysis, it is almost physically impossible to think through all the probable associations and gain insights by querying and drilling down into the data warehouse. You need a technology that can learn from past associations and results, and predict customer behavior. You need a tool that will accomplish the discovery of knowledge by itself. You want a data-driven approach and not a user-driven one. This is where data mining steps in and takes over from the users.

Progressive organizations gather enterprise data from the source operational systems, move the data through a transformation and cleansing process, and store the data in data warehouses in a form suitable for multidimensional analysis. Data mining takes the process a giant step further.

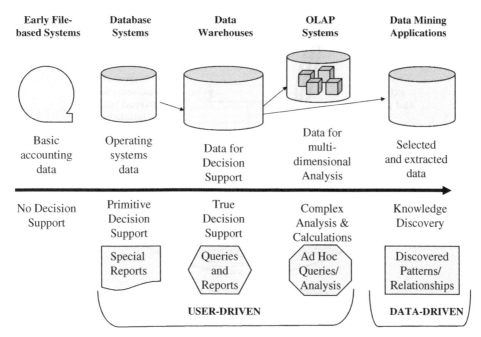

Early File-based Systems	Database Systems	Data Warehouses	OLAP Systems	Data Mining Applications
Basic accounting data	Operating systems data	Data for Decision Support	Data for multi-dimensional Analysis	Selected and extracted data
No Decision Support	Primitive Decision Support	True Decision Support	Complex Analysis & Calculations	Knowledge Discovery
	Special Reports	Queries and Reports	Ad Hoc Queries/ Analysis	Discovered Patterns/ Relationships
		USER-DRIVEN		DATA-DRIVEN

Figure 17-1   Decision support progresses to data mining.

Data Mining Defined

As an analogy, imagine a very wide and very deep repository densely packed with some important material. You use a set of sophisticated drilling tools to dig and unravel the contents. You do not know what exactly you hope to get from your effort. Nothing may turn up, or you may be fortunate to find some real gold nuggets. You may discover this valuable treasure that you never knew was there in the first place. You were not specifically looking for nuggets. You did not know they were there or if they ever existed. Figure 17-2 crudely depicts this scenario.

Now, as a change of scenery, replace the very wide and very deep repository with your data warehouse. Replace the material in the repository with the massive data content in your data warehouse and replace the drilling tools by data mining tools. The gold nuggets are the valuable pieces of information, such as patterns or relationships, you never knew existed in the data. In fact, you had applied the data mining tools to find something worthwhile you did not know existed. This is one aspect of data mining. Data mining is synonymous with knowledge discovery—discovering some aspect of knowledge you never even suspected existed.

If you do not know that some pattern or relationship even exists, how do you direct the data mining tool to find it? For a mortgage bank, how does the data mining tool know that a nugget of information exists indicating that most homeowners who are likely to default on their mortgages belong to a certain classification of customers?

If knowledge discovery is one aspect of data mining, prediction is the other. Here you are looking for a specific association with regard to an event or condition. You know that some of your customers are likely to buy upscale if they are targeted by appropriate marketing campaigns. You would like to predict the tendency to upscale. Your customer data may

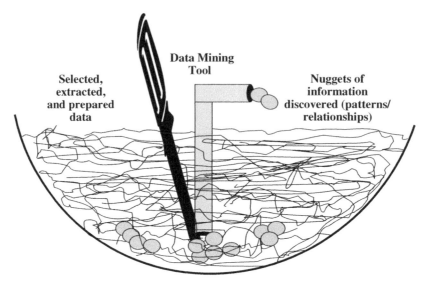

Figure 17-2   Mining for nuggets.

contain interesting associations between tendency to upscale and age, income level, and marital status. You would like to discover the factors contributing to the tendency to upscale and predict which of your customers are likely to move up in their buying patterns. Prediction is the other aspect of data mining.

So, what is data mining? It is a knowledge discovery process. Data mining helps you understand the substance of the data in a special unsuspected way. It unearths patterns and trends in the raw data you never knew existed.

"Data mining," writes Joseph P. Bigus in his book, *Data Mining with Neural Networks* (1996, p. 9), "is the efficient discovery of valuable, non-obvious information from a large collection of data." Data mining centers around the automatic discovery of new facts and relationships in data. With traditional query tools, you search for known information. Data mining tools enable you to uncover hidden information. The assumption is that more useful knowledge lies hidden beneath the surface.

The Knowledge Discovery Process

In the above discussion, we have described data mining as the process of knowledge discovery. Data mining discovers knowledge or information that you never knew was present in your data. What about this knowledge? How does it show up? Usually, the uncovered hidden knowledge manifests itself as relationships or patterns. Try to understand the kinds of relationships or patterns that are discovered.

Relationships   Take the example of your going to the nearby supermarket on the way home to pick up bread, milk, and a few other "things." What other things? You are not sure. While you fetch the milk container, you happen to see a pack of assorted cheeses close by. Yes, you want that. You pause to look at the next five customers behind you. To your amazement, you notice that three of those customers also reach for the cheese pack. Coincidence? Within a space of five minutes, you have seen milk and cheese bought together.

Now, on to the bread shelf. As you get your bread, a bag of barbecue-flavored potato chips catches your eye. Why not get that bag of potato chips? Now the customer behind you also wants bread and chips. Coincidence? Not necessarily. It is possible that this supermarket is part of a national chain that uses data mining. The data mining tools have discovered the relationships between bread and chips and between milk and cheese packs, especially in the evening rush hour. So the items may have been deliberately placed in close proximity.

Data mining discovers relationships of this type. The relationships may be between two or more different objects along with the time dimension. Sometimes, the relationships may be between the attributes of the same object. Whatever they may be, discovery of relationships is a key result of data mining.

Patterns   Pattern discovery is another outcome of data mining operations. Consider a credit card company trying to discover the pattern of usage that usually warrants increase in the credit limit or a card upgrade. They would like to know which of their customers must be lured with a card upgrade and when. The data mining tools mine the usage patterns of thousands of card-holders and discover the potential pattern of usage that will produce results in a marketing campaign.

Before you engage in data mining, you must determine clearly what you want the tool to accomplish. At this stage, we are not trying to predict the knowledge you expect to discover, but to define the business objectives of the engagement. Let us walk through the major phases and steps. First look at Figure 17-3 indicating four major phases, then read the following brief descriptions of the detailed steps.

Step 1: Define Business Objectives. This step is similar to any information system project. First of all, determine whether you really need a data mining solution. State your objectives. Are you looking to improve your direct marketing campaigns? Do you want to

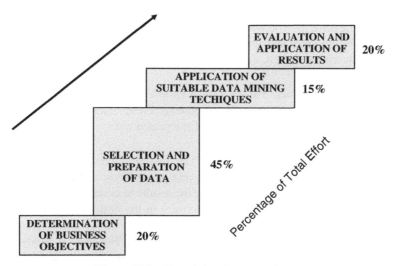

Figure 17-3 Knowledge discovery phases.

detect fraud in credit card usage? Are you looking for associations between products that sell together? In this step, define expectations. Express how the final results will be presented and used in the operational systems.

Step 2: Prepare Data. This step consists of data selection, preprocessing of data, and data transformation. Select the data to be extracted from the data warehouse. Use the business objectives to determine what data has to be selected. Include appropriate metadata about the selected data. By now, you also know what type of mining algorithm you will be using. The mining algorithm has a bearing on data selection. The variables selected for data mining are also known as active variables.

Preprocessing is meant to improve the quality of selected data. When you select from the data warehouse, it is assumed that the data is already cleansed. Preprocessing could also involve enriching the selected data with external data. In the preprocessing substep, remove noisy data, that is, data blatantly out of range. Also ensure that there are no missing values.

Clearly, if the data for mining is selected from the data warehouse, it is again assumed that all the necessary data transformations have already been completed. Make sure that this really is the case.

Step 3: Perform Data Mining. Obviously, this is the crucial step. The knowledge discovery engine applies the selected algorithm to the prepared data. The output from this step is a set of relationships or patterns. However, this step and the next step of evaluation may be performed in an iterative manner. After an initial evaluation, you may adjust the data and redo this step. The duration and intensity of this step depend on the type of data mining application. If you are segmenting the database, too many iterations are not needed. If you are creating a predictive model, the models are repeatedly set up and tested with sample data before testing with the real database.

Step 4: Evaluate Results. You are actually seeking interesting patterns or relationships. These help you in the understanding of your customers, products, profits, and markets. In the selected data, there are potentially many patterns or relationships. In this step, you examine all the resulting patterns. You will apply a filtering mechanism and select only the promising patterns to be presented and applied. Again, this step also depends on the specific kind of data mining algorithm applied.

Step 5: Present Discoveries. Presentation of knowledge discoveries may be in the form of visual navigation, charts, graphs, or free-form texts. Presentation also includes storing of interesting discoveries in the knowledge base for repeated use.

Step 6: Incorporate Use of Discoveries. The goal of any data mining operation is to understand the business, discern new patterns and possibilities, and also turn this understanding into actions. This step involves using the results to create actionable items in the business. You assemble the results of the discovery in the best way so that they can be exploited to improve the business.

These major phases and their detailed steps are shown in Figure 17-4. Study the figure carefully and note each step. Also note the data elements used in the steps. This figure illustrates the knowledge discovery process from beginning to end.

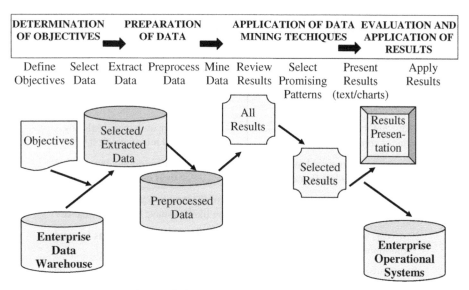

Figure 17-4 Knowledge discovery process.

OLAP Versus Data Mining

After reading the chapter on OLAP, you must now be an expert on that topic. As you know, with OLAP queries and analyses, users are able to obtain results from complex queries and derive interesting patterns. Data mining also enables users to uncover interesting patterns, but there is an essential difference in the way the results are obtained. Figure 17-5 shows the basic difference by means of a simple diagram.

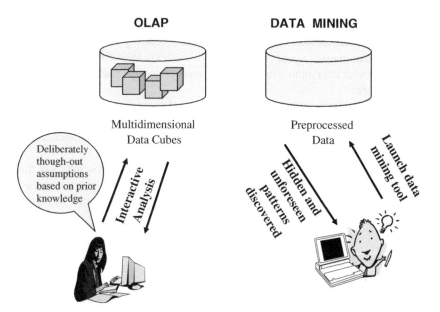

Figure 17-5 OLAP and data mining.

OLAP: Report on the past	Data Mining: Predict the future
Who are our top 100 best customers for the last three years?	Which 100 customers offer the best profit potential?
Which customers defaulted on their mortgages last two years?	Which customers are likely to be bad credit risks?
What were the sales by territory last quarter compared to the targets?	What are the anticipated sales by territory and region for next year?
Which salespersons sold more than their quota during last four quarters?	Which salespersons are expected to exceed their quotas next year?
Last year, which stores exceeded the total prior year sales?	For the next two years, which stores are likely to have best performance?
Last year, which were the top five promotions that performed well?	What is the expected returns for next year's promotions?
Which customers switched to other phone companies last year?	Which customers are likely to switch to the competition next year?

Figure 17-6   OLAP is used to analyze the past; data mining is used to predict the future.

When an analyst works with OLAP in an analysis session, he or she has some prior knowledge of what he or she is looking for. The analyst starts with assumptions deliberately considered and thought out, whereas in the case of data mining, the analyst has no prior knowledge of what the results are likely to be. Users drive OLAP queries. Each query may lead to a more complex one and so on. The user needs prior knowledge of the expected results. The process is completely different in data mining. Whereas OLAP helps the user to analyze the past and gain insights, data mining helps the user predict the future. To amplify this statement, Figure 17-6 lists the sets of questions the two methodologies can answer.

Notice how OLAP is able to give you answers to questions on past performance. Of course, from these answers you can gain a good understanding of what happened in the past. You may make guesses about the future from these answers about past performance. In contrast, notice what data mining can do. It can uncover specific patterns and relationships to predict the future.

We have said that whereas OLAP analyzes the past, data mining predicts the future. You must have guessed that there must be more to it than just this broad statement. Let us look at all the ways data mining differs from OLAP. For a comprehensive list of differences between OLAP and data mining, study Figure 17-7.

In another sense, OLAP and data mining are complementary. You may say that data mining picks up where OLAP leaves off. The analyst drives the process while using OLAP tools. In data mining, the analyst prepares the data and "sits back" while the tools drive the process.

Some Aspects of Data Mining

As we attempted to understand data mining, we compared OLAP and data mining. This comparison enabled us to getter a better grasp of data mining. As we move further in this chapter, we will be looking at some specific data mining techniques. Before doing that

Features	OLAP	DATA MINING
Motivation for information request	What is happening in the enterprise?	Predict the future based on why this is happening.
Data granularity	Summary data.	Detailed transaction-level data.
Number of business dimensions	Limited number of dimensions.	Large number of dimensions.
Number of dimension attributes	Small number of attributes.	Many dimension attributes.
Sizes of datasets for the dimensions	Not large for each dimension.	Usually very large for each dimension.
Analysis approach	User-driven, interactive analysis.	Data-driven automatic knowledge discovery.
Analysis techniques	Multidimensional, drill-down, and slice-and-dice.	Prepare data, launch mining tool and sit back.
State of the technology	Mature and widely used.	Still emerging; many parts of the technology more mature.

Figure 17-7   Basic differences between OLAP and data mining.

we would like to get a feel for some aspects of it. What are some leading methods? How and where they are useful? What are some of the goals of data mining? Let us look for some answers.

Association Rules   A common and powerful method employed in data mining is to discover rules about how variables associate among themselves. For example, if the tendency of customers in a supermarket is to buy cheese along with bread and milk, an association rule may be of the form (bread, milk) =>cheese. Such association rules, once they are found out through data mining, can be very useful for the supermarket management. The management can use the rule about bread, milk, and cheese to do promotional pricing of these products properly. They can make use of the rule in the placement of these products in close proximity on the shelves.

Outlier Analysis   Have you received a phone call from your credit card company about a charge of 55 euros on your credit card account from a bookstore in Munich, Germany? Why did they call you to verify this transaction? They called you because this transaction deviates so much from your normal transactions as to arouse suspicion that it might have been charged by someone else to your account. Flying to Munich to purchase books is not your normal practice. Therefore, that charge for 55 euros is an outlier in the charge transactions in your account. Rare, unusual, or just plain infrequent events are of interest in data mining in many contexts, including fraud in income tax, insurance, and online banking, as well as in marketing. Focus on the discovery of such unusual events is part of the method of outlier analysis in data mining.

Predictive Analytics   This encompasses a variety of methods in data mining that analyze current and historical data to make predictions about future events. In business, predictive models make use of patterns found in historical and transactional data to identify risks and opportunities. Predictive models capture relationships among many factors to allow assessment of risk or potential associated with a particular set of conditions, guiding decision making for candidate transactions. One of the most well-known applications is credit scoring, which is used in financial services. Scoring models process a customer's credit history, details on the loan application, and other customer data in order to rank-order individuals by their likelihood of making future credit payments on time. Predictive analytics are also used in insurance, telecommunications, retail, healthcare, and many other fields.

Data Mining and the Data Warehouse

The enterprise data warehouse, either as a centralized repository feeding dependent data marts or as a conglomerate of conformed data marts on a bus structure, forms a very useful source of data for data mining. It contains all the significant data you have extracted from the various source operational systems. This data has been cleansed and transformed, and stored in your data warehouse repository.

Data mining fits well and plays a significant role in the data warehouse environment. A clean and complete data warehouse forms the bedrock for data mining and the data warehouse enables data mining operations to take place. The two technologies support each other. The following are some of the major factors of this relationship.

- Data mining algorithms need large amounts of data, more so at the detailed level. Most data warehouses contain data at the lowest level of granularity.
- Data mining flourishes on integrated and cleansed data. If your ETL functions were carried out properly, your data warehouse contains such data, very suitable for data mining.
- The infrastructure for data warehouses is already robust, with parallel processing technology and powerful relational database systems. Because such scalable hardware is already in place, no new investment is needed to support data mining.

Let us point out one difference in the way data from the data warehouse is used for traditional analysis and data mining. When an analyst wants to perform an analysis, say with an OLAP tool, he or she begins with summary data at a high level, then continues through the lower levels by means of drill-down techniques. On many occasions, the analyst need not go down to the detailed levels. This is because he or she finds the suitable subsets for deriving conclusions at the higher levels. But data mining is different. As the data mining algorithm is searching for trends and patterns, it deals with lots of detailed data. For example, if the data mining algorithm is looking for customer buying patterns, it certainly needs detailed data at the level of the individual customer.

So what is a compromise approach? What is the level of granularity you need to provide in the data warehouse? Unless it is a huge burden to keep detailed data at the lowest level of granularity, strive to store detailed data. Otherwise, for data mining engagements, you may have to extract detailed data directly from the operational systems. This calls for additional steps of data consolidation, cleansing, and transformation. You may also keep light summaries in the data warehouse for traditional queries. Most of the summarized data along various sets of dimensions may reside in the OLAP systems.

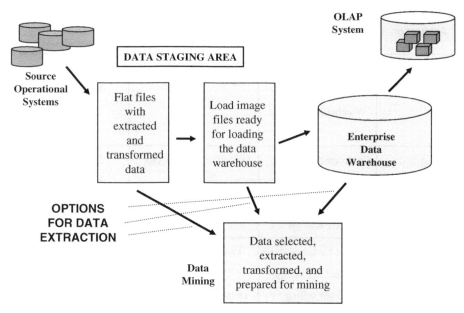

Figure 17-8   Data mining in the data warehouse environment.

The data warehouse is a valuable and easily available data source for data mining operations. Data extractions that data mining tools work on come from the data warehouse. Figure 17-8 illustrates how data mining fits in the data warehouse environment. Notice how the data warehouse environment supports data mining. Note the levels of data held in the data warehouse and the OLAP system. Also observe the flow of data from the data warehouse for the knowledge discovery process.

MAJOR DATA MINING TECHNIQUES

Now that we are at the point of getting introduced to data mining techniques, we quickly realize that there are many different ways of classifying the techniques. Someone new to data mining may be totally confused by the names and descriptions of the techniques. Even among practicing data mining consultants, no uniform terminology seems to exist. Even though no consistent set of terms seems to be available, let us try to use the more popular ones.

Many data mining practitioners seem to agree on some manner of defining data mining algorithms, data mining techniques, mining processes, mining applications, and application areas. Figure 17-9 provides examples for application areas, data mining applications, mining processes, and mining techniques. Study this figure carefully before proceeding further.

Using the figure, try to understand the connections.

- Data mining algorithms are part of data mining techniques.
- Data mining techniques are used in specific mining processes.
- Data mining processes are carried out in relation to specific data mining applications.

Application Area	Data Mining Applications	Mining Processes	Mining Techniques
Fraud Detection	Credit card frauds Internal audits Warehouse pilferage	Determination of variations from norms	Data Visualization Memory-based Reasoning
Risk Assessment	Credit card upgrades Mortgage Loans Customer Retention Credit Ratings	Detection and analysis of links	Decision Trees Memory-based Reasoning Neural Network
Market Analysis	Market basket analysis Target marketing Cross selling Customer Relationship Marketing	Predictive Modeling Database segmentation	Cluster Detection Decision Trees Link Analysis Genetic Algorithms

Figure 17-9 Data mining functions and application areas.

- Data mining applications may be categorized to fall within specific application areas.
- Each application area is a major area in business where data mining is actively used.

We will devote the rest of this section to discussing the highlights of the major applications, the processes for the applications, and the data mining techniques themselves.

Data mining covers a broad range of techniques. This is not a textbook on data mining and a detailed discussion of the data mining techniques and algorithms is not within its scope. There are a number of well-written books in the field and you may refer to them to pursue your interest further.

Let us explore the basics here. We will select six of the major techniques for our discussion. Our intention is to understand these techniques broadly without getting down to technical details. The main goal is for you to get an overall appreciation of data mining techniques.

Cluster Detection

Clustering means identifying and forming groups. Take the very ordinary example of how you do your laundry. You group the clothes into whites, dark-colored clothes, light-colored clothes, permanent press, and the ones to be dry-cleaned. You have five distinct clusters. Each cluster has a meaning and you can use the meaning to get that cluster cleaned properly. The clustering helps you take specific and proper action for the individual pieces that make up the cluster. Now think of a specialty store owner in a resort community who wants to cater to the neighborhood by stocking the right type of products. If he has data about the age group and income level of each of the people who frequent the store, using these two variables the store owner can probably put the customers into four clusters. These clusters may be formed as follows: wealthy retirees staying in resorts, middle-aged weekend golfers, wealthy young people with club memberships, and low-income clients who happen to stay in the community. The information about the clusters helps the store owner in his marketing.

Clustering or cluster detection is one of the earliest data mining techniques. This technique is designated as undirected knowledge discovery or unsupervised learning. What do we mean by this statement? In the cluster detection technique, you do not search preclassified data. No distinction is made between independent and dependent variables. For example, in the case of the store's customers, there are two variables: age group and income level. Both variables participate equally in the functioning of the data mining algorithm.

The cluster detection algorithm searches for groups or clusters of data elements that are similar to one another. What is the purpose of this? You expect similar customers or similar products to behave in the same way. Then you can take a cluster and do something useful with it. Again, in the example of the specialty store, the store owner can take the members of the cluster of wealthy retirees and target products especially interesting to them.

Notice one important aspect of clustering. When the mining algorithm produces a cluster, you must understand what that cluster means exactly. Only then you will be able to do something useful with that cluster. The store owner has to understand that one of the clusters represents wealthy retirees residing in resorts. Only then can the store owner do something useful with that cluster. It is not always easy to discern the meaning of every cluster the data mining algorithm forms. A bank may get as many as 20 clusters but may be able to interpret the meanings of only two. However, the return for the bank from the use of just these two clusters may be enormous enough so that they may simply ignore the other 18 clusters.

If there are only two or three variables or dimensions, it is fairly easy to spot the clusters, even when dealing with many records. But if you are dealing with 500 variables from 100,000 records, you need a special tool. How does the data mining tool perform the clustering function? Without getting bogged down in too much technical detail, let us study the process. First, some basics. If you have two variables, then points on a two-dimensional graph represent the values of sets of these two variables. Figure 17-10 shows the distribution of these points.

Let us consider an example. Suppose you want the data mining algorithm to form clusters of your customers, but you want the algorithm to use 50 different variables for each customer, not just two. Now we are discussing a 50-dimensional space. Imagine each customer record with different values for the 50 dimensions. Each record is then a vector defining a "point" in the 50-dimensional space.

Let us say you want to market to the customers and you are prepared to run marketing campaigns for 15 different groups. So you set the number of clusters as 15. This number is K in the K-means clustering algorithm, a very effective one for cluster detection. Fifteen initial records (called "seeds") are chosen as the first set of centroids based on best guesses. One seed represents one set of values for the 50 variables chosen from the customer record. In the next step, the algorithm assigns each customer record in the database to a cluster based on the seed to which it is closest. Closeness is based on the nearness of the values of the set of 50 variables in a record to the values in the seed record. The first set of 15 clusters is now formed. Then the algorithm calculates the centroid or mean for each of the first set of 15 clusters. The values of the 50 variables in each centroid are taken to represent that cluster.

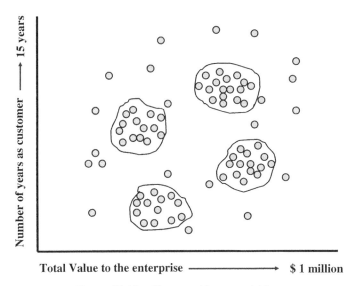

Figure 17-10 Clusters with two variables.

The next iteration then starts. Each customer record is rematched with the new set of centroids and cluster boundaries are redrawn. After a few iterations the final clusters emerge. Figure 17-11 illustrates how centroids are determined and cluster boundaries redrawn.

How does the algorithm redraw the cluster boundaries? What factors determine that one customer record is near one centroid and not the other? Each implementation of the cluster

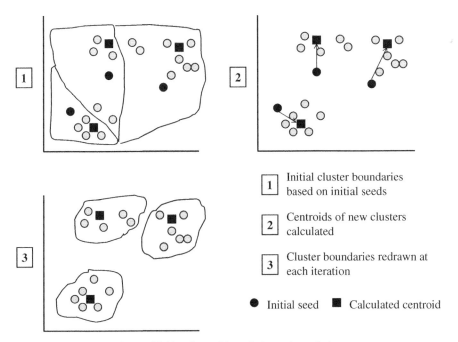

Figure 17-11 Centroids and cluster boundaries.

detection algorithm adopts a method of comparing the values of the variables in individual records with those in the centroids. The algorithm uses these comparisons to calculate the distances of individual customer records from the centroids. After calculating the distances, the algorithm redraws the cluster boundaries.

Decision Trees

This technique applies to classification and prediction. The major attraction of decision trees is their simplicity. By following the tree, you can decipher the rules and understand why a record is classified in a certain way. Decision trees represent rules. You can use these rules to retrieve records falling into a certain category. Figure 17-12 shows a decision tree representing the profiles of men and women buying a notebook computer.

In some data mining processes, you really do not care how the algorithm selected a certain record. For example, when you are selecting prospects to be targeted in a marketing campaign, you do not need the reasons for targeting them. You only need the ability to predict which members are likely to respond to the mailing. But in some other cases, the reasons for the prediction are important. If your company is a mortgage company and wants to evaluate an application, you need to know why an application must be rejected. Your company must be able to protect itself from any lawsuits of discrimination. Wherever the reasons are necessary and you must be able to trace the decision paths, decision trees are suitable.

As you have seen from Figure 17-12, a decision tree represents a series of questions. Each question determines what follow-up question is best to be asked next. Good questions produce a short series. Trees are drawn with the root at the top and the leaves at the bottom, an unnatural convention. The question at the root must be the one that best

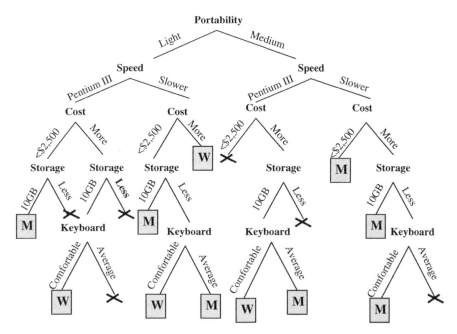

Figure 17-12 A decision tree for notebook computer buyers.

differentiates among the target classes. A database record enters the tree at the root node. The record works its way down until it reaches a leaf. The leaf node determines the classification of the record.

How can you measure the effectiveness of a tree? In the example of the profiles of buyers of notebook computers, you can pass the records whose classifications are already known. Then you can calculate the percentage of correctness for the known records. A tree showing a high level of correctness is more effective. Also, you must pay attention to the branches. Some paths are better than others because the rules are better. By pruning the incompetent branches, you can enhance the predictive effectiveness of the whole tree.

How do the decision tree algorithms build the trees? First, the algorithm attempts to find the test that will split the records in the best possible manner among the wanted classifications. At each lower level node from the root, whatever rule works best to split the subsets is applied. This process of finding each additional level of the tree continues. The tree is allowed to grow until you cannot find better ways to split the input records.

Memory-Based Reasoning

Would you rather go to an experienced doctor or to a novice? Of course, the answer is obvious. Why? Because the experienced doctor treats you and cures you based on his or her experience. The doctor knows what worked in the past in several cases when the symptoms were similar to yours. We are all good at making decisions on the basis of our experiences. We depend on the similarities of the current situation to what we know from past experience. How do we use the experience to solve the current problem? First, we identify similar instances in the past; then we use the past instances and apply the information about those instances to the present. The same principles apply to the memory-based reasoning (MBR) algorithm.

MBR uses known instances of a model to predict unknown instances. This data mining technique maintains a dataset of known records. The algorithm knows the characteristics of the records in this training dataset. When a new record arrives for evaluation, the algorithm finds neighbors similar to the new record and then uses the characteristics of the neighbors for prediction and classification.

When a new record arrives at the data mining tool, first the tool calculates the "distance" between this record and the records in the training dataset. The distance function of the data mining tool does the calculation. The results determine which data records in the training dataset qualify to be considered as neighbors to the incoming data record. Next, the algorithm uses a combination function to combine the results of the various distance functions to obtain the final answer. The distance function and the combination function are key components of the memory-based reasoning technique.

Let us consider a simple example to observe how MBR works. This example is about predicting the last book read by new respondents based on a dataset of known responses. For the sake of keeping the example quite simple, assume there are four recent bestsellers. The students surveyed have read these books and have also mentioned which they had read last. The results of four surveys are shown in Figure 17-13. Look at the first part of the figure. Here you see the scatterplot of known respondents. The second part of the figure contains the unknown respondents falling in place on the scatterplot. From where each unknown respondent falls on the scatterplot, you can determine the distance to the known respondents and then find the nearest neighbor. The nearest neighbor predicts the last book read by each unknown respondent.

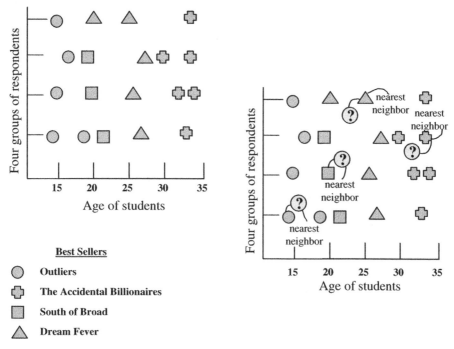

Figure 17-13   Memory-based reasoning.

For solving a data mining problem using MBR, you are concerned with three critical issues:

1. Selecting the most suitable historical records to form the training or base dataset.
2. Establishing the best way to compose the historical record.
3. Determining the two essential functions, namely, the distance function and the combination function.

Link Analysis

This algorithm is extremely useful for finding patterns from relationships. If you look closely at the business world, you clearly notice all types of relationships. Airlines link cities together. Telephone calls connect people and establish relationships. Fax machines connect with one another. Physicians prescribing treatments have links to the patients. In a sales transaction at a supermarket, many items bought together in one trip are all linked together. You notice relationships everywhere.

The link analysis technique mines relationships and discovers knowledge. For example, if you look at the supermarket sales transactions for one day, why are skim milk and brown bread found in the same transaction about 80% of the time? Is there a strong relationship between the two products in the supermarket basket? If so, can these two products be promoted together? Are there more such combinations? How can we find such links or affinities?

Pursue another example, mentioned above. For a telephone company, finding out if residential customers have fax machines is a useful proposition. Why? If a residential customer uses a fax machine, then that customer may either want a second line or want to have some kind of upgrade. By analyzing the relationships between two phone numbers established by the calls along with other stipulations, the desired information can be discovered. Link analysis algorithms discover such combinations. Depending upon the types of knowledge discovery, link analysis techniques have three types of applications: associations discovery, sequential pattern discovery, and similar time sequence discovery. Let us briefly discuss each of these applications.

Associations Discovery Associations are affinities between items. Associations discovery algorithms find combinations where the presence of one item suggests the presence of another. When you apply these algorithms to the shopping transactions at a supermarket, they will uncover affinities among products that are likely to be purchased together. Association rules represent such affinities. The algorithms derive the association rules systematically and efficiently. Figure 17-14 presents an association rule and the annotated parts of the rule. The two parts—the support factor and the confidence factor—indicate the strength of the association. Rules with high support and confidence factor values are more valid, relevant, and useful. Simplicity makes associations discovery a popular data mining algorithm. There are only two factors to be interpreted and even these tend to be intuitive for interpretation. Because the technique essentially involves counting the combinations as the dataset is read repeatedly each time new dimensions are added, scaling does pose a major problem.

Sequential Pattern Discovery As the name implies, these algorithms discover patterns where one set of items follows another specific set. The time element plays a role in these patterns. When you select records for analysis, you must have date and time as data items to enable discovery of sequential patterns.

Let us say you want the algorithm to discover the buying sequence of products. The sales transactions form the dataset for the data mining operation. The data elements in the sales transactions may consist of date and time of transaction, products bought during the transaction, and the identification of the customer who bought the items. A sample set of these transactions and the results of applying the algorithm are shown in Figure 17-15. Notice the discovery of the sequential pattern. Also notice the support factor that gives an indication of the relevance of the association.

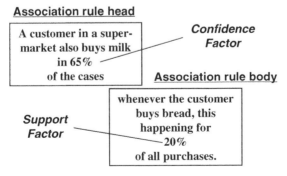

Figure 17-14 An association rule.

SALE DATE	NAME OF CUSTOMER	PRODUCTS PURCHASED
Nov. 15, 2000	John Brown	Desktop PC, MP3 Player
Nov. 15, 2000	Cindy Silverman	Desktop PC, MP3 Player, Digital Camera
Nov. 15, 2000	Robert Stone	Laptop PC
Dec. 19, 2000	Terry Goldsmith	Laptop PC
Dec. 19, 2000	John Brown	Digital Camera
Dec. 19, 2000	Terry Goldsmith	Digital Camera
Dec. 19, 2000	Robert Stone	Digital Camera
Dec. 20, 2000	Cindy Silverman	Tape Backup Drive
Dec. 20, 2000	Richard McKeown	Desktop PC, MP3 Player

**Transaction
Data File**

**Sequential Patterns –
Customer Sequence**

NAME OF CUSTOMER	PRODUCT SEQUENCE FOR CUSTOMER
John Brown	Desktop PC, MP3 Player, Digital Camera
Cindy Silverman	Desktop PC, MP3 Player, Digital Camera, Tape Backup Drive
Robert Stone	Laptop PC, Digital Camera
Terry Goldsmith	Laptop PC, Digital Camera
Richard McKeown	Desktop PC, MP3 Player

**Sequential
Pattern
Discovery with
Support
Factors**

SEQUENTIAL PATTERNS (Support Factor > 60%)	SUPPORTING CUSTOMERS
Desktop PC, MP3 Player	John Brown, Cindy Silverman, Richard McKeown

SEQUENTIAL PATTERNS (Support Factor > 40%)	SUPPORTING CUSTOMERS
Desktop PC, MP3 Player, Digital Camera	John Brown, Cindy Silverman
Laptop PC, Digital Camera	Robert Stone, Terry Goldsmith

Figure 17-15   Sequential pattern discovery.

Typical discoveries include associations of the following types:

- Purchase of a digital camera is followed by purchase of a color printer 60% of the time.
- Purchase of a desktop is followed by purchase of a tape backup drive 65% of the time.
- Purchase of window curtains is followed by purchase of living room furniture 50% of the time.

Similar Time Sequence Discovery   This technique depends on the availability of time sequences. In the previous technique, the results indicate sequential events over time. This technique, however, finds a sequence of events and then comes up with other similar sequences of events. For example, in retail department stores, this data mining technique comes up with a second department that has a sales stream similar to the first. Finding similar sequential price movements of stock is another application of this technique.

Neural Networks

Neural networks mimic the human brain by learning from a training dataset and applying the learning to generalize patterns for classification and prediction. These algorithms are effective when the data is shapeless and lacks any apparent pattern. The basic unit of an artificial neural network is modeled after the neurons in the brain. This unit is known as a node and is one of the two main structures of the neural network model. The other structure is the link that corresponds to the connection between neurons in the brain. Figure 17-16 illustrates the neural network model.

Let us consider a simple example to understand how a neural network makes a prediction. The neural network receives values of the variables or predictors at the input nodes.

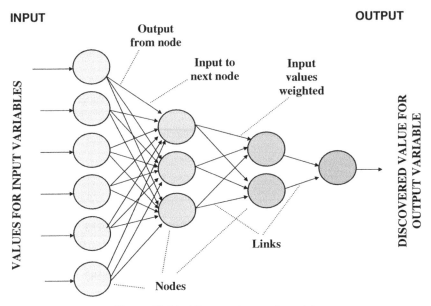

Figure 17-16 The neural network model.

If there are 15 different predictors, then there are 15 input nodes. Weights may be applied to the predictors to condition them properly. Figure 17-17 shows the working of a neural network. There may be several inner layers operating on the predictors and they move from node to node until the discovered result is presented at the output node. The inner layers are also known as hidden layers because as the input dataset is running through many iterations, the inner layers rehash the predictors over and over again.

Genetic Algorithms

In a way, genetic algorithms have something in common with neural networks. This technique also has its basis in biology. It is said that evolution and natural selection promote

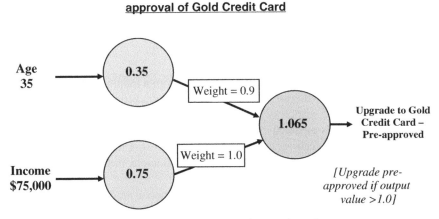

Figure 17-17 How a neural network works.

the survival of the fittest. Over generations, the process propagates the genetic material in the fittest individuals from one generation to the next. Genetic algorithms apply the same principles to data mining. This technique uses a highly iterative process of selection, cross-over, and mutation operators to evolve successive generations of models. At each iteration, every model competes with every other by inheriting traits from previous ones until only the most predictive model survives.

Let us try to understand the evolution of successive generations in genetic algorithms by using a very popular example used by many authors. This is the problem to be solved: Your company is doing a promotional mailing and wants to include free coupons in the mailing. Remember, this is a promotional mailing with the goal of increasing profits. At the same time, the promotional mailing must not produce the opposite result of lost revenue. This is the question: What is the optimum number of coupons to be placed in each mailer to maximize profits?

At first blush, it looks like mailing out as many coupons as possible might be the solution. Will this not enable the customers to use all the available coupons and maximize profits? However, some other factors seem to complicate the problem. First, the more coupons in the mailer, the higher the postal costs are going to be. The increased mailing costs will eat into the profits. Second, if you do not send enough coupons, every coupon not in the mailer is a coupon that is not used. This is lost opportunity and potential loss in revenue. Finally, too many coupons in a mailer may turn the customer off and he or she may not use any at all. All these factors reinforce the need to arrive at an optimum number of coupons in each mailer. Figure 17-18 shows the first three generations of the evolution represented by the genetic algorithm applied to the problem.

Let us examine the figure. Each simulated organism has a gene that indicates the organism's best guess at the number of coupons per mailer. Notice the four organisms in the first generation. For two of the organisms, the gene or the estimated number of coupons is abnormal. Therefore, these two organisms do not survive. Remember, only the fittest survive. Note how these two instances are crossed out. Now the remaining two surviving organisms reproduce similar replicas of themselves with distinct genes. Again, remember

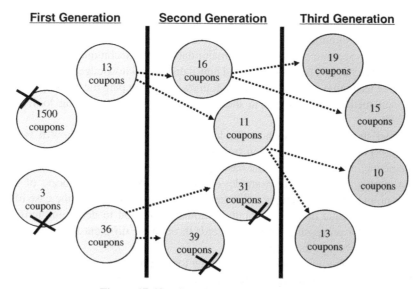

Figure 17-18   Genetic algorithm generations.

that genes represent the numbers of potential coupons in a mailer. The norm is reset at every generation and the process of evolution continues. In every generation, the fittest organisms survive and the evolution continues until there is only one final survivor. That has the gene representing the optimal number of coupons per mailer.

Of course, the above example is too simplistic. We have not explained how the numbers are generated in each generation. Also, we have not indicated how the norms are set and how you eliminate the abnormal organisms. There are complex calculations for performing these functions. Nevertheless, the example gives you a fairly good overview of the technique.

Moving into Data Mining

You now have sufficient knowledge to look in the right direction and help your company get into data mining and reap the benefits. What are the initial steps? How should your company get started in this attractive technology? First of all, remember that your data warehouse is going to feed the data mining processes. Whatever the reasons your company has for using data mining technology, the data source is your data warehouse. Before getting into data mining, a sound and solid data warehouse will put the data mining operation on a strong foundation.

As mentioned earlier, data mining techniques produce good results when large volumes of data are available. Almost all the algorithms need data at the lowest grain. Consider having data at the detailed level in your data warehouse. Another important point refers to the quality of the data. Data mining is about discovering patterns and relationships from data. Mining dirty data leads to inaccurate discoveries. Actions taken based on dubious discoveries will produce seriously wrong consequences. Data mining projects can run up the project costs. You cannot afford to launch into the technology if the data is not clean enough. Ensure that the data warehouse holds high-quality data.

When you apply a data mining technique, it is nice to discover a few interesting patterns and relationships. But what is your company going to do with the discoveries? If the discovered patterns and relationships are not actionable, it is a wasted effort. Before embarking on a data mining project, have clear ideas of the types of problems you expect to solve and the types of benefits you expect to obtain. After firming up the objectives, what next? You need a way of comparing the data mining algorithms and selecting the tool most appropriate for your specific requirements.

In the previous section, we covered the major data mining techniques. You learnt about each individual technique, how it works, and how it discovers knowledge. But the discussion dealt with one technique at a time. Is there a framework to compare the techniques? Is there a comparison method to help you in the selection of your data mining tool? Look at Figure 17-19.

The model structure refers to how the technique is perceived, not how it is actually implemented. For example, a decision tree model may actually be implemented through SQL statements. In the framework, the basic process is the process performed by the particular data mining technique. For example, decision trees perform the process of splitting at decision points. How a technique validates the model is important. In the case of neural networks, the technique does not contain a validation method to determine termination. The model calls for processing the input records through the different layers of nodes and terminate the discovery at the output node.

When you are looking for a tool, a data mining tool supporting more than one technique is worth consideration. Your organization may not presently need a composite tool with

Data Mining Technique	Underlying Structure	Basic Process	Validation Method
Cluster Detection	Distance calculations in n-vector space	Grouping of values in the same neighborhood	Cross validation to verify accuracy
Decision Trees	Binary Tree	Splits at decision points based on entropy	Cross validation
Memory-based Reasoning	Predictive structure based on distance and combination functions	Association of unknown instances with known instances	Cross validation
Link Analysis	Based on linking of variables	Discover links among variables by their values	Not applicable
Neural Networks	Forward propagation network	Weighted inputs of predictors at each node	Not applicable
Genetic Algorithms	Not applicable	Survival of the fittest on mutation of derived values	Mostly cross validation

Figure 17-19   Framework for comparing techniques.

many techniques. A multitasking tool opens up more possibilities. Moreover, many data mining analysts desire to cross-validate discovered patterns using several techniques. The most available techniques supported by vendor tools in the market today include the following:

- Cluster detection
- Decision trees
- Link analysis
- Data visualization

Before we get into a detailed list of criteria for selecting data mining tools, let us make a few general but important observations about tool selection. Please consider these tips carefully:

- The tool must be able to integrate well with your data warehouse environment by accepting data from the warehouse and be compatible with the overall metadata framework.
- The patterns and relationships discovered must be as accurate as possible. Discovering erratic patterns is more dangerous than not discovering any patterns at all.
- In most cases, you would need an explanation for the working of the model and know how the results were produced. The tool must be able to explain the rules and how the patterns were discovered.

Let us complete this section with a list of criteria for evaluating data mining tools. The list is by no means exhaustive, but it covers the essential points.

Data Access. The data mining tool must be able to access data sources such as the data warehouse and quickly bring over the required datasets to its environment. On many occasions you may need data from other sources to augment the data extracted from the data warehouse. The tool must be capable of reading other data sources and input formats.

Data Selection. While selecting and extracting data for mining, the tool must be able to perform its operations according to a variety of criteria. Selection abilities must include filtering out of unwanted data and deriving new data items from existing ones.

Sensitivity to Data Quality. Because of its importance, data quality is worth mentioning again. The data mining tool must be sensitive to the quality of the data it mines. The tool must be able to recognize missing or incomplete data and compensate for the problem. The tool must also be able to produce error reports.

Data Visualization. Data mining techniques process substantial data volumes and produce a wide range of results. Inability to display results graphically and diagrammatically diminishes the value of the tool severely. Select tools with good data visualization capabilities.

Extensibility. The tool architecture must be able to integrate with the data warehouse administration and other functions such as data extraction and metadata management.

Performance. The tool must provide consistent performance irrespective of the amount of data to be mined, the specific algorithm applied, the number of variables specified, and the level of accuracy demanded.

Scalability. Data mining needs to work with large volumes of data to discover meaningful and useful patterns and relationships. Therefore, ensure that the tool scales up to handle huge data volumes.

Openness. This is a desirable feature. Openness refers to being able to integrate with the environment and other types of tools. Look for the ability of the tool to connect to external applications where users could gain access to data mining algorithms from other applications. The tool must be able to share the output with desktop tools such as graphical displays, spreadsheets, and database utilities. The feature of openness must also include availability of the tool on leading server platforms.

Suite of Algorithms. Select a tool that provides a few different algorithms rather than one that supports only a single data mining algorithm.

DATA MINING APPLICATIONS

You will find a wide variety of applications benefiting from data mining. The technology encompasses a rich collection of proven techniques that cover a wide range of applications in both the commercial and noncommercial realms. In some cases, multiple techniques are used, back to back, to greater advantage. You may apply a cluster detection technique to identify clusters of customers. Then you may follow with a predictive algorithm applied to some of the identified clusters and discover the expected behavior of the customers in those clusters.

Noncommercial use of data mining is strong and pervasive in the research area. In oil exploration and research, data mining techniques discover locations suitable for drilling because of potential mineral and oil deposits. Pattern discovery and matching techniques have military applications in assisting to identify targets. Medical research is a field ripe for data mining. The technology helps researchers with discoveries of correlations between diseases and patient characteristics. Crime investigation agencies use the technology to connect criminal profiles to crimes. In astronomy and cosmology, data mining helps predict cosmic events.

The scientific community makes use of data mining to a moderate extent, but the technology has widespread applications in the commercial arena. Most of the tools target the commercial sector. Review the following list of a few major applications of data mining in the business area:

Customer Segmentation. This is one of the most widespread applications. Businesses use data mining to understand their customers. Cluster detection algorithms discover clusters of customers sharing the same characteristics.

Market Basket Analysis. This is a very useful application for retail. Link analysis algorithms uncover affinities between products that are bought together. Other businesses such as upscale auction houses use these algorithms to find customers to whom they can sell higher-value items.

Risk Management. Insurance companies and mortgage businesses use data mining to uncover risks associated with potential customers.

Fraud Detection. Credit card companies use data mining to discover abnormal spending patterns of customers. Such patterns can expose fraudulent use of the cards.

Delinquency Tracking. Loan companies use the technology to track customers who are likely to default on repayments.

Demand Prediction. Retail and other businesses use data mining to match demand and supply trends to forecast demand for specific products.

Benefits of Data Mining

By now you are convinced of the strengths and usefulness of data mining technology. Without data mining, useful knowledge lying buried in the mountains of data in many organizations would never be discovered and the benefits from using the discovered patterns and relationships would not be realized. What are the types of such benefits? We have already touched upon the applications of data mining and you have grasped the implied benefits.

Just to appreciate the enormous utility of data mining, let us enumerate the types of benefits. The list that follows identifies the types of benefits actually realizable in real-world situations:

- In a large company manufacturing consumer goods, the shipping department regularly short-ships orders and hides the variations between the purchase orders and the freight bills. Data mining detects the criminal behavior by uncovering patterns of orders and premature inventory reductions.

- A mail order company improves direct mail promotions to prospects through more targeted campaigns.

- A supermarket chain improves earnings by rearranging the shelves based on discovery of affinities of products that sell together.
- An airlines company increases sales to business travelers by discovering traveling patterns of frequent flyers.
- A department store hikes the sales in specialty departments by anticipating sudden surges in demand.
- A national health insurance provider saves large amounts of money by detecting fraudulent claims.
- A major banking corporation with investment and financial services increases the leverage of direct marketing campaigns. Predictive modeling algorithms uncover clusters of customers with high lifetime values.
- A manufacturer of diesel engines increases sales by forecasting sales of engines based on patterns discovered from historical data of truck registrations.
- A major bank prevents loss by detecting early warning signs for attrition in its checking account business.
- A catalog sales company doubles its holiday sales from the previous year by predicting which customers will use the holiday catalog.

Applications in CRM (Customer Relationship Management)

Customers interact with an enterprise in many ways. CRM is an umbrella term to include the management of all customer interactions so as to improve the profitability derivable from such interactions. CRM applications making use of data mining are known as analytic CRM. Analytic CRM is not confined to one industry. As it is applicable to all industries across the board, the data mining applications of analytic CRM has very broad appeal.

In general, the interactions with customers in an organization happen throughout the three phases of the customer life cycle:

- Acquisition of a customer
- Value enhancement of a customer
- Retention of a customer

Data mining applications of analytic CRM relate to all three phases of the customer life cycle.

Acquisition of a Customer In this first phase, you need to identify prospects and convert them into customers. A time-honored proven method for acquiring new customers has been the direct mail campaign. In fact, businesses conduct several direct mail campaigns in a year. When mailings are sent to prospective customers, only a small fraction of the prospects show interest and respond. The rate of return from the mailings may be increased if you are able to identify good prospects to whom you can target your mailings. Data mining is effective in identifying such good prospects and help focus the marketing efforts much more cost effectively.

Value Enhancement of a Customer The value of a customer to an enterprise is based on the purchases of goods and services by that customer. How can you increase the value of a customer? By selling more to the customer. You may try to increase the volume of the same goods and services the customer normally purchases from your enterprise. Also, if you are able to identify the additional goods and services the customer is likely to buy based on his usual purchases, then you may offer these additional items to the customer. This is known as cross-selling. In both cases, you may run appropriate marketing promotions. Data mining is effective to identify customers and products for such promotions. Another way in which data mining can help in promotions is to personalize your marketing effort. When a customer goes to your Web site to order a product, with the use of data mining that customer can receive a personal greeting and be presented with the specials and other related products he or she is likely to be interested in.

Retention of a Customer   For most companies, the cost of acquiring a new customer exceeds the cost of retaining a good customer. If the attrition rate in your company is high, say, 10%, then 100 of your 1000 customers leave each month. At a minimum, you need to replace these 100 customers every month. The customer acquisition costs could be quite high. This situation calls for a good customer attrition management program. For your attrition management program, you would need to identify in advance every month those 100 customers who are likely to leave. Next you need to know who of these 100 likely candidates are "good" customers providing value to your company. Then you may target these "good" customers with special promotions to entice them to stay. Data mining can be effective in customer attrition management programs.

Applications in the Retail Industry

Let us discuss very briefly how the retail industry makes use of data mining and benefits from it. Fierce competition and narrow profit margins have plagued the retail industry. Forced by these factors, the retail industry adopted data warehousing earlier than most other industries. Over the years, these data warehouses have accumulated huge volumes of data. The data warehouses in many retail businesses are mature and ripe. Also, through the use of scanners and cash registers, the retail industry has been able to capture detailed point-of-sale data.

The combination of the two features—huge volumes of data and low-granularity data—is ideal for data mining. The retail industry was able to begin using data mining while others were just making plans. All types of businesses in the retail industry, including grocery chains, consumer retail chains, and catalog sales companies, use direct marketing campaigns and promotions extensively. Direct marketing happens to be quite critical in the industry. All companies depend heavily on direct marketing.

Direct marketing involves targeting campaigns and promotions to specific customer segments. Cluster detection and other predictive data mining algorithms provide customer segmentation. As this is a crucial area for the retail industry, many vendors offer data mining tools for customer segmentation. These tools can be integrated with the data warehouse at the back end for data selection and extraction. At the front end these tools work well with standard presentation software. Customer segmentation tools discover clusters and predict success rates for direct marketing campaigns.

Retail industry promotions necessarily require knowledge of which products to promote and in what combinations. Retailers use link analysis algorithms to find affinities among products that usually sell together. As you already know, this is market basket analysis. Based on the affinity grouping, retailers can plan their special sale items and also the arrangement of products on the shelves.

Apart from customer segmentation and market basket analysis, retailers use data mining for inventory management. Inventory for a retailer encompasses thousands of products. Inventory turnover and management are significant concerns for these businesses. Another area of use for data mining in the retail industry relates to sales forecasting. Retail sales are subject to strong seasonal fluctuations. Holidays and weekends also make a difference. Therefore, sales forecasting is critical for the industry. The retailers turn to the predictive algorithms of data mining technology for sales forecasting.

What are the other types of data mining uses in the retail industry? What are the questions and concerns the industry is interested in? Here is a short list:

- Customer long-term spending patterns
- Customer purchasing frequency
- Best types of promotions
- Store plan and arrangement of promotional displays
- Planning mailers with coupons
- Types of customers buying special offerings
- Sales trends, seasonal and regular
- Manpower planning based on busy times
- Most profitable segments in the customer base

Applications in the Telecommunications Industry

The next industry we want to look at for data mining applications is telecommunications. This industry was deregulated in the 1990s. In the United States, the cellular alternative changed the landscape dramatically, although the wave had already hit Europe and a few pockets in Asia earlier. Against the background of an extremely competitive marketplace, the companies scrambled to find methods to understand their customers. Customer retention and customer acquisition have become top priorities in their marketing. Telecommunications companies compete with one another to design the best offerings and entice customers. No wonder this climate of competitive pressures has driven telecommunications companies to data mining. All the leading companies have already adopted the technology and are reaping many benefits. Several data mining vendors and consulting companies specialize in the problems of this industry.

Customer churn is of serious concern. How many times a week do you get cold calls from telemarketing representatives in this industry? Many data mining vendors offer products to contain customer churn. The newer cellular phone market experiences the highest churn rate. Some experts estimate the total cost of acquiring a single new customer is as high as $500.

Problem areas in the communications network are potential disasters. In today's competitive market, customers are tempted to switch at the slightest problem. Customer retention under such circumstances becomes very fragile. A few data mining vendors specialize in data visualization products for the industry. These products flash alert signs on the network maps to indicate potential problem areas, enabling the employees responsible to take preventive action.

Below is a general list of questions and concerns of the industry where data mining applications are helping:

- Retention of customers in the face of enticing competition
- Customer behavior indicating increased line usage in the future
- Discovery of profitable service packages
- Customers most likely to churn
- Prediction of cellular fraud
- Promotion of additional products and services to existing customers
- Factors that increase the customer's propensity to use the phone
- Product evaluation compared to the competition

Applications in Biotechnology

In the last decade or so, biotech companies have risen and progressed to the leading edge. They have been busy accumulating enormous volumes of data. It has become increasingly difficult to rely on older techniques to make sense of the mountains of data and derive useful results. No wonder the biotech industry is leaning towards the use of data mining to find patterns and relationships from the tons of available data. Data mining techniques have become indispensable components in today's biological research.

We cannot touch upon all the numerous data mining applications in biotechnology. Several textbooks and journal articles deal with such applications in detail. For our purposes here, we will briefly observe a few biotechnology applications supported by data mining.

Data Mining in the Biopharmaceutical Industry   This industry collects huge amounts of biological data of various types. A sample of these types of data would include clinical trial results, annotated databases of disease profiles, chemical structures of combinatorial libraries of compounds, molecular pathways to sequences, structure–activity relationships, and so on. Data mining has become the centerpiece to deal with the information overload.

The biopharmaceutical industry is generating much more biological and chemical data than the industry knows what to do with. Accordingly, deciding which target and lead compound to develop further is long, tedious, and expensive. Data mining is brought in to address this situation and enables the users to make better use of the collected data and improve the bottom line for the company. Several vendors offer data mining tools and services specifically for the biopharmaceutical industry.

Data mining applications for the biopharmaceutical industry generally fall into the following major approaches based on the category of biological data analysis desired.

Influence-Based Mining. In this case, complex data in large databases are scanned for influences between specific sets of data along several dimensions. Usually, this type of data mining is applied where there are significant cause-and-effect relationships between the data sets. An example of this would be large and multivariant gene expression studies.

Affinity-Based Mining. This case is similar to influence-based mining in that data in large and complex data sets is analyzed across several dimensions. However, in this case the mining technique identifies data points or sets that have affinity for one another and tend to be grouped together. This approach is useful in biological motif analysis for distinguishing accidental motifs from motifs with biological significance.

Time-Delay Mining. In this case, the subject data set is not available immediately in complete form. The set is collected over time and the mining technique identifies patterns that are confirmed or rejected as the data set increases and become more robust over time. This approach is useful for analysis of long-term clinical trials.

Trends-Based Mining. In this case, the mining technique analyzes large data sets for changes or trends over time in specific data sets. Changes are expected to occur because of cause-and-effect considerations in experiments on responses to particular drugs or other stimuli over time. The responses are collected and analyzed.

Comparative Mining. This approach focuses on overlaying large, complex, and similar data sets for comparison. As an example, this is useful for clinical trial meta-analysis where data might have been collected at different sites, at different times, under similar but not necessarily exactly the same conditions. The objective is to find dissimilarities, not similarities.

Data Mining in Drug Design and Production   Data mining is becoming more and more useful for pharmaceutical companies in design and production of prescription and generic drugs. By and large, drug manufacturing processes may be categorized into two methods: synthetic and fermentation. Data mining is used by manufacturers in both methods. Let us briefly note how data mining assists in these two methods of production.

Synthetic Method. Generally the production is guided by a production flowchart usually consisting of many steps. In the initial step of the production process, you begin with the raw material. At the subsequent steps the raw material is converted into a series of intermediary products through a number of chemical reactions with other compounds. The yield of the process is the quantity of product per unit of raw material used. The goal of the optimal production process is to increase the yield. In this synthetic method of production, the production process is usually very long with numerous steps. At each step, you obtain an intermediate yield, and at the end you get the overall yield. Even if you are able to increase the intermediate yield at each step by a reasonable percentage, your final yield will increase dramatically. So, it is important to find ways to increase the intermediate yields at each step. Data mining is used to work on the chemical synthesis data in each step to find the best conditions for yield enhancement at that step. Data mining has helped to optimize chemical processes involving organic chemical reactions resulting in great economic benefits to manufacturers.

Fermentation Method. Processes using this method produce drugs such as antibiotics in a fermentation tank. Generally fermentation processes are very sensitive to numerous affecting factors. As such, fermentation processes are too complicated. It is extremely difficult to find an optimization model to improve the overall production yield. Data mining assists the production process by determining the most optimal operation parameters to increase the overall yield significantly.

Data Mining in Genomics and Proteomics   In today's biotech environment, post-genomic science and its numerous studies are producing mountains of high-dimensional data. All this data will remain as mere data unless patterns and relationships—in fact, knowledge—are discovered from the data and used effectively. An encouraging phenomenon is the rapidly increasing use of data mining at all levels of genomics and proteomics.

Genomics is the branch of genetics that studies organisms in terms of their genomes. Proteomics, on the other hand, is the branch of genetics that studies the full set of proteins encoded by a genome. As you know, in recent years, both branches of genetics have gained enormous importance and are areas of intensive research. Already there are several applications of data mining to studies in genomics and proteomics. There is a concerted effort in the scientific community pushing for more sophisticated data mining approaches to genomics and proteomics.

Applications in Banking and Finance

This is another industry where you will find heavy usage of data mining. Banking has been reshaped by regulations in the past few years. Mergers and acquisitions are more pronounced in banking and banks have been expanding the scope of their services. Finance is an area of fluctuation and uncertainty. The banking and finance industry is fertile ground for data mining. Banks and financial institutions generate large volumes of detailed transactions data. Such data is suitable for data mining.

Data mining applications at banks are quite varied. Fraud detection, risk assessment of potential customers, trend analysis, and direct marketing are the primary data mining applications at banks.

In the financial area, requirements for forecasting dominate. Forecasting of stock prices and commodity prices with a high level of approximation can mean large profits. Forecasting of potential financial disaster can prove to be very valuable. Neural network algorithms are used in forecasting, options and bond trading, portfolio management, and in mergers and acquisitions.

CHAPTER SUMMARY

- Decision support systems have progressed to data mining.
- Data mining, which is knowledge discovery, is data-driven, whereas other analysis techniques such as OLAP are user-driven.
- The knowledge discovery process in data mining uncovers relationships and patterns not readily known to exist.
- Six distinct steps comprise the knowledge discovery process.
- In information retrieval and discovery, OLAP and data mining can be considered to be complementary as well as different.
- The data warehouse is the best source of data for a data mining operation.
- Major common data mining techniques are cluster detection, decision trees, memory-based reasoning, link analysis, neural networks, and genetic algorithms.

REVIEW QUESTIONS

1. Give three broad reasons why you think data mining is being used in today's businesses.
2. Define data mining in two or three sentences.

3. Name the major phases of a data mining operation. Of these phases, pick two and describe the types of activities in them.

4. How is data mining different from OLAP? Explain briefly.

5. Is the data warehouse a prerequisite for data mining? Does the data warehouse help data mining? If so, in what ways?

6. Briefly describe the cluster detection technique.

7. How does the memory-based reasoning (MBR) technique work? What is the underlying principle?

8. Name the three common applications of the link analysis technique.

9. Do neural networks and genetic algorithms have anything in common? Point out a few differences.

10. What is market basket analysis? Give two examples of this application in business.

EXERCISES

1. Match the columns:

1. knowledge discovery process	**A.**	reveals reasons for the discovery
2. OLAP	**B.**	neural networks
3. cluster detection	**C.**	distance function
4. decision trees	**D.**	feeds data for mining
5. link analysis	**E.**	data-driven
6. hidden layers	**F.**	fraud detection
7. genetic algorithms	**G.**	user-driven
8. data warehouse	**H.**	forms groups
9. MBR	**I.**	highly iterative
10. banking application	**J.**	associations discovery

2. As a data mining consultant, you are hired by a large commercial bank that provides many financial services. The bank already has a data warehouse that it rolled out two years ago. The management wants to find the existing customers who are most likely to respond to a marketing campaign offering new services. Outline the knowledge discovery process, list the phases, and indicate the activities in each phase.

3. Describe how decision trees work. Choose an example and explain how this knowledge discovery process works.

4. What are the basic principles of genetic algorithms? Give an example. Use the example to describe how this technique works.

5. In your project you are responsible for analyzing the requirements and selecting a toolset for data mining. Make a list of the criteria you will use for the toolset selection. Briefly explain why each criterion is necessary.

PART 6

IMPLEMENTATION AND MAINTENANCE

CHAPTER 18

THE PHYSICAL DESIGN PROCESS

CHAPTER OBJECTIVES

- Distinguish between physical design and logical design as applicable to the data warehouse
- Study the steps in the physical design process in detail
- Understand physical design considerations and know the implications
- Grasp the role of storage considerations in physical design
- Examine indexing techniques for the data warehouse environment
- Review and summarize all performance enhancement options

As an IT professional, you are familiar with logical and physical models. You have probably worked with the transformation of a logical model into a physical model. You also know that completing the physical model has to be tied to the details of the computing platform, the database software, hardware, and any third-party tools.

As you know, in an OLTP system you have to perform a number of tasks for completing the physical model. The logical model forms the primary basis from which the physical model is derived. But, in addition, a number of factors must be considered before you can get to the physical model. You must determine where to place the database objects in physical storage. What is the storage medium and what are its features? This information helps you define the storage parameters. Then you have to plan for indexing, an important consideration. On which columns in each table must the indexes be built? You need to look into other methods for improving performance. You have to examine the initialization parameters in the DBMS and decide how to set them. Similarly, in the data warehouse environment, you need to consider many different factors to complete the physical model.

Data Warehousing Fundamentals for IT Professionals, Second Edition. By Paulraj Ponniah
Copyright © 2010 John Wiley & Sons, Inc.

We have considered the logical model for the data warehouse in sufficient detail. You have mastered the dimensional modeling technique that helps you design the logical model. In this chapter, we will use the logical model of a data warehouse to develop and complete the physical model. Physical design gets the work of the project team closer to implementation and deployment. Every task so far has brought the project to the grand logical model. Now, physical design moves it to the next significant phases.

PHYSICAL DESIGN STEPS

Figure 18-1 is a pictorial representation of the steps in the physical design process for a data warehouse. Note the steps indicated in the figure. In the following subsections, we will broadly describe the activities within these steps. You will understand how at the end of the process you arrive at the completed physical model. After the end of this section, the rest of the chapter elaborates on all the crucial aspects of the physical design.

Develop Standards

Many companies invest a lot of time and money to prescribe standards for information systems. The standards range from how to name the fields in the database to how to conduct interviews with the user departments for requirements definition. A group in IT is designated to keep the standards up to date. In some companies, every revision must be updated and authorized by the CIO. Through the standards group, the CIO ensures that the standards are followed correctly and strictly. Usually the practice is to publish the standards on the company's intranet. If your IT department is one of the progressive ones giving due attention to standards, then be happy to embrace and adapt the standards for the data warehouse.

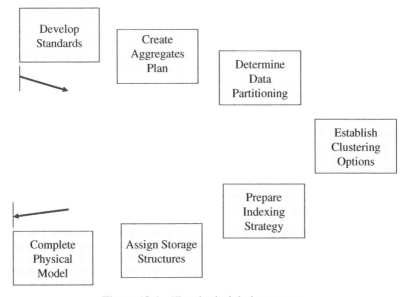

Figure 18-1   The physical design process.

In the data warehouse environment, the scope of the standards expands to include additional areas. Standards ensure consistency across the various areas. If you have the same way of indicating names of the database objects, then you are leaving less room for ambiguity. Let us say the standards in your company require the name of an object to be a concatenation of multiple words separated by dashes and that the first word in the group indicates the business subject. With these standards, as soon as someone reads an object name, that person can know the business subject.

Standards take on greater importance in the data warehouse environment. This is because the use of the object names is not confined to the IT department. Users will also be referring to the objects by names when they formulate and run their own queries. As standards are quite significant, we will come back to them a little later in this chapter. Now let us move on to the next step in the physical design.

Create Aggregates Plan

Let us say that in your environment more than 80% of the queries ask for summary information. If your data warehouse stores data only at the lowest level of granularity, every such query has to read through all the detailed records and sum them up. Consider a query looking for total sales for the year, by product, for all the stores. If you have detailed records keeping sales by individual calendar dates, by product, and by store, then this query needs to read a large number of detailed records. So, what is the best method to improve performance in cases like this? If you have higher levels of summary tables of products by store, the query could run faster. But how many such summary tables must you create? What is the limit?

In this step, review the possibilities for building aggregate or summary tables. You get clues from the requirements definition. Look at each dimension table and examine the hierarchical levels. Which of these levels are more important for aggregation? Clearly assess the trade-off. What you need is a comprehensive plan for aggregation. The plan must spell out the exact types of aggregates you must build for each level of summarization. It is possible that many of the aggregates will be present in the OLAP system. If OLAP instances are not for universal use by all users, then the necessary aggregates must be present in the main warehouse. The aggregate database tables must be laid out and included in the physical model. We will have some more to say about summary levels in a later section.

Determine the Data Partitioning Scheme

Consider the data volumes in the warehouse. What about the number of rows in a fact table? Let us make some rough calculations. Assume there are four dimension tables with 50 rows each on average. Even with this limited number of dimension table rows, the potential number of fact table rows exceeds six million. Fact tables are generally very large. Large tables are not easy to manage. During the load process, the entire table must be closed to users. Again, back up and recovery of large tables pose difficulties because of their sheer sizes. Partitioning divides large database tables into manageable parts.

Always consider partitioning options for fact tables. It is not just the decision to partition that counts. Based on your environment, the real decision is about how exactly to partition the fact tables. Your data warehouse may be a conglomerate of conformed data marts. You must consider partitioning options for each fact table. Should some be partitioned vertically and the others horizontally? You may find that some of your dimension tables are also candidates for partitioning. Product dimension tables are especially large. Examine each of your dimension tables and determine which of these must be partitioned.

In this step, come up with a definite partitioning scheme. The scheme must include:

- The fact tables and the dimension tables selected for partitioning
- The type of partitioning for each table—horizontal or vertical
- The number of partitions for each table
- The criteria for dividing each table (for example, by product groups)
- A description of how to make queries aware of partitions

Establish Clustering Options

In the data warehouse, many of the data access patterns rely on sequential access of large quantities of data. Whenever you have this type of access and processing, you will realize much performance improvement from clustering. This technique involves placing and managing related units of data in the same physical block of storage. This arrangement causes the related units of data to be retrieved together in a single input operation.

You need to establish the proper clustering options before completing the physical model. Examine the tables, table by table, and find pairs that are related. This means that rows from the related tables are usually accessed together for processing in many cases. Then make plans to store the related tables close together in the same file on the storage medium. For two related tables, you may want to store the records from both files interleaved. A record from one table is followed by all the related records in the other table while storing in the same physical file.

Prepare an Indexing Strategy

This is a crucial step in the physical design. Unlike OLTP systems, the data warehouse is query-centric. As you know, indexing is perhaps the most effective mechanism for improving performance. A solid indexing strategy results in enormous benefits. The strategy must lay down the index plan for each table, indicating the columns selected for indexing. The sequence of the attributes in each index also plays a critical role in performance. Scrutinize the attributes in each table to determine which attributes qualify for bitmapped indexes.

Prepare a comprehensive indexing plan. The plan must indicate the indexes for each table. Further, for each table, present the sequence in which the indexes will be created. Describe the indexes that are expected to be built in the very first instance of the database. Many indexes can wait until you have monitored the data warehouse for some time. Spend enough time on the indexing plan.

Assign Storage Structures

Where do you want to place the data on the physical storage medium? What are the physical files? What is the plan for assigning each table to specific files? How do you want to divide each physical file into blocks of data? Answers to questions like these go into the data storage plan.

In an OLTP system, all data resides in the operational database. When you assign the storage structures in an OLTP system, your effort is confined to the operational tables accessed by the user applications. In a data warehouse, you are not just concerned with the physical files for the data warehouse tables. Your storage assignment plan must include other types of storage such as the temporary data extract files, the staging area, and any storage needed for front-end applications. Let the plan include all the types of storage structures in the various storage areas.

Complete Physical Model

This final step reviews and confirms the completion of the prior activities and tasks. By the time you reach this step, you have the standards for naming the database objects. You have determined which aggregate tables are necessary and how you are going to partition the large tables. You have completed the indexing strategy and have planned for other performance options. You also know where to put the physical files.

All the information from the prior steps enables you to complete the physical model. The result is the creation of the physical schema. You can code the data definition language statements (DDL) in the chosen RDBMS and create the physical structure in the data dictionary.

PHYSICAL DESIGN CONSIDERATIONS

We have traced the steps for the physical design of the data warehouse. Each step consists of specific activities that finally lead to the physical model. When you look back at the steps, one step relates to the physical storage structure and several others deal with the performance of the data warehouse. Physical storage and performance are significant factors. We will cover these two in sufficient depth later in the chapter.

In this section, we will firm up our understanding of the physical model itself. Let us review the components and track down what it takes to move from the logical model to the physical model. First, let us begin with the overall objectives of the physical design process.

Physical Design Objectives

When you perform the logical design of the database, your goal is to produce a conceptual model that reflects the information content of the real-world situation. The logical model represents the overall data components and the relationships. The objectives of the physical design process do not center on the structure. In physical design, you are getting closer to the operating systems, the database software, the hardware, and the computing platform. You are now more concerned about how the model is going to work than on how the model is going to look.

If you want to summarize, the major objectives of the physical design process are improving performance on the one hand, and improving the management of the stored data on the other. You base your physical design decisions on the usage of data. The frequency of access, the data volumes, the specific features supported by the chosen RDBMS, and the configuration of the storage medium influence the physical design decisions. You need to pay special attention to these factors and analyze each to produce an efficient physical model. Now let us present the significant objectives of physical design.

Improve Performance   Performance in an OLTP environment differs from that of a data warehouse in the online response times. Whereas a response time of less than three seconds is almost mandatory in an OLTP system, the expectation in a data warehouse is less stringent. Depending on the volume of data processed during a query, response times varying from a few seconds to a few minutes are reasonable. Let the users be aware of the difference in expectations. However, in today's data warehouse and OLAP environments, response time beyond a few minutes is not acceptable. Strive to improve performance to keep the response time at this level. Ensure that performance is monitored regularly and the data warehouse is kept fine-tuned.

Monitoring and improving performance must happen at different levels. At the foundational level, make sure attention is paid by appropriate staff to performance of the operating system. At the next level lies the performance of the DBMS. Monitoring and performance improvement at this level rests on the data warehouse administrator. The higher levels of logical database design, application design, and query formatting also contribute to the overall performance.

Ensure Scalability   This is a key objective. As we have seen, the usage of the data warehouse escalates over time, with a sharper increase during the initial period. We have discussed this supergrowth in some detail. During the supergrowth period, it is almost impossible to keep up with the steep rise in usage.

As you have already observed, the usage increases on two counts. The number of users increases rapidly and the complexity of the queries intensifies. As the number of users increases, the number of concurrent users of the data warehouse also increases proportionately. Adopt methods to address the escalation in the usage of the data warehouse on both counts.

Manage Storage   Why is managing storage a major objective of physical design? Proper management of stored data will boost performance. You can improve performance by storing related tables in the same file. You can manage large tables more easily by storing parts of the tables at different places in storage. You can set the space management parameters in the DBMS to optimize the use of file blocks.

Provide Ease of Administration   This objective covers the activities that make administration easy. For instance, ease of administration includes methods for proper arrangement of table rows in storage so that frequent reorganization is avoided. Another area for ease of administration is in the back up and recovery of database tables. Review the various data warehouse administration tasks. Make it easy for administration whenever it comes to working with storage or the DBMS.

Design for Flexibility   In terms of physical design, flexibility implies keeping the design open. As changes to the data model take place, it must be easy to propagate the changes to the physical model. Your physical design must have built-in flexibility to satisfy future requirements.

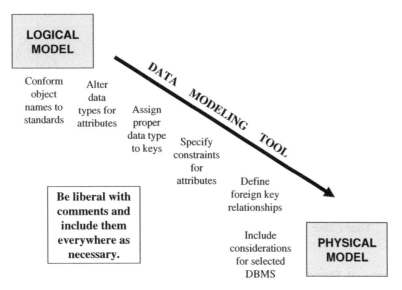

Figure 18-2   From logical model to physical model.

From Logical Model to Physical Model

In the logical model you have the tables, attributes, primary keys, and relationships. The physical model contains the structures and relationships represented in the database schema coded with the data definition language (DDL) of the DBMS. What are the activities that transform a logical model into a physical model? Figure 18-2 displays the activities marked alongside the arrow that follows the transformation process. At the end on the right side, notice the box indicated as the physical model.

This is the result of carrying out the activities mentioned alongside the arrow. Review this set of activities and adapt it for your data warehouse environment.

Physical Model Components

Having talked about the physical model in general terms and how to get to it through the physical design steps, let us now explore it in detail. The physical model represents the information content at a level closer to the hardware. That means you should have details such as file sizes, field lengths, data types, primary keys, and foreign keys all reflected in the model. Figure 18-3 indicates the major components of the physical model. Make note of the components, one by one. As you know, the components are described to the data dictionary (also known as the data catalog) of the DBMS through schemas and sub-schemas. You use the data definition language of the DBMS to write the schema definitions. Figure 18-4 gives you an example of schema definitions. Note the different types of schema statements. Notice the statements defining the database, the tables, and the columns within each table. Observe how data types and field sizes are defined. Those of you who have worked in database administration are quite familiar with the schema statements.

Let us tie it all together. Let us relate the components of the logical model to those of the physical model. Figure 18-5 presents such a combined view. Notice how these relate to the schema definition shown in Figure 18-4.

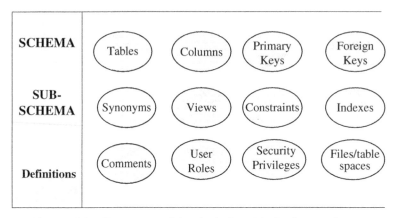

Figure 18-3 Components of the physical model of a data warehouse.

Significance of Standards

Standards in a data warehouse environment cover a wide range of objects, processes, and procedures. With regard to the physical model, the standards for naming the objects take on special significance. Standards provide a consistent means for communication. Effective communication must take place among the members of the project. In a data warehouse project, the presence of user representatives is more pronounced. As you know, users are more directly involved in accessing information from a data warehouse than they are in an OLTP environment. Clear communication with the users becomes more significant.

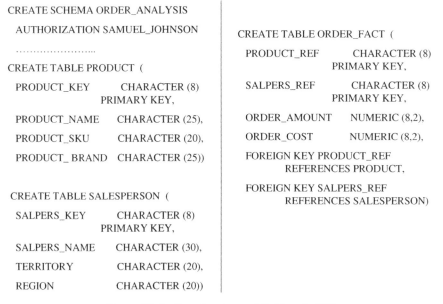

Figure 18-4 Sample schema definitions in SQL.

LOGICAL MODEL   **PHYSICAL MODEL**

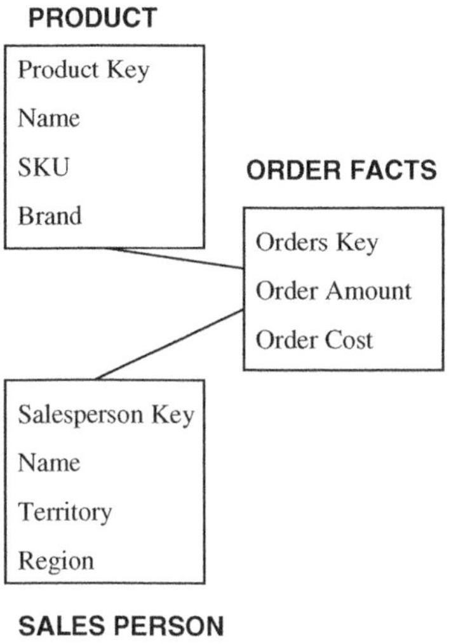

Table/Column Name	Data Type	Nulls allowed?	Comments
PRODUCT			Product dimension table including all of company's products
product_key	integer	N	Primary key
product_name		N	Name of product as used by marketing
product_sku		N	Stock Keeping Unit in source systems
product_brand		N	Name of brand as used by marketing
SALESPERSON			Sales Person dimension table includes all sales persons from all regions
salpers_key	integer	N	
salpers_name	char(30)	N	
territory	char(20)	N	
region	char(20)	N	
ORDER_FACT			Fact table containing metrics about all the orders received by the company
product_ref	integer	N	Partial primary key, also foreign key referencing product dimension table
salpers_ref	integer	N	Partial primary key, also foreign key referencing salesperson dimension table
order_amount	num (8,2)	N	Sales amount of order in dollars
order_cost	num (8,2)	N	Cost amount for the order in dollars

Figure 18-5   Logical model and physical model.

A few tips on standards follow.

Naming of Database Objects

Components of Object Names   Have a clear method for composing names of the objects. The name itself must be able to convey the meaning and description of the object. For example, look at the name of a column: customer_loan_balance. This naming convention immediately identifies the column as containing values of balance amounts. What type of balance amounts? Loan balances. Is it a total loan balance amount? Whose loan balance amount? The first word denotes that it is the customer balance and not total balance. Object names made up of multiple words generally convey the meanings better. You can standardize the function of each word in the group of words indicating the name. In our example, the first word denotes the primary subject, the third word the general class of the object, and the second word qualifies the class. Many companies adopt this type of naming standard. You may take the standard already in use in your company and enhance it for clarity and conciseness.

Word Separators   Standardize the separators that are also called the delineators. Dashes (-) or underscores (_) are commonly used. If your DBMS has specific conventions or requirements, follow those conventions.

Names in Logical and Physical Models   Names for objects such as tables and attributes may include both the logical model versions and the physical model versions. You need naming standards for both versions. More than the user community, IT professionals use the logical model names. Analysts and logical model designers communicate with each other through the logical model names. When the users need to refer to the tables and columns for data retrieval, they are communicating at the level of the physical model. Therefore, you need to adapt the standards for the physical model for the users. A better approach is to keep the logical and physical model versions of the name of a given object the same. If you need more qualifiers to further clarify the definition of the object, add them. Do not hesitate to have the definitions declared in business terminology.

Naming of Files and Tables in the Staging Area   As you know, the staging area is a busy place in the data warehouse environment. A lot of data movement happens there. You create many intermediary files from the data extracted from the source systems. You transform and consolidate data in this area. You prepare the load files in the staging area. Because of the number of files in the staging area, it is easy to lose track of them. In order to avoid confusion, you have to be clear about which files serve what purposes. It is necessary to adopt effective standards for naming the data structures in the staging area. Consider the following suggestions.

Indicate the Process   Identify the process to which the file relates. If the file is the output from a transformation step, let the name of the file denote that. If the file is part of the daily incremental update, let that be clear from the name of the file.

Express the Purpose   Suppose you are setting up the scheduling of the weekly update to the product dimension table. You need to know the input load file for this purpose. If the name of the file indicates the purpose for which it was created, that will be a big help when you are setting up the update schedule. Develop standards for the staging area files to include the purpose of the file in the name.

Examples   Given below are the names of a few files in the staging area. See if the following names are meaningful and the standards are adequate:

    sale_units_daily_stage
    customer_daily_update
    product_full_refresh
    order_entryinitial_extract
    all_sources_sales_extract
    customer_nameaddr_daily_update

Standards for Physical Files   Your standards must include naming conventions for all types of files. These files are not restricted to data and index files for the data warehouse database. There are other files as well. Establish standards for the following:

- Files holding source codes and scripts
- Database files
- Application documents

PHYSICAL STORAGE

Consider the processing of a query. After the query is verified for syntax and checked against the data dictionary for authorization, the DBMS translates the query statements to determine what data is requested. From the data entries about the tables, rows, and columns desired, the DBMS maps the requests to the physical storage where the data access take place. The query gets filtered down to physical storage and this is where the input operations begin. The efficiency of the data retrieval is closely tied to where the data is stored in physical storage and how it is stored there.

What are the various physical data structures in the storage area? What is the storage medium and what are its characteristics? Do the features of the medium support any efficient storage or retrieval techniques? We will explore answers to questions such as these. From the answers you will derive methods for improving performance. First, let us understand the types of data structures in the data warehouse.

Storage Area Data Structures

Take an overall look at all the data related to the data warehouse. First, you have the data in the staging area. Though you may look for efficiency in storage and loading, arrangement of the data in the staging area does not contribute to the performance of the data warehouse from the point of view of the users. Looking further, the other sets of data relate to the data content of the warehouse. These are the data and index tables in the data warehouse. How you arrange and store these tables definitely has an impact on the performance. Next you have the multidimensional data in the OLAP system. In most cases, the supporting proprietary software dictates the storage and the retrieval of data in the OLAP system.

Figure 18-6 shows the physical data structures in the data warehouse. Observe the different levels of data. Notice the detail and summary data structures. Think further how the data structures are implemented in physical storage as files, blocks, and records.

Optimizing Storage

You have reviewed the physical storage structures. When you break each data structure down to the physical storage level, you find that the structure is stored as files in the physical storage medium. Take the example of the customer dimension and the salesperson dimension tables. You have basically two choices for storing the data of these two dimension tables. Store records from each table in one physical file. Or, if the records from these tables are retrieved together most of the time, then store records from both the tables in a single physical file. In either case, records are stored in a file. A collection of records in a file forms a block. In other words, a file comprises blocks and each block contains records.

In this subsection, let us examine a few techniques for optimizing storage. Remember any optimizing at the physical level is tied to the features and functions available in the DBMS. You have to relate the techniques discussed here with the workings of your DBMS. Study the following optimizing techniques.

Set the Correct Block Size   As you understand, a set of records is stored in a block. What is special about the block? A data block in a file is the fundamental unit of input/output

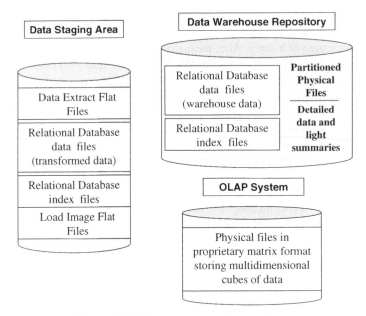

Figure 18-6   Data structures in the warehouse.

transfer from the database to memory where the data gets manipulated. Each block contains a block header that holds control information. The block header is not open to keeping data. Too many block headers means too much wasted space.

Assume that the block size for the customer file is 2 KB and that an average of 10 customer records can fit in a single block. Each DBMS has its own default block size—2 KB and 4 KB are common default block sizes. If the data records requested by a query reside in block number 10, then the operating system reads that entire block into memory to get the required data records.

What is the effect of increasing the block size in a file? More records or rows will fit into a single block. Because more records may be fetched in one read, larger block sizes decrease the number of reads. Another advantage relates to space utilization by the block headers. As a percentage of the space in a block, the block header occupies less space in a larger block. Therefore, overall, all the block headers put together occupy less space. But here is the downside of larger block sizes. Even when a smaller number of records are needed, the operating system reads too much extra information into memory, thereby impacting memory management.

However, because most data warehouse queries request large numbers of rows, memory management as indicated rarely poses a problem. There is another aspect of data warehouse tables that could cause some concern. Data warehouse tables are denormalized and therefore the records tend to be large. Sometimes a record may be too large to fit in a single block. Then the record has to be split across more than one block. The broken parts have to be connected with pointers or physical addresses. Such pointer chains affect performance to a large extent.

Consider all the factors and set the block size at the appropriate size. Generally, increased block size gives better performance but you have to find the proper size.

Set the Proper Block Usage Parameters   Most of the leading DBMSs allow you to set block usage parameters at appropriate values and derive performance improvement. You will find that these usage parameters themselves and the methods for setting them are dependent on the database software. Generally, two parameters govern the usage of the blocks, and proper usage of the blocks enhances performance. Let us start with a generic example of these two parameters and then try to understand the implications.

Example:

Block Percent Free   20
Block Percent Used   40

Block Percent Free   The DBMS leaves a percentage of each block empty so that the records in the block can expand into it. The records can use this reserved area in the block only when they expand on update. When a record is modified and expands, then the reserved area may be used. In the example, this parameter is set at 20. That means 20% of each block is reserved for expansion of records while being updated. In a data warehouse, there are hardly any updates. The initial load is all inserts of data records. The incremental loads are also mostly inserts. A few updates may take place while processing slowly changing dimension tables. Therefore, setting this parameter at a high value results in too much wasted space. The general rule is to set this parameter as low as possible.

Block Percent Used   This parameter sets a watermark level below which the amount of space used in a block must fall before new records are accepted in that block. Take the example where this parameter is set at 40. As rows are deleted from a block, the freed space is not reused until at least 60% of the block is empty. Only when the amount of storage used falls below 40% is the freed space reused. What is the situation in a data warehouse? Mostly, addition of new records. There are hardly any deletes except when archiving out of the data warehouse. The general rule, therefore, is to set this parameter as high as possible.

Manage Data Migration   When a record in a block is updated and there is not enough space in the same block for storing the expanded record, then most DBMSs move the entire updated record to another block and create a pointer to the migrated record. Such migration affects the performance, requiring multiple blocks to be read. This problem may be resolved by adjusting the block percent free parameter. However, migration is not a major problem in data warehouses because of the negligible number of updates.

Manage Block Utilization   Performance degenerates when data blocks contain excessive amounts of free space. Whenever a query calls for a full table scan, performance suffers because of the need to read too many blocks. Manage block underutilization by adjusting the block percent free parameter downward and the block percent used parameter upward.

Resolve Dynamic Extension   When the current extent on disk storage for a file is full, the DBMS finds a new extent and allows an insert of a new record. This task of finding a new extension on the fly is referred to as dynamic extension. However, dynamic extension comes with significant overhead. Reduce dynamic extension by allocation of large initial extents.

Employ File Striping Techniques You perform file striping when you split the data into multiple physical parts and store these individual parts on separate physical devices. File striping enables concurrent input/output operations and improves file access performance substantially.

Using RAID Technology

Redundant array of inexpensive disks (RAID) technology has become common to the extent that almost all of today's data warehouses make good use of this technology. These disks are found on large servers. The arrays enable the server to continue operation even while they are recovering from the failure of any single disk. The underlying technique that gives the primary benefit of RAID breaks the data into parts and writes the parts to multiple disks in a striping fashion. The technology can recover data when a disk fails and reconstruct the data. RAID is very fault tolerant. Here are the basic features of the technology:

Disk mirroring—writing the same data to two disk drives connected to the same controller.

Disk duplexing—similar to mirroring, except here each drive has its own distinct controller.

Parity checking—addition of a parity bit to the data to ensure correct data transmission.

Disk striping—data spread across multiple disks by sectors or bytes.

RAID is implemented at six different levels: RAID 0 through RAID 5.

Figure 18-7 gives you a brief description of RAID. Note the advantages and disadvantages. The lowest level configuration, RAID 0, will provide data striping. At the other end of the range, RAID 5 is a very valuable arrangement.

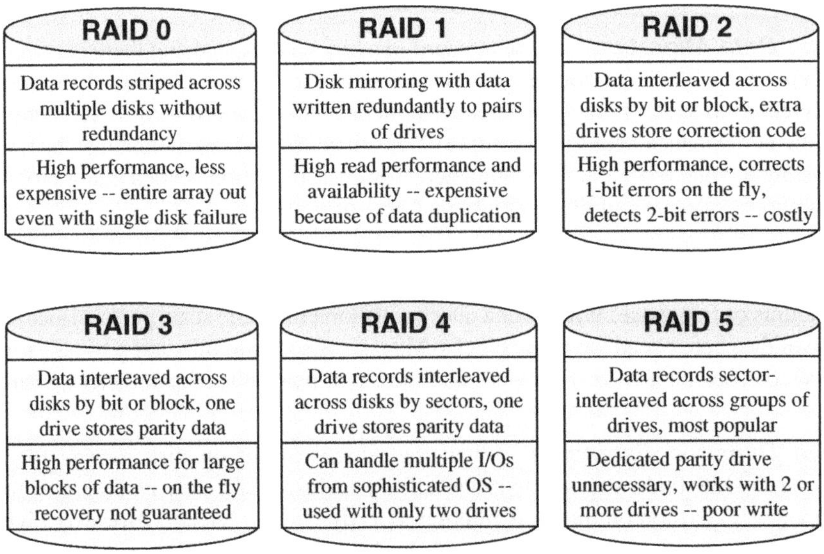

Figure 18-7 RAID technology.

Estimating Storage Sizes

No discussion of physical storage is complete without a reference to estimation of storage sizes. Every action in the physical model takes place in physical storage. You need to know how much storage space must be made available initially and on an ongoing basis as the data warehouse grows.

Here are a few tips on estimating storage sizes:

For each database table, determine
- Initial estimate of the number of rows
- Average length of the row
- Anticipated monthly increase in the number of rows
- Initial size of the table in megabytes (MB)
- Calculated table sizes in 6 months and in 12 months

For all tables, determine
- The total number of indexes
- Space needed for indexes, initially, in 6 months, and in 12 months

Estimate
- Temporary work space for sorting, merging
- Temporary files in the staging area
- Permanent files in the staging area

INDEXING THE DATA WAREHOUSE

In a query-centric system like the data warehouse environment, the need to process queries faster dominates. There is no surer way of turning your users away from the data warehouse than by unreasonably slow queries. For the user in an analysis session going through a rapid succession of complex queries, you have to match the pace of the query results with the speed of thought. Among the various methods to improve performance, indexing ranks very high.

What types of indexes must you build in your data warehouse? DBMS vendors offer a variety of choices. The choice is no longer confined to sequential index files. All vendors support B-Tree indexes for efficient data retrieval. Another option is the bitmapped index. As we will see later in this section, this indexing technique is very appropriate for the data warehouse environment. Some vendors are extending the power of indexing to specific requirements. These include indexes on partitioned tables and index-organized tables.

Indexing Overview

Let us consider the technique of indexing from the perspective of the data warehouse. The data tables are read-only. This feature implies that you almost never update the records or delete records. And records are not inserted into the tables after the loads. When you do adds, updates, or deletes, you incur additional overhead for manipulating the index files. But in a data warehouse this is not the case. So you can create a number of indexes for each table.

How many indexes can you create per table? Most of the indexing is done on the dimension tables. Generally, you will see a lot more indexes in a data warehouse than in an OLTP system. When a table grows in volume, the indexes also increase in size, requiring more storage. The general rule is that the maximum number of indexes varies inversely with the size of the table. Large numbers of indexes affect the loading process because indexes are created for new records at that time. You have to balance the various factors and decide on the number of indexes per table. Review the tables, one by one.

In the rest of this section, we will study specific indexing techniques in greater depth. Before doing so, please note the following general principles.

Indexes and Loading   When you have a large number of indexes, the loading of data into the warehouse slows down considerably. This is because when each record is added to a data table, every corresponding index entry must be created. The problem is more acute during initial loads. You can address this problem by dropping the indexes before running the load jobs. By doing so, the load jobs will not create the index entries during the load process. After the loading process completes, you can run separate jobs to construct the index files. Construction of the index files takes substantial time, but not as much as creating index entries during the load process.

Indexing for Large Tables   Large tables with millions of rows cannot support many indexes. When a table is too large, having more than just one index itself could cause difficulties. If you must have many indexes for the table, consider splitting the table before defining more indexes.

Index-Only Reads   As you know, in the data retrieval process the index record is read first and then the corresponding data read takes place. The DBMS selects the best index from among the many indexes. Let us say the DBMS uses an index based on four columns in a table and many users in your environment request data from these four columns and one more column in the table. How does the data retrieval take place? The DBMS uses this index record to retrieve the corresponding data record. You need at least two input–output (I/O) operations. In this instance, the DBMS has to retrieve the data record just for one additional column. In such cases, consider adding that extra column to the index. The DBMS will read the index and find that all the information needed is contained in the index record itself, so it will not read the data record unnecessarily.

Selecting Columns for Indexing   How do you select the columns in a table as most suitable for indexing? Which columns will produce the best performance if indexed? Examine the common queries and note the columns that are frequently used to constrain the queries. Such columns are candidates for indexing. If many queries are based on product line, then add product line to your list of potential columns for indexing.

A Staged Approach   Many data warehouse administrators are puzzled about how to get started with indexing. How many indexes are needed for each table and which columns must be selected for indexing for the initial deployment of the data warehouse? They do a preliminary review of the tables, but have no experience with real-world queries yet. This is precisely the point. Experience cannot be a guideline. You need to wait for the users to exercise the data warehouse for some time. A staged approach to indexing seems to be prudent. Start with indexes on just the primary and foreign keys of each table.

Keep monitoring the performance carefully. Make a special note of any queries that run for an inordinately long time. Add indexes as more and more users come on board.

B-Tree Index

Most database management systems have the B-Tree index technique as the default indexing method. When you code statements using the data definition language of the database software to create an index, the system creates a B-Tree index. DBMSs also create B-Tree indexes automatically on primary key values. The B-Tree index technique is superior to other techniques because of its data retrieval speed, ease of maintenance, and simplicity. Figure 18-8 shows an example of a B-Tree index. Notice the tree structure with the root at the top. The index consists of a B-Tree (a balanced binary tree) structure based on the values of the indexed column. In the example, the indexed column is Name. This B-Tree is created using all the existing names that are the values of the indexed column. Observe the upper blocks that contain index data pointing to the next lower block. Think of a B-Tree index as containing hierarchical levels of blocks. The lowest-level blocks or the leaf blocks point to the rows in the data table. Note the data addresses in the leaf blocks.

If a column in a table has many unique values, then the selectivity of the column is said to be high. In a territory dimension table, the column for City contains many unique values. This column is therefore highly selective. B-Tree indexes are most suitable for highly selective columns. Because the values at the leaf nodes will be unique they will lead to distinct

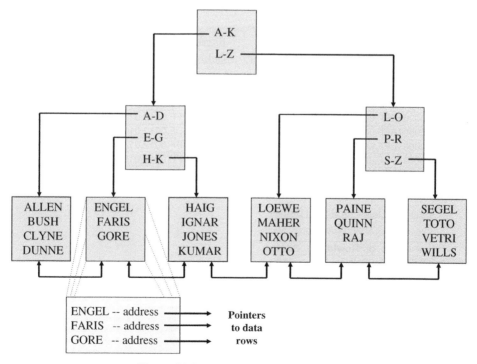

Figure 18-8 Example of a B-Tree index.

data rows and not to a chain of rows. What if a single column is not highly selective? How can you make use of B-Tree indexing in such cases? For example, the first name column in an employee table is not highly selective. Many common first names exist. But you can improve the selectivity by concatenating the first name with the last name. The combination is much more selective. Create a concatenated B-Tree index on both the columns together.

Indexes grow in direct proportion to the growth of the indexed data table. Wherever indexes contain concatenation of multiple columns, they tend to increase sharply in size. As the data warehouse deals with large volumes of data, the size of the index files can be cause for concern. What can we say about the selectivity of the data in the warehouse? Are most of the columns highly selective? Not really. If you inspect the columns in the dimension tables, you will notice a number of columns that contain low-selectivity data. B-Tree indexes do not work well with data whose selectivity is low. What is the alternative? That leads us to another type of indexing technique.

Extract of Sales Data

Address or Rowid	Date	Product	Color	Region	Sale($)
00001BFE.0012.0111	15-Nov-00	Dishwasher	White	East	300
00001BFE.0013.0114	15-Nov-00	Dryer	Almond	West	450
00001BFF.0012.0115	16-Nov-00	Dishwasher	Almond	West	350
00001BFF.0012.0138	16-Nov-00	Washer	Black	North	550
00001BFF.0012.0145	17-Nov-00	Washer	White	South	500
00001BFF.0012.0157	17-Nov-00	Dryer	White	East	400
00001BFF.0014.0165	17-Nov-00	Washer	Almond	South	575

Bitmapped Index for Product Column

Ordered bits: Washer, Dryer, Dishwasher

Address or Rowid	Bitmap
00001BFE.0012.0111	001
00001BFE.0013.0114	010
00001BFF.0012.0115	001
00001BFF.0012.0138	100
00001BFF.0012.0145	100
00001BFF.0012.0157	010
00001BFF.0014.0165	100

Bitmapped Index for Color Column

Ordered bits: White, Almond, Black

Address or Rowid	Bitmap
00001BFE.0012.0111	100
00001BFE.0013.0114	010
00001BFF.0012.0115	010
00001BFF.0012.0138	001
00001BFF.0012.0145	100
00001BFF.0012.0157	100
00001BFF.0014.0165	010

Bitmapped Index for Region Column

Ordered bits: East, West, North, South

Address or Rowid	Bitmap
00001BFE.0012.0111	1000
00001BFE.0013.0114	0100
00001BFF.0012.0115	0100
00001BFF.0012.0138	0010
00001BFF.0012.0145	0001
00001BFF.0012.0157	1000
00001BFF.0014.0165	0001

Figure 18-9 Example of a bitmapped index.

Bitmapped Index

Bitmapped indexes are ideally suitable for low-selectivity data. A bitmap is an ordered series of bits, one for each distinct value of the indexed column. Assume that the column for color has three distinct colors, namely, white, almond, and black. Construct a bitmap using these three distinct values. Each entry in the bitmap contains three bits. Let us say the first bit refers to white, the second to almond, and the third to black. If a product is white in color, the bitmap entry for that product consists of three bits, where the first bit is set to 1, the second bit is set to 0, and the third bit is set to 0. If a product is almond in color, the bitmap entry for that product consists of three bits, where the first bit is set to 0, the second bit is set to 1, and the third bit is set to 0. You get the picture. Now study the bitmapped index example shown in Figure 18-9. The figure presents an extract of the sales table and bitmapped indexes for the three different columns. Notice how each entry in an index contains the ordered bits to represent the distinct values in the column. An entry is created for each row in the base table. Each entry carries the address of the base table row.

How do the bitmapped indexes work to retrieve the requested rows? Consider a query against the sales table in the above example: Select the rows from the Sales table where product is "Washer" and color is "Almond" and division is "East" or "South."

Figure 18-10 illustrates how Boolean logic is applied to find the result set based on the bitmapped indexes shown in Figure 18-9.

As you may observe, bitmapped indexes support queries using low-selectivity columns. The strength of this technique rests on its effectiveness when using predicates on low-selectivity columns in queries. Bitmapped indexes take significantly less space than B-Tree indexes for low-selectivity columns. In a data warehouse, many data accesses are based on low-selectivity columns. Also, analysis using "what-if" scenarios require queries involving several predicates. You will find that bitmapped indexes are more suitable for a data warehouse environment than for an OLTP system.

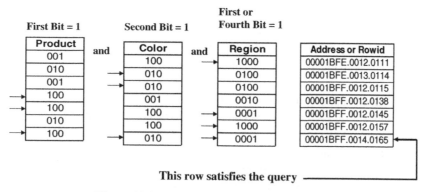

Figure 18-10   Bitmapped indexes: data retrieval.

On the other hand, if new values are introduced for the indexed columns, the bit-mapped indexes have to be reconstructed. Another disadvantage relates to the necessity to access the data tables all the time after the bitmapped indexes are accessed. B-Tree indexes do not require table access if the requested information is already contained in the index.

Clustered Indexes

Some RDBMSs offer a new type of indexing technique. In the B-Tree, bitmapped, or any sequential indexing method, you have a data segment where the values of all columns are stored and an index segment where index entries are kept. The index segment repeats the column values for the indexed columns and also holds the addresses for the entries in the data segment. Clustered tables combine the data segment and the index segments; the two segments are one. Data is the index and index is the data.

Clustered tables improve performance considerably because in one read you get the index and the data segments. Using the traditional indexing techniques, you need one read to get the index segment and a second read to get the data segment. Queries run faster with clustered tables when you are looking for exact matches or searching for a range of values. If your RDBMS supports this type of indexing, make use of this technique wherever you can in your environment.

Indexing the Fact Table

What do you normally have inside a fact table? What is the nature of the columns? Revisit the STAR schema. The primary key of the fact table consists of the primary keys of all the connected dimensions. If you have four dimension tables of store, product, time, and promotion, then the full primary key of the fact table is the concatenation of the primary keys of the store, product, time, and promotion tables. What are the other columns? The other columns are metrics such as sales units, sales dollars, cost dollars, and so on. These are the types of columns to be considered for indexing the fact tables.

Please study the following tips and use them when planning to create indexes for the fact tables:

- If the DBMS does not create an index on the primary key, deliberately create a B-Tree index on the full primary key.
- Carefully design the order of individual key elements in the full concatenated key for indexing. In the high order of the concatenated key, place the keys of the dimension tables frequently referred to while querying.
- Review the individual components of the concatenated key. Create indexes on combinations based on query processing requirements.
- If the DBMS supports intelligent combinations of indexes for access, then you may create indexes on each individual component of the concatenated key.
- Do not overlook the possibilities of indexing the columns containing the metrics. For example, if many queries look for sales dollars within given ranges, then the column "sales dollars" is a candidate for indexing.
- Bitmapped indexing does not apply to fact tables. There are hardly any low-selectivity columns.

Indexing the Dimension Tables

Columns in the dimension tables are used in the predicates of queries. A query may run like this: How much are the sales of product A in the month of March for the northern division? Here the columns product, month, and division from three different dimension tables are candidates for indexing. Inspect the columns of each dimension table carefully and plan the indexes for these tables. You may be not be able to achieve performance improvement by indexing the columns in the fact tables but the columns in the dimension tables offer tremendous possibilities to improve performance through indexing.

Here are a few tips on indexing the dimension tables:

- Create a unique B-Tree index on the single-column primary key.
- Examine the columns that are commonly used to constrain the queries. These are candidates for bitmapped indexes.
- Look for columns that are frequently accessed together in large dimension tables. Determine how these columns may be arranged and used to create multicolumn indexes. Remember that the columns that are more frequently accessed or the columns that are at the higher hierarchical levels in the dimension table are placed at the high order of the multicolumn indexes.
- Individually index every column likely to be used frequently in join conditions.

PERFORMANCE ENHANCEMENT TECHNIQUES

Apart from the indexing techniques we have discussed in the previous section, a few other methods also improve performance in a data warehouse. For example, physically compacting the data when writing to storage enables more data to be loaded into a single block. That also means that more data may be retrieved in one read. Another method for improving performance is the merging of tables. Again, this method enables more data to be retrieved in one read. If you purge unwanted and unnecessary data from the warehouse in a regular manner, you can improve the overall performance.

In the remainder of this section, let us review a few other effective performance enhancement techniques. Many techniques are available through the DBMS, and most of these techniques are especially suitable for the data warehouse environment.

Data Partitioning

Typically, the data warehouse holds some very large database tables. The fact tables run into millions of rows. Dimension tables like the product and customer tables may also contain a huge number of rows. When you have tables of such vast sizes, you face certain specific problems. First, loading of large tables takes excessive time. Then, building indexes for large tables also runs into several hours. What about processing of queries against large tables? Queries also run longer when attempting to sort through large volumes of data to obtain the result sets. Backing up and recovery of huge tables takes an inordinately long time. Again, when you want to selectively purge and archive records from a large table, wading through all the rows takes a long time.

What if you are able to divide large tables into manageable chunks? Will you not see performance improvements? Performing maintenance operations on smaller pieces is easier and faster. Partitioning is a crucial decision and must be planned up front. Doing this after the data warehouse is deployed and goes into production is time-consuming and difficult.

Partitioning means deliberate splitting of a table and its index data into manageable parts. The DBMS supports and provides the mechanism for partitioning. When you define the table, you can define the partitions as well. Each partition of a table is treated as a separate object. As the volume increases in one partition, you can split that partition further. The partitions are spread across multiple disks to gain optimum performance. Each partition in a table may have distinct physical attributes, but all partitions of the table have the same logical attributes.

What are the criteria for splitting a table into partitions? You can split a large table vertically or horizontally. In vertical partitioning, you separate out the partitions by grouping selected columns together. Each partitioned table contains the same number of rows as the original table. Usually, wide dimension tables are candidates for vertical partitioning. Horizontal partitioning is the opposite. Here you divide the table by grouping selected rows together. In a data warehouse, horizontal partitioning based on calendar dates works well. You can split a table into partitions of recent events and past history. This gives you the option to keep the recent events up and running while taking the historical component off-line for maintenance. Horizontal partitioning of the fact tables produces great benefits.

As you observe, partitioning is an effective technique for storage management and improving performance. Let us summarize the benefits:

- A query needs to access only the necessary partitions. Applications can be given the choice to have partition transparency or they may explicitly request an individual partition. Queries run faster when accessing smaller amounts of data.
- An entire partition may be taken off-line for maintenance. You can separately schedule maintenance of partitions. Partitions promote concurrent maintenance operations.
- Index building is faster.
- Loading data into the data warehouse is easy and manageable.
- Data corruption affects only a single partition. Backup and recovery on a single partition reduces downtime.
- The input–output load gets balanced by mapping different partitions to the various disk drives.

Data Clustering

In the data warehouse, many queries require sequential access of huge volumes of data. The technique of data clustering facilitates such sequential access. Clustering fosters sequential prefetch of related data.

You achieve data clustering by physically placing related tables close to each other in storage. When you declare a cluster of tables to the DBMS, the tables are placed in neighboring areas on the disk. How you exercise data clustering depends on the features of the DBMS. Review the features and take advantage of data clustering.

Parallel Processing

Consider a query that accesses large quantities of data, performs summations, and then makes a selection based on multiple constraints. It is immediately obvious that you will achieve major performance improvement if you can split the processing into components and execute the components in parallel. The simultaneous concurrent executions will produce the result faster. Several DBMS vendors offer parallel processing features that are transparent to users. As a designer of the query, the user need not know how a specific query must be broken down for parallel processing. The DBMS will do that for the user.

Parallel processing techniques may be applied to data loading and data reorganization. Parallel processing techniques work in conjunction with data partitioning schemes. The parallel architecture of the server hardware also affects the way parallel processing options may be invoked. Some physical options are critical for effective parallel processing. You have to assess propositions like placing two partitions on the same storage device if you need to process them in parallel, Parallel processing and partitioning together provide great potential for improved performance. But the designer must decide how to use them effectively.

Summary Levels

As we have discussed several times, the data warehouse needs to contain both detailed and summary data. Select the levels of granularity for the purpose of optimizing the input–output operations. Let us say you keep the sales data at the levels of daily detail and monthly summaries. If the users frequently request weekly sales information, then consider keeping another summary at the weekly level. On the other hand, if you only keep weekly and monthly summaries and no daily details, any query for daily details cannot be satisfied from the data warehouse. Choose your summary and detail levels carefully based on user requirements.

Also, rolling summary structures are especially useful in a data warehouse. Suppose in your data warehouse you need to keep hourly data, daily data, weekly data, and monthly summaries. Create mechanisms to roll the data into the next higher levels automatically with the passage of time. Hourly data automatically gets summarized into the daily data, daily data into the weekly data, and so on.

Referential Integrity Checks

As you know, referential integrity constraints ensure the validity between two related tables. The referential integrity rules in the relational model govern the values of the foreign key in the child table and the primary key in the parent table. Every time a row is added or deleted, the DBMS verifies that the referential integrity is preserved. This verification ensures that parent rows are not deleted while child rows exist and that child rows are not added without parent rows. Referential integrity verification is critical in the OLTP systems, but it reduces performance.

Now consider the loading of data into the data warehouse. By the time the load images are created in the staging area, the data structures have already gone through the phases of extraction, cleansing, and transformation. The data ready to be loaded has already been verified for correctness as far as parent and child rows are concerned. Therefore, there is no further need for referential integrity verification while loading the data. Turning off referential integrity verification produces significant performance gains.

Initialization Parameters

DBMS installation signals the start of performance improvement. At the start of the installation of the database system, you can carefully plan how to set the initialization parameters. Many times you will realize that performance degradation is to a substantial extent the result of inappropriate parameters. The data warehouse administrator has a special responsibility to choose the right parameters.

For example, if you set the maximum number of concurrent users too low, the users will run into bottlenecks. Some users may have to wait to get into the database even though resources are available, simply because the parameter was set too low. On the other hand, setting this parameter too high results in unnecessary consumption of resources. Next, consider the checkpoint frequency. How often must the DBMS write checkpoint records? If the range between two consecutive checkpoints is too narrow, too much system resources will be used up. Setting the range too wide may affect recovery. These are just a couple of examples. Review all the initialization parameters and set each appropriately.

Data Arrays

What are data arrays? Suppose in a financial data mart you need to keep monthly balances of individual line accounts. In a normalized structure, the monthly balances for a year will be found in 12 separate table rows. Assume that in many queries users request the balances for all the months together. How can you improve the performance? You can create a data array or repeating group with 12 slots, each to contain the balance for one month.

Although creating arrays is a clear violation of normalization principles, this technique yields tremendous performance improvement. In the data warehouse, the time element is interwoven into all data. Frequently, users look for data in a time series. Another example is the request for monthly sales figures for 24 months for each salesperson. If you analyze the common queries, you will be surprised to see how many need data that can be readily stored in arrays.

CHAPTER SUMMARY

- Physical design takes the data warehouse implementation closer to the hardware. Physical design activities may be grouped into seven distinct steps.
- The importance of standards cannot be overemphasized. Adopt sound standards during the physical design process.
- Optimizing storage allocation ranks high in the physical design activities. Make use of RAID technology.
- Data warehouse performance is heavily dependent on proper indexing strategy. B-Tree indexes and bitmapped indexes are suitable.
- Other performance improvement schemes that are part of the physical design include the following: data partitioning, data clustering, parallel processing, creation of summaries, adjusting referential integrity checks, proper setting of DBMS initialization parameters, and use of data arrays.

REVIEW QUESTIONS

1. Name the physical design objectives. Which objective do you think ranks as the most important?

2. What are the components that make up the physical model? How are these related to components of the logical model?

3. Give two reasons why naming standards are important in a data warehouse environment.

4. List any three techniques for optimizing storage. Describe these briefly.

5. What is index-only read? How does it improve performance?

6. Give two reasons why B-Tree indexing is superior to other indexing methods.

7. What is meant by the selectivity for a column in a physical table? What type of indexing technique is suitable for low-selectivity data? Why?

8. What is data partitioning? Give two reasons why data partitioning is helpful in a data warehousing environment.

9. What is data clustering? Give an example.

EXERCISES

1. Match the columns:

1.	fact table	A.	set at high level
2.	dynamic extension	B.	data address in each entry
3.	file striping	C.	repeating data group
4.	block percent used	D.	combined data and index segments
5.	B-Tree index	E.	DBMS finds new extent
6.	referential integrity check	F.	set at low level
7.	clustered index	G.	candidate for partitioning
8.	block percent free	H.	data addresses in leaf nodes
9.	bitmapped index	I.	store on separate devices
10.	data array	J.	suspend for loading

2. Prepare an outline for a standards manual for your data warehouse. Consider all types of objects and their naming conventions. Indicate why standards are important. Produce a detailed table of contents.

3. Refer back to the STAR schema for orders analysis shown in Figure 10.7. Transform it into a physical model. Show all the components of the physical model. Relate the physical model to the logical model.

4. What are the two common block usage parameters? Using appropriate examples, describe how storage utilization may be improved in the data warehouse by setting these parameters properly. How are the settings different from OLTP systems? Why?

5. As the data warehouse administrator, performance enhancement is high on your list. Highlight the techniques you plan to adopt. For each technique, indicate tasks necessary to implement the technique.

CHAPTER 19

DATA WAREHOUSE DEPLOYMENT

CHAPTER OBJECTIVES

- Study the role of the deployment phase in the data warehouse development life cycle.
- Review the major deployment activities and learn how to get them done.
- Examine the need for a pilot system and classify the types of pilots.
- Consider data security in the data warehouse environment.
- Survey the data backup and recovery requirements.

You have now arrived at a point where you are ready to roll out the initial version of the data warehouse. Deployment is the next phase after construction. In the deployment phase, you attend to the last few details, turn the data warehouse on, and let the users reap the benefits. By the time you reach the deployment phase, the majority of the functions are completed. The main concerns in the deployment phase relate to the users getting the training, support, and the hardware and tools they need to get into the warehouse.

To find our place in the whole life cycle of data warehouse development, let us summarize the functions and operations that have been completed up to this point. Here is the list of major activities already completed in the construction phase:

- The infrastructure is in place with the components fully tested.
- The validity of the architecture is already verified.
- The database is defined. Space allocation for the various tables is completed.
- The staging area is fully set up with file allocations.
- The extract, transformation, and all other staging area jobs are tested.

Data Warehousing Fundamentals for IT Professionals, Second Edition. By Paulraj Ponniah
Copyright © 2010 John Wiley & Sons, Inc.

- The creation of the load images is tested in the development environment. Testing of initial loads and incremental loads is done.
- Query and reporting tools are tested in the development environment.
- The OLAP system is installed and tested.
- Web-enabling the data warehouse is completed.

Before proceeding to a complete discussion of purely deployment activities, we want to highlight and reiterate some points relating to testing the data warehouse. Once you are ready to launch and deploy the data warehouse, it is assumed all testing except user acceptance have been successfully carried out.

DATA WAREHOUSE TESTING

Unit testing and system testing in a data warehousing environment consist of testing the back-end functions and the front-end provisions. During the discussion on physical design process, we had implied data warehouse testing.

Although software testing has several common features that apply to data warehouse testing, we just want to highlight a few special points. As an IT professional, you must be quite familiar with software testing procedures and how verifications of test results are conducted.

Front-End

At the front-end where the users interact with the environment and obtain business intelligence, most of the functions are usually provided through solutions obtained from third-party vendors. Therefore, the testing at the front-end is really testing of the integration of vendor tools with your data warehouse. Vendors themselves provide the interfaces that need to be tested. Testing the interfaces is not substantial.

ETL Testing

Data warehouse testing really focuses on the back-end processes, namely, the ETL functions. We can come up with a few general goals for testing ETL applications and group the goals as follows:

Data extraction. Ensure that all the data marked for extraction from various source systems are completely and correctly extracted. Data completeness is the goal here.

Data transformation and cleansing. Ensure that all data transformations are correctly performed according to the business rules for conversions. Data quality is the goal here.

Data loading. Verify that all load modules are correct based on the transformed and cleansed data. Ensure that all data for dimension, fact, and summary tables are correctly placed in appropriate files.

Audit trails. Trace the data movements and control totals throughout the steps of ETL and ensure that nothing is lost or corrupted on the way from data extraction through transformation and finally loading.

Integration. Ensure that the entire ETL process works well with all other upstream and downstream processes.

MAJOR DEPLOYMENT ACTIVITIES

Let us continue from the end of the construction phase. As you observe, a large number of critical activities have been completed. All the components have been tested. The pieces are in place. Figure 19-1 shows the activities in the deployment phase. Observe the primary tasks in each box representing the activities in this phase. In the deployment phase, establish a feedback mechanism for users to let the project team know how the deployment is going. If this is the initial rollout, most of your users will be new to the processes. Although the users must have received training, substantial handholding is essential in this phase. Be prepared to provide the support. Let us inspect each major activity in the deployment phase. As we move along, pick up tips and adapt them to your environment.

Complete User Acceptance

Proper acceptance of the system by the users is not just a formality in the deployment phase, it is an absolute necessity. Do not proceed to force the deployment before the key user representatives express their satisfaction about the data warehouse. Some organizations have procedures for a formal sign-off. Others conduct a series of user acceptance tests in which each function is accepted. It does not matter how the user acceptance activity is completed but do complete it in the manner in which such acceptances are usually done in your environment.

Who should do the acceptance testing from the side of the users? Remember the users who are already on the project team? Start with these people. If you have a user liaison manager in your project team, then this person must be made responsible. Get the end-user applications specialists to perform the acceptance testing for their own areas. In addition to the user representatives on the project team, include a few other users for a few final test sessions.

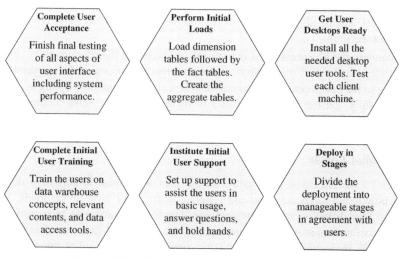

Figure 19-1   The data warehouse deployment phase.

How should the user acceptance testing be conducted? Which particular users should be testing at this final phase of deployment? Here are a few tips:

- In each subject area or department, let the users select a small number of typical queries and reports, ones for which they can verify the results without too much work or difficulty, but substantial ones involving combinations of dimension table constraints. Let the users run the queries and produce the reports. Then produce reports from the operational systems for verification. Compare the reports from the operational systems to the results from the data warehouse. Resolve and account for all seeming discrepancies. Verify and make sure that the reports from the operational systems are free of errors before matching them up with the results from the warehouse.

- This is a good time to test some of the predefined queries and reports. Have each user group pick a small number of such queries and reports and test the executions.

- Have the users test the OLAP system. Create the multidimensional cubes needed for the test and store the cubes in the OLAP multidimensional database if you are adopting the MOLAP approach. Let the users select about five typical analysis sessions to try out. Again, verify the results with reports from the operational systems.

- As you know, in almost every warehouse, users need to learn about and be comfortable with the functioning of the new front-end tools. The majority of the users must be able to use the tools with comparative ease. Design acceptance tests for the user representatives to sign off on the usability of the tools. Of course, most of this type of testing would have been done at the time of tool selection. But at that time, the testing would have been done at vendor sites or in the system development environment. Now the verification is being done in the production environment. This is a big difference.

- If your data warehouse is Web-enabled, have the users test the Web features. If Web technology is used for information delivery, let the users test this aspect.

- No user acceptance testing is complete without acceptance of the system performance. The project must have set the expectation of the users at an agreed level of performance. Query response time expectations are usually at the level of about 3 to 5 seconds. In fact, individual queries may deviate from the average, and that is understandable. The users will be able to accept such variations provided that these are exceptional and not the norm.

- Remember, the acceptance test is useful if conducted in the production environment. You may conduct all the previous individual module testing and the overall system testing in the development environment. When all the acceptance testing is completed successfully, get the sign off formally or by any other acceptable method. This is a signal that the project is ready for full deployment.

Perform Initial Loads

In Chapter 12 we discussed the loading of the data warehouse in sufficient depth. We reviewed how initial loads are done and covered methods for incremental loads. We also covered the four different modes for applying data to the warehouse repository. By the time the project arrives at the deployment phase, the team must have tested sample initial loads and mock incremental loads. Now is the time to do the complete initial load. Also, now the time is also close for doing the first incremental load, which normally takes place in 24 hours after the deployment. Recalling what we studied in Chapter 12 as background information, let us review the steps of the complete initial load. If you need to go back to Chapter 12 for a brief refresher, please do so now. Especially review how load images are created for dimension and fact tables. The initial load process picks up these load images that are already in the format of the table records themselves.

Here are the major steps of the complete initial load:

- Drop the indexes on the data warehouse relational tables. As you know, index building during the loading consumes an enormous chunk of time. Remember that the initial load deals with very large volumes of data, hundreds of thousands and even millions of rows. You cannot afford to have anything slowing down the load process.

- As you know, each dimension table record is in a one-to-many relationship with the corresponding fact table records. That means referential integrity is enforceable by the DBMS on this relationship. But we assume that the load images have been created carefully and that we can suspend this restriction to speed up the load process. This is up to each team, based on the confidence level for the creation of the load images.

- In some cases, the initial loads may run for a number of days. If your initial load aborts after a few days of processing because of some system failure, then you have a disaster on your hands. What is the solution? Should you go back to the beginning and start all over again? No. Make sure you have proper checkpoints in place so that you can pick up from the latest checkpoint and continue.

- Load the dimension tables first, for the reasons given in Chapter 12. Remember how the keys are built for the dimension table records. Recall how the keys for the fact table records are formed from those of the dimension table records. That is why you need to load the dimension tables first and then the fact tables. Some data warehouse teams opt to load the smaller dimension tables first and verify the load process before starting the loads of the larger tables.

- Load the fact tables next. The keys for the fact table records would already have been resolved before creating load images in the staging area.

- Based on your already established plan for aggregate or summary tables, create the aggregate tables based on the records in the dimension and fact tables. Sometimes, load images are created for the aggregate tables beforehand in the staging area. If so, apply these load images at this time to create the aggregate tables.

- You had suspended index creation during the loads; now build the indexes.

- If you had opted not to suspend the enforcement of referential integrity, all the referential violations would have recorded on the system log during the load process. Examine the log files and resolve the load exceptions.

Get User Desktops Ready

Getting the user machines ready for the data warehouse is a comparatively small part in terms of the overall effort from beginning to end. Although the effort may be much less than 10% of the total activities, what the users see and experience at their desktops is what counts for them. The set of desktop tools is the data warehouse for the users. Therefore, pay special attention to the installation of the data access tools, the network connections that link up the user machines to the servers, and the configuration of the middle tiers. Depending upon the method of deployment, consider allocating enough time for getting the desktops ready.

Before starting this activity, make a list of configuration needs for the client machines, all the information delivery software to be installed, the hardware setup for the desktop machines, and the entire spectrum of requirements for network connections. Let us itemize a few practical suggestions:

- Remote deployment of the data access tools for the client machines is a faster method. The data warehouse administrators are able to install the software on the various machines from a central location, thus avoiding individual visits to the user workstations. On the other hand, if you plan to install and test the access tools on the client machines one by one, plan for longer lead time.
- Irrespective of whether the deployment method is by remote installation or by individual visits to user areas, this is a unique opportunity to upgrade the workstations with other relevant types of software that may be lacking at the user sites.
- Desktop tools cannot function without the appropriate server and middle-tier components. Plan for proper timing, installation, and testing of these other components.
- Test each client machine to ensure that all components are properly installed and work well together.
- Completion of the desktop readiness activity means that the users can get to their machines and start accessing the data warehouse information. This activity necessarily includes establishing and acquiring the user passwords and logon user IDs. Ensure this is done and tested.

Complete Initial User Training

The importance of training and orientation for the users cannot be overemphasized. IT professionals may think of the separate components of data, applications, and tools. From an IT department's point of view, training is thought of as training about these three components. But to the users, it is all one. They do not distinguish between applications and tools. The training program must be designed from the users' point of view. An essential difference exists between training users in operational system implementations and data warehouse implementations. The capabilities offered in the data warehouse have a much wider potential. Users are not aware of how much they can really do with the tools in the data warehouse.

To get started, plan to train the users in the following areas:

- Basic database and data storage concepts.
- Fundamental features of a data warehouse.
- Contents of the data warehouse as applicable to each user group.
- Browsing through the warehouse contents.
- Use of data access and retrieval tools.
- Applicability of Web technology for information delivery.
- Set of predefined queries and reports.
- Types of analysis that can be performed.
- Query templates and how to use them.

- Report scheduling and delivery.
- Data load schedule and currency of the data.
- The support structure, including first line of contact.

Institute Initial User Support

In the early days of post-deployment, every member of the data warehouse support staff is usually very busy. Users may have a wide range of questions from basic sign-on to performing complex drill-down analysis. Many questions may just relate to the hardware issues. The users need an extensive degree of handholding, at least during the initial stages.

Figure 19-2 depicts a set-up for the initial user support. Note the basic support centers. The user representative in each department is the first point of contact. This person must have been trained well enough to answer most of the questions on the applications and data content. The user representative is also knowledgeable about the end-user tools on the desktops. The hotline support comes after the user representative is unable to provide answers. At least in the initial deployment, this procedure seems to work well. Also, note the type of support provided by the technical support group.

Deploy in Stages

Building and deploying a data warehouse is a major undertaking for any organization. This is a project that calls for many different types of skills. The data warehouse encompasses several different technologies. You are faced with new techniques of design. Dimensional modeling is a very different approach not previously used by designers in any operational

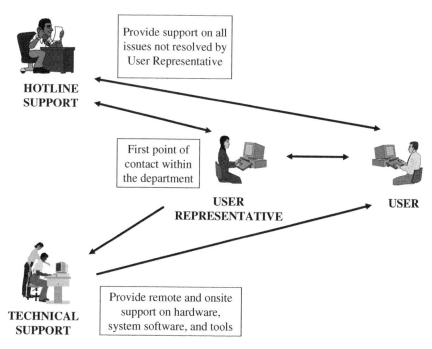

Figure 19-2   Initial user support.

systems. The process of data extraction, transformation, and loading is tedious and labor intensive. Users receive information in vastly new ways. The effort is big, possibly bigger than most of the previous information projects any enterprise has ever launched before.

Under these circumstances, what is a reasonable method for deploying your data warehouse? Most decidedly, if you parcel the deployment into manageable parts, you can bring in the data warehouse at a comfortable pace. Make the deployment happen in stages. Chalk out the stages clearly. Plan a schedule that is most effective from the point of view of the users as well as the project team.

In Chapter 2, we discussed three approaches for building a data warehouse. The top-down approach started out with a corporate normalized data warehouse feeding several departmental data marts. The bottom-up approach relates to building a group of data marts without the idea of melding the data marts together. Then the practical approach leads to a set of supermarts that form a conglomerate of conformed data marts.

Irrespective of the approach your project team is adopting for whatever reasons most plausible for your environment, divide and stage your deployment. For all the approaches, the overall requirements definition, the architecture, and the infrastructure take the corporate view. You plan for the entire enterprise but you deploy the pieces in well-defined stages. Figure 19-3 shows the staging of the deployment. Notice the suggested stages under the different approaches. Note how you build the overall enterprise-wide data warehouse first in the top-down approach. Then the dependent data marts are deployed in a suitable sequence. The bottom-up approach is less structured and less refined. In the practical approach, you deploy one data mart at a time.

You remember how conforming the dimensions is the key to the success of the practical approach. Let us reconsider this important concept. The reason for this requirement is to be

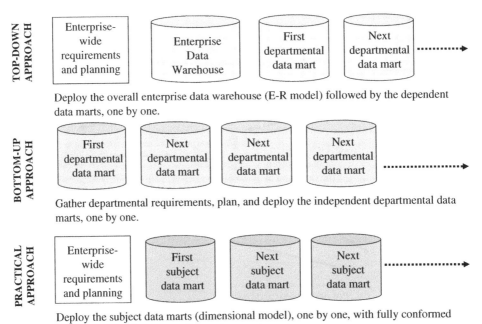

Figure 19-3   Staged data warehouse deployment.

able to preserve the cohesion of all the data marts that comprise the enterprise data warehouse. At the fundamental level, conforming of dimensions simply means this: when we say "product" in two different data marts, it means the same thing. In other words, the product dimension table in every subsequently deployed data mart is the same as the product dimension table in the first data mart. The tables must he identical in terms of all the attributes and keys.

CONSIDERATIONS FOR A PILOT

Most companies consider deploying a pilot system before the full deployment of the entire warehouse. This is not a matter of substituting the first full-fledged data mart as the pilot. The pilot is separate and distinct, with specific purposes. There are several good reasons for deploying a pilot first. The pilot enables your project team to gain broad experience, gain specific experience with the new technologies, and demonstrate proof-of-concept to your users.

If your project team opts for a pilot, concentrate on the basics from the beginning. Clarify the purpose and goal of the pilot and choose a proper subject area for it. Remember that hardly any pilot deployments are throw-away projects. Treat the pilot with all due respect as a regular project.

When is a Pilot Data Mart Useful?

Embarking on a data warehouse deployment is fraught with potential risks for failure. If you do not strike it right the first time, you may not have a second chance to convince your users about the merits of the new paradigm. Success is a primary goal; you cannot risk a failure. You must be able to demonstrate the potential positive results within a reasonably short time and you must be able to manage this activity quite easily. A pilot deployment to a small group of users in a limited and closed environment is quite appealing.

This does not, however, imply that a pilot deployment is always necessary. Your environment may be different. The group of your users may just consist of highly sophisticated analysts, and your IT team may be made up of seasoned veterans for whom any system is easy. If this is the case in your deployment of the data warehouse, then a pilot may be unnecessary. But most companies are different. Please go over the following list that indicates the conditions where pilot deployments are useful:

- The user community is totally new to the data warehousing concept.
- The users must be shown and convinced of the ease with which they themselves can retrieve information.
- The users need to gain experience with new tools and technologies.
- The analysts need to perceive the strengths of the analytical features in the data warehouse.
- The sponsors and upper management must observe the benefits of the data warehousing concept before getting into it further in a big way.
- The IT designers and architects need to gain experience in dimensional modeling techniques and in the working of the database on this model.
- The project team needs to ensure that all the ETL functions work well.

- The project team wants to confirm the working together of all the new infrastructure components such as parallel processing, replication, middleware connections, Web-based technologies, and OLAP elements.

Types of Pilot Projects

From the list of conditions that warrant consideration for a pilot, you must have inferred that there could be different types of pilot deployments. When a project team considers a pilot, some set of the reasons dominate and, therefore, the pilot would be slanted towards those needs. Frequently, pilots are not built for just one set of reasons but many different requirements are meshed together to form the pilot deployment. In this subsection, let us briefly review six types of pilots. Each pilot stands on a dominating set of reasons but each may also be serving other purposes as well in small measures. Figure 19-4 illustrates the six types of pilots, indicating the major purpose of each type.

Proof-of-Concept Pilot   The data warehouse is the viable solution for decision support. Establishing this proposition is the primary goal of the proof-of-concept pilot. You may have to prove the concept to a broad range of users, including top management. Or, you may have to justify the concept to the sponsors and senior executives for them to approve funding for the full data warehouse. You define the scope of the pilot based on the audience. Regardless of the scope, this type of pilot must provide a sampling of all the major features to show the utility of the warehouse and how easy it is to get information. You focus on the

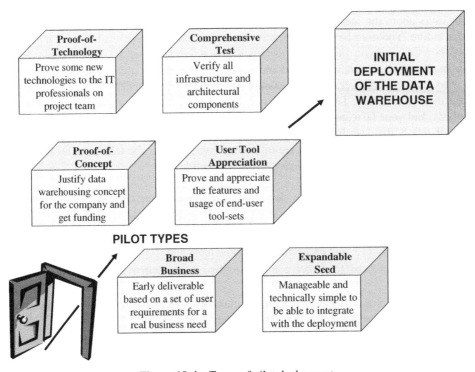

Figure 19-4   Types of pilot deployment.

interaction of the information delivery system with the users. Proof-ofconcept pilots work with limited amounts of data.

The project team thinks of this type of pilot much earlier in the development scheme. Do not take an inordinately long time. The main goal here is to impress on the minds of the users that the data warehouse is a very effective means for information delivery. Generally, no proof-of-concept pilot should take longer than six months to build and explore. You need to keep the focus on effectively presenting the concepts and quickly gaining the approval.

Proof-of-Technology Pilot   This is perhaps the simplest and easiest to build, but as it is mainly built for IT to prove one or two technologies at a time, this type of pilot is of little interest to the users. You may just want to test and prove a dimensional modeling tool or a data replication tool. Or, you may want to prove the validity and usefulness of the ETL tools. In this type of pilot, you want to get beyond the product demonstrations and claims of the vendors and look for yourself.

The utility of the proof-of-technology pilots lies in your ability to concentrate and focus on one or two technologies and prove them to your satisfaction. You can check the applicability of a particular type of replication tool to your data warehouse environment. However, as the pilot is confined to proving a small part of the collection of all the technologies, it does not indicate anything about how all the pieces will work together. This brings us to the next type.

Comprehensive Test Pilot   This is developed and deployed to verify that all the infrastructure and architectural components work together and well. It is not as complete in scope as a full-fledged data warehouse and works with a smaller database, but you verify the data flow throughout the data warehouse from all the source operational systems through the staging area to the information delivery component.

This pilot enables the IT professionals and the users on the project team to appreciate the complexities of the data warehouse. The team gains experience with the new technologies and tools. This pilot cannot be put together and deployed within a short time. The scope of the pilot encompasses the entire spectrum of data warehouse functions. It is also deployed to benefit the project team more than the users.

User Tool Appreciation Pilot   The thrust of this type of pilot is to provide the users with tools they will see and use. You place the emphasis on the end-user information delivery tools. In this type of pilot, you keep the data content and the data accuracy in the background. The focus is just on the usability of the tools. The users are able to observe all the features of the end-user tools for themselves, work with them, and appreciate their features and utility. If different tool sets are provided to different groups of users, you have to deploy a few versions of this type of pilot.

Note that there is little regard for the integrity of the data, nor does this type of pilot work with the entire data content of the data warehouse. User tool appreciation pilots have rather limited applications. One area where this type is more useful is in the OLAP system.

Broad Business Pilot   In contrast to the previous type, this type of pilot has a broader business scope. Try to understand how this type of pilot gets started. Management identifies some pressing need for decision support in some special business. They are able to define the requirements fairly well. If something is put together to meet the requirements, the potential for success is great. Management wants to take advantage of the data warehousing initiatives in the organization. The responsibility rests on the project team to come up with this highly visible early deliverable business pilot.

This type of pilot based on a specific set of requirements has a few problems. First, you are under time pressure. Depending on the requirements, the scope of the pilot could be too narrow to get integrated with the rest of the data warehouse later on. Or, the pilot could turn out to be too complex. A complex project cannot be considered as a pilot.

Expandable Seed Pilot   First, note the motivations for this type of pilot. You want to come up with something with business value. The scope must be manageable. You want to keep it as technically simple as possible for the users. Nevertheless, you have a choice of suitable simple subjects. Simple does not mean useless. Choose a simple, useful, and fairly visible business area but plan to go through the length and breadth of the data warehouse features with the pilot. This is like planting a good seed and watching it germinate and then grow.

The project team benefits from such a pilot because they will observe and test the working of the various parts. Users gain an appreciation of the tools and understand how they interact with the data warehouse. The data warehouse administration function may also be tested.

Choosing the Pilot

There is no industry-standard naming convention for the pilot types. One data warehouse practitioner may call a specific type an infrastructure test pilot and another an architectural planning pilot. The actual names do not matter. The scope, content, and motivations count. Also note that these groupings or types are arbitrary. You may very well come up with another four types. However, the major thrust of any pilot comes from the same motivations as one of the types described above. Remember that no actual pilot falls exclusively within one specific type. You will see traces of many types in the pilot you want to adopt. As the project team is building the data warehouse, it is introducing the new decision support system in a particular technical and business environment. The technical and business environment of the organization influences the choice of the pilot. Again, the choice also depends on whether the data warehouse project is primarily IT-driven, user-driven, or driven by a truly joint team.

Let us examine the conditions in the organization and determine if we can match them with the type of pilot that is suitable. Study the guidelines described below.

If your organization is totally new to the concept of data warehousing and your senior management needs convincing and first-hand proof, adopt a proof-of-concept pilot. But most companies are not in this condition. With so much literature, seminars, and vendor presentations about data warehousing, practically everyone is at least partially sold on the concept. The only question may be the applicability of the concept to your organization.

Proof-of-technology and comprehensive test pilots serve the needs of IT. Users do not gain directly from these two types. If you are expanding your current infrastructure extensively to accommodate the data warehouse, and if you are adopting new parallel processing hardware and MOLAP techniques, then these two types merit your consideration.

The importance of user involvement and user training in a data warehouse cannot be overstated. The more the users gain an appreciation of the data warehouse and its benefits, the better it is for the success of the project. Therefore, the user tool appreciation pilot and the broad business pilot pose substantial advantages. Although the user tool appreciation pilot is very limited in scope and application, it has its place. Usually it is a throw-away pilot. It cannot be integrated into the main warehouse deployment but it can continue to be used as a training tool. A word about the broad business pilot: this type has the potential for great success and can elevate the data warehouse project in the eyes of the top management, but be careful not to bite off more than you can chew. If the scope is too complex and large, you could risk failure.

At first blush, the expandable seed pilot appears to be the best choice. Although the users and the project team can both benefit from this type of pilot because of its controlled and limited scope, this pilot may not traverse all the functions and features. But a pilot is not really meant to be elaborate. It serves its purpose well if it touches all the important functions.

Expanding and Integrating the Pilot

The question arises about what you do with a pilot after it has served its intended primary purpose. What exactly is the purpose and shelf-life of a pilot? Do you have to throw the pilot away? Is all the effort expended on a pilot completely wasted? Not so. Every pilot has specific purposes. You build and deploy a pilot to achieve certain defined results. The proof-of-concept pilot has one primarily goal, and one goal only—prove the validity of the data warehousing concept to the users and top management. If you are able to prove this proposition with the aid of the pilot, then the pilot is successful and serves its purpose.

Understand the place of a pilot in the whole data warehouse development effort. A pilot is not the initial deployment. It may be a prelude to the initial deployment. Without too much modification, a pilot may be expanded and integrated into the overall data warehouse. Figure 19-5 illustrates each type of pilot and shows how some may be integrated into the

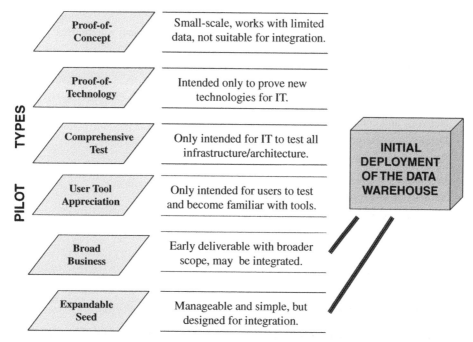

Figure 19-5 Integrating the pilot into the warehouse.

data warehouse. Note that the expandable seed pilot stands out as the best candidate for integration. In each case, observe what needs to be done for integration to occur.

SECURITY

A data warehouse is a veritable gold mine of information. All of the organization's critical information is readily available in a format that is easy to retrieve and use. In a single operational system, security provisions govern a smaller segment of the corporate data but data warehouse security extends to a very large portion of the enterprise data. In addition, the security provisions must cover all the information that is extracted from the data warehouse and stored in other data areas such as the OLAP system.

In an operational system, security is ensured by authorizations to access the database. You may grant access to users by individual tables or through database views. Access restrictions are difficult to set up in a data warehouse. The analyst at a data warehouse may start an analysis by getting information from one or two tables. As the analysis continues, more and more tables are involved. The entire query process is mainly ad hoc. Which tables must you restrict and which ones must you keep open to the analyst?

Security Policy

The project team must establish a security policy for the data warehouse. If you have a security policy for the organization to govern the enterprise information assets, then make the security policy for the data warehouse an add-on to the corporate security policy. First and foremost, the security policy must recognize the immense value of the information contained in the data warehouse. The policy must provide guidelines for granting privileges and for instituting user roles.

Here are the usual provisions found in the security policy for data warehouses:

- The scope of the information covered by the policy
- Physical security
- Security at the workstation
- Network and connections
- Database access privileges
- Security clearance for data loading
- User roles and privileges
- Security at levels of summarization
- Metadata security
- OLAP security
- Web security
- Resolution of security violations

Managing User Privileges

As you know, users are granted privileges for accessing the databases of OLTP systems. The access privilege relates to individuals or groups of users with rights to perform the operations to create, read, update, or delete data. The access restrictions for these operations may be set at the level of entire tables or at the level of one or more columns of an individual table.

Most RDBMSs offer role-based security. As you know, a role is just a grouping of users with some common requirements for accessing the database. You can create roles by executing the appropriate statements using the language component of the database management system. After creating the roles, you can set up the users in the appropriate roles. Access privileges may be granted at the level of a role. When this is done, all the users assigned to that role receive the same access privileges granted at the role level. Access privileges may also be granted at the individual user level.

How do you handle exceptions? For example, let us say user JANE is part of the role ORDERS. You have granted a certain set of access privileges to the role ORDERS. Almost all these access privileges apply to JANE with one exception. JANE is allowed to access one more table, namely, the promotion dimension table. How do you work out this exception? You separately grant privilege to JANE to access the promotion table. From this granting of the additional privilege, JANE can access the promotion table. For everything else, JANE derives the privileges from the role ORDERS.

Figure 19-6 presents a sample set of roles, responsibilities, and privileges. Observe the responsibilities as they relate to the data warehousing environment. Also, notice how the privileges match up with the responsibilities.

Password Considerations

Security protection in a data warehouse through passwords is similar to how it is done in operational systems. Updates to the data warehouse happen only through the data load jobs. User passwords are less relevant to the batch load jobs. Deletes of the data warehouse records happen infrequently. Only when you want to archive old historical records do the

ROLES	RESPONSIBILITIES	ACCESS PRIVILEGES
End-Users	Run queries and reports against data warehouse tables	System: none; Database Admin: none; Tables and Views: selected
Power Users / Analysts	Run ad hoc complex queries, design and run reports	System: none; Database Admin: none; Tables and Views: all
Helpdesk / Support Center	Help user with queries and reports; analyze and explain	System: none; Database Admin: none; Tables and Views: all
Query Tool Specialists	Install and trouble-shoot end-user and OLAP tools	System: none; Database Admin: none; Tables and Views: all
Security Administration	Grant and revoke access privileges; monitor usage	System: yes; Database Admin: yes; Tables and Views: all
Systems / Network Admin	Install and maintain Operating Systems and networks	System: yes; Database Admin: no; Tables and Views: none
Data Warehouse Administration	Install and maintain DBMS; provide backup and recovery	System: yes; Database Admin: yes; Tables and Views: all

Figure 19-6   Roles, responsibilities, and privileges.

batch programs delete records. The main issue with passwords is to authorize users for read-only data access. Users need passwords to get into the data warehouse environment.

Security administrators can set up acceptable patterns for passwords and also the expiry period for each password. The security system will automatically expire the password on the date of expiry. A user may change to a new password when he or she receives the initial password from the administrator. The same must be done just before the expiry of the current password. These are additional security procedures.

Follow the standards for password patterns in your company. Passwords must be cryptic and arbitrary, not easily recognizable. Do not let your users have passwords with their own names or the names of their loved ones. Do not let users apply their own exotic patterns. Have a standard for passwords. Include text and numeric data within a password.

The security mechanism must also record and control the number of unauthorized attempts by users to gain access with invalid passwords. After a prescribed number of unauthorized attempts, the user must be suspended from the data warehouse until the administrator reinstates the user. Following a successful sign-on, the numbers of illegal attempts must be displayed. If the number is fairly high, this must be reported. It could mean that someone is trying to work at a user workstation while that user is not there.

Security Tools

In the data warehouse environment, the security component of the database system itself is the primary security tool. We have discussed role-based security provided by the DBMSs. Security protection goes down to the level of columns in most commercial database management systems.

Some organizations have third-party security and management systems installed to govern the security of all systems. If this is the case in your organization, take advantage of the installed security system and bring the data warehouse under the larger security umbrella. Such overall security systems provide the users with a single sign-on feature. A user then needs only one sign-on user ID and password for all the computer systems in the organization. Users need not memorize multiple sign-ons for individual systems.

Some of the end-user tools come with their own security system. Most of the OLAP tools have a security feature within the toolset. Tool-based security is usually not as flexible as the security provided in the DBMS. Nevertheless, tool-based security can form some part of the security solution. Once you set the users up on the security systems in the toolset, you need not repeat it at the DBMS level, but some data warehouse teams go for double protection by invoking the security features of the DBMS also.

The tool-based security, being an integral part of the toolset, cannot be suspended. Just to get into the toolset for accessing the data, you need to get security clearance from the toolset software. If you are already planning to use the DBMS itself for security protection, then tool-based security may be considered redundant. Each set of tools from a certain vendor has its own way of indicating information interfaces. Information is organized into catalogs, folders, and items as the hierarchy. You may provide security verification at any of the three levels.

BACKUP AND RECOVERY

You are aware of the backup and recovery procedures in OLTP systems. Some of you, as database administrators, must have been responsible for setting up the backups and have probably been involved in one or two disaster recoveries.

In an OLTP mission-critical system, loss of data and downtime cannot be tolerated. Loss of data can produce serious consequences. In a system such as airlines reservations or online order taking, downtime even for a short duration can cause losses in the millions of dollars.

How critical are these factors in a data warehouse environment? When an online order-taking system is down for recovery, you probably can survive for a few hours using manual fall-back procedures. If an airlines reservation system is down, there can be no such manual fall-back. How do these compare with the situation in the data warehouse? Is downtime critical? Can the users tolerate a small loss of data?

Why Back Up the Data Warehouse?

A data warehouse houses huge amounts of data that has taken years to gather and accumulate. The historical data may go back 10 or even up to 20 years. Before the data arrives at the data warehouse, you know that it has gone through an elaborate process of cleansing and transformation. Data in the warehouse represents an integrated, rich history of the enterprise. The users cannot afford to lose even a small part of the data that was so painstakingly put together. It is critical that you are able to recreate the data if and when any disaster happens to strike.

When a data warehouse is down for any length of time, the potential losses are not as apparent as in an operational system. Order-taking staff is not waiting for the system to come back up. Nevertheless, if the analysts are in the middle of a crucial sales season or racing against time to conduct some critical analytical studies, the impact could be more pronounced.

Observe the usage of a data warehouse. Within a short time after deployment, the number of users increases rapidly. The complexity of the types of queries and analysis sessions intensifies. Users begin to request more and more reports. Access through Web technology expands. Very quickly, the data warehouse gains almost mission-critical status. With a large number of users intimately dependent on the information from the warehouse, backing up the data content and ability to recover quickly from malfunctions reaches new heights of importance.

In an OLTP system, recovery requires the availability of backed up versions of the data. You proceed from the last backup and recover to the point where the system stopped working. But you might think that the situation in a data warehouse differs from that in an OLTP system. The data warehouse does not represent an accumulation of data directly through data entry. Did not the source operational systems produce the data feeds in the first place? Why must you bother to create backups of the data warehouse contents? Can you not re-extract and reload the data from the source systems? Although this appears to be a natural solution, it is almost always impractical. Recreation of the data from the source systems takes enormous lengths of time and your data warehouse users cannot tolerate such long periods of downtime.

Backup Strategy

Now that you have perceived the necessity to back up the data warehouse, several questions and issues arise. What parts of the data must be backed up? When to back up? How to back up? Formulate a clear and well-defined backup and recovery strategy. Although the strategy for the data warehouse may have similarities to that for an OLTP system, still you need a separate strategy. You may build on the one that is available in your organization for OLTP systems, but do take into account the special needs for this new environment.

A sound backup strategy comprises several crucial factors. Let us go over some of them. Here is a collection of useful tips on what to include in your backup strategy:

- Determine what you need to back up. Make a list of the user databases, system databases, and database logs.
- The enormous size of the data warehouse stands out as a dominant factor. Let the factor of size govern all decisions in backup and recovery. The need for good performance plays a key role.
- Strive for a simple administrative setup.
- Be able to separate the current from the historical data and have separate procedures for each segment. The current segment of live data grows with the feeds from the source operational systems. The historical or static data is the content from the past years. You may decide to back up historical data less frequently.
- Apart from full backups, also think of doing log file backups and differential backups. As you know, a log file backup stores the transactions from the last full backup or picks up from the previous log file backup. A variation of this is a full differential backup. A differential backup contains all the changes since the last full backup.
- Do not overlook backing up system databases.
- Choosing the medium for backing up is critical. Here, size of the data warehouse dictates the proper choice.
- Commercial RDBMSs adopt a "container" concept to hold individual files. A container is a larger storage area that holds many physical files. The containers are known as table spaces, file groups, and the like. RDBMSs have special methods to back up the entire container more efficiently. Make use of such RDBMS features.
- Although the backup functions of the RDBMSs serve the OLTP systems, data warehouse backups need higher speeds. Look into backup and recovery tools from third-party vendors.
- Plan for periodic archiving of very old data from the data warehouse. A good archival plan pays off by reducing the time for backup and restore and also contributes to improvement in query performance.

Setting up a Practical Schedule

Without question, you need to back up the data warehouse properly. Many users will eventually depend on the data warehouse for constant flow of information. But the enormous size is a serious factor in all decisions about backup and recovery. It takes an inordinately long time to back up the full data warehouse. In the event of disasters, re-extracting data from the source operational systems and reloading the data warehouse does not seem to be an option. So, how can you set up a practical schedule for backups? Consider the following issues for making the decisions:

- As you know, backups for OLTP systems usually run at night. But in the data warehouse environment, the night slots get allocated for the daily incremental loads. The backups will have to contend with the loads for system time.
- If your user community is distributed in different time zones, finding a time slot becomes even more difficult.

- Mission-critical OLTP systems need frequent backups. In forward recovery, if you do not have regular full backups and frequent log file backups, the users must reenter the portion of the data that cannot be recovered. Compare this with the data warehouse. Reentering of data by the users does not apply here. Whatever portion cannot be recovered will have to be reloaded from the source systems provided that is possible. The data extraction and load systems do not support this type of recovery.
- Setting up a practical backup schedule comes down to these questions. How much downtime can the users tolerate before the recovery process is completed? How much data are the users willing to lose in the worst case scenario? Can the data warehouse continue to be effective for a long period until the lost data is somehow recovered?

A practical backup schedule for your data warehouse certainly depends on the conditions and circumstances in your organization. Generally, a practical approach includes the following elements:

- Division of the data warehouse into active and static data
- Establishing different schedules for active and static data
- Having more frequent periodic backups for active data in addition to less frequent backups for static data
- Inclusion of differential backups and log file backups as part the backup scheme
- Synchronization of the backups with the daily incremental loads
- Saving of the incremental load files to be included as part of recovery if applicable

Recovery

Let us conclude with a few pointers on the recovery process. Figure 19-7 illustrates the recovery process in the data warehouse environment. Notice the backup files and how they are used in the recovery process. Also, note how the possibility of some loss of data exists. Here are a few practical tips:

- Have a clear recovery plan. List the various disaster scenarios and indicate how recovery will be done in each case.
- Test the recovery procedure carefully. Conduct regular recovery drills.
- Considering the conditions in your organization and the established recovery procedure, estimate an average downtime to be expected for recovery. Get a general agreement from the users about the downtime. Do not surprise the users when the first disaster strikes. Let them know that this is part of the whole scheme and that they need to be prepared if it should ever happen.
- In the case of each outage, determine how long it will take to recover. Keep the users properly and promptly informed.
- Generally, your backup strategy determines how recovery will be done. If you plan to include the possibility of recovering from the daily incremental load files, keep the backups of these files handy.
- If you have to go to the source systems to complete the recovery process, ensure that the sources will still be available.

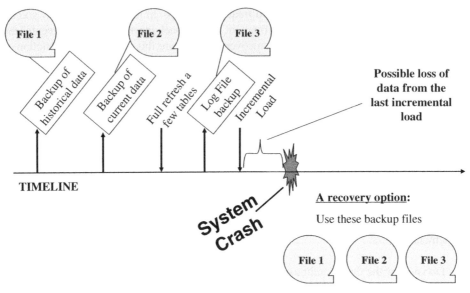

Figure 19-7 Recovery in a data warehouse.

CHAPTER SUMMARY

- Deployment of the first version of the data warehouse follows the construction phase.
- Major activities in the deployment phase relate to user acceptance, initial loads, desktop readiness, initial training, and initial user support.
- Pilot systems are appropriate in several sets of circumstances. Common types of pilots are proof-of-concept, proof-of-technology, comprehensive test, user tool appreciation, broad business, and expandable seed.
- Although data security in a data warehouse environment is similar to security in OLTP systems, providing access privileges is more involved because of the nature of data access in the warehouse.
- Why back up the data warehouse? Even though there are hardly any direct data updates in the data warehouse, there are several reasons for backing up. Scheduling backups is more difficult and recovery procedures are also more difficult because of the data volume in the warehouse.

REVIEW QUESTIONS

1. List four major activities during data warehouse deployment. For two of these four activities, describe the key tasks.

2. Describe briefly the user acceptance procedure. Why is this important?

3. What are the significant considerations for the initial data load?

4. Why is it a good practice to load the dimension tables before the fact tables?

5. What are the two common methods of getting the desktops ready? Which method do you prefer? Why?

6. What topics should the users be trained on initially?

7. Give four common reasons for a pilot system.

8. What is a proof-of-concept pilot? Under what circumstances is this type of pilot suitable?

9. List five common provisions to be found in a good security policy.

10. Give reasons why the data warehouse must be backed up. How is this different from an OLTP system?

EXERCISES

1. Indicate if true or false:

   A. It is a good practice to drop the indexes before the initial load.
   B. The key of the fact table is independent of the keys of the dimension tables.
   C. Remote deployment of desktop tools is usually faster.
   D. A pilot data mart is necessary when the users are already very familiar with data warehousing.
   E. Backing up the data warehouse is not necessary under any conditions because you can recover data from the source systems.
   F. Passwords must be cryptic and arbitrary.
   G. Always checkpoint the load jobs.
   H. It is a good practice to load the fact tables before loading the dimension tables.
   I. Initial training of the users must include basic database and data storage concepts.
   J. Role-based security provision is not suitable for the data warehouse.

2. Prepare a plan for getting the user desktops ready for the initial deployment of your data warehouse. The potential users are spread across the country in 30 major centers. Overseas users from four centers will also be tapping into the data warehouse. Analysts at five major regional offices will be using the OLAP system. Your data warehouse is Web-enabled. Make suitable assumptions, considering all aspects, and work out a plan.

3. What are the considerations for deploying the data warehouse in stages? Under what circumstances is staged deployment recommended? Describe how you will plan to determine the stages.

4. What are the characteristics of the type of pilot system described as a broad business pilot? What are its advantages and disadvantages? Should this type of pilot be considered at all? Explain the conditions under which this type of pilot is advisable.

5. As the data warehouse administrator, prepare a backup and recovery plan. Indicate the backup methods and schedules. Explore the recovery options. Describe the scope of the backup function. How will you ensure the readiness to recover from disasters?

CHAPTER 20

GROWTH AND MAINTENANCE

CHAPTER OBJECTIVES

- Clearly grasp the need for ongoing maintenance and administration.
- Understand the collection of statistics for monitoring the data warehouse.
- Perceive how statistics are used to manage growth and continue to improve performance.
- Discuss user training and support functions in detail.
- Consider other management and administration issues.

Where are you at this point? Assume the following plausible scenario. All the user acceptance tests were successful. There were two pilots; one was completed to test the specialized end-user toolset and the other was an expandable seed pilot that led to the deployment. Your project team has successfully deployed the initial version of the data warehouse. The users are ecstatic. The first week after deployment there were just a few teething problems. Almost all the initial users appear to be fully trained. With very little assistance from IT, the users seem to take care of themselves. The first set of OLAP cubes proved their worth and the analysts are already happy. Users are receiving reports over the Web. All the hard work has paid off. Now what?

This is just the beginning. More data marts and more deployment versions have to follow. The team needs to ensure that it is well poised for growth. You need to make sure that the monitoring functions are all in place to constantly keep the team informed of the status. The training and support functions must be consolidated and streamlined. The team must confirm that all the administrative functions are ready and working. Database tuning must continue at a regular pace.

Data Warehousing Fundamentals for IT Professionals, Second Edition. By Paulraj Ponniah
Copyright © 2010 John Wiley & Sons, Inc.

Immediately following the initial deployment, the project team must conduct review sessions. Here are the major review tasks:

- Review the testing process and suggest recommendations.
- Review the goals and accomplishments of the pilots.
- Survey the methods used in the initial training sessions.
- Document highlights of the development process.
- Verify the results of the initial deployment, matching these with user expectations.

The review sessions and their outcomes form the basis for improvement in the further releases of the data warehouse. As you expand and produce further releases, let the business needs, modeling considerations, and infrastructure factors remain as the guiding factors for growth. Follow each release close to the previous release. You can make use of the data modeling done in the earlier release. Build each release as a logical next step. Avoid disconnected releases. Build on the current infrastructure.

MONITORING THE DATA WAREHOUSE

When you implement an OLTP system, you do not stop with the deployment. The database administrator continues to inspect system performance. The project team continues to monitor how the new system matches up with the requirements and delivers the results. Monitoring the data warehouse is comparable to what happens in an OLTP system, except for one big difference. Monitoring an OLTP system dwindles in comparison with the monitoring activity in a data warehouse environment. As you can easily perceive, the scope of the monitoring activity in the data warehouse extends over many features and functions. Unless data warehouse monitoring takes place in a formalized manner, desired results cannot be achieved. The results of the monitoring gives you the data needed to plan for growth and to improve performance.

Figure 20-1 presents the data warehousing monitoring activity and its usefulness. As you can observe, the statistics serve as the life-blood of the monitoring activity. That leads into growth planning and fine-tuning of the data warehouse.

Collection of Statistics

What we call monitoring statistics are indicators whose values provide information about data warehouse functions. These indicators provide information on the utilization of the hardware and software resources. From the indicators, you determine how the data warehouse performs. The indicators present the growth trends. You understand how well the servers function. You gain insights into the utility of the end-user tools.

How do you collect statistics on the working of the data warehouse? Two common methods apply to the collection process. Sampling methods and event-driven methods are generally used. The sampling method measures specific aspects of the system activity at regular intervals. You can set the duration of the interval. If you set the interval as 10 minutes for monitoring processor utilization, then utilization statistics are recorded every 10 minutes. The sampling method has minimal impact on the system overhead.

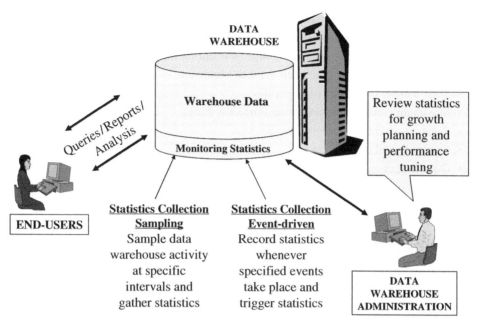

Figure 20-1   Data warehouse monitoring.

The event-driven methods work differently. The recording of the statistics does not happen at intervals, but only when a specified event takes place. For example, if you want to monitor the index table, you can set the monitoring mechanism to record the event when an update takes place to the index table. Event-driven methods add to the system overhead but are more thorough than sampling methods.

Which tools collect statistics? The tools that come with the database server and the host operating system are generally turned on to collect the monitoring statistics. Over and above these, many third-party vendors supply tools especially useful in a data warehouse environment. Most tools gather the values for the indicators and also interpret the results. The data collector component collects the statistics; the analyzer component does the interpretation. Much of the monitoring of the system occurs in real time.

Let us now make a note of the types of monitoring statistics that are useful. The following is a random list that includes statistics for different uses. You will find most of these applicable to your environment. Here is the list:

- Physical disk storage space utilization.
- Number of times the DBMS is looking for space in blocks or causes fragmentation.
- Memory buffer activity.
- Buffer cache usage.
- Input–output performance.
- Memory management.
- Profile of the warehouse content, giving number of distinct entity occurrences (for example, number of customers, products).
- Size of each database table.

- Accesses to fact table records.
- Usage statistics relating to subject areas.
- Numbers of completed queries by time slots during the day.
- Time each user stays online with the data warehouse.
- Total number of distinct users per day.
- Maximum number of users during time slots daily.
- Duration of daily incremental loads.
- Count of valid users.
- Query response times.
- Number of reports run each day.
- Number of active tables in the database.

Using Statistics for Growth Planning

As you deploy more versions of the data warehouse, the number of users increases and the complexity of the queries intensifies, you then have to plan for the obvious growth. But how do you know where the expansion is needed? Why have the queries slowed down? Why have the response times been degraded? Why was the warehouse down for expanding the table spaces? The monitoring statistics provide you with clues as to what is happening in the data warehouse and how you can prepare for the growth.

We indicate below the types of action that are prompted by the monitoring statistics:

- Allocate more disk space to existing database tables.
- Plan for new disk space for additional tables.
- Modify file block management parameters to minimize fragmentation.
- Create more summary tables to handle large number of queries looking for summary information.
- Reorganize the staging area files to handle more data volume.
- Add more memory buffers and enhance buffer management.
- Upgrade database servers.
- Offload report generation to another middle tier.
- Smooth out peak usage during the 24-hour cycle.
- Partition tables to run loads in parallel and to manage backups.

Using Statistics for Fine-Tuning

The next best use of statistics relates to performance. You will find that a large number of monitoring statistics prove to be useful for fine-tuning the data warehouse. In a later section, we will discuss this topic in more detail. For now, let us indicate below the data warehouse functions that are normally improved based on the information derived from the statistics:

- Query performance
- Query formulation
- Incremental loads

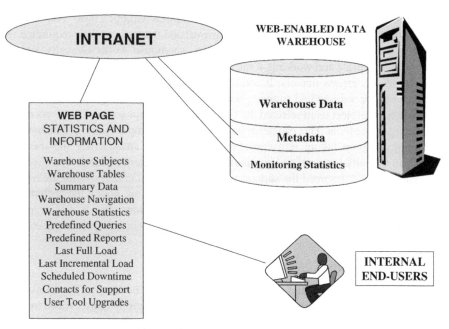

Figure 20-2 Statistics for the users.

- Frequency of OLAP loads
- OLAP system
- Data warehouse content browsing
- Report formatting
- Report generation

Publishing Trends for Users

This is a new concept not usually found in OLTP systems. In a data warehouse, the users must find their way into the system and retrieve the information by themselves. They must know about the contents. Users must know about the currency of the data in the warehouse. When was the last incremental load? What are the subject areas? What is the count of distinct entities? The OLTP systems are quite different. These systems readily present the users with routine and standardized information. Users of OLTP systems do not need the inside view. Figure 20-2 lists the types of statistics that must be published for the users.

If your data warehouse is Web-enabled, use the company's intranet to publish the statistics for users. Otherwise, provide the ability to inquire into the dataset where the statistics are kept.

USER TRAINING AND SUPPORT

Your project team has constructed the best data warehouse possible. Data extraction from the source systems was carefully planned and designed. The transformation functions cover all the requirements. The staging area has been laid out well and it supports every function carried out there. Loading of the data warehouse takes place without a flaw. Your end-users have the most effective tools for information retrieval and the tools fit their requirements as closely as possible. Every component of the data warehouse works correctly and well. With everything in place and working, if the users do not have the right training and support, none of the team's efforts matters. It could be one big failure. You cannot overstate the significance of user training and support, both initially and on an ongoing basis.

True, when the project team selected the vendor tools, perhaps some of the users received initial training on the tools. This can never be a substitute for proper training. You have to set up a training program taking into consideration all of the areas where the users must be trained. In the initial period, and continuing after deployment of the first version of the data warehouse, the users need the support to carry on. Do not underestimate the establishment of a meaningful and useful support system. You know about the technical and application support function in OLTP system implementations. For a data warehouse, because the workings are different and new, proper support becomes even more essential.

User Training Content

What should the users be trained on? What is important and necessary? Try to match the content of the training to the anticipated usage. How does each group of users need to interact with the data warehouse? If one group of users always uses predefined queries and preformatted reports, then training these users is easier. If, however, another group of analysts needs to formulate their own ad hoc queries and perform analysis, the content of the training program for the analysts becomes more intense.

While designing the content of user education, you have to make it broad and deep. Remember, the users to be trained in your organization come with different skills and knowledge levels. Generally, users preparing to use the data warehouse possess basic computer skills and know how computer systems work. But to almost all of the users, data warehousing must be novel and different.

Let us repeat what was mentioned in the previous chapter. Among other things, three significant components must be present in the training program. First, the users must get a good grasp of what is available for them in the warehouse. They must clearly understand the data content and how to get to the data. Second, you must tell the users about the applications. What are the preconstructed applications? Can they use the predefined queries and reports? If so, how? Next, you must train the users on the tools they need to employ to access the information. Having said this, please note that users do not comprehend such divisions of the training program as data content, applications, and tools. Do not plan to divide the training program into these distinct, arbitrary compartments, but keep these as the underlying themes throughout the training program. Figure 20-3 shows the important topics to be included in the training program. Again, a word of caution. The figure groups the topics under the three subjects of data content, applications, and tools, just to ensure that no topics are overlooked. While preparing the course syllabus for the training sessions, let the three subjects run through all the items covered in the course.

Preparing the Training Program

Once you have decided on the course contents, you are ready to prepare the training program itself. Consider what preparation entails. First, the team must decide on the types of training programs, then establish the course content for each type. Next, determine who has the

DATA CONTENT	APPLICATIONS	TOOLS
Subjects available in the warehouse.	Predefined queries.	Features and functions of the end-user tools.
Data warehouse dimension and fact tables.	Query templates.	Tool interface with the warehouse metadata.
Data warehouse navigation.	Preformatted reports.	Procedures to sign-on and get into the tool software.
Data granularity and aggregate tables.	Report writer options.	Use of tools to navigate and browse warehouse content.
Source systems and data extractions.	Data feeds to downstream applications	Use of tools to formulate queries and obtain results.
Data transformation and cleansing rules.	Pre-developed applications.	Use of tools to run reports.
Business terms and meanings.	OLAP summaries and multidimensional analysis.	
	Executive Information System.	

Figure 20-3   User training content.

responsibility of preparing the course materials. Organize the actual preparation of the course materials. Training the trainers comes next. A lot of effort goes into putting together a training program. Do not underestimate what it takes to prepare a good training program.

Let us go over the various tasks needed to prepare a training program. The training program varies with the requirements of each organization. Here are a few general tips for putting together a solid user training program:

- A successful training program depends on the joint participation of user representatives and IT. The user representatives on the project team and the subject area experts in the user departments are suitable candidates to work with IT.
- Let both IT and users work together in preparing the course materials.
- Remember to include topics on data content, applications, and tool usage.
- Make a list of all the current users to be trained. Place these users into logical groups based on knowledge and skill levels. Determine what each group needs to be trained on. By doing this exercise, you will be able to tailor the training program to exactly match the requirements of your organization.
- Determine how many different training courses would actually help the users. A good set of courses consists of an introductory course, an in-depth course, and a specialized course on tool usage.
- The introductory course usually runs for one day. Every user must go through this basic course.
- Have several tracks in the in-depth course. Each track caters to a specific user group and concentrates on one or two subject areas.
- The specialized course on tool usage also has a few variations, depending on the different tool sets. OLAP users must have their own course.

- Keep the course documentation simple and direct and include enough graphics. If the course covers dimensional modeling, a sample STAR schema helps the users to visualize the relationships. Do not conduct a training session without course materials.
- As you already know, hands-on sessions are more effective. The introductory course may just have a demo, but the other two types of courses go well with hands-on exercises.

How are the courses organized? What are the major contents of each type of course? Let us review some sample course outlines. Figure 20-4 presents three sample outlines, one for each type of course. Use these outlines as guides. Modify the outlines according to the requirements of your organization.

Delivering the Training Program

Training programs must be ready before the deployment of the first version of the data warehouse. Schedule the training sessions for the first set of users closer to the deployment date. What the users learned at the training sessions will be fresh in their minds. How the first set of users perceive the usefulness of the data warehouse goes a long way to ensure a successful implementation; so pay special attention to the first group of users.

Ongoing training continues for additional sets of users. As you implement the next versions of the data warehouse, modify the training materials and continue offering the courses. You will notice that in the beginning you need to have a full schedule of courses available. Some users may need refresher courses. Remember that users have their own responsibilities to run the business. They need to find the time to fit into the training slots.

Because of the hectic activity relating to training, especially if you have a large user community, the services of a training administrator become necessary. The administrator

Introductory Course	In-depth Course	End-User Tool Usage
Introduction to Data Warehousing.	Refresher on Data Warehousing.	Tool overview.
Introduction to the Data Warehouse and how data is stored.	Review of all subjects.	Detailed review of tool functions.
Data Warehouse navigation.	Detailed review of selected subject – fact tables, dimension tables, data granularity, and summaries.	Tool feature highlights.
Dimension and fact tables.		Usage of tool to navigate and browse data warehouse content.
Predefined queries and preformatted reports.	Review of source systems and data extractions.	Hands-on usage of tool for queries, reports, and analysis.
End-user applications.	Review of transformations.	Extra tool features such as drill-down, export of data.
Hands-on session to view warehouse contents.	Hands-on session.	

Figure 20-4   Sample training course outlines.

schedules the courses, matches the courses with the trainers, makes sure that the training materials are ready, arranges for training locations, and takes care of the computing resources necessary for hands-on exercises.

What must you do about training the executive sponsors and senior management staff? In OLTP systems, the senior management and executive staff rarely have a need to sit down at their desktop machines and get into the systems. That changes in the data warehouse environment. This new environment supports all decision makers, especially the ones at the higher levels. Of course, the senior officials need not know how to run every query and produce every report. But they need to know how to look for the information they are interested in. Most of these interested senior managers do not wish to take part in courses with other staff. You need to arrange separate training sessions for these executives, sometimes one-on-one sessions. You may modify the introductory course and offer another specialized course for the executives.

As the training sessions take place, you will find that some users who need to use the data warehouse are still not trained. Some users are too busy to be able to get away from their responsibilities. Some analysts and power users may feel that they need not attend any formal course and can learn by themselves. Your organization must have a definite policy regarding this issue. When you allow a user into the data warehouse without even minimal training, two things usually happen. First, they will disrupt the support structure by asking for too much attention. Second, when they are unable to perform a function or interpret the results, they will not attribute it to the lack of training but will blame the system. Generally, a "no training, no data warehouse access" policy works effectively.

User Support

User support must commence the minute the first user clicks on her or his mouse to get into the data warehouse. This is not meant to be dramatic, but to emphasize the significance of proper support to the users. As you know, user frustration mounts in the absence of a good support system. The support structure must be in place before the deployment of the first version of the data warehouse. If you have a pilot planned or an early deliverable scheduled, make sure users will have access to support.

As an IT professional having worked on other implementations and ongoing OLTP systems, you are aware of how the support function operates. So let us not try to cover the same ground you are already familiar with. Let us just go over two aspects of support. First, let us present a tiered approach to user support in a data warehouse environment. Figure 20-5 illustrates the organization of the user support function. Notice the different tiers. Note how the user representatives within each user group act as the first point of contact.

Now let us survey a few points especially pertinent to supporting the data warehouse environment. Please note the following points:

- Make clear to every user the support path to be taken. Every user must know whom to contact first, whom to call for hardware-type problems, whom to address for the working of the tools, and so on.
- In a multi-tiered support structure, clarify which tier supports what functions.
- If possible, try to align the data warehouse support with the overall user support structure in the organization.

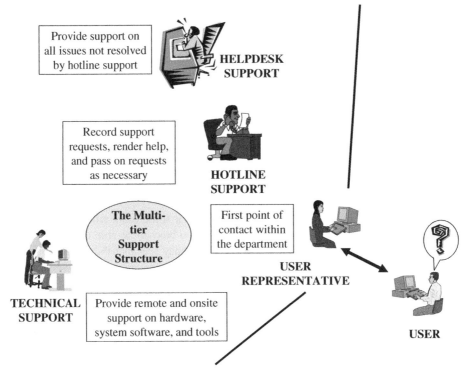

Figure 20-5   User support structure.

- In a data warehouse environment, you need another type of support. Frequently, users will try to match the information retrieved from the data warehouse with results obtained from the source operational systems. One segment of your support structure must be able to address such data reconciliation issues.

- Very often, at least in the beginning, users need handholding for browsing through the data warehouse contents. Plan for this type of support.

- Include support on how to find and execute predefined queries and preformatted reports.

- The user support can serve as an effective conduit to encourage the users based on successes in other departments and to get user feedback on their specific concerns. Ensure that communications and feedback channels are kept open.

- Most enterprises benefit from providing a company Website specially designed for data warehouse support. You can publish information about the warehouse in general, the predefined queries and reports, the user groups, new releases, load schedules, and frequently asked questions (FAQs).

MANAGING THE DATA WAREHOUSE

After the deployment of the initial version of the data warehouse, the management function switches gear. Until now, the emphasis remained on following through the steps of the data warehouse development life cycle. Design, construction, testing, user acceptance, and deployment were the watchwords. Now, at this point, data warehouse management is concerned with two principal functions. The first is maintenance management. The data warehouse administrative team must keep all the functions going in the best possible manner. The second is change management. As new versions of the warehouse are deployed, as new releases of the tools become available, as improvements and automation take place in the ETL functions, the administrative team's focus includes enhancements and revisions.

In this section, let us consider a few important aspects of data warehouse management. We will point out the essential factors. Post-deployment administration covers the following areas:

- Performance monitoring and fine-tuning
- Data growth management
- Storage management
- Network management
- ETL management
- Management of future data mart releases
- Enhancements to information delivery
- Security administration
- Backup and recovery management
- Web technology administration
- Platform upgrades
- Ongoing training
- User support

Platform Upgrades

Your data warehouse deployment platform includes the infrastructure, the data transport component, end-user information delivery, data storage, metadata, the database components, and the OLAP system components. More often, a data warehouse is a comprehensive cross-platform environment. The components follow a path of dependency, starting with computer hardware at the bottom, followed by the operating systems, communications systems, the databases, GUIs, and then the application support software. As time goes on, upgrades to these components are announced by the vendors.

After the initial rollout, have a proper plan for applying the new releases of the platform components. As you have probably experienced with OLTP systems, upgrades cause potentially serious interruption to the normal work unless they are properly managed. Good planning minimizes the disruption. Vendors try to force you into upgrades on their schedule based on their new releases. If the timing is not convenient for you, resist the initiatives from the vendors. Schedule the upgrades at your convenience and based on when your users can tolerate interruptions.

Managing Data Growth

Managing data growth deserves special attention. In a data warehouse, unless you are vigilant about data growth, it could get out of hand very soon and quite easily. Data warehouses already contain huge volumes of data. When you start with a large volume of data, even a small percentage increase can result in substantial additional data.

In the first place, a data warehouse may contain too much historical data. Data beyond 10 years may not produce meaningful results for many companies because of the changed business conditions. End-users tend to opt for keeping detailed data at the lowest grain. At least in the initial stages, the users continue to match results from the data warehouse with those from the operational systems. Analysts produce many types of summaries in the course of their analysis sessions. Quite often, the analysts want to store these intermediary datasets for use in similar analysis in the future. Unplanned summaries and intermediary datasets add to the growth of data volumes.

Here are just a few practical suggestions to manage data growth:

- Dispense with some detail levels of data and replace them with summary tables.
- Restrict unnecessary drill-down functions and eliminate the corresponding detail-level data.
- Limit the volume of historical data. Archive old data promptly.
- Discourage analysts from holding unplanned summaries.
- Where genuinely needed, create additional summary tables.

Storage Management

As the volume of data increases, so does the utilization of storage. Because of the huge data volume in a data warehouse, storage costs rank very high as a percentage of the total cost. Experts estimate that storage costs are still a substantial percentage of overall costs, yet you find that storage management does not receive sufficient attention from data warehouse developers and managers. Here are a few tips on storage management to be used as guidelines:

- Additional rollouts of the data warehouse versions require more storage capacity. Plan for the increase.
- Ensure that the storage configuration is flexible and scalable. You must be able to add more storage with minimum interruption to the current users.
- Use modular storage systems. If not already in use, consider a switchover.
- If yours is a distributed environment with multiple servers having individual storage pools, consider connecting the servers to a single storage pool that can be intelligently accessed.
- As usage increases, plan to spread data over multiple volumes to minimize access bottlenecks.
- Ensure ability to shift data from bad storage sectors.
- Look for storage systems with diagnostics to prevent outages.

ETL Management

This is a major ongoing administrative function, so attempt to automate most of it. Install an alert system to call attention to exceptional conditions. The following are useful suggestions on ETL (data extraction, transformation, loading) management:

- Run daily extraction jobs on schedule. If source systems are not available under extraneous circumstances, reschedule extraction jobs.

- If you employ data replication techniques, ensure that the result of the replication process checks out.
- Ensure that all reconciliation is complete between source system record counts and record counts in extracted files.
- Make sure all defined paths for data transformation and cleansing are traversed correctly.
- Resolve exceptions thrown out by the transformation and cleansing functions.
- Verify load image creation processes, including creation of the appropriate key values for the dimension and fact table rows.
- Check out the proper handling of slowly changing dimensions.
- Ensure completion of daily incremental loads on time.

Data Model Revisions

When you expand the data warehouse in future releases, the data model changes. If the next release consists of a new data mart on a new subject, then your model gets expanded to include the new fact table, dimension tables, and also any aggregate tables. The physical model changes. New storage allocations are made. What is the overall implication of revisions to the data model? Here is a partial list that may be expanded based on the conditions in your data warehouse environment:

- Revisions to metadata
- Changes to the physical design
- Additional storage allocations
- Revisions to ETL functions
- Additional predefined queries and preformatted reports
- Revisions to the OLAP system
- Additions to the security system
- Additions to the backup and recovery system

Information Delivery Enhancements

As time goes on, you will notice that your users have outgrown the end-user tools they started out with. In the course of time, users become more proficient at locating and using the data. They get ready for more and more complex queries. New end-user tools appear in the market all the time. This is especially true in the business intelligence market during the past decade. Why deny your users the latest and the best if they really can benefit from them? Why keep dashboards and scorecards away from your users and force them to stick to old-fashioned querying mechanisms?

What are the implications of enhancing the end-user tools and adopting a different tool set? Unlike a change to ETL, this change relates to the users directly, so plan the change carefully and proceed with caution.

Review the following tips:

- Ensure compatibility of the new tool set with all data warehouse components.
- If the new tool set is installed in addition to the existing one, switch your users over in stages.

- Ensure integration of end-user metadata.
- Schedule training on the new tool set.

If there are any data stores attached to the original tool set, plan for the migration of the data to the new tool set.

Ongoing Fine-Tuning

As an IT professional, you are familiar with the techniques for fine-tuning OLTP systems. The same techniques apply to the fine-tuning of the data warehouse, except for one big difference: the data warehouse contains a lot more, in fact, many times more data than a typical OLTP system. The techniques will have to be applied to an environment containing mountains of data.

There may not be any point in repeating the indexing and other techniques that you already know from the OLTP environment. Let us just go over a few practical suggestions:

- Have a regular schedule to review the use of indexes. Drop indexes that are no longer used.
- Monitor query performance daily. Investigate long-running queries. Work with the user groups that seem to be executing long-running queries. Create indexes if needed.
- Analyze the execution of all predefined queries on a regular basis. RDBMSs have query analyzers for this purpose.
- Review the load distribution at different times every day. Determine the reasons for large variations.
- Although you have instituted a regular schedule for ongoing fine-tuning, from time to time, you will come across some queries that suddenly cause grief. You will hear complaints from a specific group of users. Be prepared for such ad hoc fine-tuning needs. The data administration team must have staff set apart for dealing with these situations.

CHAPTER SUMMARY

- Immediately following the initial deployment, the project team must conduct review sessions.
- Ongoing monitoring of the data warehouse requires collection of statistics on a variety of indicators. Use the statistics for growth planning and for fine-tuning.
- The user training function consists of determining the content of the needed training, preparation of the training program, and delivering the training program.
- The user support function needs to have multiple tiers to deliver the appropriate support relating to data content, applications, and tools.
- Ongoing management and administration includes the following: platform upgrades, managing data growth, storage management, ETL management, data model revisions, information delivery enhancements, and ongoing fine-tuning.

REVIEW QUESTIONS

1. List the types of statistics collected for monitoring the functioning of the data warehouse.

2. Describe any six different types of action for growth planning prompted by the statistics collected.

3. How do the statistics help in fine-tuning the data warehouse?

4. Do you think publishing the statistics and similar data for the users is helpful? If so, why?

5. What are the three main subjects in user training content? Why are these essential?

6. Describe any four major tasks needed to prepare a training program.

7. What are the responsibilities of the training administrator?

8. Do you think a multi-tier user support structure is suitable for the data warehouse environment? What are the alternatives?

9. What role can the company's intranet play in training and user support?

10. List any five factors that are part of ETL management.

EXERCISES

1. Set up a procedure for gathering statistics from the data warehouse following the deployment. List all the types of statistics to be gathered. Indicate how each type of statistics will be used for ongoing support and improvements.

2. You are specifically assigned to improve the query performance in your data warehouse, deployed about six months ago. How will you plan for the assignment? What are the types of statistics you will need? Create a detailed plan.

3. You are hired as the new training administrator for the data warehouse in a nationwide automobile dealership. The data warehouse is Web-enabled. The analysts in the head-quarters work with the OLAP system based on the MOLAP model. Establish an improved ongoing training program. Describe the highlights of the program.

4. Review the user support structure illustrated in Figure 20-5. Is this support structure adequate for a Web-enabled data warehouse with about 250 internal users and 150 outside business partners accessing the data warehouse? About 20 full-time analysts use the OLAP system for complex analysis and studies. What improvements would you want to make to the support structure? Indicate the highlights.

5. As the manager for the data warehouse project, write a project completion report to your CIO and the executive project sponsor. List the major activities completed. Mention the plan for staged deployment of future releases. Indicate the plans for ongoing maintenance. Briefly highlight each topic on growth and maintenance.

ANSWERS TO SELECTED EXERCISES

CHAPTER 1 THE COMPELLING NEED FOR DATA WAREHOUSING

1 Match the columns

1-D, 2-G, 3-I, 4-F, 5-H, 6-A, 7-J, 8-E, 9-B, 10-C

CHAPTER 2 DATA WAREHOUSE: THE BUILDING BLOCKS

1 Match the columns

1-H, 2-G, 3-J, 4-F, 5-B, 6-I, 7-C, 8-A, 9-E, 10-D

CHAPTER 3 TRENDS IN DATA WAREHOUSING

1 Indicate if true or false

A-T, B-F, C-T, D-F, E-F, F-T, G-F, H-T, I-F, J-F

CHAPTER 4 PLANNING AND PROJECT MANAGEMENT

1 Match the columns

1-D, 2-E, 3-G, 4-H, 5-F, 6-I, 7-J, 8-A, 9-C, 10-B

CHAPTER 5 DEFINING THE BUSINESS REQUIREMENTS

1 Indicate if true or false

A-F, B-T, C-F, D-T, E-T, F-F, G-F, H-F, I-F, J-T

Data Warehousing Fundamentals for IT Professionals, Second Edition. By Paulraj Ponniah
Copyright © 2010 John Wiley & Sons, Inc.

CHAPTER 6   REQUIREMENTS AS THE DRIVING FORCE FOR DATA WAREHOUSING

1 Match the columns

1-H, 2-F, 3-J, 4-A, 5-I, 6-B, 7-E, 8-D, 9-G, 10-C

CHAPTER 7   THE ARCHITECTURAL COMPONENTS

1 Indicate if true or false

A-F, B-T, C-F, D-F, E-F, F-F, G-T, H-F, I-T, J-F

CHAPTER 8   INFRASTRUCTURE AS THE FOUNDATION FOR DATA WAREHOUSING

1 Match the columns

1-F, 2-D, 3-J, 4-A, 5-G, 6-E, 7-B, 8-C, 9-H, 10-I

CHAPTER 9   THE SIGNIFICANT ROLE OF METADATA

1 Indicate if true or false

A-F, B-T, C-F, D-F, E-T, F-T, G-F, H-T, I-T, J-F

CHAPTER 10   PRINCIPLES OF DIMENSIONAL MODELING

1 Match the columns

1-F, 2-I, 3-G, 4-A, 5-J, 6-B, 7-E, 8-C, 9-D, 10-H

CHAPTER 11   DIMENSIONAL MODELING: ADVANCED TOPICS

1 Indicate if true or false

A-T, B-F, C-T, D-F, E-T, F-F, G-T, H-T, I-F, J-T

CHAPTER 12   DATA EXTRACTION, TRANSFORMATION, AND LOADING

1 Match the columns

1-E, 2-G, 3-B, 4-F, 5-J, 6-A, 7-C, 8-H, 9-D, 10-I

CHAPTER 13   DATA QUALITY: A KEY TO SUCCESS

1 Match the columns

1-D, 2-J, 3-I, 4-F, 5-H, 6-C, 7-A, 8-G, 9-E, 10-B

CHAPTER 14   MATCHING INFORMATION TO THE CLASSES OF USERS

1 Match the columns

1-J, 2-G, 3-I, 4-H, 5-A, 6-C, 7-D, 8-B, 9-F, 10-E

CHAPTER 15   OLAP IN THE DATA WAREHOUSE

1 Indicate if true or false

A-T, B-F, C-T, D-F, E-F, F-T, G-T, H-F, I-F, J-F

CHAPTER 16 DATA WAREHOUSING AND THE WEB

1 Indicate if true or false

A-F, B-T, C-F, D-F, E-T, F-T, G-T, H-F, I-F, J-T

CHAPTER 17 DATA MINING BASICS

1 Match the columns

1-E, 2-G, 3-H, 4-A, 5-J, 6-B, 7-I, 8-D, 9-C, 10-F

CHAPTER 18 THE PHYSICAL DESIGN PROCESS

1 Match the columns

1-G, 2-E, 3-I, 4-A, 5-H, 6-J, 7-D, 8-F, 9-B, 10-C

CHAPTER 19 DATA WAREHOUSE DEPLOYMENT

1 Indicate if true or false

A-T, B-F, C-T, D-F, E-F, F-T, G-T, H-F, I-T, J-F

APPENDIX A

PROJECT LIFE CYCLE STEPS AND CHECKLISTS

DATA WAREHOUSE PROJECT LIFE CYCLE: MAJOR STEPS AND SUBSTEPS

Note: The substeps indicated here are at a high level. Expand these substeps as necessary to suit the requirements of your environment.

Project Planning

Definition of scope, goals, objectives, and expectations

Establishment of implementation strategy

Preliminary identification of project resources

Assembling of project team

Estimation of project schedule

Requirements Definition

Definition of requirements gathering strategy

Conducting interviews and group sessions with users

Review of existing documents

Study of source operational systems

Derivation of business metrics and dimensions needed for analysis

Data Warehousing Fundamentals for IT Professionals, Second Edition. By Paulraj Ponniah
Copyright © 2010 John Wiley & Sons, Inc.

Design

Design of the logical data model

Definition of data extraction, transformation, and loading functions

Design of the information delivery framework

Establishment of storage requirements

Definitions of the overall architecture and supporting infrastructure

Construction

Selection and installation of infrastructure hardware and software

Selection and installation of the DBMSs

Selection and installation of ETL and BI (business intelligence) tools

Completion of the design of the physical data model

Completion of the metadata component

Deployment

Completion of user acceptance tests

Performance of initial data loads

Making user desktops ready for the data warehouse

Training and support for the initial set of users

Provision for data warehouse security, backup, and recovery

Maintenance

Ongoing monitoring of the data warehouse

Continuous performance tuning

Ongoing user training

Provision of ongoing support to users

Ongoing data warehouse management

CHECKLISTS FOR MAJOR ACTIVITIES

Note: Break the following major activities down into detailed tasks. Prepare your own checklists for the tasks in each major activity.

Project Planning

Complete definition of project scope and objectives

Prepare project initiation document

Conduct project initiation sessions with sponsor and user representatives

Complete selection of project team members

Prepare project schedule

Complete project plan document

Requirements Definition

Complete summaries of interviews and group sessions

Summarize available information on data from source systems

Document requirements for information delivery to user groups

Discuss and agree with users on system performance

Complete information package diagrams showing metrics and dimensions

Prepare and publish requirements definition document

Design

Complete the E-R and dimensional diagrams for the logical data model

Document all data extraction and data staging functions

Estimate data storage requirements

Classify users and determine information delivery criteria for each class

Document desired features needed in all types of tools

Create design specifications for any in-house programs for data staging, loading, and information delivery

Construction

Install and test infrastructure hardware and software

Install and test selected DBMSs

Install and test selected tools

Complete the physical data model and allocate storage

Test initial and ongoing data loads

Complete overall system test

Deployment

Complete user acceptance documents

Load initial data

Install and test all the required software on the client machines

Train initial set of users

Grant authorizations for data warehouse access to various classes of users

Establish backup and recovery procedures

Maintenance

Establish procedures to gather statistics for ongoing monitoring

Fine-tune the data warehouse as necessary

Complete materials for training of users and establish training schedule

Establish user support structure

Establish procedures for data warehouse management

Upgrade infrastructure as needed from time to time

APPENDIX B

CRITICAL FACTORS FOR SUCCESS

- Do not launch the data warehouse unless and until your company is ready for it.
- Find the best executive sponsor. Ensure continued, long-term, and committed support.
- Emphasize the business aspects, not the technological ones, of the project. Choose a business-oriented project manager.
- Take an enterprise-wide view for the requirements.
- Have a pragmatic, staged implementation plan.
- Communicate realistic expectations to the users; deliver on the promises.
- Do not overreach to cost-justify and predict ROI.
- Institute appropriate and effective communication methods.
- Throughout the project life cycle, keep the project as a joint effort between IT and users.
- Adopt proven technologies; avoid bleeding-edge technologies.
- Recognize the paramount importance of data quality.
- Do not ignore the potential of data from external sources.
- Do not underestimate the time and effort for the data extraction, transformation, and loading (ETL) functions.
- Select the architecture that is just right for your environment; data warehousing is not a one-size-fits-all proposition.
- Architecture first, technology next, and only then, tools.
- Determine a clear training strategy.

Data Warehousing Fundamentals for IT Professionals, Second Edition. By Paulraj Ponniah
Copyright © 2010 John Wiley & Sons, Inc.

- Be wary of "analysis paralysis."
- Begin deployment with a suitable and visible pilot to deliver early benefits.
- Do not neglect the importance of scalability. Plan for growth and evolution.
- Focus on queries, not transactions. The data warehouse is query-centric, not transaction-oriented.
- Emphasize and distinguish between the data warehousing and analytical environments.
- Clearly define and manage data ownership considerations.

APPENDIX C

GUIDELINES FOR EVALUATING VENDOR SOLUTIONS

Here are a few practical guidelines. These are general guidelines relating to all types of products that perform various functions, from data extraction through information delivery. Adapt and apply these to your specific environment.

- First and foremost, determine the functions in your data warehouse that absolutely need vendor tools and solutions.
- For each type of product you need, carefully list the features that are expected. Divide the features into groups by importance—high, medium, and low. Use these groups of features to grade the products you are considering.
- Allocate enough time to research available solutions and vendors thoroughly.
- If you try to incorporate solutions from too many different vendors, you must be prepared to face serious challenges of incompatibilities and restrictions for integration. Stay with two or three vendors whose products are most appropriate for your needs.
- Metadata is a key component of a data warehouse. Ensure that the vendor products you choose can handle metadata satisfactorily.
- The standing and stability of the vendor are equally important as the effectiveness of the products themselves. Even when the products are suitable for your environment, if you are concerned about the staying power of the vendor, have second thoughts on selecting these products.
- Never rely solely on vendor demonstrations as the basis for your selection, nor should you check only the references furnished by the vendors themselves.
- Test the tools and products in your environment, with subsets of your own data.

Data Warehousing Fundamentals for IT Professionals, Second Edition. By Paulraj Ponniah
Copyright © 2010 John Wiley & Sons, Inc.

- Arrange for both user representatives and IT members of the project team to test the products, jointly and independently.
- Establish a definitive method for comparing and scoring competing products. You may devise a point system to score the various features you are looking for in a product type.
- The success of your data warehouse rides on the end-user tools. Pay special attention to the choice of the end-user tools. You may compromise a bit on the other types, but not on the end-user tools.
- Most of your end-users will be new to data warehousing. Good, intuitive and easy-to-use tools go a long way in winning them over.
- Users like tools that seamlessly incorporate online queries, batch reporting, and data extraction for analysis.

APPENDIX D

HIGHLIGHTS OF VENDORS
AND PRODUCTS*

Here is a list of vendors and products for data warehousing/business intelligence. Although this list contains several vendors, the list is by no means exhaustive and complete. As needed, the readers may do their own research on the Internet and elsewhere to find vendors and products in specific areas of data warehousing/business intelligence.

In this list the product information is shown in italics. Only one or two products of each vendor are mentioned. For detailed offerings of each vendor please consult the respective Website.

Large vendors have several product offerings. Therefore, for such vendors, only their Website information is given. Please visit the Websites of these large vendors for complete information on their product offerings.

Actuate

(www.actuate.com)

> **BIRT** *(Open Source Business Intelligence and Reporting Tools)—full spectrum of products to develop and deploy Rich Information Applications for any organization from a simple startup to a global enterprise. Applications can range from individual reports and Business Intelligence and Performance Management applications for departments to dynamic, interactive applications for hundreds of thousands of users outside the firewall. Included in company's end-to-end information-driven solutions are products for Rich Information Application development, data integration and application deployment.*

---

* Sources: Websites of respective vendors, other literature, and usage experience.

Data Warehousing Fundamentals for IT Professionals, Second Edition. By Paulraj Ponniah
Copyright © 2010 John Wiley & Sons, Inc.

ADVIZOR Solutions, Inc.

(www.advizorsolutions.com)

> **ADVIZOR Analyst**—*Analyst is a Microsoft.NET client-based solution that enables business users to visually analyze desktop and enterprise data, create dashboards that can be shared with other ADVIZOR Analyst users, publish dashboards to ADVIZOR Desktop Navigator (client-based) and ADVIZOR Server AE (thin Web-based) deployment, and export findings to Microsoft Office and Adobe PDF products. The Analyst contains the full suite of interactive ADVIZOR Charts with Visual Discovery. It is ideal for performing interactive analysis on all types of business data to drive fact-based decision making.*

agileDSS Inc.

(www.agiledss.com)

> **agileWORKFLOW**—*A process automation platform that enables enterprises to manage and control their business intelligence and data warehousing processes in an easy and reliable way.*

Applix, Inc.

(www.applix.com)

> **TM1**—*A MOLAP database server, and related presentation tools, including Applix Web and Applix Executive Viewer. Together, Applix TM1, Applix Web, and Applix Executive Viewer were the three core components of the Applix Business Analytics Platform. [In 2007, Applix was acquired by Cognos, an IBM company. Cognos has rebranded all Applix products under its name.]*

arcplan, Inc.

(www.arcplan.com)

> **arcplan Enterprise**—*Delivers real-time, interactive analytics that go beyond just reports. With arcplan Enterprise, you deliver actionable, contextual knowledge to decision makers at every level so that you have the intelligence to understand and change how you operate. With arcplan Enterprise, you get business intelligence when you need it, cost effectively. arcplan Enterprise's complementary approach analyzes information from multiple data sources such as ERP, OLAP, relational databases, and Web services simultaneously.*

Arkidata Corporation

(www.arkidata.com)

> **Daetaective Office 6.0**—*With powerful new features making the technology much more efficient as a data cleansing technology tool. Such developmental efforts also permit the company to broaden applications of the technology to data mining and the ETL marketplace.*

Ascential Software Corporation

(www.ascential.com)

> **DataStage**—*A data extraction and transformation program that is used to pull data from legacy databases, flat files and relational databases and convert them into data marts and data warehouses. Formerly a product from Ascential Software Corporation,*

which IBM acquired in 2005, DataStage became a core component of the IBM WebSphere Data Integration suite.

Attensity

(www.attensity.com)

Semantic Applications Suite (Voice of the Customer, Cloud, Response Management, E-Service, Research & Discovery, Risk & Compliance, Intelligence Analysis)—*Business is built on conversations. These customer, partner, and employee conversations are captured in e-mails, call notes, letters, surveys, forums, and social media. Attensity's semantic applications suite enables you to monitor, analyze, respond to, and reuse these conversations—transforming them into actionable facts and insights that you can use to drive your business.*

Business Objects

(www.businessobjects.com)

BusinessObjects XI—*Set of components that provide performance management, planning, reporting, query and analysis, and enterprise information management.*

Celequest Corporation

(www.celequest.com)

On-Demand Business Intelligence—*Celequest is the leading provider of on-demand business intelligence (BI). Delivered as an appliance or as Software-as-a-Service (SaaS), Celequest enables companies to deliver enterprise-class BI without the cost and complexity of other approaches to operational BI. Celequest's innovative technology includes data integration, analytics, and dashboards/reporting in a single integrated product. Critical application areas for Celequest technology include financial performance management, risk mitigation, manufacturing operations, demand visibility, inventory monitoring, continuous sales analysis, margin optimization, and logistics monitoring.*

ClearForest

(www.clearforest.com)

Text-Driven Business Intelligence—*ClearForest, a Reuters company, provides text-driven business intelligence solutions that supply the analytical bridge between two previously disconnected worlds of information—unstructured text and enterprise data. Its solutions offer manufacturers, publishers, federal, chemical, and financial service organizations critical links to situational context buried in text for use in business intelligence systems. Adding this situational context to enterprise data systems empowers organizations to uncover hidden relationships, evaluate events, discover unforeseen patterns, and facilitate problem identification for rapid resolution. Applying this intelligence enables organizations to avoid loss of profit margins due to preventable write-offs, customer churn, legal settlements, warranty claims, or inefficient product development cycles.*

Cognos

(www.cognos.com)

IBM Cognos 8 Business Intelligence—*Delivers the complete range of BI capabilities on a single, service-oriented architecture (SOA). Enables businesses to set targets,* *see results, understand what drives the numbers, identify trends that may be benefits or threats, and take action with a common context for decision making across every department.*

Corda Technologies, Inc.
(www.corda.com)

CenterView—*Business Performance Dashboard delivers greater control of an organization's performance with its powerful performance dashboard technology. With CenterView, not only can one visualize the data in the most meaningful way, but one can also quickly take action. Corda's patented Datafunnel rapidly connects to virtually any data source.*

Crystal Decisions, Inc.
(www.crystaldecisions.com)

Crystal Reports—*Allows report designers to create highly formatted reports, connected to virtually any data source—interactivity empowers business users to manipulate data, while decreasing the number of reports IT needs to maintain.*

DATAllegro
(www.datallegro.com)

DATAllegro v3—*Goes beyond the low cost and high performance of first generation data warehouse appliances and adds the flexibility and scalability that only an enterprise-class platform can offer. The result is a complete data warehouse appliance that enables companies to rapidly query large volumes of data (up to several hundreds of terabytes) at a very affordable price.*

DataFlux
(www.dataflux.com)

DataFlux Data Quality Integration Platform—*Comprised of dfPower Studio, the Dataflux Integration Server, and DataFlux adapters, offers a unique, award-winning approach built on a single, flexible code base. DataFlux offers industry-leading technology for data governance, master data management, data quality, and data integration.*

DataLever Corporation
(www.datalever.com)

DataLever Enterprise Suite—*Datalever's cutting edge data integration and data quality management solutions enable organizations to harness the power of their data to effectively drive their business and stay one step ahead of the competition. DataLever is a visual process designer that makes it easy to create and run high-performance data-transformation processes. Using a modular approach, you select components from a palette. Each component performs a specialized operation. By connecting the components, you can create custom data processing engines—complex processes tailored to meet your specific needs. The framework encompasses a broad range of functions: data reengineering, data profiling, geocoding, matching, householding, text parsing, pattern matching, and so on.*

DataMentors, Inc.

(www.datamentors.com)

Software Solutions Suite—*Includes a variety of software solutions designed to address the data quality and business intelligence issues of the marketplace. Specific products include ValiData (Data Discovery and Profiling), DataFuse (Data Quality and Integration), PinPoint (Data Mining, Analysis, and Database Marketing), and NetEffect (Real-Time Transactional Data Cleansing and Matching).*

DataMirror

(www.datamirror.com)

IBM InfoSphere Change Data Capture—*Detects and delivers information across heterogeneous data stores in real time. Log-based Change Data Capture (CDC) technology, acquired by IBM in the DataMirror acquisition, detects and delivers mission-critical data events in real time without impacting system performance.*

Endeca

(www.endeca.com)

Endeca Commerce Suite—*Includes Merchandising Workbench, Search Engine Marketing, and Social Navigation. Endeca provides a platform for search applications that enables more millions of people around the world to access information quickly and easily. Endeca-powered solutions give customers and employees clear visibility into any information, driving up measurable cost savings and increasing revenue.*

FAST

(www.fastsearch.com)

FAST ESP—*A best-in-class enterprise search solution for the most demanding enterprise search needs. FAST ESP can be extended through FAST ESP Add-Ons to provide additional business value and enhanced user experiences. Together, these solutions offer an extensible and scalable search platform that helps deliver intuitive user experiences and positive business results.*

Firstlogic

(www.firstlogic.com)

Information Quality Suite—*Identifies data quality problems and business rule violations within the organization's database. The data quality software parses and standardizes both customer and operational data, corrects the data based on secondary data sources to improve matching, and appends additional information such as phone numbers to provide a more complete base of customer knowledge. The core of the Information Quality Suite is the matching and consolidation technology, which identifies duplicate records, consolidates data, builds relationships, and creates a single customer view across databases. A complete data quality strategy offers powerful tools for data profiling, data cleansing, data enhancement, and data consolidation.*

HP

(www.hp.com)

For this large vendor, refer to the vendor's official Website for products and solutions.

Hummingbird Ltd.

(www.hummingbird.com)

BI/Query—*Enterprise query and reporting application. BI/Query (formerly Hummingbird GQL) features a graphical ad hoc query interface. Together with its integrated report writer, BI/Query's unparalleled ease of use helps users make faster and better strategic decisions.*

Hyperion

(www.hyperion.com)

Oracle Hyperion Performance Scorecard—*A balanced scorecard collaborative certified application that helps companies clearly articulate strategy and goals, communicate them across the enterprise, monitor key performance indicators, and improve business alignment. The software offers companies complete strategy- and accountability-mapping capabilities, as well as Web-based message boards, forums, and discussion threads.*

IBM

(www.ibm.com)

For this large vendor, refer to the vendor's official Website for products and solutions.

iDashboards

(www.iDashboards.com)

iDashboards Enterprise Edition—*Leading software for business intelligence dashboards. Organizations are adopting iDashboards as the corporate standard to deliver performance management, scorecards, and business alerts. iDashboards helps companies leverage information assets through visually rich, real-time, and personalized business intelligence dashboards to analyze, track, and drill down through a wealth of information. The security framework provides role-based user privileges and access control. Because iDashboards complies with industry standards (J2EE, XML, JDBC, ODBC, LDAP), installation is simplified. Features include user-level customization of dashboards, drill down to charts, dashboards, and web URLs, real-time analytics to perform data calculations and track statistical outliers, and seamless connectivity to relational databases.*

InetSoft

(www.inetsoft.com)

InetSoft Style Intelligence—*Is an operational business intelligence platform that uses a visualization-driven approach to address reporting, analysis, and dashboard needs, in a unified, easy-to-use business intelligence solution. It has been deployed by enterprises all around the world and embedded in other solution provider's applications serving dozens of verticals to meet their dashboard, reporting, and visual analysis needs. InetSoft's unique user-driven data approach yields good self-service, benefiting business users, administrators, and developers.*

Informatica Corporation

(www.informatica.com)

Informatica PowerCenter—*A single, unified enterprise data integration platform for accessing, discovering, and integrating data from virtually any business system, in* *any format, and delivering that data throughout the enterprise at any speed. Informatica is a leader in data integration software. Several companies rely on the Informatica Platform to lower IT costs and gain greater business value from all their information assets both on-premise in traditional IT computing systems and in the Internet cloud.*

Information Builders

(www.ibi.com)

WebFOCUS—*A comprehensive and fully integrated enterprise business intelligence platform whose architecture, integration, and simplicity permeate every level of the global organization—executive, analytical, and operational—and make any data available, accessible, and meaningful to every person or application who needs it, when and how they need it. The vendor is a leader in enterprise business intelligence and Web reporting software solutions.*

Interactive Edge

(www.interactiveedge.com)

XP3 Suite—*Combines a powerful data analysis engine with flexible end-user tools to summarize and illustrate useful, compelling information on demand; and has proven itself highly effective as a point-of-impact solution for distributed sales and management teams.*

Jaspersoft

(www.jaspersoft.com)

Jaspersoft Business Intelligence Suite—*A comprehensive, open source suite of products for reporting, data analysis (OLAP), and data integration (ETL). It is easy to deploy incrementally, which makes it especially cost effective for enterprise departments, small and mid-sized businesses, and independent software vendors (ISVs). The suite includes JasperReports, iReport, JasperServer, JasperAnalysis, and JasperETL.*

LogiXML Inc.

(www.LogiXML.com)

LogiXML business intelligence software (BI) solutions—*Offer easy to use and quick to deploy business intelligence software and Web-based reporting tools. Solutions include reporting, analysis, and dashboard software for developers (Logi Info), for end-users (Logi Ad Hoc), and Web-based ETL/data integration (Logi ETL).*

Melissa Data Corp

(www.melissa.com)

Data Quality Suite—*Multiplatform toolkit to verify, correct, and standardize address, phone, e-mail, and names at point of entry.*

Microsoft

(www.microsoft.com)

For this large vendor, refer to the vendor's official Website for products and solutions.

MicroStrategy, Inc.

(www.microstrategy.com)

MicroStrategy 9—*Most feature-rich release in a decade, allows companies to support all levels of BI initiatives, and helps companies to consolidate islands of BI gradually into a cohesive enterprise BI framework. The MicroStrategy Platform is a business intelligence architecture that delivers high performance, sophisticated analytics, low cost of ownership, rapid report creation, and good end-user self-service. The enterprise-caliber technology is based on Relational OLAP (ROLAP) architecture and is one of the earliest to offer both a highly scalable and fully interactive BI environment. Leading independent provider of Business Intelligence, Performance Management, and Dashboard Reporting Solutions.*

Oracle Corporation

(www.oracle.com)

For this large vendor, refer to the vendor's official Website for products and solutions.

OutlookSoft Corporation

(www.outlooksoft.com)

OutlookSoft 5—*Provides a single performance management platform for strategic planning, budgeting, forecasting, statutory consolidation, reporting, analysis, predictive analytics, scorecarding, and dashboards.*

PivotLink Inc.

(www.pivotlink.com)

Business Intelligence as SaaS—*Analytic Software as a Service (SaaS) that provides every department the power, flexibility, and simplicity to answer critical business questions and make profitable decisions for the company—all at a lower cost and in less time. It's easy to get started, easy to add data, and easy to use. PivotLink delivers data analysis, reporting, and dashboard solutions so that business users can analyze the data that matters most to their business.*

ProClarity Corporation

(www.proclarity.com)

ProClarity Analytics—*A Microsoft business intelligence platform. Other offerings include Analytics Server, which manages analysis activities; Dashboards that monitor business conditions; Scorecard, which exhibits business intelligence; reporting services; development platform that supports high-performing analytics for OEMs, software developers, and corporations.*

QlikTech Inc.

(www.qlikview.com)

QlikView 9—*A complete BI solution that allows companies to build, deploy, and distribute analysis applications. It uses next generation in-memory association technology to simplify the creation, deployment, use, and maintenance of visually interactive multidimensional analysis of data held in disparate information systems.*

Relational Solutions, Inc.

(www.relationalsolutions.com)

POSmart—*A leading, multi-retailer solution. It automates the data integration and harmonization of point-of-sale data, syndicated data, and internal data. The integration and analytics engine pulls in demand-level data (retailer POS) with its built-in retailer-specific data connectors, along with shipments and other internal ERP data, internal master data, and syndicated data, then applies Dynamic Matching Technology and industry algorithms that validate and harmonize the data and delivers the actionable information needed to change the way business is done.*

SAP America Inc.

(www.sap.com/analytics)

For this large vendor, refer to the vendor's official Website for products and solutions.

SAS Institute

(www.sas.com)

For this large vendor, refer to the vendor's official Website for products and solutions.

Sybase, Inc.

(www.sybase.com)

Sybase Analytic Appliance—*Configured and tuned out of the box, providing analytics capabilities for overburdened enterprise data warehouse systems. Combining technologies, including Sybase IQ, PowerDesigner, IBM Power Systems, and MicroStrategy business intelligence technology, the Analytic Appliance provides all the benefits of a custom-built enterprise data warehouse, but is easy, fast, and affordable.*

Syncsort Inc.

(www.syncsort.com)

DMExpress—*Data integration solution to help drive ROI with a combination of high performance, optimal hardware utilization, and ease of use. DMExpress brings speed and ease of use to processes and applications like ETL, data warehousing, and BI, while leveraging inexpensive and commodity hardware.*

Teradata

(www.teradata.com)

For this large vendor, refer to the vendor's official Website for products and solutions.

Trillium Software

(www.trilliumsoftware.com)

Data Cleansing and Standardization—*Automatically does the hard work for you, without time and labor-consuming preformatting or preprocessing. The tool understands, interprets, and reorganizes data within any context, from any source, even free text disassociated from relevant fields. Once the initial cleansing has been done, data is now standardized to work effectively with all applications and systems, including*

CRM, ERP, MDM, CDI, SOA, eCommerce platforms, and more. Plus, any rules created or modified may be reused within any system in the organization.

Truviso Inc.

(www.truviso.com)

Truviso Continuous Analytics—*Software is based on a revolutionary technology that completely eliminates the need to batch, store, organize, and retrieve data before it is analyzed. Continuous Analytics enables organizations to instantly query large volumes of both live and stored data to provide actionable insight moments after events occur. Truviso immediately processes and analyzes data as soon as it becomes available, completely eliminating batch processing delays. The traditional data warehouse approach to analytics—store first, query later—can't keep up with the unique demands of network-driven businesses. Online advertising, streaming video, content delivery, and mobile providers depend on instant analysis across multiple data sources to maximize their revenue. Continuous Analytics software can process massive amounts of historical and live data in real time, helping these types of companies make the most of their content and inventory, command higher CPM, and provide live dashboards to their customers.*

Unisys Corporation

(www.unisys.com)

For this large vendor, refer to the vendor's official Website for products and solutions.

Visual Mining

(www.visualmining.com)

NetCharts Performance Dashboards (NCPD)—*A dynamic, interactive dashboard solution that enables one to analyze data, gain insight, and make better business decisions. With NCPD, end-users can quickly and easily design and create dashboards that incorporate advanced data visualizations and adapt to constantly changing business requirements. NCPD allows one to be agile—one can create and deploy dashboards quickly and refine them on the fly—and NCPD is designed for the everyday end-user. Users control design and layout, so they don't need a programmer or IT department to implement the solution and won't need IT to customize the dashboard(s) for personal preferences. With its built-in ease-of-use features, dashboards can be used as effectively for a three-week project as for a three-year project.*

APPENDIX E

REAL-WORLD EXAMPLES
OF BEST PRACTICES*

This appendix contains a few typical examples of best practices in the application of data warehousing and business intelligence. Many more such examples may be found by researching on the Internet and elsewhere.

AIRLINES

American Airlines serves more than 250 cities in 41 countries, with 1100 airplanes and about 4400 daily flights. The airline processes about 125 million transportation documents on an annual basis. It is important for the company to detect fraudulent ticket processing, track ticket sales properly, and ensure that proper revenue is flowing in. But because of the complexity of the airline industry and the amount of data involved in ticket transactions, accomplishing this is no small task. With the amount of data created by all these ticket documents, American Airlines needed a more efficient system that would help ensure proper amounts of earned revenue on ticket sales.

American Airlines now has the data warehouse named RADAR (Revenue Account Data Access Resource) to detect fraudulent ticket processing, track ticket sales properly, and ensure that proper revenue is flowing into the company. RADAR enables expert business analysts to quickly query and sort through large amounts of data. RADAR has produced savings to American Airlines in millions of dollars through detection of fraudulent ticketing.

*Sources: Publications of the Data Warehousing Institute, other literature, and the Internet.

SPECIALTY TEXTILES

SAERTEX GmbH & Co. KG is a specialist manufacturer of high-tech textiles for the aviation, automotive, shipbuilding, and utilities sectors. With its headquarters and main production facilities at Saerbeck in Germany, the company has grown internationally and now operates from seven locations on four continents. With employees working in numerous locations and time zones across the globe, it was not easy for subsidiaries to communicate and collaborate effectively. Gradually, each site began to adopt slightly different working practices, making it difficult to access and share sales and business data across the company. SAERTEX senior management wanted to define a global set of business processes that the whole company would follow, which would help speed the flow of information throughout the business. The company wanted a solution that would allow users to log in from any location easily and efficiently, using nothing more than a Web browser.

A data warehouse and Web portal capable of managing, sharing, and controlling the data as required has provided what SAERTEX needed. The configuration provides data mining, online analytical processing (OLAP), and extract, transform, and load (ETL) functionality to create multidimensional data cubes within the data warehouse. These are then analyzed and presented to users via Web access. The portal provides a dashboard with easy access to reports, helping users understand the current status of the business and identify trends. The sales teams can easily view month-on-month or year-on-year percentage changes in revenue and this helps them analyze performance and respond more effectively. SAERTEX now has access to a single source of truth for business intelligence reporting, and the IT team can maintain and manage the data centrally, which saves costs.

TRAVEL

ARC provides data and analytical services to the travel industry. Traditionally, travel agency fraud was identified by auditing volumes of paper coupons and weekly reports at the agency physical location. Thirteen weeks of data took two days or more to analyze, spot trends and patterns, and to report on findings.

The ARC industry data warehouse with predictive fraud modeling has dramatically cut down the time for analysis and reporting. Huge volumes of data for even 39 months can now be analyzed in minutes (as compared to 24 days) and findings reported expeditiously.

HEALTH CARE

Ingenix, a wholly owned subsidiary of United Health Group, is a global health care information company. The company offers a rapidly evolving portfolio of tools and services to help health care organizations transform data into actionable information. Its solutions help drive disease prevention programs, enhance the efficiency of claims processes, detect and deter fraudulent and erroneous claims, and much more. With data scattered across myriad data silos, business decisions were often subject to incomplete and inconsistent information. And because multiple versions of the same data existed in different locations, staff would often obtain different results from the same queries. As a result, much time was spent determining what information was correct.

Today, the company's enterprise data warehouse named Galaxy is at the heart of the organization's business intelligence and performance management activities. It enables the company to integrate information from diverse subject areas, such as claims, membership, and provider directories, across multiple data sources. And Galaxy drives many of the organization's scoring and predictive models, rules engines, reporting, functional data marts, analytical models, normative data sets, and transaction engines. These are critical for pricing, marketing, customer reporting, underwriting, clinical analytics, research, fraud and abuse auditing, and regulatory reporting. Information is made available to users at the transaction level so that staff can view each specific claim, not simply a summary of claims. Delivery of information as a service goes to more than 2000 registered users. Between 10,000 and 15,000 queries are processed each day and more than 15 trillion rows are read from the database each week. Cost cuts are in millions of dollars.

SECURITIES

RBC Wealth Management, a subsidiary of Royal Bank of Canada, has over 2300 financial consultants and 5000 employees. The company, one of Canada's largest full-service securities firms, had been providing a stale and inadequate sales development Excel-based tool to its field advisors. Reports were run manually.

The new RBC Dashboard changed all of this and provides tremendously greater visibility and offers growth possibilities. Field advisors immediately perceived how the dashboard had empowered them. The use of the dashboard has spread to hundreds of field advisors.

INTERNATIONAL SHIPPING AND DELIVERY

DHL leads the world in developing innovative, tailored solutions in international express shipping and logistics delivery. Although making extensive use of IT in operations, DHL did not have a comprehensive solution for current and future needs that reported or monitored business processes. The company also needed to organize its administration to create a better, transparent overview of administrative costs and case handling. DHL Express Sweden needed an environment for improved decision making and enhanced customer experience.

A data warehouse and reporting application were built to monitor DHL's Nordic activities. The system provides DHL with an overview of all product areas. DHL now has a data warehouse that provides major benefits in its daily operational activities. A drastic drop in IT costs and significantly better information to make critical decisions provide added value of the business intelligence (BI) solution.

RAIL SERVICES

GE Rail Services (GERS) provides repairs and maintenance services for leased railcars in North America. Repair shop selections were made by customer service representatives without proper knowledge of shop capacity, railcar movement patterns, and so on. Railcars could wait for weeks before repairs may be scheduled.

Now, Shoptimizer, a real-time BI operational analytical tool can match and locate the optimal shop to provide repairs subject to more than 20 constraints and parameters. It has cut down the wait-time for repairs and eliminated unnecessary shipping and leasing costs.

PHONE SERVICE

Reliance Communication, India's second-largest communications company, has a digital network covering over 14,000 towns and 400,000 villages. The company's subscriber base exceeded 40 million and was growing at an annual rate of 50%. The increase in demand for Reliance's services was producing explosive growth in the systems and infra-structure required to operate the business. The need to provide accurate, timely analytics to all parts of the business was becoming more acute. One area of the company that required rapid delivery of relevant analysis was Reliance's Law Enforcement Department.

The company selected the approach of using a Data Warehouse Appliance. As a result of deploying the DW Appliance, the time required to turn around a request for detailed call records shrank by over 80%, from multiple days to a few hours. In addition to the company's issues with information retrieval, the inability to load data into the data warehouse quickly enough was becoming increasingly problematic. Compared to Reliance's previous database system, the DW Appliance solution reduced the average time to load a day's worth of data by over 90%, from 2 hours to under 10 minutes.

HOME IMPROVEMENT RETAIL

Lowe's Companies, Inc. serves approximately 13 million customers a week at more than 1375 home improvement stores in 49 states. Based in Mooresville, North Carolina, the 60-year-old company is the second-largest home improvement retailer in the world. Lowe's has been committed to information-driven decision making and used decision support and data warehousing for more than a decade.

Enhancement to Lowe's BI initiatives has come in the implementation called DART (Data Access and Reporting Tool). This provides employees greater insight into key per-formance metrics. More than 150,000 reports are run each week, and Lowe's employees from multiple business areas use the data to manage inventory, improve margins, review market specificity, and identify sales opportunities. Lowe's also uses BI to analyze demo-graphic attribute data to better anticipate the products that its customers will buy. Lowe's primary data warehouse contains more than 20 terabytes of data and has grown by more than 20% per year over the past few years.

CREDIT UNION

With more than $1 billion in assets, Spokane Teachers Credit Union is a large, full-service organization serving 80,000 members through 13 branch locations. It employs 350 people. As the membership grew, the ability to service members effectively dwindled.

STCU, being a progressive institution, dramatically changed and improved its service mechanism through its data warehouse as the analytical engine behind an in-house front-end. This "Conversation Engine" Solution enables each member's individual portfolio of services and behaviors to be analyzed and specific opportunities identified. The simplicity of the tool produced widespread adoption in the company resulting in a service revolution for STCU.

LIFE INSURANCE

Like many insurance and financial services companies, the basic sales philosophy of face-to-face contact with customers has been a cornerstone of Western and Southern Life's history. In addition to the issue of customer information not making it back to the company from sales representatives, there have been other areas that prevented Western and Southern from fully capitalizing on the strength of its customer base. These issues include the segmentation of data into various legacy systems, not being able to effectively determine which customers are high value customers, and not being able to obtain a global view of the various products that customers own. Western and Southern decided to focus on the strategic business processes that were the core of the business. These processes included customer retention, customer service, cross-selling, lead generation, target marketing, and product generation. The vision proved to be the driving force behind the creation of a marketing data warehouse.

Prior to Western and Southern Life's data warehouse, marketing campaigns generally focused on saturating an undifferentiated client population with direct marketing materials so there would be enough responses to generate an acceptable return. Western and Southern Life's strategy has changed from a mass-marketing approach to a focused, targeted approach. By using data mining with a data warehouse to identify the most likely responding segments, Western and Southern Life is able to achieve phenomenal ROI results, while only marketing to a limited portion of the customer base. This targeted approach dovetails with Western and Southern's larger corporate CRM initiative of offering relevant products to the right people at the right time.

TELECOMMUNICATIONS

France Telecom is one of the world's leading telecommunications carriers, with over 91 million customers on five continents in 220 countries and territories. Recording more than a 500 million calls per day, France Telecom required a solution that would provide a unique view for each of its customers. The call data included length, frequency, and amount, as well as information about cancellations and payment types. France Telecom needed quick data analysis to accurately understand customer behavior in order to adapt products and services for each unique customer. Faced with more than 50 separate databases, increasing traffic and escalating requirements from internal staff, France Telecom needed a new system that would become the online repository for all telecom traffic, support fraud detection efforts, improve customer service, and enable effective network traffic analysis.

France Telecom's data warehouse, named Symphonie, supports 1145 users who generate global traffic of 23 requests per second, with more than 600 concurrent users during peak hours. Standard online CDR queries complete in less than 4 seconds. As many as 65 million new CDRs are added hourly to the data warehouse, resulting in up to 100 gigabytes of new data added daily. The Symphonie data warehouse holds more than 200 billion CDRs. This 42-terabyte data warehouse is one of the largest data warehouses in the world.

REFERENCES

Adamson, Christopher, and Michael Venerable, *Data Warehouse Design Solutions*, New York: Wiley, 1998.

Adriaans, Pieter, and Doff Zantinge, *Data Mining*, Harlow, UK: Addison Wesley, 1996.

Ambler, Scott W., *Agile Database Techniques*, Hoboken, NJ: Wiley, 2003.

Barquin, Ramon C., and Herb Edelstein, *Planning and Designing the Data Warehouse*, Upper Saddle River, NJ: Prentice-Hall PTR, 1997.

Berson, Alex, and Stephen J. Smith, *Data Warehousing, Data Mining, and OLIP*, New York: McGraw-Hill, 1997.

Berry, Michael J. A., and Gordon Linoff, *Data Mining Techniques*, New York: Wiley, 1997.

Bigus, Joseph P., *Data Mining with Neural Networks*, New York: McGraw-Hill, 1996.

Bischoff, Joyce, and Ted Alexander, *Data Warehouse: Practical Advice from the Experts*, Upper Saddle River, NJ: Prentice-Hall, 1997.

Cabena, Peter, et al., *Discovering Data Mining: From Concept to Implementation*, Upper Saddle River, NJ: Prentice-Hall PTR, 1998.

Codd, E. F., *Providing On-Line Analytical Processing to User Analysts*, San Jose: Codd & Date, Inc., 1993.

Craig, Robert S., et al., *Microsoft Data Warehousing*, New York: Wiley, 1999.

Debevoise, Nielson Thomas, *The Data Warehouse Method: Integrated Data Warehouse Support Environments*, Upper Saddle River, NJ: Prentice-Hall PTR, 1999.

Devlin, Barry, *Data Warehouse from Architecture to Implementation*, Boston, MA: Addison Wesley, 1997.

Eckerson, Wayne, *Performance Dashboards*, Hoboken, NJ: Wiley, 2006.

Eckerson, Wayne, *Dashboard or Scorecard: Which Should You Use?* Date Warehousing Institute, January 2005, www.tdwi.com.

English, Larry P., *Improving Data Warehouse and Business Information Quality: Methods for Reducing Costs and Increasing Profits*, New York: Wiley, 1999.

Gill, Harjinder S., and Prakash C. Rao, *The Official Client/Server Computing Guide to Data Warehousing*, Indianapolis, IN: Que Corporation, 1996.

Groth, Robert, *Data Mining: A Hands-On Approach for Business Professionals*, Upper Saddle River, NJ: Prentice-Hall PTR, 1998.

Hammergren, Tom, *Data Warehousing Strategies, Technologies, and Techniques*, New York: McGraw-Hill, 1996.

Humphries, Mark, et al., *Data Warehousing: Architecture and Implementation*, Upper Saddle River, NJ: Prentice-Hall PTR, 1999.

Inmon, W. H., *Building the Data Warehouse* (2nd Edition), New York: Wiley, 1996.

Inmon, W. H., et al., *Data Warehouse Performance*, New York: Wiley, 1999.

Inmon, W. H., et al., *Managing the Data Warehouse: Practical Techniques for Monitoring Operations and Performances, Administering Data and Tools, Managing Change and Growth*, New York: Wiley, 1997.

Kelly, Sean, *Data Warehousing in Action*, Chichester, UK: Wiley, 1997.

Kimball, Ralph, and Richard Merz, *The Data Webhouse Toolkit: Building the Web-Enabled Data Warehouse*, New York: Wiley, 2000.

Kimball, Ralph, *The Data Warehouse Toolkit: Practical Techniques for Building Dimensional Data Warehouses*, New York: Wiley, 1996.

Kimball, Ralph, et al., *The Data Warehouse Lifecycle Toolkit: Expert Methods for Designing, Developing, and Deploying Data Warehouses*, New York: Wiley, 1998.

Malone, Thomas W., and Rockart, John F., *Computers, Networks, and the Corporation*, Center for Information Systems Research, Sloan School of Management, Massachusetts Institute of Technology, August 1991.

Mattison, Rob, *Data Warehousing Strategies, Technologies, and Techniques*, New York: McGraw-Hill, 1996.

Meyer, Don, and Casey Cannon, *Building a Better Data Warehouse*, Upper Saddle River, NJ: Prentice-Hall PTR, 1998.

Morse, Stephen, and David Isaac, *Parallel Systems in the Data Warehouse*, Upper Saddle River, NJ: Prentice-Hall PTR, 1998.

Poe, Vidette, et al., *Building a Data Warehouse for Decision Support* (2nd Edition), Upper Saddle River, NJ: Prentice-Hall PTR, 1998.

Singh, Harry, *Interactive Data Warehousing*, Upper Saddle River, NJ: Prentice-Hall PTR, 1999.

Thomsen, Erik, *OLAP Solutions: Building Multidimensional Information Systems*, New York: Wiley, 1997.

Westphal, Christopher, and Teresa Blaxton, *Data Mining Solutions*, New York: Wiley, 1998.

Witten, Ian H., and Eibe Frank, *Data Mining*, San Francisco, CA: Morgan Kaufmann, 2005.

GLOSSARY

Ad Hoc Query. A query that is not predefined or anticipated, usually run just once. Ad hoc queries are typical in a data warehouse environment.

ADO. ActiveX Data Objects. Microsoft's software interface mechanism for distributed Web applications.

Agent Technology. A technology where specialized software modules act to produce desired results based on specified events. The software is structurally transparent to users.

Agile Development. A term coined in 2001 with the formulation of the Agile Manifesto to refer to software development methodologies based on iterative development where requirements and solutions evolve through collaboration among self-organizing, cross-functional teams.

Alert System. A software system that notifies and alerts users when particular events take place, such as some business indicator exceeding a preset threshold value.

API. Application Program Interface. A functional interface, usually supplied by the operating system, that allows one application program to communicate with another program for receiving services. APIs are generally implemented through function calls.

ASCII. American Standard Code for Information Interchange. A standard code, consisting of a set of 7-bit coded characters, used for information exchange between computer and communication systems.

BAM. Business Activity Monitoring refers to the collection, aggregation, analysis, and presentation of real-time information about activities within an organization.

Bitmapped Indexing. A sophisticated and fast indexing technique using the binary values of individual bits to indicate values of attributes in relational database tables. This technique is very effective in a data warehouse for low-selectivity data, that is, for attributes that have only a few distinct values.

Data Warehousing Fundamentals for IT Professionals, Second Edition. By Paulraj Ponniah
Copyright © 2010 John Wiley & Sons, Inc.

BLOB. Binary Large Object. Very large binary representation of multimedia objects that can be stored and used in some enhanced relational databases.

B-Tree Indexing. A hierarchical indexing technique based on an inverted tree of nodes containing ranges of indexed values. Going down the hierarchical levels, the nodes progressively contain smaller numbers of index values, so that any value may be searched for in a few trials by starting at the top.

Buffer. A region of computer memory that holds data being transferred from one area to another. Data from database tables are fetched into memory buffers. Memory buffer management is crucial for system performance.

Business Intelligence (BI). Generally used synonymously with the information available in an enterprise for making strategic decisions.

Cache. A method for improving system performance by creating a secondary memory area with access speeds closer to the processor speed. A disk cache is a section of main memory set apart to cache data from the disk. A memory cache is a section of high-speed memory to cache data from main memory.

CASE. Computer-Aided Software Engineering. CASE tools or programs help develop software applications. A set of tools may include code generators, data modeling tools, analysis and design tools, and tools for documenting and testing applications.

CGI. Common Gateway Interface. A standard program interface in Web servers to connect different computer applications. In Web technology, the interface is designed to connect client applications to remote relational databases.

CIO. Chief Information Officer. The executive who heads the information services division of an organization. The CIO, usually reporting directly to the Chief Executive Officer, has the responsibility for all the organization's computing and data communications.

Clickstream. Recording of what the user clicks on while browsing the Web. Clickstream data provides insight into what a visitor is interested in at a Website.

Clustering. A method of keeping database files physically close to one another on the storage media for improving performance through sequential pre-fetch operations.

Composite Key. A key for a database table made up of more than one attribute or field.

Conformed Dimensions. Two sets of business dimensions represented in dimension tables are said to be conformed if both sets are identical in their attributes or if one set is an exact subset of the other. Conformed dimensions are fundamental in the bus architecture for a family of STARS.

CORBA. Common Object Request Broker Architecture. Developed by the Object Management Group (OMG) to provide interoperability and portability for objects over a network of heterogeneous, distributed systems in a multiplatform environment. The object request broker is a software mechanism for switching messages between objects.

CRM. Customer Relationship Management. Refers to the set of procedures and computer applications designed to manage and improve customer service in an enterprise. Data warehousing, with integrated data about each customer, is eminently suitable for CRM.

Crosstab. Refers to cross tabulation of data in tabular format with totals of columns and rows for summarization and analysis.

C/S (Client/Server) Computing. A distributed methodology for building applications where the server machines provide services to users at the client machines. The servers may manage communications, run applications, or provide database services.

Dashboard. A visual display mechanism to enable business users at every level to receive the information they need to make better decisions that improve business performance.

Database. A repository where an ordered and integrated collection of the enterprise data is stored for computer processing and information sharing.

Data Mart. A collection of related data from internal and external sources, transformed, integrated, and stored for the purpose of providing strategic information to a specific set of users in an enterprise.

Data Mining. A data-driven approach to analysis and prediction by applying sophisticated techniques and algorithms to discover knowledge.

Data Visualization. Technique for presentation and analysis of data through visual objects, such as graphs, charts, images, and specialized tabular formats.

Data Warehouse. A collection of transformed and integrated data, stored for the purpose of providing strategic information to the entire enterprise. In the top-down approach of implementation, it represents a centralized repository along with a set of dependent data marts. In the bottom-up approach of implementation, it may represent a set of independent data marts. In a practical approach built with conformed dimensions and facts, it represents a unified set of conformed data marts.

Data Warehouse Appliance. Consists of an integrated set of servers, storage, operating systems, DBMS, and software specifically pre-installed and pre-optimized for data warehousing.

DBMS. Database Management System. A software system to store, access, maintain, manage, and safeguard data in databases.

DD. Data Dictionary. A catalog or directory in a database management system that stores the data structures and relationships.

DDL. Data Definition Language. A component in a database management system used for defining data structures in the data dictionary.

Dimension Table. In the dimensional data model, each dimension table contains the attributes of a single business dimension. Product, store, salesperson, and promotional campaign are examples of business dimensions along which business measurements or facts are analyzed.

DOLAP. Desktop OLAP. A variation of ROLAP (relational online analytical processing). In the DOLAP model, multidimensional cubes are created and sent to the desktop machine where the DOLAP software exists to process the cubes.

Drill Down. Method of analysis for retrieving lower levels of detailed data starting from summary data.

DSS. Decision Support System. Application that enables users to make strategic decisions.

EAI. Enterprise Application Integration is a set of technologies and services that form a framework to enable integration of systems and applications across the enterprise.

EBCDIC. Extended Binary-Coded Decimal Interchange Code. A coded character set of 256 eight-bit characters commonly used in mainframe systems.

EII. Enterprise Information Integration is a process using data abstraction to provide a single interface for viewing all the data within an organization so that heterogeneous data sources may appear to a user as a single, homogeneous data source.

EIS. Executive Information Systems. Applications specially designed for senior executives to perform information look-up and trend analysis.

E-R Data Modeling. A popular data modeling technique used for representing business entities and the relationships among them.

ERP Systems. Enterprise Resource Planning Systems. Large packaged applications offered by leading vendors, such as SAP and PeopleSoft. ERP applications are built with proprietary software and they usually cover the entire range of a company's business.

Extranet. Enterprise network using Web technologies for collaboration of internal users and selected external business partners.

Fact Table. In the dimensional data model, the middle table that contains the facts or metrics of the business as attributes in the table. Sales units, sales dollars, costs, and profit margin are examples of business metrics that are analyzed.

Fat Client. In the client/server architecture, a client workstation that can process both application logic and presentation services.

Fine-tuning. The application of software and procedures for performance improvement of a computing system.

Firewall. A computer system placed between the Internet and an internal subnet of an enterprise to prevent unauthorized outsiders from accessing internal data.

Foreign Key. An attribute in a relational table used for establishing the direct relationship with another table, known as the parent table. The values for the foreign key attribute are drawn from the primary key values of the parent table.

Forward Engineering. The process of transforming a logical data model into a physical schema of a target database. CASE tools used for data modeling have facilities for forward engineering.

4GL. Fourth Generation Language. High-level, nonprocedural language for data manipulation, generally used with relational databases.

Gateway. A generic term referring to a computer system that routes data or merges two dissimilar services together.

Granularity. Indicates the level or grain of data. Detailed data have low granularity.

GUI. Graphical User Interface. An intuitive user interface consisting of windows, pointing devices, pull-down menus, drag-and-drop facilities, and icons. GUI has replaced the earlier CUI (Character User Interface).

HOLAP. Hybrid Online Analytical Processing. An approach to analytical processing that combines the MOLAP and ROLAP techniques.

Homonyms. Two or more data elements having the same name but containing different data.

HTML. HyperText Markup Language. A standard for defining and creating Web documents.

HTTP. HyperText Transfer Protocol. A communications protocol of the Web that governs the exchange of HTML-coded documents between a Website and a browser.

IMS. Information Management System. IBM's hierarchical database management system. Old applications in several companies are still supported by IMS databases.

Indexing. The method for speeding up database access by creating index files that point to data files.

Intranet. The enterprise network using Web technologies for collaboration of internal users.

I/O. Input/Output. Abbreviation used to indicate a database read/write operation. Excessive I/O degrades system performance.

IT. Information Technology. Covers all the computing and data communications in an enterprise. The CIO is responsible for IT operations of the enterprise.

JAD. Joint Application Development. A methodology for developing computer applications in which IT professionals and end-users cooperate and participate in the development.

Java. An object-oriented programming language that offers full interactivity with the Web.

JDBC. Java Database Connectivity. Java provides access to SQL through JDBC.

Join. A database operation used to merge data from two related tables that have common attributes.

KDD. Knowledge Discovery in Data. The process for discovering knowledge from prepared data by using data mining algorithms.

KM. Knowledge Management. A computing environment for accumulating, encoding, storing, and managing enterprise knowledge.

LAN. Local Area Network. The physical network links that connect computing devices located within a small area.

Legacy Systems. Old computer applications on disparate platforms, supported by outdated database systems that are still in use in many companies, as legacies from the past.

Load Image. Record layout in a flat file for loading a database table generally by using database utility programs. The record layout of the flat file is an exact match or image of the table.

Log. A file used by the database management system to record all database transactions. The log file is used for recovery of the database in case of failures.

Mainframe. A large computer system with extensive capabilities and resources, usually housed in a large computer center.

MDAPI. Multi-Dimensional Application Programmers Interface. The standard developed by the OLAP Council.

MDDB. Multidimensional Database. A proprietary database meant to store multidimensional data cubes. MDDBs use multidimensional arrays to store data.

MDM. Master Data Management comprises a set of processes and tools that consistently define and manage the nontransactional data entities of an organization such as Customers and Products.

Metadata. Data about data itself. For example, in a database metadata refers to the data type, length, format, default values, and so on—all information or data about the data itself.

Middleware. The term refers to software services that are placed between applications and database servers to make the data interchange transparent and efficient.

Mission Critical System. A software application that is absolutely essential for the continued operation of an organization.

MOLAP. Multidimensional Online Analytical Processing. An analytical processing technique in which multidimensional data cubes are created and stored in separate proprietary databases.

MPP. Massively Parallel Processing. Shared-nothing architecture for parallel server hardware where memory and disks are not shared among the processor nodes.

NUMA. Nonuniform Memory Architecture. Recent architecture for parallel server hardware, which is like a big SMP broken down into smaller SMPs.

ODBC. Open Database Connectivity. A programming interface from Microsoft that provides a common language interface for Windows applications to access databases on a network.

OLAP. Online Analytical Processing. Covers a wide spectrum of complex multidimensional analysis involving intricate calculations and requiring fast response times.

OLTP. Online Transaction Processing. Processes in applications that collect data online during the execution of business transactions. Order processing is an OLTP application.

Operational System. An application that supports the day-to-day operations of a business.

Outlier. In analysis, an outlier is an observation or member of a sample that deviates significantly from the rest of the sample.

Partitioning. The method for dividing a database into manageable parts for the purpose of easier management and better performance.

Portability. Refers to the ability of a piece of software to be moved around and made to function on different computing platforms.

Predictive Analysis. Includes a variety of statistical and data mining techniques to analyze historical and current data to make predictions about the future.

Primary Key. One or more fields or attributes that uniquely identify each record in a database table.

Punch Card. A card medium that was used to store data in old computer systems. Each card had 80 columns and several rows to store data.

Query. A computing function that requests data from the database, stating the parameters and constraints for the request.

Query Governor. A mechanism, usually in the DBMS, used to monitor and intercept runaway queries that might bring down the database system.

RAID. Redundant Array of Inexpensive Disks. A system of disk storage where data is distributed across several drives for faster access and improved fault tolerance.

RDBMS. Relational Database Management System. A software system for relational databases.

Referential Integrity. Refers to two relational tables that are directly related. Referential integrity between related tables is established if non-null values in the foreign key field of the child table are primary key values in the parent table.

Replication. A method for creating copies of the database, either in real time or in a deferred mode.

Reverse Engineering. The process of transforming the physical schema of any particular database into a logical model. Data modeling CASE tools have facilities for reverse engineering.

ROA. Return on Assets. Measure of payback from a project for assets deployed.

ROI. Return on Investment. Measure of payback from a project for investment made.

ROLAP. Relational Online Analytical Processing. An analytical processing technique in which multidimensional data cubes are created on the fly by the relational database engine.

Roll Up. Method of analysis for retrieving higher levels of summary data starting from detailed data.

Scalability. The ability to support increasing numbers of users in cost-effective increments without adversely affecting business operations.

Schema. A collection of tables that forms a database.

Scorecard. Online, real time reporting to monitor performance against targets.

Slice and Dice. The term commonly used for a method of analysis where multidimensional data is presented in many ways, by rotating the presentation between columns, rows, and pages.

SMP. Symmetric Multiprocessing. Shared-everything architecture for parallel server hardware where memory and disks are shared among the processor nodes.

Snowflake Schema. A normalized version of the STAR schema in which dimension tables are partially or fully normalized. Not generally recommended because it compromises query performance and simplicity for understanding.

Sparsity. Indicates the condition in the data warehouse in which every fact table record in a dimensional model is not necessarily filled with data.

SQL. Structured Query Language. Has become the standard interface for relational databases.

Standardized Facts. Two sets of facts represented in fact tables in a family of STARS are said to be standardized if both sets are identical in their attributes or if one set is an exact subset of the other. Standardized facts are fundamental in the bus architecture for a family of STARS.

STAR Schema. The arrangement of the collection of fact and dimension tables in the dimensional data model, resembling a star formation, with the fact table placed in the middle surrounded by the dimension tables. Each dimension table is in a one-to-many relationship with the fact table.

Stored Procedure. A software program stored in the database itself to be executed on the server based on stipulated conditions.

Subschema. A collection of external user views of a database.

Supermart. The term commonly applied to a data mart with conformed dimensions and standardized facts.

Surrogate Key. An artificial key field, usually with system-assigned sequential numbers, used in the dimensional model to link a dimension table to the fact table. In a dimension table, the surrogate key is the primary key which becomes a foreign key in the fact table.

Syndicated Data. Data that can be purchased from outside commercial sources to augment the data in the enterprise data warehouse.

Synonyms. Two or more data elements containing the same data but having different names.

Table Space. Refers to an area on a physical medium where one or more relational database tables can exist.

TCP/IP. Transmission Control Protocol/Internet Protocol. Basic communication protocol with an applications layer (TCP) and a network layer (IP).

Thin Client. In the client/server architecture, a client workstation that manages only the graphical user interface.

Threads. A thread is a unit of task under the control of a single computing process that can be implemented within a server process, or by means of an operating system service.

Time Stamping. In applications, the procedure of marking each database record with the date and time of the database operation such as insert, update, or designation to delete.

Trigger. A stored procedure that can be triggered and executed automatically when a database operation such as insert, update, or delete takes place.

UDF. User-Defined Functions in advanced database systems.

UDT. User-Defined Data Types in advanced database systems.

UNIX. A multiuser, multitasking robust operating system originally developed by Bell Laboratories.

Volatility. Data are said to be highly volatile if they are subject to frequent additions, updates or deletes.

VSAM. Virtual Storage Access Method. A powerful storage and data access method, very popular on mainframes before databases became prevalent.

WAN. Wide Area Network. The physical network links that connect computing devices spread out across a large area. In a global organization, a WAN connects the users across continents.

XML. eXtensible Markup Language. Was introduced to overcome the limitations of HTML. XML is extensible, portable, structured, and descriptive.

INDEX

Data Warehousing Fundamentals for IT Professionals, Second Edition. By Paulraj Ponniah
Copyright © 2010 John Wiley & Sons, Inc.

Printed and bound by CPI Group (UK) Ltd, Croydon, CR0 4YY

27/10/2024

14580259-0004